T0313780

IN THIS SERIES

Socio-Economic Surveys of Three Villages in Andhra Pradesh:
A Study of Agrarian Relations
Edited by V. K. Ramachandran, Vikas Rawal, Madhura Swaminathan

Socio-Economic Surveys of Two Villages in Rajasthan:
A Study of Agrarian Relations
Edited by Madhura Swaminathan and Vikas Rawal

Socio-Economic Surveys of Three Villages in Karnataka:
A Study of Agrarian Relations
Edited by Madhura Swaminathan and Arindam Das

Socio-Economic Surveys of Three Villages in Tripura:
A Study of Agrarian Relations
Edited by Madhura Swaminathan and Ranjini Basu

Socio-Economic Surveys of Three Villages in West Bengal:
A Study of Agrarian Relations
Edited by Aparajita Bakshi and Tapas Singh Modak

SOCIO-ECONOMIC SURVEYS OF
Three Villages in West Bengal

A STUDY OF AGRARIAN RELATIONS

Edited by

Aparajita Bakshi and Tapas Singh Modak

Published by

Tulika Books

www.tulikabooks.in

in association with

Foundation for Agrarian Studies

www.agrarianstudies.org

© Foundation for Agrarian Studies 2021

First published in India 2021

ISBN: 978-81-947175-5-3

Printed at Chaman Enterprises, Delhi 110 002

Foreword

Post-liberalisation changes in agrarian relations in West Bengal have been crucial in influencing recent political developments in the State. This book is an important contribution to understanding those changes.

The 1980s were a period of rapid growth in rural West Bengal and in agricultural production in the State. This period of growth was powered by land reform. In particular, it was powered by the new opportunities for surplus generation and the enthusiasm for cultivation caused by the redistribution of land and Operation Barga. Growth was possible also because of the expansion of irrigation, particularly groundwater irrigation, in the decade following the land reform.

The growth that was stimulated by land reform began to tail off by the early 1990s; that this tailing-off coincided with the period of accelerated introduction of policies of liberalisation and financial austerity was to have profound consequences for the future of growth in the West Bengal countryside.

The study in this book is of the West Bengal countryside after 2010, and the core data come from surveys conducted in 2010 and 2015 in three villages, one each in Bankura, Maldah, and Koch Bihar districts.

A salient finding of the study is the progress of differentiation in the West Bengal countryside. A clear section of households have emerged as the group that Surjya Kanta Mishra has called the "rural neo-rich." In class terms, these are rich capitalist farmers that have benefited from and enriched themselves over the long period of Left Front rule and, in some cases, landlord remnants that continued to retain and build on their social and economic advantage.

These households own the biggest and best landholdings in the villages, they have the highest incomes from the land, they make a profit in all years, and earn new crop incomes from varied sources. Although many of them owe their present commercial success and wealth to the freeing of the productive forces subsequent to the land reform, they also formed the bulwark of the opposition to the Left and support to the Trinamool Congress in 2011.

At the other end of the class spectrum, the surveys showed the difficult conditions of production and poor crop incomes among the poor peasantry, the lack of adequate employment in non-crop employment in the villages, and low incomes among poor peasants and rural manual workers. Indeed, an important development of the period was large-scale migration by workers from all the villages, but particularly from Kalmandasguri village in Koch Bihar district, for employment to different parts of India. The data show that while the absolute levels of wealth and investment among the rich were lower than in many (or most) parts of India, the unequalising effects of differentiation in the countryside were as evident.

Agricultural policy was weak on multiple fronts. Public and private investment in infrastructure, production, and mechanisation was inadequate, as was the system of public procurement of agricultural produce at guaranteed minimum prices. Research and extension work by the agricultural research and education system, and directly by the government, lagged far behind States such as Punjab or Tamil Nadu. The supply of formal credit was limited. No measures were taken to introduce new institutional structures – cooperative or otherwise – to mitigate the ill effects of small-scale production.

Thus, by the second decade of the twenty-first century, the situation in the West Bengal countryside was one of high levels of capitalist differentiation and low growth of productivity.

These were changes of great historical moment in West Bengal. This collection of studies of how three villages fared, particularly with respect to production, incomes, and poverty, provides an invaluable insight into the economics of rural Bengal at a crucial period in its recent history.

V. K. Ramachandran
Series Editor
August 2021

Acknowledgements

This book is a result of the collective and collaborative efforts of field investigators, data processing and analysis teams, and researchers who have authored the individual chapters. We are grateful to the many persons who have contributed to the making of this book.

Census surveys were conducted in the three selected villages in West Bengal in 2010. In 2015, we revisited the villages and conducted a sample survey. We are thankful to all the investigators who participated in both surveys.

Data entry and processing was supervised by Arindam Das, Tapas Singh Modak, and T. Sivamurugan. We are thankful to the staff of the Foundation for Agrarian Studies (FAS) for their crucial support at various stages of the project.

The preliminary findings of the surveys were presented at a symposium in Durgapur on September 11–13, 2015. We are grateful to A. Bheemeshwar Reddy, Deepak Kumar, Madhura Swaminathan, Rahul Kumar, R. Ramakumar, R. V. Bhavani, Sanjukta Chakraborty, T. Sivamurugan, Venkatesh Athreya, Vijay Kumar, V. K. Ramachandran, Yasodhara Das, and Yoshifumi Usami for presenting papers along with the authors of this book, and providing valuable comments and suggestions. Kalyan Das helped us translate the relevant materials into Bengali for the symposium. We are grateful to the participants of the symposium for their inputs. Participants from the All India Kisan Sabha, All India Democratic Women's Association, and All India Agricultural Workers Union gave us detailed comments on our presentations. Our special thanks to Surjya Kanta Mishra, Madan Ghosh, Amiya Patra, Kabita Kayal, Tushar Ghosh, Amal Haldar, and Nurul Huda.

The chapters of the book were peer-reviewed, and we are grateful to the reviewers. We owe special thanks to Madhura Swaminathan who read most of the chapters and gave detailed comments. Mansi Goyal assisted us in editing and preparing the manuscript.

We are grateful to the Rosa Luxemburg Stiftung (RLS) for providing funding support to the FAS at various stages of the surveys and book project. We thank Indira Chandrasekhar and the team at Tulika Books for their efforts in giving the manuscript its final shape. TNQ Technologies Pvt. Ltd. designed the cover.

APARAJITA BAKSHI
TAPAS SINGH MODAK
March 2021

Contents

III INCOME, EMPLOYMENT, AND CREDIT

Tables and Figures

1. Introduction

2. The Contemporary Agricultural Economy of West Bengal

3. Nature of Classes in Rural West Bengal

4. The Impact of Land Reforms on the Ownership and Distribution of Land

5. Household Crop Incomes among Small Farmers

6. Fertilizer Use in West Bengal: A Case Study of Three Villages

7. Development of Groundwater Irrigation in West Bengal since 1990

8. Climate and Agriculture in West Bengal

9. A Contemporary Study of Rural Credit in West Bengal

10. Labour and Employment in Rural West Bengal

11. Wage Rates in Rural West Bengal

12. Income Diversification in West Bengal Villages

13. Aspects of Poverty in the Three Villages

SECTION I

The General Context of Production and Agrarian Relations

1

Introduction

Aparajita Bakshi and Tapas Singh Modak

This is the fifth book in the Socio-Economic Survey of Villages series of the Foundation for Agrarian Studies (FAS). The series reports the findings from village surveys conducted by FAS under its Project on Agrarian Relations in India (PARI), and this book documents findings from surveys of three villages in West Bengal.

The 2010 PARI survey of villages in West Bengal portrays agrarian relations in the State during the last year of the Left Front government, and throws light on some of the problems of the economy that had manifested by then. The gains achieved through land reforms, which changed power relations in the countryside by breaking the social, economic, and political dominance of the *jotedars* or large landowners, and empowering the small peasants, were beginning to be threatened by neoliberalism. In the late 1970s and early 1980s, the small peasants had gained substantially from land and tenancy reforms, through measures such as provision of formal credit and subsidised inputs, rural electrification, and public investment in irrigation. These were instrumental in sustaining a high agricultural growth rate in West Bengal, one of the highest among Indian States, for a decade and a half from the 1980s onwards (Saha and Swaminathan 1994; Rawal and Swaminathan 1998; Rawal, Swaminathan, and Ramachandran 2002).[1] This was a major success of the Left Front government and its pro-poor policies. As Sen (1992, p. 12) has noted,

---

[1] "West Bengal, with a growth rate of over 7 per cent per annum in agricultural value added – more than two-and-a-half times the national average – can be described as the agricultural success story of the eighties." – Sen (1992, p. 10)

the West Bengal example, where value added has grown faster than gross output, contrary to the trends elsewhere, suggests that greater efficiency in input use is possible through reform and devolution.

However, by 2010, the problem of scale began to surface in West Bengal's agriculture. Demographic pressures caused further fragmentation and subdivision of already small landholdings. According to the Agricultural Census of 2010–11, the average size of individual landholdings in West Bengal was only 0.74 hectare, and 96 per cent of all agricultural holdings were marginal and small, less than five acres (GoI 2015). The Land and Livestock Holdings Survey of 2012–13 reported that 43.4 per cent of rural households in West Bengal were landless, an increase of 8 per cent since 2003 (Bansal, Usami, and Rawal 2018). Neoliberalism had weakened the State's economy and limited its capacity to protect the interests of its small farmers. National policies withdrawing agricultural investment and subsidies for inputs and credit had serious implications for Bengal's peasantry. Increased costs of production rendered agriculture unviable for farmers with small and marginal holdings. Rapid proletarianisation of the peasantry was underway, and there was increased out-migration of workers seeking manual wage employment in other States. The 2010 surveys in the three study villages capture this situation of agricultural stress as well as the undercurrents of the political churning that were taking shape in West Bengal. In 2011, the Trinamool Congress (TMC) defeated the 34-year-old Left Front government and came to power in West Bengal. In 2015, as the TMC government was completing its first term, the FAS team revisited the three study villages and conducted surveys in a sample of households. The purpose was to see if any major changes at the ground level were arresting the decline in agriculture.

The methodology used in this book is that of village studies. Detailed statistical data at the household level on various aspects of production and living standards were collected through interviews using a structured questionnaire. The collected data are rich in content, and great care has been taken to maintain quality and accuracy. However, it should be noted that these are data from three villages in West Bengal, and the results cannot be generalised for the State as a whole. Though we do comment in detail on the production systems, economic and social relations, and changes occurring in the villages, and try to understand these within the socio-economic context of West Bengal, we are cautious about drawing a metanarrative for the State as a whole based on the experiences of the three villages.

One of the objectives and strengths of the PARI studies is to identify the classes in the villages, and to understand economic and social processes through the lens of class relations. The impact of economic policies is felt differently by different classes, and the method of analysis followed in this book attempts to capture that reality.

Project on Agrarian Relations in India (PARI)

PARI was conceived by FAS in 2005 to understand the rapid changes taking place in the Indian countryside in contemporary times. According to FAS,

> Historically, there has been in India a tradition of urging scholarship to turn its face to the countryside, to conduct specific studies of social and economic changes there and to assess and evaluate these changes. In recent years, however, such detailed study and social science research have lagged behind the rapid and complex changes that are occurring in the countryside.[2]

This need for a deeper understanding of the rapidly changing rural scenario of India based on rigorous statistical and socio-economic surveys in villages provided the motivation for PARI, whose objectives are as follows:

(i) to analyse village-level production, production systems and livelihoods, and the socio-economic characteristics of different strata of the rural population;

(ii) to conduct specific studies of sectional deprivation in rural India, particularly with regard to the Scheduled Caste (SC) and Scheduled Tribe (ST) populations, women, specific minorities, and the income-poor; and

(iii) to report on the state of basic village amenities and rural people's access to the facilities of modern life.

The first PARI surveys were initiated in 2006, in three villages of (erstwhile) Andhra Pradesh.[3] Since then, one or two States have been selected each year, and two or three villages in different agroecological regions of that

---

[2] http://fas.org.in/category/research/project-on-agrarian-relations-in-india-pari/, October 21, 2020.

[3] Two villages in Andhra Pradesh and one village in Telangana.

State are surveyed. State-level mass organisations suggest the regions and districts for study, and assist in selecting the final villages from a shortlist prepared by FAS. The survey team comprises members of the FAS team, and students and researchers from the respective States. Till 2019, 27 villages in 12 States have been surveyed under PARI, as given in Table 1.

The FAS team generally conducts a census-type survey that covers every household and individual in each village. In five of the 27 villages surveyed under PARI, sample surveys were conducted after initial house-listing surveys. A village-level questionnaire is canvassed in each village. In addition, a village profile, based on the existing sources of secondary data, is constructed. The information collected in the census questionnaire covers the following information, which can be further disaggregated:

- Demographic data
- Education levels
- Occupation and work status
- Ownership and operational landholdings of households
- Tenurial status
- Cropping pattern and crop production
- Ownership of assets
- Participation in government schemes
- Household electricity, sanitation, and water facilities
- Housing
- Incomes and earnings
- Patterns and levels of employment
- Indebtedness.

It is noteworthy that there are no official sources of serial data on household incomes in rural India. The National Sample Survey provides regular data on monthly per capita household expenditure, and the Comprehensive Scheme for the Study of Cost of Cultivation of Principal Crops in India (CCPC) provides regular data on farm business incomes for selected crops. Our village data, by contrast, include data on household incomes from all sources of tangible household income, under the following categories:

- Income from crop production[4]
- Income from animal resources

---

[4] Data on crop production and the cost of cultivation, though based on the CCPC methodology, are somewhat more detailed in the PARI database. The detailed methodology for income calculation can be found in FAS (2015).

Table 1 *PARI study villages and their location details, year and type of survey, and number of households*

Village	Sub-district	District	State	Year of survey	Type	Number of households
Ananthavaram	Kollur	Guntur	Andhra Pradesh	2005–06	Census, Sample	664
Bukkacherla	Raptadu	Anantapur	Andhra Pradesh	2005–06	Census, Sample	292
Kothapalle	Thimmapur	Karimnagar	Telangana	2005–06	Census, Sample	370
Harevli	Najibabad	Bijnor	Uttar Pradesh	2006	Census	109
Mahatwar	Rasra	Ballia	Uttar Pradesh	2006	Census	156
Warwat Khanderao	Sangrampur	Buldhana	Maharashtra	2007	Census	250
Nimshirgaon	Shirol	Kolhapur	Maharashtra	2007	Sample	137
25 F Gulabewala	Karanpur	Sri Ganganagar	Rajasthan	2007	Census	204
Dungariya	Kotra	Udaipur	Rajasthan	2007	Census	111
Rewasi	Sikar	Sikar	Rajasthan	2010	Census	219
Gharsondi	Bhitarwar	Gwalior	Madhya Pradesh	2008	Census	263
Badhar	Pushprajgarh	Anuppur	Madhya Pradesh	2008	Census	118
Alabujanahalli	Maddur	Mandya	Karnataka	2009	Census	243
Siresandra	Kolar,	Kolar	Karnataka	2009	Census	79
Zhapur	Kalaburagi	Kalaburagi	Karnataka	2009	Census	109
Panahar	Kotulpur	Bankura	West Bengal	2010, 2015	Census, Sample	248
Amarsinghi	Ratua-I	Maldah	West Bengal	2010, 2015	Census, Sample	127
Kalmandasguri	Cooch Behar- II	Koch Bihar	West Bengal	2010, 2015	Census, Sample	147
Tehang	Phillaur	Jalandhar	Punjab	2011	Census	681
Hakamwala	Budhlada	Mansa	Punjab	2011	Census	500
Katkuian	Bagaha II	West Champaran	Bihar	2012	Census	358
Nayanagar	Hasanpur	Samastipur	Bihar	2012	Sample	1205
Mainama	Manu	Dhalai	Tripura	2016	Sample	1451
Khakchang	Dasda	North	Tripura	2016	Sample	589
Muhuripur	Julaibari	South	Tripura	2016	Sample	1054
Venmani	Kilvelur	Nagapattinam	Tamil Nadu	2019	Census	416
Palakurichi	Kilvelur	Nagapattinam	Tamil Nadu	2019	Census	390

- Income from agricultural and non-agricultural wage labour
- Income from salaries
- Income from business and trade, rent, interest earnings, pensions, remittances, scholarships, and all other sources.

PARI Surveys in West Bengal

Three villages were selected for the West Bengal round of PARI surveys: Panahar in Bankura district, Amarsinghi in Maldah district, and Kalmandasguri in Koch Bihar district (Figure 1). The villages span from the south to the north of the State, representing different agroclimatic features and cropping systems, though rice was the main crop in all three. All three village surveys were resurveys, as they were previously studied

Figure 1 *Location of three study regions representing different agroclimatic zones*

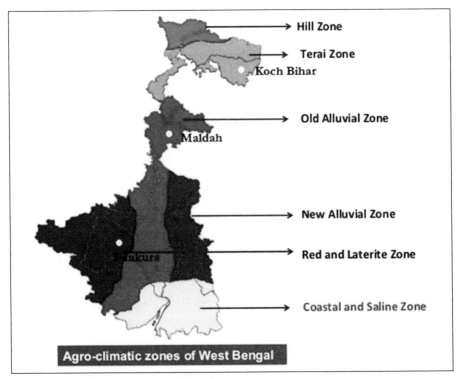

Source: http://agricoop.nic.in/sites/default/files/WestBengal%2013-North%2024%20 Parganas-31-12-2011_0.pdf, viewed on January 12, 2020.

by scholars associated with FAS at different points of time. A rich archive of data from several villages in West Bengal was available to FAS before the 2010 surveys were conducted.

Amarsinghi and Kalmandasguri were among the eight villages surveyed as part of a UNU-WIDER (United Nations University World Institute for Development Economics Research) study titled "Rural Poverty, Social Change and Public Policy in West Bengal" in 1989–90. This was a special study of schooling and literacy in the State, and V. K. Ramachandran was a part of these surveys (Ramachandran 1995; Ramachandran, Swaminathan, and Rawal 2003).

In 1994–95, V. K. Ramachandran conducted a study in five villages on literacy, primary education, and child labour after the initiation of the Total Literacy Campaign in the State (Ramachandran, Swaminathan, and Rawal 2003). This study was supported by the UNICEF, and Panahar and Kalmandasguri were among the villages surveyed. In 1995–96, Rawal followed up with a detailed household-level survey on irrigation use in Panahar (Rawal 1999).

In May and June 2005, Ramachandran and Rawal conducted a study of "Landlessness and Debt in Seven Villages in West Bengal" for the Development and Planning Department, Government of West Bengal (Rawal 2006a, 2006b). Amarsinghi and Kalmandasguri were again selected for this study. Following this, Bakshi (2010) conducted a detailed sample survey on household incomes in Amarsinghi in 2005–06.

Table 2 shows the years in which the three villages were surveyed by scholars associated with FAS prior to the PARI surveys; archival data for most of these surveys were available with FAS. It should be noted that the

Table 2 *Details of surveys conducted in the three study villages before the 2010 PARI survey*

Village	Year of survey	Details of survey
Panahar	1994–95	Literacy, primary education, and child labour (UNICEF)
	1995–96	Irrigation development (doctoral research)
Amarsinghi	1989–90	Schooling and literacy (UNU-WIDER project)
	2005	Landlessness and debt (Government of West Bengal)
	2005–06	Household incomes (doctoral research)
Kalmandasguri	1989–90	Schooling and literacy (UNU-WIDER)
	1994–95	Literacy, primary education, and child labour (UNICEF)
	2005	Landlessness and debt (Government of West Bengal)

purpose of each of these surveys was different, and detailed data on all the aspects covered in the PARI surveys were not collected in the earlier surveys.

The West Bengal rounds of the PARI surveys were conducted in May and June 2010, and covered all households in the villages – the detailed PARI questionnaire was canvassed in every household.[5] A total of 247 households in Panahar, 127 in Amarsinghi, and 147 in Kalmandasguri were covered in these surveys.[6] In 2015, surveys of a sample of households were conducted in the three villages using the same interview schedule to assess if there were any notable changes in the intervening period of five years during which the State underwent major political changes. Acknowledging the rising trend of migration from West Bengal in recent years, a separate short questionnaire on migration was canvassed among all sampled households in 2015, and case studies on migration were also conducted by a few scholars during the survey.

The 2015 samples were selected using the 2010 household list as the sampling frame and a stratified sampling method. A simple stratification based on landholdings and social groups was used to draw samples. The households were first stratified according to their landholding status – those with and without operational holdings. The second stage of stratification was done according to the social groups specific to each village using a probability-proportionate sampling method. Multipliers were used to arrive at population estimates. The household sample sizes were 106 in Panahar, 55 in Amarsinghi, and 52 in Kalmandasguri.[7] Further details of the samples drawn in each village are given in Appendix Tables 1a–c.

Between 2010 and 2015, and even after 2015, scholars associated with FAS continued their study of these villages and conducted detailed research on specific topics. Basu (2015) studied the history of land reforms in Kalmandasguri, and Modak and Bakshi (2017) studied groundwater

---

[5] The PARI survey schedule is available at http://fas.org.in/wp-content/themes/zakat/pdf/Survey-method-tool/Schedule%20for%20Survey%20of%20Households.pdf, viewed on October 10, 2018.

[6] We follow the same definition of a "household" as the Census of India and National Sample Survey: a household comprises members usually staying together and having food from the same kitchen. However, we also noted migrant members who were away from the family for six months or more for work or education, though these members were not included in calculations pertaining to demographics in the village.

[7] In case it was found that a household selected in the sample had been subdivided in 2015, all units of the old household were surveyed.

markets in Amarsinghi. The doctoral theses of Sarkar (2017), Das (2019), Basu (2020), and Modak (2020) are based on these villages. This emphasises FAS's long-standing and continued research engagement in studying the agrarian economy of West Bengal through detailed village surveys.

Introducing the Three Villages

Panahar

Panahar is situated in the Vindhyan Alluvial region in the southern part of West Bengal, in Deshra-Koalpara, Kotulpur block of Bankura district. The village is in a fairly urbanised region, well connected to nearby urban centres and Kolkata. It is located 3 km from the block headquarters of Kotulpur, which is also the major agricultural market for the village, and 6 and 12 km respectively from the towns of Jayrambati and Kamarpukur, both well-known pilgrimage sites receiving a regular stream of visitors. All-weather roads and regular bus services connect Panahar to these towns, and the nearest railways stations are at Arambagh (28 km) and Bishnupur (48 km). Panahar is connected to Kolkata (108 kms) by bus and train routes through Arambagh. The village shares its boundaries with two other villages, Koalpara and Palpuskarini. At the time of the 2010 survey, the high school and primary health centres were in Koalpara.

Figure 2 *Location of Panahar village*

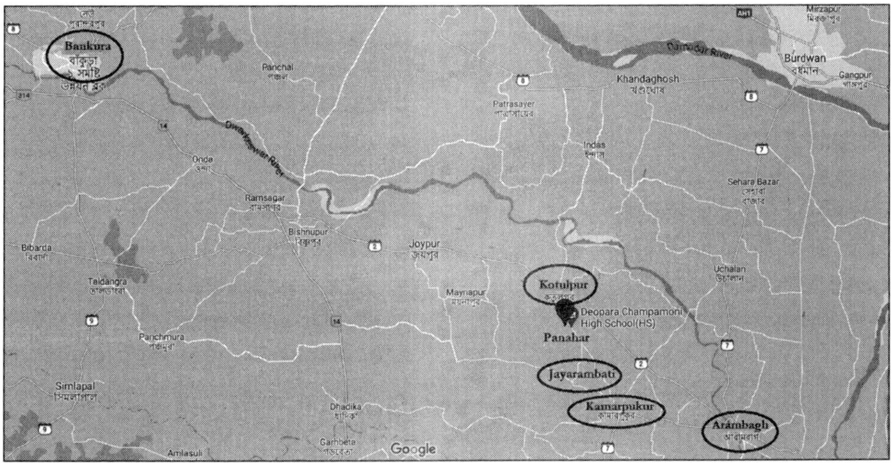

Source: maps.google.com

At the time of the survey, Panahar was an irrigated village, and much of the land was triple-cropped. An *aman* (kharif) crop of paddy, a winter crop of potato, and summer crops of *boro* paddy or sesame were the major crops. In 2010, mustard, rapeseed, and wheat were also cultivated on a small scale. Though the village is in the command area of the Kangsabati project,[8] and canal and river lift irrigation were important sources of irrigation in 1995–96, these sources of irrigation had declined and been replaced by electrified deep tubewells by 2010.

In an earlier study of Panahar, Rawal (1999) revealed substantial public intervention in agriculture through land reforms, provision of electricity for agriculture, and support in agricultural marketing since 1977–78. These led to the transformation of agricultural production and high agricultural growth till the mid-1990s. In 2010, Panahar was the most advanced among the three study villages in terms of area irrigated, mechanisation of agriculture, and the functioning of a cooperative society providing agricultural inputs and marketing services.

In 2010, Panahar had 248 households and a total population of 1,083. The households belonged to various castes and social groups including Goala, Baishnab, Modak, Majhi, Tanti, and Kumbhakar (officially designated as Other Backward Classes/OBCs); Bagdi, Kaibarta, Kotal, and Teli (Scheduled Castes/SCs); Santhal (Scheduled Tribes/STs); and Brahmin, Baishnab, Sadgop, and Muslim households.[9] According to the

Table 3 *Demographic features of the population, Panahar*

	Census (2011)	PARI (2010)
Households	237	248
Total population	1,104	1,083
Sex ratio	1,000	987
SC	53%	49%
ST	6%	6%
Literacy rate	60%	55.7%

Source: Census of India (2011); PARI survey (2010).

[8] The Kangsabati Project was started in the year 1956–57 with the specific aim of providing irrigation to the laterite regions across the districts of Bankura, erstwhile Medinipur, and Hughli.
[9] See Appendix Table 2a.

Table 4 *Distribution of workers, Panahar, 2011*

Description	Male	Female
Workers (as % of total population)	55.1	4.3
Main workers (as % of all workers)	97.7	95.8
Distribution of main workers		
Cultivators	25.3	4.3
Agricultural labourers	56.6	73.9
Household industry	2.4	0
Other workers	15.8	21.7
All main workers	100	100

Source: Census of India (2011).

PARI data, 49 per cent of the population belonged to SCs and 6 per cent were ST. The overall literacy rate was 55.7 per cent.

According to the Census of India 2011, the work participation rate in Panahar was 55.1 for males and 4.3 for females (Table 4). More than 95 per cent of both male and female workers were main workers, that is, they worked for more than six months in the year. About 25.3 per cent of male workers and only 4.3 per cent of female workers were cultivators, whereas 56.6 and 73.9 per cent of male and female workers were agricultural labourers, respectively. Inequality of land ownership was high in this village, compared to the other two study villages.

Amarsinghi

Amarsinghi is situated in Samsi Village Panchayat, Ratua-I block of Maldah district and five km from Samsi town, the nearest railhead and market centre. There was a regulated agricultural produce market in Samsi, and most of the agricultural commodities of the village – vegetables, jute, and paddy – were sold in the weekly *haat* on Thursdays. However, connectivity between Amarsinghi and Samsi was poor, with no buses or public transport. The nearest buses were available from Motiganj, about 3 km away, and cycle vans fitted with motors ferried passengers at regular intervals. The village is 16 km from the block headquarters and 65 km from Maldah town, both of which can be reached by bus from Samsi. The primary school was located in the adjacent village Bandhakuri and the nearest secondary and higher secondary schools were in Samsi and Baidyanathpur, both within 5 km from the village. The village did not have

Figure 3 *Location of Amarsinghi village*

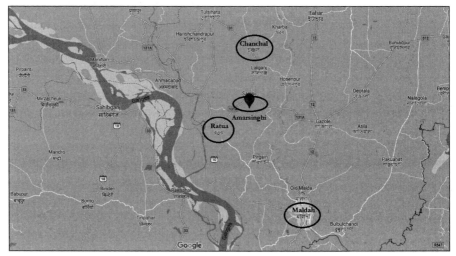

Source: maps.google.com

any primary health centres in 2015 – the nearest one was in Bandhakuri. Amarsinghi and Bandhakuri villages formed an integrated unit; many Bandhakuri residents owned land in Amarsinghi and vice versa.

Located in the fertile plains fed by the Ganges and its tributaries in the New Alluvial Plain region of West Bengal, Amarsinghi had a wide variety of crops, with *aman* and *boro* paddy and jute as the main ones. In addition, potato, mustard, and pulses (lentils and gram) as well as different kinds of vegetables were cultivated, although under minimal acreage. Many households also owned mango orchards – Maldah district is famous for mangoes in the State. A few households also grew sugarcane and sold sugarcane juice in nearby Samsi. The village is irrigated by tubewells during the summer season, and diesel pumps were used to draw water until 2007, when electrification for agriculture began. At the time of the survey in 2010, very few farmers used diesel pumps for irrigation, and a small acreage was irrigated by river lift irrigation.

In many ways, Amarsinghi is an atypical village. The data showed land distribution to be fairly equal, and most households were small farmers – there were no rich-landlord or large-landowner households. Inequality between castes and social groups was also not very high. Though all households in the village were Hindus, large Muslim populations resided in the adjoining villages. At the time of the 2010 survey, Amarsinghi had 127 households and a total population of 575 (Table 5). The major caste groups were Tanti (OBC), Tiyar (SC), Napit (OBC), and Goala (OBC), and there was one Santhal (ST) household.[10] Forty-five per cent of the population belonged to the SCs, 0.7 per cent ST, and the remaining OBCs.

According to the Census of India 2011, 57.3 per cent of the male and 9.2 per cent of the female population in the village were workers. The proportion of main workers was 76.5 and 43.8 per cent of male and female workers, respectively, and the remaining were marginal workers who worked for less than six months in the year. Seasonal outmigration of workers from the village to Delhi and other States were observed in the

Table 5 *Demographic features of the population, Amarsinghi*

	Census (2011)	PARI (2010)
Households	150	127
Population	704	575
Sex ratio	977	1,010
SC	36%	45%
ST	0.5%	0.7%
Literacy	51.7%	63.2%

Source: Census of India (2011); PARI survey (2010).

Table 6 *Distribution of workers, Amarsinghi, 2011*

Description	Male	Female
Workers as % of total population	57.3	9.2
Main workers as % of all workers	76.5	43.8
Distribution of main workers		
Cultivators	26.3	7.1
Agricultural labourers	41	14.3
Household industry	4.5	0
Other workers	28.2	78.6
All main workers	100	100

Source: Census of India (2011).

[10] See Appendix Table 2a.

surveys. Sixty-seven per cent of the male workers were in agriculture –
26.3 per cent as cultivators and 7.1 per cent as agricultural labourers. The
Census of India reported 78.6 per cent of female main workers as other
workers, only 7.1 per cent as cultivators, and 14.3 per cent as agricultural
labourers.

Kalmandasguri

Located in the Terai Teesta region, Kalmandasguri village is a part of
the Bararangras Village Panchayat, Cooch Behar-II block of Koch Bihar
district and 17 km from the district town of Koch Bihar. At the time of the
2010 survey, the nearest markets were 3 and 7 km away in Bararangras
and Pundibari, respectively, and the village did not have electricity or any
all-weather roads. Though it had electrified by the 2015 sample survey,
there was no available public transport. The nearest bus stop was 3 km
away in Baudiardanga, where the bus frequency was five times a day. The
nearest primary health centre was 3 km away in Thanesar. Kalmandasguri
had one primary school and one child learning centre (*shishu shiksha
kendra*), and the nearest secondary school was in Baudiardanga.

As per the 2005 survey data, only 33 per cent of net sown area in the
village was irrigated by diesel-powered shallow tubewells. There was no
major expansion of irrigation facilities in the village between 2005 and
2010. Although a substantial part of the land in the village was double-

Figure 4 *Location of Kalmandasguri village*

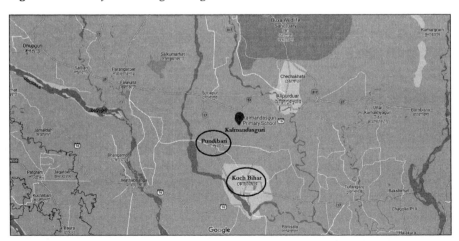

Source: maps.google.com

cropped because of high rainfall (jute in pre-monsoon and *aman* paddy in monsoon), agricultural yields remained low. The major crops were paddy and jute, and more recently, potato, which was cultivated in irrigated plots. With electrification in the village, some farmers reported to have invested in electric-powered pumps and borewells during the 2015 survey. However, the impact of full-scale irrigation was yet to be achieved.

Fishing was an important occupation among Muslim households in Kalmandasguri in addition to substantial migration for non-agricultural employment. The migration trend visible even in 2005 had only strengthened in the subsequent survey years.

At the time of the 2010 survey, Kalmandasguri had 147 households and population of 712 persons, and the major social groups were Muslim, Jogi, Napit, and Baishya Kapali (all classified as OBCs in West Bengal); Rajbangshi and Muchi (classified as SCs in West Bengal); Oraon, Munda, and Nagesiya (STs); and Kayastha.[11] Of the total population, 34 per cent were SC and 6 per cent ST.

According to the Census, the worker-to-population ratio in the village was 55.4 for males and 22.9 for females in 2011. The majority of main workers were employed in agriculture as cultivators and agricultural labourers. Similar to Amarsinghi, Kalmandasguri had a predominance of medium and small peasants, and there were no landlords or large farmers in the village. The largest landowning households owned only 5.33 acres of land, and the average landholding size was 0.95 acres. Rajbangshis were the major landowning social group.

Table 7 *Demographic features of the population, Kalmandasguri*

	Census (2011)	PARI (2010)
Households	152	147
Population	712	701
Sex ratio	913	910
SC	34%	34%
ST	5.5%	6%
Literacy rate	64.4%	58.1%

Source: Census of India (2011); PARI survey (2010).

[11] See Appendix Table 2c.

Table 8 *Distribution of workers, Kalmandasguri, 2011*

Description	Male	Female
Workers as % of total population	55.4	22.9
Main workers as % of all workers	77.2	12.8
Distribution of main workers		
Cultivators	17	20
Agricultural labourers	58.5	60
Household industry	0	0
Other workers	24.5	20
All main workers	100	100

Source: Census of India (2011).

Organisation of the Book

The 13 chapters of this book are divided into four sections. The first section establishes the broad agrarian context of the State of West Bengal and the three study villages. Here, the present and first chapter introduces the villages and the village surveys. Chapter 2 examines various aspects of the rural economy since 1990 and uses official sources of data to analyse the growth of agricultural production, which had largely stagnated in West Bengal since the 2000s. The chapter also explores some of the present challenges facing the agrarian economy. Chapter 3 describes the socio-economic classes in the study villages including the criteria used for such classification. It also briefly discusses the nature of differentiation of classes in the villages and characteristics of the peasantry. Chapter 4 discusses the landholding pattern of the study villages in light of the changes brought by land reforms in West Bengal. It also highlights the contemporary challenges of landholdings in the study villages in particular and West Bengal in general. These four chapters provide the context for the analytical chapters in the following sections.

The second section focuses on various aspects of the crop economy. Chapter 5 examines the cropping pattern, yields, and returns from farming across socio-economic classes and highlights the challenges faced by the poor peasantry. Chapter 6 investigates the use of fertilizers in West Bengal and the study villages in terms of quantity, cost, and efficiency. Given the crucial role of the groundwater irrigation in West Bengal's high agricultural growth in the 1980s and early 1990s, chapter 7 analyses the pattern of groundwater irrigation development in the State after 1990 by drawing upon secondary data. This chapter also discusses the evolution of water markets, public and private sources of irrigation, and their implications for farm households in two study villages. Chapter 8 raises some important issues pertaining to climate and West Bengal agriculture. The authors establish the State's increasing vulnerability to flooding due to climatic factors that has serious consequences for small farmers, and emphasise the need for adaptive climate policies.

The third section of the book deals with rural credit, employment, and incomes. Chapter 9 analyses the development of rural credit in the contemporary period in West Bengal and access to agricultural credit in the study villages. Chapter 10 discusses the employment situation in the villages and examines work participation and days of wage employment of poor-peasant and manual-worker households for whom manual wage employment is the main source of income and livelihoods. It also discusses labour absorption in agriculture and male migration from the three villages. Chapter 11 examines the changes in wage rates in the study villages between 2009–10 and 2014–15, the different types of agricultural wage contracts, and the gender gap in wage rates. Chapter 12 analyses the level of household income and diversification of incomes.

The final section on poverty consists of chapter 13, which examines the different forms of deprivation experienced by the surveyed households in the study villages using four dimensions – incomes, assets, education, and housing and basic amenities. It concludes the book by trying to understand these deprivations in light of the findings from the previous chapters.

References

Bakshi, Aparajita (2010), "Rural Household Income," unpublished PhD thesis, University of Calcutta, Kolkata.

Bansal, Vaishali, Usami, Yoshifumi, and Rawal, Vikas (2018), *Agricultural Tenancy in Contemporary India: An Analytical Report and A Compendium of Statistical Tables based on NSSO Surveys of Land and Livestock Holdings*, SSER Monograph 18/1, Society for Social and Economic Research, New Delhi, available at http://archive. indianstatistics.org/sserwp/sserwp1801.pdf, viewed on October 20, 2020.

Basu, Ranjini (2015), "Land Tenures in Cooch Behar District, West Bengal: A Study of Kalmandasguri Village," *Review of Agrarian Studies*, vol. 5, no. 1, pp. 88–111.

Basu, Ranjini (2020), "Land Reforms in West Bengal: A Study of its Movement and Implementation," PhD thesis, Tata Institute of Social Sciences, Mumbai.

Das, Yasodhara (2019), "Socio-Economic Aspects of Migration from Rural India: A Study of West Bengal," PhD thesis, University of North Bengal, West Bengal.

Foundation for Agrarian Studies (FAS) (2015), "Calculation of Household Incomes - A Note on Methodology," available at http://fas.org.in/wp-content/themes/zakat/pdf/Survey-method-tool/Calculation%20of%20Household%20Incomes%20-%20A%20Note%20on%20Methodology.pdf, viewed on August 16, 2018.

Government of India (GoI) (2015), *All-India Report on Agriculture Census, 2010–11*, Department of Agriculture and Cooperation, Ministry of Agriculture and Farmers' Welfare, Government of India, New Delhi, available at http://agcensus.nic.in/document/ac1011/ac1011rep.html, viewed on June 15, 2018.

Modak, Tapas, and Bakshi, Aparajita (2017), "Changes in Groundwater Markets: A Case Study of Amarsinghi Village 2005 to 2015," *Review of Agrarian Studies,* vol. 7, no. 2, pp. 91–110.

Modak (2020), "Groundwater Irrigation in West Bengal after 1990: Policies, Institutional Arrangements and Its Implications for Farm Households," PhD thesis, Tata Institute of Social Sciences, Mumbai.

Ramachandran, V. K. (1995), "Universalising School Education: A Case Study of West Bengal," Draft paper, Indira Gandhi Institute of Development Research, Mumbai.

Ramachandran, V. K., Swaminathan, Madhura, and Rawal, Vikas (2003), "Barriers to Expansion of Mass Literacy and Primary Schooling in West Bengal: A Study Based on Primary Data from Selected Villages," CDS Working Paper No. 345, Centre for Development Studies, Thiruvananthapuram.

Rawal, Vikas (1999), "Irrigation Development in West Bengal, 1977–78 to 1995–96," unpublished PhD thesis, Indira Gandhi Institute of Development Research, Mumbai.

Rawal, Vikas (2006a), "Landlessness in Rural West Bengal," Report submitted to Development and Planning Department, Government of West Bengal.

Rawal, Vikas (2006b), "Indebtedness in Rural West Bengal," Report submitted to Development and Planning Department, Government of West Bengal.

Rawal, Vikas, and Swaminathan, Madhura (1998), "Changing Trajectories: Agricultural Growth in West Bengal, 1950 to 1996," *Economic and Political Weekly*, vol. 33, no. 40, October 3–9, pp. 2595–2602.

Rawal, Vikas, Swaminathan, Madhura, and Ramachandran, V. K. (2002), "Agriculture in West Bengal: Current Trends and Directions for Future Growth," background paper submitted for West Bengal State Development Report and Perspective, Kolkata.

Saha, Anamitra, and Swaminathan, Madhura (1994), "Agricultural Growth in West Bengal in the 1980s: A Disaggregation by Districts and Crops," *Economic and Political Weekly*, vol. 29, no. 13, March 26, pp. A2–A11.

Sarkar, Biplab (2017), "The Economics of Household Farming: A Study with Special Reference to West Bengal," unpublished PhD thesis, University of North Bengal, West Bengal.

Sen, Abhijit (1992), "Economic Liberalisation and Agriculture in India," *Social Scientist*, vol. 20, no. 11, pp. 4–12.

Appendix 1

Sampling Methodology for 2015 Surveys

Appendix Table 1a *Description of sample stratification, Panahar*

Strata I (operational holding)	Strata II (social group)	Census (2010)	Sample (2015)	Sampling probabilities of each stratum (C/A)
		A	B	C
Capitalist farmer		7	6	0.857
With operational holdings	Caste Hindu	67	31	0.463
	Muslim	2	1	0.5
	SC	94	39	0.415
	ST	14	6	0.429
Zero operational holdings	Caste Hindu	21	8	0.381
	Muslim	1	0	0
	SC/ST	42	15	0.357
Total		248	106	

Appendix Table 1b *Description of sample stratification, Amarsinghi*

Strata I (operational holding)	Strata II (social group)	Census (2010)	Sample (2015)	Sampling probabilities of each stratum (C/A)
		A	B	C
With operational holdings	Caste Hindu	60	28	0.467
	SC	34	12	0.353
Zero operational holdings	Caste Hindu	9	5	0.556
	SC/ST	24	10	0.417
Total		127	55	

Appendix Table 1c *Description of sample stratification, Kalmandasguri*

Strata I (operational holding)	Strata II (social group)	Census (2010)	Sample (2015)	Sampling probabilities of each stratum (C/A)
		A	B	C
With operational holdings	Caste Hindu	23	7	0.304
	Muslim	38	14	0.368
	SC	47	17	0.362
	ST	8	3	0.375
Zero operational holdings	Caste Hindu	4	2	0.5
	Muslim	23	7	0.304
	SC/ST	4	2	0.5
Total		147	52	

Appendix 2

Appendix Table 2a *Distribution of population by caste, Panahar, 2010*, in number and per cent

Caste/Tribe/Religion	Social group	Females	Males	Total	As percentage of total population
Bene	Caste Hindu	6	5	11	1
Brahmin		15	22	37	3.4
Goala		53	50	103	9.5
Karmakar		2	2	4	0.4
Kumbhakar		12	13	25	2.3
Majhi		16	21	37	3.4
Moira/Modak (Halwai)		14	11	25	2.3
Pallav Gope		3	3	6	0.6
Sadgop		50	49	99	9.1
Tanti		6	6	12	1.1
Teli		6	6	12	1.1
Vaishnava		42	40	82	7.6
Muslim	Muslim	14	15	29	2.7
Bagdi	SC	259	265	524	48.4
Kaibarta		5	7	12	1.1
Santhal	ST	35	30	65	6
All		538	545	1,083	100

Appendix Table 2b *Distribution of population by caste, Amarsinghi, 2010,* in number and per cent

Caste/Tribe/Religion	Social group	Females	Males	Total	As percentage of total population
Goala	Caste Hindu	3	2	5	0.9
Napit		6	6	12	2.1
Tanti	SC	149	147	296	51.5
Tiyar		129	129	258	44.9
Santhal	ST	2	2	4	0.7
All		289	286	575	100

Appendix Table 2c *Distribution of population by caste, Kalmandasguri, 2010,* in number and per cent

Caste/Tribe/Religion	Social group	Females	Males	Total	As percentage of total population
Baishya Kapali	Caste Hindu	3	5	8	1.1
Jogi		27	37	64	9.1
Kayastha		18	24	42	6.0
Napit		6	3	9	1.3
Muslim	Muslim	142	154	296	42.2
Muchi	SC	3	1	4	0.6
Rajbanshi		117	119	236	33.7
Nagesia	ST	8	16	24	3.4
Oraon		10	8	18	2.6
All		334	367	701	100

2

The Contemporary
Agricultural Economy of West Bengal

Aparajita Bakshi and Tapas Singh Modak[1]

Introduction

In this chapter, we try to identify and understand the dynamics of the rural economy of West Bengal in the period after 1990, and more specifically after 2000. The entire chapter is based on official sources of secondary data, to the extent that it might resemble a data compendium. Given that the three villages studied in great detail are microcosmic illustrations, the effort is to describe their general context as accurately and vividly as possible, in its multifaceted plurality.

With 23 districts and an area of 88,752 sq. km, the State of West Bengal comprises 2.2 per cent of the total geographical area of the country, and is home to 7.55 per cent of the Indian population. It is the fourth most populous and second most densely populated State in India at 1,029 persons per sq. km, which is much higher than the national average (382 persons per sq. km). The rural remains an important segment of the State, with 61.83 per cent of the population residing in rural areas in 2011. Though the pace of urbanisation has not been very rapid – the urban population increased only by 4.39 per cent between 1991 and 2011 – the rural economy of West Bengal has not remained unchanged (Census of India 2011).

In 2013–14, the sector of agriculture and allied activities contributed about 16.8 per cent of the net state domestic product (NSDP) of West Bengal. Though this share is higher than the national average of 13.9

[1] We thank R. Ramakumar for his initial analysis in the paper that he presented at the Symposium on Results from Three Study Villages in West Bengal in Durgapur, September 11–13, 2015, and also his extensive comments on the draft of this chapter.

per cent, West Bengal witnessed a rapid decline in the sectoral share of agriculture and allied activities in NSDP from 25 per cent in 2004–05 to 16.2 per cent in 2014–15. This trend of falling share of agriculture is observed all over India; however, in West Bengal, it is in contrast to the remarkable growth in agriculture in the 1980s that contributed significantly to the NSDP and the State economy. The estimated annual growth rate of the State's income from agriculture was 6.1 per cent between 1981 and 1990, double that in the previous decade (3 per cent in the 1970s) (Das 2010). After 1990, however, the growth in agricultural income decelerated – it was only 3.4 per cent between 1991 and 2006 (*ibid.*) – contributing to the fall in the share of agricultural NSDP. In more recent years, the NSDP growth rate in West Bengal has been driven by the growth of the services sector, and agricultural growth has fallen further. According to our estimates, the annual average growth rate of NSDP from agriculture and allied activities was only 2 per cent between 2004–05 and 2014–15, whereas the economy grew at 6.5 per cent per annum, largely led by the high growth in services sector (8.7 per cent per annum).

In the first section of this chapter, we examine the trends in agriculture in West Bengal with specific emphasis on the period after 2000. There is a large body of literature establishing the fact that West Bengal achieved high levels of growth in agricultural production in the 1980s, which could be attributed to specific technological and institutional changes in the State that were initiated in the late 1970s. The high levels of agricultural growth, particularly in the production of rice which is the main crop grown in West Bengal, decelerated in the 1990s and stagnated after 2000. In the second section of the chapter, we discuss some of the recent challenges facing the agrarian economy, which may have implications for the stagnation in agricultural production and decline in agriculture.

We have relied on official statistics published by Government of India and Government of West Bengal for the analysis, which is thus limited in terms of availability of data. We have tried to use the most recently published data, and hence, yearly end points in different tables may vary.

West Bengal Agriculture: From Impasse to Golden Age to Stagnation

Agricultural growth in West Bengal followed a unique trajectory in the post-Independence era. Till the late 1970s, in spite of favourable natural conditions, agricultural development in the State was characterised by stagnation. Estimates by Boyce (1987) showed that the growth rate of agricultural output was 1.74 per cent per annum between 1949 and 1980, which was below the annual population growth rate in the State (2.42 per cent). Official documents such as the S. R. Sen Committee report (1984) and the Seventh Five-Year Plan document (1985) mentioned that the gap between the potential and actual yields of rice, the major crop in the State, was very high in West Bengal and in eastern India in general (Mishra and Rawal 2002). It has been argued that the main causes for the agricultural stagnation from Independence through the 1970s were backward relations of production, a highly unequal agrarian structure retaining remnants of the colonial zamindari system, and stagnation in the forces of production in terms of poor infrastructural development, poor irrigation, and agricultural technology (Bhaduri 1973; Boyce 1987; Rawal and Swaminathan 1998; Mishra and Rawal 2002).[2]

In the 1980s, however, there was rapid growth in agricultural production. Sen and Sengupta (1995) found a trend break in the growth rate of total production and yield of rice and, in aggregate, foodgrains in 1981–82: the growth rate of agricultural value added per annum was 6.85 per cent in the 1980s as compared to 2.3 per cent in the 1970s. The divergence between regions and districts in the State with respect to production and yield of major crops also declined in this period; that is, agricultural growth was witnessed across all districts (Saha and Swaminathan 1994; Ramachandran, Swaminathan, and Bakshi 2010).

The State's high agricultural growth rate since the 1980s was on account of high growth in rice production brought about by two technological breakthroughs: the adoption of high-yielding and short-duration paddy varieties, and the spread of irrigation enabling summer rice cultivation (Rawal and Swaminathan 1998; Webster 1999).

The high agricultural growth in West Bengal in the 1980s was preceded by land reforms and reorganisation of the local governance system.[3] Scholars attribute these institutional reforms as a major contributing factor that led to agricultural growth (Sen and Sengupta 1995; Mukherjee and Mukhopadhyay1995; Ghatak 1995; Bhaumik 1993; Sengupta and Gazdar 1997). Ramachandran, Swaminathan, and Bakshi (2010, p. 234) state that

---

[2] See Mishra and Rawal (2002) for a detailed discussion.
[3] See chapter 4 of this book for a detailed discussion on land reforms and their implications on the agrarian structure of the State in general and the three villages in particular.

. . . the West Bengal path to agricultural growth was unique in the post-Independence era. In those parts of the rest of India that saw a rapid and substantial growth in agricultural incomes, the major sources of surplus accumulation were capitalist landlords, rich peasants, and, in general, the rural rich. In West Bengal, by contrast, the moving force of agricultural change and of the dynamism of the rural economy in the 1980s and 1990s were small cultivators. Agricultural growth in West Bengal was made possible because of the removal, by means of land reform and the establishment of panchayati raj, of institutional fetters to growth.

There has however been deceleration in the growth of agricultural output since the early 1990s (Ramachandran, Swaminathan, and Bakshi 2010; Bhattacharyya and Bhattacharyya 2007; Dasgupta and Bhaumik 2014). Bhattacharyya and Bhattacharyya (2007) found both a trend break and a decline in agricultural growth in West Bengal in 1992–93.

In the following sections we analyse the trends in production of rice and other important crops in West Bengal. Though the primary objective of the analysis is to understand the trajectory of agricultural growth after 2000, we have analysed data from the 1980s in order to be able to contrast the period after 2000 with previous decades of high agricultural growth. For the analysis, we have divided our study period (1980–81 to 2013–14) into three distinct sub-periods, 1980–81 to 1989–90, 1990–91 to 1999–00, and 2000–01 to 2013–14.[4]

Trends in Rice Production

Table 1 shows the exponential rates of growth of the area under rice cultivation, and its production and yield, for the period 1980–81 to 2013–14. We have used a three-year moving average method and then fitted a semi-logarithmic trend to calculate the growth rates. The growth rate of production of rice was the highest in the 1980s at 7.33 per cent per annum, which declined to 2.07 per cent in the 1990s and stagnated at 0.32 per cent in the subsequent period. A decomposition of the total growth of rice production into area sown with rice and yield of rice shows that growth in yield had contributed significantly to growth in the 1980s (Rawal and Swaminathan 1998). In the 1990s and 2000s, growth in yield

---

[4] Foodgrains, particularly rice, have been the primary crops in the State. From the trends of index numbers of foodgrains (particularly area and production), three different phases of agricultural growth in the State can be identified – rapid growth in 1980s, slowdown in 1990s, and stagnation between 2000–01 and 2013–14.

Table 1 *Exponential trend growth rates of area, production, and yield of rice, West Bengal, 1980–2014*, in per cent

Period	Area	Production	Yield
1980–81 to 1989–90	1.4	7.33	5.99
1990–91 to 1999–00	0.37	2.07	1.7
2000–01 to 2013–14	−0.75	0.32*	1.08

Note: * Estimates are not significant at a five per cent level of confidence.
Source: GoWB (various years).

declined but remained positive. The decrease in growth in yield combined with a reduction in area (at −0.75 per cent) resulted in stagnation of rice production in the 2000s.

In the 1980s, production of all three varieties of rice – *aus, aman,* and *boro* – grew at substantially high rates of 5.39 per cent, 6 per cent, and 13.54 per cent per annum, respectively (Table 2).[5] The high growth in production of *aus* and *aman* rice in this period was primarily due to significant growth in yield, whereas in the case of *boro* rice, rapid expansion of area was the primary contributor to growth in production. In the 1990s, however, there was a sharp decline in the growth rate of area, production, and yield of rice in all three seasons, in comparison to the previous decade. The slowdown of total rice production in the State in the 1990s was mainly on account of stagnation in the production of *aman* rice, which accounted for about two-thirds of the total net sown area under paddy. In the case of *boro* rice, the annual growth rates of area and production were still high at 5.71 per cent and 6.34 per cent per annum, respectively, but nevertheless was less than half the growth rate achieved in the 1980s. Between 2000–01 and 2013–14, there was a sharp decline in the production of *boro* rice, primarily due to decline in area, whereas yield growth had already decelerated since the 1990s. Area and production of *aus* rice continued to fall, while area and production of *aman* rice stagnated. Thus, the stagnation in rice production after the 2000s can be attributed to stagnation in *boro* yield and decline in area in all three seasons.

In general, district-level growth rates of rice show a similar trend as the State (see Appendix Table 1, Appendix Figure 1). Nevertheless, large variations are observed across districts. In the 1980s, all districts

---

[5] See Saha and Swaminathan (1994), Rawal and Swaminathan (1998).

Table 2 *Exponential trend growth rates of area, production, and yield of rice, by season, West Bengal, 1980–2014*, in per cent

Period	Aus			Aman			Boro		
	Area	Production	Yield	Area	Production	Yield	Area	Production	Yield
1980–81 to 1989–90	−0.36*	5.39	5.68	0.38	6	5.67	11.31	13.54	2.18
1990–91 to 1999–00	−3.98	−2.35	1.6	−0.54	0.66*	1.19	5.71	6.34	0.62
2000–01 to 2013–14	−5.66	−4.42	1.24	−0.37	0.91	1.3	−0.84	−0.31*	0.54
1980–81 to 2013–14	−3.97	−1.19	2.76	−0.19	2.15	2.35	3.86	4.4	0.54

Note: * Estimates are not significant at five per cent level of confidence. All others are highly significant.
Source: GoWB (various years).

experienced an annual growth in rice production above five per cent, with Jalpaiguri (2.4 per cent per annum) and Darjiling (3.21 per cent per annum) being the only exceptions. The highest annual growth rate of rice production was observed for districts located in the Old and New Alluvial agroclimatic zones,[6] whereas the growth rate of rice production in the districts of the Terai agroclimatic zone, such as Jalpaiguri, Koch Bihar, and Dinajpur, was moderate. In the 1990s, all districts experienced lower growth of rice production than in the 1980s. Yield growth declined significantly across all districts in the 1990s, though most districts saw positive growth ranging from one to three per cent per annum. Reduction in area under rice was already under way in many districts in the 1990s, while it stagnated for the State as a whole. The period between 2000–01 and 2013–14 showed further decline in the growth rate of rice production in the State as whole. All districts witnessed a decline or stagnation in area under rice. Yield growth stagnated in most districts, except for some in the Terai and the northern part of New Alluvial agroclimatic zone, such as Dinajpur, Maldah, Jalpaiguri, Koch Bihar, and Darjiling.

To sum up, rice production stagnated after 2000 and area under rice cultivation declined; yield growth almost stagnated for *boro* paddy and was low for *aman* and *aus* paddy.

---

[6] Both agroclimatic regions are rich in groundwater resources.

Other Features of Agricultural Growth after 2000

Stagnation in rice production and decline in rice area are important but not the only features accounting for poor performance of agriculture in West Bengal since the 2000s. There was a decline in the growth of cropping intensity that can be primarily attributed to slowdown in the growth of irrigation.[7] In West Bengal, a remarkable expansion of irrigation from the early 1980s led to an increase in gross cropped area and subsequently in cropping intensity. As shown in Figure 1, cropping intensity increased significantly in the 1980s and 1990s – from 139, 168, and 185 in 1980–81, 2000–01, and 2014–15, respectively. After 2005–06, however, the growth rate of cropping intensity slowed down in the State and across districts. The districts of Barddhaman, Haora, Nadia, Uttar Dinajpur, and Maldah experienced a decline in cropping intensity between 2005–06 and 2014–15, while it increased in Birbhum, Purba Medinipur, Paschim Medinipur, Hugli, North 24 Parganas, South 24 Parganas, and Puruliya districts.

Rice was and remains the dominant crop of West Bengal, though its share in total area has been declining over the years. As discussed in the previous section, the area under rice declined in all three seasons after 2000. Here, the decline in area under *boro* crop may be an important

Figure 1 *Cropping intensity, West Bengal, 1980–81 to 2014–15,* in per cent

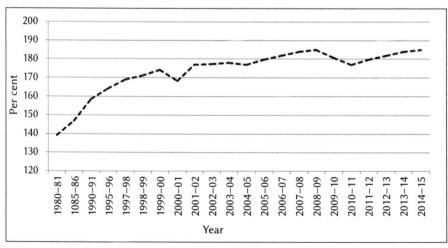

Source: GoWB (various years).

[7] See chapter 7 for a detailed analysis of irrigation in West Bengal.

constituent factor for stagnation in cropping intensity, as it is the major irrigated crop in the State.

While area and production of rice in particular and foodgrains in general stagnated after 2000, the good performance of crops such as oilseeds, potato, fruits, and vegetables in the 1980s and 1990s was also not sustained in the subsequent decades.

The production of oilseeds, mainly mustard and rapeseed, grew rapidly in the 1980s, at a rate of 12.02 per cent per annum (Table 3). Oilseeds have replaced to a large extent rabi cultivation of pulses in various districts since the 1980s. The growth rate of oilseed production was one of the highest among all crops after *boro* rice in the 1980s, and based on significant expansion in area under oilseeds and improvement in yields across all districts. For example, in the leading districts of Medinipur, Haora, Hugli, Birbhum, and West Dinajpur, oilseed production grew at more than 24 per cent per annum in the 1980s (Saha and Swaminathan 1994). This was due to the shorter duration of oilseeds compared to pulses, which allowed for cultivation of *boro* in the next season on triple-cropped, irrigated land. In subsequent years, however, oilseed production slowed down, and the growth rate of both area and yield declined. Though the 2000s saw some revival of growth in yield, growth of area declined. Barddhaman, Koch Bihar, Maldah, and Puruliya districts experienced negative growth in area under oilseeds in this period.

West Bengal is the second highest producer of potato in India, after Uttar Pradesh. In 2014–15, the State comprised about 20 per cent of the area under potato in the country but contributed about 25 per cent of total potato production. In the 1980s, the area under potato grew steadily in West Bengal at a rate of 6.62 per cent per annum, and resulted in an annual growth in production of 9 per cent (Table 4). Potato is largely an

Table 3 *Exponential trend growth rates of area, production, and yield of oilseeds, West Bengal, 1980–2014, in per cent*

Period	Area	Production	Yield
1980–81 to 1989–90	12.02	18.2	6.11
1990–91 to 1999–00	1.77*	2.09*	0.26*
2000–01 to 2013–14	1.16	3.75	2.17

Note: * Estimates are not significant at five per cent level of confidence; all others are highly significant.
Source: GoWB (various years).

irrigated rabi crop, and hence, the expansion of irrigation in the 1980s was instrumental in the expansion of the crop. In the 1990s, the growth rate of both area and production of potato declined to about 5 per cent in the State as whole, and further to 4.18 per cent after 2000. However, it must be noted that the area under potato continued to expand in most districts after 2000 (Appendix Table 2).

As one of the leading producers of vegetables in the country, the State produced about 2.6 million metric tons of vegetables in 2016–17, according to National Horticultural Board (NHB) estimates. Contributing to 14 per cent of total vegetable production in the country, West Bengal ranked second after Uttar Pradesh in area and production of total vegetables.

Unlike data on field crops where there are well-established methods of estimation, and regular collection and dissemination of statistics, the statistics on vegetables and fruits are neither as reliable nor regularly published. Statistics on horticultural crops are available only from 2000–01 onwards in the West Bengal Statistical Abstracts. As an alternate source, NHB data suggest rapid growth in area and production of vegetables in the 1990s (Table 5).[8] In 1991–92, the area under vegetables in the State was 4,56,000 hectares, and total production was about 46,80,000 metric tons. By 2001–02, the area under vegetables reached 11,39,000 hectares, about 15 per cent growth rate per annum, and total production increased to 1,80,75,000 metric tons, about 29 per growth rate per annum.[9] In the following decade, however, the growth rate in both area and production of vegetables was much lower, further dropping after 2010 (Table 5). In the case of fruits, growth of area and production in the 1990s was not as high

Table 4 *Exponential trend growth rates of area, production, and yield of potato, West Bengal, 1980–81 to 2013–14*, in per cent

Period	Area	Production	Yield
1980–81 to 1989–90	6.62	9	2.4
1990–91 to 1999–2000	5	5.61	0.58*
2000–02 to 2013–14	2.28	4.18	1.82*

Note: * Estimates are not significant at five per cent level of confidence; all others are highly significant.
Source: GoWB (various years).

[8] Due to data limitations, we could not analyse the data on fruits and vegetables in the 1980s.
[9] These are end point estimates; we could not undertake trend analysis.

Table 5 *Average annual growth rate of area and production of fruits and vegetables, West Bengal, 1991–92 to 2016–17,* in per cent

Year	Fruits		Vegetables	
	Area	Production	Area	Production
1991–92 to 2001–02	3.33	7.46	14.98	28.62
2001–02 to 2011–12	4.59	5.39	1.69	2.95
2011–12 to 2016–17	3.43	3.47	0.84	1.79

Note: These are end point estimates.
Source: National Horticultural Board (various years).

as that of vegetables and further declined over time. Nevertheless, the area under fruits increased by 3.43 per cent per annum between 2011–12 and 2016–17.

Thus, the post-2000 period in West Bengal witnessed not only stagnant production in rice, its major crop, but also deceleration in growth of area and production of other important crops such as oilseeds, potato, fruits, and vegetables.

Contemporary Challenges Facing the Agrarian Economy

Farm Size

Land reform measures implemented in the late 1970s and early 1980s democratised land ownership in the State to a large extent.[10] Though the measures provided ownership and tenancy rights to a large number of small farmers and incentivised production in the 1980s, small farm size has posed specific challenges for the agrarian economy in more recent years. There has been a rapid rise in landlessness, as the size of farms has become too small for cultivation.

---

[10] One important part of the land reform programme in West Bengal was to redistribute land to poor and landless households. Under the programme, by 2008, about 11,22,116 acres were redistributed to 29,71,875 landless and marginal-cultivator households. This constituted about 22.6 per cent of total land distributed in India (Ramachandran 2008). Scheduled Caste (SC), Scheduled Tribe (ST), and Muslim landless households were major beneficiaries of the programme, which led a significant reduction in inequalities of land ownership (Bakshi 2008, 2014). By 2011, among the total beneficiaries of land redistribution, 36 per cent were SC, 18 per cent were ST, and 44 per cent belonged to other groups of which Muslims were a major section (GoWB 2012).

Most of the agricultural land in West Bengal is owned and operated by small and marginal farmers. According to National Sample Survey Office (NSSO) estimates (2012–13), about 90.53 per cent of total households were marginal (owning less than or equal to one hectare), and their share in total land ownership holdings was 73.32 per cent (Table 6). At the all-India level for the same year, 73 per cent of total households were marginal and constituted only 28 per cent of land ownership holdings; the higher figures in Bengal was a result of the implementation of land reforms. There was not a single large landowner (owning more than 10 hectares) in the State in 2013. Furthermore, the average size of ownership holdings was much below the national average (0.592 hectare), and this too has been rapidly declining (Table 7). The distribution of ownership holdings in West Bengal is more equal than that of other States. According to NSSO estimates, the

Table 6 *Distribution of ownership landholdings by land-size class, West Bengal and India, 2013, in per cent*

Land-size class	West Bengal		India	
	Number	Area	Number	Area
Landless	6.55	0.01	7.41	0.01
Marginal (0.005–2.47 acres)	90.53	73.32	75.42	29.75
Small (2.47–4.94 acres)	2.44	18.9	10	23.54
Semi-medium (4.94–9.88 acres)	0.43	6.43	5.01	22.07
Medium (9.88–24.7 acres)	0.05	1.35	1.93	18.83
Large (>24.7 acres)	0	0	0.24	5.81
All	100	100	100	100

Note: Till 2002–03, the marginal category of landholdings included the landless. In 2012, the landless category was defined as owning less than or equal to 0.002 hectare.
Source: NSSO (2015).

Table 7 *Average size of household ownership holdings, West Bengal and India, 1992–2013, in hectare*

Year	West Bengal	India
1992	0.46	1.01
2003	0.295	0.725
2013	0.174	0.592

Source: NSSO (2015).

Table 8 *Proportion of households not cultivating land,*
West Bengal and India, 1999–2000 to 2011–12, in per cent

Year	West Bengal	India
1999–2000	48.1	40.9
2004–05	47.8	43.4
2009–10	62.2	47.1
2011–12	65	48.5

Source: Rawal (2013); computed from unit-level data, NSS Employment and Unemployment Surveys, various rounds.

value of Gini coefficient of operational landholdings in West Bengal has consistently declined since 1970 (Appendix Table 3 in Appendix).

Since the 2000s, however, farmers have been rapidly departing from agriculture, and there has been an increase in landlessness. Table 8 shows the sharp increase in the proportion of households not cultivating land in West Bengal, from 47.8 per cent to 62.2 per cent in 2004–05 and 2009-10, respectively. This is a distinct shift from previous decades in West Bengal, as well as from the general trend in India.

Proletarianisation of the Agricultural Workforce

There is a tendency of proletarianisation of the agricultural workforce in West Bengal, even though agricultural workers comprising cultivators and agricultural labourers still constitute the largest share of the workforce in the rural economy of West Bengal (Table 9). In 2011, the proportion of agricultural workers was 61.5 per cent – 20.6 per cent of whom were cultivators and 40.9 per cent agricultural labourers. From 2001 to 2011, the share of cultivators declined from 26 to 21 per cent of rural workers, while the share of agricultural labour increased from 33 to 41 per cent. As a matter of fact, taking the rural economy as a whole, the share of agricultural workers increased, while that of all other types of workers decreased. We also observe an increase in the proportion of marginal workers in general, from 26 to 32 per cent; this is primarily on account of an increase in the share of marginal agricultural labourers.

These trends in the composition of workforce are replicated in every district of the State. There is a decline in the percentage of main workers and a corresponding increase in marginal workers in all districts except Nadia and Uttar Dinajpur, where the shares have remained unchanged

Table 9 *Distribution of rural workforce, by category of worker, West Bengal, 2001 and 2011,* in per cent

Category of worker	2001			2011		
	Main worker	Marginal worker	Total	Main worker	Marginal worker	Total
Cultivator	21	5	26	17	4	21
Agricultural labourer	20	13	33	23	17	40
Household industry worker	5	3	8	4	3	7
Other	28	6	34	24	7	31
Total	74	26	100	68	32	100

Source: Census of India (2001, 2011).

Figure 2 *Share of cultivators (main and marginal) in total workers, West Bengal and districts, 2001 and 2011,* in per cent

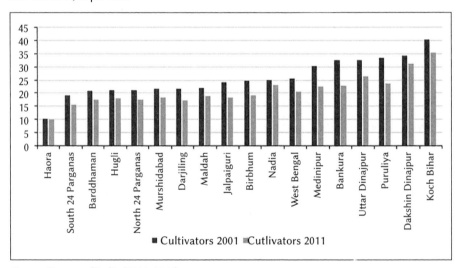

Source: Census of India (2001, 2011).

(see Appendix Table 4). All districts showed a decline in the share of cultivators (main and marginal) between 2001 and 2011 (Figure 2). The decline was high in districts in the lateritic belt – Puruliya, Medinipur, Bankura, and Birbhum, and the hilly districts of Koch Bihar and Jalpaiguri; these are regions that face limitations of groundwater potential and use.[11]

---

[11] See chapter 7 in this book.

There was an increase in the proportion of agricultural labourers in total workers in all districts between 2001 and 2011 (Appendix Figure 2). At the same time, there were not enough days of employment available for agricultural workers, and hence, there was an increase in marginal workers in this category. Census data also have shown that there has been an increase in out-migration of workers from West Bengal to other parts of the country.[12]

Increase in Non-Agricultural Employment[13]

In recent years there has been a shift away from agriculture in the occupational structure of rural West Bengal. Though such change is observed in India as a whole, the decline in agricultural employment in West Bengal is more pronounced than the national trend.

Tables 10 and 11 indicate the distribution of workers by industry in rural West Bengal and rural India during the last decade, by using usual principal status. Workers in agriculture are divided into self-employed (code no. 11) including employers (12), family helpers (21), and agricultural labourers (31 and 51). From 2004–05 to 2015–16, both the shares of male workers in agricultural self-employment and male agricultural labourers in the total workforce in rural West Bengal declined – the former from 32 to 23.6 per cent and the latter from 32.1 to 25.4 per cent. The decline in the shares of agricultural workers in both categories was much lower than those for India. Furthermore, West Bengal had a lower proportion of male workers in agriculture than the national average.

In the case of female workers, the share of those self-employed in agriculture sharply declined from 31.5 to only 16.7 per cent in 2004–05 and 2015–16, respectively, whereas the share of female agricultural labourers increased marginally from 28 to 31.3 per cent. These changes differ from the all-India trends, showing a smaller decline in the share of female workers self-employed in agriculture and a larger increase in the share of female agricultural labourers. A major proportion (71.6 per cent) of the rural female workforce in India is employed in agriculture. However, the occupational structure of rural West Bengal is distinct, with less than half (48 per cent) of rural female workers employed in agriculture (Table 11).

Thus, non-agricultural employment is the dominant form of employment for both male and female workers in rural West Bengal. In

---

[12] See chapter 10 in this book.
[13] This section is written with inputs from Arindam Das.

the decade after 2004–05, employment in construction and manufacturing increased rapidly for both male and female workers. Female employment in manufacturing is remarkably high (29.6 per cent) in West Bengal and is also increasing in services.

The occupational shift in rural West Bengal may be related to low levels of income for households employed in agriculture. Estimates from the NSS Situation Assessment of Agricultural Households, 2013 show that

Table 10 *Distribution of male workers (by usual principal status), by industry, rural West Bengal and India, 2004–16,* in per cent

Sector	West Bengal			All India			Average growth, 2004–15	
	2004–05	2011–12	2015–16	2004–05	2011–12	2015–16	West Bengal	India
Agriculture (self-employment)	32	21.7	23.6	42.2	38.9	35	−35.6	−10
Agricultural labour	32.1	35.2	25.4	24.1	20.4	19.3	−26.4	−5.4
Manufacturing	9	12.6	13.9	8.8	8.9	8.7	35.3	−2.2
Construction	4.9	10.2	13.4	6.9	13	13.6	63.4	4.6
Services	22	20.3	23.8	18	18.7	23.4	7.6	25.1

Note: Mining and electricity/gas/water are included in manufacturing.
Source: NSSO (2013, 2006).

Table 11 *Distribution of female workers (by usual principal status), by industry, rural West Bengal and India, 2004–16,* in per cent

Sector	West Bengal			All India			Average growth 2004–15	
	2004–05	2011–12	2015–16	2004–05	2011–12	2015–16	West Bengal	India
Agriculture (self-employment)	31.5	14.5	16.7	53.8	48.1	36.9	−88.6	−23.3
Agricultural labour	28	27.4	31.3	29.7	26.8	34.7	10.5	29.5
Manufacturing	28.2	41.7	29.6	8.6	10	8.2	4.7	−18
Construction	0.5	3	5.5	1.5	6.7	7.2	90.9	7.5
Services	11.8	13.4	16.9	6.6	8.4	13	30.2	54.8

Note: Mining and electricity/gas/water are included in manufacturing.
Source: NSSO (2013, 2006).

the average annual income for agricultural households in West Bengal was only Rs 47,760 in 2012–13, much lower than the national average of Rs 77,112. Further, income from cultivation accounted for only 24.6 per cent of total household income of agricultural households, lower than the national average of 47.9 per cent.

State Expenditure in Agriculture and Rural Development

Public expenditure on agriculture and components related to the agrarian economy has been low in West Bengal since the 1990s, and remains so till today. Despite being a major producer of agricultural goods, expenditure in agriculture and allied activities was less than one per cent of total government expenditure and around 0.05 per cent of the State's NSDP in 2017–18.

In an analysis of public expenditures on the "rural economy" (comprising expenditures on agriculture and allied activities, rural development, fertilizer subsidies, cooperation, and irrigation), Jha and Acharya (2011) delineated the following three broad phases for India: a slackening of public expenditure on the rural economy after the First Five-Year Plan, a revival of expenditure after the mid-1970s, and relative neglect since the early 1990s. In their analysis of Indian States, the authors pointed out that West Bengal's budgetary expenditure for the rural economy in the 1990s and 2000s was quite poor compared to other States. The average share of expenditure on the rural economy in total expenditure declined from 19.39 to 16.34 per cent during the 1990s, and further to only 9.07 per cent during the 2000s. The State's share of this expenditure has always been below the national average, and in the 2000s, its spending was among the lowest of Indian States.

To understand State investment in agriculture, we examined the trends in four expenditure components from 2004-05 onwards: expenditures in agriculture and allied activities, rural development, irrigation, and panchayati raj institutions (PRIs) that indirectly support agriculture. Each of these components constitutes a very small fraction – less than one per cent – of total expenditure (Figure 3).

Expenditure on agriculture and allied activities has remained below one per cent throughout the period, with minor fluctuations. Though it increased in real terms after 2013–14 (Figure 4), from 20,588 million (at 2014–15 prices) in 2013–14 to 29,690 million in 2017–18, its share in total expenditure only increased from 0.6 to 0.9 per cent, in 2013–14 and 2015–16 respectively, and dropped below 0.5 per cent in the subsequent years.

Expenditure in rural development increased from Rs 34,638 million to

Rs 1,37,636 million (both figures at 2014–15 prices) as did its share in total expenditure, from 1 to 2.9 per cent in 2013–14 and 2015–16, respectively, which further settled below 2 per cent in subsequent years. In the case of irrigation, expenditure increased marginally from Rs 13,947 million to Rs 18,071 million, while its share in total expenditure remained below 0.5 per cent. Expenditure on PRIs decreased in real terms throughout the decade.

Though expenditure in agriculture and rural development has somewhat increased in the last few years, we should not overemphasise the numbers. Expenditure on agriculture and components indirectly related to it remained low over the entire period. None of the components, except rural development, surpassed one per cent of the total State expenditure. Rural employment formed the major component of expenditure on rural development – the increase in this, till 2014–15, was on account of increase in expenditure in rural employment.[14] A cursory check of West Bengal's performance in MGNREGA showed that there was no consistent increase in person days generated.[15] Increase in wages may be the driving

Figure 3 *Share of agriculture and allied activities, rural development, irrigation, and PRIs in total expenditure, West Bengal, 2004–05 to 2017–18, in per cent*

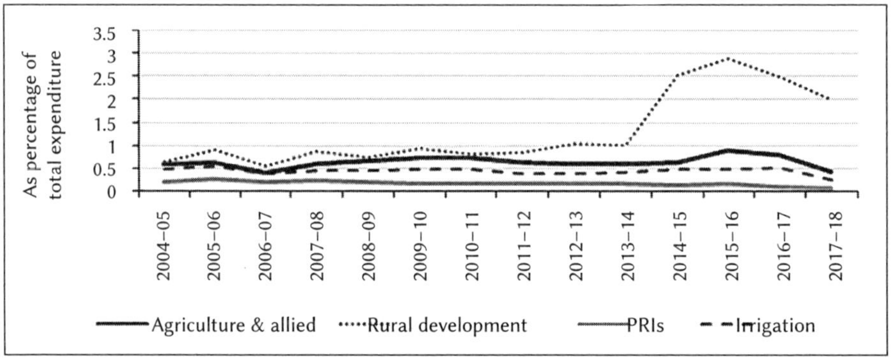

Source: Reserve Bank of India (various years).

[14] RBI does not provide disaggregated data on the components of rural development. Statistical Abstracts published by the GoWB however provide disaggregated data on revenue expenditure showing that increase in rural development expenditure was on account of increase in expenditure on rural employment. The 2015 Statistical Abstract provides data on revenue expenditure till 2014–15 but not on capital expenditures.

[15] Person days generated under MGNREGA in West Bengal in fact declined from 229,634,013 in 2013–14 to 169,497,114 in 2014–15 and then increased to 286,403,332 the next year (data sourced from MGNREGA MIS).

Figure 4 *Budgetary expenditure on agriculture and allied activities, rural development, irrigation, and PRIs, West Bengal, 2004-05 to 2017–18*, in million Rs at 2014–15 prices

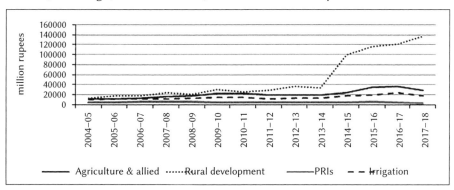

Note: Expenditures have been adjusted to 2014–15 prices using implicit SDP deflator, which is the ratio of SDP at current and constant (2014–15 base) prices.
Source: Reserve Bank of India (various years).

factor behind the increase in expenditure on rural employment and, consequently, rural development.

Conclusion

In this chapter, we have attempted to outline the major features of the agrarian economy of West Bengal after 2000. The most visible feature of this period, in our view, is the decline and near stagnation of agriculture, particularly in terms of the physical production of major crops. The stagnation in agricultural production is largely due to a decline in cropped area and a tapering-off of major crop yields. The agricultural economy is overwhelmingly dependent on the production of rice, the major crop of the State. After the golden age of rice production in the 1980s, when both area under rice cultivation and rice yields increased significantly, the growth of rice production declined in the 1990s and stagnated after 2000. The stagnation was on account of decline in area and near stagnation in yield growth. Other crops such as oilseeds, potato, fruits, and vegetables that showed promising trends of growth in the 1980s and 1990s also slowed down after 2000.

The agricultural economy of West Bengal faces serious challenges as of recent times, even as farmers are rapidly exiting agriculture (suggested by an increase in the proportion of non-cultivating households after 2004–

05). Agriculture is dominated by extremely small-sized farms, wherein the average size of ownership holdings is less than half an acre. The small size of holdings poses two types of challenges for farming households. First, there is an inability to diversify production due to land constraints, as seen by a rice-dominated cropping pattern. Though there is some diversification to fruits and vegetables, which may fetch higher incomes, their share in cropped area remains small. Secondly, small farmers are capital-constrained. When state support to agriculture reduces, adverse impacts such as reduction in profits and investments manifest more acutely in small farmer economies. West Bengal's budgetary expenditure on the rural economy has always been below the national average, and such expenditure has been declining since the 1990s. This means that the State's support to agriculture and the rural economy shrank at a time when small producers were increasingly feeling the pressure of competitive market forces. Since 2013–14, there has been a slight increase in expenditure on rural development on account of rising wages, but its share in total expenditure remains low. The secondary data point to the problem of capital accumulation in agriculture, particularly the stagnation of cropping intensity and gross irrigated area. Our village data provide a deeper understanding of the problem.

References

Bakshi, Aparajita (2014), "Land Reform and Access to Land among Dalit Households in West Bengal" in V. K. Ramachandran, and Madhura Swaminathan (eds.), *Dalit Households in Village Economies*, Tulika Books, New Delhi., pp. 111–132.

Bakshi, Aparajita (2008), "Social inequality in land ownership in India: A study with particular reference to West Bengal," *Social Scientist*, vol. 39, no. 9–10, pp. 95-116

Bhaduri, Amit (1973), "Agricultural Backwardness under Semi-Feudalism," *The Economic Journal*, vol. 83, vol. 329, pp. 120–37.

Bhattacharyya, Maumita and Bhattacharyya, Sudipta (2007), "Agrarian Impasse in West Bengal in the Liberalisation Era," *Economic and Political Weekly*, vol. 42, no. 52, pp. 65–71.

Bhaumik, Sankar Kumar (1993), *Tenancy Relations and Agrarian Development: A Study of West Bengal*, Sage Publications, New Delhi.

Boyce, James K. (1987), *Agrarian Impasse in Bengal: Agricultural Growth in Bangladesh and West Bengal, 1949-1980*, Oxford University Press, New York.

Census of India (2011), "Primary Census Abstract," Office of the Registrar General & Census Commissioner, Ministry of Home Affairs, Government of India.

Census of India (2001), "Primary Census Abstract," Office of the Registrar General & Census Commissioner, Ministry of Home Affairs, Government of India.

Das, Panchanan (2010), "Growth and Structural Changes," *West Bengal Development Report*, Planning Commission, Government of India, New Delhi.

Dasgupta, Suranjana and Bhaumik, Sankar Kumar (2014), "Crop Diversification and Agricultural Growth in West Bengal," *Indian Journal of Agricultural Economics*, vol. 69, no. 1, January–March, pp. 108–24.

Ghatak, Maitreesh (1995), "Reforms, Incentives and Growth in West Bengal Agriculture," Paper presented at Workshop on Agricultural Growth and Agrarian Structure in Contemporary West Bengal and Bangladesh, Calcutta, January 1995.

Government of India (GoI) (2016), *Report on Fifth Annual Employment–Unemployment Survey 2015–16*, Ministry of Labour and Employment, Labour Bureau, Chandigarh

Government of West Bengal (GoWB) (2012), *Economic Review 2010-11*, Bureau of Statistics and Planning, Kolkata.

Government of West Bengal (GoWB) (various years), *Statistical Abstract 1980–81 to 2014–15*, Bureau of Statistics and Planning, Kolkata.

Jha, Praveen and Acharya, Nilachala (2011), "Expenditure on the Rural Economy in India's Budgets since the 1950s: An Assessment," *Review of Agrarian Studies*, vol. 1, no. 2, pp. 134–56.

Mishra, Surjya Kanta and Rawal, Vikas (2002), "Agrarian Relations in Contemporary West Bengal and Tasks for the Left," in V. K. Ramachandran and Madhura Swaminathan (eds.), *Essays on Agrarian Relations in Less-Developed Countries*, Tulika Books, New Delhi., pp. 329–55.

Mukherjee, Badal and Mukhopadhyay, Swapna (1995), "Impact of Institutional Change on Productivity in a Small-Farm Economy–Case of Rural West Bengal," *Economic and Political Weekly*, vol. 33, no. 34, pp. 2134–37.

National Horticultural Board (NHB) (various years), *Horticultural Statistics at a Glance 1991–91 to 2016–17*, Department of Agriculture Cooperation and Farmers Welfare, Ministry of Agriculture and Farmers Welfare, Government of India.

National Sample Survey Office (NSSO) (2015), *Household Ownership and Operational Holdings in India, NSS 70th Round, Report No. 571*, Ministry of Statistics and Programme Implementation, Government of India.

National Sample Survey Office (NSSO) (2013), Key Indicators of the *Employment and Unemployment in India 2011-12, NSS 68th Round, Report No. 68/10*, Ministry of Statistics and Programme Implementation, Government of India.

National Sample Survey Office (NSSO) (2006), *Employment and Unemployment Situation in India 2004-05, NSS 61st Round, Report No. 515 (61/10/1)*, Ministry of Statistics and Programme Implementation, Government of India.

Ramachandran, V. K., Swaminathan, Madhura, and Bakshi, Aparajita (2010), "Food Security and Crop Diversification: Can West Bengal Achieve Both Simultaneously?," in Banasri Basu, Bikash K. Chakrabarti, Satya R. Chakravarty, and Kaushik Gangopadhyay (eds.), *Econophysics and Economics of Games, Social Choices and Quantitative Techniques*, Springer, Segrate, pp. 233–40.

Ramachandran, V. K (2008), "Land Reform Continues in West Bengal", *The Hindu*, August 22, http://www.thehindu.com/2008/08/22/stories/2008082255051100.htm

Rawal, Vikas (2013), "Changes in the Distribution of Operational Landholdings in Rural India: A Study of National Sample Survey Data," *Review of Agrarian Studies*, vol. 3, no. 2, pp. 73–104.

Rawal, Vikas, and Swaminathan, Madhura (1998), "Changing Trajectories: Agricultural Growth in West Bengal, 1950 to 1996," *Economic and Political Weekly*, vol. 33, no. 40, pp. 2595–2602.

Reserve Bank of India (RBI) (various years), *State Finances: A Study of Budgets*, Mumbai.

Saha, Anamitra and Swaminathan, Madhura (1994), "Agricultural Growth in West Bengal in the 1980s: A Disaggregation by Districts and Crops," *Economic and Political Weekly*, vol. 19, no. 13, pp. A2–A11.

Sen, Abhijit and Sengupta, Ranja (1995), "The Recent Growth in Agricultural Output in Eastern India, with Special Reference to the case of West Bengal," Paper presented at Workshop on Agricultural Growth and Agrarian Structure in Contemporary West Bengal and Bangladesh, Calcutta, January 1995.

Sengupta, Sunil and Gazdar, Haris (1997), "Agrarian Politics and Rural Development in West Bengal," in Jean Drèze and Amartya Sen (eds.), *Indian Development Selected Regional Perspectives*, Oxford University Press, Delhi, pp. 129–204.

Webster, Neil (1999), "Institutions, Actors and Strategies in West Bengal's Rural Development-A Study on Irrigation," in Ben Rogaly, Barbara Harriss-White, and Sugata Bose (eds.), *Sonar Bangla: Agricultural Growth and Agrarian Change in West Bengal and Bangladesh*, Sage Publications, New Delhi, pp. 329–56.

Appendix

Appendix Table 1 *Exponential trend growth rates of area, production, and yield of rice, West Bengal districts, 1980–81 to 2013–14*, in per cent

District	1980–81 to 1989–90			1990–91 to 1999–2000			2000–01 to 2013–14		
	Area	Produc-tion	Yield	Area	Produc-tion	Yield	Area	Produc-tion	Yield
Barddhaman	1.56	7.21	5.75	2.33	3.58	1.23	−0.66	0*	0.67
Birbhum	0.82	7.86	7.19	0.97	3.85	2.83*	−0.52*	0.15*	0.7
Bankura	1.66	8.69	7.22	−0.32*	2.03	2.31	−0.78*	−0.52*	0.21*
Medinipur	0.93	8.25	7.39	0.6	2.06	1.45	0.15*	0.97	0.83
Haora	3.71	8.74	5.09	−0.83*	−1.49*	−0.68*	−1.39	−0.81*	0.58*
Hugli	1.4	5.04	3.72	0.54*	1.45	0.94	−0.14*	0.95	1.11
24 Parganas	0.84	7.15	6.31	0.77	1.38	0.61*	−1.73	−0.84	0.9
Nadia	3.56	10.59	7.08	0.99	1.7	0.72	−2.4	−1.84	0.54
Murshidabad	1.93	8.45	6.64	−0.30*	1.58	1.89	−0.54*	0.3*	0.87
Dinajpur	0.43*	6.07	5.64	0.42	3.38	2.97	−1.62	0.23*	1.86
Maldah	2.52	6.24	3.69	−1.09	1.57	2.68	−0.52*	1.58	2.11
Jalpaiguri	0.18*	2.4	2.32	−0.78	0.15*	0.87*	−1.26	2.02	3.28
Darjiling	3.78	3.21	−0.57*	−4.84	−6.49	−1.73*	−0.96	2.33	3.29
Koch Bihar	1.47	5.12	3.65	−1.21	0.09*	1.29	−0.05*	3.02	3.09
Puruliya	2.22	7.47	5.57	−0.36*	2.09	2.3	−0.40*	0.63*	0.89
West Bengal	1.4	7.32	5.99	0.37	2.07	1.7	−0.75	0.32	1.08

Note: * Estimates are not significant at five per cent level of confidence; all others are highly significant.
Source: GoWB (various years).

Appendix Table 2 *Exponential trend growth rates of area, production and yield of potato, West Bengal districts, 1980–81 to 2013–14*, in per cent

District	1980–81 to 1989–90			1990–91 to 1999–2000			2000–01 to 2013–14		
	Area	Produc-tion	Yield	Area	Produc-tion	Yield	Area	Produc-tion	Yield
Barddhaman	5.32	6.35	1.01	2.18*	2.67	0.56*	2.2	3.23	0.99*
Birbhum	8.57	13.87	5.3	5.74	6.33	0.5*	4.09	6.83	2.75*
Bankura	10.42	15.07	4.19	4.94	3.48	−1.51	3.2	5.29	1.97*
Medinipur	11.58	15.55	4.03	5.18	6.48	1.32	−0.26*	0.37*	0.57*
Haora	7.19	10.4	3.53	13.39	12.17	−1.18*	−0.52*	0.93*	1.38*
Hugli	6.01	7.16	1.2*	3.34	2.17*	−1.27*	1.46	4.03	2.43*
24 Parganas	−1.57*	5.12	7.21	8.72	12.79	4.06	1.3*	4.82	3.49
Nadia	−4.25*	0.96*	5.42	8.02	10.19	2.13	3.08	5.36	2.3
Murshidabad	−2.23*	2.24*	4.55	3.91	5.52	1.63	3.85	5.58	1.74*
Dinajpur	1.88*	2.7*	0.84*	6.02	19	12.86	3.15	7.72	4.57
Maldah	4.16	9.13	4.98	4.99	10.58	5.67	6.51	12.38	5.88
Jalpaiguri	13.95	18.1	4.01	13.07	20.76	7.54	6.22	8.81	2.55
Darjiling	3.58	3.2	−0.48*	1.18*	7.12	5.12	0.54	2.08	1.53
Koch Bihar	13.47	16.94	3.84	13.72	22.63	8.89	7.94	9.35	1.37*
Puruliya	22.61	14.2	−8.5	0.45*	3.65	3.13	−2.02*	0.98*	2.83
West Bengal	6.62	9	2.4	5	5.61	0.58*	2.28	4.18	1.82*

Note: * Estimates are not significant at five per cent level of confidence; all others are highly significant.
Source: GoWB (various years).

Appendix Table 3 *Gini coefficient of distribution of operational holdings, West Bengal and India, 1970–71 to 2013*

	1970–71	1982	1992	2003	2013
West Bengal	0.433	0.494	0.43	0.313	0.223
India	0.567	0.596	0.591	0.557	0.516

Source: NSSO (2015).

Appendix Table 4 *Share of main workers in total workers, West Bengal and districts, 2001 and 2011,* in per cent

District	2001	2011
Bankura	65	61
Barddhaman	74	72
Birbhum	72	66
Dakshin Dinajpur	75	73
Darjiling	80	72
Haora	79	75
Hugli	78	75
Jalpaiguri	76	72
Koch Bihar	77	78
Maldah	71	66
Medinipur	66	57
Murshidabad	83	76
Nadia	86	86
North 24 Parganas	83	79
Puruliya	55	46
South 24 Parganas	73	63
Uttar Dinajpur	75	75
West Bengal	74	68

Source: Census of India (2001, 2011).

Appendix Figure 1 *District-wise yield of paddy, West Bengal, 1981–82, 1995–96, 2005–06, and 2013–14*

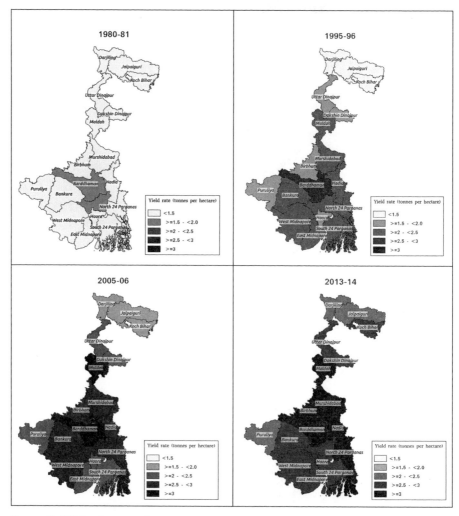

Source: GoWB (various years)

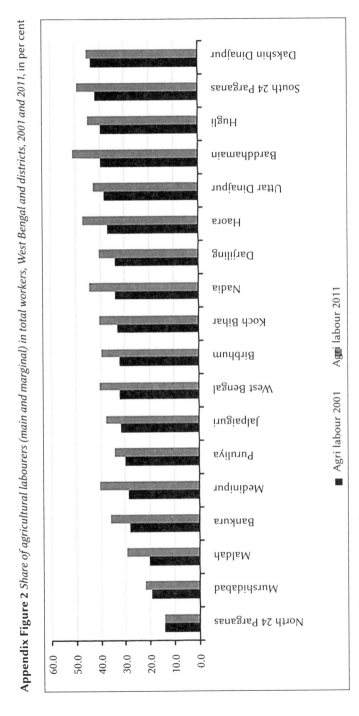

Appendix Figure 2 *Share of agricultural labourers (main and marginal) in total workers, West Bengal and districts, 2001 and 2011, in per cent*

Source: Census of India (2001, 2011).

3

Nature of Classes in Rural West Bengal, with Insights from Three Villages

Aparajita Bakshi, Tapas Singh Modak, and Arindam Das

Introduction

This chapter describes the socio-economic classes in the three villages surveyed in West Bengal and the criteria used for such classification. This classification is used by authors for their analyses in subsequent chapters. We use the term "socio-economic class" in the Marxist sense, to understand differentiation that emanates from varied ownership and control over the means of production and the relationships that emerge thereof.

In the classical Marxist literature on class differentiation in agriculture, three criteria are used to identify different classes: ownership of the means of production (of which land is an important but not exclusive component), relative use of hired and family labour or the labour ratio, and the surplus generated in the process of production (Mao Tse Tung 1933; Lenin 1972). These criteria need to be adapted and interpreted when applied to differing local contexts. The parameters that could enable us to capture a historical and dynamic concept such as class also need to be dynamic in nature – changing over time and space. Hence, in our analysis, the criteria we use to identify different classes may vary across villages to reflect the differences in local production conditions and historical circumstances.[1]

---

[1] See Ramachandran (2010, 2011, 2017) for the identification and classification of socio-economic classes in village surveys conducted by the Foundation for Agrarian Studies.

Classes in West Bengal in a Historical Perspective

The question of class and class struggle has featured prominently in the political history of rural West Bengal since the colonial era. The colonial legacy of the Permanent Settlement land revenue system led to the emergence of the most exploitative form of *zamindari* and clearly divided the rural polity into rent-seeking zamindars (most often absentee landlords settled in cities) and their retinue of rack-rentiers on one side, and exploited cultivators and sharecroppers on the other. During this time, the Bengal famine was the worst manifestation of this class conflict. The acute poverty and desperation of the peasantry led to the militant Tebhaga movement in 1946, when the cultivators, led by the Bengal Provincial Kisan Sabha, demanded that a two-thirds share of the produce be given to the tenant.[2] There were also other peasant struggles before and during the Tebhaga movement that demanded the removal of market taxes (*haat-tola*) collected by landlords, the lowering of interest rates on paddy loans (*karja*) taken by sharecroppers from landlords, and that protested against the increase in canal tax in Barddhaman district (Bakshi 2014a; Sen 1972). These struggles were a reflection of rising class antagonism between the zamindars (and their sub-tenants), who were in close contact with the colonial government, and the actual cultivators, who were burdened by high rents and taxes and falling production.

The class antagonism that emerged from the exploitative *zamindari* system also created fertile ground for the rise of left politics in Bengal and the emergence of the Krishak Sabha (see Sen 1972; Bakshi 2014a, 2014b). After Independence, land reforms – initiated during the two brief United Front governments (of which the Communist Party of India was a major constituent) in 1967 and 1969, and taken forward during the uninterrupted 34-year office of the Left Front government from 1977 – had its historical roots in the peasant struggles of the 1940s. The demands raised in those struggles – land to the tiller, security of tenure, and a fixed share for sharecroppers – were rights granted through land reforms. Major institutional reforms made through the devolution of powers to local governments, the panchayats, broke the economic and political

---

[2] The literal translation of *tebhaga* is "three shares". The demand of the Tebhaga movement was that the produce be divided into three equal shares – one each for land (landowner), labour (tenant cultivator), and all other inputs (the one who incurs the costs, usually the tenant). This was previously recommended by the Floud Commission in 1940.

stronghold of the erstwhile rentier classes and brought the movement for land reforms to fruition. According to Surjya Kanta Mishra, erstwhile Minister of Panchayats and Rural Development of West Bengal, "There could not have been a panchayat in 1978 without land reforms. Without panchayats there could not have been Operation Barga."[3]

The land reform measures undertaken by the Left Front government were able to break up the land monopoly and extreme class antagonism in the Bengal countryside. Between 1970–71 and 2002, the share of large and medium operational holdings in West Bengal declined from 0.1 and 3 per cent of all operational holdings to 0 and 0.2 per cent, respectively; their combined share in total operated area decreased from 15.2 to 2.7 per cent (Mishra 2007; NSSO 2006). Mishra and Rawal (2002) summarised the changes in agrarian relations in West Bengal triggered by land reforms as follows. A large number of agricultural workers acquired small parcels of land through land reforms and were also able to purchase ceiling-surplus land from landowners. At the same time, agricultural wages and agricultural employment improved in the period of high agricultural growth following land reforms. Sharecroppers gained permanent and heritable sharecropping rights (*barga*) to land, which increased their bargaining power vis-à-vis landlords. They were also able to purchase land and grow multiple crops on the same land with the development of irrigation. Introduction of irrigated crops in the summer and rabi seasons also led to the emergence of short-term, fixed-rent contracts, which further increased land access for sharecroppers and small farmers. Small and marginal farmers also acquired land through land markets after land reforms. They were able to intensify agricultural production by purchasing irrigation water and accessing subsidised inputs such as seeds.

Land reforms weakened the large landowning classes but did not decimate them. These households lost land but benefited from the overall development of agriculture. They cultivated land more intensively and took advantage of the various opportunities outside agriculture – in services, trade, and business. This class of the "new rural rich" was

---

[3] Personal interview with Surjya Kanta Mishra, September 3, 2014. Mishra served as minister of Panchayats and Rural Development in West Bengal from 1996 to 2011. Operation Barga conferred permanent and heritable tenancy rights to registered sharecroppers or *bargadar*s. More than 1.5 million *bargadar*s cultivating 1.1 million acres of land were registered under Operation Barga (Mishra 2007). Panchayats played a major role in the identification and registration of *bargadar*s.

"neither purely feudal nor capitalist: one may actually find the existence of elements of both pre-capitalist and capitalist relationships in one and the same person" *(ibid.,* p. 344).

The achievements of land reforms were significant, but they did not completely transform production and production relations. Though there was rapid agricultural growth, commercialisation, and increased use of modern inputs and irrigation, agricultural production in West Bengal was and remains primarily small peasant production. The small size of landholdings and subdivision and fragmentation of land continued to pose significant challenges to the agrarian economy. The contractionary economic policies of the 1990s did not augur well for such a production system. As government support declined, the problems of smallholding agriculture emerged and agricultural growth stagnated. These changes accentuated tendencies of proletarianisation and the rise of a large informal non-agricultural sector. Based on National Sample Survey (NSS) data of various Employment and Unemployment Surveys, Rawal (2013) estimated that the proportion of households not cultivating any land in rural West Bengal increased from 39.6 per cent in 1987–88 to 65 per cent in 2011–12. These developments led to substantive changes in the class configuration of rural West Bengal.

In an article written for a special issue of the Bengali newspaper *Ganashakti,* Mishra (2013) identified changing features of classes in rural West Bengal in contemporary times, based on his observation and political experience. He emphasised that the proletarian and semi-proletarian classes, who participated in both the agricultural and the informal, non-agricultural economy, were numerically the largest and a growing section of the rural population. However, landlords remained the most economically powerful class in the villages of the State, and had gained much political power in recent years. Presently, in West Bengal, agricultural and non-agricultural incomes are increasingly concentrated in the hands of this class. Members of this class, from erstwhile landlord households or capitalist farmer households, used two methods of exploitation – the feudal method of rent extraction and the capitalist method of exploitation of wage labour; they successfully resisted the second and third amendments to the West Bengal Land Reforms Act, 1955 as well as the redistribution of ceiling-surplus land acquired during the Congress regime (before the amendments were enacted by the Left Front government in 1977). After 2011, they were also successful in re-registering some of the land under litigation in their names and evicting existing cultivators.

Mishra (2013) further noted the expansion of several non-agricultural classes in recent times. Among them are landowners who own land but receive income from salaries and other sources, or those who may own homesteads and land in the village but reside and work at low-income jobs in nearby towns and semi-urban areas. Neoliberal changes increased the number of such non-cultivating households and expanded the urban, lower-middle class with roots in rural areas, but there was not much expansion of the upper-middle classes in rural areas. However, the difference between these non-agricultural classes and the rural poor has been increasing in recent years. Rural households engaged in trade and businesses were generally of low- and middle-income classes (though a section of rich- and capitalist-farmer households also engaged in such occupations), whereas an emerging section of non-agricultural capitalists in the countryside owned petty capital and small production units such as cold storages, paper mills, sponge iron factories, food processing units, large poultries, fish ponds, and trawlers in coastal areas. Among the landlords and capitalist and rich farmers were members of the "new rural rich" class who were large construction contractors, and involved in microfinance institutions and chit funds.

Mishra's analysis brings out the rising importance of non-agricultural income sources within the rural economy of the State, a trend observed across India but more acutely in West Bengal. At the same time, most households exiting agriculture seem to languish or earn meagre gains as manual workers or petty producers in the rural or semi-urban informal economy. During the 2010 survey, it was observed that important changes were taking place in the rural economy, polity, and class structures, as indicated by Mishra (2013). The agrarian economy was experiencing near stagnation of agricultural production and yield, and a decline in net sown area.[4] At the same time, attempts by the Left Front government to promote industrialisation in the State during its last term were strongly resisted by the peasantry and the rural population.

Identification of Rural Classes

The identification of classes in the West Bengal study villages, particularly among the peasantry, proved to be a complex task, given the distribution of land and asset holdings, extensive use of hired labour for agricultural

---

[4] See chapter 2 in this book.

operations by cultivator households, and extensive wage labour performed by cultivator households (including some rich cultivator households).[5]

Similar to the landholding structure in the State, a majority of landholdings in the villages were held by marginal farmers. In Panahar, 84 per cent of ownership holdings were below 2.5 acres, whereas in Amarsinghi and Kalmandasguri, 96 per cent and 92 per cent of ownership holdings were below 2.5 acres, respectively. There were no medium and large holdings in Amarsinghi and Kalmandasguri, i.e. all ownership holdings were below 5 acres. In Panahar, 5 per cent of the holdings were above 5 acres. As land was the major asset in the villages, small landholdings indicated low value of assets for most households. Assets were valued at only one lakh rupees (Rs 100,000) for the bottom 50 per cent of households, and below five lakh rupees for 70 per cent of all households. Secondary data sources such as the All India Debt and Investment Surveys of the NSS confirm the fact that the value of asset holdings of rural households in West Bengal are far below the national average.

The clustering of land size and value of assets within a tight range for most households presents a challenge to the classification of the peasantry by land and asset holdings. In addition, there was extensive use of wage labour in all three villages. Most cultivating households hired wage labour for agricultural operations; at the same time, they were engaged in agricultural and non-agricultural wage employment. There was little correlation between landownership and the labour ratio.[6] In other PARI villages outside West Bengal, different classes of peasants were identified using the value of asset holdings and labour ratio. Because such an exercise proved difficult in the case of the West Bengal villages, we used a different methodology, described in Appendix Note 2.

In our analysis, manual workers and the non-agricultural classes are distinguished based on the share of income that households received from manual wages and non-agricultural sources. Households receiving a major share of their income from cultivation and animal husbandry were defined as agricultural households and formed either the landlord/

---

[5] The broad scheme used by FAS to identify classes in the PARI villages is described briefly in Appendix Note 1.

[6] This result is similar to earlier attempts at classification of the peasantry in West Bengal by Bhattacharyya (2001). Classifying peasants by Patnaik's (1976) labour exploitation (E) criteria, Bhattacharyya (2001) showed that the association between land size and labour use in villages was not absolute.

capitalist-farmer class or the peasantry comprising upper-/poor-peasant classes.

Landlords/Capitalist Farmers

The class of landlords/capitalist farmers was present only in Panahar. These households wielded substantial influence in the village economy through their control over land and other means of production, particularly irrigation. Landlords and capitalist farmers were similar in most aspects: they did not participate in manual-labour operations in agriculture and hired labour to cultivate their land, hired agricultural workers on annual contracts, leased out land on seasonal leases, owned modern machinery, used modern agricultural inputs, and all of them owned tubewells and sold groundwater. Thus, they exploited surplus through both feudal and capitalist means. An important difference between landlords and capitalist farmers was that the former had historically controlled land and agriculture in the village, whereas the latter rose from the ranks of the peasants and increased their control over land through accumulation in agriculture.

The class of landlords/capitalist farmers was distinct from the rest of the cultivating households due to their ownership of land and other means of production and incomes.

Upper Peasantry

The upper peasantry in the three villages operated small landholdings. They cultivated their land using both family and hired labour; some even worked for others in agricultural and non-agricultural operations. The upper peasantry generally owned larger landholdings and higher-value assets, invested more in agricultural production, and received higher incomes from agriculture than poor peasants. In addition, they engaged less in manual labour as compared to poor peasants.[7]

A small section of the upper peasantry in Panahar and Amarsinghi were rich peasants owning higher-value assets and with increased ownership of land and means of production than the rest of the upper peasantry. Out of nine rich-peasant households in Panahar, two owned a tractor/tiller and three owned a tubewell with a pump – these three also sold water for irrigation in the village.

---

[7] See chapter 12 for the income composition of different classes.

In Amarsinghi, two rich-peasant households owned tubewells, of whom one earned substantial income from sale of water, and both shifted from diesel- to electric-powered pumpsets.

In Kalmandasguri, where accumulation in agriculture was minimal compared to the other villages and use of agricultural machinery limited, we did not further differentiate the upper peasantry. At the time of the 2010 survey, agricultural production in Kalmandasguri was in decline and there was no electricity for agriculture or domestic use. The few diesel-powered, shallow tubewells in the village were either defunct or used for irrigation sparingly due to high diesel costs – only 40 per cent of the area was irrigated. In addition, there was high outmigration of male workers for manual wage work. Given this context, differentiation among the peasantry was minimal. Village electrification in 2015 afforded the potential to initiate a process of differentiation and the rise of a rich peasantry, but this could not be captured by our survey.

It is important to note that though there was substantial differentiation of the peasantry in the three villages, the landlords/capitalist farmers and the upper peasantry in West Bengal operated smaller landholdings than elsewhere in India (Appendix Table 1).

Poor Peasants

Poor peasants had meagre operational holdings and hired out their labour in different kinds of agricultural and non-agricultural manual work. In Kalmandasguri, with few opportunities for manual wage employment, some poor-peasant households undertook various self-employment occupations such as street vending, and catching and selling fish. The quality of employment and level of income received from such activities were similar to manual wage employment. We divided the class of poor peasants in Kalmandasguri into two groups: those undertaking manual-wage employment and those engaged in petty self-employment; both belonged to the large, semi-proletarianised workforce of rural West Bengal.

Description of Classes in the Three Villages

Panahar

Class formation in Panahar differed from that in the other villages in important ways. First, inequalities in landownership was comparatively higher in Panahar, which possessed a substantially high proportion of landless households (43.1 per cent) as well as a few households owning medium and large landholdings. Secondly, Panahar and its surrounding region were among the forerunners in the agricultural transformation witnessed in West Bengal since the 1970s. Thus, mechanisation of agriculture and use of modern inputs was more prevalent in Panahar than in Amarsinghi and Kalmandasguri.

Landlords/capitalist farmers
Panahar was the only West Bengal village surveyed where a class of landlords/capitalist farmers was identified. There were seven households belonging to this class – three Muslim households comprised the erstwhile landlords and four caste-Hindu households were capitalist farmers who had emerged from the rich-peasant class (see Appendix Table 3a). The caste Hindus were from the Goala and Kumbhakar castes. Furthermore, the Krishak Sabha was active in the region, and led significant political struggles to implement land reform measures.[8] During the land reforms period, landlord households lost large tracts of land, some of which came under litigation and were later returned (see Box 1) but still retained the largest and most optimal land in the village. Public interventions in the form of subsidies for diesel-operated tubewells and electrification for irrigation in 1986 allowed these households to modernize their agriculture.[9] They were among the first in the village to invest in groundwater irrigation and take advantage of multiple cropping by cultivating short-duration, high-yielding varieties of paddy. In addition, they diversified to other non-agricultural sources of income. We observed two kinds of propensities within this class: the younger members of households had a weak interest in agriculture and worked in various non-agricultural jobs with many not residing in the village, and members of households with active interest in agriculture took advantage of new agricultural opportunities while also working at non-agricultural jobs. Both are illustrated in the following case studies.

The largest landlord household owned 32 acres. Traditionally, this Muslim household had multiple business interests in Bankura and Murshidabad, particularly in the cattle and hide markets. They own the cattle market (*haat*) in Kotulpur town as well as a paddy mill, and employed

[8] See chapter 4 in this book.
[9] See chapter 7 in this book.

long-term workers to cultivate their agricultural land. Land was given out on lease during *boro* and rabi seasons, and some of the land remained fallow. On a portion of land, the household cultivated the Atlanta variety of potato using seeds and fertilizers provided by PepsiCo. AK, a family member of another Muslim landlord household, owned about 10 acres of land and lost a portion of his holdings to land reforms. The head of the household was a retired school teacher, and his son owned a computer business in Kolkata. The household did not possess any tubewell or agricultural machinery; their land was leased out or cultivated by hiring long-term workers.

SK was a capitalist farmer belonging to a traditional landowning caste-Hindu family. At the time of the survey, SK owned about 13.5 acres of land, shares in several ponds, a borewell, and other agricultural machinery including a power tiller. He cultivated a variety of crops including vegetables, sold water from his tubewell, and also farmed fish in the ponds. Regularly conferring with agricultural officers, he obtained the best seeds and is locally known to achieve the highest crop yields. In addition, he was a paddy and potato trader in the local market.

The class of landlords/capitalist farmers in Panahar constituted only 2.8 per cent of all households but owned 42.5 per cent of total asset value and 40 per cent of total land in the village (Tables 1 and 2). Though there was substantial concentration of wealth in this class, their average per household landholding was 11.6 acres, modest in comparison to their counterparts in other parts of India. As mentioned above, the largest landholding was 32 acres. The scale of capital accumulation in agriculture was not particularly high. Of the 7 landlord/capitalist-farmer households, 3 owned irrigation equipment, 5 owned tractors or tillers, and only 1 had purchased land in the past ten years (Appendix Table 2a).

The peasant classes
The peasantry comprised 58.4 per cent households in Panahar: 3.6 per cent were classified as "upper peasant 1," 17.3 per cent as "upper peasant 2," and the remaining 37.5 per cent as poor peasants. Upper-peasant 1 households consisted of rich peasants owning 20 per cent of total asset value and 14.3 per cent of the agricultural land in the village. Thus, their control over land and assets in the village was much higher than their representation in population, indicating a concentration of wealth in the upper-peasant 1 class. However, the size of their landholdings and value of their assets as well as incomes were substantially lower than those of

Box 1
Case study of the largest landlord household in Panahar

Ranjini Basu

The Khans were one of the traditional landowning families of Panahar. In the pre-land-reforms period, the head of the household, Abdul Baset Khan, owned up to 187 *bighas* (93 acres) of land and multiple ponds, spread across Panahar and Koalpara villages. The family also owned many properties and commercial establishments in the towns of Bankura and Murshidabad, most of which are now shut or were donated to the Wakf board in later periods. They received earnings from trade in raw hides, and even today, the family owns the 0.8 acre of land in Kotulpur town where the weekly cattle market is held, from which they continue to receive a commission on raw hide sales. Abdul Baset Khan's lands were inherited by his two sons and ultimately by his three grandsons – Abdul Saleem Khan, Anwar Ali Khan, and Asaduzamman Khan. In 2010, the eldest grandson Abdul Saleem Khan passed away. His widow and other immediate family members resided mostly outside the village and had leased out their shares of land, having minimal interest in agriculture and their main income was from salaries. The second grandson, Anwar Ali Khan, a primary school teacher, joined the Krishak Sabha and served as the panchayat pradhan from 1978 to 1991. During Operation Barga, he voluntarily registered his sharecroppers, and in 2010, he owned 10 acres of land. He had not purchased any land, and his son, who ran a computer business, preferred a salaried profession rather than agriculture.

The third grandson, Asaduzamman Khan, was the largest landowner in the village during our survey of 2010, owning 32 acres of land. His father's 40 acres of land was posthumously divided into holdings registered in the names of Asaduzamman (the only son), six daughters and widow. Despite the division in ownership, the lands, for all practical purposes, were operated by Asaduzamman Khan (we therefore considered the land as part of his ownership holding). Around 2005, a portion of his land was declared as ceiling surplus by the block development officer. Almost 20 acres of these vested lands were distributed among 250 families, spread across Panahar and Koalpara, under the leadership of the Krishak Sabha. In response, Asaduzamman Khan filed a case, resulting in an injunction. The sub-divisional land and land reforms officer reversed the decision, and in June 2009, the declared ceiling-surplus lands were repossessed by Asaduzamman Khan. He justified his repossession of these lands using conditions of Muslim personal law, stating that the lands were registered in the name of his divorced wife. In addition to his agricultural lands and ponds, he also owned a rice mill in 2010 and had invested in fish cultivation in his ponds. One of his sons runs a business, whereas the other holds a PhD and teaches at a college.

landlords/capitalist farmers. The average size of their ownership holding was 3.3 acres. All nine upper-peasant 1 households were caste Hindus belonging to the following castes: Goala, Sadgope, Kumbhakar, Vaishnav, and Teli.

Upper-peasant 2 households were essentially medium peasants owning 21.3 per cent of total asset value and 31.2 per cent of agricultural land in the village. The average size of their landholding was 1.47 acres, and they engaged in manual labour, petty trade, and other non-farm activities. Lastly, this class was more caste heterogeneous than the upper-peasant 1 class; 34 of the 43 households were caste Hindus from different castes,

---

Box 2
Case studies of peasant households in Panahar

NG belonged to the upper-peasant 1 class, owning 3 acres of cropland and 0.24 acre of a water body. NG's household had multiple sources of income: cultivation of *aman* and *boro* paddy, potato, and sesame; water sales throughout the year (they owned a submersible tubewell, in addition to a thresher machine); a fertilizer shop; and trading in potato and paddy procured from Panahar and neighbouring villages.

BP, belonging to a typical upper-peasant 2 household in Panahar, owned 1.26 acres of land with *barga* rights over 0.16 acres, and cultivated *aman* and *boro* paddy, potato, and sesame. With his five brothers, he jointly owned a tubewell and several agricultural machinery, and their income from water sales served as a second source of income after crop production.

SM's family of five were poor peasants, owning a tiny plot of land (0.4 acre) in 2010. Along with SM, his wife and eldest son also worked on the land, only cultivating *aman* paddy and earning a net income of Rs 2,000. Because of these low earnings from crop production, the household largely depended on manual wage employment. SM was a long-term worker (about 10 months in 2009–10) for a household in Jairambati town where he operated a tractor and performed other non-agricultural tasks. His wife worked as an agricultural labourer for a landlord household in the village, whereas his son worked as a daily wage labourer in agriculture throughout the year. In addition, SM's wife and son also did MGNREGA (Mahatma Gandhi National Rural Employment Guarantee Act, 2005) work in the village. On aggregate, about 93 per cent of their total household income was derived from wage earnings in 2010.

6 were Scheduled Castes (SCs) (Bagdi), 2 were Scheduled Tribes (STs) (Santhal), and 1 was Muslim.

Capital accumulation in agriculture among the upper-peasant classes was lower than that among landlords. Among the 52 upper-peasant households, only 9 owned irrigation equipment, 7 owned power tillers, and only 18 had taken a formal sector loan – the average principal borrowed being Rs 24,300.

The poor-peasant class in Panahar constituted 37.5 of all households, which owned meagre assets and land (about half an acre on average). They owned only 6.6 per cent of total asset value and 5.6 per cent of land in the village. Thus, there were sharp differences between the poor and upper-peasant classes in terms of land and asset ownership. The difference is also visible in capital accumulation – poor peasants barely had the wherewithal to invest in agriculture or elsewhere. Only 2 of the 93 households owned irrigation equipment (mainly diesel pumps), none owned tractors or tillers, and 2 had taken formal sector loans. Apart from cultivation, these households depended heavily on manual wage earnings – 60 per cent of their household income was from agricultural and non-agricultural wages. This class was caste heterogeneous, though a majority (73.1 per cent) were SCs from Bagdi and Kaibartta castes, 12.9 per cent were STs (Santhal), and 14.0 per cent were caste Hindus.

Manual workers

Landless and near-landless manual-worker households constituted 25 per cent of all households, owning only 1.8 per cent of total asset value and 0.5 per cent of land in the village. About 89 per cent of SC and 88 per cent of the ST households in Panahar belonged to this class. Of the 63 manual-worker households, only 7 were caste Hindus. They worked as agricultural labourers throughout the year in Panahar and nearby villages. Because the village was well connected to urban centres, many members of manual-worker households worked as non-agricultural wage workers such as carpenters, masons, construction workers, drivers, loaders/unloaders at brick kilns and cold storages, *pandal* workers, and NREGA (National Rural Employment Guarantee Act, 2005) workers in the village and the nearby towns.

Non-agricultural classes

The remaining 13 per cent of households in Panahar were non-agricultural households: 5.3 per cent had major income from businesses; 4.9 per cent

Table 1 *Households and share in total asset value, by socio-economic class, Panahar, 2010,* in number and per cent

Class	Households	Share in total households	Share in total asset value
Landlord/capitalist farmer	7	2.8	42.5
Upper peasant 1	9	3.6	20
Upper peasant 2	43	17.3	21.3
Poor peasant	93	37.5	6.6
Manual worker	63	25.4	1.8
Major income from business	13	5.3	3.7
Major income from remittances/rent	3	1.2	0.2
Major income from salaries	12	4.9	3.8
Major income from other sources	5	2	0.1
All	248	100	100

Source: : PARI survey (2010).

Table 2 *Household ownership holding and share in total ownership holding, by socio-economic class, Panahar, 2010,* in number, acres, and per cent

Class	Households	Ownership holding (acres)	Share in total ownership holding
Landlord/capitalist farmer	7	81.2	40.0
Upper peasant 1	9	29.94	14.7
Upper peasant 2	43	63.46	31.2
Poor peasant	93	11.5	5.6
Manual worker	63	0.9	0.5
Major income from business	13	7.8	3.8
Major income from remittances/rent	3.0	1.0	0.5
Major income from salaries	12	7.1	3.5
Major income from other sources	5.0	0.4	0.2
All	248	203.3	100

Source: : PARI survey (2010).

from salaries; and the remaining from transfers, remittances, and other sources. Importantly, their share in total asset value was a mere 7 per cent, less than their population share, indicating that those who were not engaged with agriculture were by no means better off than peasant households. Household members primarily engaged in petty trade and jobs in the village and nearby towns, and households receiving major income from business and salaries also owned some land – all except three were all caste Hindus. Households with major income from other sources were near landless – four out of five such households were SCs.

Amarsinghi

There were no landlords or large farmers residing in Amarsinghi. Land here and in surrounding villages belonged to a large zamindar family – the Chowdhurys of Nurpur. With the abolition of *zamindari* and later implementation of land reforms, the cultivators received land titles. Subdivision of land in subsequent generations further reduced the size of holdings. At the time of the 2010 survey, the largest landowning family owned no more than five acres of land.

The peasant classes

We identified the three peasant classes in the village – upper peasant 1, upper peasant 2, and poor peasant. The former constituted 3.9 per cent of the households in the village, owned 20.2 per cent of total asset value and 19 per cent of total land, and had an average landholding size of 2.6 acres. Even though there is some concentration of wealth in this class, the magnitude of concentration is less than that seen in Panahar. All upper-peasant 1 households were caste Hindus, belonging to the Tanti caste. The upper-peasant 2 class constituted 10.2 per cent of all households, owned 31.2 per cent of total asset value and 31 per cent of land, and had an average ownership holding size of 1.3 acres. Of the 13 upper-peasant 2 households, 10 were from the Tanti caste and the remaining 3 belonged to the Tiyar caste (SC) (see Appendix Table 3b).

Upper-peasant households had larger landholdings than the poor-peasant households, and these households cultivated a variety of crops including mangoes and vegetables, invested in groundwater irrigation, and received the major share of their household income from cultivation. Of the 18 upper-peasant households, 5 owned tubewells. Income from groundwater sales were important, motivating investments in groundwater irrigation. No households owned tractors or power tillers, and only four had availed formal sector loans. Only four households had purchased land in the previous ten years, with the average value of land transaction being Rs 60,000 in 2010. Thus, apart from investments in groundwater irrigation, which yielded good returns from water sales, capital accumulation in agriculture was limited (Appendix Table 2b). Lastly, the upper peasantry did not participate in manual wage labour in agriculture, but members of these families did participate in non-agricultural wage work and sometimes owned petty businesses or had salaried jobs.

The poor peasant class owned smaller landholdings (average of 0.75 acre) and participated in agricultural and non-agricultural wage labour, though cultivation was the major source of income. This class constituted 28.3 per cent of all households in the village, owning 28.8 per cent of total asset value and 38.0 per cent of land. Thus, their access to land and assets was similar to their share in population – this is a distinct feature of poor

---

Box 3
Case studies of peasant households in Amarsinghi

The largest landowner BM owned 4.25 acres of cropland and shares in pond and seasonally leased out a small portion of his land. In addition to cultivating paddy, jute, pulses, and oilseeds, he owned an electric-powered tubewell and received significant income from selling irrigation water. PM, belonging to another upper-peasant 1 household, jointly owned 3.5 acres with his brother. Though he received a salary from working as an accountant in Ratua town, his brother cultivated paddy, jute, potato, oilseed, and mango and participated in NREGA when employment was available. These two peasant households had the largest landownership in the village.

JM belonged to upper-peasant 2 household owning 1.66 acres of cropland and 0.25 acres of a water body. This household's sole income sources was from paddy, jute, and rapeseed cultivation.

SM belonged to a poor-peasant household, operating 0.92 acre of land on which he cultivated *aman* and *boro* paddy, mustard, potato, and jute in 2010. The net earnings from crop production was very low in 2010. He laboured out in agricultural and non-agricultural wage work within the village. In addition, he engaged in selling of fish and trading jute fibre within and outside village. His wife was a MDM (mid-day meal) cook in a primary school.

peasants in Amarsinghi compared to Panahar and PARI villages outside of West Bengal. In most villages, poor peasants owned a significantly lower share in total asset value and land than their share in population in the village; the similarity between shares in total asset value and in population points to the remarkable achievement of land reforms in West Bengal wherein poor peasants had improved access to land, despite small holding sizes. Capital accumulation in agriculture among poor peasants in Amarsinghi was low: only two of the 36 households owned irrigation equipment (shallow tubewells with diesel pumps) and seven borrowed from formal sources (the average principal borrowed was less than Rs 10,000) (Appendix Table 2b). Three-fourths of poor peasants were caste Hindus (Tanti), and the remaining were SCs (Tiyar).

Manual workers

The class of manual workers constituted 37.8 per cent of all households in Amarsinghi. They owned 10.7 per cent of total village asset value and 6.1 per cent of land. They worked in agricultural and non-agricultural wage work in and around the village, though some also owned small parcels of land. A majority of manual-worker households (73 per cent) were SCs, 25 per cent were caste Hindus, and there was one ST (Santhal) household. Members of manual-worker and poor-peasant classes also migrated seasonally to various cities in India. For example, short-term migration to Delhi was an established feature when the village was studied in 2005 and 2006 (see Bakshi 2010). At the time of the 2010 survey, three households had members who had migrated to Delhi.[10]

Non-agricultural classes

The non-agricultural classes comprised 20 per cent of all households. They owned small shops and businesses, traded in agricultural inputs and outputs such as jute, were petty vendors such as those selling sugarcane juice, and worked as barbers (a caste-based occupation) and MDM cooks through self-help groups (SHGs) in nearby villages. Because their businesses yielded low and irregular incomes, they were in a similar condition to that of manual-worker households.[11] The class receiving major income from business constituted 10.2 per cent of all households,

---

[10] See chapter 10 for a description of migration of male workers from Amarsinghi and Kalmandasguri.

[11] See chapter 12 on household incomes for further elaboration of this point.

Table 3 *Households and share in total asset value, by socio-economic class, Amarsinghi, 2010*, in number and per cent

Class	Households	Share in total households	Share in total asset value
Upper peasant 1	5	3.9	20.2
Upper peasant 2	13	10.2	31.2
Poor peasant	36	28.3	28.8
Manual worker	48	37.8	10.7
Major income from business	13	10.2	3.6
Major income from remittances/rent	4	3.1	1
Major income from salaries	3	2.4	3.9
Major income from pension	3	2.4	0.2
Income from artisanal work	2	1.6	0.4
All	127	100	100

Source: PARI survey (2010).

Table 4 *Household ownership holding and share in total ownership holding, by socio-economic class, Amarsinghi, 2010*, in number, acres, and per cent

Class	Households	Ownership holding (in acres)	Share in total ownership holding
Upper peasant 1	5	13.5	19.3
Upper peasant 2	13	21.7	31
Poor peasant	36	26.6	38.0
Manual worker	48	4.3	6.1
Major income from business	13	1.9	2.8
Major income from remittances/rent	4	0.5	0.7
Major income from salaries	3	1.2	1.7
Major income from pension	3	0.1	0.1
Income from artisanal work	2	0.2	0.3
All	127	70.1	100

Source: PARI survey (2010).

but their share in total asset value was a mere 3.6 per cent. Only three households received major income from salaries (two were caste Hindu and one was SC). The remaining nine households received major income from rent and remittances (four), pension (three), and artisanal earnings (two). This class was the most caste heterogeneous, with households from the Napit, Goala, Tanti, and Tiyar castes.

Kalmandasguri

There were no landlords or rich capitalist farmers in Kalmandasguri. Before land reforms, most land here was owned by a few Muslim households who lost most of their land during land reforms.[12] Rajbanshi (SC) and Muslim households were the major beneficiaries of land reforms. At the time of and even prior to the 2010 survey, agriculture was on the decline. The few diesel-powered shallow tubewells operating in the 1990s had become mostly defunct, and agriculture was limited to two unirrigated crops: jute in pre-monsoon, followed by monsoon paddy. Households were exiting agriculture, and the tendencies of proletarianisation and migration observed in the 2010 survey were accentuated in the 2015 survey. Though there were important developments in productive forces in agriculture after 2010, they did not yield significant results in 2015.[13]

The peasant classes

The peasant classes in the village were categorised in two classes of upper (19 per cent) and poor peasants (33.4 per cent) (Table 5).[14] The former had larger landholdings compared to the latter, though the average size of ownership holding was a mere 2.4 acres per household. The 19 upper-peasant households in the village constituted 12.9 per cent of all households, owning 37.1 per cent of total asset value and 41.3 per cent of land (Table 6). This was the only class in the village that commanded a substantially higher share in land and asset value than their population share.

Among these households, 10 were SC (Rajbanshi), 4 were Muslims, 4 were caste Hindus (Jogi and Baishya Kapali), and 1 was ST – this caste heterogeneity at the upper peasant level is a unique feature of the village

---

[12] See chapter 4 of this book, for a detailed history of land reforms in this village.

[13] See the postscript in chapter 5 on production.

[14] In Kalmandasguri, we did not differentiate the upper peasantry into upper peasant 1 and upper peasant 2, because accumulation in agriculture was minimal compared to the other villages and use of agricultural machinery was limited.

(see Appendix Table 3c). Importantly, the SC households belonging to the Rajbanshi caste were the major landholders of the village, a legacy of land reforms in West Bengal.

Even though agricultural production in Kalmandasguri was severely limited by high irrigation costs and the lack of electrification in 2010, the upper peasantry reflected a distinct dynamism. Their possession of the means of production was widespread, as 10 of the 19 households owned irrigation equipment (mostly shallow tubewells and diesel pumps) and 1 owned a power tiller.[15] Furthermore, 11 households had purchased land in the last 10 years and 12 had borrowed from banks (Appendix Table 2c).

Though the upper-peasant class received a major share of their income from cultivation, they also received a portion from wage labour, non-agricultural self-employment, and other sources.

Most poor-peasant households owned less than an acre of land. We observed that, in addition to crop production, these households depended on manual wage work or small self-employment. Accordingly, we separated the households into two groups: those with small self-employment in non-agriculture (11) and semi-proletarians (38). Similar to Amarsinghi, poor peasants in Kalmandasguri owned assets and land in the village roughly in proportion to their population share. They constituted 33.4 per cent of households, and owned 31.7 per cent of total asset value and 34.1 per cent of land in the village. Improved access of poor peasants to land and assets in the State, being a major achievement of land reforms, cannot be emphasised enough.[16]

The class of poor peasants was also caste heterogeneous: 34.7 per cent belonged to the Rajbanshis (SC), 28.6 per cent were Muslims, 10.2 per cent were STs (Nagesia and Oraon), and the remaining were caste Hindus. In addition, there was an important distinction between the two poor peasant groups: all but two SC and all ST households were largely dependent on manual wage work and thus classified in the semi-proletarian group, whereas caste Hindu and Muslim poor peasants were present in both the small self-employment and semi-proletarian groups.

---

[15] In 2010, the low average cost of installation for a shallow tubewell in Kalmandasguri (below Rs 10,000) was mainly due to the high water table, about 50 feet below ground level. In addition, some respondents reported that the total installation cost was borne by the village panchayat or that they received a subsidy for tubewell installation.

[16] Earlier work by Bakshi (2008), using data from NSS surveys, also showed that SCs in West Bengal had better access to land, roughly proportionate to their population share.

Box 4

Case studies of peasant households in Kalmandasguri

The upper-peasant household with the largest ownership holding was that of AR. He cultivated 3.5 acres of land, a part of which was irrigated by a diesel-powered, shallow tubewell. AR leased out an acre on seasonal-share rent for paddy cultivation; cultivated paddy, potato, ginger, and turmeric on the remaining land; and raised cows, goats, ducks, and chickens. Members of his household did not engage in any kind of manual labour or other non-agricultural activities.

SR, a poor peasant with small self-employment, owned 1.5 acres of unirrigated land in which he cultivated paddy, jute, lemon, and chillies. He also sold tea in trains between the towns of Cooch Behar and Alipurduar. Members of his family participated in agricultural labour and NREGA work.

IM, a semi-proletarian poor peasant, owned 0.57 acre of land on which he cultivated paddy, jute, and mustard. He did not hire any labourers for cultivation but laboured out himself within the village during the agricultural season. For the rest of the year, he engaged in different types of non-agricultural wage work within and outside the village such as in brick kilns and small construction work.

Capital accumulation in agriculture among poor peasants was less than that among upper peasantry. Of the 49 poor-peasant households, though 6 households owned irrigation equipment, only 4 owned diesel pumps. Only 3 had accessed bank loans and 12 had purchased land in the last 10 years.

Manual workers

The 55 manual-worker households (37.4 per cent) in Kalmandasguri owned 13.5 per cent of the total asset value and 9.5 per cent of the land. Participation in and income shares from non-agricultural wage employment was higher here than those in the other two villages. Workers worked in brick kilns, construction, and NREGA work within the village and in nearby towns and semi-urban areas. Members from manual-worker classes reported to have family members who were migrant workers, particularly in the construction sector in distant places such as Kerala, Delhi, Jaipur, Goa, Bhutan, and Arunachal Pradesh. The majority of manual-worker households were Muslim.

Table 5 *Households and share in total asset value, by socio-economic class, Kalmandasguri, 2010, in number and per cent*

Class	Households	Share in total households	Share in total asset value
Upper peasant	19	12.9	37.1
Poor peasant	49	33.4	31.7
a) small self-employment	11	7.5	8.1
b) semi-proletarian	38	25.9	23.6
Manual worker	55	37.4	13.5
Major income from business	15	10.2	7.4
Major income from salaries	6	4.1	10.0
Major income from pension	3	2.0	0.3
All 147	100	100	

Source: PARI survey (2010).

Table 6 *Household ownership holding and share in total ownership holding, by socio-economic class, Kalmandasguri, 2010 in number, acres, and per cent*

Class	Households	Ownership holding (in acres)	Share in total ownership holding
Upper peasant	19	46.3	41.3
Poor peasant	49	38.2	34.1
a) small self-employment	11	9.6	8.6
b) semi-proletarian	38	28.6	25.5
Manual worker	55	10.6	9.5
Major income from business	15	7.2	6.4
Major income from salaries	6	9.8	8.7
Major income from pension	3	0	0
All	147	112.2	100

Source: PARI survey (2010).

Non-agricultural classes

A total of 16 per cent of households were classified as non-agricultural classes, of which 10.2 per cent derived income from small businesses, 4.1 per cent from salaries, and 2 per cent from pensions. The small businesses owned by most of these households did not yield high incomes and included petty shops; small trade in agricultural products such as bamboo,

---

Box 5
Case study of fishing businesses run by SHGs
in Kalmandasguri

In Kalmandasguri, landless and poor residents (mostly Muslim) formed groups of 10–12 members and collectively engaged in fish harvesting. Throughout the year, these groups usually took contracts for harvesting fish from pond owners in the village and surrounding areas and sold the catch in the nearby towns. AM and his son, belonging to a landless Muslim household in Kalmandasguri, were part of a group and engaged in the fish business for 10–12 months in 2009–10 and both earned an average of Rs 100 per day.

---

betel nuts, and fruits; and working in carpentry and as barbers. A sizeable section sold fish after purchasing it from the market or local ponds. Nine of the 15 households with major income from business were Muslim.

Households receiving major income from salaries were clearly better off among the non-agricultural classes in the village. There were six such households (4.1 per cent), and their share in total land and asset value was higher than their population share. Four of these households were Rajbanshis (SC), one was Oraon (ST), and one was Muslim, and there were no salaried households among caste Hindus. Salaried employees had government jobs as teachers at primary schools, clerks in government offices, police constables, and peons at post offices in Kalmandasguri, Baudiardanga, Darjeeling, and Bararangras.

Changes between 2010 and 2015

In 2015, a sample survey was conducted in all the three villages to understand changes in the village over a span of five years.[17] In this section, we discuss important changes in the characteristics of the socio-economic classes observed in the surveyed villages. These observations are based on an analysis of data from the panel of households surveyed in both 2010 and 2015.

In Panahar, where the incidence of landlessness had already been high in 2010, demographic pressures further reduced size of landholdings. The proportion of marginal landholdings within the panel of households

---

[17] The methodology used for this sample survey is described in chapter 1.

increased, and the average size of landholdings further reduced from 1.3 to 1.05 acres of subdivided land. These changes further accelerated the process of proletarianisation of the peasantry. We found that, between 2010 and 2015, poor-peasant households witnessed a decline in income from crop production, and their dependency on income from wage employment increased.[18]

In addition, there may have been further concentration of land at the top, among the landlords and capitalist farmers. In 2009, the largest landlord won a court case wherein 16 acres of his land, earlier vested by the government as ceiling surplus, was returned to him, and he regained control over this land after 2010.

In Amarsinghi, though subdivision of land and decline in landholding were not as pronounced, there was an important development of productive forces: Even though electrification of irrigation had occurred in 2007, a few diesel-operated tubewells had continued to function in 2010, but by 2015, all were replaced with electric pumpsets. Of the four privately owned, electric-operated tubewells, three were owned by an upper-peasant 1 household in 2015. The relatively higher capital cost of tubewell installation discouraged other peasants to invest in irrigation.[19] Thus, a single household had gained control over a large part of the water market and reaped rich dividends from water sales, though there was also a cooperatively owned deep tubewell in the village. Our analysis showed that irrigation costs were higher for those purchasing water from private water sellers than from members of the water cooperative.

BM, the largest landowner in Amarsinghi (with an operational holding of 4.5 acres in 2015), had installed two electric submersible tubewells in 2010 and 2014, purchased with a formal loan from UBI bank, Samsi branch. Since then, income from irrigation water sales became his major source of income, and in 2015, he sold water that irrigated 67 acres of cropland and earned a net income of Rs 2,50,000.

In Kalmandasguri, the subdivision of landholdings for demographic reasons and increase in marginal landholdings were visible. The average size of landholdings among the panel of households declined from 1.05 to 0.88 acres in the five years. However, there were important changes in the productive forces, and that had implications for the differentiation

[18] See chapter 12 for a detailed analysis.
[19] See chapter 7 for a detailed description of the operation of water markets and costs of irrigation in Amarsinghi.

of the peasantry. Electricity for both domestic use and agriculture was introduced in 2013, and subsequently, a few electric-operated tubewells were introduced by the upper-peasant households, leading to an expansion of irrigated area between 2010 and 2015. In addition, a tractor and thresher were introduced in this period, a development which had been absent in 2010.

SR, belonging to a peasant household, operated 3.33 acres of land in 2015, whereas his three sons diversified to different non-agricultural work. The eldest had migrated to Jaipur (Rajasthan) in 2010 but returned and engaged in agricultural activities in 2015. The middle son ran a small construction business, whereas the youngest son had worked as an insurance agent at a microfinance company in 2010 and later as a peon in a post office. From the surplus income of these various sources, SR's household made a substantial investment between 2010 and 2015 on agricultural machinery including an electrified tubewell, a tractor, a rotavator, and a thresher. Through renting out their machinery, they earned Rs 2,65,000 in 2015.

The analysis here reflects the increased differentiation of the peasantry in the villages after 2010. The tendencies of proletarianisation continued in Panahar and Kalmandasguri. In all three villages, the richest further accumulated wealth. In Panahar, the richest landlord regained ceiling-surplus land, whereas in Amarsinghi and Kalmandasguri, the few rich peasants cornered the benefits of the electrification of groundwater irrigation.

Conclusion

This chapter described the socio-economic classes in the three villages of West Bengal and the process of differentiation among the peasantry. There was limited presence of the landlord/capitalist-farmer class in the villages due to effective implementation of land reforms. This class was present only in Panahar, where a significant proportion of its land and asset value was concentrated in this class. The landlords here belonged to a traditional landowning Muslim family who lost much of their land in land reforms but still owned sufficiently large holdings, albeit, within the land-ceiling limits. Our survey in 2015 showed that this household even managed to regain some ceiling-surplus land through litigation. Notably, in terms of landownership and ownership of other means of production, the landlord/capitalist-farmer households in Panahar operated on a lower scale than their counterparts in other parts of India. However, true to their counterparts, they took advantage of the best agricultural and non-agricultural sources of income available: potato cultivation under contract with PepsiCo, investments in groundwater irrigation for own crop production as well as water sales, education investments due to which the younger generation held salaried jobs, and business activities.

In Panahar and Amarsinghi, a small section of peasantry was rich peasants – the upper-peasant 1 class. Though smallholders in terms of landownership, they were among the better-off class within the village. In both villages, some rich peasants owned groundwater irrigation equipment and other machinery. In most cases, investments in irrigation were made to accrue rent, as groundwater markets provided rich dividends to tubewell owners. Electrification of irrigation in Amarsinghi disproportionately benefited a few upper-peasant households who could make large investments and monopolise water markets. However, the small size of holdings dampened the vigour of most rich-peasant households, as capital accumulation in terms of owning machinery, purchasing land, and borrowing from banks was not very high within this class.

There were no rich peasants in Kalmandasguri. In spite of the limitations of agriculture in the village, a large proportion of the upper-peasant class owned small irrigation equipment such as diesel pumps (used to produce potato in a small area), purchased land, and borrowed from banks. The economic potential of these households was dampened by factors such as the small size of farms and the lack of electricity for irrigation. By the 2015 survey, the village had been electrified, and we observed members of the upper peasantry investing income gained from non-agricultural sources into purchasing agricultural machinery.

Poor peasants in all three villages depended heavily on manual wage work in addition to cultivation. In Kalmandasguri, a section of poor peasants also engaged in small businesses. An important feature of poor-peasant households in Amarsinghi and Kalmandasguri was that despite having small landholdings and low-value assets as compared to the upper peasantry, their share in total land and asset value in the village was proportionate to their representation in the village population. This was in contradistinction to the poor peasants in Panahar, and in most other villages in India. The relatively equitable distribution of resources, and poor peasants' better access to land and assets in the two villages are certainly remarkable achievements of land reforms in the State.

Manual-worker and poor-peasant households with small parcels of land formed the largest sections in the villages. A decline in landholding size due to subdivision of land and increased income from manual wage employment were observed between 2010 and 2015. Thus, the analysis of classes in the three villages confirm the growing de-peasantisation and proletarianisation of the agrarian economy of West Bengal, further confirmed by secondary data.

The non-agricultural classes mainly consisted of petty traders and producers, and salaried employees in formal and semi-formal jobs. Some households, particularly the salaried, may be seen as the "rural rich" in a relative sense, given that their incomes and asset values were higher than or similar to upper-peasant households. Most non-agricultural households engaged in small businesses with negligible capital investments, and their relative position in the village in terms of ownership of land and assets was no better than that of poor peasants and manual workers. Non-agricultural employment is an important source of income and employment in rural West Bengal. Our analysis of classes also shows that poor peasants, manual workers, and a section of the asset poor depend on various non-agricultural wage work and self-employment in the three villages.

To conclude, the distinct characterisation of classes in the three villages was due to West Bengal's history of land reforms. The class of landlords and capitalist farmers had limited presence in the villages, being present only in Panahar. The landlords, capitalist farmers, and rich peasants operated smaller landholdings compared to those of their counterparts in other parts of the country. The poor peasantry in Amarsinghi and Kalmandasguri owned meagre parcels of land, but their share in total land and asset value was proportionate to their share in population. In spite of these features, there was significant differentiation in the villages. The class of manual workers and poor peasants, heavily dependent on manual work, constituted the largest section in the villages. Between 2010 and 2015, the size of landholdings declined, whereas manual wage incomes increased, indicating further proletarianisation of the peasantry. Ownership of the means of production other than land such as irrigation equipment, tractors, and tillers were concentrated among the landlords/ capitalist farmers and rich-peasant classes; this tendency intensified over time in all three villages.

References

Bakshi, Aparajita (2014a), "Land Reform and Access to Land Among Dalit Households in West Bengal" in V. K. Ramachandran and Madhura Swaminathan (eds.), *Dalit Households in Village Economies*, Tulika Books, New Delhi, pp. 111–30.

Bakshi, Aparajita (2014b), "Contextualising Land Reform in West Bengal: An Interview with Benoy Konar," *Review of Agrarian Studies*, vol. 4, no. 2, pp. 123–36.

Bakshi, Aparajita (2010), "Rural Household Incomes," unpublished PhD thesis, University of Calcutta, Kolkata.

Bakshi, Aparajita (2008), "Social Inequality in Land Ownership: A study with special reference to West Bengal," *Social Scientist*, Volume 39(9-10), September, pp. 95–116

Bhattacharyya, Sudipta (2001), "Capitalist Development, Peasant Differentiation and the State: Survey Findings from West Bengal," *Journal of Peasant Studies*, vol. 28, no. 4, 95–126.

Lenin, V. I. (1972), "The Development of the Capitalism in Russia", in *Collected Works*, vol. 3, Progress Publishers, Moscow, available at https://www.marxists.org/archive/lenin/works/1899/devel/, viewed on October 30, 2020.

Mishra, Surjya Kanta (2007), "On Agrarian Transition in West Bengal," *The Marxist*, vol. 23, no. 2, pp. 1–22.

Mishra, Surjya Kanta (2013), "Gramanchale Shreni Samparka o Ganatantrik Aikyer Sandhane," *Ganashakti Shaarad Sankhya*, 1420, p.29-36.

Mishra, Surjya Kanta, and Rawal, Vikas (2002), "Agrarian Relations in Contemporary West Bengal and Tasks for the Left," in V. K. Ramachandran and Madhura Swaminathan (eds.), *Essays on Agrarian Relations in Less-Developed Countries*, Tulika Books, New Delhi, pp. 329–55.

National Sample Survey Organisation (NSSO) (2006), *Some Aspects of Operational Land Holdings in India, 2002–03, National Sample Survey 59th Round (January–December 2003)*, National Sample Survey Report No. 492(59/18.1/3), NSSO, Ministry of Statistics and Programme Implementation, Government of India, New Delhi.

Patnaik, Utsa (1976), "Class Differentiation within the Peasantry: An Approach to Analysis of Indian Agriculture," *Economic and Political Weekly*, vol. 11, no. 39, pp. A82–A87.

Ramachandran, V. K. (2017), "Socio-economic Classes in the Three Villages," in Madhura Swaminathan and Arindam Das (eds.), *Socio-economic Surveys of Three Villages in Karnataka: A Study of Agrarian Relations*, Tulika Books, New Delhi, pp. 69–85.

Ramachandran, V. K. (2011), "The State of Agrarian Relations in India Today", *The Marxist*, vol. 27, nos. 1–2, Jan–Jun, pp. 51–89.

Ramachandran, V. K. (2010), "A Note on Socio-economic Classes in the Survey Villages," in V. K. Ramachandran, Vikas Rawal and Madhura Swaminathan (eds.), *Socio-economic Surveys of Three Villages in Andhra Pradesh: A Study of Agrarian Relations*, Tulika Books, New Delhi, pp. 24–33.

Rawal, Vikas (2013), "Changes in the Distribution of Operational Landholdings in Rural India: A Study of National Sample Survey Data," *Review of Agrarian Studies*, vol. 3, no. 2, pp. 73–104.

Tse Tung, Mao (1933), "How to Differentiate the Classes in the Rural Areas," in *Selected Works of Mao Tse Tung*, vol. 1, Foreign Languages Press, Beijing, available at https://www.marxists.org/reference/archive/mao/selected-works/volume-1/mswv1_8.htm viewed on October 30,2020.

Appendix Note 1

Characterisation of Classes in Contemporary Rural India
(Extracted from Ramachandran 2017)

Landlords

Landlord households own the most land and generally the best land in most Indian villages, and the members of landlord households do not participate in the major agricultural operations on the land. Their land is cultivated either by tenants, to whom land is leased out on fixed rent or share, or by means of the labour power of hired workers.[20] Landlord families are, in general, historical participants in the system of land monopoly in the village. Landlords dominate not just economic, but also traditional social and modern political hierarchies in the village. It is absolutely essential to remember that – to quote E. M. S. Namboodiripad – "landlordism is not only an economic category but also social and political."

Capitalist farmers also do not participate in the major manual operations on the land. The main difference between capitalist farmers and landlords is that the former did not traditionally belong to the class of landlords. Some of them came from rich peasant or upper-middle peasant families that had a tradition of family labour, whose members, in fact, actually worked at major manual tasks even in the present or previous generation. Such families invested the surplus they gained from agriculture or other activities – including moneylending, salaried employment, trade and business – in land. Agriculture was or became the focal point of their activity, and the basis of their economic power. The basis of the power of landlords and rich capitalist farmers is their control over land.

---

[20] Those landlords whose surpluses come mainly from the labour of hired manual workers are called capitalist landlords.

Manual Workers

At the other end of the spectrum of classes involved in agricultural production is the class of manual workers, whose major income comes from working as hired workers on the land of others and at tasks outside crop production.

In general, manual workers work on a wide range of tasks, and the set of skills necessary for most tasks in, say, a village are found among most manual labourers in that village.

Notably, I use the term "manual workers" rather than "agricultural workers," because it is no longer possible (nor particularly helpful) to separate a *class* of non-agricultural workers from the larger pool of manual workers – that is, to recognise rural farm and non-farm workers as discrete categories – in most villages. The typical rural manual worker today can be characterised more as a "miscellaneous worker in rural society" than as solely an agricultural worker.

Most manual workers are casual workers who work at daily-rated tasks or for piece-rates. Some, however, are annual workers: farm servants who do agricultural, non-agricultural, and some domestic tasks for a single employer for a monthly wage (and generally on an annual contract).

Manual workers can also have other sources of income. These can include, for instance, animal husbandry, petty vending, domestic work, and miscellaneous low-remuneration jobs in the private sector.

For historical reasons, in most regions, a majority or a large proportion of Dalit households and households belonging to other region-specific oppressed castes belong to the class of manual workers. Nevertheless, since manual work remains the rural occupation of last resort, manual labour tends to be the most caste-heterogeneous class in village society.

The Peasantry

Peasant households, whose members work on all or some of the major manual operations on the land, constitute the sector of petty producers that lies between landlords and rich capitalist farmers on the one hand, and manual workers on the other. While peasants have shown great resilience as a social category, having existed continually under different historical social formations, the hallmark of the modern peasantry is its subjugation to the capitalist market.

As part of our research, using the classical texts as guideposts, we have tried to work out broad criteria for the classification of peasants in the modern rural Indian context into different class categories. These criteria are as follows:

1. Ownership of the means of production and other assets.
2. The labour ratio – defined as the ratio between the sum of number of days of family labour and the number of days of labouring out – of members of the household in agricultural and non-agricultural work (in the numerator), and the number of days of labour hired in by the household (in the denominator).
3. Rent exploitation: that is, rent received or paid by the household.
4. Net income of the household, making separate note of the gross value of output from agriculture and the investment in agriculture per hectare.
5. The sources of income of the household.

We emphasise here the problems of classifying the peasantry on the basis of a single year's data, when socio-economic circumstances typically fluctuate from year to year. We use, in other words, static data to study dynamic circumstances. This problem affects income particularly, since peasant incomes typically fluctuate from year to year.

With regard to the labour ratio, the extent of participation of working members of peasant households in the labour process in agriculture depends on the nature of land use and cropping pattern in each village, on economic and social status. In every village, cropping pattern and technological processes are such that there are substantial variations in labour absorption per crop, and the relative ratios in which family labour, exchange labour (if it exists at all), and different types of hired labour are deployed.[21]

We then classified households into rich, upper-middle, lower-middle, and poor, on the basis of their ownership of the means of production, labour ratios, and incomes. This was in itself a complex effort, and the point to remember is that the purpose here is not to provide a universal, one-size-fits-all scheme, but to try to apply the existing Marxist literature, and village-level data and observation, to construct criteria (or identify guidelines) for identifying classes in different socio-economic and agricultural environments.

Rich peasant households have the highest levels of ownership of means of production, particularly land and other productive assets, while, at the other end of the spectrum, poor peasants hardly have any productive assets at all other than small plots of land. In some villages, poor and

---

[21] Labour ratios are also affected by year-to-year fluctuations.

lower-middle peasants are tenants, so do not own any land. With respect to the labour ratio, in general, the coefficient is above 0 but very low for rich peasants, generally in the vicinity of 1 among middle peasants (less than 1 for upper-middle and greater than 1 for lower-middle peasants), and greater than 1 among poor peasants.

Incomes can vary from high surpluses based on relatively heavy investments among the rich, to subsistence and even negative incomes among the poor. The income criterion was particularly important in resolving borderline problems in the classification of the middle peasantry into upper and lower sections.

APPENDIX NOTE 2

Classification of Households in the Three Villages

It is important to note at the very outset that the exercise of identifying and categorising households in different socio-economic classes was conducted only using the FAS–PARI 2010 census-type survey data. We did not attempt to reclassify households using the 2015 data, though it is methodologically possible; that is to say that the data exist, if one is tempted to study class mobility in the villages.

Non-Agricultural Classes

As the first step in the identification of classes using the PARI data, the non-agricultural classes are first identified and classified. In the West Bengal villages, two broad non-agricultural classes were identified: manual-worker households and others.

Manual-worker households had no operational holdings and the majority of their income was sourced from manual work. Given the miscellaneous nature of employment of these households, no further attempt was made to classify them by specified types of manual work (such as agricultural and non-agricultural labour). Others were households where the majority of income was sourced from remittances, business activities, salaries earned, and other sources. These households were further classified by the major source of household income.

Agricultural Classes

The agricultural classes mainly consisted of landlords and different peasant classes. The peculiarities of West Bengal villages and legacy of land reforms meant that agriculture was dominated by petty peasantry – two of the villages had no landlords. The class of rich capitalist farmers were also absent. In only one village, Panahar, we categorised seven households as landlords/capitalist farmers. These households owned the most and best land and had historically dominated the social and economic life in the village.

The peasantry

Identification and classification of peasant households presented us with specific challenges not experienced in other PARI villages. In other PARI studies, peasant classes could be distinguished based on their landholding and asset value, including ownership of productive assets and the labour exploitation ratio.[22] In West Bengal, as mentioned earlier, a large majority of households owned very small landholdings. There was high use of hired labour, even among the petty peasantry, and differentiation of the peasantry could not be captured using one or two simple indicators. To classify households under peasant categories, we thus took the following variables into consideration:

1. Operational landholding
2. Cost A2 (all paid out agricultural costs incurred by the household)
3. Total value of household asset holdings
4. Total number of labour days per household
5. Manual income

We formed quartile classes of all households (except the manual worker and others category) for each of the variables mentioned above and assigned quartile scores to each household for each variable. Thus, a household could achieve any score between 1 and 4 for each indicator, 1 being the lowest score and 4 the highest. The quartile scores for "total number of labour days" and "manual income" were logically reversed. The final score for each household was the sum of individual variable scores.

Mathematically, if the rank of operational holding = a_1, rank of cost A2 = a_2, rank of total asset value = a_3, rank of total labour days = a_4, rank of manual income = a_5, then the final score = $a_1 + a_2 + a_3 + a_4 + a_5$. The final score that can be achieved by a household can vary between 5 and 20.

Households with lower ranks would characterise poorer-/smaller-peasant households than ones with higher ranks. Households with scores

---

[22] See Appendix Note 1 for an explanation of the labour ratio.

between 5 and 7 were examined on a case-by-case basis to ascertain their categorisation in one of the non-agricultural classes. In most cases, these households had low participation in agriculture and high shares of income from manual labour. They were merged with the class of manual-worker households (see previous para). In a few cases, if the major source of income for these households was from sources other than manual labouring out, we categorised them accordingly.

The rest were peasant households and ranked based on their quartile scores in two variables – asset value and cost A2. Households with lower scores were classified as poor peasants, as they had lower asset values and agricultural investments (cost A2), whereas those with higher scores were classified as upper peasants. The exact cut-offs of the scores were decided based on the distribution in the respective villages. In Panahar and Amarsinghi, upper peasants were classified in two groups based on their asset holdings: upper-peasant 1 households were rich peasants that owned assets valued at more than Rs 25,00,000, whereas upper-peasant 2 households were medium peasants with assets valued at less than Rs 25,00,000. Kalmandasguri had no peasant households owning assets above Rs 25,00,000.

APPENDIX TABLES

Appendix Table 1 *Average ownership holding and value of assets of landlord and rich peasant classes, PARI villages,* in acres and rupees (at 2009–10, prices)

Village	Year of survey	Landlord/capitalist classes		Rich peasant class*	
		Average ownership holding	Average value of assets (in lakhs)**	Average ownership holding	Average value of assets (in lakhs)**
Ananthavaram, Andhra Pradesh	2005–06	16.59	64.6	9.67	33.1
Kothapalle, Andhra Pradesh	2005–06	20.1	58.3	4.93	12.8
Bukkacherla, Telangana	2005–06	51.78	207.2	27.3	73.9
Alabujanahalli, Karnataka	2009	19.55	384.4	10.07	70.3
Siresandra, Karnataka	2009	NA	NA	20.68	98.7
Zhapur, Karnataka	2009	56.09	128.9	40.12	45.5
Rewasi, Rajasthan	2010	28.63	74.1	15.65	34.5
Panahar, West Bengal	2010	13.12	94.2	1.8	34.7
Amarsinghi, West Bengal	2010	NA	NA	2.7	22.7
Kalmandasguri, West Bengal	2010	NA	NA	2.43	8.5
Katkuian, Bihar	2012	89.91	292.6	14.05	81.5
Nayanagar, Bihar	2012	104.37	721.2	24.89	100.6

Note: * Rich peasant class denotes the highest class within the peasantry in each village
** Asset values are deflated using the wholesale price index at the all-India level (base year 2004–05).
1 lakh is equivalent to Rs 100 thousand.
Source: PARI Surveys.

Appendix Table 2a *Capital accumulation in agriculture, by class, Panahar, 2010, in number and rupees*

Class	House-holds	Land purchased in last 10 years		Irrigation equipment owned		Tractors/tillers owned		Crop loans taken from banks	
		House-holds	Average value of transaction	House-holds	Average value	House-holds	Average value	House-holds	Average principal borrowed
Landlord/capitalist farmer	7	1	5,22,200	3	18,933	5	62,000	5	56,600
Upper peasant 1	9	6	1,48,333	3	11,333	2	53,000	6	29,667
Upper peasant 2	43	9	85,000	6	3,979	3	1,08,333	12	21,617
Poor peasant	93	8	42,525	2	3,490	0	0	2	6,000
Manual worker	63	2	8,250	0	0	0	0	0	0
Major income from business	13	0	0	3	2,333	0	0	2	10,000
Major income from salaries	12	3	34,333	0	0	0	0	1	10,000
Major income from remittances/rent	3	0	0	0	0	0	0	0	0
Major income from other sources	5	0	0	0	0	0	0	0	0
All	248	29	90,928	17	7,568	10	74,100	28	27,229

Source: PARI survey (2010).

Appendix Table 2b *Capital accumulation in agriculture, by class, Amarsinghi, 2010, in number and rupees*

Class	House-holds	Land purchased in last 10 years		Irrigation equipment owned		Tractors/tillers owned		Crop loans taken from banks	
		House-holds	Average value of transaction	House-holds	Average value	House-holds	Average value	House-holds	Average principal borrowed
Upper peasant 1	5	1	39,765	2	28,750	0	0	3	49,000
Upper peasant 2	13	3	66,667	3	28,120	0	0	1	44,000
Poor peasant	36	7	21,911	2	8,250	0	0	7	9,286
Manual worker	48	5	31,260	0	0	0	0	0	0
Major income from business	13	2	55,000	0	0	0	0	0	0
Major income from salaries	3	1	35,500	0	0	0	0	0	0
Major income from remittances/rent	4	0	0	0	0	0	0	0	0
Major income from pensions	3	0	0	0	0	0	0	0	0
Income from artisanal work	2	0	0	0	0	0	0	0	0
All	127	19	36,576	7	22,623	0		11	23,273

Source: PARI survey (2010).

Appendix Table 2c *Capital accumulation in agriculture, by class, Kalmandasguri, 2010, in number and rupees*

Class	House-holds	Land purchased in last 10 years		Irrigation equipment owned		Tractors/tillers owned		Crop loans taken from banks	
		House-holds	Average value of transaction	House-holds	Average value	House-holds	Average value	House-holds	Average principal borrowed
Upper peasant	19	11	54,825	10	4,199	1	150,000	12	28,917
Poor peasant: small self-employment	11	2	62,500	1	1,800	0	0	1	10,000
Poor peasant: semi-proletarian	38	10	28,413	5	904	0	0	2	14,000
Manual worker	55	8	25,125	1	300	0	0	4	19,250
Major income from business	15	4	49,158	1	2,600	1	100,000	1	50,000
Major income from salaries	6	3	61,083	3	2,217	0	0	1	14,000
Major income from pensions	3	0	0	0	0	0	0	0	0
All	147	38	41,923	21	2,755	2	125,000	21	25,048

Source: PARI survey (2010).

Appendix Table 3a *Distribution of households, by socio-economic class and social group, Panahar, 2010, in number and per cent*

Class	SC		ST		Muslim		Caste Hindu		All	
	Number	% of column total	Number	% of column total	Number	% of column total	Number	% of column total	Number	% of column total
Landlord/capitalist farmer	0	0	0	0	3	50	4	4.3	7	2.8
Upper peasant 1	0	0	0	0	0	0	9	9.8	9	3.6
Upper peasant 2	6	4.5	2	11.8	1	16.7	34	37	43	17.3
Poor peasant	68	51.1	11	64.7	1	16.7	13	14.1	93	37.5
Manual worker	51	38.3	4	23.5	1	16.7	7	7.6	63	25.4
Major income from business	3	2.3	0	0	0	0	10	10.9	13	5.2
Major income from remittances/rent	1	0.8	0	0	0	0	2	2.2	3	1.2
Major income from salaries	0	0	0	0	0	0	12	13	12	4.8
Major income from other sources	4	3	0	0	0	0	1	1.1	5	2
All	133	100	17	100	6	100	92	100	248	100

Source: PARI survey (2010).

Appendix Table 3b *Distribution of households, by socio-economic class and social group, Amarsinghi, 2010, in number and per cent*

Class	SC		ST		Caste Hindu		All	
	Number	% of column total	Number	% of column total	Number	% of column total	Number	% of column total
Upper peasant 1	0	0	0	0	5	7.2	5	3.9
Upper peasant 2	3	5.3	0	0	10	14.5	13	10.2
Poor peasant	9	15.8	0	0	27	39.1	36	28.3
Manual worker	35	61.4	1	100	12	17.4	48	37.8
Major income from business	4	7	0	0	9	13	13	10.2
Major income from remittances/rent	1	1.8	0	0	3	4.3	4	3.1
Major income from salaries	1	1.8	0	0	2	2.9	3	2.4
Major income from pensions	2	3.5	0	0	1	1.4	3	2.4
Income from artisanal work	2	3.5	0	0	0	0	2	1.6
All	57	100	1	100	69	100	127	100

Source: PARI survey (2010).

Appendix Table 3c *Distribution of households, by socio-economic class and social group, Kalmandasguri, 2010, in number and per cent*

Class	SC		ST		Muslim		Caste Hindu		All	
	Number	% of column total	Number	% of column total	Number	% of column total	Number	% of column total	Number	% of column total
Upper peasant	10	20.4	1	10	4	6.6	4	14.8	19	12.9
Poor peasant: small self-employment	2	4.1	0	0	4	6.6	5	18.5	11	7.5
Poor peasant: semi-proletarian	16	32.7	5	50	10	16.4	7	25.9	38	25.9
Manual worker	15	30.6	2	20	30	49.2	8	29.6	55	37.4
Major income from business	2	4.1	1	10	9	14.8	3	11.1	15	10.2
Major income from salaries	4	8.2	1	10	1	1.6	0	0	6	4.1
Major income from pensions	0	0	0	0	3	4.9	0	0	3	2
All	49	100	10	100	61	100	27	100	147	100

Source: PARI survey (2010).

4

The Impact of Land Reforms on the Ownership and Distribution of Land

A Study of Three Villages in West Bengal

Ranjini Basu[1]

Introduction

Land reforms played a pivotal role in transforming the landholding structure of the rural countryside in West Bengal. State-led land reforms received a push during the late 1960s under the two United Front governments and later became a major policy thrust of the Left Front government first elected in 1977 (Sengupta and Gazdar 2003). This was preceded by a history of organised peasant struggles in the State focusing on ending landlordism, redistributing land among the rural poor, and ensuring security of tenure for sharecroppers (Dasgupta 1984; Konar 2002; Bakshi 2008, 2015).

The ambitious land reforms programme in West Bengal was one of the largest redistributive programmes undertaken by any State in independent India. According to 2015 data, West Bengal had a share of 54 per cent of all land redistribution beneficiaries in the country.[2] The redistributive

---

[1] The author would like to acknowledge the detailed comments received from Aparajita Bakshi and an anonymous reviewer, which have greatly benefited this chapter. The author is thankful to Mansi Goyal for her intensive copy-editing, which made this chapter more readable.

[2] Statistical data on the implementation of land ceiling laws across India, once publicly available, have now been removed, and their publication has been discontinued by the Land Reforms Division under the Ministry of Rural Development (MoRD). Even among the previously available data on State-wise area declared as ceiling-surplus land, the surplus land under State possession, the area distributed, and the number of beneficiaries is incomplete and, for some States, not updated. No national-level dataset exists on the implementation of tenancy laws. The data cited here was obtained through a Right to Information (RTI) request response dated January 13, 2016 from the Department of Land Resources and Land Reforms

programme directly benefited half of rural households in the State (Ramachandran and Ramakumar 2001). Through these reforms, Scheduled Caste (SC), Scheduled Tribe (ST), and Muslim households, forming the largest section of the landless population, gained greater access to agricultural land and homestead plots, which in turn led to significant reduction in inequality (Bakshi 2008). By 2011, among the total number of land reforms beneficiaries, 36 per cent and 18 per cent belonged to SCs and STs, respectively. Muslims were included in the remaining 44 per cent. Of the total number of *bargadar*s (sharecroppers) registered in the State, 30 per cent and 11 per cent belonged to SCs and STs, respectively. Of the remaining 59 per cent, one section comprised Muslims (GoWB 2012).

The land reform programme in West Bengal had three components, namely surplus land redistribution, tenancy reforms, and, later, the redistribution of homestead land. The intensity in implementation of each of these varied across different regions of the State and depended on the nature of pre-existing tenurial relations. Success of the land reforms programme can be largely attributed to its two-pronged approach of combining administrative legal measures with political mobilisation of beneficiaries. The involvement of peasant organisations and local-level institutions challenged the feudal hold of the landlords. This created an environment for beneficiaries to claim and retain their rights over the redistributed land and attain tenurial security through registering themselves as sharecroppers under Operation Barga (Dasgupta 1984; Surjeet 1992; Bakshi 2015). This "walking-on-two-legs" policy of ensuring both distributive growth through land reforms and pro-poor programmes undertaken by local self-government bodies became the defining approach of the Left Front government (Mishra and Rawal 2002).

Furthermore, land reforms succeeded in ending the long-standing agricultural stagnation in West Bengal. The 1980s recorded impressive agricultural growth, which took the State out of food insecurity (Sen 1992; Lieten 1992; Saha and Swaminathan 1994; Banerjee, Gertler, and Ghatak 2002; Ghatak and Roy 2007; Mishra 2007; Ramachandran, Swaminathan, and Bakshi 2010). Land reforms were also accompanied by a broader approach of extending rural electrification and irrigation in the State (Rawal 2001b).

Division, MoRD, available in Chaturvedi (2016). The RTI response is available at https://docs.google.com/document/d/1nwu_Vm4Ch04lqKiL8RX2iIoQAS8sSh1u9aej-c-hv3w/edit (viewed on June 16, 2019).

This chapter will examine the landholding pattern in three villages in West Bengal studied by the Foundation for Agrarian Studies (FAS) under its Project on Agrarian Relations in India (PARI). It will try to contribute to the literature and existing macro-level studies by presenting a micro perspective of the impact of land reforms in these villages. The chapter is divided into four broad sections. For each of the study villages, the first and second sections discuss their landholding pattern and their history of the implementation and impact of land reforms, respectively. The third section discusses contemporary challenges facing land reform beneficiaries after nearly four decades of its implementation, and the last offers a conclusion to the study.

Multiple sources and types of data were used to understand differences in land tenure and the process of implementing land reforms across the villages. Colonial land settlement and administrative reports, along with documents of the Krishak Sabha[3] were used to study land tenure in the districts at the time of Independence. Accounts from village residents formed an oral history of the pre-land reforms land system, and interviews conducted with Krishak Sabha activists, panchayat representatives, and beneficiaries illuminated the process of implementing land reforms in the three villages. Finally, data from village surveys conducted between 1989 and 2015 by various organisations and scholars are an important source for examining the impact of land reforms on the land ownership pattern in the villages as well as contemporary issues of landholdings.[4]

Landholding Pattern in the State and the Study Villages

West Bengal

Scholars have raised methodological problems of estimating ownership and operational landholdings using NSSO survey rounds (Rawal 2013; Kumar 2016). However, there are stark trends emerging from the 2012–13 NSSO 70th Round data that may help describe the present distribution

---

[3] The Paschim Banga Pradeshik Krishak Sabha (West Bengal Provincial Kisan Sabha) has been referred to as Krishak Sabha in this chapter. The Krishak Sabha is the provincial front of the All Indian Kisan Sabha (AIKS). AIKS was formed in 1936 as a class-based mass organization in response to the colonial rule and upholding economic freedoms of the peasantry. Before partition, the Krishak Sabha was known as the Bangiya Pradeshik Krishak Sabha (Bengal Provincial Kisan Sabha).

[4] See chapter 1 for details of different surveys carried out in the study villages.

Table 1 *Distribution of land-size class of operational holdings, by household and area operated, West Bengal and India, 2012–13*, in per cent

Land-size class	West Bengal		India	
	Household	Area	Household	Area
Landless (≤ 0.005acre)	0	0	0.03	0
Marginal (0.005–2.47 acres)	95.17	73.05	73.17	27.71
Small (2.47–4.94 acres)	4.05	18.79	15.3	23.44
Semi-medium (4.94–9.88 acres)	0.67	6.15	8.1	23.5
Medium (9.88–24.7 acres)	0.11	1.88	3.04	19.33
Large (>24.7 acres)	0	0.12	0.37	6.02
All	100	100	100	100

Source: NSSO (2015, p. 62)

of landholdings in rural West Bengal. Table 1 shows the land-size distribution of operational holdings among households and area operated in West Bengal and India, based on the NSSO 70th Round data. The land-size categories are those used in the NSSO surveys of Land and Livestock Holdings, wherein land ownership included all land under possession of the household, including homestead land. In the 70th Round, area operated refers to land used for agricultural production by the household and is thus a better marker to study distribution of agricultural land.

In West Bengal, 95 per cent of households operated less than 2.47 acres of land, compared to 73 per cent at the all-India level. Significantly, though 73 per cent of the total operated area in West Bengal consisted of marginal holdings, the corresponding figure at the all-India level was only 28 per cent. This predominance of small cultivators indicated the breakdown of land concentration in rural West Bengal, after nearly four decades since the implementation of land reforms.[5] By contrast, in States like Punjab, 1.2 per cent of households had operational holdings in the largest land-size category but controlled 12.6 per cent of the total area operated. Finally, the data also revealed that West Bengal had the smallest average ownership holding of 0.186 hectares (0.46 acre), as compared to the all-India average of 0.639 hectares (1.58 acres).

In addition to the predominance of marginal landholdings in the State,

---

[5] In this chapter, land concentration refers to the control of land by a few as well as the presence of large holdings.

Table 2 *Average number of plots by land-size class of operational holdings, West Bengal, 2012–13*, in number

Land-size class	Average number of plots
Marginal (0.005–2.47 acres)	4
Small (2.47–4.94 acres)	7
Semi-medium (4.94–9.88 acres)	13
Medium (9.88–24.7 acres)	13
Large (>24.7 acres)	15
All	4

Source: NSSO (2015).

there was increasing fragmentation of landholdings. Table 2 presents the average number of plots under each land-size class of operational holdings in West Bengal as reported by the NSSO. The largest number of rural households operating in the marginal land-size category had four plots on average, meaning that the majority of small cultivators farmed on meagre plots of unconsolidated land.

The NSSO landholding dataset highlights the absence of concentration of landholdings in contemporary rural West Bengal and the overwhelming presence of small-cultivator households. This condition was an outcome of the land reforms programme undertaken in the State since the late 1970s. In the following sections, the landholding pattern in each of the three study villages is discussed.

Panahar

In 2010, 56.4per cent of Panahar households owned land (Table 3), and 48 per cent owned less than 2.5 acres. The largest landholding, also the largest among the study villages, was 32 acres and owned by a Muslim household. This was an exception among the Bengal villages, as will be discussed later, and, interestingly, was smaller than most of large landholdings in other villages surveyed in the rest of the country under PARI.[6]

Forty-four per cent of Panahar households were landless, the highest

[6] For instance, the largest ownership holding was 280 acres in Bukkacherla, a dry village in Anantapur district of Andhra Pradesh surveyed in 2005–06;150 acres in Gharsondi of Madhya Pradesh surveyed in 2008; and 57 acres in Tehang of Punjab's Jalandhar district surveyed in 2011 (Swaminathan and Baksi 2017).

among the three villages. Landlessness was concentrated among the socially-deprived SC households (64 per cent were landless), which also formed the largest section of the village population. In addition, of the 17 ST households in the village, 6 were landless, whereas the rest owned less than 2.5 acres of land.

The proportion of households that were landless in terms of ownership (Table 3) and that of households operationally landless (Table 4) were 44 per cent and 26 per cent, respectively. The smaller proportion of operationally landless households indicates the presence of an active lease market in Panahar. In other words, landless households gained land to operate through the lease market. In fact, acreage under operational holdings (215 acres) was greater than that under ownership holdings (201 acres); Panahar households leased in land from landowners outside the village. In 2010, 30 per cent of SC households were operationally landless, indicating that a fair proportion of SC households gained land through the lease market.

The proportion of operationally landless households in Panahar, as well as the other two villages, was less than that in West Bengal as a whole, as calculated from various rounds of the NSSO's Employment and Unemployment Surveys. Rawal (2013) calculated that in 2011–12, 65 per cent of rural households in West Bengal were operationally landless. He also contended that NSSO surveys have consistently overestimated landlessness in West Bengal – this remains unsubstantiated by the results of various empirical village studies conducted in the State. The largest operational holding in Panahar was 19.2 acres, a result of the largest landowning household leasing out substantial amounts of agricultural land. The smallest and average operational holdings were 0.03 and 1.2 acres, respectively, and 65 per cent of cultivators operated less than 2.5 acres of land.

Of the study villages, only Panahar had a landlord/capitalist-farmer class (Table 5). This socio-economic class comprised only 7 households (2.8 per cent) but together owned 40 per cent of the total agricultural land in the village. Of these 7 households, 3 were descendants of the traditional Muslim *jotedar* or rich, landed-peasant family of the village (one of which dominated with 32 acres out of the total 81 acres owned by this class) and 4 acquired land through purchase. Of the remaining agricultural land in Panahar, 45 per cent was owned by upper-peasant households, which comprised 21 per cent of the village population. The manual-worker and poor-peasant households, forming the majority at 63 per cent, owned only 6 per cent of the land.

Table 3 *Distribution of cropland ownership holdings, by social group, Panahar, 2010, in number and acre*

Landsize	General		SC		ST		OBC		Muslim		All	
	Number	Acre	Number	Acre	Number	Acre	Number	Acre	Number	Acre	Number	Acre
Landless	5 (10.4)	0	85 (63.9)	0	6 (35.3)	0	11 (25)	0	1 (16.7)	0	108 (43.5)	0
0.01–2.5 acres	37 (77.1)	38 (64.3)	48 (36.1)	12.1 (100)	11 (64.7)	5.3 (100)	20 (45.5)	10.8 (14.5)	2 (33.3)	1.3 (2.6)	118 (47.6)	67.5 (33.5)
2.5–5 acres	5 (10.4)	15.9 (26.9)	0	0	0	0	10 (22.7)	35.7 (48)	0	0	15 (6)	51.6 (25.6)
5–10 acres	1 (2.1)	5.2 (8.8)	0	0	0	0	2 (4.5)	14.6 (19.7)	2 (33.3)	17.1 (33.9)	5 (2)	36.9 (18.3)
>10 acres	0	0	0	0	0	0	1 (2.3)	13.2 (17.8)	1 (16.7)	32 (63.5)	2 (0.8)	45.2 (22.5)
Total	48 (100)	59.1 (100)	133 (100)	12.1 (100)	17 (100)	5.3 (100)	44 (100)	74.3 (100)	6 (100)	50.4 (100)	248 (100)	201.2 (100)

Note: Figures in parenthesis denote the percentage share of the column totals.
Source: PARI survey (2010).

Table 4 *Distribution of cropland operational holdings, by social group, Panahar, 2010, in number and acre*

Landsize	General		SC		ST		OBC		Muslim		All	
	Number	Acre	Number	Acre	Number	Acre	Number	Acre	Number	Acre	Number	Acre
Landless	10 (20.8)	0	40 (30.1)	0	3 (17.6)	0	10 (22.7)	0	1 (16.7)	0	64 (25.8)	0
0.01–2.5 acres	32 (66.7)	35.02 (60.3)	93 (69.9)	35.9 (100)	13 (76.5)	8.5 (73.9)	21 (47.7)	12.9 (17.2)	2 (33.3)	1.3 (3.7)	161 (64.9)	93.62 (43.5)
2.5–5 acres	5 (10.4)	17.9 (30.8)	0	0	1 (5.9)	3 (26.1)	10 (22.7)	35.4 (47.3)	0	0	16 (6.5)	56.3 (26.2)
5–10 acres	1 (2.1)	5.2 (8.9)	0	0	0	0	2 (4.5)	13.3 (17.8)	2 (33.3)	14.2 (40.9)	5 (2)	32.7 (15.2)
>10 acres	0	0	0	0	0	0	1 (2.3)	13.2 (17.6)	1 (16.7)	19.2 (55.3)	2 (0.8)	32.4 (15.2)
Total	48 (100)	58.12 (100)	133 (100)	35.9 (100)	17 (100)	11.5 (100)	44 (100)	74.8 (100)	6 (100)	34.7 (100)	248 (100)	215.02 (100)

Note: Figures in parenthesis denote the percentage share of the column totals.
Source: PARI survey (2010).

Table 5 *Distribution of households and cropland ownership and operational holdings, by socio-economic class, Panahar, 2010,* in per cent

Class	Share households	Share in area in under ownership holdings	Share in area under operational holding
Capitalist landlord/farmer	2.8	40.0	30.0
Upper peasant I	3.6	14.7	13.0
Upper peasant II	17.3	31.2	32.7
Poor peasant	37.5	5.6	16.8
Manual worker	25.4	0.5	1.3
Others	13.4	8.0	6.2
All	100.0	100.0	100.0

Source: PARI survey (2010).

The landlord/capitalist-farmer class held 30 per cent of the operational landholdings (Table 5). The household with the largest landholding in this class leased out substantial acreage of land, which explains the difference in shares of ownership and operational holdings by this class. The availability of leased land particularly benefitted poor-peasant households, whose share in the total land under operational holdings rose to 17 per cent, as compared to only a 6 per cent share under ownership holdings.

Amarsinghi

In 2010, 64 per cent of Amarsinghi households owned land – the majority of which (61 per cent) held marginal landholdings of less than 2.5 acres (Table 6), and no household owned more than 5 acres. Of the 46 landless households, 31 belonged to the SCs, one was the only ST household, and the rest were OBC (Other Backward Classes) households. As will be discussed in later sections, most SC households in Amarsinghi were more recent settlers, whereas the OBCs, the largest landed social group, were the earliest settlers of the village. Landlessness was restricted to 20 per cent among OBC households – 75 per cent of these households owned less than 2.5 acres of land.

In 2010, there was no concentration of land among a few owners in Amarsinghi, which historically was under the control of the *zamindari* system in the pre-Independence period and the jotedars in the pre-land reforms period (see section "Implementation of Land Reforms and Its Impact").

Table 6 *Distribution of cropland ownership holdings, by social group, Amarsinghi, 2010, in number and acre*

Land size	SC		ST		OBC		All	
	Number	Acre	Number	Acre	Number	Acre	Number	Acre
Landless	31	0	1	0	14	0	46	0
	(54.4)		(100)		(20.3)		(36.2)	
0.01–2.5 acres	26	12.91	0	0	52	38.93	78	51.84
	(45.6)	(100)			(75.4)	(79.6)	(61.4)	(83.9)
2.5–5 acres	0	0	0	0	3	9.98	3	9.98
					(4.3)	(20.4)	(2.4)	(16.1)
Total	57	12.91	1	0	69	48.91	127	61.82
	(100)	(100)	(100)		(100)	(100)	(100)	(100)

Note: Figures in parenthesis denote the percentage share of the column totals.
Source: PARI survey (2010).

Table 7 *Distribution of cropland operational holdings, by social group, Amarsinghi, 2010, in number and acre*

Land size	SC		ST		OBC		All	
	Number	Acre	Number	Acre	Number	Acre	Number	Acre
Landless	27	0	1	0	12	0	40	0
	(47.4)		(100)		(17.4)		(31.5)	
0.01–2.5 acres	30	17.47	0	0	53	41.85	83	59.32
	(52.6)	(100)			(76.8)	(76.2)	(65.4)	(81.9)
2.5–5 acres	0	0	0	0	4	13.07	4	13.07
					(5.4)	(23.8)	(3.1)	(18.1)
Total	57	17.47	1	0	69	54.92	127	72.39
	(100)	(100)	(100)		(100)	(100)	(100)	(100)

Note: Figures in parenthesis denote the percentage share of the column totals.
Source: PARI survey (2010).

Operational holdings falling under the land-size class of 0.01–2.5 acres were held by 65 per cent of households, which were largely marginal cultivators (Table 7). Households belonging to the smallest land-size class held 82 per cent of the total acreage under operational holdings. The total operational land of 72.39 acres, higher than the total ownership holding, indicated the presence of a lease market, wherein Amarsinghi households leased in land from landowners outside the village.

Operational landlessness in Amarsinghi was 31.5 per cent, lower than ownership landlessness by five per cent. It was mostly concentrated in SC households, whose operational landlessness was lower than their ownership landlessness (47 vs. 54 per cent). Operational holdings reduced landlessness in the case of OBC households (17 per cent), whereas the single ST household was operationally landless. The largest, smallest, and average operational landholding sizes were 4, 0.096, and 0.8 acres, respectively.

The socio-economic class distribution of ownership holdings in Amarsinghi in 2010 shows no presence of landlords or an emerging capitalist-farmer class (Table 8). The majority of land had been distributed among the upper-peasant and poor-peasant classes. The relatively affluent upper-peasant households, constituting 14 per cent of the village, owned over 50 per cent of the land. Poor peasants, comprising 28 per cent of the village, owned 38 per cent of the land. However, the inequality in landholding distribution was seen among manual-worker households – they formed the largest section of the village at 38 per cent but owned only 6 per cent of the land.

In 2010, the distribution of land under both operational and ownership holdings was similar. Though upper-peasant households leased out some of their owned land, such was not the case for poor-peasant households. The proportion of land under poor-peasant households ownership compared to their operational holdings was 38 and 42 per cent. In the case of manual-worker households, their share of area under operational holdings was marginally higher than that under ownership holdings. However, their shares were lower than their share in the total population.

Table 8 *Distribution of cropland ownership and ownership holdings, by socio-economic class, Amarsinghi, 2010*, in per cent

Class	Share in households	Share in area under ownership holdings	Share in area under operational holdings
Landlord/capitalist farmer	0	0	0
Upper peasant I	3.9	19.3	19.7
Upper peasant II	10.2	31.0	26.0
Poor peasant	28.3	38.0	41.6
Manual worker	37.8	6.1	8.1
Others	19.8	5.6	4.6
All	100.0	100.0	100.0

Source: PARI survey (2010).

Kalmandasguri

In 2010, Kalmandasguri consisted of mostly small and marginal landholders, with no household owning more than 5 acres of land (Table 9). Having had only four resident landowning households until the 1970s, the village now had 78 per cent of households owning some agricultural land, according to the 2010 survey data (see section "Implementation of Land Reforms and Its Impact"). Furthermore, 71 per cent of households owned between 0.01 and 2.5 acres of agricultural land. The share of acreage under ownership holdings of the smallest land-size class, 71.7 per cent, was similar to the proportion of its number of holdings. The average size of ownership landholding was less than one acre per household.

Landlessness prevailed in 22 per cent of households. The share of landlessness among Muslim and SC households was 43 per cent and 9 per cent, respectively, and only one of the 10 ST households was landless. Muslim households in Kalmandasguri have historically been the most socially deprived section.

The distribution of operational holdings is similar to that of ownership holdings (Table 10). No household operated more than 5 acres of land, and 75 per cent of households operated less than 2.5 acres. Seventy-nine per cent of the total land under operational holdings belonged to the smallest land-size category. Of the study villages, Kalmandasguri had the lowest level of operational landlessness at 21 per cent, however, 39 per cent of Muslim households were operationally landless.

Unlike the other two study villages, total acreage under ownership and operational holdings was similar (108.5 and 107.8 acres, respectively), indicating a weak tenancy market in the village. The largest, smallest, and average operational holdings were 5, 0.05, and 0.9 acres, respectively.

The 2010 survey found no households in Kalmandasguri belonging to the landlord class (Table 11), and most of the land in the village was owned by peasant households. This shows that older patterns of land concentration were not present, and land was largely controlled by small cultivators.

The distribution of acreage under ownership and operational holdings were similar. Upper-peasant households, comprising 13 per cent of all households and whose primary source of income was from crop production, held 41 per cent of the total land each under ownership and operational holdings, respectively. Households belonging to the "poor peasant: small employment" and "poor peasant: semi-proletarian" socio-

Table 9 *Distribution of cropland ownership holdings, by social group, Kalmandasguri, 2010, in number and acre*

Land size	General		SC		ST		OBC		Muslim		All	
	Number	Acre	Number	Acre	Number	Acre	Number	Acre	Number	Acre	Number	Acre
Landless	1 (16.7)	0	5 (9.4)	0	1 (10)	0	0	0	26 (42.6)	0	33 (22.4)	0
0.01–2.5 acres	5 (83.3)	2.09 (100)	41 (77.4)	33.47 (59.9)	9 (90)	10.46 (100)	15 (88.2)	13.2 (61.3)	35 (57.4)	18.64 (100)	105 (71.4)	77.86 (71.7)
2.5–5 acres	0	0	7 (13.2)	22.36 (40.1)	0	0	2 (11.8)	8.33 (38.7)	0	0	9 (6.1)	30.69 (28.3)
Total	6 (100)	2.09 (100)	53 (100)	55.83 (100)	10 (100)	10.46 (100)	17 (100)	21.53 (100)	61 (100)	18.64 (100)	147 (100)	108.55 (100)

Note: Figures in parenthesis denote the percentage share of the column totals.
Source: PARI survey (2010).

Table 10 *Distribution of cropland operational holdings, by social group, Kalmandasguri, 2010, in number and acre*

Land size	General		SC		ST		OBC		Muslim		All	
	Number	Acre	Number	Acre	Number	Acre	Number	Acre	Number	Acre	Number	Acre
Landless	1 (16.7)	0	4 (7.5)	0	2 (20)	0	0	0	24 (39.3)	0	31 (21.1)	0
0.01–2.5 acres	5 (83.3)	1.84 (100)	45 (84.9)	41.49 (75.2)	8 (80)	8.13 (100)	15 (88.2)	13.49 (61.1)	37 (60.7)	20.65 (100)	110 (74.8)	85.6 (79.4)
2.5–5 acres	0	0	4 (7.5)	13.65 (24.8)	0	0	2 (11.8)	8.58 (38.9)	0	0	6 (4.1)	22.23 (20.6)
Total	6 (100)	1.84 (100)	53 (100)	55.14 (100)	10 (100)	8.13 (100)	17 (100)	22.07 (100)	61 (100)	20.65 (100)	147 (100)	107.83 (100)

Note: Figures in parenthesis denote the percentage share of the column totals.
Source: PARI survey (2010).

Table 11 *Distribution of cropland ownership and operational holdings, by class, Kalmandasguri, 2010*, in per cent

Class	Share in households	Share in area under ownership holdings	Share in area under operational holdings
Landlord/capitalist farmer	0	0	0
Upper peasant	12.9	41.3	40.6
Poor peasant: small self-employment	7.5	8.6	10.3
Poor peasant: semi-proletarian	25.9	25.5	28.2
Manual worker	37.4	9.5	10.6
Others	16.3	15.1	10.3
All	100	100	100

Source: PARI survey (2010).

economic classes held shares of land comparable to their shares in the population. In contrast, inequality in landholdings existed for manual-worker households, which comprised 37 per cent of the village population but owned and operated only 10 per cent and 11 per cent of the total land under possession of households, respectively.

The current distribution of landholdings in all the three villages discussed in this section is an outcome of the implementation of land reforms on the previous land tenure structure. In the following section, I will discuss this implementation and its impact on the distribution of landholdings in the study villages.

Implementation of Land Reforms and Its Impact

Panahar

Implementation

Panahar village of Kotulpur block is situated on the eastern fringes of Bankura district, which was created by the British government by merging two distinct geographical and territorial divisions. The northern and western parts were formed from the forested Jungle Mahals, whereas the eastern and central parts were part of the erstwhile Bishnupur Raj. The eastern parts possessed fertile alluvial soil, whereas the rest of the district was characterised by undulating highlands with loamy soil. Another distinction between these two parts was in the size of landholdings – the eastern and central parts had smaller holdings compared to the western part (Robertson 1926).

The district was divided into estates under the Permanent Settlement agreement. Under this, zamindars were given the right to collect revenue and retain a share as profit, however, in many estates, a class of absentee landlords who subleased their revenue-collecting rights to inferior intermediaries emerged. Within the estates, there were the *raiyati* or cultivating tenures and a few rent-free tenures. Despite the presence of intermediaries in Bankura in 1926, 42 per cent of the land was under the direct control of the tenure holders, unlike in other western districts of the Bengal Presidency (*ibid.*).

The growing control of moneylenders over land and resources was established by the end of the colonial period. Tenure holders entered into the money lending business, extending loans to their subordinate tenants. Tenants failing to pay the heavy interest on borrowed sums immediately lost control over their lands. The moneylenders usually retained portions of the most fertile lands under their direct control and resettled dispossessed tenants on the remaining lands (*ibid.*).Their increasing control of land was seen through the increase in *raiyat*s (cultivators) paying produce-based rents, known as *sanja* and *bhag*,[7] which were higher than the fixed rents paid in cash. The moneylender class increasingly dispossessed *raiyat*s holding occupancy rights, followed by settling these lands with former proprietors of these lands at high *sanja* and *bhag* rates. The first census survey undertaken in independent India in 1950–51 reported that 26.6 per cent of the total agricultural land in Bankura was being cultivated by tenants paying produce-shared rents (Mitra 1953).

During colonial times, a large proportion of landless agricultural labourers in the district belonging to the socially backward Bauri caste and tribal Santhal groups supplied wage labour to the tenure holders directly controlling the land. This landholding system in colonial Bankura persisted in the post-Independence period and was ultimately altered after the implementation of land reforms.

Panahar's proximity to Kotulpur town, an important commercial centre in the region even before Independence, influenced the pre-land reforms land tenure structure of the village. The size of landholdings in this part of Bankura was relatively smaller than that in the rest of the district, and landowners directly supervised the sharecroppers and

---

[7] Under the *bhag* tenure the rent was half of the gross produce.

agricultural labourers. The movement for land reforms gained traction in Bankura during the first United Front government in West Bengal. Led by the Krishak Sabha, the push for identifying and distributing *benami*[8] land was largely restricted to the southern parts of the district that had larger landholdings and an already established base of popular support for the Krishak Sabha.[9]

The registration of the *bargadar*s began in Bankura even before 1977 – those from Panahar registered as early as 1972. The most daunting hurdle to this process was the political clout and administrative support of the erstwhile Congress government enjoyed by landowners. Sudeb Mondal, a sharecropper, describes how his father Rupchand, one of Panahar's first registered bargadars, was once picked up and harassed by police to forego his *bargadar* claims on the land.[10] Numerous instances of administrative, bureaucratic, and judicial favour towards landlords prior to 1977 are well documented. For example, Mitra (1977) narrated the anguish of sharecropper Indra Lohar's loss of land, and Bandyopadhyay (1971) recorded a case in Salihan village (Onda block of Bankura) where *bargadars'* harvest was captured by landlords with the help of police – an outright denial of tenants' rights as granted under the West Bengal Land Reforms Act. Similar cases of bargadars denied justice and faults within the legal system were scrutinised in the district's Gangajalghati and Hinjuri villages under Bishnupur police station (Directorate of Land Records and Surveys 1975).

With the election of the Left Front government in 1977, policy shifted in favour of the sharecroppers and towards agrarian reforms. The simultaneous process of political decentralisation through the panchayats ensured greater representation of small cultivators, sharecroppers, and landless agricultural labourers in these bodies. Supported by the Krishak Sabha, panchayats' role was crucial in the successful implementation of land reforms.

Gour Hari Pal, a 75-year-old resident of Banmukho village of Kotulpur panchayat, is a veteran Krishak Sabha leader and elected gram panchayat member in 1978. He revealed that one of the priority functions of the elected

---

[8] The land that large *landowners and jotedar*s divided under different family members, relatives, and others to escape the stipulated land ceiling came to be known as *benami* land. Under the United Front government of 1967–70, there were drives to identify these *benami* possessions and acquire them for redistribution.

[9] Interview with Nakul Mahato on July 20, 2017.

[10] Interview with Sudeb Mondal on July 18, 2017.

panchayats under the Left rule was to impart administrative training of the elected members, many of whom were illiterate, to enable them to better perform their duties.[11] Badal Sadra, a resident of neighbouring Muidara village, has been a Krishak Sabha activist since 1970–71 and was a panchayat member during 1993–98. He stated that the movement for the registration of *bargadar*s occurred during 1978 and 1982–83 in the region.[12] However, the process of identifying and redistributing ceiling-surplus land, which started around the same time, continued until 1990. Panahar's Chandi Charan Pal, a Krishak Sabha activist since 1990–91 and its current *anchal-sabhadhipati* (area president), added that some land redistribution in the village continued till as late as 2011.[13]

Operation Barga[14]
Operation Barga was the field-based programme undertaken by the Left Front government during 1978–81 to fast-track the registration of sharecroppers by organising rural camps. In Kotulpur block, registration camps for sharecroppers were located in Gopinathpur (11 km away from Kotulpur town) and Madanmohanpur (10 km from Deshra-Koalpara village panchayat) villages. The panchayat bodies played the role of a "sahayak" (assistant) to sharecroppers in the process of filing their claims to the record of rights by writing applications and remaining present during land reforms officials' field visits for investigating claims.[15]

The Krishak Sabha organised *para-baithak*s (hamlet meetings) to inform residents of various land reform policies undertaken by the State government. Sharecroppers were encouraged to register during these interactive sessions. Gour Hari Pal remarked that the Krishak Sabha's role was to organise the movement in the fields ("mathe andolon porichalona kora"). Furthermore, landowners filed legal cases against the sharecroppers' claims; in turn, the sharecroppers refused to part with the landowners' share of the produce and utilised it to defray their legal costs.[16]

Swapan Bhangi started sharecropping in 1972–73 and registered under Operation Barga in 1982–83. After obtaining the plot markings from the revenue department officer (also referred to as the *amin* and was also

---

[11] Interview with Gour Hari Pal on July 19, 2017.
[12] Interview with Badal Sadra on July 18, 2017.
[13] Interview with Chandi Charan Pal on July 19, 2017.
[14] *Barga* refers to the sharecropping contract.
[15] Interview with Gour Hari Pal on July 19, 2017.
[16] *Ibid.*

responsible for land surveys), he submitted his self-completed application at the Joyrambati Settlement Camp established by the Government of West Bengal. The land reforms officials then conducted a field investigation and provided him a registration certificate. He considered Operation Barga as a watershed event that altered the relationship between landowners and sharecroppers. Despite tensions with the landlords, he noted that sharecroppers chose to register themselves because they felt that they would be evicted regardless. During this time, landowners stopped extending loans to sharecroppers.[17]

Madan Mahanto, a Krishak Sabha member since 1978 and Panahar panchayat member during 1993–97, described how the Krishak Sabha played an active role in identifying ceiling-surplus land and in following up on the redistribution process with the Kotulpur block land reforms officer (BLRO). The Krishak Sabha generated a list of landless households, which was announced at the *para-baithak*, and divided the ceiling-surplus land among them. These beneficiaries were asked to occupy their designated plot on the specified day when the land surveyor would be present. On this day, Krishak Sabha leaders assisted the beneficiaries in identifying their exact plots. The officials, along with the activists then prepared beneficiaries' documents, mentioning their designated plot numbers, and submitted them to the panchayat. Panchayat leaders forwarded the documents to the BLRO, who would then issue legal *pattas* (land deeds) to the beneficiaries.[18]

Stressing the importance of mobilisation during the occupation of the ceiling-surplus land to resist eviction by landowners, Gour Hari Pal stated that peasants' only strength was in their numbers, "not in the power of the sticks in their hands" ("hatey lathi chhilo na").[19] Led by the Krishak Sabha along with the administrative support of the decentralised panchayats, these mobilisations played an important role in the implementation of land reforms in Panahar.

Impact
The scope of land reforms in Panahar can be seen from Vikas Rawal's 1995 village study. He found that 22 per cent of households received a total of 14 acres of agricultural land under redistribution, wherein mostly landless

---

[17] Interview with Swapan Bhangi on July 17, 2017.
[18] Interview with Madan Mahanto on July 18, 2017.
[19] Interview with Gour Hari Pal on July 19, 2017.

and land-poor households received *pattas*. In addition, the majority of the leased-in land under operation (12 per cent of the total operational land) was cultivated by registered sharecroppers. Also, nine households had received homestead plots of 4 katha (one katha= 1/60 of an acre) each under the agrarian reforms programme (Rawal 1999).

The largest landholding family in pre-land reforms Panahar were the Khans. Abdul Baset Khan, owned a combined 187 *bighas* (62.3 acres) of agricultural land in the village and neighbouring Koalpara village, non-agricultural land including multiple ponds, and 0.8 acre in Kotulpur – here, the Khans continued to receive a commission on the sale of raw hides at the weekly cattle market. They donated their property in Sagardighi of Murshidabad district to the Wakf Board.[20] Abdul Khan's grandsons, Anwar Ali Khan and Asaduzamman Khan, and their families presently reside in the village. Asaduzamman Khan, the largest landowner in 2010, shifted to non-agricultural business in the post-land reforms period. He bought a rice mill four years ago, now managed by his elder son, whereas his younger son, a PhD holder, teaches in Rasulpur in Barddhaman district. Though his land was demarcated as ceiling surplus, he was able to legally retain it. In 2010, he leased out a substantial amount of land to sharecroppers.[21]

Satya Narayan Koley belongs to the other pre-land reforms landlord family in Panahar. Having lost land under the land ceiling laws, his family presently owns 13.2 acres of cropland. About 12–13 acres was vested between 1977 and 2006 in four stages; in each of the first three acquisitions, he lost 4 acres, followed by 5 *shataks* (one *shatak* = 1/100 of an acre) in the last acquisition. The surplus lands also included two ponds – one measuring 2.77 acres and the other 0.69 acre. He contested the first three acquisitions in both the Bishnupur district civil court and the high court, with the cases active from 1977 to 1990. When the fourth acquisition occurred, he decided to avoid the expensive legal route and entered into negotiations with the BLRO, which resulted in his family relinquishing outlying land and retaining land closer to their house. He mentioned that there was no difference in the quality of these lands – all were irrigated and triple-cropped.[22]

In the pre-land reforms period, a section of landless agricultural

[20] Interview with Anwar Ali Khan on July 18, 2017.
[21] Interview with Asaduzamman Khan on July 17, 2017.
[22] Interview with Satya Narayan Koley on July 17, 2017.

labourers were employed in both agricultural and non-agricultural work, with wages as low as Rs 4–5 per day. These landless agricultural-labour households primarily belonged to the SCs. Satya Narayan Koley stated that his vested lands were redistributed among these sections of landless SC households in Panahar, adding that most beneficiaries could not retain the redistributed land they were assigned. Though this point could not be corroborated from the survey data, the *District Human Development Report for Bankura* reported that by the end of 2005, 15.5 per cent of the *pattadars* (beneficiaries of redistributed land) had alienated their land. This was higher than the State figure of 13.2 per cent, however only 0.4 per cent of *pattadars* sold the land received through land reforms (GoWB 2007a). Since losing his land under land reforms, Satya Narayan Koley has not bought any new land but has attempted to consolidate his existing landholdings, stating that small holdings were economically unviable. In the last two years, he and his sons have started a dairy business.[23]

The region under the Deshra-Koalpara panchayat, of which Panahar is a part, traditionally had a section of non-cultivating landholders, settled in Kotulpur town, who hired sharecroppers to cultivate their lands.[24] These sharecroppers formed a substantial population of the village and cultivated on a 50:50 crop-sharing basis. Kanai Panja, a 70-year-old SC resident and sharecropper stated that in the early 1970s, he had to give half the share of produce to the landowner, who shared half the cost of cultivation. With only a single crop cycle, he sought employment in non-agricultural activities during the lean season, resorting to jobs such as mending straw-roofs and other construction work at a daily wage of one rupee and four annas (Rs 1.25).[25]

At times of financial crisis in the pre-land reforms period, landowners served as moneylenders for sharecroppers. For example, Kanai Panja stated that he took loans from his landowner, Gopal Chatterjee, when he was in dire straits. These loans carried an exorbitant interest rate of ten rupees for every hundred rupees borrowed. He preferred taking grain loans, as he had young children and there was overall scarcity of food in the village. For every 20 kg of paddy ("char sholi dhan") borrowed, 20 kg of paddy was charged as interest ("char sholi barie dite hoto").[26] Sudeb

---

[23] *Ibid.*

[24] Interviews with Badal Sadra on July 18, 2017 and Gour Hari Pal on July 19, 2017.

[25] Interview with Kanai Panja on July 17, 2017.

[26] *Ibid.*

Mondal recalled that there was no relaxation in paying the landowner's share of half the produce, even in times of drought.[27]

Some large landowners voluntarily registered their sharecroppers and agreed to the stipulated arrangement of crop-sharing under Operation Barga. Such is the case of Anwar Ali Khan, a 75-year-old retired primary school teacher and panchayat pradhan from 1978 to 1991, owned over 10 acres of agricultural land, some of which he has leased out on a shared rent contract. He narrated how his association with the Krishak Sabha since 1967 led him to voluntarily register his sharecroppers during Operation Barga. The 2010 village survey showed that 1.5 acres of his land was leased out on shared rent to two registered sharecroppers, one Muslim and one SC.[28]

Sharecroppers such as Sudeb Mondal gained from the agrarian reforms. His family of traditional sharecroppers had been cultivating lands belonging to the Laha family, the erstwhile zamindars of Joypur in Bankura district who presently live in Jharkhand and annually visit Panahar to collect rent. Sudeb Mondal's father was the first registered sharecropper in the village and presently sharecrops on two acres of land. After land reforms and improvements in irrigation, Sudeb Mondal was able to buy land. According to the 2010 survey, he owned 4.68 acres of land and was categorised as a capitalist farmer, growing *aus* paddy, potato, and *boro* paddy. Sudeb Mondal stated that the latter two crops were introduced into the cropping cycle with the expansion of irrigation in the village and had contributed towards raising incomes and savings and investments in agricultural land. Though he wanted to purchase the land that he sharecropped, the landowners refused to make the sale, as they considered their annual visit as a leisure trip which they wanted to continue making ("berate jachhi").[29]

However, there were instances where the sharecroppers and landowners negotiated *barga* land sales. Badal Sadra, the local Krishak Sabha activist, stated that some landlords wished to sell land owing to financial stress but could not legally do so without sharecroppers' consent.[30] Swapan Bhangi reported that his landowner sold a portion of the *barga* land he was cultivating and that each of them received half of the sale proceeds. He explained that tenancy reforms required landowners to obtain

[27] Interview with Sudeb Mondal on July18, 2017.
[28] Interview with Anwar Ali Khan on July 18, 2017.
[29] Interview with Sudeb Mondal on July 18, 2017.
[30] Interview with Badal Sadra on July 18, 2017.

sharecroppers' consent. So, the landowner first transferred all the land to Swapan Bhangi, who in turn sold it to the purchaser.[31] The tenancy reforms have ensured that sharecroppers are consulted in all matters related to the land they cultivate. Furthermore, Rawal's (2001a) study on land markets in Muidara and Panahar villages between 1977 and 1995 supported the finding that, in the post-land reforms period, the landless and land-poor gained from land markets as net purchasers of agricultural land. The existing political, social, and economic conditions contributed towards the rural poor and sharecroppers becoming owners of small landholdings.

In the pre-land reforms period, Panahar saw an influx of tribal migrant agricultural workers, travelling from the drought-hit western parts of Bankura, Purulia, and Medinipur districts where irrigation was poorly developed in these areas and people faced abject poverty. Till the 1980s, the village saw a steady inflow of these labourers, who would live in landowners' houses or build makeshift huts. They arrived during the sowing season and left by February, around the time of their festival of Parab, though some eventually settled in Panahar.[32] Even before the agrarian reforms programme was undertaken, this seasonal labour migration during times of drought, from the water-scarce western and central parts of the district to the fertile eastern parts, was an established migration circuit in Bankura, locally known as "pube-jawa" (migrating to the east).[33] In 2010, there were 17 resident ST households in Panahar, 11 of which owned 0.01–2.5 acres of agricultural land. Therefore, in the post-land reforms period, these families, which had migrated from other parts of Bankura and neighbouring districts, were no longer only agricultural labourers but also became small landowners settled in Panahar.[34]

Amarsinghi

Implementation
Maldah district was carved from parts of Purnia, Dinajpur, and Rajshahi districts in 1813, when the Permanent Settlement was in operation. The district comprised three distinctive physio-geographic regions – the Barind, Tal, and Diara – formed by the criss-crossing Mahananda and

---

[31] Interview with Swapan Bhangi on July 17, 2017.
[32] Interview with Satya Narayan Koley on July 17, 2017.
[33] Interview with Achintya Ray on July 21, 2017
[34] Other village studies (Rogaly 1996) have also reported that in the post-land reforms period there was a trend among the seasonal migrant labourers to settle in the agriculturally advanced

Figure 1 *Physiographic divisions of Maldah district*

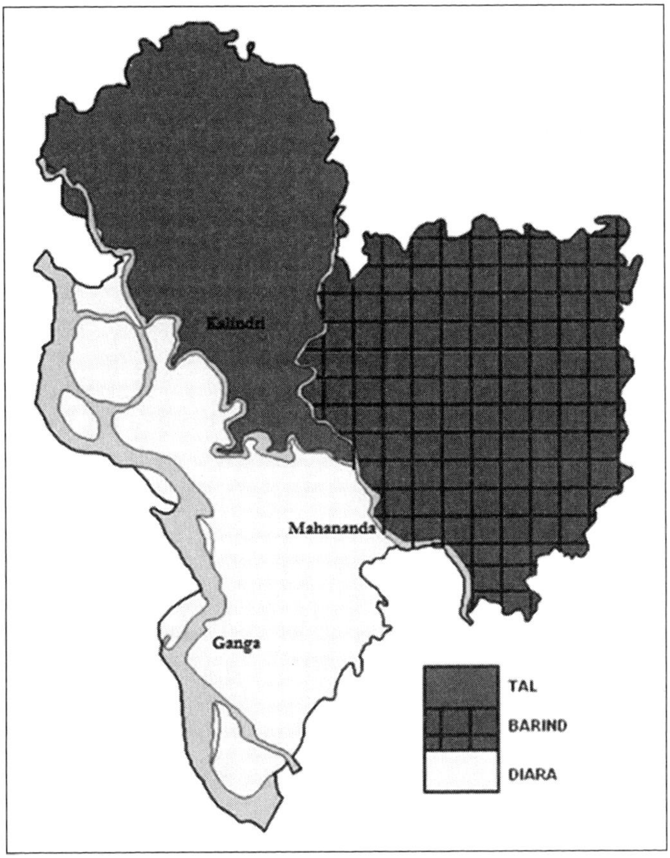

Source: Siddiqui (2013)

Kalindi rivers (see Figure 1). Barind has undulating lands with red alluvial soil, the Tal is characterised by its low-lying marshy lands with swamps and frequent floods, and the Diara consists of the most fertile lands of the district. Amarsinghi village is in Ratua block and situated in the Tal. These geographical divisions of the district were an important factor in shaping agrarian relations and the implementation of land reforms.

---

regions of West Bengal. This was associated with the increased labour requirement in these regions as certain sections of the untouchable castes moved out of the labour force, as feudal obligations between the employer and workers weakened.

The British divided the district into estates controlled by different zamindars with revenue-collecting rights, many of whom were also non-residents and of aristocratic lineage. The *raiyati* tenure holders were settled in these estates and held heritable rights over their lands – they cultivated 72 per cent of all the land surveyed in the district during 1928–1935. Forty-four per cent of *raiyati* holdings were less than one acre, whereas another 24 per cent was between one and two acres (Lambourn 1918; Carter 1938).

The Barind area was a newly reclaimed region of the district and had a greater proportion of *adhi* or sharecropping tenures held by Santhal cultivators, the first settlers of these lands. These sharecropping cultivators faced increasing indebtedness, which led them to alienate their possessed lands. The landlords, officials, and moneylenders were complicit in exacting *abwab*s or illegal taxes from the Santhal cultivators (Carter 1938; Barman 1938). The Census Report of 1951 noted that 30 per cent of the total land in the district was cultivated by sharecroppers (Dhanagare 1991). Sharecropping was also found to be prevalent in regions outside the Barind, under the various estates, although to a lesser extent.

The Report on the Lower Classes in Bengal suggested the presence of a class of agricultural labourers in the *zamindari* estates during the colonial period (Government of Bengal 1888). It noted that agricultural labourers received employment for no more than six months of the year, and, for the rest of the time, did odd jobs such as collecting jungle produce, weaving bamboo baskets, and husking and parching rice. They were paid monthly wages, along with a morning meal of dry paddy and midday meal of rice and fish or pulses. Long-term labourers were generally given advance payments for two to three years, which bonded them to their employers for that period. Because agricultural labourers did not receive rent-free land, they paid rent for their homesteads; debt was common among them.

The Tebhaga movement, which started on the eve of Independence and demanded a two-thirds share of the produce for sharecroppers, was restricted to the Barind area in pre-partitioned Maldah. In Barind, the exploitation of the sharecropper class – Rajbanshi, Santhal, and Poli groups – provided fertile ground for raising demands for Tebhaga.[35] In the Tal region, movements immediately after Independence were against illegal exactions on *haat*s or markets.[36]

---

[35] See Sen (1972) for details regarding the significant participation of Santhals and Rajbangshis in the Tebhaga movement.
[36] Interview with Salimuddin on January 14, 2018.

When the Estates Acquisition Act was passed in 1953 and the zamindars realised that they could not retain their properties, they started selling their lands and ponds. The large *jotedar*s and *mahajan*s took advantage of this to expand their land ownership.[37]

The movement to identify *benami* or fraudulently held lands began in Maldah as early as 1962 in a part of Barind known as the Habibpur region. Later, the movement to identify benami lands gained momentum in the rest of West Bengal under the United Front in 1967.[38] Due to the short terms of the two subsequent United Front governments, the redistribution of *patta*s could not be undertaken. Nevertheless, the following slogans remained: "barti jomi dakhol koro" ("occupy ceiling-surplus land") and "dakhole rekhe chas koro" ("occupy and cultivate the ceiling-surplus land").[39] The *benami* land movement also took place in Amarsinghi and surrounding regions. Paresh Basak, a resident of the neighbouring Baidyanathpur village of Samsi village panchayat and a former panchayat member, stated that the *benami* lands belonging to Gaffur Haji, a large *jotedar* owning about 2,200 *bigha*s of land in the region, were identified during the United Front government rule.[40] In Amarsinghi, the redistribution of land through *patta*s began after 1977, and the implementation of land reforms continued till the early 1990s.[41]

Paresh Basak became an active Krishak Sabha member in 1976 and was a Samsi village panchayat member from 1978 to 1988, during which he also became vice chairman of the panchayat samiti. During his tenure, he oversaw the process of land redistribution. He explained that the panchayat samiti chairman would decide the day that panchayat officials would visit different village panchayats to record the amount of vested land available for distribution and the persons already occupying and cultivating the ceiling-surplus land. The next stage involved preparing the priority list.[42] The ceiling-surplus land was redistributed according to this priority list, prepared according to the State guidelines and usually included all probable beneficiary households of a panchayat who met the eligibility criteria for receiving *patta*s. The government established the

[37] Interviews with Paresh Basak on January 13, 2018 and Salimuddin on January 14, 2018.
[38] Interview with Tushar Bhattacharya on January 16, 2018.
[39] Interview with Najimul Haque on January 25, 2018.
[40] Interview with Paresh Basak on January 13, 2018.
[41] Interview with Anukul Mandal on January 12, 2018.
[42] Interview with Paresh Basak on January 13, 2018.

limit of distributed ceiling-surplus land to either *bargadars* or *raiyats* at one acre or three *bighas*.[43] Under this limit, a landless family was eligible to receive up to one acre of land, whereas in the case of a *bargadar*, half the sharecropped land was considered when deciding the amount of ceiling-surplus land (Board of Revenue 1991).

Paresh Basak further described that the priority list he handled included about a dozen categories, with landless households at the fore. Social group was also taken into consideration when making the priority list – ST landless households were followed by SC and OBC households. The *bargadars* and other *raiyats* who had already occupied ceiling-surplus land were considered for *patta* redistribution. Paresh Basak added that the amount of land allotted to a household depended on the total acreage of ceiling-surplus land available for redistribution as well as the number of eligible beneficiaries residing close to the land. Before being finalised, the list would be discussed with the local Krishak Sabha members, who assisted the panchayat officials when they conducted field visits to the villages, similar to the process in Panahar.[44] Once the list was prepared, the proposed beneficiaries had to file a written application to the village panchayat, which would then forward it to the BLRO along with its recommendation. *Pattas* had to be approved by the sub-divisional officer and would finally be distributed either from the BLRO's office or at special block-level meetings organised with the assistance of the panchayats.[45]

There were instances in Amarsinghi of large landowners using fraudulent methods to evade the ceiling laws. Anukul Mondal, a veteran Krishak Sabha activist from the village and a panchayat representative for three continuous terms since 1983, narrated the following case: Ananta Mondal, one of the largest landowners of Amarsinghi, donated one *bigha* of land to a local school to evade the ceiling law. A widow had been cultivating this plot as a sharecropper, and when it was identified as ceiling surplus, the authorities issued her a notice to vacate. Anukul Mondal and other Krishak Sabha leaders intervened and presented the case to the BLRO to protect her rights. Her deceased husband's sharecropping rights had not been transferred to her in absence of a male heir. The intervention

---

[43] File No. 13846 (17)- GE/ 251/81, dated November 26, 1981, issued by the Office of Board of Revenue, Government of West Bengal, Department of Panchayat and Rural Development, Compendium II (GoWB, undated).

[44] Interview with Paresh Basak on January 13, 2018.

[45] Interview with Najimul Haque on January 25, 2018.

was successful, and the BLRO issued a notice allowing her to continue cultivating the land. She was asked to submit the landowner's legal share of the produce at the BLRO's office and to keep a receipt, according to the usual practice in case of a dispute.[46]

Impact

According to village elders, colonial Amarsinghi formed a part of the estate belonging to the Pathans of Nurpur.[47] Colonial reports also mention the Khan zamindars of Nurpur belonging to an old Pathan family; commenting on the status of these landlords, a British administrator wrote, "Their property has been considerably reduced, but their bearing and local influence indicates their aristocratic origin" (Carter 1938). The neighbouring Chanchal Estate (the largest in the district) was outside the control of the Pathans. This led some Amarsinghi residents to migrate to the neighbouring estate and take up *raiyati* holdings, despite its marshy and poor-quality lands to evade the authoritarian rent collectors appointed by the Pathan zamindars.[48]

In pre-land reforms Amarsinghi, the largest landholders were three brothers – Kalachand, Ananta Mondal, and Panchanan Mondal – who collectively held almost 100 acres or 300 *bigha*s of land and whose house was the only permanent structure in the whole village. All three have passed away, and none of their family members presently live in the village. Residents stated that they increased their land ownership through the interests on loans they gave. Their lands were spread across Amarsinghi and the neighbouring Gopalpur *mouja* or revenue village, as was the case with the other landholding families of the village.[49] The Mondal brothers died without any heirs to their property, so their relatives such as Subhashini Mondal, an Amarsinghi resident, inherited the land. The brothers lost the largest amounts of land under the ceiling laws, and after 1977, when they realised they would not be able to retain their surplus lands, they cooperated in the process of land redistribution. Gokul Pradhan, who received 32 *shatak*s of *patta* land formerly belonging

---

[46] Interview with Anukul Mondal on January 12, 2018. One of the critiques of the West Bengal land reforms programme was its failure to recognise women as sharecroppers and legitimate heirs of tenancy rights.

[47] *Ibid.*

[48] Interviews with Anukul Mondal and Prafulla Chandra Mondal on January 12, 2018.

[49] *Ibid.*

to Ananta Mondal in 1980, stated that the plot was shown to him by the "malik" (owner) himself.[50]

The United Nations-World Institute of Development Economics and Research (UN-WIDER) survey conducted in 1990 in Amarsinghi revealed that 14 of all 57 households had received ceiling-surplus agricultural land and, of these 14 households, 7 belonged to the SCs. An average of 0.11 acre of agricultural land was redistributed among the beneficiary households, and the total acreage of redistributed land (6.35 acres) formed 11 per cent of the total ownership holding of the village. Four previously landless households became landholders through land reforms, and an additional four households, including the lone ST household, received homestead land. The 2005 survey showed that of Amarsinghi's 107 households, 35 were SC, 71 were OBC, and one was ST; there were no Muslim households. Furthermore, 31 per cent of the households received the average 0.11 acre under land reforms, with OBC households (85 per cent) as the largest section of beneficiaries. Homestead land was redistributed to 19 per cent of households, the majority of which were SC – 8 of the 12 SC households that received homestead land owned no agricultural land. Six other households received either bamboo orchards or ponds under land reforms.

Prafulla Chandra Mondal, a 68-year-old resident, recalled that since he began cultivating at the age of 20, besides the three Mondal brothers, there were other landed families in Amarsinghi whose land ownership consisted of 30–70 *bigha*s (10–23.3 acres). Out of these landed families, all of which were OBC, the ones with relatively fewer male heirs managed to retain large landholdings in subsequent generations by avoiding inter-generational fragmentation of land.[51] He added that in the pre-land reforms period, Amarsinghi had a greater proportion of landed households than the other villages of the region. Large landholders had their lands cultivated by sharecroppers who were from Amarsinghi or the surrounding villages. Sharecroppers had no occupancy rights to the land, and their contracts were almost always oral. The common practice of shifting the sharecroppers to other plots of land every one or two years was done to prevent them from making occupancy claims. The prevalent sharecropping arrangement was a 50:50 share of the produce, with the cost of cultivation entirely borne by the sharecropper.[52] Landowners,

---

[50] Interview with Gokul Pradhan on January 13, 2018.
[51] Interview with Prafulla Chandra Mondal on January 12, 2018.
[52] Interview with Nimai Das on January 13, 2018.

called "morol," would take their share from the field, or in other cases, it had to be transported to their "bhite bari" (barn). Many landowners in the region were not residents and would visit the village only during the harvest season to collect rent.[53]

The 2005 survey found only three households that leased out land on shared-lease contracts to registered sharecroppers and only five sharecropper households that cultivated 2.5 per cent of the total operational land. Both findings indicate that previous sharecropper households became small landholders through land redistribution by land reforms. This was a major transformation from the pre-land reforms period when Amarsinghi households were major lessors of surplus lands to sharecropper households within and outside the village.

In the post-Independence period, there was a rise in the population of landless agricultural labourers in Amarsinghi. Before land reforms, they would migrate from the southern parts of Ratua *thana* to work in the paddy fields of the village.[54] Mostly belonging to Das, Tiyar, and Parihar SC groups, they migrated from low-lying regions that were prone to frequent flooding and covered by mango orchards. Initially, they performed harvesting and threshing activities and temporarily remained in the village with relatives; some eventually settled in Amarsinghi and even bought homestead land.[55]

One such landless household that settled in Amarsinghi was that of Ashok Parihar's, who moved to the village when he was a child and is now in his mid-fifties. His mother was from Amarsinghi and his father belonged to a village in Katihar district of Bihar – both belonged to landless families. Within a few years of marriage, amidst general food scarcity in his father's village, the couple decided to relocate to Amarsinghi with their children. Not having a residence there, they initially shifted from one house to another, living with relatives such as Ashok Parihar's maternal uncle. Ashok Parihar remarked that they led an existence of vagabonds. His father started working as a daily wage labourer, whereas his mother was forced to do paddy threshing, even immediately after giving birth

---

[53] Interviews with Prafulla Chandra Mondal on January 12, 2018 and Paresh Basak on January 13, 2018.

[54] Historically, parts of Ratua thana, under which Amarsinghi is located, had a large proportion (49 per cent) of double-cropped area, known as *do-fasili* land – *aman* and *aus* paddy were the two main crops grown in this region (Carter 1938).

[55] Interview with Prafulla Chandra Mondal on January 12, 2018.

to her third son –this work earned her about 0.93 kg of rice per day.[56] In the early 1990s, 1–1.5 *bighas* belonging to *jotedar* Ananta Mondal was redistributed as homestead plots among landless, agricultural-labourer households.[57] Ashok Parihar was one of the beneficiaries of this homestead redistribution. The homestead *patta* was originally received by his father, Buddha Parihar; currently, Ashok Parihar and his two brothers, along with their families, live on 5 *katha* of land. Ashok Parihar said, "ei bhite jomi tai amader parthakko" ("this homestead land has made the difference").[58] The homestead *patta* provided relief from the insecurity of homelessness.

In the 1960s, the daily wage of agricultural labourers was around 8 *anna*s and their share of daily meals consisted of 2.5 *powa* or about 700 gm of paddy. In case labourers opted out of receiving meals, they would receive one *seer* (1.25 kg) of paddy to take home, along with their daily wage. There was also a type of long-term worker, referred to as "laga thaka" ("at constant disposal"), who remained attached to a landowner; this worker worked on the landowner's lands and contributed to the household chores and, on days there was no work, could work on others' lands. This worker would start working at the break of dawn and continue till noon, take a break between 12 pm and 3 pm for lunch and bathing, and resume work till sundown.[59] After the implementation of land reforms, this labour contract disappeared.

Additionally, in the post-land reforms period, wages of agricultural labourers rose due to the spread of irrigation and high-yielding variety (HYV) seeds. As part of the support given to small producers, the State, through its decentralised local government system, played an important role in extending irrigation, electricity, and input packages (Saha and Swaminathan 1994). Due to the introduction of HYV seeds and a subsequent rise in paddy production, the share of produce received by agricultural labourers increased as kind-wages also rose. Piece-rated wages for harvesting, carrying, and threshing operations rose to four *dhara* of paddy (approximately 20 kg) for every five *bighas* of land due to production increasing to 10–15 *mon* (one mon is approximately 38

[56] Interview with Ashok Parihar on January 13, 2018; Speaking of his childhood, Parihar said that on most days they would survive on rice starch. He remembered the relatively sweeter starch of the paddy harvested in the *bhadoi* season (*aus* paddy) and that, occasionally, generous residents would offer puffed rice to the children. He never attended school.

[57] Interview with Anukul Mondal on January 12, 2018.

[58] Interview with Ashok Parihar on January 13, 2018.

[59] Interview with Prafulla Chandra Mondal on January 12, 2018.

kg) per *bigha* (1,140–1,710 kg per acre). Labourers collectively received 76 kg of paddy in the agricultural season, much higher than the wage rate paid in kind during the pre-land reforms period.[60]

Some agricultural labourers also received ceiling-surplus land, which enabled their economic mobility. In 1998, Manik Das received 61 *shatak*s (0.61 acre) of agricultural land and a homestead *patta* of 12 *shatak*s. Before receiving the patta land, he was a landless agricultural labourer and lived with his three brothers and father; his share in his father's previous homestead plot was only one shatak. He informed that since receiving the *patta* land, he has been cultivating *boro* paddy, which became possible in the village with expansion of irrigation; this has greatly improved his situation. He receives irrigation water from the river lift irrigation scheme and grows three cycles of crop – *aus* paddy, mustard, and *boro* paddy. He additionally bought two *bigha*s of land around 2008 and reconstructed his mud house into a permanent structure, with the help of the Indira Awaas Yojana and a loan. He labours out only when he has time.[61]

Kalmandasguri[62]

Implementation
Kalmandasguri village is located in the Bararangras block of Cooch Behar district, which was a princely state till 1948 when it joined the Indian Union. At this time, agrarian relations here were different from other parts of British-ruled Bengal where the Permanent Settlement was applied. Previously, the ruler of Cooch Behar had supreme control over land, followed by the *jotedar*s or revenue-paying landholders, then six levels of inferior subtenants, and finally the masses of sharecroppers, or *adhiar*s, as they were called in this part of Bengal. These sharecroppers had no right over the cultivated land, cultivated on a 50:50 crop-sharing arrangement, faced frequent evictions, and lived on landlords' lands. The failure of tenurial legislations to curb growing sub-infeudation resulted in the creation of a class of illegal tenants called *krishipraja*s (Chaudhuri 1903; Ganguli 1930; Todarmal 2002). Backward agricultural productivity and low levels of production (Sircar 1990) added to the poverty and indebtedness

---

[60] Interview with Ashok Parihar on January 13, 2018. Scholars have written on the role of land reforms in reducing poverty and raising calorie intake through increased agricultural wages (Besley and Burgess 1998; Ramachandran and Ramakumar 2001).

[61] Interview with Manik Das on January 13, 2018.

[62] This section is drawn from Basu (2015).

of sharecroppers (Chaudhuri 1986). In the post-Independence period, the *jotedars* emerged as the largest landholders in Cooch Behar, with some owning as much as 2,000 *bighas* (*ibid.*).

From the 1950s to the 1970s, the Krishak Sabha led mobilisations on issues of land redistribution and tenancy rights for sharecroppers. The two United Front governments in 1967 and 1969 drove the process of land reforms in the State, primarily through identifying *benami* lands and encouraging peasants to occupy them. Under the second United Front government, over 15,000 *bighas* of ceiling-surplus land, belonging to the erstwhile Cooch Behar Maharaja, was identified by the revenue department to be acquired. This ceiling-surplus land, which included 12,000 *bighas* (about 4,000 acres) of cultivable land, was then earmarked under the rules of the West Bengal Estates Acquisition Act, 1953. Harekrishna Konar, the then land revenue minister described the takeover of such princely wealth as a "big blow to feudalism."[63] The actual process of redistributing land started in 1977 when the Left Front government was elected; it ensured the agrarian reforms programme as the focal point of State administrative policies.

Similarly in Kalmandasguri, which falls under the Bararangras village panchayat, the Krishak Sabha led the first movement that aimed to identify *benami* land. Baidyanath Ray, Bhuvaneshwar Ray, and Mohammad Ali were some of the early leaders of the movement within the village. Further, the Krishak Sabha's campaigns against illegal exactions gained popular support in the village in the late 1960s. These exactions took the form of high interest rates demanded by the *jotedars* for grain loans given to sharecroppers, who were also cheated when produce was divided. The *jotedars* did not bear any of the input costs yet demanded more than 50 per cent of the produce.[64]

Taoli Oraon, a local Krishak Sabha leader and elected member of the village and district panchayats for two decades, described the process of land reform in Kalmandasguri. The Krishak Sabha first identified ceiling-surplus land, which was then acquired, often by means of mass action. The peasant movement faced physical resistance and violence from armed henchmen (*lathihar*) of the large landlords whose surplus land had been identified. The Krishak Sabha was also involved in negotiations

---

[63] "15 Hajar Bigha Jomi Dakhal: Samantabader Opor Prachanda Aghat" ("15,000 Bighas of Land Belonging to Cooch Behar Maharaj Taken Over: Big Blow for Feudalism"), *Ganashakti*, May 11, 1969.

[64] Interview with Taoli Oraon on September 7, 2013.

with the large landowners, who moved the courts for injunctions on land acquisition – this jeopardised the entire land reforms process.[65]

With regard to the redistribution of ceiling-surplus land, the Krishak Sabha, similar to the other two villages, generated lists of landless and sharecropper households, giving preference to households belonging to oppressed and minority social groups. They ensured that sharecroppers received as much land they were cultivating as possible. A plot of land identified as ceiling surplus was first allotted to the original occupiers and sharecroppers and, if there was land remaining for further redistribution, allotted among other landless households. The BLRO was then responsible for officially surveying land identified to be ceiling surplus. After that, all concerned parties were called together to implement the process of redistributing the ceiling-surplus land.[66] In spite of all the disruption by landowners, the Krishak Sabha and the elected local bodies ensured the success of land reforms.

The redistribution of homestead land was one of the important components of the land reforms programme in West Bengal.[67] In Kalmandasguri, its significance for the landless population was derived from the nature of housing in the pre-land reforms period. During that time, the *jotedar*'s house was surrounded by the stick-and-thatch huts of his sharecroppers and servants who provided services including domestic chores, maintaining the security of the *jotedar*'s property, winnowing paddy, and other menial tasks in exchange for a meagre, in-kind payment. When land reforms ensured homestead land to these households, they were freed from compulsory service to the *jotedar*.

Impact

The first study on the impact of land reforms in Kalmandasguri was through the Project on Rural Poverty and Social Change in West Bengal, under which village studies were conducted by UN-WIDER in 1987–89. Sengupta and Gazdar (2003) noted from the same survey results that one-

---

[65] *Ibid.*

[66] *Ibid.*

[67] The West Bengal Acquisition of Homestead Land for Agricultural Labourers, Artisans and Fishermen Act was passed in 1976 and aimed to provide homestead land to landless agricultural-labourer households. The majority of these households previously lived on landlords' land, which tied them to landlords' service. The Act gave agricultural-labour households the freedom to choose their employer, without the fear of losing their homes and livelihoods (Dasgupta 1984).

third of all households in the village benefited from land redistribution. New-found incomes obtained from redistributed land improved the economic condition of previously landless households, forming 28 per cent of their total incomes. Further, the second WIDER study conducted in Kalmandasguri in 1995 showed 43 out of all 100 households received 12.41 acres of land under redistribution, which constituted 23 per cent of the entire acreage under ownership holdings in the village. Thirty-one of these beneficiary households previously owned no agricultural land, and 15 received homestead land. The majority of the beneficiaries of both agricultural and homestead land were Muslims and SCs.

The 2005 survey data showed that 28 per cent of Kalmandasguri households were beneficiaries of land redistribution, receiving an average of 0.47 acres of agricultural land, and 41 per cent were homestead beneficiaries. Muslim households accounted for the largest share of beneficiaries of agricultural and homestead land, at 47 per cent and 59 per cent, respectively. This was particularly significant because Muslim households constituted the bulk of households without agricultural land (Basu 2015). Furthermore, oral histories collected from residents bear testament to the gradual decline of the *jotedar's* dominance in the village. According to Taoli Oraon, before 1977, there were only four landowning households in the village, all belonging to the same extended family.[68]

Prior to land reforms, Haji Jaliluddin Miyan of neighbouring Shibpur village was the largest landlord of the region, owning 250 *bigha*s or 83 acres of land inherited from his father, an even larger landlord in the colonial period. Though Jaliluddin Miyan passed by the time of my field study in 2013, his youngest son, Mujuriddin Haji, was still living in Shibpur and spoke about his family's landed possessions before land reforms. During that time, Jaliluddin Miyan and his brothers and their families lived in separate houses and employed several sharecroppers, whose houses surrounded theirs. However, once the implementation of land reforms marked their ceiling-surplus land for redistribution, each of Mujuriddin Haji's uncles gradually left the village. Presently, Mujuriddin Haji and his elder brother Jamaluddin Haji are the only two remaining members of the family in Shibpur.[69]

Mujuriddin Haji described how his family's land was acquired in two stages, vividly remembering the second stage in 1985–86. After the

---

[68] Interview with Taoli Oraon, September 7, 2013.
[69] Interview with Mujuriddin Haji, September 9, 2013.

government acquired the ceiling-surplus land, about 50 *bighas* or 16 acres were retained by his father and further divided between Mujuriddin Haji and his brothers. His family brought court injunctions to try halting the land redistribution process, pursued the legal case all the way to the High Court, and finally reached an agreement with the local Krishak Sabha, which was involved in identifying and redistributing ceiling-surplus land. In this agreement, the sharecroppers were provided homestead plots on a separate piece of land called the "colony." Mujuriddin Haji accused his father of being "careless" in dealing with the family's landholding and not evading the land-ceiling limit. Though his other uncles divided their landholdings and recorded them under the names of different family members, his father had not done so. His father tried to register his land under his two wives' names after the ceiling was declared, but this was illegal. As a result, according to Mujuriddin Haji, they lost more land under the land-ceiling clause than they should have. With the implementation of land reforms, the concentration of land in the hands of the *jotedars* was completely broken. In 2013, Mujuriddin owned around 2.5 acres of land, one acre of which he purchased after his family lost all the ceiling-surplus land. Remarking about life after land reforms, Mujuriddin Haji said that because he was not accustomed to doing agricultural work, he sold some of his lands and other assets to meet the needs of his household.[70]

According to Kapiluddin Miyan, a sharecropper and former labourer for Jaliluddin Miyan and later his sons, sharecroppers lived in poverty during the pre-land reforms period and had to often substitute their meagre incomes from cultivation by employment in other agricultural and non-agricultural work.[71] Mohammad Kasu Miyan, a landless sharecropper also formerly employed by Jaliluddin Miyan and had resided on his land in Shibpur, spoke of his previous difficulties when he cultivated about seven acres of land with his own draught bullocks. Due to huge debts, he lost this land as well as his bullocks. *Duna* or grain loans given by the *jotedars* were to be repaid at an exorbitant rate of three *mons* (one *mon*= approximately 38 kg) of paddy for every *mon* borrowed. The harassment faced by Kasu Miyan at the hands of the *jotedar* ultimately forced him to flee to Kalmandasguri from Shibpur.[72]

In the post-land reforms period, many previously landless sharecropper

[70] *Ibid.*
[71] Interview with Kapiluddin Miyan, September, 3, 2013.
[72] Interview with Mohammad Kasu Miyan on September 3, 2013.

households became small landowners themselves. In 2005, there was an overall decline in the levels of tenancy in Kalmandasguri – only eight households had leased-in land (covering an extent of 7.99 acres), whereas three leased land out (covering an extent of 2.25 acres). There were four registered sharecroppers who cultivated six per cent of the total operational land in the village, whereas unregistered sharecroppers operated on just one per cent of the cultivated land. This decline in tenancy was a marked shift from the past, when the majority of households were sharecroppers. Furthermore, landless sharecroppers who once lived on the *jotedar*'s land received homestead land as part of land reforms. For instance, Kapiluddin Miyan received two acres of agricultural land and a house site through land reforms.[73] Homestead land was provided on separate plots taken from the *jotedar*'s surplus possession. The 2015 village study data showed that 16 of the 53 households that received homestead land, as either original beneficiaries or inheritors, were previously landless, whereas the other 37 households owned less than two acres each of agricultural land (Basu 2015).

Therefore, not only did many of the earlier landless sharecroppers in Kalmandasguri become landowners but also attained housing security through possessing their own homesteads in the post-land reforms period.

Contemporary Challenges of Landholdings

Land reforms in the study villages transformed the earlier concentration of land towards an equitable landholding distribution and more just production relations. We now interrogate some contemporary challenges of landholdings faced by small peasant cultivators, particularly the land reforms beneficiaries. Unlike the previous sections, here, we look at the challenges of the post-land reforms period through a composite view of the three study villages.

Difficulties in Retaining Land

A 2003 study on the status of land reforms beneficiaries conducted by the West Bengal State Institute of Panchayats and Rural Development (now renamed as the B.R. Ambedkar Institute of Panchayats and Rural Development) found that 13.2 per cent of ceiling-surplus land recipients had been alienated from their lands. Only 2.7 per cent of these *pattadars* lost

---

[73] Interview with Kapiluddin Miyan on September 3, 2013.

control of their lands due to them being sold, even though the transfer of assigned land through sales was not legally recognised (Chakraborti 2003). Rawal (2006) analysed data from seven villages (including Amarsinghi and Kalmandasguri) across different agroecological zones of the State and found significant landlessness among beneficiary households due to transfer of assigned land in the case of Dalkati village of Jhargram block in Paschim Medinipur district. Here, the tribal beneficiary households had entered into 99-year-long mortgage contracts regarding their *patta* land, largely due to economic need in an agriculturally backward region.

The 2005 study showed that 10 out of the 33 Amarsinghi households that received assigned land had begun selling their lands in the previous decade. Though none of these sales rendered them landless, they sold an average of 0.31 acre of agricultural land and reduced their average ownership holding from 0.9 to 0.6 acre. The reasons for selling were largely to meet household consumption needs. For example, NT, a beneficiary of land redistribution, was forced to sell 10 *kathas* of assigned land to meet his father's funeral costs. In Kalmandasguri, the same survey reported only four of the 36 households that received assigned land sold portions of agricultural land in the previous decade to meet their consumption needs. Here too, land transactions did not result in landlessness of the beneficiary households. For example, KM, a land reforms beneficiary, had to sell portions of his two-acre assigned land to bear the costs of his medical treatment and daughter's wedding. The evidence from these two villages showed no rampant sales of assigned land. However, in the few reported cases of sold assigned land, the sales did not leave the beneficiary households landless but rather decreased their already marginal holdings.

Another factor posing a challenge to beneficiary households in retaining their assigned land was the fragmentation of land due to demographic reasons. Tables 12 and 13 present the composition of landless households and average ownership holdings by social group for Amarsinghi and Kalmandasguri in 2005 and 2010. Census household survey data from these years for these two villages showed growth in the landless population over the five-year period, more prominently in Amarsinghi than in Kalmandasguri where it was marginal.

In Amarsinghi, the proportion of landless households increased, regardless of social group, and the average size of ownership holding declined (Table 12). Increased landlessness was particularly high for SCs and OBCs. As previously mentioned, OBC households were the prime beneficiaries of land redistribution in Amarsinghi. The 2005 survey reported 39 per cent of OBC households as beneficiaries of agricultural land redistribution, receiving an average of 0.39 acre. The remaining beneficiaries included 14 per cent of SC households that received an average of 0.1 acre of vested agricultural land. The rise in landlessness among OBC households between 2005 and 2010 indicated that some beneficiary households with marginal holdings were pushed into the landless category due to subdivision of their landholdings over generations. Among SC households, landlessness grew from 46 to 54 per cent (35 to 57 households) during the five-year period. Thus, demographic pressure rather than land sales pushed more SC households into the landless category.

In Kalmandasguri, the proportion of overall landlessness grew marginally from 21.9 to 22.4 per cent between 2005 and 2010 – among Muslim households, the figure increased from 37 to 43 per cent (Table 13) . As discussed earlier, Muslim households in Kalmandasguri historically formed the landless sharecropping population and were the prime beneficiaries under land reforms. The 2005 survey reported that 33 per cent of Muslim households gained an average of 0.37 acre of agricultural land under land reforms. Between 2005 and 2010, the number of Muslim households also grew from 51 to 61, a demographic change which led to the subdivision of the lands of marginal-landholding households and increase in the number of landless households among this historically marginalized group in the village.

This increasing trend of intergenerational fragmentation of land and landlessness must be contextualised among the concerns regarding the

Table 12 *Composition of landless households and average ownership holding, by social group, Amarsinghi, 2005 and 2010*, in number and acre

	SC	ST	OBC	All
2005				
Landless households	16 (45.7)	1 (100)	10 (14.1)	27 (25.2)
Average ownership holding	0.6	0	1	0.9
2010				
Landless households	31 (54.4)	1 (100)	14 (20.3)	46 (36.2)
Average ownership holding	0.5	0	0.89	0.76

Note: Figures in parenthesis denote the percentage share of the column totals.
Source: PARI survey (2010).

Table 13 *Composition of landless households and average ownership holding, by social group, Kalmandasguri, 2005 and 2010*, in number and acre

	Hindu				Muslim	All
	General	SC	ST	OBC		
2005						
Landless households	0	7 (14.9)	1 (14.3)	1 (5.9)	19 (37.3)	28 (21.9)
Average ownership holding	0.69	1.14	1.03	1.18	0.56	0.93
2010						
Landless households	1 (16.7)	5 (9.4)	1 (10)	0	26 (42.6)	33 (22.4)
Average ownership holding	0.42	1.19	1.16	1.27	0.51	0.96

Note: Figures in parenthesis denote the percentage share of the column totals.
Source: PARI survey (2010).

contemporary rural economy of West Bengal as discussed in chapter 2 of this book. State support to agriculture in terms of inputs, prices, and overall public expenditure allocations have been declining since the 1990s and with greater pace in the 2000s, a period which has also seen stagnant agricultural growth rates. The increasing pressure of the rising cost of cultivation has most adversely affected small and marginal cultivators. The land reforms beneficiaries of the State belong to this category of cultivators, and the small size and fragmented nature of their holdings now presents a challenge in maintaining sustainable income from agriculture. Dependence on other sources of non-farm income among rural households, which is discussed in chapter 12 of this book, is also evident among the land reforms beneficiaries. In West Bengal, the current reversal of peasantisation, initially ushered in through land reforms that provided land to earlier landless sections, is largely due to the impact of market-led reforms.

Legal Hurdles for Land Reforms Beneficiaries

Legal hurdles to the implementation of land reforms in West Bengal existed in various courts wherein landowners collectively and individually filed cases against the ceiling and tenancy laws. The Left Front government instituted the West Bengal Land Reforms and Tenancy Tribunal in 1997 to hasten the redressal mechanism, but a high number of ongoing litigations persist. The government favoured marginalised beneficiaries by providing them institutional support, however in some cases, the protracted legal battles posed a disadvantage to them. Presently, the legal insecurities of many beneficiaries have increased under the policy direction of the Trinamool Congress government. Land reforms as a redistributive policy to mitigate poverty and inequality was absent from the budget speeches of this government (Bakshi 2013). In this section, we highlight some of the legal hurdles present in the study villages – these cases threaten the achievements of land reforms.

In Panahar, ceiling-surplus lands belonging to Asaduzamman Khan were identified as recently as the mid-2000s. A total of 61 *bighas* or 20 acres of surplus land spread across Panahar, and Enarchowk and Ismailchowk *moujas* were distributed among landless households of the village.[74] NP, a resident of Sahebganj *para* (hamlet) in Panahar, received 5.5 *katha* of Asaduzamman Khan's surplus lands. He belongs to a SC family dependent on his labouring out and his wife BP's work as a housemaid. After receiving the ceiling-surplus parcel of land, they began cultivating paddy and potato, but the land was repossessed after one year. Though 25–30 households in Sahebganj each received 4.5–5.5 *kathas* of ceiling-surplus land, Asaduzamman Khan challenged this in court, which brought an injunction to the acquisition based on the Muslim law of inheritance.[75] Acquiring back his former lands around 2009–10, he was thus reinstated as the largest landowner in Panahar and claimed that the "dispute" was now over.[76] NP, on the other hand, now only owned his homestead land of 0.06 acre.

Litigation on matters relating to sharecroppers' rights and acquisition of ceiling-surplus land in both Amarsinghi and Kalmandasguri are pending in the court. While conducting interviews in the village in 2013, I found 21 ongoing cases related to disputes over the takeover of ceiling-surplus land under the Bararangras village panchayat, of which Kalmandasguri is a part. Local Krishak Sabha leader Taoli Oraon stated that landowners in many cases took advantage of these protracted legal battles to repossess sharecroppers' land.[77]

Another case concerns the once migrant tribal population of agricultural labourers in Panahar. The 17 ST households surveyed in 2010 initially lived near a canal on the western end of the village. Floods in

---

[74] Interview with Chandi Charan Pal on July 19, 2017.
[75] *Ibid.*, interview with NP and BP on July 18, 2017.
[76] Interview with Asaduzamman Khan on July 17, 2017.
[77] Interview with Taoli Oraon on September 7, 2013.

1998–99 forced them to shift to their present location along the banks of a pond originally owned by Satya Narayan Koley, which was subsequently acquired as ceiling surplus.[78] KS, an agricultural worker, was among those who shifted. She stated that they still had not received homestead *patta*s and were staying as occupiers, even though they had paid for their plots.[79] Without a legal *patta* to their homestead lands, their occupation remains legally unrecognised and they are vulnerable to eviction.[80] This case explicates the changing role of the panchayats, which were envisaged as crucial links in the implementation process of the agrarian reforms programme, as has been evident in the three study villages. However, in recent years, panchayat bodies have weakened towards implementing its earlier pro-poor agenda (Bakshi 2011).

Change in Type of Tenancy

In their study on agricultural tenancy in India, Bansal, Usami, and Rawal (2018) analysed data from various rounds of the NSSO surveys of Land and Livestock Holdings from 1960–61 to 2012–13. They found that the proportion of fixed-rent tenancies had gradually attained prominence over shared-produce arrangements. At the all-India level, land under fixed-rent tenancies increased from 47 to 55 per cent between 2002–03 and 2012–13, with cash as the primary mode of payment. However, States such as West Bengal saw the continuation of sharecropping on 40.8 per cent of the total leased-in land.

The study villages displayed an increasing trend towards short-term fixed tenancies. Table 14 shows the proportion of leased-in and leased-out land according to type of contract for the study villages in 2010 and 2015. By 2015, fixed-rent tenancies emerged as the main form of tenancy contract among households both leasing in and leasing out land in all three villages. In the case of Panahar, Rawal (1999) also observed a rising trend in seasonal fixed-rent tenancies. Improvements in irrigation had enabled tenants to undertake risky seasonal contracts in potato and *boro* paddy cultivation; a similar trend was observed in the 2010 survey data. In these seasonal contracts, the entire cost of cultivation was borne by the tenants.

---

[78] Interviews with Chandi Charan Pal and KS on July 19, 2017.

[79] Interview with KS on July 17, 2017.

[80] There have also appeared instances of evictions of *bargadar*s who had not received title deeds (Bhattacharya 2011). See "For Bargadars, Land is Now Labour Lost," *The Hindu*, April 22, 2016, available at https://www.thehindu.com/elections/westbengal2016/west-bengal-assembly-polls-for-bargadars-land-is-now-labour-lost/article8505495.ece, viewed on September 17, 2020.

Table 14 *Proportion of leased-in and leased-out land, by type of contract, study villages, 2010 and 2015*, in per cent

		Panahar		Amarsinghi		Kalmandasguri	
		2010	2015	2010	2015	2010	2015
Leased-in land	Shared rent	48	50	16	24	57	9
	Fixed rent	52	50	84	76	43	91
Leased-out land	Shared rent	61	27	21	21	48	6
	Fixed rent	39	73	79	79	52	94

Source: PARI surveys (2010 and 2015).

In 2010–11, registered *bargadars* operated 9.2 per cent of the net sown area in West Bengal (GoWB 2012); however, this may be an overestimation. In the study villages, it was observed that some registered *bargadars* converted their shared contracts into fixed-rent money contracts, while still being formally registered as sharecropping tenancies. For example, the father of Kanai Panja, a registered sharecropper in Panahar, did not own any land and cultivated 5.6 acres of fellow resident Gopal Chatterjee's land on a share arrangement. After his father's death, the *barga* land was jointly cultivated by Kanai Panja and his two brothers. Twenty years ago, the land was divided among the three brothers, who cultivated independently, though on a produce-share rent arrangement. The 2010 survey revealed that Kanai Panja divided his two-acre share of leased-in land among his three sons, each receiving 0.6 acre, though the barga registration remained in his own name. By the 2015 survey, Kanai Panja's contract with the landowner became fixed, according to a per *bigha* arrangement; however, the *barga* rights still were applicable, partly because of Gopal Chatterjee's death. Now Chatterjee's grandsons, who live outside the village, have their produce share transported to their homes at the time of harvest.[81] This shift from a shared-rent to a fixed-rent arrangement can also be associated to landowners' weakening hold and their inability to supervise.

Both the 2010 and 2015 surveys in Panahar showed that about half of leased-in land was under fixed-rent tenancies, a majority of which were paid in kind through the produce of potato, paddy, and sesame. Sarkar (2018) calculated that fixed-rent tenancies led to lower farm business

---

[81] Interview with Kanai Panja on July 17, 2017; Fixed contracts continued to be paid in kind in the form of agricultural produce.

incomes in Panahar – rent costs incurred by the tenants alone comprised 30–50 per cent of the total paid-out costs.

The 2010 survey in Kalmandasguri revealed the emergence of a cashless, short-term, and fixed-lease contract in the case of potato cultivation, wherein rent included fertilizer costs borne by the lessee. Given the high fertilizer requirement of potato, the residual fertilizer in the soil suffices for the next crop grown – this enabled landowners to evade fertilizer input costs. Therefore, landowners saw these lease arrangements as a means to boost soil fertility without incurring input costs. Most fixed-term leases reported in 2010 and 2015 in Kalmandasguri were of this nature. Pradeep Nath, a Cooch Behar district committee member of the Krishak Sabha, stated that such short-term, fixed-lease arrangements for potato cultivation were relatively new in the region, arising only in the past decade.[82] They have ushered in cash crops such as potato, integrating the village economy further into the market. This presents a new challenge of protecting the rights of tenants under fixed contracts, currently unrecognised under the State tenancy laws. Our data showed that short-term tenancy contracts are increasing, and so, there must be safeguards to protect tenants from rising rents and other forms of tenurial insecurity.

Conclusion

This chapter studied the process of implementing land reforms and its impact in three study villages of West Bengal. Land reforms in these villages consisted of the redistribution of ceiling-surplus lands, tenancy reforms, and redistribution of homestead plots. The varying degrees of implementation of these components of land reforms in the villages after 1977 led to more equitable distribution of landholdings and tenurial arrangements. I undertook a longitudinal and historical study of the land tenure systems in the villages between the pre- and post-land reforms periods to provide a comprehensive assessment of the extent of change. This chapter also highlighted more contemporary challenges related to land tenures faced by land reforms beneficiaries, in particular, and small and marginal landholders in the villages.

The history of land-tenure arrangements in the pre-land reforms period revealed that specificities in each of the villages, determined by the colonial and post-Independence administrative land policies, shaped distinct

82 Interview with Pradeep Nath on September 2, 2013.

landholding patterns. However, the following commonalities among the villages could be identified: unequal distribution of landholdings, presence of a *jotedar* class, a population of sharecroppers cultivating on a 50:50 crop-sharing arrangement, and landless agricultural labourers working on paltry wages. Food insecurity in the villages was also a common feature before the implementation of land reforms.

All the three villages saw the implementation of land reforms with the active participation from the Krishak Sabha and local panchayat bodies. Surveys conducted after 1977 captured the extent and nature of the implementation in the villages. This chapter used the findings of these multiple surveys along with oral accounts of Krishak Sabha activists, panchayat representatives, and village residents to form a thorough understanding of land reforms in the villages.

In Panahar, sharecropper households, which formed a substantial section of the population in the pre-land reforms period, were mostly registered according to the 1995 survey. The same survey found that 22 per cent of households received ceiling-surplus lands – of all villages, tenancy reforms had the most significant impact in Panahar.

A 2005 survey conducted in Amarsinghi found 31 per cent of households received ceiling-surplus lands and 19 per cent were beneficiaries of homestead plot redistribution. The backward social groups in the village – the OBCs, SCs, and the lone ST household – were beneficiaries under the land reforms programme.

Kalmandasguri, also surveyed in the 2005 survey, had 21 per cent and 41 per cent of its households as beneficiaries of redistribution of ceiling-surplus agricultural land and homestead land, respectively. Muslim households, the largest landless population in the village in the pre-land reforms period, formed the largest share of the beneficiaries. In addition, Kalmandasguri experienced the greatest impact of homestead land redistribution. The 2010 survey found it was also the only village where beneficiaries of homestead redistribution cultivated vegetables on their relatively large plots. In the other villages, the redistributed homestead plots barely managed to ensure household housing security.

The 2005 survey found fewer shared-lease contracts in both Amarsinghi and Kalmandasguri than those existing during the pre-land reforms period, according to oral accounts of sharecroppers from both villages. Along with the decline in the proportion of landlessness in these villages, this indicated that many erstwhile sharecroppers have now became owners of small holdings as a result of the land redistribution programme.

Additionally, the 2010 survey showed no concentration of land in Amarsinghi and Kalmandasguri: erstwhile landlord classes and ownership holdings larger than five acres were no longer present. Panahar was an exception, as the largest landowner belonging to the former landlord class had consolidated his 32-acre holding. However, even this was small with respect to the largest landholdings of villages in other States surveyed by FAS. In Panahar, the older landlord section diversified into other non-agricultural businesses, whereas the sharecroppers attained more decision-making power through attaining tenurial security.

The 2010 survey found that the level of operational landlessness was restricted to 26 per cent households in Panahar, 32 per cent in Amarsinghi, and 21 per cent in Kalmandasguri. All the three villages were dominated by small and marginal holdings; the average operational holding was highest in Panahar at 1.2 acres, followed by Amarsinghi at 0.8 acre, and Kalmandasguri at 0.9 acre.

The challenges related to landholding and land tenure posed threats to the land reforms beneficiaries. Firstly, to deter the process of land reforms, landowners registered legal cases, many of which continue to be unresolved. For example, the largest landowner in Panahar retained his ceiling-surplus land through a protracted legal case. Similarly, the other two villages have many ongoing legal disputes between landowners and sharecroppers. In Amarsinghi, the section of beneficiaries without *pattas* remains vulnerable to eviction.

Secondly, fragmentation of land and the marginal size of holdings held by land reforms beneficiaries indicate the threat of rising landlessness along with livelihood concerns. Some beneficiaries have sold portions of their redistributed land to meet their household consumption needs. The higher incidence of landlessness among marginalised social groups is especially worrying. This landlessness and further fragmentation of landholdings threaten beneficiaries' agricultural incomes in the context of declining State support for agriculture. Small landholdings are increasingly proving inadequate, leading to greater dependence on non-farm incomes.

Lastly, all the three villages showed a trend of increased short-term fixed leases paid in cash between 2010 and 2015. These leases led to an increased cost of cultivation for the tenants and, in some cases, indicated a weakened control of the landowners. However, they also pose contemporary threats to tenants who remain unrecognised under present tenancy laws, and thus, there is a need to safeguard their rights.

References

Bakshi, Aparajita (2008), "Social Inequality in Land Ownership in India: A Study with Particular Reference to West Bengal," *Social Scientist*, vol. 39, no. 9–10, September–October, pp. 95–116

Bakshi, Aparajita (2011), "Weakening Panchayats in West Bengal," *Review of Agrarian Studies*, vol. 1, no. 2, July–December, pp. 202–14.

Bakshi, Aparajita (2013), "Assessing 'Paribartan' Reflections on Development, Politics and Change in Rural West Bengal," unpublished note.

Bakshi, Aparajita (2015), "Contextualising Land Reform in West Bengal: An Interview with Benoy Konar," *Review of Agrarian Studies*, vol. 4, no. 2, July–December, pp. 123–36.

Bandyopadhyay, D. (1971), "Bargadars of Salihan," teacher's notes presented at the Public Administration Case Workshop, Administrative Staff College of India, New Delhi, December 20–23.

Banerjee, Abhijit V., Gertler, Paul J., and Ghatak, Maitreesh (2002), "Empowerment and Efficiency: Tenancy Reform in West Bengal," *Journal of Political Economy*, vol. 110, no. 2, April, pp. 239–80.

Bansal, Vaishali, Usami, Yoshifumi, and Rawal, Vikas (2018), "Agricultural Tenancy in Contemporary India: An Analytical Report and A Compendium of Statistical Tables based on NSSO Surveys of Land and Livestock Holdings," SSER Monograph 18/1, Society for Social and Economic Research, New Delhi, available at http://archive.indianstatistics.org/sserwp/sserwp1801.pdf, viewed on September 20, 2020

Barman, Kshitis Chandra (1938), *Report on the Conditions of the Santhals in Malda, 1934*, Bengal Government Press, Alipore.

Basu, Ranjini (2015), "Land Tenures in Cooch Behar District, West Bengal: A Study of Kalmandasguri Village," *Review of Agrarian Studies*, vol. 5, no.1, January–June, pp. 88–111.

Bhattacharya, Malini (2011), "Reversing Reforms?," *Frontline*, vol. 28, no. 21, October 8–21, available at: https://frontline.thehindu.com/static/html/fl2821/stories/20111021282104500.htm, viewed on September 20, 2020.

Besley, Timothy, and Burgess, Robin (1998), "Land Reform, Poverty Reduction & Growth: Evidence from India," The Development Economics Discussion Paper Series, London School of Economics, London.

Board of Revenue (1991), *The West Bengal Land and Land Reforms Manual*, Government of West Bengal, Sree Saraswathy Press, Calcutta.

Carter, M.O. (1938), *Final Report on the Survey and Settlement Operations in the District of Malda 1928–1935*, Bengal Government Press, Alipore.

Chakraborti, Anil K., with Mukhopadhyay, Apurba Kumar, and Roy, Debesh (2003), *Beneficiaries of Land Reforms: The West Bengal Scenario*, State Institute of Panchayats and Rural Development, Kalyani, Nadia and Spandan, Kolkata

Chaturvedi, Sumit (2016), "Land Reforms Fail; 5% of India's Farmers Control 32%,"
    The Wire, May 4, available at http://thewire.in/2016/05/04/land-reforms-fail-5-of-
    indias-farmers-control-32-land-33523/, viewed on September 20, 2020

Chaudhuri, Harendra Narayan (1903), *The Cooch Behar State and its Land Revenue
    Settlements*, Cooch Behar State Press, Cooch Behar.

Chaudhuri, Shiben (1986), "Cooch Beharer Gourab-Krishaker Gourab (Cooch Behar's
    Pride-Peasant's Pride)," souvenir for 27th State Conference of the West Bengal
    Provincial Krishak Sabha held in Cooch Behar.

Dasgupta, Biplab (1984), "Sharecropping in West Bengal: From Independence to
    Operation Barga," *Economic and Political Weekly*, vol. 19, no. 26, June 30, pp. A85–
    A87 and A89–A96.

Dhanagare, D.N. (1991), "The Tebhaga Movement in Bengal, 1946–7," in *Peasant
    Movement in India: 1920–50*, Oxford University Press, New Delhi, pp. 155–77.

Directorate of Land Records and Surveys (1975), *Bargadar's Right in Law and in Fact:
    Two Case Studies*, Superintendent Government Printing, West Bengal.

Ganguli, Karali Charan (1930), *Final Report on the Survey and Settlement Operations in
    the Cooch Behar State 1913–1927*, Cooch Behar State Press, Cooch Behar.

Ghatak, Maitreesh, and Roy, Sanchari (2007), "Land Reform and Agricultural
    Productivity in India: A Review of the Evidence," *Oxford Review of Economic Policy*,
    vol. 23, no.2, Summer, pp. 251–26.

Government of Bengal (1888), *Report on the Condition of Lower Classes of Population
    in Bengal*, Bengal Secretariat Press, Calcutta.

Government of West Bengal (GoWB) (2007a), *District Human Development Report:
    Bankura*, Development and Planning Department, Sishu Sahitya Samsad Pvt.
    Limited, Kolkata.

Government of West Bengal (GoWB) (2012), *Economic Review 2010–11*, Bureau of
    Statistics and Planning, Kolkata.

Government of West Bengal (GoWB) (undated), *Compendium II*, Department of
    Panchayat and Rural Development. available at https://burdwanzp.org/images/
    gov_notification_files/1517982433WB%20Pan%20Compendium%20II.pdf, viewed
    on September 20, 2020.

Konar, Benoy (2002), "The Peasant Movement, Land Reforms, and the Left Front
    Government: An Outline of Growth," *The Marxist*, vol. 18, no. 2, April–June,
    available at http://www.cpim.org/marxist/200202_marxist_lf&peasants_bkonar.
    htm, viewed on September 20, 2020.

Kumar, Deepak (2016), "Discrepancies in Data on Landholdings in Rural India:
    Aggregate and Distributional Implications," *Review of Agrarian Studies*, vol. 6, no.
    1, January–June, pp. 39–62.

Lambourn, G.E. (1918), *Bengal District Gazetteers: Malda*, Bengal Secretariat Book
    Depot, Calcutta.

Lieten, G.K. (1992), *Continuity and Change in Rural West Bengal*, Sage Publications,
    New Delhi.

Mishra, Suryakanta (2007), "On Agrarian Transition in West Bengal," *The Marxist*, vol. 23, no. 2, April–June, pp. 1–22.

Mitra, A. (1953), *Census 1951: District Handbooks Bankura*, Sree Saraswathy Press, Calcutta.

Mitra, Ashok (1977), "The Story of Indra Lohar," in *Calcutta Diary*, Frank Cass and Company Limited, London.

National Sample Survey Office (NSSO) (2015), "Report No. 501: Household Ownership and Operational Holdings in India, NSS 70th Round," Ministry of Statistics and Program Implementation, Government of India, New Delhi, available at http://mospi.nic.in/sites/default/files/publication_reports/Report_571_15dec15_2.pdf, viewed on September 20, 2020.

Ramachandran, V. K., and Ramakumar, R. (2001), "Agrarian Reforms and Rural Development Policies in India," in *Agrarian Reform and Rural Development*, Department of Agrarian Reform, Government of the Philippines and the Philippines Development Academy, Manila.

Ramachandran,V.K., Swaminathan, Madhura, and Bakshi, Aparajita (2010), "Food Security and Crop Diversification: Can West Bengal Achieve Both?," in Banasri Basu, Bikas K. Chakrabarti, Satya R. Chakravarty, and Kausik Gangopadhyay (eds.), *Econophysics and Economics of Games, Social Choices and Quantitative Techniques*, Springer, Segrate.

Rawal, Vikas (1999), "Irrigation Development in West Bengal, 1977–78 to 1995–96," unpublished PhD thesis, Indira Gandhi Institute of Development Research, Mumbai.

Rawal, Vikas (2001a), "Agrarian Reform & Land Markets: A Study of Land Transactions in Two Villages of West Bengal, 1977–1995,"*Economic Development & Cultural Change*, vol. 49, no. 3, April, pp. 611–29.

Rawal, Vikas (2001b), "Expansion of Irrigation in West Bengal: Mid-1970s to Mid-1990s," *Economic and Political Weekly*, vol. 36, no. 42, October 20–26, pp. 4017–24.

Rawal, Vikas (2006), *Landlessness in Rural West Bengal*, unpublished manuscript.

Rawal, Vikas (2013), "Changes in the Distribution of Operational Landholdings in Rural India: A Study of National Sample Survey Data," *Review of Agrarian Studies*, vol. 1, no. 2, July–January, pp.73–104.

Robertson, F.W. (1926), *Final Report of the Survey and Settlement Operations in the District of Bankura 1917–1924*, Bengal Secretariat Book Depot, Calcutta.

Rogaly, Ben (1996), "Agricultural growth and the structure of "casual" labour-hiring in rural West Bengal," *Journal of Peasant Studies*, vol. 23, no. 4, July, pp. 141–65.

Sarkar, Biplab (2018), "The Economics of Household Farming: A Study with Special Reference to West Bengal," unpublished PhD thesis, University of North Bengal.

Saha, Anamitra, and Swaminathan, Madhura (1994), "Agricultural Growth in West Bengal," *Economic and Political Weekly*, vol. 29, no. 13, March 26, pp. A2–A11

Sen, Abhijit (1992), "Economic Liberalisation and Agriculture in India," *Social Scientist*, vol. 20, no. 11, November, pp. 4–19.

Sengupta, Sunil, and Gazdar, Haris (2003), "Agrarian Politics and Rural Development in West Bengal," in Jean Drèze and Amartya Sen (eds.), *Indian Development Selected Regional Perspectives*, Oxford University Press, Delhi.

Siddiqui, Farasat Ali (2013), "Dimensions of Education, Employment and Fertility Status of Muslim Population in Malda District (West Bengal)," PhD thesis, Aligarh Muslim University, available at https://shodhganga.inflibnet.ac.in/handle/10603/12906, viewed on September 20, 2020.

Sircar, Sekhar (1990), "Land Settlement and Revenue Administration and Taxation under the Maharajas of Cooch Behar State (1773–1949)," unpublished PhD thesis, University of North Bengal.

Surjeet, Harkishan Singh (1992), *Land Reforms in India: Promises and Performance*, National Book Agency, Delhi.

Swaminathan, Madhura, and Baksi, Sandipan (eds.) (2017), *How Do Small Farmers Fare? Evidence from Village Studies in India*, Tulika Books, New Delhi.

Todarmal (2002), *Evolution of the Indian Land Revenue System: Analysis of Land in West Bengal*, Anima Prakashani, Kolkata.

SECTION II

The Crop Economy

5

Household Crop Incomes among Small Farmers

A Study of Three Villages in West Bengal

Biplab Sarkar[1]

Introduction

Farmers in India have contributed greatly to the country's transformation from a state of food insecurity to one of surplus cereal production (NCF 2004a, 2004b, 2006a, 2006b, 2006c). Between 1950–51 and 2015–16, the production of foodgrain in the country increased from 51 million tonnes to 252 million tonnes, while oilseed production increased from 5 million tonnes to 25 million tonnes (GoI 2016). Similar growth was also achieved in the production of sugarcane, cotton, fruit, vegetables, and other crops.

Despite tremendous gains in agricultural development after Independence, problems of indebtedness, crop failure, non-remunerative prices for crops, poor returns over costs of cultivation, and negative crop incomes persist in the farming system (Reddy and Mishra 2009; Ramachandran 2011; Rawal and Swaminathan 2011; Dev 2012; Gaurav and Mishra 2014). The National Commission on Farmers 2004–06 appointed by the Ministry of Agriculture, Government of India, was one of the earliest official bodies to recognise the crisis in farm incomes and livelihoods. The first objective of the National Policy for Farmers formulated by the Commission was to improve the economic viability of farming by ensuring a minimum net income (NCF 2006a, 2006b, 2006c).

---

[1] An earlier version of this chapter was published in *Review of Agrarian Studies*, volume 7, number 2, and is re-published here with permission of the author and journal editors. A postscript authored by Tapas Singh Modak has been added to the original article, to discuss the changes in farm incomes in the three villages between 2010 and 2015.

The National Policy for Farmers (GoI 2007) also recognised the need to focus on the economic well-being of farm households.

> There is a need to focus more on the economic well-being of the farmers, rather than just on production. Socio-economic well-being must be a prime consideration of agricultural policy, besides production and growth. The aim of the Policy is, therefore, to stimulate attitudes and actions which should result in assessing agricultural progress in terms of improvement in the income of farm families, not only to meet their consumption requirements but also to enhance their capacity to invest in farm-related activities (GoI 2007, p. 2).

Official data (NSSO 2005) show that in 2002–3, 95 per cent of farm households cultivating less than four hectares of land were unable to earn enough to meet their consumption needs (Bhalla 2006). This means that small and marginal farmers could undertake little to no investment to improve agriculture. This is especially significant for West Bengal, where marginal and small farmers cultivate 84 per cent of agricultural land (NSSO 2015).

This article uses data from three villages in West Bengal surveyed at different points of time as part of the Project on Agrarian Relations in India (PARI). The villages are Panahar in Bankura district, Amarsinghi in Maldah district, and Kalmandasguri in Koch Bihar district.[2] The article addresses the following questions. What are the levels of income from crop production in the villages? How does crop income vary across households, and across the villages? What are the factors affecting levels of household crop income in the villages?

Village Surveys: An Introduction

Panahar in Bankura district, Amarsinghi in Maldah district, and Kalmandasguri in Koch Bihar district are located in three distinct agro-ecological regions in West Bengal. A census-type survey of all resident households in the villages was conducted in 2010. Only those households that operated some land (hereafter called farm households) are considered in this article. By this definition, farm households constituted 71 per cent of all households in Amarsinghi, 79 per cent of all households in Kalmandasguri, and 75 per cent of all households in Panahar. All farm

---

[2] A total of 25 villages across 11 States have been surveyed under PARI between 2005 and 2016 (see www.fas.org.in).

households in Amarsinghi and Kalmandasguri came under the definition of "small farmers," that is, the extent of their operational holdings was less than two hectares. In Panahar, 95 per cent of farm households (all but eight farm households) were small farmer households. Some basic characteristics of the study villages are given in Table 1.

These villages provide interesting case studies of production systems that have specific features, yet share general characteristics of agricultural production in West Bengal.

Panahar village in Bankura district is well-connected by all-weather roads to urban centres and regulated markets. The village had stable access to irrigation throughout the reference year. The average crop yield in the village was significantly higher than the State and all-India average. In contrast, Kalmandasguri in Koch Bihar district is connected by a mud and gravel road to the nearest unban centre. Agriculture here was mostly unirrigated with low agricultural yields. Amarsinghi in Maldah district is very close to the Samsi regulated market, and motor vans were the main means of transport between the village and the market. Rice yields

Table 1 *Characteristics of the study villages, West Bengal, 2009–10*

Characteristics of the villages	Panahar (Bankura district)	Amarsinghi (Maldah district)	Kalmandasguri (Koch Bihar district)
Number of households	248	127	147
Total population	1,083	579	701
Share of irrigated land in gross cropped area (in per cent)	90	89	40
Sources of irrigation (area under the source as a proportion of gross cropped area)	Tubewells (86) Canals (3) Ponds (1)	Tubewells (82) RLI* (6)	Tubewells (35) Ponds (5) Ponds (1)
Major crops in kharif season (June–July to November)	*aman* and *aus* rice	*aman* rice	*aman* rice
Major crops in rabi season (November to February–March)	potato, mustard/ rapeseed, wheat, and vegetables	mustard/ rapeseed, potato	potato, mustard/ rapeseed, and vegetables
Major crops in summer season (February–March to May–June)	*boro* rice, sesame	*boro* rice, jute	jute
Cropping intensity**	2.05	1.94	1.84

Notes: *RLI = River Lift Irrigation.
    **Cropping intensity is the ratio of gross cropped area to net sown area.
Source: PARI survey (2010).

in Amarsinghi were substantially higher than the State and all-India averages. But the average yields of major non-foodgrain crops (jute and mustard/rapeseed) in the village were lower than average yields in the district and the State.

The three villages also share some common features that characterise rural West Bengal. They are all dependent primarily on rice cultivation.[3] Secondly, there is a significant presence of smallholder agriculture in all three villages.[4]

Estimates of Household Crop Income

Calculating household crop income can be a complex process, given that a substantial part of the produce is not marketed and a large part of the inputs used in production is not purchased from markets. In fact, for some products and inputs, no markets or only very basic markets exist. In general, households cannot directly report crop income over a specified reference period; instead, income has to be derived from a detailed accounting of crop output and input costs (Bakshi 2010).

This article calculates household crop incomes from detailed data on crop inputs and outputs. I calculate the gross value of output (GVO) and two cost measures: paid-out cost (or Cost A2) and "catch-all cost" (or Cost C2). The gross value of output less paid-out cost is designated Farm Business Income, and gross value of output less catch-all cost is designated Net Income.

The values of the main crop product and the by-product together constitute the gross value of output. The main product is that part or item of the produce for which crop production is undertaken. The by-product refers to straw, plant bushes, or other plant residue. The gross value of output is the total value of produce, including output consumed and sold. Each crop produced by a household during the reference year is valued separately and aggregated to estimate the gross value of output.

The cost items considered in the Cost A2 and Cost C2 calculations are

---

[3] Village data show that the share of area under paddy in the total gross cropped area ranged from 49 per cent in Kalmandasguri to 65 per cent in Panahar and Amarsinghi. According to the Bureau of Applied Economics and Statistics, Government of West Bengal, paddy covered 58 per cent of the gross cropped area of West Bengal in 2011–12 (GoWB 2013).

[4] The village data show that all the agricultural land in Amarsinghi and Kalmandasguri were owned by marginal and small farmers. In Panahar, marginal and small farmers owned 60 per cent of the total agricultural land in the village.

listed in Appendix Table 1. The calculation methodology for each of the items comprising Cost A2 is available in a manual by the Foundation for Agrarian Studies, *Calculation of Household Incomes: A Note on Methodology* (FAS 2015). For the calculation of Cost C2, I have followed the Cost of Cultivation of Principal Crops (CCPC) methodology to impute the rental value of owned land, interest on fixed capital assets, and wages for family labour use.

The rent of owned land is imputed based on the prevailing average rate of rent in the tenancy market in the village. The average rent so calculated for each crop is then imputed as rent on owned land. Interest on fixed capital is calculated from data on means of agricultural production owned by the households. Following the CCPC scheme methodology, we calculate interest at the rate of 10 per cent per annum on the present value of fixed productive assets, which includes all machinery owned and used by the household for cultivation. Cost of family labour is imputed depending on the prevailing daily wage rate in the village.

Household Crop Income: Levels and Disparities

Our major findings follow.

First, there was a marked variation in farm business income across the study villages in 2009–10. Farm business incomes of a majority of farm households in Panahar, a village in an agriculturally advanced region (Old Alluvial Zone) were lower than those in Kalmandasguri, a village located in a relatively backward region (Terai Teesta Zone). Table 2 shows that median annual farm business income for farm households in relatively well-irrigated Amarsinghi, located in the New Alluvial region of West Bengal, was Rs 10,460. The median farm business income was Rs 1,780 in Panahar and Rs 7,996 in Kalmandasguri.

Incomes are based on a single year's observation. Even though the survey year was a good agricultural year in terms of rainfall and yield, there was a problem with potato prices (discussed later).

Mean farm business incomes were higher than median incomes, as averages were influenced by the high incomes of a few households. The mean farm business income per household over the reference year was Rs 14,538 in Amarsinghi, Rs 11,374 in Kalmandasguri, and Rs 11,606 in Panahar. It is significant that, on average, Panahar had more operated land, higher irrigation, crop yield, and higher crop intensity, yet in 2009–10 the mean annual farm business income was similar to that of Kalmandasguri,

Table 2 *Descriptive statistics of annual farm business income per household, study villages, West Bengal, 2009–10, in Rs per household*

Village name	Number of farm households	Farm business income (Rs per household)				
		Median	Mean	Minimum	Maximum	Coefficient or variation
Panahar	184	1,780	11,606	−41,184	4,89,169	4.46
Amarsinghi	91	10,460	14,538	−1,666	1,19,961	1.15
Kalmandasguri	116	7,996	11,374	−24,750	1,31,149	1.53

Note: The differences in mean annual farm business income per household across study villages are not statistically significant (Results of one-way ANOVA:$F(2,388) = 0.227$ and p value = 0.797).
Source: PARI survey (2010).

a relatively backward village, where only around 40 per cent of the gross cropped area was irrigated and crop yields were substantially lower.

In a study of 600 households in two districts of West Bengal in 1999–2000, Bhaumik (2007) observed that the mean annual farm business income was Rs 21,170 per household in an agriculturally advanced district (Hooghly) as compared to Rs 6,080 per household in a relatively backward district (Koch Bihar).[5] The data from the study villages in 2010 did not show any statistically significant difference in mean annual farm business income between advanced and backward regions in the State.

In a survey conducted in 2003–04, Rakshit (2014) found that the annual income from crop production per holding in an agriculturally advanced region was higher than in a backward region. He calculated two variables to project economic surpluses or deficits of cultivator households in Barddhaman (an advanced region) and Purulia (a backward region) districts of West Bengal. The variables were farm labour income (FLI) and farm labour surplus/deficit (FLS). FLI is the value of agricultural production less total material input cost and wages in kind and cash. FLS is FLI less imputed value of family labour. However, the cost of rent paid for leased-in land, maintenance expenses of owned animal and machinery, depreciation of implements and machinery, interest on working capital, and land revenue were not accounted for in the crop income estimation. Therefore, a comparison with the calculations made in this article must

---

[5] The consumer price incomes at 2009–10 prices (with State CPI-AL) are Rs 38,106 in Hooghly and Rs 10,994 in Koch Bihar.

be made with caution. Rakshit calculates an annual FLI per holding of Rs 17,060 in the advanced region and Rs 11,451 in the backward region (or Rs 27,807 and Rs 18,665 respectively at 2009–10 prices). The corresponding figures for annual FLS were Rs 17,225 and Rs 14,094 at 2009–10 prices.

A study conducted by Bakshi (2010) in three villages of West Bengal in 2005–06 found that mean annual farm business income per household was Rs 10,401 in Bidyanidhi village, located in the agriculturally advanced Barddhaman district. The corresponding figures for Amarsinghi (Maldah) and Dalkati (West Medinipur) villages were Rs 3,725 and Rs 1,610 respectively.[6]

Secondly, low, and even negative, farm business incomes for a majority of the households in Panahar was on account of the huge loss incurred in potato cultivation as a result of a crash in potato prices in the survey year.[7] The average farm harvest price in the district in 2010 was the lowest price, in real and nominal terms, in relation to the past five years. I recalculated farm business income for a hypothetical situation. What would be incomes if farm households received prices for a normal year? New estimates of farm business income that were arrived at by calculating

Table 3 *Descriptive statistics of annual farm business income per household after potato price adjustment, study villages, West Bengal, 2009–10, in Rs per household*

Village name	Farm business income (in Rs per household)			
	Mean	Minimum	Maximum	Coefficient of variation
Panahar	35,103	−11,165	6,94,384	2.37
Amarsinghi	14,538	−1,666	1,19,961	1.15
Kalmandasguri	18,288	−5,254	2,10,452	1.56

Note: There was a statistically significant difference in mean annual farm business income between study villages as determined by one-way ANOVA (F(2,388)=4.716, p value = 0.009). A Tukey post-hoc test revealed that the mean annual farm business income was statistically significantly higher for Panahar compared to Amarsinghi and Kalmandasguri. There was no statistically significant difference in mean annual farm business income between Amarsinghi and Kalmandasguri.
Source: PARI survey (2010).

[6] This is equivalent to Rs 15,289, Rs 5,476, and Rs 2,367 respectively at 2009–10 prices.
[7] Actual farm harvest price received (FHPs) was below paid-out cost (A2 cost) for 80 per cent of farmers in Panahar in 2010. Farmers incurred paid-out cost of Rs 286 per quintal, but received only Rs 181 per quintal for their production.

average farm harvest prices of potato for the previous three years are shown in Table 3.[8]

The estimated mean annual farm business income per household, based on triennial average farm harvest prices, was Rs 35,103 in Panahar, followed by Kalmandasguri (Rs 18,288), and Amarsinghi (Rs 14,538). Panahar now emerges as the village with a significantly higher average farm business income than Amarsinghi and Kalmandasguri.

Thirdly, income from crop production is generally low, but there are pronounced variations across farm households within a village. Take for example, Panahar, where the mean annual income from crop production was only Rs 11,606 per household but varied from minus (–) Rs 41,184 to Rs 4,89,169 per household (Table 2).

At the same time, it must also be noted that incomes from sources other than crop cultivation supplemented crop production incomes. Table 4 shows the average household incomes from different sources in the study villages. Average income from crop production was only around 18 per cent of total household incomes in Panahar (Bankura district) and Kalmandasguri (Koch Bihar district) in 2009–10. By contrast, in Amarsinghi in Maldah district, around 30 per cent of average household incomes came from crop cultivation. Other sources of income played an important role to supplement the income of farm households. However, the extent of contribution of other economic activities varied across villages and classes of cultivators. For example, income from animal

Table 4 *Average household incomes from crop production, animal husbandry, and other activities, study villages, West Bengal, 2009–10, in Rs per household*

Village name	Average farm business income	Average income from animal husbandry	Average income from other sources*	Average household income
Panahar	11,606	2,260	48,872	62,738
Amarsinghi	14,538	3,844	29,727	48,109
Kalmandasguri	11,374	7,681	42,453	61,508

Note: *Other income sources include rental income from agricultural land and machinery, wage earnings from farm and non-farm employment, salary, business, moneylending, pensions, and remittances.
Source: PARI survey (2010).

[8] I use district-level farm harvest prices for 2006–07, 2007–08, and 2008–09, connected to 2009–10 prices.

Table 5 *Descriptive statistics of annual net income (NI) over Cost C2 from crop production per household, study villages, West Bengal, 2009–10, in Rs per household*

Village name	Net income over Cost C2 from crop production (Rs per household)				
	Median	Mean	Minimum	Maximum	Standard deviation
Panahar	−1,379	−997	−90,922	3,09,004	36,088
Amarsinghi	2,520	5,267	−11,113	84,351	11,842
Kalmandasguri	−1	−151	−45,692	79,591	12,665

Note: Differences in mean annual farm business income per household across study villages are not statistically significant (Results of one-way ANOVA F $(2,388)$ = 1.809 and p value = 0.165).
Source: PARI survey (2010).

resources was 4 per cent of average household income in Panahar and around 13 per cent in Kalmandasguri in 2009–10.

Finally, farming for a majority of households is non-remunerative when the cost of family labour, rental value of own land, and interest on other productive assets are imputed (Cost C2) to estimate the income from crop production. Table 5 shows that median annual net incomes (NI) in Panahar and Kalmandasguri were negative in 2009–10. In Amarsinghi, it was positive, but low.

Dey's (2013) calculation of farm labour surplus (FLS) for sample households in Birbhum, Barddhaman, Hooghly, and Murshidabad districts includes the imputed cost of family labour. He estimated an average income of minus (−) Rs 29,525 per holding in 2010–11. He imputed the value of family labour with the cost of material inputs and the wage bill for hired labour, and subtracted it from the value of agricultural production to arrive at farm labour surplus (FLS).

The proportion of farm households that incurred a loss in crop production over Cost C2 was 65 per cent in Panahar, 50 per cent in Kalmandasguri, and 28 per cent in Amarsinghi. Accounting only for paid-out cost (Cost A2), a substantial proportion of farm households still incurred losses (Figure 1).[9]

The Lorenz curve of income from crop production shows that a cumulative 84 per cent of farm households in Panahar received zero

---

[9] Bakshi and Modak (2017) argue that loss making farmers do not give up farming because of the lack of alternative sources of employment.

Figure 1 *Proportion of farm households with negative incomes from crop production, by study villages, West Bengal, 2009–10, in per cent*

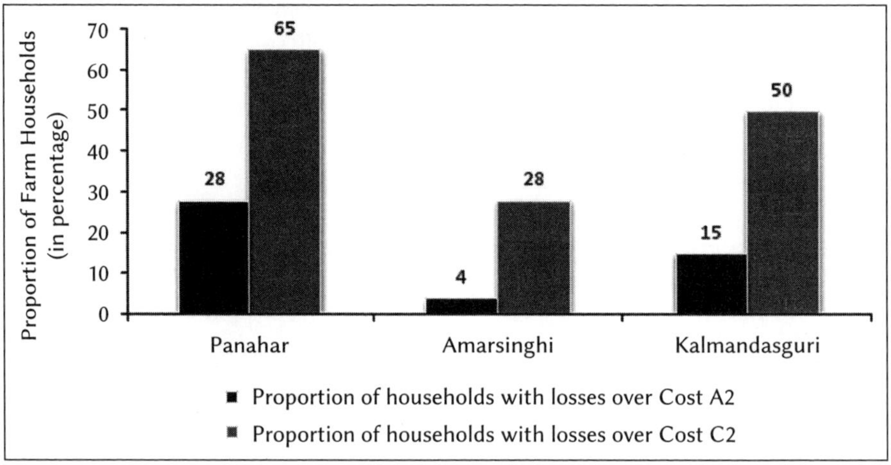

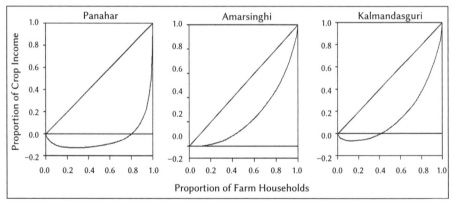

Source: PARI survey (2010).

Figure 2 *Lorenz curves of farm business income per household, by study villages, West Bengal, 2009–10*

Source: PARI survey (2010).

income over Cost A2. This proportion was 42 per cent in Kalmandasguri and 11 per cent in Amarsinghi (Figure 2).

Several factors can lead to losses from crop production. Negative incomes could be on account of low crop yields due to weather shocks, pests and diseases, high input prices, low output prices, or other factors.

In the study villages, the primary cause for losses in crop production was low agricultural output prices in general and a crash in potato prices in the survey year in particular. However, some households also incurred losses specifically because of low crop yields, particularly with regard to mustard cultivation in Panahar and jute cultivation in Kalmandasguri.

Crop insurance is a possible solution to protect farmers from losses. In reality, crop insurance schemes in India have limited coverage, especially among small farmers (Das and Swaminathan 2017).

Variations in Household Crop Income across Socio-Economic Classes

All households with operational holdings are grouped into five categories. The categories are: landlords/capitalist farmers, peasant (upper), peasant (lower), hired manual workers, and other households.[10]

Table 6 presents data on average farm business income per household across different socio-economic classes. In Panahar (Bankura district), average farm business income per household was highest for landlord/ capitalist farmers (Rs 1,67,478) and declined sharply for poorer socio-

Table 6 *Mean annual farm business income (FBI) by socio-economic class, study villages, West Bengal, 2009–10, in Rs per household*

Socio-economic class	Panahar		Amarsinghi		Kalmandasguri	
	Number	FBI	Number	FBI	Number	FBI
Landlord/big capitalist farmer	7	1,67,478				
Peasant (upper)	52	14,555	19	30,370	30	21,506
Peasant (lower)	93	1,886	36	16,058	38	12,687
Manual worker	20	1,895	24	4,477	36	3,283
Other households	12	−572	12	5,035	12	6,157
All farm households	184	11,606	91	14,538	116	11,374

Source: PARI survey (2010).

[10] There are minor differences in the classification of households in this chapter, and in other chapters in this book. The peasant (upper) refers to the class 'upper peasant' in Panahar and Amarsinghi, and the combined classes of 'upper peasant' and 'poor peasant: small self-employment' in Kalmandasguri. The class peasant (lower) in this chapter refers to the class of 'poor peasant' in Panahar and Amarsinghi and 'poor peasant: semi-proletariat' in Kalmandasguri.

economic classes. The income of peasant (lower) households from crop production was only around one per cent of the income earned by landlord/big capitalist farmers. Amarsinghi (Maldah district) and Kalmandasguri (Koch Bihar district) villages had no landlords and big capitalist farmers, but variations in average farm business income across classes were substantial. In Amarsinghi, it was Rs 30,370 for the peasant (upper) category, Rs 16,058 for the peasant (lower) category, and Rs 4,477 for hired manual worker households. In Kalmandasguri, it was Rs 21,506 for the peasant (upper) category, Rs 12,687 for the peasant (lower) category, and Rs 3,283 for hired manual worker households.

The level of farm business income depends on the extent of operated land and the return per hectare. Average operated land is directly related to the class status of households (with the exception of the "other" household category). For instance, in Panahar, the average size of household operational holding was highest for landlord/big capitalist farmers among all categories of farm households (9.24 acres), followed by peasant "upper" (1.89 acres), peasant "lower" (0.39 acres), and hired manual workers (0.15 acres). The average size of household operational holding among other households was 1.02 acres.

The relationship between socio-economic class and the return per hectare is a complex one. Table 7 shows the relationship between socio-economic class and farm business income per hectare. In Panahar, the average farm business income per hectare declines as one moves from the landlord/capitalist farmer class (Rs 33,780) to upper peasant (Rs 14,938) and lower peasant households (Rs 12,910). However, the per hectare farm business income for hired manual workers was higher (Rs 25,205) than for peasant classes. Hired manual workers in Panahar operated only one per cent (a negligible share) of the gross cropped area in the village.

There was a positive relationship between socio-economic class and farm business income per hectare in Panahar. There was no such relationship in Amarsinghi and Kalmandasguri.

It may be argued that the relationship between socio-economic class and profitability will be different if we measure returns from crop production over Cost C2. Estimates of average income from crop production over Cost C2, presented in Table 8, show that the direction of the relationship between class and net return remains unchanged. In Panahar, landlord/capitalist farmers had the highest level of net income from crop production over Cost C2. However, no such relationship was evident in Amarsinghi and Kalmandasguri.

Table 7 *Mean annual farm business income (FBI) by socio-economic class, study villages, West Bengal, 2009–10, in Rupees per hectare*

Socio-economic class	Annual farm business income (in Rupees per hectare)		
	Panahar	Amarsinghi	Kalmandasguri
Landlord/capitalist farmer	33,780	–	–
Peasant (upper)	14,938	35,500	26,768
Peasant (lower)	12,910	46,665	41,472
Manual worker	25,205	43,566	37,753
Other households	–8,163	48,840	23,419
All farm households	14,239	43,803	34,648

Note: There was a statistically significant difference in mean annual farm business income between socio-economic classes in Panahar as determined by one-way ANOVA (F(4,179)=3.751, p value = 0.006). A Tukey post-hoc test revealed that the mean annual farm business income was statistically significantly higher for landlord/capitalist farmers compared to all other classes. There was no statistically significant difference in mean annual farm business income between socio-economic classes in Amarsinghi and Kalmandasguri as determined by one-way ANOVA (Amarsinghi F(3,87)=0.463, p value=0.709 and Kalmandasguri F(3,112)=1.344, p value =0.264).
Source: PARI survey (2010).

Table 8 *Mean annual net income (NI) over Cost C2 from crop production by socio-economic class, study villages, West Bengal, 2009–10, in Rs per hectare*

Socio-economic class	Annual net income (NI) from crop production (Rs per hectare)		
	Panahar	Amarsinghi	Kalmandasguri
Landlord/capitalist farmer	9,655	–	–
Peasant (upper)	–16,912	12,156	–1,764
Peasant (lower)	–21,024	15,872	4,294
Manual worker	–887	10,355	–541
Other households	–31,526	22,505	–6,928
All farm households	–17,191	14,516	66

Note: There was a statistically significant difference in mean annual farm business income between socio-economic classes in Panahar as determined by one-way ANOVA (F(4,179)=2.648, p value=0.035). A Tukey post-hoc test revealed that the mean annual farm business income was statistically significantly higher for landlord/capitalist farmers compared to all other classes. There was no statistically significant difference in mean annual farm business income between socio-economic classes in Amarsinghi and Kalmandasguri as determined by one-way ANOVA (Amarsinghi F(3,87)=0.373, p value=0.773 and Kalmandasguri F(3,112)=0.385, p value=0.764).
Source: PARI survey (2010).

Potato Cultivation in Panahar

In Panahar, 23 per cent of the gross cropped area was under potato cultivation in 2009–10. The varieties of potato cultivated in Panahar included Jyoti, Pokhraj, and Atlantic. The first two were cultivated for sale in the open market and the third was cultivated under contract farming. The Atlantic variety was mainly cultivated by landlord/capitalist farmers, and occupied a fourth of the area they cultivated with potato. Two middle peasant households cultivated Atlantic on two per cent of the total area under potato cultivated by this socio-economic class. The Jyoti and Pokhraj varieties were cultivated by all categories of farmers and accounted for 61 per cent and 32 per cent respectively of the total area under potato cultivation.

Potato is planted in Panahar between October and December, and harvested between January and March. A perishable commodity, it cannot be stored for more than a month without cold storage. In 2009–10, 72 per cent of potato produced (Jyoti and Pokhraj) was immediately sold upon harvest, while the rest was kept in cold storage.

Cold storage facilities around Panahar were privately owned. In 2010, the cost of storage was Rs 54 per bag (50 kg of potato) for a period up to 10 months. The cold storage would issue a receipt for the potatoes, termed potato bonds. These bonds could be traded in the market as well as exchanged for potatoes at a day's notice at any time during the 10 months. If the potato was not retrieved in this period, it would be kept by the cold storage facility.

A majority of the farmers in Panahar sold potatoes to village traders. The traders resold a significant portion of the produce in neighbouring wholesale markets ("mandis" in Kotulpur) to large traders, for whom they worked as commission agents. The large traders in turn sold potato to retailers in the retail markets, or in the neighbouring States of Odisha, Bihar, Assam, and Andhra Pradesh.

Marketing channels of potato cultivators are depicted in Figure 3. Two-thirds of the marketed potato in Panahar was sold to village traders and another five per cent was sold directly to large traders in Kotulpur. A negligible quantity (less than one per cent of total production) was sold to a cooperative society.

The following are some major observations regarding potato marketing.

First, potato cultivators in Panahar, on average, received prices lower than the paid-out cost in 2009–10. As a result, a majority of the potato

Figure 3 *Potato production and marketing channels in Panahar, Bankura district, West Bengal, 2009–10*

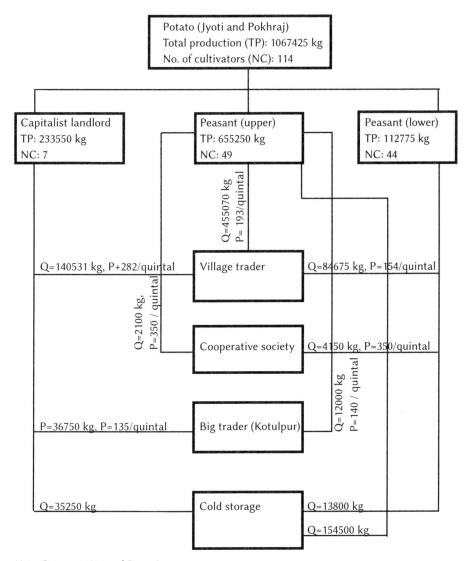

Note: Q = quantity and P = price.
Source: PARI survey (2010).

cultivators (80 per cent) made losses. A price of around Rs 300 per quintal was required for an average cultivator to break even. However, almost the entire output was sold to private traders at less than Rs 300 per quintal. The West Bengal State Co-operative Marketing Federation Limited (BENFED) purchased potatoes at Rs 350 per quintal, but acquired only one per cent of the total production in the village.

Secondly, in the absence of government support, the price of potato was influenced by negotiations between farmers and village traders. The relative bargaining power of the farmer was dependent on economic status, volume of marketed output, and dependence on traders for inputs and credit. Most village traders or input dealers have a network of farmers to whom they provide required inputs such as seed, fertilizers, or cash on credit, and from whom they buy potato on a regular basis. Payments are often delayed, which is why farmers prefer selling to traders with a good record of trade credit repayment. It has been observed that capitalist landlords received better prices than peasants from the village trader (Figure 3).

Thirdly, there is a difference between the price offered by traders to

Figure 4 *Jyoti potato prices in the village market and at Kotulpur market, Bankura district, West Bengal, February to December 2010*, in Rs per quintal

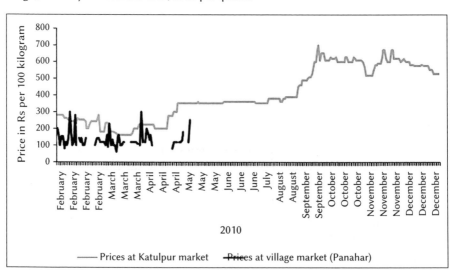

Note: 2010 potato prices at Kotulpur market were collected during a follow up visit in 2013.
Source: PARI survey (2010).

farmers in the village and the prevailing price in the nearest market at Kotulpur. Potato prices were collected from a big trader in Kotulpur market from February to December 2010 (Figure 4). Prices were relatively low (below Rs 300 per quintal) for three to four months (February–May) following the harvest. This gradually rose to Rs 400 between May and August, and increased sharply in the period September–December to Rs 500 to Rs 700 per quintal. More than two-thirds of the produce was sold in the early months after the harvest. However, it was sold at a village price lower than the prevailing market price in Kotulpur. Farmers mainly rely on village traders. The daily price uncertainty and cost of transporting produce to the market were deterrents against sale in Kotulpur. Also, a number of farmers bought inputs from local agents and in turn sold the output to them.

Given the seasonal price movement, the rational action for farmers would be to put the crop in cold storage and sell the produce several months after harvest. However, in the absence of sufficient cold storage space, some farmers were compelled to sell their output just after the harvest.[11]

Contract Farming

Though the Atlantic variety of potato was not widely cultivated in Panahar, it comprised 25 per cent of potato cultivation by landlord/capitalist farmers. This variety was grown under contract farming in agreement with Frito Lays, a subsidiary of PepsiCo Company Private Limited. The company approached potential farmers through commission agents. As per the rules of the agreement between the farmer and the commission agent, the farmer was entitled to a kit (including seed and guidelines document), credit (in kind), price insurance, and frequent inspection. Insecticides and pesticides were also provided by the company, though the farmers had to bear the cost. Contract farmers supplied land, labour, and residual inputs. Field agents of the company made frequent visits to monitor technical aspects of cultivation, such as farming practices, and to check for disease and pests. The output price was fixed before sowing. In 2009–10, the rate was Rs 490 per quintal, much higher than the break-even price of Rs 300. An "incentive price" in addition to the base price was on offer for quality produce and a good relationship with the company.

[11] On shortages of cold storage space in West Bengal, see Dahiya and Sharma (1994), GoI (2010).

Contract farming of the Atlantic variety with an assured price was profitable and the returns were higher than the production of Jyoti and Pokhraj, as both varieties registered a steep decline in prices that year.

A study by Pandit *et al.* (2009) observed that contract farming of potato in four southern districts of West Bengal resulted in good returns in 2008 in comparison to those obtained by non-contract farmers. Tripathy, Singh, and Singh (2005) also note the greater profitability of potato in Haryana due to contract farming. Similarly, Singh (2002) mentions that contract farming had led to higher farm incomes in Punjab.

These studies argue that contract farming offers greater economic viability. The scope of operation of contract farming and its suitability for small and marginal farmers, however, need further study. In Panahar, contracts were mainly undertaken with landlord/capitalist farmers. While the reasons for absence of contract farming among small and marginal farmers need more study, my present hypothesis is that company agents do not find it worthwhile to engage with those cultivating tiny plots.

Conclusion

This article explored levels of and variations in annual farm business income (gross value of output minus Cost A2) of households across socio-economic classes in three villages located in different agro-ecological zones of West Bengal. The analysis is based on household-level data from village census surveys conducted by the Foundation for Agrarian Studies in 2010.

It shows that annual farm business incomes varied substantially across villages located in different agro-ecological regions. The median annual farm business income for farm households in Amarsinghi village, located in the New Alluvial region of West Bengal, was Rs 10,460. It was Rs 7,996 in the non-irrigated Kalmandasguri village, located in the Teesta Terai region. In Panahar, an irrigated village in the Old Alluvial region of West Bengal, median annual farm business income was only Rs 1,780. The unexpected lower income in Panahar was mainly because of huge losses incurred in potato cultivation because of a crash in output prices in the survey year.

Secondly, a substantial proportion of households incurred negative crop incomes, or losses from crop production. The proportion of farm households that incurred a loss in crop production over Cost A2 was 28 per cent in Panahar and 15 per cent in Kalmandasguri. In the case of

Panahar, this loss was mainly on account of losses incurred in potato farming, whereas in Kalmandasguri, low yields for mustard and jute cultivation were important factors.

Thirdly, the variation in annual farm business incomes across households within villages was substantial. In Panahar, farm business incomes per household were highest for landlord/capitalist farmers and declined steeply as we moved down the socio-economic class hierarchy. The crop income of poor peasant households was only one per cent of the crop income of landlord/capitalist farmers. In Amarsinghi and Kalmandasguri, there were no landlords/capitalist farmers, but variations in average farm business income across classes remained.

In Panahar, where the major commercial crop was potato, diversification of potato cultivation had a negative impact on incomes, as potato prices crashed in the survey year. Diversification to commercial crops, it is argued, can be a necessary and sufficient condition to augment farmers' income. Commercial crop cultivation without adequate institutional support to mitigate high risks of cultivation, however, can lead to huge losses.

POSTSCRIPT: Changes in Farm Incomes, 2010–2015

Tapas Singh Modak

This note discusses some important changes in household crop production systems in the three villages of West Bengal between 2010 and 2015. We have analysed data from the panel of households that were surveyed in both survey years.[12]

In the period between the two surveys, some important interventions in groundwater irrigation occurred in Amarsinghi and Kalmandasguri that had specific implications for agriculture and farm incomes. By 2015, groundwater irrigation in Amarsinghi was entirely by electric pumpsets; shallow tubewells operated by diesel-powered pumpsets had been phased out. Kalmandasguri was electrified in 2013, and subsequently, some diesel-operated tubewells were replaced by electric pumpsets, which led to an expansion of irrigated area. Further, one peasant household in the village purchased a tractor and a thresher in 2012 and 2014, respectively, thus introducing mechanisation of agricultural operations in the village – a phenomenon completely absent till then.

---

[12] There are 103 households in Panahar, 54 households in Amarsinghi, and 52 households in Kalmandasguri in the data panel.

Changes in Cropping Pattern and Crop Yields

In terms of extent of cropped area, paddy remained the most important seasonal crop in all three villages in 2015 (Table 1). It was followed by potato and sesame in Panahar, mustard/rapeseed and jute in Amarsinghi, and potato and jute in Kalmandasguri.

In Panahar, the most significant change occurred in the cropped area during summer seasons. The area under *boro* paddy sharply declined from 56.5 acres in 2010 to 35.4 acres in 2015, while the area under sesame increased from 18.6 to 32.2 acres; this shift was from an irrigated, water-intensive crop to an unirrigated, dry crop. In Amarsinghi, there was no such change in the cropping pattern aside from some increase in the area under *boro* paddy. In Kalmandasguri, the shift in irrigation, as discussed, substantially increased the area under rabi crops. In particular, the area under potato, which requires frequent watering, had almost doubled, from 22.6 acres in 2009–10 to 43.7 acres in 2014–15.

Postscript Table 1 *Area under main crops for panel households, study villages, 2009–10 and 2014–15*, in acres

Village	Season	Crop name	2009–10	2014–15
Panahar	Kharif	Paddy (aman)	110.9	99.2
		Paddy (aus)	17.2	13.4
	Rabi	Potato	61.0	70.9
		Mustard/Rapeseed	9.3	2.3
	Summer	Paddy (boro)	56.5	35.4
		Sesame	18.6	32.2
Amarsinghi	Kharif	Paddy (aman)	27.4	29.8
	Rabi	Mustard/Rapeseed	8.1	10.1
		Potato	4.4	3.8
	Summer	Paddy (boro)	22.4	28.2
		Jute	8.5	4.8
Kalmandasguri	Kharif	Paddy (aman)	46.6	40.2
	Rabi	Potato	22.6	43.7
	Summer	Jute	24.5	19.4

Source: PARI surveys (2010 and 2015).

Changes in Farm Business Incomes

In this section, I examine the changes in average farm business income (FBI), both at the crop and household level in the study villages between 2009–10 and 2014–15.[13] The consumer price index for rural labour is used to convert 2010 prices to 2015 prices for comparing the FBI between the two years. Table 2 shows that, on aggregate, there was a decline in average real FBI prices in all the three villages – the decline ranged from 18.4 per cent in Amarsinghi to 78.4 per cent in Panahar to 99.1 per cent in Kalmandasguri over the five years.

To understand the decline in FBI, we examine the gross value of output (GVO), cost of cultivation (Cost A2), and income from production of

Postscript Table 2 *Changes in farm business income per household, study villages, 2009–10 and 2014–15, in Rs (at 2015 prices)*

Village	2009–10	2014–15	Change (%)
Panahar	29,924	6,455	−78.4
Amarsinghi	25,948	21,181	−18.4
Kalmandasguri	22,799	194	−99.1

Source: PARI surveys (2010 and 2015).

Postscript Table 3 *Changes in average gross value of output (GVO), paid-out cost (Cost A2), and farm business income (FBI), major crops, Panahar, 2009–10 and 2014–15, in Rs per acre (at current prices)*

Crop	Year	GVO	Cost A2	FBI	Relative profitability (GVO/Cost A2)
Paddy (*aman*)	2009–10	16,552	10,525	6,027	1.57
	2014–15	23,437	16,280	7,156	1.44
Paddy (*boro*)	2009–10	19,712	12,060	7,652	1.63
	2014–15	32,802	20,276	12,526	1.62
Potato	2009–10	21,590	26,704	−5,114	0.81
	2014–15	29,916	46,031	−16,114	0.65
Sesame	2009–10	8,442	2,825	5,618	2.99
	2014–15	7,181	4,899	2,283	1.47

Source: PARI surveys (2010 and 2015).

[13] FBI is calculated based on Cost A2, using the definition used by the Commission for Agricultural Costs and Prices.

Postscript Table 4 *Changes in average gross value of output (GVO), paid-out cost (Cost A2), and farm business income (FBI), major crops, Amarsinghi, 2009–10 and 2014–15*, in Rs per acre (at current prices)

Crop	Year	GVO	Cost A2	FBI	Relative profitability (GVO/Cost A2)
Paddy (*aman*)	2009–10	15,509	9,755	5,754	1.59
	2014–15	23,315	15,153	8,162	1.54
Paddy (*boro*)	2009–10	24,579	14,966	9,612	1.64
	2014–15	32,802	20,276	12,526	1.62
Mustard/Rapeseed	2009–10	9,149	4,725	4,424	1.94
	2014–15	12,360	6,672	5,688	1.85
Jute	2009–10	27,481	11,654	15,827	2.36
	2014–15	29,634	17,903	11,732	1.66

Source: PARI surveys (2010 and 2015).

Postscript Table 5 *Changes in average gross value of output (GVO), paid-out cost (Cost A2), and farm business income (FBI), major crops, Kalmandasguri, 2009–10 and 2014–15*, in Rs per acre (at current prices).

Crops	Year	GVO	Cost A2	FBI	Relative profitability (GVO/Cost A2)
Paddy (*aman*)	2009–10	11,590	4,193	7,398	2.76
	2014–15	18,228	8,171	10,057	2.23
Potato	2009–10	21,479	24,837	−3,358	0.86
	2014–15	30,511	39,788	−9,278	0.77
Jute	2009–10	19,173	6,936	12,237	2.76
	2014–15	15,891	8,799	7,092	1.81

Source: PARI surveys (2010 and 2015).

selected crops in the villages in 2009–10 and 2014–15 (Tables 3, 4, and 5). The major points that emerge from the analysis are as follows.

Overall, there was a decline in profitability (ratio of GVO to Cost A2) across crops. To take an example, the profitability of potato in Panahar and Kalmandasguri was 0.81 and 0.86 in 2010, respectively, indicating that farmers incurred net losses, and further declined in 2015. In addition, there was substantial decline in profitability for jute cultivation in Amarsinghi and Kalmandasguri.

The decline in the profitability across crops between 2009–10 and 2014–15 was because of the sharp increase in the cost of cultivation, which outstripped the growth in GVO. To illustrate, in the case of potato in Panahar, the average per acre GVO increased from Rs 21,590 in 2009–10 to Rs 29,916 in 2014–15, or about 39 per cent in five years, while the cost of cultivation increased from Rs 26,704 to Rs 46,031 per acre, or about 72 per cent. In Kalmandasguri, there was an absolute decline in per acre GVO for jute cultivation, but its cost of cultivation increased by 27 per cent. The increase in cost of cultivation was not only because of increase in material costs but also substantial increase in rent for leased-in land and wages for hired labour.

Despite the fact that farm households recorded higher yield in 2014–15 than that in 2009–10, the slow growth in per acre GVO between the two surveys implied that farm harvest prices of all crops did not substantially rise. For instance, for one quintal *aman* paddy, the average farm harvest

Postscript Table 6 *Changes in farm business income (FBI) per household, by socio-economic class, study villages, 2009–10 and 2014–15, in Rs (at current prices)*

Village	Socio-economic class	2010		2015		Change (%)
		Number of households	Average FBI	Number of households	Average FBI	
Panahar	Capitalist land-lord/farmer	6	2,95,492	6	1,59,173	−46
	Peasant I	7	66,209	3	22,335	−66
	Peasant II	53	3,768	30	−13,014	−445
	Manual labour	10	2,351	24	−1,352	−157
	Others	5	−7,160	10	−12,797	79
Amarsinghi	Peasant I	4	85,123	4	85,837	1
	Peasant II	22	28,506	26	18,342	−36
	Manual labour	9	7,360	8	5,045	−31
	Others	6	5,119	4	7,250	42
Kalmandasguri	Peasant I	6	63,920	8	−31,354	−149
	Peasant II	25	18,399	17	14,362	−22
	Manual labour	6	10,639	7	3,053	−71
	Others	4	6,852	9	−748	−111

Source: PARI surveys (2010 and 2015).

price increased by 13 per cent in Panahar, 31 per cent in Amarsinghi, and 19 per cent in Kalmandasguri; while the cost of cultivation (Cost A2) increased by 25 per cent, 44 cent, and 49 per cent respectively. This trend was the case for all major crops in the villages.

At the household level, all socio-economic classes witnessed a decline in FBI (Table 6). However, the decline was greater for farm households in Panahar and Kalmandasguri than those in Amarsinghi. In Panahar, the average FBI per household for capitalist landlord/farmer households declined from Rs 2,95,492 in 2009–10 (2015 prices) to Rs 1,59,173 in 2014–15, about 46 per cent in five years. Among the peasantry, Peasant II households experienced a sharper decline in average FBI in the villages.

To conclude, our surveys indicate that in spite of expansion and electrification of irrigation in Amarsinghi and Kalmandasguri, FBIs substantially declined in all three villages. Though all sections of the peasantry experienced this decline, the smaller peasantry was affected more acutely than others. The decline in FBI can be attributed to a rapid increase in the cost of cultivation, which far outstripped the growth in GVO and farm harvest prices.

References

Bakshi, Aparajita (2010), "Rural Households Income," unpublished PhD thesis, University of Calcutta, Kolkata.

Bakshi, Aparajita, and Modak, Tapas Singh (2017), "Incomes of Small Farmer Households," in Madhura Swaminathan, and Sandipan Baksi (eds.), *How Do Small Farmers Fare? Evidence from Village Studies in India*, Tulika Books, New Delhi.

Bhalla, G. S. (2006), *Condition of Indian Peasantry*, National Book Trust, New Delhi.

Bhaumik, Sankar Kumar (2007), "Diversification of Employment and Earnings by Rural Households in West Bengal," *Indian Journal of Agricultural Economics*, vol. 62, no. 4.

Central Statistical Organisation (CSO) (2008), *Manual on Cost of Cultivation Surveys*, Ministry of Statistics and Programme Implementation, Government of India, New Delhi.

Dahiya, Prem Singh, and Sharma, Hoshyar Chand (1994), "Potato Marketing in India: Status, Issues, and Outlook," Working Paper Series, Social Science Department, International Potato Centre, Lima.

Das, Arindam, and Swaminathan, Madhura (2017), "Cropping Pattern, Crop Productivity, and Incomes from Crop Production," in Madhura Swaminathan, and Sandipan Baksi (eds.), *How Do Small Farmers Fare? Evidence from Village Studies in India*, Tulika Books, New Delhi.

Dey, Rajiv (2013), "Problem of Farm Viability, Poverty and Agrarian Crisis: The Case of West Bengal," in Suman K. Chandra, Suresh V. Babu, and Pradip Kumar Nath (eds.), *Agrarian Crisis in India: The Way Out*, Academic Foundation in Association with the National Institute of Rural Development (NIRD), Hyderabad.

Dev, S. Mahendra (2012), "Small Farmers in India: Challenges and Opportunities," Working Paper 14, Indira Gandhi Institute of Development Research, Mumbai, June.

Foundation for Agrarian Studies (FAS) (2015), *Calculation of Household Incomes: A Note on Methodology*, Foundation for Agrarian Studies, available at http://fas. org.in/wp-content/themes/zakat/pdf/Survey-method-tool/Calculation%20of%20 Household%20Incomes%20-%20A%20Note%20on%20Methodology.pdf, viewed on October 24, 2016.

Gaurav, S., and Mishra, S. (2014), "Farm Size and Returns to Cultivation in India: Revisiting an Old Debate," *Oxford Development Studies*, vol. 43, no. 2, pp. 165–93.

Government of India (GoI) (2007), *National Policy for Farmers 2007*, Department of Agriculture and Cooperation, Ministry of Agriculture, Government of India, New Delhi.

Government of India (GoI) (2010), *West Bengal Development Report*, Planning Commission, Government of India, New Delhi.

Government of India (GoI) (2016), *Agricultural Statistics at a Glance 2014*, Directorate of Economics and Statistics, Department of Agriculture and Cooperation, Ministry of Agriculture, New Delhi.

Government of West Bengal (GoWB) (2013), *Statistical abstract West Bengal, 2011-12*, Bureau of Applied Economics and Statistics, Kolkata

National Commission on Farmers (NCF) (2004a), *Serving Farmers and Saving Farming (First Report)*, National Commission on Farmers, Ministry of Agriculture, Government of India.

National Commission on Farmers (NCF) (2004b), *Serving Farmers and Saving Farming: From Crisis to Confidence (Second Report)*, National Commission on Farmers, Ministry of Agriculture, Government of India.

National Commission on Farmers (NCF) (2006a), *Serving Farmers and Saving Farming: 2006, Year of Agricultural Renewal (Third Report)*, National Commission on Farmers, Ministry of Agriculture, Government of India.

National Commission on Farmers (NCF) (2006b), *Serving Farmers and Saving Farming: Jai Kisan: A Draft National Policy for Farmers (Fourth Report)*, National Commission on Farmers, Ministry of Agriculture, Government of India.

National Commission on Farmers (NCF) (2006c), *Serving Farmers and Saving Farming: Towards Faster and More Inclusive Growth of Farmers (Fifth and Final Report)*, National Commission on Farmers, Ministry of Agriculture, Government of India.

National Sample Survey Organisation (NSSO) (2005), *Income, Expenditure and Productive Assets of Farmer Households, Situation Assessment Survey of Farmers,*

National Sample Survey 59th Round, Report no. 497 (59/33/5), Ministry of Statistics and Programme Implementation, Government of India.

National Sample Survey Office (NSSO) (2015), *Household Ownership and Operational Holdings in India*, National Sample Survey 70th Round, Report no. 571, Ministry of Statistics and Programme Implementation, Government of India.

Pandit, Arun, Pandey, N. K., Rana, Rajesh K., and Lal, Barsati (2009), "An Empirical Study of Gains from Potato Contract Farming," *Indian Journal of Agricultural Economics*, vol. 64, no. 3.

Rakshit, Santanu (2014), "Output, Surpluses, and 'Stressed Commerce': A Study on Farm Viability and Agrarian Transition in West Bengal, in India, in the New Millennium," *The Journal of Peasant Studies*, vol. 41, no.3.

Ramachandran, V. K. (2011), "The State of Agrarian Relations in India Today," *The Marxist*, vol. 27, nos. 1–2.

Ramachandran, V. K. (2015), "Socio-economic Classes in the Study Villages," presented at the Symposium on Results from Village Surveys, Durgapur, September 11–13.

Rawal, Vikas, and Swaminathan, Madhura (2011), *Returns from Crop Cultivation and Scale of Production*, paper presented in a workshop on *Policy Options and Investment Priorities for Accelerating Agricultural Productivity and Development in India*, organised by Indira Gandhi Institute of Development Research and Institute for Human Development on November 10–11 at India International Centre, New Delhi.

Reddy, D. Narasimha, and Mishra, Srijit (2009), *Agrarian Crisis in India*, Oxford University Press, New Delhi.

Singh, Sukhpal (2002), "Contracting out Solution: Political Economy of Contract Farming in the Indian Punjab," *World Development*, vol. 30, no. 9.

Tripathy, R. S., Singh, Ram, and Singh, Sube (2005), "Contract Farming in Potato Production: An Alternative for Managing Risk and Uncertainty," *Agricultural Economics Research Review*, vol. 18, pp. 47–60.

Appendix

Appendix Table 1 *Items included in the cost of cultivation calculation*

Items included in the cost of cultivation calculation	
Paid-out cost (or Cost A2)	Catch-all cost (or Cost C2)
Seed (farm saved and purchased)	All items in Cost A2
Manure (home-produced and purchased)	Imputed value of rent for owned land
Chemical fertilizer	Interest on fixed capital (excluding land)
Plant protection	Imputed value of family labour
Irrigation	
Hired labour	
Animal labour (own and hired)	
Machine (owned and hired)	
Rent paid for leased-in land	
Marketing expenses	
Land revenue	
Crop insurance	
Interest on working capital	
Depreciation on own machinery	

Sources: FAS (2015) and CSO (2008)

Appendix Table 2 *Socio-economic class wise composition of households, means of production, and income, study villages, West Bengal, 2009–10, in number, per cent, acres, and Rs*

Socio-economic class	Number of cultivator households	Share of total cultivator households	Proportion in gross cropped area (in per cent)	Average operational holding (in acres)	Proportion of irrigated area in GCA (in per cent)	Average value of means of production per household (in Rs)	Income per household (in Rs)
Panahar village							
Landlord/Capitalist Farmer	7	4	31	9.24	91	76,410	4,94,931
Peasant (upper)	52	28	49	1.89	89	12,667	73,303
Peasant (lower)	93	50	14	0.39	74	569	28,899
Manual Worker	21	11	1	0.15	77	42	39,203
Other Households	12	7	5	1.02	88	3,240	71,493
All Farm Households	185	100	100	1.17	87	6,206	63,075
Amarsinghi village							
Peasant (upper)	19	21	46	1.97	78	3,603	79,028
Peasant (lower)	36	40	42	0.92	89	480	37,732
Manual Worker	24	26	8	0.26	81	20	29,699
Other Households	12	13	4	0.27	63	0	42,168
All Farm Households	91	100	100	0.87	82	2,056	48,109
Kalmandasguri village							
Peasant (upper)	30	26	50	1.89	51	3,453	77,551
Peasant (lower)	38	33	29	0.84	21	280	47,501
Manual Worker	36	31	11	0.34	27	488	42,785
Other Households	12	10	10	0.97	48	7,921	121,932
All Farm Households	116	100	100	0.96	39	2,676	61,509

Source: : PARI survey (2010).

6

Fertilizer Use in West Bengal

A Case Study of Three Villages

Kamal Kumar Murari

Introduction

Agricultural production is strongly linked to fertilizer use, one of the key factors for growth in foodgrain production in India. Given the importance of fertilizers in crop productivity, many regions in India have witnessed a significant growth in fertilizer use.

There are three key issues in relation to fertilizer use in Indian agriculture. The first is the excess use of fertilizer per hectare. In some States, particularly Punjab and Andhra Pradesh, the application of fertilizer per unit area is much higher than that of other productive regions in the world. Studies have confirmed that excess use of fertilizer resulted in local environmental pollution, particularly contaminating local water bodies including groundwater (Ladha *et al.* 2005; Vel Murugan and Dadhwal 2007; Pathak *et al.* 2010). The second issue is that fertilizer use in Indian agriculture is not uniform across India. Fertilizer use both in terms of type and quantity varies from one geography to another, being quite low in some States (Department of Fertilizers 2014). Thus, considerable scope exists to raise agricultural production by improving fertilizer use. Thirdly, in many parts of the country, fertilizers used are predominantly nitrogenous ones, mainly urea, leading to imbalance in the NPK (Nitrogen-Phosphorous-Potassium) ratio.[1] This imbalance in fertilizer nutrient use raises concerns about soil fertility, productivity, and efficient use of fertilizer.

---

[1] These are the three important micronutrients essential for proper crop growth. In NPK ratio, N stands for Nitrogen, P for Phosphorous, and K for Potassium. Different chemical combinations of fertilizers have different proportion of N, P, and K nutrients. For further details on the proportions of N, P, and K and the NPK ratio, see Murari, Jayaraman, and Chakraborty (2017).

Yield response to fertilizer application can be improved by employing better management practices and application of technology. One of the most common limitations to farmers adopting better management practices and technology, more particularly in relation to quantity and timing of application of inputs, is that they do not have adequate information on the economic benefit associated with different management practices at the farm level (Mujeri *et al.* 2012). A majority of studies on fertilizer use focus on agronomic issues that deal with increased yield and potential environmental implications rather than the costs and benefits of an individual farmer's operation. Improvements in the effective use of fertilizer are conditional not only on physiological and technical factors (such as plot area and soil condition) but also socio-economic factors (such as farmer assets, income, and access to credit facilities). At present, the relative importance of these factors at the micro as well as macro level are poorly understood. This aspect is important because farmers' options related to crop choices or fertilizer type and its application rate are mainly influenced by economic considerations (Ncube *et al.* 2006).

In the context of the above discussion, this chapter presents a descriptive account of fertilizer use practices of West Bengal. It aims to use both macro as well as village study data to present an understanding about fertilizer use and its relation to productivity and profitability in agriculture. As stated above, the literature has a clear gap in terms of relating fertilizer application, its role in productivity, and its economic benefits.

The next section gives an overview of the different types of fertilizer used in West Bengal. It begins with a physical and agricultural description of the State and includes a subsection on fertilizer use and its nutrient content in terms of NPK application per hectare. The third section begins with a description of fertilizer use and cropping pattern of the three villages surveyed in 2010 and 2015: Panahar, Amarsinghi, and Kalmandasguri. It also describes fertilizer application and gives the NPK application rate for different crops in the villages and discusses how fertilizer application is related to crop yield. The fourth section describes the economics of the cost of cultivation for different crops in the villages and looks at the relationship between fertilizer application, crop productivity, and crop profitability.[2] The chapter ends with concluding remarks.

---

[2] Crop profitability is an economic term understood as a net profit due to the sale of products and by-products of a given crop minus the expenditure on all types of input in the field. There is a variety of input that needs to be considered for growing a given crop; due to this, there

An Overview of Fertilizer Use Pattern

West Bengal is one of the major agricultural States, mainly because of its geography: it is fed by two major rivers, the Ganges and the Brahmaputra. Climatologically, a large part of West Bengal falls in the humid region making it water-abundant for the majority of the year. The cropping intensity is close to 185 per cent, indicating that a majority of net sown area is cultivated more than once. West Bengal is a major producer of rice, jute, and potato in India. However, despite such production, there has not been optimum productivity in the State. In this context, the Government of West Bengal (GoWB) has identified the following key challenges in relation to agricultural production: (1) deterioration of soil health due to imbalance in the use of chemical fertilizer, (2) a lack of suitable improved seed varieties, (3) inadequate farm mechanisation, and (4) an unorganised marketing structure.[3]

One of the concerns regarding productivity, according to the GoWB, is the imbalance in the use of fertilizer, which therefore affects soil fertility. In this section, we investigate this concern using data from the Agricultural Input Survey available from the Department of Agriculture, Cooperation & Farmers Welfare.[4]

Fertilizer Use Pattern

To attain higher productivity from cultivated land, plant nutrients from both fertilizers and organic manure is required. Because chemical fertilizer is cheap relative to the value of the extra crop produced and can be applied easily as opposed to organic forms, they are more widely used. Table 1 shows the various types of commonly applied chemical fertilizers in West Bengal: urea, DAP (Di-Ammonium Phosphate), super phosphate, and potassium-based fertilizers.

For the period between 1996–97 and 2011–12, the application rate of urea, DAP, and NPK showed a monotonically increasing trend in the State: the former doubled, the second increased five-fold, and the latter doubled.

---

are a number of measures for estimating the cost of cultivation. I define crop profitability as the difference between gross value output (GVO) (due to both products and by-products) and A2 cost. Further details about A2 cost is given in https://eands.dacnet.nic.in/Cost_Concept/Cost_Con.pdf, viewed on August 14, 2018.

[3] https://wb.gov.in/portal/web/guest/agriculture#, viewed on August 14, 2018.

[4] http://inputsurvey.dacnet.nic.in/, viewed on August 14, 2018.

Comparing the most recent figures (2011–12) of the State's NPK level of 89:55:35 with the all-India recommended level of 120:60:30 (Prasad and Pathak 2009)[5] shows that West Bengal's N application rate was lower than the recommended level and those of P and K were closer to the recommend levels. This suggests that the State focused on the latter two macronutrients, despite the fact that nitrogenous fertilizers, particularly urea and DAP, are the predominant fertilizers in the State. However, the NPK application rate suggests that complex fertilizers[6] are more popular. This contradicts the GoWB's understanding that imbalance is one of the reasons for the lower productivity in the State. Though data presented in Table 1 do not support this understanding, we can extrapolate that the lower application rate (with respect to the recommended rate) of nitrogenous fertilizer might be one of the reasons for lower agricultural productivity, particularly that of rice. However, this argument needs to be further validated with in-depth analysis.

Table 1 *Fertilizer application pattern, West Bengal, 1996–2012,* in kg/ha

	1996–97	2001–02	2006–07	2011–12
Urea application rate	72.78	126.21	134.31	137.87
DAP application rate	17.68	23.6	28.13	79.32
Super phosphate application rate	26.08	113.98	99.27	34.46
Ammonium sulphate application rate	0.43	0.18	0.13	0.08
Total N applied	44.83	66.12	72.47	89.37
Total P applied	21.22	35.09	45.9	55.76
Total K applied	16.88	31.79	34.78	35.65
NPK ratio*	2.66:1.26:1	2.08:1.1:1	2.08:1.32:1	2.51:1.56:1
Total manure applied	2,218.77	1,070.27	1,243.51	1,558.57

Note: * NPK ratio is not given in kg/ha.
Source: Agricultural Input Survey, GoI, 2007, 2008, 2012, 2016.

[5] At the national level, it has been generally recognised that an NPK consumption ratio of 4:2:1 should be attained. The NPK needs of the farm are determined by the crop, its variety, the soil's capacity to supply nutrients, and the nutrient efficiency of a location. However, a general recommendation to maintain NPK ratio to 4:2:1 is largely in tune with the NPK requirement of major crops in India, mainly wheat and paddy, which corresponds to the recommended dose of NPK as 120:60:30 kg/ha (Murari, Jayaraman, and Chakraborty 2017).
[6] Complex fertilizers are one that has a mix of different proportion of N, P, and K.

Table 2 *Cropping pattern, West Bengal, 1995–2012,* in per cent of gross cropped area

Crop	1995	2004	2012
Paddy *aman*	47.73	42.91	42.41
Paddy *boro*	12.93	14.45	12.98
Paddy *aus*	5.69	3.37	2.17
Oilseeds	3.65	7.07	7.69
Potato	2.85	3.37	4.11
Pulses	2.37	2.38	2.3
Jute	5.75	5.98	6.1

Source: Nandi (2018); GoWB (2015).

Cropping pattern in any location depends upon agroclimatic conditions, technical facilities, access to inputs, yield and market response. The agroclimatic setting of West Bengal is favourable for foodgrain production, which dominates the cropping pattern (Ghosh 2011). Table 2 shows the cropping pattern of major crops, which covered more than 80 per cent of the gross cropped area (GCA) of the State: paddy covered more than 60 per cent of the GCA and oilseeds, potato, pulses, and jute were other main crops. Potato, jute, and oilseeds showed an increasing trend, suggesting they replaced paddy and pulses.

The fertilizer application rate is influenced by the cropping pattern. Table 3 shows the pattern of fertilizer application for major crops in 2011–12. The application rates of urea and DAP were highest for the area cultivated under pulses – a surprising fact given that pulses are leguminous crops with nitrogen fixation properties. Furthermore, the nitrogen application rate for pulses was higher than the recommended rate (120 kg/ha).

The area under pulses also had a higher phosphorous application rate compared to other crops due to higher DAP application rate for pulses. The N and nitrogenous fertilizer application rate for paddy was much lower than the recommended rate. Because paddy in West Bengal is grown on more than 60 per cent of the GCA, the overall lower rate of nitrogen applied (as observed from Table 1) was due to the low application rate of urea applied in the paddy fields. Though the P application rate for paddy was also low, that of K-based fertilizer was similar to the recommended rates (30 kg/ha). This differs from the all-India fertilizer application rate as well as those of major agricultural States, where the application rate is skewed towards nitrogenous fertilizers than to P and K. Furthermore,

Table 3 *Fertilizer application rate for cultivated land under major crops, West Bengal, 2011–12,* in kg/ha

Fertilizer/nutrient	Paddy	Jute	Total oilseeds	Potato	Total pulses
Urea	116.16	172.62	162.87	208.71	272.73
DAP	43.15	84.23	131.07	90.06	206.38
Super phosphate	36.28	27.12	24.07	77.49	6.7
Ammonium sulphate	0.08	0.04	0.02	0.13	0
Total N applied	67.04	101.36	103.65	133.74	163.63
Total P applied	37.84	55.66	74.12	103.68	98.09
Total K applied	31.95	29.71	25.78	99.41	4.18
N-P-K ratio*	2.1:1.18:1	3.41:1.87:1	4.02:2.88:1	1.35:1.04:1	39.15:23.47:1
Total manure applied	1,779.96	1,116.57	636.79	2,269.14	130.98

Note: * NPK ratio is not given in kg/ha.
Source: Agricultural Input Survey 2011–12.

the Input Survey data also showed the level of manure application in ascending order: oilseeds and pulses, rice and jute, and potato.

The Cost of Cultivation of Selected Crops and Fertilizer Costs

The cost of fertilizer is significant to the total input cost for cultivating a crop. Higher fertilizer application rates not only affect the overall farm profitability but also influence farmers' choice of cropping pattern. Dev (2012) suggested that an increase in fertilizer prices did not have a significant effect on fertilizer consumption but that farmers shift the cropping pattern from fertilizer-intensive crops like wheat to less fertilizer-intensive crops. However, the reverse is also true, as the macro data at the all-India level revealed that the area under pulses did not increase significantly (Mohanty and Satyasai 2015). In fact, Dixit, Singh, and Singh (2014) observed that there was a significant shift from the area under pulses to high-yielding varieties of cereals, particularly in places like Punjab, Haryana, and Western Uttar Pradesh. This choice can be explained by farmers' anticipation of securing higher returns.

Table 4 shows the total cost of input (A2 cost) for three major crops: paddy, jute, and potato. I compared costs in 2009–10 and 2014–15; the selection of years was based on when the village survey was conducted. Further details on this household survey are given in the next section. As given in Table 4, the per hectare cost of cultivation of rice doubled in 2014–15, whereas the crop's GVO increased by 43 per cent. For jute,

Table 4 *Total input and fertilizer costs for major crops, West Bengal, 2009–15*, in Rs/ha

Particulars	Paddy		Jute		Potato		Rapeseed/ Mustard	
	2009– 10	2014– 15	2009– 10	2014– 15	2009– 10	2014– 15	2009– 10	2014– 15
Cost of cultivation (A2 cost*)	19,862	37,904	18,412	42,893	67,760	107,436	12,046	24,841
Gross value output	41,144	58,956	52,389	78,988	61,837	99,509	27,049	48,554
Total input cost#	6,585	12,142	4,594	8,406	45,406	72,912	4,746	8,254
Fertilizer and manure cost	3,190	6,034	2,446	4,828	10,609	22,740	2,244	5,092

Note: * This also covers hired labour costs. # This reflects the cost of irrigation charges, fertilizer (chemical and manure), insecticides, and seeds.
Source: CACP (2009–10) and CACP (2014–15), Department of Economics and Statistics.[7]

the cost more than doubled, whereas its GVO increased by 50 per cent. Fertilizer cost ranged between 10 to 15 per cent of the total A2 cost for the three crops. In absolute terms as well as in ratio of A2 cost, this cost was lowest for jute and highest for potato. On a per hectare land basis, fertilizer cost for potato was quadruple that of jute and double that of paddy.

GVO is an important indicator for the profitability of cultivating a particular crop. In estimating the cost of cultivation for a given crop, its GVO is estimated at the prevailing market prices during the harvest season in the village/cluster of villages where the crop is grown and harvested (Sharma and Sharma 2017). The GVO for paddy in West Bengal was double the A2 cost in 2009–10; the GVO to A2 cost ratio reduced by 155 per cent in 2014–15. The GVO for jute was 285 per cent of the A2 cost in 2009–10 and reduced to 185 per cent in 2014–15. This indicates that jute is more profitable than paddy in West Bengal, but in 2014–15, the profitability of both jute and paddy reduced from the 2009–10 levels. Interestingly, according to cost of cultivation data, the GVO for potato was less than the A2 cost for both 2009–10 and 2014–15. This indicates that potato cultivation has not been profitable in the State, even though there has been an increase in the area under cultivation for potato from 4,08,000 hectares in 2010–11 to 4,12,000 hectares in 2014–15. This anomaly

[7] CACP (Cost of cultivation and production): the datasets are available at https://eands.dacnet. nic.in/Cost_of_Cultivation.htm, viewed on September 12, 2018.

in input price and GVO for potato in the State needs corroboration with further data. It raises the question of why potato is a popular cash crop when the cost of cultivation indicates a loss in the value.

In this section, I use two main agricultural statistical datasets to understand the macro picture of agriculture in West Bengal: the Agricultural Input Survey and the CACP data. Using these datasets, I observed following points related to agriculture in the State:

1. There is a monotonically increasing trend in per unit application rate of urea and DAP.
2. The application rate for N was much lower than the recommended levels, whereas the P and K application rates were close to the recommended levels.
3. The application rates of urea and DAP were highest on the area under pulses.
4. Compared to other crops, pulses and oilseeds, which have nitrogen fixation properties, had a higher application rate of nitrogenous fertilizer. Further, the area under pulses and oilseeds had a lower application rate of manure.
5. Cost of cultivation data suggests that among paddy, jute, and potato, which cover more than 80 per cent of the GCA, jute was the most profitable.
6. According to the cost of cultivation data, potato requires very high input per unit area of cultivated land. Interestingly, GVO figures suggest it was not a profitable crop.

Many of these macro-data-based observations for West Bengal contradict our understanding of fertilizer application at the all-India level. I next explore the trends of fertilizer application at the village level using the PARI data for 2009–10 and 2014–15.

Fertilizer Use Pattern in Three Villages

This section discusses the findings from the PARI village studies regarding patterns of fertilizer application among households surveyed in 2009–10 and 2014–15. The 2010 survey was a census survey, whereas the 2015 one was a sample survey for which multipliers for each category of surveyed households were available. The estimation of crop yield and fertilizer application rate (at the village level) were obtained by employing a weighted average using multipliers for each household category. I have compared the crop yield and fertilizer application rate by using the median yield value of households. There is a possibility of deviation from the average in crop yield and fertilizer application rate for households, particularly during the 2015 survey. Therefore, I used both weighted average and median as a measure of central tendency because these measures are not affected by a large deviation or outliers in the data. This method also has a tendency to nullify the effect of extreme values of crop yield and fertilizer application rates in the villages.

Table 5 gives types of fertilizer applied – urea, NPK (10:26:26),[8] DAP, potash, and super phosphates were widely used in 2010. In Panahar, urea, DAP, and potash covered more than 90 per cent of the area under fertilizer application, whereas in Amarsinghi and Kalmandasguri, urea, NPK (10:26:26), and potash covered 85 per cent of the same. The application rates of urea and NPK (10:26:26) were much higher in Panahar and Amarsinghi than Kalmandasguri. For potash, the application rate was highest in Panahar, followed by Kalmandasguri; Amarsinghi applied the lowest amount per unit area.

The area under fertilizer application and the fertilizer application rate depend upon the cropping pattern and productivity in a village, which is discussed in the subsequent section.

Table 5 *Types of fertilizer applied, study villages, 2010,* in per cent and kg/ha

Fertilizer type	Panahar		Amarsinghi		Kalmandasguri	
	Area applied (%)	Application rate (kg/ha)	Area applied (%)	Application rate (kg/ha)	Area applied (%)	Application rate (kg/ha)
Urea	34.27	124.43	42.41	125.90	40.28	67.13
NPK (10:26:26)	6.76	267.66	27.28	199.62	27.68	89.53
DAP	29.15	277.60	3.99	153.52	6.92	67.51
Potash	28.21	192.65	15.32	61.73	15.04	120.98
Super phosphate	0	0	1.99	101	8.9	382.59

Note: Area applied refers to the area on which a particular fertilizer has been applied, expressed as a percentage of the total area on which fertilizer has been applied.
Source: PARI survey (2010).

[8] A complex fertilizer is referred to by its grade (in terms of percentages of N, P and K) present in it. For example, a fertilizer with NPK grade of 10:26:26 indicates that it has 10 per cent of nitrogen, 26 per cent each of phosphorous and potassium by weight.

Cropping Pattern of Selected Crops

Comparing the cropping pattern, particularly area coverage, between the two different survey rounds is difficult, given that the 2015 survey was a sample survey. However, as mentioned above, I have employed the weighted average method by using the available multipliers for different household categories. The results are particularly important to understanding the changes in the cropping pattern.

Figure 1 shows the area under major crops (as a percentage of GCA) for the three villages. Paddy is the dominant crop across the villages, and both *aman* and *boro* varieties cover nearly 60 per cent of the GCA. In Amarsinghi, oilseeds (mustard and rapeseed) and jute were the other major crops and vegetables, pulses, and maize were sown in pockets. A comparison of area under major crops between the 2010 and 2015 indicates an increase in area coverage for aman and *boro* paddy. Area

Figure 1 *Cropping pattern for major crops, three villages, 2010 and 2015*, in per cent of gross cropped area (GCA)

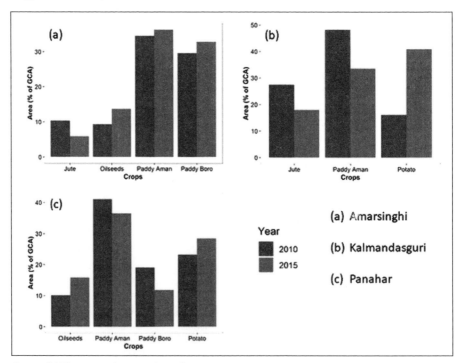

Source: PARI surveys (2010 and 2015).

under oilseeds and jute increased and decreased, respectively, during the period.

In Kalmandasguri, the dominant crops were *aman* paddy, potato, and jute, covering more than 90 per cent of the GCA. Area under *aman* paddy and jute declined during the survey period, whereas that of potato more than doubled.

Crop-Wise Fertilizer Use Pattern

Given agroclimatic conditions in the three villages favourable to cultivating paddy, the recommended NPK dose is 80:40:40.[9] For potato, the recommended dose of N in West Bengal is 145–161 kg/ha (Jaiswal and Grewal 1990). Though the P requirement for healthy crops is similar to that of cereal crops such as paddy, a healthy potato crop requires more K than cereals do. However, the P and K requirements for potato vary according to the agroclimatic region, variety, and soil type. In general, the recommended P and K doses for potato is 25–30 and 170–230 kg/ha, respectively (Trehan *et al.* 2008).

The recommended NPK dose for jute in West Bengal is 60:40:40,[10] lower than that of other crops. Most oilseed crops have nitrogen fixation properties, meaning they require less nitrogenous fertilizer than other crops. In general, the recommended NPK doses for oilseed crops range between 40–65 kg/ha N, 20–35 kg/ha P_2O_5, and 15–30 kg/ha K (Hegde 2002).

Table 6 shows the fertilizer/nutrient application rate for selected crops in Panahar. Here, the fertilizer and nutrient application rate for all crops was the highest among the three villages. For paddy, the N application rate was per the recommended limits, but the P and K rates were much higher than the recommended limits. In the case of potato and jute, the NPK application rate was much higher than the recommended limits – for jute, the P rate was particularly higher than the recommended limits.

Table 7 shows the fertilizer/nutrient application pattern for selected crops in Amarsinghi. Between the survey years, there has been an increase in urea application for the three major crops and reduction in

---

[9] This dose indicates an application rate of 80 kg/ha, 40 kg/ha, and 40 kg/ha for N, P, and K, respectively. In other words, if only urea is applied on a hectare of land, the recommended dose should be about 174 kg. Similarly, if only DAP and potash are applied, the recommended doses are 87 and 80 kg, respectively, to reach the 40 kg/ha recommendation for P and K.

[10] www.crijaf.org.in/pdf/cropcalendar/JafCropCalendar_2013.pdf, viewed on October, 20 2018.

Table 6 *Fertilizer/nutrient application rate for major crops, Panahar, 2010 and 2015*, in kg/ha

Fertilizer/nutrient	Paddy		Potato		Oilseeds	
	2010	2015	2010	2015	2010	2015
Urea	84.12	94.56	256.81	281.35	100.12	91.94
NPK	174.38	156.53	564.64	446.76	243.57	276.22
DAP	155.75	160.1	630.00	594.55	212.21	260.72
Potash	104.87	109.73	434.49	343.78	99.83	113.21
Total N	71.54	74.77	244.8	238.95	92.32	99.32
Total P	95.84	94.65	363.74	328.63	131.6	157.76
Total K	74.21	73.24	280.65	222.06	83.83	95.07

Note: Oilseeds consist of rapeseed, mustard, sesame, sunflower, and groundnut. Rapeseed/mustard covers the majority of area under oilseeds area of the village.
Source: PARI surveys (2010 and 2015).

Table 7 *Fertilizer/nutrient application rate for major crops, Amarsinghi, 2010 and 2015*, in kg/ha

Fertilizer/nutrient	Paddy		Oilseeds		Jute	
	2010	2015	2010	2015	2010	2015
Urea	135.15	184.6	109.82	122.46	63.69	66.98
NPK (10:26:26)	162.57	163.15	210.82	196.67	136.8	124.54
DAP	129.81	128.31	123.83	187.12	161.22	149.7
Potash	68.06	65.49	92.57	127.08	38.58	78.95
Total N	81.43	99.46	75.11	87.74	57.6	56.17
Total P	77.94	77.43	83.26	106.32	86.38	79.81
Total K	53.24	52.3	70.76	82.3	37.32	51.51

Note: Oilseeds consist of rapeseed, mustard, sesame, sunflower, and groundnut. Rapeseed/mustard covers the majority of area under oilseeds area of the village.
Source: PARI surveys (2010 and 2015).

NPK (10:26:26) application for all crops. Though the DAP application rate for oilseeds increased, it decreased for other crops. In terms of NPK, the N application rate for paddy in Amarsinghi was approximately the recommended dose, whereas the P and K application rates were higher than the recommended doses. For oilseeds, the NPK application rate was close to the recommended limit, whereas that for jute was higher than the recommended limit. In particular, the P and K application rates were much higher than the recommended doses.

Table 8 *Fertilizer/nutrient application rate, major crops, Kalmandasguri, 2010 and 2015,* in kg/ha

Fertilizer/nutrient	Paddy		Potato		Jute	
	2010	2015	2010	2015	2010	2015
Urea	37.3	51.24	162.72	136.69	38.38	68.14
NPK (10:26:26)	68.31	61.78	256.23	302.04	66.11	67.48
DAP	65.43	85.02	66.69	50.27	60.29	55.55
Potash	36.67	64.24	187.53	239.02	28.33	37.14
Total N	23.25	29.28	73.11	66.38	22.83	31.26
Total P	28.97	31.51	102.89	121.54	27.00	28.13
Total K	24.03	33.37	38.17	37.69	21.94	22.38

Source: PARI surveys (2010 and 2015).

Table 8 shows the fertilizer/nutrient application pattern for selected crops in Kalmandasguri. The application rates of urea, NPK (10:26:26), DAP, and potash were lower than those in Panahar and Amarsinghi. Although the urea application rate increased for paddy and jute, it decreased for potato. The NPK application rate (10:26:26) did not increase, except in the case of potato. The DAP application rate significantly increased for paddy, but not for other crops. The application rate of potash increased for all crops. The NPK application rate was lower than the recommended limits in both survey years, indicating nutrient deficiency and its effect on productivity of major crops in the village.

Tables 6, 7, and 8 indicate a specific pattern of the three studied villages. Panahar had a tendency of fertilizer application being higher than the levels recommended for that agroclimatic region, whereas Amarsinghi's rate was close to the recommended limits. The fertilizer application rate is lowest in Kalmandasguri, where the NPK application rate was less than the prescribed rate for that agroclimatic region. I now examine the notion that higher fertilizer rates are generally related to increased productivity, using the fertilizer use pattern in these villages.

The Relationship of Fertilizer Application and Crop Productivity

Figure 2 shows the distribution of household-yield values for selected crops in the three villages and compares these yields with the all-India and State average yields. Barring rice yield, which is higher in West Bengal, the average crop yields at the all-India and State level were similar. In Panahar and Amarsinghi, the median rice yield was almost equal and higher than both the State and all-India averages, respectively. In Kalmandasguri, though the distribution of rice-yield values was concentrated among low values, the median yield is the lowest among the villages and also lower than the all-India and State average yields.

In comparing yield values with fertilizer rates from the crop-wise fertilizer application tables (Tables 6, 7, and 8), both Panahar and Amarsinghi had similar NPK application rates that were close to or above the recommended limits, which explains both villages' similar median rice yields. The low rice yield in Kalmandasguri could be explained by the low NPK application rate. Comparision of Figure 2 and Table 7 indicates that Kalmandasguri was a nutrient-deficient village as reflected in its lower rice yields. Addressing the nutrient application rate here might help villagers to enhance agricultural productivity; however, this is a preliminary proposal that further requires a detailed field study.

Given that West Bengal is a major potato producing State, the average productivity of the crop is higher than that at the all-India average (Figure 2). In Kalmandasguri, low potato productivity could be explained by the low application of fertilizers compared to Panahar (Tables 7 and 8). In fact, much of the distribution of potato productivity values in Kalmandasguri lies among values lower than the all-India average, despite West Bengal being a top potato producer. Similarly, potato productivity in Panahar was also lower than the State average, however its fertilizer application rate was higher than the recommended limits. This indicates that high levels of fertilizer application (higher than the recommended limits) may not always lead to higher crop productivity. Other factors such as crop variety, irrigation and farm management should also be accounted for to attain high potato productivity.

In the case of jute, West Bengal is also a top producer State. In the year 2010, Panahar did not grow the crop in a large part of its GCA. Whereas, jute was the second dominant crop in Amarsinghi and Kalmandasguri, respectively. However, the area under the crop has considerably changed in 2015. (Figure 1). In Amarsinghi, jute productivity was higher than that of the State average (Figure 2), which can be related to the fertilizer application rate (Table 6). Though the NPK application rate here was similar to the recommended limits, it was much less than the recommend limits in Kalmandasguri. Lower jute productivity in Kalmandasguri (Figure 2) can thus be attributed to the lower fertilizer application rate.

Among oilseed crops, I consider rapeseed and mustard as they are more widely grown in the State. Oilseed production in West Bengal

Figure 2 *Yield of selected crops in the three villages*

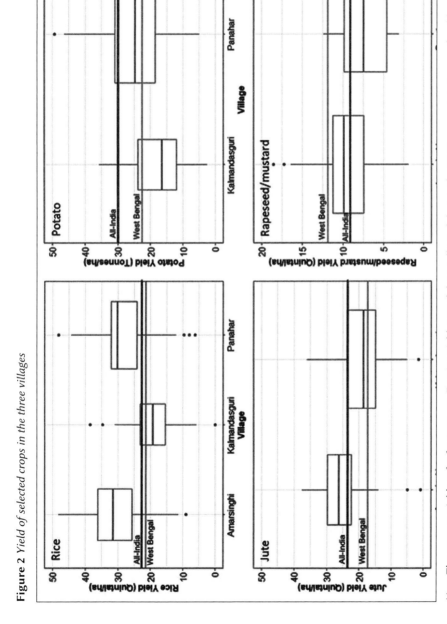

Note: The average yields refer for 2009–10. For rice yield, actual data collected during the PARI survey is in terms of paddy yield, which was converted to rice yield using a conversion factor of 0.65 (Singha 2013).

is restricted due to physical factors and certain cultivation practices, particularly late sowing due to late harvesting of *aman* (kharif) paddy that leads to inadequate moisture at sowing time. In addition, a large part of cultivated land in the State are flood-affected areas. As a result, the average productivity of rapeseed/mustard in the State was much lower than that of the all-India average. Rapeseed and mustard were grown in Panahar and Amarsinghi but not in Kalmandasguri (Figure 1). In Panahar, the productivity was lower than both the State average and the median productivity of Amarsinghi. In Amarsinghi, the productivity of oilseeds was higher than the State-level average but lower than the all-India average (Figure 2).

Economics of Fertilizer Use Pattern in Villages

As noted earlier, Kalmandasguri had the lowest fertilizer-use and crop productivity, whereas the other two villages' fertilizer rates were close to or higher than the recommended limits. Comparision of fertilizer application patterns between Panahar (with fertilizer rates higher than the recommended limits) and Amarsinghi (fertilizer rates close to recommended limits) also indicates that fertilizer use did not increase productivity beyond a certain threshold. Importantly, there is no evidence that excess fertilizer use led to a decline in productivity – in fact, there is not enough macroscale data or literature to prove this relationship. A natural question that arises is why villages have low fertilizer use if it enhances productivity or, conversely, why there is excess use if there is no evidence that it will boost productivity. This is a complex question with no straightforward answer and applies to the villages presently under study.

The answer to the above question involves understanding farmers' choice of crop and variety, their irrigation and fertilizer management practices, and the economics of cultivation practices in a given locality. Understanding the relationship between fertilizer use and economic factors for farmers in India is a domain for further research, given the fact that a large section of farmers do not have a clear choice among a variety of technological and economic options. There is minimal literature on this topic due to the lack of micro- and macro-level data. Keeping this gap in mind, I try, in this section, to understand the existing economic options available to farmers in the three villages. I do not provide a detailed economic assessment or description of the agricultural practices; rather, the economic discussion is limited to inputs for selected crops. Based on this discussion, I compare village-level input costs with their State-level counterparts using cultivation data. This comparison will elucidate the relevancy of village-level data on the cost of cultivation, an important indicator for framing minimum support price policy. In addition, I compare the share of input costs and the GVO for a given crop to provide insight on farmers' choice of a particular cropping pattern in a region.

Figure 3 shows the distribution of fertilizer prices (for 50 kg) as reported by household respondents in 2010. As discussed earlier, there are four types of fertilizer – urea, DAP, complex NPK (10:26:26 grade), and muriate of potash (potash) – applied on the fields. The median price of urea among the three villages is Rs 300 per 50 kg bag. Village data indicate variation in urea prices for Panahar, and less variation for Amarsinghi and Kalmandasguri. In Panahar, the distribution of urea prices suggest that a sizable proportion of famers paid less than the median value of Rs 300.

In the case of the complex fertilizer with NPK (10:26:26 grade), the reported median cost was around Rs 1,000 in Panahar and Amarsinghi, where the median cost was about Rs 100 higher than the median cost of Kalmandasguri. As discussed earlier, this fertilizer was widely applied in Amarsinghi and Kalmandasguri. The box-and-whisker plot suggests a wide variation in the reported cost of NPK (10:26:26) among all the three villages, but the distribution of reported prices is wider in Kalmandasguri and concentrated among higher values. This suggests that many farmers pay more than the median price of fertilizer in that village.

DAP is the third most important type of fertilizer and is widely used in Panahar, whereas its use was limited in the other two villages. DAP's reported cost per 50 kg bag was similar to that of urea and NPK (10:26:26) and lowest in Panahar. The box-and-whisker plot indicates low variation of reported DAP prices for Panahar, whereas there is significant variation in Amarsinghi and Kalmandasguri. For the latter village, the box-and-whisker plot for DAP prices is concentrated around higher values.

The reported median price of muriate of potash was the same in Panahar and Amarsinghi, and Rs 100 higher in Kalmandasguri. The box-and-whisker plot suggests minimal variation in the price of potash in Amarsinghi and higher variation in the same in the other two villages; Kalmandasguri had the highest reported prices.

Figure 3 suggests that, not only is the average pricing of all fertilizer grades highest in Kalmandasguri, but also that a large section of cultivators paid very high prices for fertilizers. It also indicates that all fertilizers

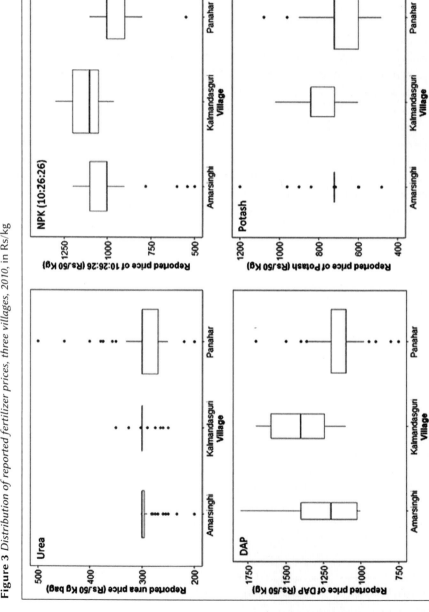

Figure 3 *Distribution of reported fertilizer prices, three villages, 2010, in Rs/kg*

were available at high prices in this village, thus possibly explaining the low application rate of fertilizers, which further relates to the low productivity of major crops. This observation is consistent with findings from Murari *et al.* (2017), who stated that small farmers were paying more than the big farmers for fertilizer.

Table 9 shows the cost of major inputs for selected crops in Panahar. The estimated values of all costs and GVO were higher than the corresponding State figures, except in the case of fertilizer and input costs for paddy and input costs for potato in 2010. As discussed earlier, agriculture in Panahar is fertilizer-intensive, which increases the input cost, and therefore, the per hectare A2 cost as well. Like Kalmandasguri and average figures of the State, the cost analysis suggests that the potato is a loss-making crop, although its productivity in Panahar is higher than that in Kalmandasguri.[11] The cost of cultivation indicates a per hectare loss of Rs 20,000 in 2010, increasing to Rs 50,000 in 2015 – this is aligned to the State-level cost of cultivation estimate as well. This raises concerns about what motivates farmers in the studied villages (and the State) to grow potato in their plots. It is possible that 2010 and 2015 are isolated

Table 9 *Cost of cultivation and other major inputs for selected crops, Panahar, 2010 and 2015, in Rs/ha*

	Paddy		Rapeseed/Mustard		Potato	
	2010	2015	2010	2015	2010	2015
Cost of cultivation (A2 cost)	26,699	39,501	18,058	33,977	59,277	112,451
	(19,861)	(37,904)	(12,593)	(24,841)	(67,760)	(107,436)
Gross value output	44,108	58,457	16,302	18,679	39,863	62,522
	(41,143)	(58,956)	(27,048)	(48,554)	(61,837)	(99,509)
Input cost[#]	8,873	16,034	7,811	24,021	40,308	79,781
	(6,184)	(10,756)	(4,382)	(7,952)	(44,450)	(69,389)
Fertilizer and manure cost	3,328	8,089	4,619	10,930	11,763	26,305
	(3,190)	(6,034)	(2,244)	(5,092)	(10,609)	(22,740)

Notes: (i) [#] Input cost covers of major inputs such as seeds, fertilizers and manure, and irrigation charges; values reflect the median statistics.

(ii) Values in the parentheses indicate the average cost of cultivation for West Bengal.

Source: PARI surveys (2010 and 2015).

[11] See chapter 5 in this book for a detailed analysis of the economics of potato cultivation in Panahar.

events, and in general, there are years when farmers do earn sufficient profits from potato cultivation – further evidence is required to support this speculation.

In the case of paddy, net profitability in Panahar was low compared to the State-level cost of cultivation estimate. The cost of fertilizer doubled in 2015 and was higher than the corresponding State-level cost by Rs 2,000 per hectare. For oilseeds, the GVO was low compared to the corresponding State average, showing the crops' low productivity (Figure 2). Importantly, oilseed productivity is not related to the application rate of fertilizer. For potato, the cost of cultivation estimates clearly indicate that it is an input-intensive crop, with one-third of input costs being fertilizer costs; this is true despite reported fertilizer costs for potato being the lowest in Panahar.

Table 10 shows the cost of major inputs for selected crops in Amarsinghi. All input costs and values of products and by-products were estimated following Swaminathan and Rawal (2011). In Amarsinghi, the median A2 cost for paddy and jute was higher than the State average cost. Although the GVO for both crops was also high in the village, State-level values showed lower net profits in paddy and jute. Paddy and jute input costs and GVO in 2015 were very close to the State values. Jute was more profitable than paddy and rapeseed/mustard in 2010; however, this profitability did not continue in 2015, possibly due to increased labour costs and a lack of increase in crop market prices. In all cases, the cost of fertilizer and manure more than doubled over the period, whereas the State-level costs did not show a similar increase. This suggests that inputs have become much costlier in Amarsinghi than what is described by the cost of cultivation estimates.[12]

Table 11 shows the cost of major inputs for selected crops in Kalmandasguri. The median values of all costs and GVO were less than the State average values. The GVO of all crops being less than the State averages further corroborates the low productivity of the crops as indicated earlier. Interestingly, the GVO for potato was Rs 4,000 and Rs 28,000 less than the A2 cost in 2010 and 2015, respectively; this is similar to the State-level average values, which also indicate that the GVO is less than the A2 cost, indicating that the market price for potato did not offset the input costs. However, it is important to note that for potato

---

[12] Also see chapter 5 for an analysis of changes in crop production and incomes in the three villages.

Table 10 *Median estimates of cost of cultivation and other major inputs for selected crops, Amarsinghi, 2010 and 2015,* in Rs/ha

	Paddy		Jute		Rapeseed/Mustard	
	2010	2015	2010	2015	2010	2015
Cost of cultivation (A2 cost)	25,691	37,478	29,349	44,654	8,244	16,472
	(19,861)	(37,904)	(18,411)	(42,893)	(12,593)	(24,841)
Gross value output	48,139	53,432	75,045	79,339	20,748	31,248
	(41,143)	(58,956)	(52,389)	(78,987)	(27,048)	(48,554)
Input cost[#]	8,908	11,616	5,514	11,054	3,537	13,669
	(6,184)	(10,756)	(4,594)	(8,129)	(4,382)	(7,952)
Fertilizer and manure cost	2,086	7,061	1,478	7,282	2,066	9,182
	(3,190)	(6,034)	(2,446)	(4,828)	(2,244)	(5,092)

Notes: (i) [#] Input cost covers of major inputs such as seeds, fertilizers and manure, and irrigation charges.
(ii) Values in the parentheses indicate the average cost of cultivation for West Bengal.
Source: PARI surveys (2010 and 2015).

Table 11 *Median estimates of cost of cultivation and other major inputs for selected crops, Kalmandasguri, 2010 and 2015,* in Rs/ha

	Paddy		Jute		Potato	
	2010	2015	2010	2015	2010	2015
Cost of cultivation (A2 cost)	8,676	16,549	14,534	20,335	53,479	94,232
	(19,861)	(37,904)	(18,411)	(42,893)	(67,760)	(107,436)
Gross value output	28,571	45,466	43,531	35,193	49,378	68,337
	(41,143)	(58,956)	(78,987)	(78,987)	(61,837)	(99,509)
Input cost[#]	2,685	11,850	9,506	9,880	33,827	71,190
	(6,184)	(10,756)	(4,594)	(8,129)	(44,450)	(69,389)
Fertilizer and manure cost	1,515	4,249	4,147	3,679	15,213	28,234
	(3,190)	(6,034)	(2,446)	(4,828)	(10,609)	(22,740)

Notes: (i) [#] Input cost covers of major inputs such as seeds, fertilizers and manure, and irrigation charges.
(ii) Values in the parentheses indicate the average cost of cultivation for West Bengal.
Source: PARI surveys (2010 and 2015).

in Kalmandasguri, the difference between the A2 cost and GVO was much higher than the estimated State-level costs, especially in 2015. This difference indicates the economic loss in potato cultivation and raises the same question posed earlier about why farmers continue to grow potato.

Like in Amarsinghi, jute in Kalmandasguri was profitable in 2010, providing a net profit of Rs 29,000 per hectare; in 2015, paddy was most profitable, at Rs 22,000 per hectare.[13] Except for paddy, the cost of fertilizer and manure more than doubled in 2015, whereas, the corresponding State-level costs did not show a similar increase. Again similar to Amarsinghi, this suggests that the inputs in Kalmandasguri have become more expensive than the cost of cultivation estimates.

Figure 2 indicated that paddy productivity in Amarsinghi was higher than the other villages; consequently, the profitability was also higher than the other villages, for both years. The fertilizer application rate in Amarsinghi for paddy was close to the recommended limits, whereas in Panahar, it was higher than that in Amarsinghi and even exceeded the recommended limits. This suggests that intensive fertilizer application does not always lead to increased productivity and profitability. In fact, this provides evidence to encourage optimum fertilizer use as useful intervention to enhance profitability for both paddy and rapeseed/ mustard cultivation in Amarsinghi and Kalmandasguri. Comparing these two villages, as discussed in the previous section, the former had a fertilizer application rate close to recommended limits, whereas the latter was characterised by limited fertilizer use and having lower nutrients to soil. Particularly in the case of jute, its productivity and GVO were much higher in Amarsinghi than in Kalmandasguri. Extrapolating from this, optimum fertilizer use can help to attain higher productivity and profitability. For example, Kalmandasguri, being limited in nutrients because of minimal fertilizer use, requires a boost in fertilizer application rates to optimum levels to attain increased value per hectare.

Concluding Remarks

For both West Bengal and three of its villages, this chapter aimed to (1) discuss fertilizer use patterns, particularly from an environmental and sustainability point of view, and (2) understand the relationship between fertilizer use and agricultural productivity and profitability. The three

---

[13] Currently, the net profit is considered as the difference between the GVO and A2 cost.

main data sources were (1) Agricultural Input Survey for West Bengal, (2) Cost of Cultivation and Production for major crops in West Bengal, and (3) PARI village survey data. The main findings are as follows:

1. In West Bengal, the N application rate was lower than the recommended levels, but those of P and K were close to the recommend levels. This diverges from the all-India trend as well as that of other major agricultural States, wherein the application rate is skewed towards nitrogenous fertilizers rather than P and K.

2. According to the cost of cultivation figures for West Bengal, the potato GVO is less than the A2 cost for both 2009–10 and 2014–15, thus potato cultivation has not been profitable. This anomaly in input price and GVO needs to be corroborated with further data to understand why potato continues to be a popular cash crop in the State.

3. Among the three studied villages, the fertilizer application pattern in Amarsinghi indicated that the NPK application rate was close to the recommended limits for most major crops. In Kalmandasguri, the fertilizer application rates for major crops were much lower than the recommended limits, whereas they were higher in Panahar for all crops. In summary, Amarsinghi nearly attained the optimum application of macronutrients, Kalmandasguri was characterised as macronutrient-deficient village, and Panahar had very high fertilizer/nutrient application rates.

4. Kalmandasguri had the lowest yields for major crops, which could be explained due to lower NPK application rates in its rice fields. The productivity of main crops (paddy and rapeseed/mustard) was higher in Amarsinghi than Panahar, suggesting that high doses of fertilizer (higher than the recommended limits) do not necessarily relate to increased productivity.

5. The distribution of reported fertilizer costs among households suggests that not only was the average pricing of all fertilizer grades highest in Kalmandasguri but also a large section of cultivators pay these high prices. Given most farmers in Kalmandasguri were small or marginal, the higher cost of fertilizer is consistent with Murari et al. (2017), who stated that small farmers paid higher for the fertilizer. This may be due to these farmers lacking cash in the beginning of the crop season.

6. Paddy productivity was highest in Amarsinghi; consequently, its profitability was also the highest here in both years. The fertilizer application rate in Amarsinghi for paddy was close to the recommended

limits, whereas it was higher in Panahar and even exceeding the recommended limits. This suggests intensive fertilizer application did not always lead to increased productivity and profitability, and thus encourages optimum fertilizer use to enhance profitability.

7. The cost of cultivation for jute in Amarsinghi and Kalmandasguri shows that optimum fertilizer application is related to increased productivity and profitability; this relation can thus be generalised for any given village. Kalmandasguri, being a nutrient-deficient village in terms of fertilizer application, requires boosting fertilizer rates to an optimum level to attain increased value per hectare.

The findings of the chapter emphasise the role of fertilizer application in crop productivity as well as realising profits. Fertilizer is an important input for productivity and profitability, and an increase in its price will impact net economic gains. Although the chapter provides a descriptive account of crop productivity and fertilizer use in three villages, further detailed study is required to confirm the conclusions drawn. Though preliminary, the main findings identify areas of interventions in the studied villages to attain enhanced agricultural productivity and profitability. For example, the fertilizer application rate should be improved in Kalmandasguri, mainly in terms of accessibility and ensuing low-cost fertilizers. At the same time, increasing fertilizer application rates do not necessarily lead to increased productivity and profitability, as in the case of Panahar. In such villages, interventions should lead towards more awareness to implement optimum levels of fertilizer use.

References

Department of Fertilizers (2014), "Indian Fertilizer Scenario 2013," Ministry of Chemicals and Fertilizers, Government of India, available at http://fert.nic.in/sites/default/files/Indian%20Fertiliser%20SCENARIO-2014.pdf, viewed on July 31, 2018.

Dev, S. Mahendra (2012), "Small Farmers in India: Challenges and Opportunities," IGIDR working paper no. WP-2012-014, June, available at http://www.igidr.ac.in/pdf/publication/WP-2012-014.pdf, viewed on July 10, 2018.

Dixit G. P., Singh, Jagdish, and Singh, N. P. (eds.) (2014), "Pulses: Challenges and Opportunities Under Changing Climate Scenario," Proceedings of the National Conference on Pulses: Challenges and Opportunities Under Changing Climate Scenario, JNKVV Jabalpur, September 29–October 1.

Government of India (GoI) (2007), *All-India Report on Input Survey, 1996–97*, Department of Agriculture and Co-operation, Ministry of Agriculture, Government of India, New Delhi, available at http://agcensus.nic.in/document/input9697/input96rep.htm

Government of India (GoI) (2008), *All-India Report on Input Survey, 2001–02*, Department of Agriculture and Co-operation, Ministry of Agriculture, Government of India, New Delhi, available at http://agcensus.nic.in/document/input2001/input2001rep.htm

Government of India (GoI) (2012), *All-India Report on Input Survey, 2006–07*, Department of Agriculture and Co-operation, Ministry of Agriculture, Government of India, New Delhi, available at http://agcensus.nic.in/document/is2006/is2006rep.html

Government of India (GoI) (2016), *All-India Report on Input Survey, 2011–12*, Department of Agriculture and Co-operation, Ministry of Agriculture, Government of India, New Delhi, available at http://agcensus.nic.in/document/is2011/is2011rep.html

Government of West Bengal (GoWB) (2015), *West Bengal Statistical Abstract 2012*, Bureau of Statistics and Planning, Kolkata.

Ghosh, Bidyut Kumar (2011), "Essence of Crop Diversification: A Study of West Bengal Agriculture," *Asian Journal of Agricultural Research*, vol. 5, no. 1, pp. 28–44.

Hegde, D. M. (2002), "Integrated Nutrient Management for Oilseed Crops," Directorate of Oilseed Research, Indian Council of Agricultural Research, p. 20.

Jaiswal, V. P., and Grewal, J. S. (1990), "Agronomic Studies on Potato Under All India Coordinated Potato Movement Project," Technical bulletin no. 20, Central Potato Research Institute, Shimla.

Ladha, Jagdish K., Pathak, Himanshu, Krupnik, Timothy J., Six, J., and van Kessel, Chris (2005), "Efficiency of Fertilizer Nitrogen in Cereal Production: Retrospects and Prospects," *Advances in Agronomy*, vol. 87, pp. 85–156.

Mohanty, S., and Satyasai, K. S. (2015), "Feeling the Pulse: Indian Pulse Sector," *NABARD Rural Pulse*, vol. 5, pp. 2–4.

Mujeri, M. K., Shahana, S., Chowdhury, T. T., and Haider, K. T. (2012), "Improving the Effectiveness, Efficiency and Sustainability of Fertilizer Use in South Asia," Briefing Paper, Global Development Network, New Delhi, India, available at http://www.gdn.int/sites/default/files/WP/WP67-SA-Fertilizer-Use_5ee.pdf, viewed on July 31, 2018.

Murari, Kamal Kumar, Jayaraman T., and Chakraborty, Sanjukta (2017), "Fertilizer Use and the Small-Scale Farms," in Madhura Swaminathan and Sandipan Baksi (eds.), *How do Small Farmers Fare? Evidence from Village Studies in India*, Tulika Books, New Delhi, pp 201–29.

Nandi, Moitreyee (2018), "Agricultural Growth in West Bengal from 1995 to 2012: An Analysis of Trends," unpublished MA dissertation, Tata Institute of Social Sciences, Mumbai.

Ncube, Bongani, Dimes, John P., Twomlow, Steve J., Mupangwa, Walter, and Giller, Ken E. (2006), "Raising Productivity of Smallholder Farms Under Semi-Arid

Conditions by Use of Small Doses of Manure and Nitrogen: A Case of Participatory Research," *Nutrient Cycling in Agroecosystems*, vol. 77, no. 1, pp. 53–67.

Pathak, H., Mohanty, S., Jain, Niveta, and Bhatia, Arti (2010), "Nitrogen, Phosphorous, and Potassium Budgets in Indian Agriculture," *Nutrient Cycling in Agroecosystems*, vol. 86, pp. 287–99.

Prasad, Rajendra, and Pathak, P. S. (2009), "Crop Response and Nutrient Ratio," Policy Paper No. 42, National Academy of Agricultural Sciences, New Delhi, available at http://naasindia.org/Policy%20Papers/policy%2042.pdf, viewed on September 3, 2018.

Sharma, V. P., and Sharma, S. (2017), "Price Policy for Rabi Crops: The Marketing Season 2018–19," Commission for Agricultural Costs and Prices, Department of Agriculture Cooperation and Farmers' Welfare, Government of India.

Singha, Komol (2013), "Paddy Processing Mills in India: An Analysis," *Rice Research: Open Access*, vol. 1, no. 2, pp. 1–5, available at http://dx.doi.org/10.4172/jrr.1000115, viewed on August 18, 2018.

Swaminathan, Madhura, and Rawal, Vikas (2011), "Is India Really a Country of Low Income-Inequality? Observations from Eight Villages," *Review of Agrarian Studies*, vol. 1, no. 1, January–June, pp. 1–22, available at http://ras.org.in/is_india_really_a_country_of_low_income_inequality_observations_from_eight_villages, viewed on August 18, 2018.

Trehan, S. P., Upadhayay, N. C., Sud, K. C., Kumar, Manoj, Jatav, Mukesh K, and Lal, S. S. (2008), "Nutrient Management in Potato," CPRI Technical Bulletin No. 90, Central Potato Research Institute, Shimla, Himachal Pradesh.

Vel Murugan, A., and Dadhwal, V. K. (2007), "Indian Agriculture and Nitrogen Cycle," in Y. P. Abrol, N. Raghuram, and M. S. Sachdev, (eds.), *Agricultural Nitrogen Use & Its Environmental Implications*, I.K. International Publishing House Pvt. Ltd., New Delhi, pp. 9–28.

7

Development of Groundwater Irrigation in West Bengal since 1990

With Special Reference to Water Markets in Two Villages

Tapas Singh Modak

Introduction

This chapter describes and analyses groundwater irrigation development and its implications for agricultural growth and agrarian relations in West Bengal, particularly after 1990. More specifically, it tracks groundwater irrigation development in the State and its districts from 1990 to 2016, examines the factors that led to the decline of groundwater irrigation expansion after 1990, and examines the actual impact of groundwater irrigation development and policies on farm households in two villages located in different agroecological zones. I have used available secondary data on irrigation and primary data from two villages in West Bengal, which were surveyed in 2010 and 2015 by the Foundation for Agrarian Studies (FAS) as part of its Project on Agrarian Relations in India (PARI).

West Bengal provides a unique site to study irrigation development and growth in agriculture. The State is rich in groundwater resources. It has large expanses of fertile alluvial soil and receives abundant rainfall in a normal year, averaging 1,500 mm per year. Despite these advantages, the growth of groundwater irrigation was slow till the late 1970s, unlike the pattern in India as a whole. It was argued by scholars and official reports that the main cause for agricultural stagnation in West Bengal since Independence through the 1970s was the underdevelopment of water control (RBI 1984; Boyce 1987; Rawal 2001b). Rawal and Swaminathan (1998) argued that the technological changes necessary to develop irrigation required large capital investments and involved high risks – major constraints for marginal and small farmers. Further, inequality in the agrarian structure and absence of institutional mechanisms to mobilise cooperation in irrigation practices posed a serious obstacle to the development of irrigation till the late 1970s (*ibid.*). After the Left Front government came to power in 1977, two important institutional changes were initiated: the implementation of land reforms, and decentralisation of power and resources to be the local governments. In the 1980s, there was remarkable growth in tubewell irrigation, which led to high agricultural growth rates (Saha and Swaminathan 1994; Rawal and Swaminathan 1998; Rawal 2001b). Rawal (1999) argued that public action, particularly in the form of expanding rural electrification and empowering local governance, created appropriate conditions for private investment in irrigation. Agricultural production and yields, however, decelerated from the early 1990s onwards (Bhattacharyya and Bhattacharyya 2007; Ramachandran, Swaminathan, and Bakshi 2010; Dasgupta and Bhaumik 2014).

In addition, the agrarian structure of the State, characterised by a predominance of small farms and extreme fragmentation of land, led to the development of informal groundwater markets. The water market is an arrangement wherein a small number of better-off farmers owning tubewells sell water to a large number of poor farmers. Different kinds of informal institutional arrangements have also evolved with the expansion of water markets.[1] There is, however, no secondary data available on water markets, and thus, in general, it is not possible to estimate the actual area irrigated by means of water markets, much less to specifically understand institutional problems with respect to informal arrangements in water markets. Thus, one has to take recourse to detailed village studies to understand the dynamics of groundwater access and exchange systems. This chapter, based on primary data from two study villages located in different agroecological zones, tries to understand the institutional arrangements in ownership and access to groundwater irrigation and its implications for farmer households.

Development of Irrigation in West Bengal

After Independence, West Bengal lagged behind in irrigation development in comparison to the agriculturally developed States or the country as

---

[1] See Modak (2020) for details.

a whole. There was a significant increase in net irrigated area (NIA) by tubewells in Punjab, Haryana, and Tamil Nadu, particularly after the introduction of the Green Revolution in India during the late 1960s. In West Bengal, the growth of irrigation was slow until the mid-1970s. Boyce (1987) estimates that three-year averages of irrigated area as a proportion of net sown area increased by only 2.1 per cent between 1949–51 and 1971–72. According to data from the Agricultural Census 1970–71, only 16.4 per cent of total operational land was irrigated in West Bengal, whereas it was 72.1 per cent in Punjab, 46.1 per cent in Haryana, 19.5 per cent in Bihar, and 18 per cent in India as whole (GoI 1975).

Though statistics on irrigation in the State are largely inconsistent and limited, the Agricultural Census provides a profile of irrigation development by all sources at five-year intervals.[2] It shows that there was an increase in NIA in West Bengal after the late 1970s. The proportion of NIA in total operational holdings was 24.1 per cent in 1980–81 that increased to 53.3 per cent in 1995–96 and further to 62.2 per cent in 2010–11. The NIA, for these years, was 1.3 million hectares, 3 million hectares, and 3.4 million hectares, respectively.

Figure 1 shows a shift in the share of area irrigated by different sources in the total NIA. Groundwater emerged as a major source of irrigation and contributed to major expansion of irrigated area in the State, similar to the country as a whole (Modak 2018). Surface water irrigation, including canals and tanks, accounted for 87 per cent of total NIA in 1970–71, but sharply declined to only 21 per cent in 2010–11. In the same period, there was a remarkable increase in the share of groundwater irrigation in total NIA, from 6 per cent in 1970–71 to 66 per cent in 2010–11. Data from NSSO Land and Livestock Holdings Survey, 2013 (NSSO 2014) also indicate that groundwater irrigation accounted for 63 per cent of total irrigated land. Tubewell irrigation, in particular, contributed the largest share in total NIA.

Table 1 shows the growth rate of area irrigated by different sources of irrigation between 1975 and 2011. The trend clearly indicates that there are

---

[2] Generally, these problems pertain to conceptual difficulties in the definition of irrigation acreage, data on quality of irrigation, and absence of an overall integrated system of data collection on irrigation (Boyce 1987, p. 167; Rawal 2001a). Although data sources provide many aspects of statistics on irrigation of West Bengal, they fail to provide a holistic picture at the country level. There are large discrepancies in the data on irrigation across data sources (See Appendix Table 1 and Modak 2020).

Figure 1 *Proportion of net irrigated area, by source, West Bengal, 1970–71 to 2010–11*, in per cent

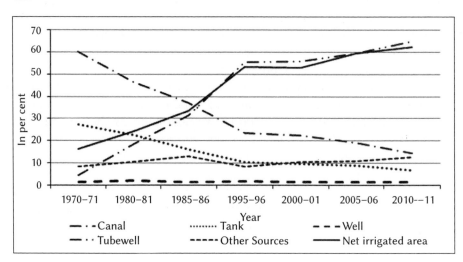

Source: All–India Report on Agriculture Census (GoI 1975, 1987, 1992, 1998, 2003, 2008, 2012, 2015).

Table 1 *Annual average growth of net irrigated area, by source, West Bengal, 1976–77 to 2010–11*, in per cent

Sources	1975–85	1985–95	1995–2005	2005–11
Canal	1.3	0	−1	−4.1
Tank	4.4	0.4	−0.5	−4.4
Well	−3.5	10.8	−1.2	−1.3
Tubewell	57.5	17.7	1.8	2.8
Other sources	20.1	0.2	4	4.1
All sources	7.4	5.7	1	0.9

Source: Modak and Bakshi (2017).

two distinct phases in the expansion of irrigation. During the first phase, between 1975 and 1995, the State underwent high growth in annual NIA at 7.4 per cent and 5.7 per cent during 1975–85 and 1985–95, respectively. It is noteworthy that the expansion in tubewell irrigation was highest among all sources – 57.5 per cent in annual NIA between 1975 and 1985 – but slowed down to 17.7 per cent per annum between 1985 and 1995.

The second phase, between 1995 and 2011, showed a significant decline in the growth of irrigation development, wherein the annual growth rate of NIA reduced to only one per cent. Surface water (canal and tank) and well irrigation had experienced negative growth. Importantly, the growth rate of groundwater irrigation development stagnated in this period.

Thus, to summarise, after the period of stagnation that lasted till the late 1970s, the State experienced a remarkable expansion in irrigation in the 1980s. However, the growth rate of irrigation development declined significantly from the mid-1990s, primarily due to the slowdown of groundwater irrigation expansion. To understand further, the next two subsections examine the development of groundwater irrigation across districts, in terms of the number of structures and area irrigated.

Groundwater Irrigation after 1990

There are three types of groundwater structures in the State: (1) dug wells, (2) shallow tubewells, and (3) deep tubewells.[3] As West Bengal is rich in groundwater resources and has a high water table on average, shallow tubewells are the primary sources of groundwater irrigation, accounting for about 90 per cent of the total gross irrigated area (GIA) by groundwater structures.

To measure the growth of groundwater irrigation, this section uses data from five Census of Minor Irrigation Schemes for the reference years of 1986–87, 1993–94, 2000–01, 2006–07, and 2013–14 to analyse the number of groundwater structures and area irrigated by groundwater (Tables 2 and 3). Several major important findings emerged from the analysis.

First, between 1986–87 and 1993–94, there was a decline in groundwater irrigation expansion in comparison with the early 1980s. In the early 1980s, the number of tubewells grew at a rate of 23 per cent in per annum, primarily a result of the increased number of private shallow tubewells (Rawal 2001b). In comparison, both the number of tubewells and area irrigated increased by about 5 per cent between 1986–87 and 1993–94. However, the growth rate of electric shallow tubewells was higher than

---

[3] Dug wells are ordinary open wells of varying dimensions, dug or sunk from the ground surface into the water-bearing stratum to extract water for irrigation purposes. These are broadly masonry wells, kuchcha wells, and dug-cum-bore wells. A shallow tube well consists of a bore hole built into the ground with the purpose of tapping groundwater from porous zones. In sedimentary formations, the depth of a shallow tubewell does not exceed 60–70 metres. Deep tubewells usually extend to a depth of 100 metres or more and are designed to give a water discharge 100 to 200 cubic metres per hour. Their annual output is roughly 15 times that of an average shallow tubewell (GoI 2014).

Table 2 *Annual average growth of number of tubewells, West Bengal, 1987–2007, in per cent*

Source	1987–94	1994–2001	2001–07	2007–14
Shallow tubewell	5.1	2.6	−2.5	0.7
Deep tubewell	8.7	4.1	1	22.4
All	5.1	2.6	−2.4	0.9

Source: Census of Minor Irrigation Schemes, Government of India (GoI 1993, 2001, 2005, 2014, and 2017).

Table 3 *Annual average growth of gross irrigated area, by groundwater structure, West Bengal, 1987–2007, in per cent*

Source	1987–94	1994–2001	2001–07	2007–14
Dug well	−4.3	−0.4	−1.6	−5.4
Shallow tubewell	5.1	0.7	4.7	−1.7
Deep tubewell	6.3	0.9	5.4	9
All	4.9	0.7	4.6	−0.6

Source: Census of Minor Irrigation Schemes, Government of India (GoI 1993, 2001, 2005, 2014, and 2017).

that of diesel-powered shallow tubewells during this period – data from the Census of Minor Irrigation Schemes shows that the number of electric tubewells increased at 13 per cent per annum compared to 5 per cent per annum for diesel tubewells. Furthermore, data from the West Bengal State Electricity Board (WBSEB) shows that electrified tubewells increased at 10.6 per cent per annum between 1987 and 1996, in contrast to 18.3 per cent per annum between 1981 and 1987 (Rawal 2001b).

Secondly, between 1993–94 and 2000–01, the growth of groundwater structures further declined to 2.6 per cent annually, and consequently, the area irrigated by groundwater grew only by 0.7 per cent annually. According to data from the Census of Minor Irrigation Schemes, GIA increased from 1,332 to 1,396 thousand hectares in 1993–94 and 2000–01, respectively (GoI 2001, 2005). However, the data from the Agricultural Census for the same period shows that there was a decline in NIA by tubewells, from 1,664 to 1,647 thousand hectares in 1995 and 2001, respectively (GoI 2003, 2008).

Thirdly, between 2000–01 and 2006–07, there was a moderate revival in the growth of GIA by groundwater despite a decline in growth of groundwater structures. The data from 2000–01 and 2005–06 in the

Table 4 *Distribution of shallow tubewells, by source of energy, West Bengal, 1986–87 to 2013–14, in per cent*

Year	Electric	Diesel	Other	All
1986–87	9.1	88.3	2.6	100
1993–94	12.5	85.5	1.9	100
2006–07	18.2	79.3	2.5	100
2013–14	32.1	64.9	2.9	100

Source: Census of Minor Irrigation Schemes, Government of India (GoI 1993, 2001, 2005, 2014, and 2017).

Agricultural Censuses also indicate a similar pattern of growth in NIA and number of groundwater structures (GoI 2008, 2012).

Fourthly, the most important feature during 2006–07 and 2013–14 is a significant increase in the number of deep tubewells and the area irrigated by them. The number of deep tubewells increased on average by 22.4 per cent per annum in this period (Table 2). It is important to note that, data from Census of Minor Irrigation Schemes for the reference year of 1993–94, 2000–01, and 2006–07 showed that 98 per cent of all deep tubewells were publicly owned or run by a cooperative society. However, the recent 5th Census of Minor Irrigation Schemes (2013–14) showed a substantial increase in the number of private deep tubewells, from only 31 in 2006–07 to 5,984 in 2013–14, as well as a large number of these tubewells installed at depths greater than 100 meters.

Lastly, between 2006–07 and 2013–14, the share of electric tubewells among shallow tubewells increased substantially (Table 4). Data from the All India Electricity Statistics also show that there was high growth in the number of electrified tubewells in agriculture between 2011 and 2016 (GoI 2017).

Inter-District Pattern of Groundwater Irrigation Development

This section examines the inter-district pattern of groundwater irrigation development between 1981 and 2007 using data from the Census of Minor Irrigation Schemes. This exercise is not extended to 2013–14 (5th Census of Minor Irrigation Schemes) because district-level statistics are not available. Based on the maps in Figures 2a–2e showing the district-wise distribution of tubewells (number per 100 sq. km of net sown area) (see Appendix Table 2), a few important patterns emerge and are discussed below.

First, the eastern districts, which fall under the groundwater-rich Old

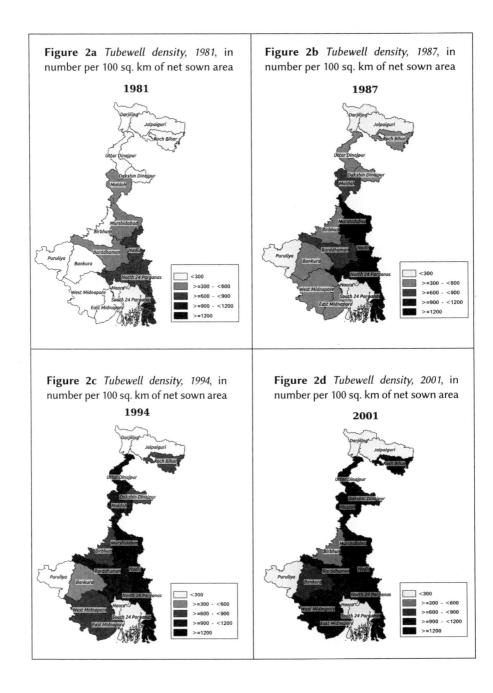

Figure 2a *Tubewell density, 1981, in* number per 100 sq. km of net sown area

Figure 2b *Tubewell density, 1987, in* number per 100 sq. km of net sown area

Figure 2c *Tubewell density, 1994, in* number per 100 sq. km of net sown area

Figure 2d *Tubewell density, 2001, in* number per 100 sq. km of net sown area

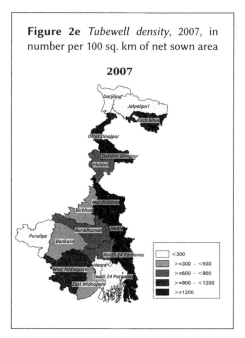

Figure 2e *Tubewell density*, 2007, in number per 100 sq. km of net sown area

2007

Sources: Data for 1981 and 1986–87 are from Rawal (2001b); data on the number of tubewells are from Census of Minor Irrigation Schemes, Government of India (GoI 2001, 2005, 2014, and 2017); data on net sown area are from the Agricultural Census 2003, 2008, 2012.

Alluvial agroclimatic zone (according to the classification by National Agricultural Research Zone), saw the initial development of groundwater irrigation – in 1981, districts such as North 24 Parganas, Nadia, and Hugli had high tubewell densities. Gradually, groundwater irrigation diffused towards the northern and western districts; data from first Census of Minor Irrigation Schemes for the reference year of 1986–87 showed more tubewell-dense districts, particularly those in the New Alluvial agroclimatic zone (GoI 1993). Table 5 shows the growth in the density of tubewells per annum was significant for the districts of Medinipur (51.6 per cent), Bankura (42.8 per cent), Birbhum (37.9), and West Dinajpur (26 per cent) between 1981 and 1987.[4]

Secondly, the data between 1993–94 and 2000–01 showed that the trend

---

[4] Medinipur district was bifurcated into the Purba (East) Medinipur and Paschim (West) Medinipur districts in January 2002. West Dinajpur district was divided into Uttar (North) Dinajpur and Dakshin (South) Dinajpur districts in April 1992.

of increased tubewell density continued across districts, but with lower annual growth rates. Nonetheless, in three northern districts – Uttar Dinajpur, Koch Bihar, and Maldah – tubewell density was higher than the State average in 2000–01 (until 1986–87, the density in these districts had been lower than the State average).

Thirdly, the period between 2000–01 and 2006–07 showed a progressive decline in tubewell density for all districts except Dakshin Dinajpur. The annual growth in tubewell density ranged from –6.7 per cent in Haora to –0.1 per cent in Koch Bihar, with –2.8 per cent for the State as a whole.

It is also important to note that there was a significant decline in the

Table 5 *Annual average growth of tubewell density, by district, West Bengal, 1981–2007*, in per cent

District	1981–87	1987–94	1994–2001	2001–07
Bankura	42.8	11.3	3.8	−6.2
Barddhaman	21.9	4.1	1.9	−5.7
Birbhum	37.9	4.3	−1.3	−6.1
Dakshin Dinajpur	26	4.8	7.9	4.1
Uttar Dinajpur	0	0	8.3	−2.5
Darjiling	0	0	−3.6	−5.1
Haora	0.3	0.8	1.8	−6.7
Hugli	5.6	−0.3	0.3	−4
Jalpaiguri	9.6	52.6	5.3	−2.6
Koch Bihar	20.1	25.7	11.3	−0.1
Maldah	16.3	8.3	3.5	−5.1
Murshidabad	21.2	6.8	1.5	−3.1
Nadia	19	5.7	1.8	−0.2
North 24 Parganas	20.4	1.3	1.5	−2.7
South 24 Parganas	17	6.5	7.8	−4.4
Medinipur*	51.6	8.3	3.6	−0.2
Puruliya	–	–	–	–
West Bengal	21.6	5.4	3.1	−2.8

Notes: * Medinipur district was bifurcated into Purba Medinipur and Paschim Medinipur districts on January 1, 2002. – Negligible.
Sources: Data for 1981 and 1986–87 are from Rawal (2001b); data on the number of tubewells are from Census of Minor Irrigation Schemes, Government of India (GoI 2001, 2005, 2014, and 2017); data on net sown area are from the Agricultural Census 2003, 2008, 2012.

inter-district variation of tubewell density – the coefficient of variation of it across districts was 0.91 in 1981 and continued to decline: 0.84 in 1986–87, 0.80 in 1993–94, and further to 0.77 in 2000–01. However, the gap between districts with respect to tubewell density widened in 2006–07, wherein the coefficient of variation increased to 0.867 in 2006–07.

It is clear from the secondary data on irrigation that the period after the mid-1990s was associated with a decline in the number of tubewells as well as stagnation in the area irrigated by groundwater across districts. This can be understood from the following two possible explanations.

First, the scope of further groundwater irrigation development was restricted due to the natural limits of groundwater exploitation. Topography, geological formations, soil water retention capacity, and rainfall play a key role in the development of groundwater use. West Bengal has diverse geographical characteristics, ranging from extra-peninsular in the north to peninsular mass in the southwest and further to alluvial and delta plains in the south and east. Table 6 shows that the districts of Nadia, Hugli, Barddhaman, Uttar Dinajpur, and Murshidabad were highly irrigated – more than 85 per cent of operational holdings were irrigated in 2011. In these districts, most agricultural lands are located in the Gangetic alluvial region and where groundwater irrigation contributed to a major share of irrigated area. In contrast, Purba Medinipur, Paschim Medinipur, Jalpaiguri, Bankura, South 24 Parganas, Darjiling, and Puruliya districts lagged behind in terms of NIA. A large extent of geographical area of these districts consists of undulating plateaus or hilly areas and is where expansion of groundwater irrigation is restricted by topographical factors such as rocky top layers and deep aquifers.

The stage of groundwater development in the State as a whole, that is, the ratio between annual withdrawal and recharge of groundwater, was only 45 per cent in 2013 (CGWB 2017) (Appendix Table 3). This implies that overuse of groundwater in West Bengal is not of much concern as it is in Punjab, Haryana, Karnataka, Rajasthan, and Tamil Nadu. Thus, there is scope for further groundwater use in various districts, particularly those which have moderate irrigation levels. However, arsenic contamination of groundwater is often a serious quality problem for some parts of the State and must also be considered.

Secondly, economic factors and policy constraints have contributed to the slowdown of irrigation development after the mid-1990s. Several studies have shown that the continuously rising cost of diesel, low rates of tubewell electrification, and bureaucratic hurdles in getting permission

Table 6 *Proportion of net irrigated area (NIA) in total operational holding, by source and district, West Bengal, 2011,* in per cent

District	NIA						Unirrigated
	Canal	Tank	Well	Tubewell	Other sources	All	
Nadia	0.5	2	0.7	64.4	23.6	91.2	8.8
Hugli	24.1	4.8	1.3	54.4	5.7	90.2	9.8
Barddhaman	37.6	2.1	1.5	40.9	6.3	88.4	11.6
Uttar Dinajpur	0.5	1	0.8	79.4	4.2	85.9	14.1
Murshidabad	3	3	0.8	74.8	3.9	85.6	14.4
Dakshin Dinajpur	0.2	10.1	1.6	56.8	2.4	71	29
North 24 Parganas	1.7	2	0.8	61.8	2.6	68.9	31.1
Haora	37.7	5.4	0	7.2	16.5	66.9	33.1
Maldah	0.4	5.8	0.2	46.8	10.7	63.8	36.2
Birbhum	18.3	7.4	0.1	33.8	3.8	63.5	36.5
Koch Bihar	0.7	3.6	1.2	45.6	9.7	60.8	39.2
Paschim Medinipur	5.8	2.4	0.7	43.3	7.8	60	40
Purba Medinipur	14.3	5.6	0.1	31.8	4.2	56	44
Jalpaiguri	2.2	3.9	1	18.3	18.3	43.7	56.3
Bankura	9.2	4.4	1.3	22.8	5.2	42.9	57.1
South 24 Parganas	9.5	8.1	0.2	9	4.9	31.6	68.4
Darjiling	1.3	0.1	0.9	1.8	7.8	12	88
Puruliya	0.5	7.1	0.3	0.1	2.2	10.1	89.9
West Bengal	9.1	4.2	0.8	40.4	7.7	62.2	37.8

Source: All-India Report on Agriculture Census, GoI (2015).

for tubewell installation were responsible for the deceleration of tubewell irrigation in West Bengal after the 1990s (Bakshi 2010; Modak and Bakshi 2017; Mukherji, Banerjee, and Biswas 2018).

Contributory Factors for the Deceleration of Groundwater Irrigation Development after 1990

Rising diesel prices
In the early 1980s, the rapid growth of diesel-pump-operated shallow tubewells was a response to abundant groundwater resources, low diesel prices, and support from the local government. However, after

Figure 3 *Retail price of diesel in Kolkata, 1980–2014*, in Rs per litre

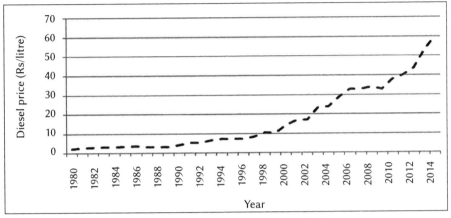

Source: Ministry of Petroleum and Natural Gas, Government of India.

liberalisation in 1991, the price of diesel increased rapidly throughout the country as well as in West Bengal. For instance, the retail price of diesel oil in Kolkata, the State capital, was Rs 2.25 in 1980, Rs 4.2 in 1990, Rs 16.9 in 2001, Rs 40 in 2011, and Rs 60 in 2014 (Figure 3). Given that a large share of tubewells in West Bengal was operated by diesel-operated pumpsets, the rapid increase in the price of diesel adversely affected the development of irrigation.

Stagnation of electrification in agriculture

In India, one important feature of agriculture is the complementarity between public and private investment. Ramakumar (2012) argued that "in a growing economy, public investment induces or 'crowds in' private investment by farmers" (p. 95). Rural electrification is one of the most important components of indirect public investment in irrigation development and has important consequences in mobilising private finance for investment in irrigation (Rawal 1999). The Government of West Bengal (GoWB) had invested substantially in the power sector in the 1980s – annual expenditure on the power sector increased from Rs 4 crores in 1980–81 to Rs 14.6 crores (at 1980 prices) in 1990–91 (*ibid.*).

As a result, there was a significant increase in the number of electrified pumpsets between 1977 and 1995 in West Bengal (Table 7) – 10,701 in 1976–77 to 99,252 in 1995–96. The growth rate during this period was 10.3 per cent, the third highest among major States, whereas the country-wide figure was 7.3 per cent. Similarly, the electricity load supplied to the agricultural sector increased substantially between 1980 and 1995 (Figures 4a and 4b). In the same period, the compound annual rate of growth of electricity supplied to agriculture was about 20 per cent. Among total electricity consumption, the share consumed by the agricultural sector increased from only 1.2 per cent in 1980–81 to 10.3 per cent in 1998–99.

After 1995, however, West Bengal could not continue the pace of electrification for agriculture. The compound annual growth rate of electrification of pumpsets in West Bengal reduced to only 1.1 per cent between 1995 and 2010, lower than the country average of 2.8 per cent. As a result, the compound annual growth rate of electricity consumption in

Table 7 *Annual compound growth rate of electrified pumpsets, West Bengal, 1977–2011, in per cent*

Year	Growth of electrified pump sets
1977–1995	10.3
1995–2010	1.1

Source: All India Electricity Statistics, Ministry of Power, Government of India.

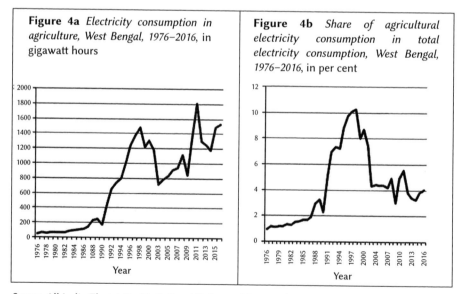

Figure 4a *Electricity consumption in agriculture, West Bengal, 1976–2016, in gigawatt hours*

Figure 4b *Share of agricultural electricity consumption in total electricity consumption, West Bengal, 1976–2016, in per cent*

Source: All India Electricity Statistics, Ministry of Power, Government of India.

agriculture declined to only 1.7 per cent between 1995 and 2011, whereas it was about 20 per cent between 1980 and 1995. Of total electricity consumption in the State, the share consumed by the agriculture sector declined by half, from 10.3 per cent in 1998–99 to 4.9 per cent in 2010–11.

Policy for Regulation of Groundwater Use

By the early 1990s, the major policy prescription with regard to groundwater development in India was to restrict the unregulated growth of groundwater structures and groundwater exploitation. This directive was based on the situation in the northern, western, and southern regions of India. The main reasons for the introduction of such regulatory measures in these regions (and particularly in Punjab, Haryana, Karnataka, Tamil Nadu, Gujarat, and Rajasthan) were the falling water tables and overexploitation of aquifers, and consequent water shortages for agriculture and other purposes. This restriction of groundwater exploitation became national policy and was enforced by means of different measures in different States.

In West Bengal, the same policy was ushered in even though there was no water shortage or overexploitation of groundwater resources. The stage of groundwater development (that is, the ratio of annual groundwater draft to net annual groundwater availability) was less than 45 per cent, therefore nowhere near overexploitation. The GoWB regulated groundwater usage, particularly for agriculture through direct control of installing groundwater structures and indirect control through regulating electricity connections and pricing. Starting from April 1993, the State government directed the State Water Investigate Directorate (SWID), the authority responsible for regulating groundwater use, to place restrictions on electricity connections of privately owned, low-duty tubewells fitted with submersible pumps. West Bengal was also one of the first States to follow the Central Government's "Model Bill" to regulate and control the use of groundwater when the Legislative Assembly enacted the West Bengal Groundwater Resources (Management, Control and Regulation) Act in 2005. This Act requires any groundwater user in the State to obtain a registration certificate from SWID to sink a new tubewell as well as for existing tubewells.

Researchers have often argued that getting permission from SWID for installing new or existing tubewells created bureaucratic hurdles for farmers (Mukherji *et al.* 2009; Mukherji, Shah, and Banerjee 2012; Jayaraman 2015; Modak and Bakshi 2017; Mukherji, Banerjee and Biswas

2018). The electricity department made the registration certificate from SWID mandatory for any electrification of tubewells. In addition, tubewell electrification was not economically viable for a large number of small and marginal farmers because a tubewell owner had to pay full capital costs for an electricity connection, including the costs of wire, cement poles, and a 10-kva transformer. Tubewell owners were thus discouraged to shift from diesel-operated tubewells to electric ones. Therefore, it can be argued that the effect of these policies halted the development of groundwater irrigation and, consequently, the growth of agricultural production.

Changes in Policies on Groundwater Use for Agriculture after 2011

To address the low rates of tubewell electrification, the GoWB removed the restrictions on issuing permits for tubewell installation in 2011. The Water Resources Investigation and Development Department (WRIDD) issued a notification on November 3, 2011 stating that the installation of tubewells with a discharge limit of 30 cubic meters per hour and using five-horsepower pumps did not require permits from the district authority of the SWID. However, this was not applicable for 38 blocks of the State that were categorised as semi-critical as per Central Ground Water Board (CGWB) in 2008–09 (SWID 2011).[5]

At the same time, the West Bengal State Electricity Distribution Company Limited (WBSEDCL) reduced the electricity connection fee ranging from Rs 1,000 to Rs 30,000, depending on the connection load, whereas previously farmers had to bear the full capital costs, as mentioned above (Mukherji, Shah, and Banerjee 2012). In addition, the Department of Agriculture, GoWB launched a scheme called the One Time Assistance for Electrification of Agricultural Pumpsets (OTS-EAP) on November 30, 2012, under which small and marginal farmers received a one-time assistance of Rs 8,000 to meet electricity connection charges for five-horsepower agricultural pumps.

These changes in policy significantly increased the number of electrified tubewells. Between 2011 and 2016, data from the Ministry of Power, Government of India show that the number of electrified

---

[5] The assessment units for groundwater development are based on four categories: "safe," "semi-critical," "critical," and "overexploited." This is determined by two criteria: a) stage of groundwater development and b) the long-term trend of pre- and post- monsoon water levels (CGWB 2017).

tubewells more than doubled (Table 8). In addition, the share of electric shallow tubewells increased from 18.2 per cent in 2006–07 to 32.1 per cent in 2013–14 (Census of Minor Irrigation Schemes, GoI 2014, 2017).

Though the number of electrified tubewells in the State increased after the implementation of the policy changes – WRIDD notification,

Table 8 *Number of electrified pump sets, West Bengal, 2011–16*

Year	Number of electrified pumpsets	Annual percentage increase
2011	116,343	–
2012	116,348	0.004
2013	116,458	0.1
2014	212,745	82.7
2015	243,027	14.2
2016	269,395	10.8

Source: All India Electricity Statistics, Ministry of Power, Government of India.

Figure 5 *Average power tariff for agriculture, West Bengal, 2008–09 to 2015–15,* in paisa per kWh

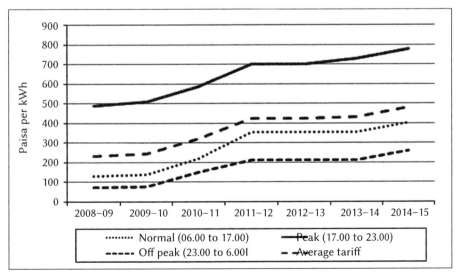

Note: The three time segments for tariffs in agriculture are the following: normal hours (6 am–5 pm), peak hours (5 pm–11 pm), and off-peak hours (11 pm–6 am). The objective of this time-based system is to encourage the use of tubewells during off-peak hours.

Source: West Bengal Electricity Regulatory Commission, 2008–09 to 2014–15.

WBSEDCL fee reduction, and the OTS-EAP scheme – other problems have since emerged. There has been a rapid hike in electricity tariffs for irrigation in the recent period in West Bengal (Figure 5). After assigning equal weights to the three tariff segments based on time of day, it is observed that the average tariff increased by about 50 per cent, from Rs 3.19 per kWh in 2010–11 to Rs 4.81 per kWh in 2014–15. In addition, the yearly flat-rate electricity cost for unmetered tubewells with submersible pumps also increased from Rs 13,176 in 2010–11 to Rs 21,600 in 2015–16. The power tariff for agriculture in West Bengal is now the highest among all major groundwater-irrigated States, thus rendering the abolition of State control over the allocation of electric pumps of no benefit to farmers.

Results from Two Study Villages

This section tries to establish the link between changes in groundwater irrigation policy in the State and survey results from two villages – Panahar in Bankura district and Amarsinghi in Maldah district. Both villages have been surveyed at different points of time by the FAS and other researchers.[6] The survey data spanning over a decade for both villages also allow for the examination of various factors responsible for the slowdown of groundwater irrigation development in the State. Though groundwater was the primary source of irrigation in both villages in 2010, they followed different trajectories of irrigation development.

Panahar, Bankura District

Panahar village is situated in the eastern part of Bankura district and falls in the Old Alluvial Zone of West Bengal. Eastern Bankura primarily consists of porous alluvial sediments of the Ganga and Brahmaputra river systems, and hence, the region is rich in groundwater resources.[7] SWID data also showed that the district water level was between 1.5 and 15 meters below ground level (bgl) in 2011. In spite of these favourable conditions, the development of irrigation in Panahar was limited until the

---

[6] See chapter 1.

[7] The hydrogeology of Bankura district, based on geology and presence of groundwater, is broadly divided into three regions – western, middle, and eastern. The western and middle regions of the district primarily consist of crystalline and laterite rocks, which limits the groundwater use. The eastern part of the district mainly comprises porous, alluvial sediments and is rich in groundwater (CGWB 2016).

late 1970s due to minimal public and private intervention in expanding the area under irrigation as was the case for the State as a whole (Rawal 1999).

As in the State overall, substantial development of irrigation in Panahar occurred after 1977. Rawal (1999) and my interviews with different stakeholders in 2017 revealed that there were two phases of irrigation development in the village – first, between 1977 and 1986, and second, after 1986. In the first phase, diesel-powered shallow tubewells were installed mostly by the large landowners of the village. These tubewells irrigated a limited area and were primarily used only to irrigate owners' agricultural land. As the water discharge from these tubewells was limited, they failed to introduce a significant multiple cropping system including *boro* paddy cultivation. One of the owners of a diesel-powered shallow tubewell in early 1980s, SK, reported that the low discharge from these tubewells, particularly during *boro* paddy cultivation season, was mainly due to the seasonal fall in the water table. Because of this, operating these tubewells required much effort; owners had to dig about 20 feet and sink pumpsets in the pits to reach the water table.[8,9]

During this period, substantial efforts were undertaken by the State government through panchayats to repair public irrigation systems. Ponds were desilted under the National Rural Employment Programme, which was implemented through the panchayat. In addition, part of the village was under the command area of Kangsabati Canal Project through which the village received water though an unlined canal. Anwar Ali Khan, the former *pradhan* of Deshra-Koalpara Gram Panchayat during 1978–91 and also a resident of Panahar, reported that the panchayat also undertook different initiatives under rural development programmes to revive the canal channels.[10] However, as a whole, these public interventions could not greatly increase the area irrigated in the village, particularly during the rabi or summer seasons. These were served as supplementary water resources in the kharif season.[11]

There was a remarkable change in irrigation development after 1986 when the introduction of electricity led to the replacement of diesel-

---

[8] We also found a similar experience of diesel-powered shallow tubewell use in Amarsinghi village.
[9] Interview with SK on July 18, 2017
[10] Panahar village falls under the jurisdiction of Deshra-Koalpara Gram Panchayat.
[11] Interview with Anwar Ali Khan on July 17, 2017

operated shallow tubewells with electrified submersible deep tubewells. This technological shift substantially increased the efficiency of tubewells, as it enabled water discharge from a greater depth, water availability throughout the year, and increased potential area irrigated by tubewells. Along with increased efficiency of tubewells, the number of electrified submersible tubewells also rose substantially from the mid-1980s. Overall, irrigated area expanded, which led to a shift in cultivation practices from a single paddy crop to multiple cropping.

The PARI census survey showed that 92 per cent of gross cropped area (GCA) was irrigated in 2010 (Table 9). Private tubewells, the main of source of irrigation, irrigated 88 per cent of the total GCA.[12] In 2015, the share of tubewell irrigation increased to 92.5 per cent, according to a sample-based estimate. Between 2010 and 2015, however, the share of irrigated area by the Kangsabati Canal Project declined further in Panahar.

Since the mid-1980s, the expansion of electric-powered submersible tubewells for irrigation was undertaken primarily by large landowners, as installation of these tubewells required high investment (Rawal 1999). In 2010, there were 16 electrified submersible tubewells in the village, all owned by cultivator households; this ownership was skewed in favour of large-farmer households. Of the 16 electrified submersible tubewells, eight were owned by the seven landlord/capitalist households. The remaining eight tubewells were owned by eight households belonging to the peasant class (consisting of 52 households), whereas the poorest

Table 9 *Proportion of gross irrigated area, by source, Panahar, 2010 and 2015,* in per cent

Source of irrigation	2010	2015
Tubewell/borewell	88.1	92.5
Canal/river	2.9	0.2
Pond	0.9	0.4
Rainfed	8.1	6.9
All	100	100

Source: PARI surveys (2010 and 2015).

[12] There was a large discrepancy between the village survey data and official statistics. The 2011 Census data showed that 71 per cent of the total NIA in Panahar was irrigated by canals, whereas only 10 per cent by tubewells and the remaining 19 per cent by ponds.

section of peasantry (small-peasant/semi-proletarian households) did not own any tubewells.[13]

Similar to West Bengal overall, agricultural land in Panahar is characterised by small farms and fragmented landholdings.[14] Given that a tubewell has a fixed location and can only irrigate land to a certain distance, tubewell owners cannot fully use the potential of their tubewells by only irrigating their own lands. On the other hand, poor-peasant households cannot invest in tubewells because of high installation costs. These aspects led to the emergence of an informal private water market, which farmers revealed to be widespread after the introduction of electric-powered submersible tubewells in the mid-1980s.

Despite the concentration in ownership of tubewells, all farm households had access to irrigation in all seasons from an active water market (Table 10). All tubewell owners sold water in 2010 and most sold it for a much larger area of agricultural land than they themselves owned and irrigated. In 2010, 84 per cent of households that operated land bought water for irrigation, and 55 per cent of GIA in the village was irrigated by purchased water. Because tubewell ownership was concentrated among landlord/capitalist farmers, major water buyers belonged to upper-peasant and poor-peasant households (Table 10). Purchased water irrigated 72 and 96 per cent of the GIA of upper-peasant and poor-peasant households, respectively. Landlord/capitalist households, however, also bought water – 13 per cent of their GIA was irrigated by purchased water – primarily due to land fragmentation.

In Panahar, water was sold primarily on two kinds of fixed-rate contracts

Table 10 *Proportion of households purchasing water and of gross irrigated area (GIA) irrigated by purchased water, by socio-economic class, Panahar, 2010,* in per cent

Socio-economic class	Households purchasing water	GIA irrigated by purchased water
Landlord/capitalist farmer	29	13
Upper peasant	90	72
Poor peasant	83	96
All	84	55

Source: PARI survey (2010).

[13] See chapter 3 for a description of socio-economic classes in the study villages.

[14] In 2010, the average size of an operational holding in Panahar was only 1.1 acres.

– crop-acreage and time-rates. Water was sold at hourly rates in the case of time-rate contracts, whereas in crop-acreage contracts, tubewell owners were entrusted to ensure adequate irrigation for a successful crop and charged water buyers based on the area irrigated. There were no fixed norms for the volume of water or number of waterings to be supplied for specific crops. Crop-acreage fixed contracts were more common in Panahar in 2010 and 2015. In addition, water sellers reported in 2017 that some of their buyers, mostly poor peasants, exchanged wage labour in different agricultural operations on the sellers' fields in place of cash payments.[15] However, the crop-sharing payment contract wherein water sellers received a share of total production as payment was totally absent in Panahar. Notably, these crop-sharing contracts were also popular in the water market of other parts of West Bengal and other States (Shah 1991; Janakarajan 1993; Fujita and Hussain 1995; Rawal 2002; Sarkar 2011; Modak and Bakshi 2017).

Changes in tubewell irrigation, 2010–2017
Based on a follow-up survey of 106 sample households in 2015 and case studies conducted in 2017, there were important changes in tubewell irrigation in Panahar, which can be linked with contemporary changes in policy on groundwater irrigation in West Bengal after 2010. The major changes are discussed below.

Number of tubewells
Like the rest of the State, there was significant increase in the number of tubewells in Panahar between 2010 and 2017. It was also revealed from the 2017 case studies that the number of electric-powered tubewells increased in the village primarily due to an easier process of installing a tubewell and reduced costs of an electricity connection.[16,17] The number of electrified tubewells in the village increased from 16 in 2010 to 30 in

---

[15] Interview with SK and RM in July 2017.

[16] Interview with SM and RG in July 2017.

[17] In an interview on July 18, 2017, RG reported that before 2011, installing an electric-powered submersible tubewell in the village required permission from the district SWID office. As per the rule, he applied for permission to install a tubewell in 2008, but only received it in 2010. However, he did not drill a tubewell in 2010 and eventually installed an electric-powered submersible tubewell in 2013. He paid Rs 20,000 to the electricity department to get an electricity connection – Rs 8,000 was the quotation fee for the connection and Rs 12,000 as a bribe to the contractor.

2017. Notably, poorer sections of peasants as well as non-farm households invested in tubewell irrigation, a phenomenon absent in 2010.

Water rates
Although the relaxations given for tubewell installation have significantly contributed towards more tubewells in the village, the hike in the electricity tariff increased water rates substantially. Table 11 shows the per acre water rates for major crops paid by the water buyers.[18] There was significant increase in water rates for all major crops between 2010 and 2017. For example, the water rates for the most water-intensive crop, *boro* paddy, increased from Rs 3,000 to Rs 5,000 per acre, and later to Rs 6,500 per acre in 2010, 2015, and 2017, respectively. In other words, water rates for a typical buyer more than doubled in seven years.

During interviews in July 2017, water sellers reported that they increased water rates primarily on account of the rapid increase in electricity bills since 2011. Anwar Ali Khan, the former *pradhan* of the gram panchayat, revealed that before 2010, he paid a flat rate of Rs 10,000 to operate one tubewell in a year, whereas in 2016–17, he paid a Rs 40,000 electricity bill.

Table 11 *Water rates for major crops irrigated by purchased water, Panahar, 2010, 2015, 2017,* in Rs per acre

Year	*Aman* paddy	*Boro* paddy	Potato
2010	1,000	3,000	1,500
2015	2,000	5,000	2,500
2017	2,000	6,250	3,000

Source: PARI surveys (2010 and 2015); case studies, 2017.

Irrigation cost
Due to increased power tariffs, there was significant increase in the average per acre irrigation cost between 2010 and 2015 (Table 12). Taking the example of the main irrigated crop, *boro* paddy, the average irrigation cost per acre increased from Rs 2,843 to Rs 5,045 for the households purchasing water from private tubewells in the respective years. The

---

[18] It is notable that there are some variations in water rates reported by different buyers on account of factors like the relationship between water sellers and buyers, and the distance from the tubewell.

increase in average per acre irrigation cost during this time was much higher for water buyers than for tubewell owners. During the five-year period, the average irrigation cost per acre for *aman* paddy increased by 19 per cent for tubewell-owner households and by 107 per cent for water-buyer households.

As shown in Figure 6, statistics published by the Commission for Agricultural Costs and Prices (CACP) also indicated an increase in irrigation costs for paddy cultivation in West Bengal – from Rs 1,963 to Rs 2,912 per hectare in 2009–10 and 2014–15, respectively.[19]

Table 12 *Average irrigation cost for major crops, for tubewell owners and water buyers, Panahar, 2010 and 2015,* in Rs at current prices

Crop	Tubewell owners			Water buyers		
	2010	2015	Increase (%)	2010	2015	Increase (%)
Aman paddy	688	820	19	978	2021	107
Boro paddy	1049	1800	72	2843	5045	77
Potato	732	797	9	1680	2491	48

Source: PARI surveys (2010 and 2015).

Figure 6 *Estimated irrigation cost for paddy cultivation, West Bengal, 2000–15,* in Rs per hectare of operational holding

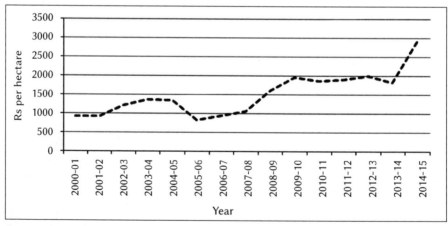

Source: Data in the reports of the Commission for Agricultural Costs and Prices (CACP).

[19] Here, the irrigation cost for paddy cultivation is estimated in aggregate for all three seasons in West Bengal.

To summarise, though the number of electrified tubewells in Panahar, as in the rest of the State, increased after the implementation of policy changes in 2011, other problems have since emerged. This is due to the fact that despite the reduction in fixed irrigation costs, including those for pump installation and electricity connections, there has been no decline in the variable costs, that is, electricity prices. In the following section, I argue that the rapid hike in the electricity tariff has adversely affected agriculture.

Changes in cropping pattern, 2010–2015
In 2010, Panahar primarily had triple-cropped agriculture with the following major crops: *aman* paddy in kharif, potato in winter, and *boro* paddy or sesame in summer. Of the 65 per cent of total GCA under paddy cultivation in 2009–10, the shares of *aus* paddy (pre-kharif), *aman* paddy, and *boro* paddy were 5, 41, and 19 per cent, respectively. Cultivation of *aus* and *aman* paddy were primarily rainfed and used supplementary irrigation and, thus, had low water requirements. In contrast, *boro* paddy was completely dependent on irrigation, requiring frequent watering. Potato constituted 23 per cent of total GCA and required frequent watering, albeit less than that needed in the case of *boro* paddy.

More strikingly, data from two surveys conducted in 2010 and 2015 suggested that there has been a shift in cropping pattern, particularly in the pre-kharif season (Table 13). The area under *boro* paddy declined from 19 to 12 per cent of the total GCA. *Boro* paddy was largely replaced by sesame – because the latter is suited for dry cultivation and requires minimal water. For instance, in 2015, the water rate for sesame was only Rs 1,250 per acre, whereas it was Rs 5,000 per acre for *boro* paddy. The estimation from panel households, which were surveyed in both survey years, also showed a reduction in area under *boro* paddy (from 57 to 36 acres) and increased area under sesame (from 19 to 32 acres) during pre-kharif season.

Importantly, there was also decline in area under *aman* paddy between 2009–10 and 2014–15 in Panahar, from 181.7 acres (41 per cent of total GCA) to 169.4 acres (37 per cent of total GCA). To understand further, I examine the changes in cultivation practices of both tubewell owners (9 households) and water buyers (44 households) among the panel in 2010 and 2015. Table 14 shows that the area under *boro* paddy cultivation declined for both types of cultivating households. However, interestingly, in the same period, the area under *aman* paddy declined only for the water buyers, from 37.4 acres to 31.3 acres, whereas the area under *aman* paddy

Table 13 *Area under specified crops as a proportion of gross cropped area, Panahar, 2009–15*

Crop season	Crop	Share of GCA (in per cent)*		Area (in acres)**	
		2009–10	2014–15	2009–10	2014–15
Kharif	Paddy (*aman*)	41	37	111	100
Rabi	Potato	23	29	61	71
	Mustard/rapeseed	3	1	9	2
	Rabi vegetables	1	2	3	4
Pre-kharif	Paddy (*aus*)	5	5	17	14
	Paddy (*boro*)	19	12	57	36
	Sesame	7	15	19	32
	Pre-kharif vegetables	1	1	1	2
	GCA	100	100	279	261

Notes: * Proportions of GCA in 2014–15 are sample-based estimates.
　　** Data in the last two columns are for households sampled in 2010 and 2015 and constitute a panel.
Source: Sarkar (2015).

remained unchanged for tubewell owners. One of the main reasons for this could be that water sellers doubled the water rates for *aman* paddy in 2015, from Rs 1,000 to Rs 2,000 per acre.

To elaborate the relationship between the increasing cost of irrigation and changes in the cropping pattern, three case studies from Panahar, discussed below, each present a different situation:

1. CA, belonging to a joint family, is a small farmer who operated two acres of land in 2015. Crop land under his ownership was irrigated by water purchased from private tubewells. At the time of both surveys, he reported cultivating his crop land thrice a year. Between 2010 and 2015, interestingly, there was no change in the area under *aman* paddy (a monsoon crop) and potato, whereas the area under *boro* paddy fell from 0.8 acre in 2010 to only 0.2 acre in 2015. In contrast, he cultivated sesame on 1.8 acres in 2015, which he did not do in 2010. The shift from *boro* paddy to sesame was primarily due to increased water rates for *boro* paddy, which subsequently increased the total paid-out cost. [20] For example, in 2010, he paid Rs 2,750 per acre for water in *boro* paddy

---

[20] Paid-out cost is calculated using the definition of cost A2 used by the CACP.

Table 14 *Area under specified crops as a proportion of gross cropped area, for tubewell owners and water buyers, Panahar, 2010 and 2015*, in acres

Crop season	Crop	Tubewell owner		Water buyer	
		2010	2015	2010	2015
Kharif	Paddy (*aman*)	56.8	56.3	37.4	31.3
Rabi	Potato	29	30.9	24	28.7
	Mustard/rapeseed	6.8	0.5	1.7	1
	Vegetables	2.6	2.7	0.2	0.5
Pre-kharif	Paddy (*aus*)	14.2	10	2	2.6
	Paddy (*boro*)	36.7	23.7	14.1	9.1
	Sesame	10.9	7.1	5.9	16.9
	Vegetables	0.4	–	0.6	–

Note: Data are for households sampled in 2010 and 2015 and constitute a panel. There were 9 tubewell owners and 44 water buyers in the panel.
Source: PARI surveys (2010 and 2015).

cultivation, which increased to Rs 5,000 per acre in 2015. The cost of irrigation as a proportion of total paid-out cost was 12 per cent in 2010, increasing to 30 per cent in 2015. In contrast, the water rate for sesame cultivation was only Rs 1,100 per acre in 2015, as it was not a water-intensive crop.

2. SM was a medium farmer operating six acres of irrigated crop land in 2015 – four acres were owned and two acres were sharecropped. An important feature of his household was that it accessed irrigation water from the private water market in 2010, but installed two electrified submersible tubewells in 2014 and 2015. In 2017, SM was one of the largest water sellers in the village. However, even after acquiring ownership of tubewells, his household's area under *boro* paddy declined from 4 acres in 2010 to 2.86 acres in 2015. In contrast, their area under sesame increased from 1.2 acres in 2010 to 2.86 acres in 2015 during the pre-kharif season.

3. SK, a traditional landlord farmer in the village, owned 18 acres of irrigated crop land in 2015. Under the land reform programme between 1977 and 2002, he lost 13.31 acres of crop land and ponds. SK was one of the large landowners who introduced submersible tubewells in the village. The extent of area cultivated by SK for *boro* paddy fell from 7 acres in 2010 to 4.8 acres in 2015. Even more striking is the difference in the annual

electricity bill for irrigation during the period. In 2010, he paid Rs 9,000 for the whole year, which covered 32 acres of GCA under his ownership, and another 21 acres for which he sold water. This increased to Rs 30,000 in 2015 for the same 32 acres of GCA under his ownership.[21] The estimated irrigation cost for *boro* cultivation was an average of Rs 300 per acre in 2010 (3.6 per cent of total paid-out cost) which increased to Rs 1,650 per acre in 2015 (12 per cent of the total paid-out cost). In 2017, he affirmed that the rapid hike in power tariff in agriculture had adversely affected the cultivation of summer crops, particularly *boro* paddy.

Along with increased irrigation costs, market conditions were also one of the determinants for changes in the agricultural production system in Panahar. Table 15 shows the average farm harvest prices (FHP) for *aman* and *boro* paddy in 2010 and 2015. In the five-year period, the FHP for *aman* paddy increased from Rs 850 to Rs 1,000 per quintal, and that of *boro* paddy increased from Rs 900 to Rs 1,000 per quintal. In real prices, strikingly, FHPs declined between 2010 and 2015 and were much lower than the official minimum support prices (MSPs) in both years. Only 1 out of 148 households cultivating *aman* paddy and 4 out of 121 cultivating *boro* paddy received prices higher than the MSP in 2010.

The decline in *boro* paddy area in Panahar is of a piece with the declining trend in the State as a whole. In West Bengal, the area under *boro* paddy declined from 1,430 hectares in 2009–10 to 1,290 hectares in 2014–15, at –2.03 per cent annual compound growth rate. The area under *aus* and *aman* paddy remained unchanged in the review period, whereas interestingly, the area under water-intensive *boro* paddy has been substituted by mostly dry cultivation of sesame, green gram, and maize (Table 17).

Table 15 *Average farm harvest prices for paddy, Panahar, 2010 and 2015,* in Rs per 100 kg at current prices

Crop name	2010	2015
Paddy (*aman*)	850	1,000
Paddy (*boro*)	900	1,000
Minimum support price (MSP)	1,050	1,360

Source: PARI survey (2010 and 2015).

[21] Previously, he was a water seller in Panahar. In the 2015 survey, he reported that he had stopped selling water since 2014 on account of difficulties in collecting rent from water buyers.

Table 16 *Area under paddy cultivation, by season, West Bengal, 2009–14*, in '000 hectares

Year	*Aus* paddy (pre-kharif)	*Aman* paddy (kharif)	*Boro* paddy (summer)
2009	214	3,986	1,430
2010	212	3,362	1,370
2011	212	3,999	1,221
2012	205	4,010	1,228
2013	210	4,016	1,286
2014	227	4,008	1,290

Source: GoWB (2017).

Table 17 *Area under various summer crops, West Bengal, 2009–14*, in '000 hectares

Year	Groundnut	Maize	Green gram	Potato	*Boro* paddy	Sesame	All
2009	50	38	13	2	1,430	184	1,717
2010	48	39	15	2	1,370	180	1,654
2011	53	41	17	2	1,221	180	1,514
2012	55	49	20	2	1,228	194	1,548
2013	55	53	21	2	1,287	211	1,629
2014	55	55	28	2	1,290	222	1,652

Source: GoWB (2017).

Therefore, in a situation wherein rising power tariffs substantially increased water rates for water buyers cultivating *boro* or summer paddy, and that consequently led to an increase in the cost of cultivation without suitable remunerative prices, cultivators were discouraged from sowing *boro* paddy. The shift from paddy to sesame also affected employment, as the cultivation of sesame is less labour-intensive than *boro* paddy and usually performed by family labour (see chapter 10).

Amarsinghi, Maldah district [22]

Amarsinghi is situated in Ratua I block in Maldah district in the New Alluvial plains of West Bengal. Groundwater was the main source of irrigation in the village. As discussed earlier, the introduction of technological advances

[22] This section is taken from Modak and Bakshi (2017).

in irrigation was delayed in Amarsinghi in comparison to Panahar. Till the late 2000s, agricultural land was primarily irrigated by diesel-powered shallow tubewells, after which two major government interventions – electrification for irrigation and the installation of a cooperative-run deep tubewell – took place in the village. This section analyses how these two State interventions changed the ownership of tubewells, terms of exchange, and water rates. It also examines the impact of these changes on the cost of irrigation and net returns from agriculture. This section uses data from the 2005, 2010, and 2015 surveys and my case studies from 2016.[23]

The development of irrigation in the village was minimal as it was in much of the State until the mid-1970s. Modern and mechanical irrigation was introduced through the establishment of a public river lift irrigation (RLI) scheme in the late 1970s. However, the scheme did not fall within the village boundaries, and only some crop land belonging to Amarsinghi cultivators was irrigated by water that scheme. In the early 1980s, farmers started installing self-operated, diesel-powered, shallow tubewells (locally known as mini-tubewells). The geographical location,[24] abundant groundwater, low diesel prices, and support from the gram panchayat[25] played a favourable role in the expansion of shallow tubewell irrigation both in terms of the number of tubewells and area irrigated. Both private shallow tubewells and the RLI scheme increased the extent of *boro* paddy cultivation and led to a change in the cultivation practice from mono-cropping to multiple cropping.

From the late 1990s, the increased use of groundwater had a negative impact on the groundwater level, particularly in summer. Diesel-powered shallow tubewells could not extract sufficient water during *boro* paddy cultivation.[26] In addition, there was a sharp increase in the diesel price,

---

[23] A detailed sample survey was conducted by Aparajita Bakshi in 2005–06. FAS conducted a census survey in 2010 and a sample survey in 2015, as part of PARI. I undertook case studies on specific questions of irrigation development through semi-structured interviews in 2016. Semi-structured interviews were conducted with water sellers, buyers, members of tubewell cooperatives, and elected representatives from the village to understand the historical trajectories of irrigation development and forms of water exchange.

[24] The village is located in the Gangetic fluvial region where farmers can easily access groundwater throughout the year.

[25] In an interview on August 11, 2016, the former *upa-pradhan* (deputy head) of the panchayat reported that the panchayat had initiated the process of granting permission for installing private, diesel-powered shallow pumps.

[26] Farmers had to dig 7–10 feet near the shallow tubewell and place the pump down to reach the water level during summer. This was an extremely laborious work.

particularly after 1990 (see previous section, "Factors for the Deceleration of Groundwater Irrigation Development after 1990"). The increasing cost of diesel and the inability of diesel tubewells to extract water from greater depths, particularly in summer, led to diesel tubewell owners abandoning shallow tubewells in the mid-2000s.[27] In the late 2000s, two major government interventions took place in the village. First, electricity for irrigation in the village arrived in 2007, causing shallow tubewell owners to gradually shift to electric-powered submersible tubewells. In 2017, there was not a single diesel-powered shallow tubewell in the village. Secondly, a deep tubewell was installed in 2008 by the GoWB and is currently managed by a cooperative.

A major proportion of the cultivated land in Amarsinghi is irrigated. In 2005–06, according to the sample-based estimate, 88.6 per cent of the GCA was irrigated, and in 2010, the figure recorded in the census-type survey was 89.7 per cent. In 2005, 82 per cent of the total irrigated area was irrigated by diesel-powered shallow tubewells, and the remaining area was irrigated by government-owned RLI (Bakshi 2010). By 2010, the share of tubewell irrigation increased to 90.3 per cent of the GIA (Table 18).

Village survey data show that a majority of cultivators bought water for irrigation. In 2010, 82 of the 90 households operating land in Amarsinghi

Table 18 *Proportion of gross irrigated area, by different sources, Amarsinghi, 2005 and 2010, in per cent*

Source of irrigation	2005	2010
Tubewell/borewell	82	90.3
River lift irrigation	18	4.5
Multiple sources	–	4.6
Pond	–	0.7
Total	100	100
NIA	88.6	89.7

Sources: Bakshi (2010) for 2005 data; PARI survey (2010).

[27] In an interview on August 12, 2016, AM, a cultivator, reported that water buyers had to bear the total cost of diesel used for irrigation. To buy diesel for irrigating *boro* paddy, water buyers sold mustard, which would otherwise have been used for their annual domestic supply of mustard oil. In addition, the supply of diesel was very low in nearby towns. Farmers had to queue for long hours to buy diesel during *boro* paddy cultivation, as demand was very high.

Table 19 *Share of households purchasing water and gross irrigated area, by source of irrigation, Amarsinghi, 2010*

Source	Household		GIA	
	Total (number)	Share (per cent)	Total (in acres)	Share (per cent)
Cooperative deep tubewell	33	39	41.56	33
Private shallow tubewell	56	62	54.66	43
All tubewells	82	91	96.22	76
River lift irrigation	10	11	8.64	7
All sources*	82	91	104.86	83
All cultivating households	90	100	125.82	100

Note: * Farmers purchased water from multiple sources as crop lands were distributed across the command area of irrigation sources.
Source: PARI survey (2010).

purchased water, and 83 per cent of the GIA was irrigated by purchased water. Tubewell irrigation was the predominant source of irrigation. Thirty-nine per cent of households purchased water from the cooperative tubewell, and the remaining households purchased from private water sellers in 2010 (Table 19).

Changes in private ownership of tubewells
In the 1980s and 1990s, all tubewells were diesel operated. After electrification for irrigation in 2007, only a few tubewell owners were able to shift from diesel- to electric-powered tubewells using submersibles. Though the potential command area of an electric tubewell with a submersible is much higher than that of a diesel-powered tubewell,[28] the high capital cost of tubewell installation and the process of obtaining permission for electric tubewells have made the shift from diesel- to electric-powered tubewells difficult and expensive for tubewell owners.[29] This has led to significant changes

[28] An interview with AM on August 12, 2016 revealed that the command area of an electric-powered submersible is about 25 acres of land, whereas it is only six to seven acres for a diesel-powered shallow tubewell. The depth of an electric-powered submersible is also much higher than a diesel-operated shallow tubewell.
[29] Mukherji, Shah, and Banerjee (2012) have pointed out that bureaucratic hurdles for getting permission and corruption in tubewell installation were the major reasons for the decline in tubewell irrigation in West Bengal after the 1990s. An interview with AD on August 11, 2016

in ownership, water use, prices, and exchange relations in the private water market.

In 2005, there were 10 tubewells in the village, owned individually or jointly, and all tubewells used diesel pumps. In 2010, the number of tubewells fell to six, of which four were powered by diesel pumps and two shifted to electric-powered submersible tubewells. Two of the tubewells (one diesel pump[30] and one electric submersible) were jointly owned by two households each (Table 20). In 2010, all six tubewell owners reported having sold water to irrigate a much larger area than they themselves irrigated.

In 2015, there were no diesel tubewells in the village, and only four tubewells, all of which used electric submersible pumps. The richest household in the village owned two of these tubewells. Of the remaining two, one was owned jointly by two households. The data show a clear fall in the number of tubewells between 2005 and 2015, reflecting a tendency towards concentrated ownership and control over water sources. To further illustrate this phenomenon, the case study of BM, the largest landowner in the village, is elaborated.

Table 20 *Ownership of tubewells by source of power, Amarsinghi, 2005–15, in number*

Year	Total number of tubewells	Source of power		Ownership	
		Diesel	Electric	Individual	Joint
2005	10	10	–	–	–
2010	6	4	2	4	2
2015	4	–	4	3	1

Sources: Bakshi (2010) for 2005 data; PARI survey (2010 and 2015).

---

revealed the unpleasant and frustrating experience of obtaining permission for an electricity connection for a tubewell. AD installed an electric submersible pump jointly with another farmer as the capital cost for the submersible tubewell installation was too high for him to cover alone. A sum of Rs 80,000 was given to a middleman in 2007 for procuring relevant documents for drilling a tubewell, as per the requirements of the SWID and Electricity Department. The latter assigned a contractor for the electricity connection who asked for a bribe. Up to the time of last field visit in 2016, AD had paid Rs 15,000 to the contractor as a bribe, but the work remained incomplete. AD reported that the contractor would want more money to finish the remaining work and that the Electricity Department was not willing to take any responsibility for it.

[30] This tubewell was inherited and owned by two brothers.

BM had an operational holding of 4.5 acres in 2015 and was also one of the richest households in terms of net household income in the village in 2010. His income was solely from agriculture and sale of water, the latter becoming his major source of income in 2015. His tubewells irrigated 67 acres of crop land in both Amarsinghi and surrounding villages. In 2015, he earned a total of Rs 2,50,000 net income from water sales, out of his total household net income of Rs 3,80,000.

He installed two electric submersible tubewells in 2010 and 2014. For the installation of both tubewells, he received a loan from UBI bank, Samsi branch. However, he installed his second tubewell in 2014 within the existing command area of another tubewell owner's submersible tubewell. A uniform water rate for each crop had been decided by the tubewell owners of all villages under Samsi Gram Panchayat.[31] BM ignored this informal agreement and reduced the water rate to increase the command area of his second tubewell. As a result, the area irrigated under the other tubewell was reduced to only five to seven acres of crop land, whereas the capacity of an electric submersible tubewell is about 25 acres. The other tubewell owner (a marginal farmer) was unable to compete with BM in reducing the water rate and failed to recover his investment from installation of a tubewell.

Though the literature on water markets often encourages competition to drive down water rates, in this case, we see that BM, being wealthier than his competitor, was able to drive him away through predatory pricing. Though, at present, BM has reduced the water rate for water buyers, he will surely increase the water rates once the loss-incurring tubewell owner ceases to sell water.

Changes in contracts and water prices in private groundwater market
In the 1980s, when water was first sold, it was purchased on a time-rate contract for all crops, that is, payment was made for the number of hours the cultivator received water. An interview with AM revealed that under a time-rate contract, the total irrigation cost was very high, particularly

[31] In interviews conducted during August 11–12, 2016, tubewell owners in Amarsinghi reported that a uniform water rate for each crop was decided among all tubewell owners in Samsi Gram Panchayat. The rate was fixed in such a way that it would profit water sellers, and there was no space for the water buyer in deciding water rates. But in discussions with other tubewell owners, it was reported that BM decreased the water rate to increase his command area without any discussion with the other tubewell owners.

for water-intensive *boro* paddy. Later there was a shift to share contracts and then, by 2016, to fixed contracts.

In 2005, before the electrification of tubewells, water was purchased on the basis of share contracts. Bakshi (2010) observes that

> In Amarsinghi, *boro* paddy was irrigated by shallow tubewells and diesel pumps. Rent for water was high and households paid one-fifth to one-sixth share of total produce as rent. In addition, households had to meet all expenses for diesel. Irrigation costs amounted to 42 per cent of the gross value of output of *boro* paddy in Amarsinghi. (p. 164)

Payment for water as a share of total produce provided an incentive for diesel tubewell owners selling water, who were themselves also marginal or small farmers, to provide water on a regular basis and oversee cultivation. However, after electrification and concentration of tubewell ownership, the contract shifted to fixed rates. One explanation for this is that share contracts required maintaining many records and monitoring the cultivation of water buyers, a difficult and complex task for water sellers.

At the time of the 2010 survey, all water charges were paid in fixed rates, and of the two types of contracts – crop-acreage and time-rate – the former was more common. In these contracts, water buyers usually received adequate water throughout the crop cycle, and they were charged based on the area irrigated. The volume of water supplied or hours of irrigation were not specified. In time-rate contracts, water was purchased at hourly rates. About 95 per cent of the area irrigated by private water sellers involved crop-acreage contracts and the remaining had time-rate contracts in 2010. Time-rate contracts were only used for *aman* paddy, jute, and mustard cultivation, where irrigation water requirements were low. For *boro* paddy and rabi crops, crop-acreage contracts were used, but prices were not uniform across buyers.

Forms of payment were either cash and in kind and depended on the timing of the payment. In cash contracts, water buyers had to pay at the beginning of the crop season, whereas in kind contracts, payment was made after harvest. The rate for in kind payment per acre was about 15 per cent higher than for cash payments; thus, tubewell owners preferred in kind payment.[32] About 90 per cent of the irrigated area was under this type of payment in 2010.

In the private water market, there was a difference in water rates. For

---

[32] Interview with AD on August 11, 2016

example, water charges ranged from Rs 1,500 to Rs 9,581 per acre for *boro* paddy in the private water market in 2010. Differences in water rates were mainly due to the type of tubewell used for irrigation (diesel or electric pump), terms of contract (crop-acreage or time-rate), and forms of payment (cash or in kind). In addition, location of the crop land,[33] distance from the tubewell, and personal relationships were also key factors in determining water rates.

Table 21 shows the average per acre water charges for major crops paid by water buyers in 2010 and 2015 (all in kind payments are valued at FHPs of produce in this calculation). The shift from diesel to electric tubewells lowered water rates for all crops in 2010, as the rates for buying water from diesel tubewells were higher due to high diesel prices.

During the 2015 sample survey, it was seen that all payments to private water sellers had shifted to crop-acreage contracts as time-rates required rigorous monitoring and account-keeping. Water buyers also preferred crop-acreage contracts as this ensured water supply throughout the crop period. Diesel pumps were no longer used for irrigation in the village, and hence no additional diesel charge was necessary. However, there was an increase in water rates for all major crops except jute. The shift from temporary to metered connections in electric tubewells did not reduce water rates.[34] Water charges for *boro* paddy ranged from Rs 4,500 to

Table 21 *Average water charges paid by water buyers, by crop and source of irrigation, Amarsinghi, 2010 and 2015*, in Rs per acre (at current prices)

Crop	2010		2015
	Private tubewell water seller (diesel)	Private tubewell water seller (electric)	Private tubewell water seller (electric)
Jute	1,228	1,018	1,025
Paddy (*aman*)	1,575	1,291	2,402
Paddy (*boro*)	5,678	3,994	5,386
Potato	1,061	1,027	1,656
Mustard/rapeseed	780	477	664

Source: : PARI survey (2010 and 2015).

[33] High land requires more frequent water during *boro* cultivation than low land.

[34] In 2007, when electrification was first introduced, tubewell owners received temporary connections for 105 days, particularly for *boro* paddy cultivation. They had to pay a considerable sum of Rs 22,500 to the Electricity Department as an advance payment at the beginning of the

Rs 6,000 per acre, or three to six quintals of paddy in 2015, which was higher than the charges for electric tubewells in 2010. This is likely due to the rise in power tariffs for agriculture in West Bengal (see previous section, "Changes in policies on groundwater use for agriculture after 2011").

Irrigation costs and agricultural profitability
Irrigation costs accounted for a significant proportion of the total cost of cultivation in Amarsinghi. As discussed in the previous section, different prices were charged in the water markets for different sources of irrigation. In this section, I examine cost of irrigation, particularly for *boro* paddy and potato, which are water-intensive crops by dividing households' own tubewells and hired irrigation from private tubewells into two categories based on the source of power of the tubewells – diesel and electric.

Table 22 shows that for the main irrigated crop, *boro* paddy, the average per acre irrigation cost and total paid-out cost[35] were much higher for households purchasing water from private electric and diesel-powered tubewells than those using the cooperative tubewell or their own tubewells in 2010. As a result, irrigation cost constituted 27.2 per cent of total paid-out cost for households dependent on private electric tubewells and 39.3 per cent of paid-out cost for households dependent on diesel-powered tubewells. In contrast, households using the cooperative tubewell paid only 14.3 per cent of paid-out cost for irrigation. RLI irrigation cost was lower than all other sources of purchased irrigation for *boro* paddy. For potato cultivation, the difference between the share of the irrigation cost in total cost when water was purchased from the cooperative tubewell and that from private water sellers was not significant.

The same pattern is reflected in the ratio of irrigation cost to gross value of output (GVO). Table 23 shows that the share of irrigation cost in GVO was much higher for households receiving water from private electric- and diesel-powered tubewells, at 18.6 per cent and 24.7 per cent, respectively, whereas it was only 8.1 per cent for households receiving water from the cooperative tubewell.

We measure the profitability of crops using the GVO (including by-products) to cost per acre ratio. Bakshi (2010) estimated that the profitability of *boro* paddy in Amarsinghi was 0.76 in 2005–06, indicating

---

crop season. By 2015, all electric tubewells were metered and the tubewell owners received electricity supply throughout the year, and payment was made according to use.
[35] Paid-out cost was calculated using the definition of cost A2 by the CACP.

Table 22 *Average irrigation cost, total paid-out cost, and irrigation costs as a proportion of total paid-out cost, by crop and source of irrigation, Amarsinghi, 2010*

Irrigation source	*Boro* paddy			Potato		
	Irrigation cost (Rs per acre)	Total paid-out cost (Rs per acre)	Share of irrigation cost in total input cost (per cent)	Irrigation cost (Rs per acre)	Total paid-out cost (Rs per acre)	Share of irrigation cost in total input cost (per cent)
Own tubewell (diesel)	2,383	15,925	15	–	–	–
Own tubewell (electric)	751	10,160	7.4	–	–	–
Cooperative deep tubewell	1,883	13,123	14.3	945	24,004	3.9
Private tubewell (diesel)	5,678	14,448	39.3	–	–	–
Private tubewell (electric)	3,994	14,681	27.2	1,027	29,832	3.4
RLI	909	11,950	7.6	–	–	–

Source: : PARI survey (2010).

Table 23 *Share of irrigation cost in total gross value of output (GVO), by crop and source of irrigation, Amarsinghi, 2010*

Irrigation source	Paddy (boro)		Potato	
	GVO (Rs per acre)	Share of irrigation cost in GVO (per cent)	GVO (Rs per acre)	Share of irrigation cost in GVO (per cent)
Cooperative deep tubewell	24,475	8.1	28,585	4.7
Private tubewell (diesel)	24,385	24.7	–	–
Private tubewell (electric)	23,427	18.6	30,313	5.8
RLI	23,688	3.9	–	–

Source: : PARI survey (2010).

that farmers incurred net losses. She argued that in the 2000s, the cultivation of rice in the *boro* season on groundwater-irrigated fields where tubewells were driven by diesel-operated pumpsets became almost completely unprofitable because of a sharp and continuous rise in fuel prices, increased the irrigation cost significantly (*ibid.,* p. 242). By 2010, the profitability of *boro* paddy increased across farmer households in Amarsinghi primarily due to an increase in productivity and fall in irrigation cost. The profitability of *boro* paddy, however, was highest for households using RLI and cooperative tubewells for irrigation (Table 24). The higher profitability in cooperative tubewell-irrigated *boro* paddy was partly due to the lower cost of irrigation, but also due to increased production, a likely result of higher-quality irrigation.[36] The profitability of potato was highest for cooperative-tubewell-irrigated plots. There was no such difference in profitability between unirrigated and irrigated monsoon crops (such as mustard/rapeseed and *aman* paddy) where supplementary irrigation was used.

In 2015, there was a decline in the share of irrigation cost in total paid-out cost for households purchasing water from the cooperative tubewell for *boro* paddy and potato, whereas it remained unchanged for cultivators who purchased water from private tubewells (Table 25). However, for *boro* paddy cultivation in 2015, the percentage of irrigation cost to GVO declined to 7.4 per cent for households purchasing water from the cooperative tubewell and to 15.9 per cent for those purchasing water from private tubewells. This could be attributed to either increased irrigation cost, productivity, or FHPs. The irrigation cost for *boro* paddy cultivation increased between 2010 and 2015, particularly for households purchasing water from private tubewells. In addition, the productivity of all major crops also increased in the same period; for example, *boro* paddy per hectare increased from 5,503 kg in 2010 to 6,205 kg in 2015. However, the farm harvest price of *boro* paddy had not risen – the average per quintal price of *boro* paddy was Rs 1,000 during both survey years. Hence, the increase in productivity did not translate to any increase in profitability across farmer households.

---

[36] Sarkar (2017), using an analysis of covariance (ANCOVA), found that the source of irrigation contributed significantly to productivity differences of *aman* and *boro* paddy among farmers in Amarsinghi in 2010. He found that the households using public deep tubewells had received much higher productivity per hectare in these crops than those receiving water from privately owned shallow tubewell. This may be due to higher-quality irrigation supplied by public deep tubewell in 2010.

Table 24 *Gross value of output to cost per acre ratio, by crop and source of irrigation, Amarsinghi, 2010*

Crop	Unirrigated	Own tubewell		Purchased irrigation			
		Diesel	Electric	Coopera-tive deep tubewell	Private tubewell (diesel)	Private tubewell (electric)	RLI
Paddy (*boro*)	–	1.68	2.96	1.94	1.77	1.75	2.63
Potato	–	–	–	1.23	–	1.17	–
Jute	–	–	–	3.1	2.49	3.18	3.43
Mustard/rapeseed	2.71	–	–	2.07	2.6	2.49	–
Paddy (*aman*)	1.85	1.79	1.93	1.91	2	1.95	1.96

Source: : PARI survey (2010).

Table 25 *Share of irrigation cost in total cost and gross value of output (GVO), by crop and irrigation source, Amarsinghi, 2015,* in per cent

Crop	Irrigation cost in total paid-out cost			Irrigation cost in GVO		
	Cooperative deep tubewell	Private tubewell water seller	River lift irrigation	Cooperative deep tubewell	Private tubewell water seller	River lift irrigation
Paddy (*boro*)	11.8	26.5	7.8	7.4	15.9	3.5
Potato	2.3	3.7	–	2	2.5	–

Source: PARI survey (2015).

Conclusion

Using primary and secondary data sources, this chapter focuses on groundwater irrigation in West Bengal, a water-abundant State in India. It specifically examines the pattern of groundwater irrigation expansion and the inter-district variations after 1990 and the factors that led to a slowdown in groundwater irrigation from the mid-1990s onwards. The major points that emerge from the chapter are summarised below.

Despite limitations with statistics on irrigation in West Bengal, available statistics indicate that there are two distinct phases in the development of irrigation in West Bengal between 1975 and 2011. First, between 1975 and 1995, the State showed remarkable development in groundwater irrigation that led to a significant increase in irrigated area. The NIA was 1.3 million hectares in 1980–81, which increased to 3 million hectares in 1995–96.

In other words, the share of NIA in total operational holdings increased from 24.1 per cent in 1980–81 to 53.3 per cent in 1995–96. In the second phase between 1995 and 2011, development of groundwater irrigation slowed down significantly, and as a result, overall irrigation development stagnated. For example, data from the Census of Minor Irrigation Schemes show that the number of tubewells and NIA by groundwater increased by about five per cent per annum between 1986–87 and 1993–94, whereas it was negligible between 2006–07 and 2013–14.

District-wise analysis of the expansion of groundwater irrigation shows interesting features. In the 1980s, groundwater irrigation was more developed in the eastern districts, located in the Old Alluvial agroclimatic zone, and gradually diffused to the northern and western districts, spreading everywhere except for hilly and island regions. As a result, inter-district disparity in the development of groundwater irrigation, in terms of the number of tubewells per 100 sq. km, also reduced in the 1980s and 1990s. In the recent period (1995–96 to 2013–14), however, the growth of groundwater irrigation stagnated across districts and in the State as a whole.

From 1993 to 2011, policies that regulated groundwater use and restricted the electrification of tubewells had the effect of decelerating groundwater irrigation in West Bengal. Although the State is rich in groundwater resources, the government regulated groundwater use through two interlinked policies. First, in 1993, it became mandatory to avail a clearance certificate from SWID to install a tubewell in seven districts – this was subsequently introduced across all districts in 2006 by the passage of the West Bengal Groundwater Resources (Management, Control and Regulation) Act, 2005. Furthermore, the Electricity Board stated that the clearance certificate from SWID was mandatory for any electrification of tubewell. Additionally, the electrification of a tubewell was not cost-effective for farmers because they had to bear the capital cost of installation including that for wire, cemented poles, and transformers. In light of West Bengal's experience since the mid-1990s to 2011, I argue that regulatory polices of groundwater irrigation should be region-specific, watershed-specific, and sometimes even aquifer-specific.

In order to address these problems, the GoWB removed restrictions on issuing permits for tubewell installation and reduced the cost for electricity connection in 2011. As a result, the number of electrified tubewells increased between 2011 and 2016. However, other problems have since emerged, namely a rapid hike in the electricity tariff for irrigation. Thus, in practice, though the fixed cost of irrigation, that is pump installation charges and bureaucratic hurdles, have reduced, there has been no decline in variable costs, that is, electricity prices.

The findings from survey data in Panahar village suggest that the rise in power tariffs substantially increased the irrigation cost, particularly for those households buying water from private water markets. Consequently, cultivators were discouraged from cultivating the main irrigated crop, *boro* paddy, because of increasing costs of cultivation on one hand and not receiving suitable remuneration for paddy on the other.

Amarsinghi village differs from Panahar in terms of technological advance in irrigation. Till the late 2000s, agricultural land in Amarsinghi was primarily irrigated by diesel-powered shallow tubewells. Two public interventions in the late 2000s – the introduction of electricity in 2007 and installation of a public deep tubewell by the government in 2008 – facilitated the expansion of irrigation and reduced the cost of irrigation significantly. In the past decade (2005–15), both the rising cost of diesel and the shift from diesel- to electric-powered tubewells led to dynamic changes in water markets in Amarsinghi, in terms of ownership of tubewells, terms of exchange, and water rates. Changes in forms of irrigation led to changes in contracts. In 2005, share contracts prevailed in the water market. Electrification changed contracts in the private water market, with share contracts giving way to fixed water rates. It can be argued that the concentration of tubewell ownership rapidly led to the use of fixed rates, as share contracts required sellers to maintain records and keep track of cultivation, a difficult and complex task. However, the analysis suggests that compared to households purchasing water from private market, households receiving water from public deep tubewells obtained higher net returns from *boro* paddy cultivation in 2010 – they had higher crop productivity and incurred lower costs of irrigation.

In conclusion, this chapter argues that the need for public intervention in groundwater irrigation, particularly in water-abundant and small-farmer dominated regions of eastern India, to reduce the cost of irrigation.

References

Bakshi, Aparajita (2010), "Rural Household Incomes," unpublished PhD thesis, University of Calcutta, Kolkata.

Bhattacharyya, Maumita and Bhattacharyya, Sudipta (2007), "Agrarian Impasse in West Bengal in the Liberalisation Era," *Economic and Political Weekly*, vol. 42, no. 52, December–January, pp. 65–71.

Boyce, Joyce (1987), *Agrarian Impasse in Bengal: Agricultural Growth in Bangladesh and West Bengal, 1949–1980*, Oxford University Press, New York.

Central Ground Water Board (CGWB) (2016), "Ground Water Year Book of West Bengal and Andaman and Nicobar Islands (2014–2015)," Ministry of Water Resources, Government of India, Faridabad.

Central Ground Water Board (CGWB) (2017), "Dynamic Groundwater Resources in India (As on March 31, 2013)," Ministry of Water Resources, River Development, and Ganga Rejuvenation, Government of India, Faridabad.

Commission for Agricultural Costs and Prices (CACP) Reports, Ministry of Agriculture, Government of India, New Delhi, various issues.

Dasgupta, Suranjana and Bhaumik Sankar Kumar, "Crop Diversification and Agricultural Growth in West Bengal," *Indian Journal of Agricultural Economics*, vol.69, no.1, January.-March, pp. 107–124.

Fujita, K., Hossain, F. (1995), "Role of the Groundwater Market in Agricultural Development and Income Distribution: A Case Study in a North-West Bangladesh Village," *The Developing Economies*, 33(4), 442–463.

Government of India (GoI) (1975), *All-India Report on Agricultural Census, 1970–71*, Department of Agriculture, Ministry of Agriculture and Irrigation, Government of India, New Delhi, available at http://agcensus.nic.in/document/ac7071/ac7071rep.html, viewed on June 15, 2018.

Government of India (GoI) (1987), *All-India Report on Agricultural Census, 1980–81*, Department of Agriculture and Co-operation, Ministry of Agriculture, Government of India, New Delhi, available at http://agcensus.nic.in/document/ac8081/ac8081rep.html, viewed on June 15, 2018.

Government of India (GoI) (1992), *All-India Report on Agricultural Census, 1985–86*, Department of Agriculture and Co-operation, Ministry of Agriculture, Government of India, New Delhi, available at http://agcensus.nic.in/document/ac8586/ac8586rep.html, viewed on June 15, 2018.

Government of India (GoI) (1993), *Report on Census of Minor Irrigation Schemes 1986–87*, Minor Irrigation Division, Ministry of Water Resources, Government of India, New Delhi, available at http://micensus.gov.in/sites/default/files/First-MI-report.pdf, viewed on June 15, 2018.

Government of India (GoI) (2001), *Report on Census of Minor Irrigation Schemes 1993–94*, Minor Irrigation Division, Ministry of Water Resources, Government of India, New Delhi, available at http://micensus.gov.in/sites/default/files/Second-MI-report-I_2.pdf, viewed on June 15, 2018.

Government of India (GoI) (2003), *All-India Report on Agricultural Census, 1995–96*, Department of Agriculture and Co-operation, Ministry of Agriculture, Government of India, New Delhi, available at http://agcensus.nic.in/document/agcensus9596/agcensusrep9596.htm, viewed on June 15, 2018.

Government of India (GoI) (2005), *Report on 3rd Census of Minor Irrigation Schemes 2000–01*, Minor Irrigation Division, Ministry of Water Resources, Government of

India, New Delhi, available at http://micensus.gov.in/sites/default/files/Third-MI-report.pdf, viewed on June 15, 2018.

Government of India (GoI) (2008), *All-India Report on Agricultural Census, 2000–01*, Department of Agriculture and Co-operation, Ministry of Agriculture, Government of India, New Delhi, available at http://agcensus.nic.in/document/agcenrep01.htm, viewed on June 15, 2018.

Government of India (GoI) (2012), *All-India Report on Agricultural Census, 2005–06*, Department of Agriculture and Co-operation, Ministry of Agriculture, Government of India, New Delhi, available at http://agcensus.nic.in/document/agcenrep01.htm, viewed on June 15, 2018.

Government of India (GoI) (2014), *4th Census of Minor Irrigation Schemes Report 2006–07*, Minor Irrigation (Statistics Wing), Ministry of Water Resources, River Development and Ganga Rejuvenation, Government of India, New Delhi, available at http://164.100.229.38/sites/default/files/4thmicensusreport.pdf, viewed on June 15, 2018.

Government of India (GoI) (2015), *All-India Report on Agriculture Census, 2010–11*, Department of Agriculture and Cooperation, Ministry of Agriculture and Farmers' Welfare, Government of India, New Delhi, available at http://agcensus.nic.in/document/ac1011/ac1011rep.html, viewed on June 15, 2018.

Government of India (GoI) (2017), *5th Census of Minor Irrigation Schemes Report 2013–14*, Minor Irrigation (Statistics Wing), Ministry of Water Resources, River Development and Ganga Rejuvenation, Government of India, New Delhi, available at http://164.100.229.38/sites/default/files/5th-MICensusReport.pdf, viewed on June 15, 2018.

Government of India (GoI) (various years), *All India Electricity Statistics: General Review*, Central Electricity Authority, Ministry of Power, Government of India, available at https://www.indiastat.com/power-data/26/electrification/84/pumpset-tubewells-energisation-1983-2019/452515/stats.aspx, viewed on June 20, 2018.

Government of India (GoI) (various years), Ministry of Petroleum and Natural Gas, Government of India, https://www.indiastat.com/petroleum-data/25/petroleum-prices/222/build-up-retail-selling-prices-of-petroleum-products/379339/stats.aspx, viewed on January 20, 2021.

Government of West Bengal (GoWB) (2017), *West Bengal Statistical Abstract 2014–15*, Bureau of Statistics and Planning, Kolkata.

Janakarajan, S. (1993), "Triadic Exchange Relations: An Illustration from South India," *Institute of Development Studies Bulletin*, vol. 24, no. 3, July, pp. 75–82.

Jayaraman, T. (2015), "Climate Change and Agriculture: Some considerations for West Bengal," Paper presented at the Symposium on Results from Village Surveys, Foundation for Agrarian Studies, Durgapur, September 11–13.

Modak, Tapas Singh (2020), "Groundwater Irrigation in West Bengal after 1990: Policies, Institutional Arrangements and Its Implications for Farm Households," PhD thesis, Tata Institute of Social Sciences, Mumbai.

Modak, Tapas Singh (2018), "From Public to Private Irrigation: Implications for

Equity in Access to Water," *Review of Agrarian Studies*, vol. 8, no. 1, January–June, pp. 28–61, available at http://ras.org.in/f071c902dea772c447c66730b0cb911c, viewed on July 2, 2018.

Modak, Tapas Singh and Bakshi, Aparajita (2017), "Changes in Groundwater Markets: A Case Study of Amarsinghi Village, 2005 to 2015," *Review of Agrarian Studies*, vol. 7, no. 2, July–December, pp.92–110, available at http://ras.org.in/599ee0d68d0c6ca20dc6db5649b7ea4d, viewed on July 2, 2018.

Mukherji, Aditi, Banerjee, Partha Sarathi, and Biswas, Durba (2018), "Private Investments in Groundwater Irrigation and Smallholder Agriculture in West Bengal: Opportunities and Constraints" in Abhijit Mukherjee (eds.), *Groundwater of South Asia*, Springer, Singapore, pp. 657–74.

Mukherji, A., Das, B., Majumdar, N., Nayak, N. C., Sethi, R. R., and Sharma, Bharat R. (2009), "Metering of Agricultural Power Supply in West Bengal, India: Who Gains and Who Loses?" *Energy Policy*, vol. 37, no. 12, December, pp. 5530–39.

Mukherji, Aditi, Shah, Tushaar, and Banerjee, Partha Sarathi (2012), "Kick-starting a Second Green Revolution in West Bengal," *Economic and Political Weekly*, vol. 47, no. 18, May, pp. 27–30.

National Sample Survey Office (NSSO) (2014), "Land and Livestock Holdings Survey, 2013," Ministry of Statistics and Programme Implementation, Government of India, New Delhi, available at http://mospi.nic.in/sites/default/files/publication_reports/KI_70_18.1_19dec14.pdf, viewed on June 16, 2018.

Ramachandran, V. K., Swaminathan, Madhura, and Bakshi, Aparajita (2010), "Food Security and Crop Diversification: Can West Bengal Achieve Both Simultaneously?" in Banasri Basu, Bikash K. Chakrabarti, Satya R. Chakravarty, and Kaushik Gangopadhyaya (eds.), *Econophysics and Economics of Games, Social Choices and Quantitative Techniques*, Springer, Dordrecht, pp. 233–40.

Ramakumar, R. (2012), "Large-scale Investments in Agriculture in India," *IDS Bulletin*, vol. 43, July.

Rawal, Vikas (1999), "Irrigation Development in West Bengal: 1977–78 to 1995–96," unpublished PhD thesis, Indira Gandhi Institute of Development Research, Mumbai.

Rawal, Vikas (2001a), "Irrigation Statistics in West Bengal," *Economic and Political Weekly*, vol. 36, no. 27, July, pp. 2537–44.

Rawal, Vikas (2001b), "Expansion of Irrigation in West Bengal: Mid-1970s to Mid-1990s," *Economic and Political Weekly*, vol. 36, no. 42, October, pp. 4017–24.

Rawal, Vikas (2002), "Non-Market Interventions in Water-Sharing: Case Studies from West Bengal, India," *Journal of Agrarian Change*, vol. 2, no. 4, October, pp. 545–569.

Rawal, Vikas and Swaminathan, Madhura (1998), "Changing Trajectories: Agricultural Growth in West Bengal, 1950 to 1996", *Economic and Political Weekly*, vol. 33, no. 40, October, pp. 2595–2602.

Reserve Bank of India (RBI) (1984), "Agricultural Productivity in Eastern India: Report of the Committee on Agricultural Productivity in Eastern India," vol. I, Reserve Bank of India, Bombay.

Saha, Anamitra and Swaminathan, Madhura (1994), "Agricultural Growth in West Bengal in the 1980s: A Disaggregation by Districts and Crops," *Economic and Political Weekly*, vol. 19, no. 13, March, pp. A2–A11.

Sarkar, Anindita (2011), "Socio-economic Implications on Depleting Groundwater Resource in Punjab: A Comparative Analysis of Different Irrigation System," *Economic and Political Weekly*, vol. 46, no. 7, March, pp. 59–66.

Sarkar, Biplab (2015), "Cropping Pattern, Yields and Farm Business Incomes: Some Findings from Surveys of Three Study Villages in West Bengal," Paper presented at the Symposium on Results from Three Study Villages in West Bengal, Durgapur, September 11–13.

Sarkar, Biplab (2017), "The Economics of Household Farming: A Study with Special Reference to West Bengal," PhD thesis, University of North Bengal, West Bengal.

Shah, Tushaar (1991), "Water Markets and Irrigation Development in India," *Indian Journal of Agricultural Economics*, vol. 46, no. 3, July–December, pp. 335–48.

Shah, Tushaar and Ballabh, Vishwa (1997), "Water Markets in North Bihar: Six Village Studies in Muzaffarpur District," *Economic and Political Weekly*, vol. 37, no 18, December, pp. A183–A190.

State Water Investigation Directorate (SWID) (2011), *Notification Order no. 189/WRIDD/SECY dated 3rd November, 2011*, available at http://wbwridd.gov.in/swid/appellate.html, viewed on June 27, 2018.

West Bengal Electricity Regulatory Commission (2008), *Order of the West Bengal Electricity Regulatory Commission for the years of 2008–09*, available at http://www.wberc.gov.in/sites/default/files/WBSEDCL%20Tariff%20Order.pdf, viewed on June 28, 2018.

West Bengal Electricity Regulatory Commission (2009), *Order of the West Bengal Electricity Regulatory Commission for the years of 2009–10*, available at http://www.wberc.gov.in/sites/default/files/wbsedcl%20merge.pdf, viewed on June 28, 2018.

West Bengal Electricity Regulatory Commission (2011), *Order of the West Bengal Electricity Regulatory Commission for the years of 2010–11*, available at http://www.wberc.gov.in/sites/default/files/WBSEDCL_2010_11.pdf, viewed on June 28, 2018.

West Bengal Electricity Regulatory Commission (2012), *Order of the West Bengal Electricity Regulatory Commission for the years of 2011–12 and 2012–13*, available at http://www.wberc.gov.in/sites/default/files/WBSEDCL2011-12TO2013-14.pdf, viewed on June 28, 2018.

West Bengal Electricity Regulatory Commission (2013), *Order of the West Bengal Electricity Regulatory Commission for the years of 2013–14*, available at http://www.wberc.gov.in/sites/default/files/WBSEDCL_Tariff_2013-14%20with%20corrigendum.pdf, viewed on June 28, 2018.

West Bengal Electricity Regulatory Commission (2015), *Order of the West Bengal Electricity Regulatory Commission for the years of 2014–15*, available at http://www.wberc.gov.in/sites/default/files/WBSEDCL_MYT_14-15%20TO%2016-17%20WITH%20CORRIGENDUM%20new.pdf, viewed on June 28, 2018.

APPENDIX

Appendix Table 1 *Dug wells and tubewells, by data source, West Bengal, 1985–86 to 2014*, in number

Year	Sources	Dug well	Diesel tubewell	Electric tubewell	All
1985–86	Agricultural Census	77,000	4,13,000	98,000	5,11,000
1986–87	Census of Minor Irrigation Schemes	57,783	3,23,621	36,195	3,69,500
1987	All India Electricity Statistics			52398	
1995–96	Agricultural Census	98,000	8,23,667	2,34,001	1,,57,668
1993–94	Census of Minor Irrigation Schemes	49,862	4,31,553	67,293	5,08,677
1994	All India Electricity Statistics	–	–	96,988	–
2000–01	Agricultural Census	1,26,649	9,56,382	3,56,416	13,12,798
2000–01	Census of Minor Irrigation Schemes	35,316	–	–	6,08,806
2001	All India Electricity Statistics	–	–	111,513	–
2005–06	Agricultural Census	1,30,348	6,08,385	2,86,575	8,94,960
2006–07	Census of Minor Irrigation Schemes	11,448	3,97,668	96,091	5,06,972
2007	All India Electricity Statistics	–	–	114,490	–
2010–11	Agricultural Census	98,498	6,04,272	3,07,548	9,11,820
2013–14	Census of Minor Irrigation Schemes	5,754	2,66,155	1,31,724	3,97,879
2014	All India Electricity Statistics	–	–	2,12,745	–

Sources: All–India Report on Agricultural Census, Government of India 1992, 2003, 2008, 2012, 2015; Census of Minor Irrigation Schemes, Government of India 1993, 2001, 2005, 2014, and 2017; All India Electricity Statistics, Ministry of Power, Government of India.

Appendix Table 2 *Density of tubewells, by district, West Bengal, 1981–2007, in number of tubewells per 100 sq. km of net sown area*

District	1981			1986–87			1993–94			2001	2006–07		
	Electric	Diesel	Total	Electric	Diesel	Total	Electric	Diesel	Total	Total	Electric	Diesel	Total
Bankura		92.8	92.8	23.4	307.6	331	66.2	515.8	591.9	750.9	107.6	347.3	470
Barddhaman	48.5	285.1	333.6	66.1	705.8	771.8	188.7	796.4	995.4	1,125.1	348.3	361.4	740.3
Birbhum	27.1	122.2	149.3	75.7	412.8	488.5	179.4	452.6	636.7	578.3	253.8	91.7	365.7
Dakshin Dinajpur	19.9	173.1	193	14.9	479.2	494.1	26.5	630.4	661.5	1025	170.1	1,084.7	1,276.3
Uttar Dinajpur							75.4	1,280.3	1360	2,149.7	63.3	1,750.8	1,831.1
Darjiling							4	50.7	194.3	145.9	2.3	80.9	100.8
Haora	13.9	95.8	109.7	6.1	105.6	111.7	25.1	88.8	118.1	133.2	42	29.9	79.3
Hugli	54.9	689.6	744.5	132.7	862.9	995.6	301.8	621.9	971.4	993.4	498.3	231	755
Jalpaiguri	7.8	21.3	29.1	2.3	43.6	45.9	33.3	154	215.1	294.9	12.7	195.2	249.3
Koch Bihar	23.5	119.6	143.1	9.1	306.6	315.8	39.1	766.4	883.5	1,581.7	68.6	1479	1,574.7
Maldah	39.2	290.7	330	35.7	617.8	653.6	69.5	960.6	1,032.8	1,285.6	90.6	798.6	895.2
Murshidabad	60.6	467.8	528.5	73.8	1,126.6	1,200.3	207.3	1,558.9	1768	1,952.7	287	1,271.4	1,592.9
Nadia	178	637.4	815.4	299.2	1447	1,746.2	423.4	2,009.9	2,446.6	2,761.2	347.3	2,362.8	2,726.1
North 24 Parganas	80.9	772.8	853.7	144.6	1,754.9	1,899.6	218.6	1827	2,067	2,286.7	201	1,690.7	1,915.6
South 24 Parganas	0.9	58.4	59.2	0.1	119.5	119.5	2.2	169.6	173.6	268.1	11	185.6	198.1
Paschim Medinipur	17	104.1	121.1	44.1	452.2	496.2	87.9	676.5	784	980.3	235.4	655	967
Purba Medinipur											172	158.3	338.4
Puruliya							0	0	0.4	0.1	0	0.5	0.6
West Bengal	38.9	259	297.9	63.7	620.4	684.1	124.5	799.7	942.7	1,146.6	181.2	749.9	956
Coefficient of variation	1.054	0.912	0.912	1.229	0.822	0.842	1.051	0.835	0.801	0.772	0.889	1.02	0.867

Sources: Data for 1981 and 1986–87 are from Rawal (2001b); data on the number of tubewells are from Census of Minor Irrigation Schemes, Government of India (GoI 2001, 2005, 2014, and 2017); data on net sown area are from the Agricultural Census 2003, 2008, 2012.

Appendix Table 3 *Stage of groundwater development,*
by district, West Bengal, 2013, in per cent

District	Stage of groundwater development
Nadia	92
Murshidabad	87
North 24 Parganas	66
Uttar Dinajpur	62
Dakshin Dinajpur	54
Hugli	49
Maldah	48
Bankura	46
Barddhaman	44
Paschim Medinipur	36
Birbhum	34
Purba Medinipur	34
Haora	25
Koch Bihar	20
Puruliya	9
Darjiling	6
Jalpaiguri	5
West Bengal	45

Source: CGWB (2017).

8

Climate and Agriculture in West Bengal

T. Jayaraman, Sandeep Mahato, and Dibyendu Sen[1]

Introduction

Climate change, or more precisely, the impact of global warming of anthropogenic origin, constitutes one of the most significant challenges for agriculture across the world. For India, a land where the farmer has always had to struggle to adapt to climate variability, this new challenge is a particularly serious one that merits close consideration in any discussion on the future of agriculture and agricultural production. A large body of literature – both from scholarly and scientific sources as well as from climate and environmental activists, informed lay persons, media persons, and policymakers – has emerged on the subject (IPCC 2014; Aggarwal 2008; Hillel and Rosenzweig 2011; see Jayaraman 2011 and references therein). Significant findings and learnings have emerged from this literature that have provided us with an idea of the scale and scope of the potential impact of global warming and its collateral effects on agriculture across the world. Such impact arises not only from direct climate effects such as rising temperatures, changes in precipitation and precipitation patterns, variations in solar irradiance due to changes in cloud cover, and changes in the frequency and intensity of climate extremes. There is also significant indirect impact due to such climatic changes. For instance, crop production is likely to be affected by climate change-induced changes in the geosphere including soil and water, as

[1] We gratefully acknowledge the assistance of Dr Kamal Kumar Murari for useful discussions. We also acknowledge Mr Isaac Manah for providing us with the district-wise figures of temperature trends as well as the table on district-wise yield gaps.

well as on the biosphere, especially on weeds and pests. Other sectors in agriculture, including fisheries and livestock, are also likely to undergo such changes both directly and indirectly arising from climate change (for an overview, see Barange *et al.* 2018; Rojas-Downing *et al.* 2017; Sirohi and Michaelowa 2007).

A significant part of this new knowledge, however, despite its volume, is still tentative and exploratory, especially in relation to countries like India which are hampered by lack of adequate data, expertise, and resources. Some of these lacunae are being fixed currently, but the lack of time-series data is not something that can easily be remedied for a few years. One of the key gaps is the lack of a sufficiently rigorous understanding of the relation between climate variability and climate change on the one hand, and agricultural productivity and production on the other. Such a gap was no doubt a global problem a couple of decades ago, especially since climate variability was always seen independent of any context set by climate change. Despite the scientific advances since then, the gap certainly persists in the Indian context as a consequence of which current climate variability is routinely conflated with climate change and the increasing climate variability that can follow (Jayaraman and Murari 2014). While this problem is difficult enough even in the context of climate science itself, it becomes even more complex when considering the impact of climate change in agriculture.

These difficulties are also compounded by the diversity of agriculture in the semi-tropical regions. In crop production for instance, across many regions and even across different sections of the cultivating classes, there is considerable variation in the choice of crops through one full crop cycle, which makes the quantitative assessment of climate-change impact quite complex. Translating the results of the science of agronomy into estimates of the impact of climate change across agricultural landscapes or agro-ecosystems in a country like India is a challenging task.

Another important aspect of our knowledge of climate change and agriculture is the various uncertainties that are intrinsic to the nature of the subject itself, even at the scientific level. The possible trajectory of climate change itself is a first source of uncertainty, arising both from the uncertainties of future emissions and the ability of the world to undertake the necessary mitigation action as well as the scientific uncertainties in the behaviour of global and regional climate as a consequence of the warming that results. The second source of uncertainty is the study of climate impacts on agriculture, where a variety of methods are used, including modelling techniques and the study of ongoing trends in impacts, each one of them having their own particular limitations (Iizumi *et al.* 2013; Lobell and Burke 2008).

The third source of uncertainty relates to the socio-economic aspects of agriculture as a productive sector of the economy. Agriculture production and productivity, as is well established, is not merely determined by the technical aspects of production but also by the social and economic conditions under which it is undertaken (Jayaraman and Murari 2014). In particular, perhaps the most understudied aspect is how climate change will impact the lives and livelihoods of the millions of small producer households engaged in various sectors of agriculture. It is this aspect, as a recent survey of the literature on climate change and agriculture has revealed, that has been missing in the burgeoning literature on this subject, an aspect that is of considerable importance for India (Laborde, Porciello, and Smaller 2020). Hence the importance in the Indian context of studying the differential impact of climate change across various socio-economic strata of cultivators or fisherfolk, pastoralists, and those earning through livestock rearing.

One way of dealing with such uncertainties in the context of Indian agriculture is to focus on two dimensions of the issue in the present that may provide robust evidence of the nature of agriculture in the future. The first is to study the impact of current climate variability, especially climate extremes, on agricultural production and productivity. The second is to examine the socio-economic conditions of production to ascertain the ability of small farmers to cope with climate shock that provides important indication of the kind of adaptive capacity that will be required in the future.

This is, of course, not to rule out the importance of laboratory and field experiments, and techniques like crop models to determine future climate impacts. There is also considerable room for qualitative leaps forward in adapting to climate change such as path-breaking technological innovations. However, the two directions of enquiry suggested above are not easily understood through these methods, while, nevertheless, being significant aspects to study.

In this chapter, we turn to examine some of these issues in the context of West Bengal (in this chapter 'Bengal' and 'West Bengal' has been used interchangeably to refer to the state of West Bengal), especially in relation to the themes of climate extremes and their consequences as well as the extraordinarily widespread prevalence of small holders in agriculture.

Climate Change and West Bengal

In the first part of this section, we briefly consider the climatic setting of West Bengal and the current indications of climate variability and climate change that can be inferred from meteorological data, while locating these facts within the all-India context. Meteorologically, the State may be divided into two regions – Gangetic West Bengal and Himalayan West Bengal – and, where possible, we will cite results for the two regions separately. In the second part, we provide a short summary of expected trends in the future.

Temperature

Climate change is associated with a number of temperature-related changes. One may calculate the shift in the annual average temperature, an indicator that is reconstructed from the annual data. However, such a number may be useful in broad climatological considerations, but hardly of use for sectors like agriculture where seasonal variations including the potential independent variation of maximum and minimum temperatures in different seasons are also important.

Annual mean, maximum, and minimum temperatures averaged over India during 1986–2015 show significant warming trend of 0.15 °C, 0.15 °C, and 0.13 °C per decade, respectively (Sanjay *et al.* 2020).

For Himalayan West Bengal the increase in temperature is shown in Figure 1 below: The temperature data used for the analysis here is from (Srivastava *et al.* 2009) available with the Indian Meteorological Department (IMD).

The trend is clearly slower than the all-India average daily maximum temperature. For Gangetic West Bengal, we do not see any trend that is statistically significant.

Similarly, in Figure 2 (a, b and c) below, we describe the trends in temperature at district level which further illustrates the difference between spatial averages versus spatially disaggregated measures of temperature increase. Temperature trends are a particularly significant measure for climate change and agriculture as they have a direct effect on productivity, though such effects are more visible in rabi than the kharif crops. Traditionally, and even today, the role of temperature is not as readily recognized, unlike rainfall, for its impact on crop productivity. We will return to this issue shortly.

Figure 1 *Trend in area average annual maximum temperature of Himalayan West Bengal region and Gangetic West Bengal region*

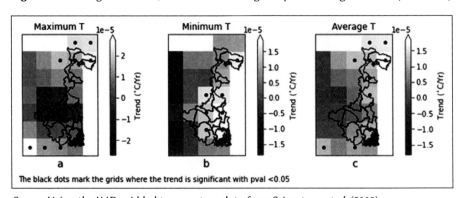

Source: Using the IMD gridded temperature data from Srivastava *et al.* (2009).

Figure 2 *West Bengal maximum, minimum and average temperature long term trend (1951–2015)*

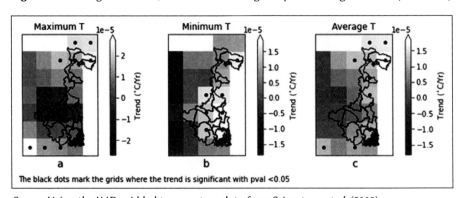

Source: Using the IMD gridded temperature data from Srivastava *et al.* (2009).

Precipitation

Rainfall has been traditionally the climatic variable of interest, par excellence, for agriculture in the Indian subcontinent. Unlike temperature, however, trends in precipitation changes are more difficult to establish, and even more so, the extent to which such changes may be attributed to climate change. The dynamics of rainfall over the Indian subcontinent is rendered more complicated due to the complex nature of the monsoon, and the, as yet, tentative nature of its scientific understanding. Many climate models used in the fifth assessment report of the (IPCC AR5) have considerable difficulty in reproducing even the current characteristics of the monsoon (Chaturvedi *et al.* 2012), and so the study of current rainfall trends is of particular importance. However, the ability of models to reproduce the characteristics of the Indian summer monsoon have improved in the sixth phase of the Coupled Model Intercomparison Project (CMIP-6) class of models (Gusain, Ghosh, and Karmakar 2020; Katzenberger *et al.* 2020). So the study of current rainfall trends remains important. There are a number of rainfall-related parameters that are relevant to climate change and agriculture. These include total quantum of rainfall, the inter-seasonal distribution including the active/break spells, the distribution for extreme rainfall events, and precipitation associated with cyclonic events to name some obvious ones.

To briefly summarise, rainfall trends for India, one may note the following, based on a careful reading of the authoritative "Assessment of Climate Change Over the Indian Region" published by the Ministry of Earth Sciences, Government of India (Raghavan *et al.* 2020).[2] Overall, all-India rainfall as well as the summer monsoon (active during June–September) precipitation has decreased by about 6 per cent from 1951 to 2015, most notably over the Indo-Gangetic Plain and the Western Ghats. However, the decline in all-India rainfall is not statistically significant. On the time-scale of 1901–2015, no decreasing trend in annual and summer monsoon rainfall is observed. These changes are not uniform over the subcontinent, and hence, spatially disaggregated trends are important. The same assessment notes the following:

i) Monsoon rainfall has shown moderate increasing trends in 27 (out of 36) subdivisions across India.
ii) The linear trend in annual as well as seasonal rainfall shows a statistically significant decreasing trend over Jharkhand, Chhattisgarh, and Kerala.
iii) Eight subdivisions, namely Gangetic West Bengal, West Uttar Pradesh, Jammu and Kashmir, Konkan and Goa, Madhya Maharashtra, Rayalaseema, Coastal Andhra Pradesh and North Interior Karnataka show increasing trends.

---

[2] In the authors' opinion the executive summary of the report does not provide sufficient clarity and the summary provided here is based on a careful reading of the relevant chapter – chapter 3 – by Kulkarni *et al.* (2020).

iv) Based on high-resolution gridded data for 1901–2015, there are statistically significant decreasing trends in annual as well as seasonal rainfall over Kerala, Western Ghats, and some parts of central India including Uttar Pradesh, Madhya Pradesh, and Chhattisgarh, as well as some parts of the North-Eastern States.

v) Rainfall over Gujarat, Konkan coast, Goa, Jammu and Kashmir, and east coast shows a significant increasing trend.

With regard to the annual distribution of rainfall for West Bengal, the authors' own independent analysis of the rainfall data shows that over more than 100 years, there has been no significant changes. This is true for both Gangetic and Himalayan West Bengal IMD sub-divisions. This also shows that there have been some changes in the variability of the rainfall over this period. This is shown in Figure 3, below. The rainfall data used for the analysis here is from Pai *et al.* (2014) available with the IMD.

Figure 3 *Distribution of monthly rainfall and coefficient of variation of area averaged annual rainfall in Gangetic West Bengal and Himalayan West Bengal region*

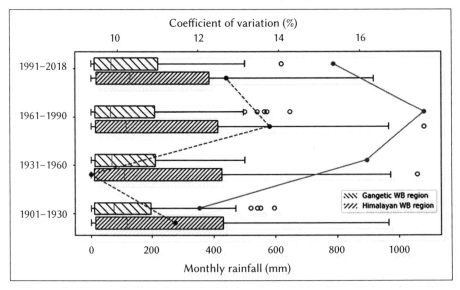

Note: The solid and dotted lines refer to the coefficient of variation for each time period for the Gangetic WB region and the Himalayan WB region respectively. The values are in the top axis.

Source: Using the IMD gridded rainfall data from Pai *et al.* (2014).

Climate Extremes and Extreme Events – Floods and Cyclones

In any climatic region, there are a number of potential climatic extremes that can manifest themselves. Typically, though, there are only a few that are the most frequent and pronounced in their impact. In the case of West Bengal, these are floods and cyclonic storms. We will include floods in the discussion as a climatologically related extreme event even though they are not, strictly speaking, a climatic extreme as well as cyclones. Drought does occur in a couple of districts in south-western Bengal, but that is limited in scope.

West Bengal, along with Assam and Bihar, is among the most flood-prone States in the country. For instance, between the years 1960 and 2000, there were only five years when less than 500 sq km of the State was affected by floods. Table 1 gives the number of flood events classified by area affected over the same period published in WBDMD (2020).

Floods arise due to a number of causes, but there is an important distinction to be made between origin of floods in northern West Bengal and in the southern Gangetic region. Roughly speaking, the Ganga–Padma divides the State into two parts. The cause of floods in the northern part of the State (including the Terai–Tista plains and the Old Vindhyan flood plains) is primarily due to heavy rainfall and landslides, aggravated by deforestation and agricultural expansion, though this has been called into question by other authors (Hofer 1993). The primary cause of floods in the southern part, namely the Gangetic flood plain, is due to high rainfall in the river-basin areas – the major part of it is outside the State – synchronised

Table 1 *Area flooded and years of occurrence*

Flood affected area (in sq.km)	Years during which the flood occurred	Total no. of years
Below 500	1985, 1989, 1992, 1994, and 1997	5
500–2000	1962, 1963, 1964, 1965, 1966, 1972, 1975, and 1996	8
2000–5000	1960, 1961, 1967, 1969, 1970, 1974, 1976, 1980, 1981, and 1982	10
5000–10000	1973, 1977, 1993, 1995, and 1998	5
10000–15000	1968, 1979, 1983, 1990, and 1999	5
15000–20000	1971, 1986, 1987, and 1988	4
Above 20000	1978, 1984, 1991, and 2000	4

Source: Reproduced from WBDMD (2020).

with high-tide conditions in the Bhagirathi and the Hooghly into which these rivers flow. The floods in the northern part of the State are early in the season and tend to be intense and of short duration. The floods in the southern part are later in the season.[3]

Several of the particular features that lead to floods in both the northern and southern parts of West Bengal are likely to be exacerbated by the effects of global warming. The bulk of the flow in the northern part is from the snowmelt-fed rivers in the Ganga–Brahmaputra basin. The flow in these rivers abruptly decelerates on reaching the plains leading to heavy siltation and consequent rise of the river bed. In the short and medium terms, rising temperatures are likely to lead to greater flow from snowmelt due to higher summer temperatures while in the long term, flows could actually diminish with eventual glacier retreat. Sudden surges in volumes can occur due to both extreme rainfall events that are likely in this region where total rainfall is set to increase. Sudden surges can also arise from the floods due to glacial lake outbursts which can cause substantial damage downstream. Such flows may also occur due to the collapse of lakes created by landslides and slope failures.

The flood pattern in the southern part is likely to be altered by both increased rainfall in the river basin areas and the slow rise of sea-levels. The outflow of these rivers being dependent on tidal conditions the effects of sea-level rise on the tides is a critical parameter in assessing the potential for floods in the southern part. As is well-understood by now, areas such as the Sunderbans which are in the deltaic region of the Ganga-Padma river system would be particularly vulnerable to flooding and the attendant consequences.[4]

Apart from floods, the erosion of river banks is also a particular cause for concern. High levels of erosion are found in the left bank of the Ganga upstream from the Farakka barrage, and in other parts of the Ganga–Padma and Bhagirathi–Hooghly river systems (See, for instance, GoI 2005). Several towns on the banks are threatened with annihilation in future if bank erosion continues unchecked.

A study assessing the flood-hazard vulnerability in Ganga, Jalangi and

---

[3] See Irrigation Department, Government of West Bengal at the website at http://www.wbiwd. gov.in/.

[4] The policy literature and the activity centred around the Sunderbans run the risk of focusing on an important but easily understood issue in climate-change adaptation while turning attention away from the larger, more complex and yet urgent questions faced by region as a whole.

Churni river basins , identifies 66 administrative blocks that are prone to flood hazards (Sanyal and Lu 2003). The same study also categorises the blocks in terms of severity of hazard-proneness based on a composite flood-hazard index. Seventeen blocks are shown to be very high in flood proneness.

The overlap of the agro-climatic zones and flood hazards suggests that there is variability in terms of flood severity even within a single agro-climatic region. While most of the Vindhyan Alluvial region falls within high flood-hazardous zone, there are blocks within the same zone that are relatively less hazard-prone. It is clear that estimates of vulnerability can sharply vary even on sub-regional scales, and vulnerability indicators that are averaged spatially over large scales may miss many important sources of loss and damage.

Thus, it is clear that one of the foremost issues in the climate-change impacts on West Bengal is that of floods. The State appears highly vulnerable to the effects of high flows and impairment of the natural drainage mechanism of its rivers due climatic changes and extreme weather events inside and outside the State boundary.

What is the extent of the economic impact of floods in West Bengal? To examine this, it is useful to study the data on floods and their impact from the Flood Forecast and Monitoring, Directorate of the Central Water Commission (FFM 2018). Based on this data, the frequency distribution of the crop area affected by floods is given in Figure 4 below. It is important to note the fat-tailed character of the distribution, namely that there is a non-vanishing probability of very large-scale floods (Strictly speaking such a conclusion should be drawn from the kernel smoothing of this distribution). There also appears to be no statistically significant trend overall in the crop losses due to floods (see Figure 5), though the year-on-year variations can be considerable, with the bulk of the losses ranging anywhere between Rs 100 crore to Rs 1,000 crore and above, on a logarithmic scale, at constant 2012 prices. There is also considerable variation between the crop area affected and crop losses as seen in Figure 6. It is not possible to determine clearly the causes of high losses in particular years and the considerable variability in losses for the same extent of area affected without spatially and seasonally disaggregated data that is not readily available. The very lack of such readily available data and the lack of frequent update of the same speak to the continuing lack of attention and awareness of the seriousness of the problem of floods to the agrarian economy of Bengal.

Figure 4 *Frequency distribution of crop area affected by floods*

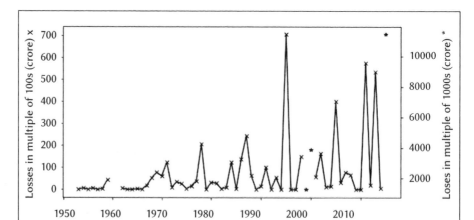

Source: Based on data in FFM (2018).

Figure 5 *Crop losses*, in Rs crore at 2018 prices

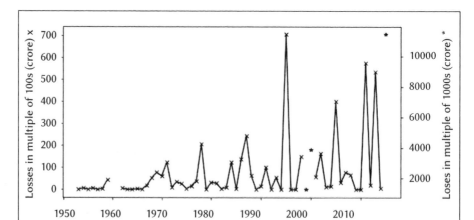

Source: Author's calculations based on data from FFM (2018).

Figure 6 *Real value of crop losses by crop area affected*

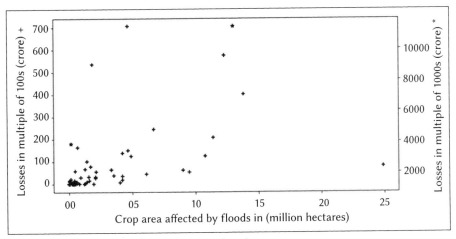

Source: Authors' calculations based on FFM (2018).

There are a number of other impacts of floods that require probing beyond the simple overall narrative of overall loss and damage. Floods in Bengal typically exacerbate the loss of valuable agricultural or human settlement land to the river, an ongoing process in itself. This introduces a peculiar vulnerability to floods in the era of climate change that merits further study. The link between the social and ecological dimensions of vulnerability due to floods is graphically illustrated in the District Human Development Report for Maldah (GoWB 2007). The example of Maldah has been relatively less cited in the climate change literature compared to the Sunderbans (in conjunction with Bangladesh) despite the fact that it offers some of the most potent illustrations of the relationship between current vulnerability and the impact of climate change in the future.

Maldah is one of the most flood-prone districts in West Bengal, apart from the damage incurred by the long-term shifting course of the Ganga and the consequent issues like river bank erosion etc. According to the District Human Development Report for Maldah (GoWB 2007), between 1971 and 2005, there have been 21 occurrences of floods, of which the 1998 and 1999 floods were the most damaging. The extraordinary severity of the 1998 floods was the consequence of several factors whereby all regional rivers acted in conjunction. Significant damage to non-land assets was reported resulting in the loss of almost half the value of assets held prior to the floods, as evidenced by later surveys. Significant loss of land had also occurred both due to floods and due to the continuing loss of land to riverine erosion. As a result a significant number of cultivators have been reduced to the status of landless labour. The typical coping/adaptation strategy of the poor, namely migration, has also been in evidence, with large-scale migration being a feature of the district.

Bandyopadhyay, Ghosh, and Dutta (2006) graphically illustrates the problem of permanent displacement of people due to riverine erosion in the districts of Maldah and Murshidabad. These accounts illustrate the travails of a section that may be regarded with some qualifications as "climate refugees." But even if this description is not fully appropriate, the study sheds light on the potential problem in the future of "climate refugees" in West Bengal.

It is clear that current global warming trends will exacerbate the conditions of ecological vulnerability currently in evidence in Maldah district. A further detailed study of the current status of vulnerability in Maldah district in conjunction with a study of the cost and impact of several flood control measures that are underway in this region would also offer a unique opportunity to evaluate some aspects of climate adaptation costs for the future. It also appears that the early attention to the vulnerability of agriculture, and agriculture in Bengal and India as a whole, is now waning, with an increasing focus on mitigation in agriculture (Giller *et al.* 2015). However, the brief account of floods and crop losses above illustrates the need to maintain continued emphasis on agriculture as primarily the site of climate change adaptation.

West Bengal's location on the eastern coast of India, at the head of the Bay of Bengal, makes it vulnerable to cyclones. Overall for India, the frequency of medium- and low-intensity cyclones have been decreasing while there is some increase in high-intensity cyclones (Vellore *et al.* 2020). The recent cyclones in the Bay of Bengal have indicated the potential severity of future cyclone impacts for the coastal region. However, the actual intensity distribution and frequency of cyclones in the future, especially at the regional scale, is subject to several uncertainties. West Bengal has suffered 69 cyclones between 1891 and 2013 (Mishra 2014). Between 2009 and 2020 some of the high-intensity cyclones include Aila (2009), Mora (2017), Fani (2019), and Amphan (2020). All of them have led to significant evacuations prior to their arrival, along with considerable damage to houses, other buildings, trees and crops, alongside the impact of flooding wherever it occurred on infrastructure.

Future Climate Trends

Some projections are available at the regional scale for future climate trends in West Bengal. A useful set of observations is provided in WBSAPCC (2017), the second edition of WBSAPCC (2012). Such projections are provided with respect to particular scenarios of future global warming known as Representative Concentration Pathways (RCP) that are associated with a numerical label that indicates the extent of atmospheric warming in watts/square metre.

For West Bengal, the results as summarized in WBSAPCC (2017) are given in the table below (as in the original).

Table 2 *Annual changes in projected maximum temperature (Tmax), minimum temperature (Tmin), and precipitation 2021–30 w.r.t. baseline 1961–90*

District	Simulated observed average Tmax (^{0}C)	Change in average annual Tmax w.r.t base line (^{0}C)	Simulated observed average Tmin (^{0}C)	Change in average annual Tmin w.r.t base line (^{0}C)	Simulated observed average annual rainfall intensity (mm)	Change in rainfall intensity (%)
	1961–90	2021–30	1961–91	2021–31	1961–92	2021–32
RCP 2.6	30.49	1	19.66	1.17	5.3	−8.98
RCP 4.5	30.49	1.04	19.66	1.22	5.3	−10.91
RCP 8.4	30.49	2.33	19.66	2.65	5.3	−22.25

Source: WBSAPCC (2017).

These results are drawn from an ensemble of climate models (WBSAPCC 2017 and references therein). These estimates are supplemented by district-wise estimates up to year 2100. However, there are considerable uncertainties again associated with such forecasts of the possible impact of global warming. But the broad consistent trend across these models is the decline in rainfall intensity (in mm/day) that increases rapidly for extreme warming, while temperatures increase by approximately 1^{0}C to 2^{0}C in the short term for both maximum and minimum temperatures.

Crop Production, Climate Variability, and Climate Change

As we have noted earlier, it is important to review both the current status of agricultural production and agricultural productivity with respect to climate variability in the present, as well as future trends in climate and its impact on productivity and production.

In the case of India, we must recognize first the generally lowered levels of productivity across many regions and crops with respect to both the potential yield (as agronomically or experimentally determined) as well as the maximum achievable yield[5] (determined with respect to the maximum yield in districts with similar climate characteristics). Unfortunately, an incorrect picture of climate-change impact is projected by estimating how current yields will be affected by global warming, which ignore the potential for improving productivity from current levels (Jayaraman 2011). However, outside of the specific literature on climate change and agriculture, the issue of yield gaps in agriculture in India and other countries is well recognized (Global Yield Gap Atlas 2020; Licker *et al.* 2010; Manah and Jayaraman 2020).

The second issue of relevance for Indian agriculture and climate change is the widespread prevalence and role of small producers in agricultural production. One part of the literature tends to project the current vulnerability of small producers to climate shocks as the impact of climate change (Jayaraman and Murari 2014). They, thus, tend to argue that the current vulnerability of agricultural production is due to the impact of climate change, without taking note of the socio-economic determinants of agricultural productivity with respect to small and marginal farmers. Another part of the literature tends to ignore the specific conditions of productions particular to small farmers and tend to project climate and agriculture as a purely technical question (Giller *et al.* 2015; Shiferaw and Holden 2001). More recently, this second stream in the academic and policy advocacy literature, has turned to emphasizing agriculture as the site of mitigation, even at the cost of allowing what is politely referred to as "yield penalties" (*ibid*). Since such mitigation efforts may lead to loss of income for farmers, the argument is made that farmers need to be incentivised for the adoption of such cultivation practices, through so-called "payment for ecosystem services."

Current Productivity in Bengal Agriculture

Having noted the above, it is of course important to determine the impact of both current climate variability and future climate change on

---

[5] The terminology is drawn from Licker *et al.* (2010).

agricultural production and productivity, to the extent possible in the case of the latter due to the large uncertainties that we have referred to in the introduction. In this section, we will be able to provide only a snapshot of some of the issues referred to here with reference to West Bengal. Much of our analysis will be focused on the case of paddy, the pre-eminent crop in Bengal, with only brief remarks on the others. A comprehensive assessment has to await further more detailed research studies.

In general, given the initial historically low base of agriculture productivity, yields of all major crops show a secular increasing trend. In the case of Bengal, some jumps in productivity are noted in particular districts at different rates, indicating that productivity growth has not been uniform across regions. The figures below show the increase in rice productivity for the three main paddy growing seasons in Bengal, namely *aus*, *aman* and *boro*. In the last few years, there is however an apparent slowdown in yield growth.

Notably in Bengal, the yield gap in terms of achievable yield is fairly low by all-India standards, as is evident in Table 3 below. The climatic zones are based on the revised classification described in Raju *et al.* (2013). However, the fact that we are speaking of achievable yield must be kept

Figure 7 *Rice yield for main paddy growing seasons of West Bengal*

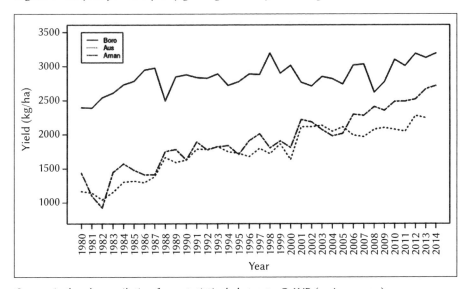

Source: Authors' compilation from statistical abstracts, GoWB (various years).

in mind, namely with respect to the highest yield achieved in districts of the same climatic characteristics. The fact that the rice yield is below 3 tonnes/ha in a region of high rainfall and ample water availability speaks to the gap in productivity with respect to international standards. This data also does not reflect the season-wise variation in yields, which, as we can see from the earlier figure, varies substantially between *boro* and other two seasons. There is also some anomaly for the figures for Maldah which requires a separate explanation that we do not enter into here.

We have not examined in detail the situation with respect to other crops in this brief chapter, but the case of rice, Bengal's pre-eminent crop, amply illustrates the issue.

Table 3 *District-wise yields and yield gaps with respect maximum achievable yield (averaged over 2009–11)*

District	Climatic zone	Yield gap (kg/ha)	Yield gap (%)	Yield (kg/ha)
Darjiling	Per-humid	482.8	17.2	2,318.7
Koch Bihar	Per-humid	590.8	21.1	2,210.8
Jalpaiguri	Per-humid	733.3	26.2	2,068.3
Barddhaman	Moist sub-humid	0.0	0.0	2,990.2
Hugli	Moist sub-humid	31.5	1.1	2,958.6
Birbhum	Moist sub-humid	136.3	4.6	2,853.9
Murshidabad	Moist sub-humid	209.5	7.0	2,780.7
Bankura	Moist sub-humid	226.4	7.6	2,763.7
Pashchim Medinipur	Moist sub-humid	293.7	9.8	2,696.4
Purba Medinipur	Moist sub-humid	448.9	15.0	2,541.3
Haora	Moist sub-humid	8,46.6	28.3	2,143.6
Maldah	Moist sub-humid	2,262.4	75.7	727.7
Nadia	Dry sub-humid	2,011.7	41.5	2,834.5
Puruliya	Dry sub-humid	2,534.8	52.3	2,311.4
North 24 Parganas	Humid	84.9	3.0	2,737.4
Dakshin Dinajpur	Humid	167.0	5.9	2,655.3
Uttar Dinajpur	Humid	327.1	11.6	2,495.2
South 24 Parganas	Humid	582.0	20.6	2,240.3

Source: Authors' calculation from data downloaded from Directorate of Economics and Statistics, Ministry of Agriculture, Government of India, available at https://eands.dacnet.nic. in/, viewed on January 19, 2021..

Climate Sensitivity of Current Agricultural Production

Despite the strong indications provided by crop models, determining the impact of climate variability on productivity and production is not easy. As was noted by Gadgil (1995) and Gadgil and Gadgil (2006), one may broadly take the view that while the general trend of growth in yields is a consequence of technological advance, it is the year-on-year fluctuations that are the signal of climate variability. Other economic factors are more likely to be reflected in the area sown, and hence production, while productivity itself is not affected by them. While this may not be fully so in all cases it is nevertheless a good working hypothesis with which to examine the time-series data on productivity in relation to temperature and rainfall indicators.

In practice however, at the district level, extracting the signal of climate variability is fairly complex and emerges clearly only in a few instances. We illustrate this in the case of rice production once again.

In the figure above, the choice of independent variables, the average night-time temperature has been taken as rice is sensitive to this variable. The other variables, season average temperature and total season rainfall, are of course prima facie the ones to choose. We do not also see any clear argument why we should also include higher-order effects in these variables beyond the linear, though this merits further investigation. Further, the data consists of the yield of every individual district, for every year between 1980 and 2014. Since we are interested in year-on-year variation as the signal of climate variability, we have taken the first difference for both independent and dependent variables.

However, we can obtain further insight if we go beyond visual examination to a regression analysis, where first difference in yield is the dependent variable with respect to the other first difference of the other independent variables.

The figure below shows the results for a linear regression with district fixed-effects with respect to season average temperature, with and without total seasonal rainfall (all first differences[diffs]) (See Table 4 – a, b, and c) .The effect of climate variability appears very small, as is clear from the R-squared values that are quite small, even though the regression coefficients are significant. This, of course, applies only to *aman* productivity, with both *boro* and *aus* showing no significant trends. This is somewhat surprising, since we might expect *boro* to be more temperature-sensitive as it is a summer crop.

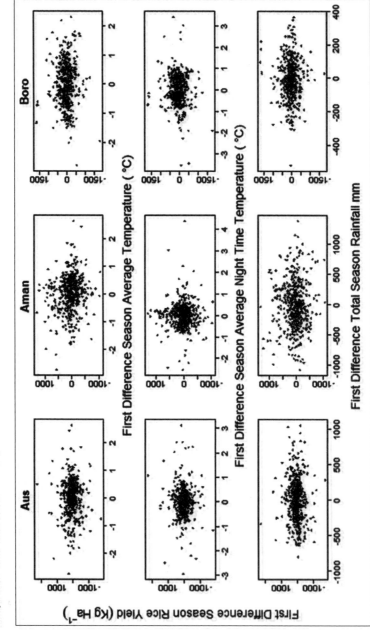

Figure 8 *First difference of rice yields with respect to first difference of season average temperature, season average night time temperature, and total seasonal rainfall*

Source: Based on the IMD gridded data on rainfall from Pai et al. 2014 and temperature data from Srivastava et al. 2009. The rice yield data is from the Department of Economics and Statistics, Government of West Bengal.

We note here that this simple regression model is the only one giving consistent results. With other variants of models, significant coefficients do appear, but the sign is the opposite of what is to be expected from simple agronomic considerations. Even in the model below while there is

Table 4 *Results for linear regression with district fixed-effects with respect to season average temperature, with and without total seasonal rainfall (all first diffs)*

(a) Rice yield with season average temperature for all the rice-growing season

	Aus	Aman	Boro
Season avg temp (1st diff)	−5.874	−77.630 ***	−6.842
(27.096)	(23.330)	(21.349)	
Observations	503	525	525
R-Squared	0.000	0.021	0.000

(b) Rice yield with season average temperature total season rainfall for all the rice-growing season

	Aus	Aman	Boro
Season avg temp (1st diff)	13.639	−91.323 ***	−14.024
(30.198)	(25.018)	(25.793)	
Total season rainfall (1st diff)	0.091	−0.061	−0.080
(0.063)	(0.040)	(0.162)	
Observations	503	525	525
R-Squared	0.004	0.025	0.001

(c) Rice yield with GDD, EDD and total rainfall for the growing season

	Aus	Aman	Boro
GDD	−0.269	0.329	−0.117
(0.602)	(0.313)	(0.116)	
EDD	3.869 *	−7.293 ***	0.489
(1.785)	(1.419)	(0.732)	
Total season rsainfall	0.110	−0.062	−0.015
(0.061)	(0.039)	(0.160)	
Observations	503	525	525
R-Squared	0.014	0.048	0.003

Note: *** $p < 0.001$; ** $p < 0.01$; * $p < 0.05$.
Source: Based on the IMD gridded data on rainfall from Pai *et al.* (2014) and temperature data from Srivastava *et al.* (2009). The rice yield data is from the Department of Economics and Statistics, Government of West Bengal.

some consistency with *aman* results, the model does not tell us anything particular about *aus* and *boro* productivity.

We also try another variant of this regression where we attempt to separate out extreme temperature effects. We do this in terms of a regression model that we have successfully applied to wheat production in the Indo-Gangetic plain (Murari, Mahato, and Jayaraman 2014). Using 34^0C as the critical temperature for rice, the growing degree-days (GDD) and the extreme degree-days (EDD) were calculated. For this model too, the temperature effect shows up only for the *aman* crop, though it is now more explicitly the effect of extreme temperatures rather than the normal heat exposure over the entire season for the crop. A significant source of uncertainty in these calculations is the need to approximate the season length based on the approximate months of cultivation. Other work suggests that getting the precise length of the growing season is important to capture variability in yields (Pathak 2017), which however we cannot do here for want of accurate data on growing season lengths across different districts and so on.

The absence of strong and easily visible evidence of the impact of climate variability suggests that there is considerable scope for what is termed in the literature as autonomous adaptation (Kavi Kumar 2010). The incremental changes in climatic conditions are fairly readily taken care of by the slight shifts in cultivation practices that do not perhaps register significantly on a meso or macro scale. Moreover, as we have constantly underlined, technological advance over a low productivity base is capable of significantly suppressing any signal of climate variability.[6] Similar analysis needs to be extended to the case of the other crops, most notably potato, jute, and also wheat and maize (Dibyendu Sen, PhD thesis, in preparation).

Future Impact of Climate Change on Crop Productivity

The 2012 edition of the West Bengal SAPCC provides some relevant data on the future impact of climate change. These results are derived typically from crop model based studies that are cited in the SAPCC. One study based on the Infocrop model estimates that a 1 degree C rise in temperature (whether it is local season average temperature increase

---

[6] For a macro-level analysis of this type of effect, see Lobell, Schlenker, and Costa-Roberts 2011; Pattanayak and Kavi Kumar 2014, 2017.

or a global increase is unclear), would lead to yield declines of 830 kg/ha for kharif rice, 450 kg/ha for mustard and 640 kg/ ha for wheat (WBSAPCC 2012). It is clear that such declines would seriously impact current productivity of the *aman* paddy crop, if further efforts at yield enhancement are not undertaken. However, such figures have to be seen in the context of current productivity gaps.

In one scenario, potato production is projected to decline by 4–16 per cent by the 2030s in Bengal. In another study productivity of potato cultivation is projected to decline by 2 per cent to 19 per cent by 2020 and 9 to 55 per cent by 2050. However, the assumptions of this calculation are unclear. Unfortunately, the bulk of the section on agriculture and climate change in the WBSPACC of 2012 is taken up by purely qualitative discussion attributed to experts. In the WBSPACC of 2017, the major gaps in the discussion of the earlier edition are not taken up, and there is even less of a comprehensive quantitative assessment of climate change impact on crop production.

The absence in the public domain of a serious compendium of quantitative climate impact on crop production for particular States is a major lacuna and should be one of the foremost policy tasks of any government that is serious about climate change adaptation. In the case of Bengal, there are important specific features that run counter to the standard discourse on climate-change adaptation in India, the vulnerability to floods being the foremost among them.

In this brief survey, detailed considerations of other sectors in agriculture would be outside its scope. However, we cannot end without mention of the important signals of climate-change impact on agriculture in India that has been observed in Bengal, namely the impact of rising temperatures on tank breeding of carps. The increase in temperatures has shifted the start of the breeding season from June to March, extending the breeding season by 40–60 days (Jayaraman 2011; WBSAPCC 2012).

Small Farmers and Climate Change

As has been explored at some length in other chapters in this volume, Bengal is characterized by the dominant presence of small and marginal farmers. The differential impact of climate change on small farmers still needs to be explored in the literature. The data from the PARI surveys however provide important information on the primary socio-economic characteristics of small producers in Bengal agriculture and other parts of India (Swaminathan and Baksi 2017). The relevance of these results to understanding the impact of climate change has been discussed in Jayaraman and Murari (2014). As however they have no specific comments particular to Bengal we will refer the interested reader to the original article.

One important difference between the wide prevalence of small farmers in Bengal and the rest of the country though needs to be commented on. In general, across all major rice-producing districts in the country, we have found that the presence of small farmers is positively correlated with increasing yield gap, across all climatic zones. But in the specific case of Bengal, we have already observed that the yield gaps are relatively low in the districts which are in the moist sub-humid category, though these are only in terms of achievable yield. This suggests that expanding productivity requires overcoming barriers of scale, though for a more definite statement we would need further investigation.

But to go beyond the basic features to a deeper understanding of the impact of climate and weather shocks on the marginal, small and medium farmer categories requires time-series data of a kind that is not available and must await other future studies. It is clear though that the fate of the small farmer is a critical aspect of climate adaptation in Bengal agriculture.

Conclusion

We will only be brief here in keeping with nature of our overview in this chapter. But some important points need to be re-emphasised. First is the surprising persistence of major knowledge gaps (or simply, absence of any knowledge) on important aspects of Bengal agriculture. These include the continuing inadequacy of quantitative information on the impact of climate variability and climate change on Bengal agriculture, in both the sense of agricultural science as well as the socio-economic conditions of agricultural production. It is indeed surprising that little progress has been made between the two versions of the SAPCC for the State. Regrettably, one is left to ask whether this is also partly a consequence of an increasing emphasis on mitigation rather than adaptation. This, for Bengal, would be a very negative development given the conditions that prevail in the State.

Second, one of the frontlines of climate adaptation in Bengal is the vulnerability to floods. In terms of scale and resources, dealing with floods is among the most challenging aspects of climate-resilient infrastructure.

This merits further detailed study of all the various dimensions of this problem. Third, any trajectory of development in Bengal, needs to confront the question of petty production in agriculture. The data on productivity illustrates, we believe, the natural limits of petty production, and without serious efforts to diversify livelihoods, employment, and sources of income in the countryside, the burden of climate change on agriculture could be truly magnified in its impact.

We hope to return to some of these issues in more detail in the future.

References

Aggarwal, P. K. (2008), "Global Climate Change and Indian Agriculture: Impacts, Adaptation and Mitigation," *Indian Journal of Agricultural Sciences*, vol. 78, pp. 911–19.

Bandyopadhyay, Krishna, Ghosh, Soma, and Dutta, Nilanjan (2006), *Eroded Lives*, Mahanirban Calcutta Research Group, Kolkata, West Bengal.

Barange, Manuel, Bahri, Tarûb, Beveridge, Malcolm C. M.., Cochrane, Kevern, L., Funge-Smith, Simon, and Poulain, Florence (2018), *Impacts of Climate Change on Fisheries and Aquaculture: Synthesis of Currrent Knowledge, Adaptation and Mitigation Options*, Food and Agriculture Organization, United Nations, Rome.

Chaturvedi, Rajiv, Joshi, Jaideep, Jayaraman, Mathangi, Govindasamy, Balasubramanian, and Ravindranath, N. H. (2012), "Multi-Model Climate Change Projections for India under Representative Concentration Pathways," *Current Science*, vol. 103, pp. 791–802.

Flood Forecast and Monitoring (FFM) (2018), Statewise Flood Damage Statistics - Regarding, Letter No.3/38/2012-FFM/0657-1165, retrieved from http://cwc.gov.in/sites/default/files/statewiseflooddatadamagestatistics.pdf, viewed on January19, 2021.

Gadgil, Sulochana (1995), "Climate Change and Agriculture – An Indian Perspective," *Current Science*, vol. 69, no. 8, pp. 649–59.

Gadgil, Sulochana, and Gadgil, Siddhartha (2006), "The Indian Monsoon, GDP and Agriculture," *Economic and Political Weekly*, vol. 41, no. 47, pp. 4887–95.

Giller, Ken E., Andersson, Jens A., Corbeels, Marc, Kirkegaard, John, Mortensen, David, Erenstein, Olaf, and Vanlauwe, Bernard (2015), "Beyond Conservation Agriculture," *Frontiers in Plant Science*, vol. 6, doi: 10.3389/fpls.2015.00870.

Government of West Bengal (GoWB) (2007), *District Human Development Report Malda*, Development and Planning Department, Government of West Bengal.

Global Yield Gap Atlas (2020), "Global Yield Gap Atlas," retrieved from http://www.yieldgap.org /, viewed on January 12, 2021.

Gusain, A., Ghosh, S., and Karmakar, S. (2020), "Added Value of CMIP6 over CMIP5

Models in Simulating Indian Summer Monsoon Rainfall," *Atmospheric Research*, vol. 232, article no. 104680, doi: 10.1016/j.atmosres.2019.104680.

Hillel, D., and Rosenzweig, C. (2011), *Handbook of Climate Change and Agroecosystems: Impacts, Adaptation, and Mitigation*, Imperial College Press, London.

Hofer, Thomas (1993), "Himalayan Deforestation, Changing River Discharge, and Increasing Floods: Myth or Reality?," Mountain Research and Development, vol. 13, no. 3, pp. 213, doi: 10.2307/3673653.

Iizumi, Toshichika, Sakuma, Hirofumi, Yokozawa, Masayuki, Luo, Jing-Jia, Challinor, Andrew, J., Brown, Molly, E., Sakurai, Gen, and Yamagata, Toshio (2013), "Prediction of Seasonal Climate-Induced Variations in Global Food Production," Nature Climate Change, vol. 3, no. 10, pp. 904–8, doi: 10.1038/nclimate1945.

Intergovernmental Panel on Climate Change (IPCC) (2014), *Climate Change 2014: Impacts, Adaptation, and Vulnerability. Part A: Global and Sectoral Aspects*, Contribution of Working Group II to the Fifth Assessment Report of the Intergovernmental Panel on Climate Change, Cambridge and New York.

Jayaraman, T. (2011), "Climate Change and Agriculture: A Review Article with Special Reference to India," *Review of Agrarian Studies*, vol. 1, no. 2, pp. 16–78, Foundation for Agrarian Studies, Bangalore.

Jayaraman, T., and Murari, Kamal, K.. (2014), "Climate Change and Agriculture: Current and Future Trends, and Implications for India," *Review of Agrarian Studies*, vol. 4, no. 1, pp. 1–48, Foundation for Agrarian Studies, Bangalore.

Katzenberger, Anja, Schewe, Jacob, Pongratz, Julia, and Levermann, Anders (2020), *Robust Increase of Indian Monsoon Rainfall and Its Variability under Future Warming in CMIP-6 Models*, Earth Syst. Dynam. Discuss. [preprint], available at https://doi. org/10.5194/esd-2020-8, in review, 2020.

Kavi Kumar, K. S. (2010), "The Challenge of Adaptation," *Seminar*, vol. 606.

Kulkarni, Ashwini, Sabin, T. P., Chowdary, Jasti, S., K. Rao, Koteswara, Priya, P., Gandhi, Naveen, Bhaskar, Preethi, Buri, Vinodh K., Sabade, S. S., Pai, D. S., Ashok, K., Mitra, A. K., Niyogi, Dev, and Rajeevan, M. (2020), "Precipitation Changes in India," in R. Krishnan, J. Sanjay, C. Gnanaseelan, M. Mujumdar, A. Kulkarni, and S. Chakraborty (eds.), *Assessment of Climate Change over the Indian Region: A Report of the Ministry of Earth Sciences (MoES)*, Government of India, Singapore: Springer Singapore, pp. 47–72.

Laborde, David, Murphy, Sophia, Parent, Marie, Porciello, Jaron, and Smaller, Carin (2020), *Ceres2030: Sustainable Solutions to End Hunger Summary Report*, Cornell University, International Food Policy Research Institute (IFRI) and International Institute for Sustainable Development (IISD).

Licker, Rachel, Johnston, Matt, Foley, Jonathan A., Barford, Carol, Kucharik, Christopher J., Monfreda, Chad, and Ramankutty, Navin (2010), "Mind the Gap: How Do Climate and Agricultural Management Explain the 'Yield Gap' of Croplands around the World?," *Global Ecology and Biogeography*, vol. 19, no. 6, pp. 769–82, doi: 10.1111/j.1466-8238.2010.00563.x.

Lobell, David B., and Burke, Marshall B. (2008), "Why Are Agricultural Impacts of Climate Change so Uncertain? The Importance of Temperature Relative to Precipitation," *Environmental Research Letters*, vol. 3, no. 3, article no. 034007, doi: 10.1088/1748-9326/3/3/034007.

Lobell, David B., Schlenker, Wolfram, and Costa-Roberts, Justin (2011), "Climate Trends and Global Crop Production Since 1980," Science 333 (6042), pp. 616–20, doi: 10.1126/science.1204531.

Manah, Isaac, and Jayaraman, T. (2020), "Development Deficits and Climate Change Adaptation: Yield Gaps in Agriculture," unpublished manuscript.

Mishra, Ashutosh (2014), "Temperature Rise and Trend of Cyclones over the Eastern Coastal Region of India," *Journal of Earth Science & Climatic Change*, vol. 5, no. 9, pp. 1–5, doi: 10.4172/2157-7617.1000227.

Murari, K. K., Mahato S., and Jayaraman, T. (2014), "Empirical Evidence of the Direct Impact of Extreme Temperatures on Wheat Yield in the Major Wheat-Growing Region of India," American Geophysical Union (AGU), Fall meeting, December 15–19, San Francisco, USA.

Pai, D. S., Latha Sridhar, Rajeevan M., Sreejith O.P., Satbhai, N. S., and Mukhopadhyay, B., (2014), "Development of a New High Spatial Resolution (0.25° X 0.25°) Long Period (1901–2010) Daily Gridded Rainfall Data Set Over India and Its Comparison With Existing Data Sets Over The Region," *MAUSAM*, vol. 65, no. 1, January, pp. 1–18.

Pathak, Himanshu (2017), "Application of Decision Support System for Agrotechnology Transfer (DSSAT – a Crop Simulation Model) to Assess Impacts of Mean Temperature Increase on Wheat Yield in Raisen, Madhya Pradesh," Tata Institute of Social Sciences, Mumbai, Maharashtra.

Pattanayak, Anubhab, and Kavi Kumar, K. S. (2014), "Weather Sensitivity of Rice Yield: Evidence from India," *Climate Change Economics*, vol. 5, no. 4, article no. 1450011, doi: 10.1142/S2010007814500110.

Pattanayak, Anubhab, and Kavi Kumar K. S. (2017), *Does Weather Sensitivity of Rice Yield Vary Across Regions? Evidence from Eastern and Southern India*, Madras School of Economics, Chennai, India.

Government of India (GoI) (2005), *Half-Yearly Performance Review of West Bengal's Annual Pland 2006*, Planning Commission, Government of India.

Raghavan, Krishnan, Jayanarayanan, Sanjay, Gnanaseelan, Chellappan, Mujumdar, Milind, Ashwini, and Chakraborty, Supriyo (eds.) (2020), *Assessment of Climate Change over the Indian Region: A Report of the Ministry of Earth Sciences (MoES)*, Government of India, Springer, Singapore.

Raju, B. M. K., Rao, K. V., Venkateswarlu, B., Rao, A. V. M. S., Rao, Rama, C. A., Rao, V. U. M., Rao, Bapuji, B., Kumar, Ravi, N., Dhakar, R., Swapna, N., and Latha, P. (2013), "Revisiting Climatic Classification in India: A District-Level Analysis," *Current Science*, vol. 105, no. 4, pp. 492–95.

Rojas-Downing, M. Melissa, Nejadhashemi, Pouyan, A., Harrigan, Timothy, and Woznicki, Sean A. (2017), "Climate Change and Livestock: Impacts, Adaptation, and Mitigation," *Climate Risk Management*, vol. 16, pp. 145–63, doi: 10.1016/j. crm.2017.02.001.

Sanjay, J., Revadekar, J. V., Ramarao, M. V. S., Borgaonkar, H., Sengupta, S., Kothawale, D. R., Patel, Jayashri, Mahesh, R., Ingle, S., AchutaRao, K., Srivastava, A. K., and Ratnam, J. V. (2020), "Temperature Changes in India," in R. Krishnan, J. Sanjay, C. Gnanaseelan, M. Mujumdar, A. Kulkarni, and S. Chakraborty, (eds.), *Assessment of Climate Change over the Indian Region: A Report of the Ministry of Earth Sciences (MoES)*, Government of India, pp. 21–45.

Sanyal, Joy, and Lu, Xi Xi (2003), "Application of GIS in Flood Hazard Mapping: A Case Study of Gangetic West Bengal, India," poster presented at Map Asia 2003, Kuala Lumpur.

Shiferaw, Bekele, and Holden, Stein T. (2001), "Farm-Level Benefits to Investments for Mitigating Land Degradation: Empirical Evidence from Ethiopia," *Environment and Development Economics*, vol. 6, no. 3, pp. 335–58, doi: 10.1017/S1355770X01000195.

Sirohi, Smita, and Michaelowa, Axel (2007), "Sufferer and Cause: Indian Livestock and Climate Change," *Climatic Change*, vol. 85, no. 3, pp. 285–98, doi: 10.1007/ s10584-007-9241-8.

Srivastava, A. K., Rajeevan, M., and Kshirsagar, S. R. (2009), "Development of High Resolution Daily Gridded Temperature Data Set (1969–2005) for the Indian Region," *Atmospheric Science Letters*, doi: 10.1002/asl.232.

Swaminathan, Madhura, and Baksi, Sandipan (eds.) (2017), *How Do Small Farmers Fare? Evidence from Village Studies in India*, Tulika Books, New Delhi.

Vellore, Ramesh K., Deshpande, Nayana, Priya, P., Singh, Bhupendra B., Bisht, Jagat, and Ghosh, Subimal (2020), "Extreme Storms," in R. Krishnan, J. Sanjay, C. Gnanaseelan, M. Mujumdar, A. Kulkarni, and S. Chakraborty, *Assessment of Climate Change over the Indian Region: A Report of the Ministry of Earth Sciences (MoES)*, Government of India, Springer, Singapore, pp. 155–73.

West Bengal Disaster Management and Civil Defence Department (WBDMD) (2020), "Natural Disaster: Flood," West Bengal Disaster Management & Civil Defence Department, available at http://wbdmd.gov.in/pages/flood2.aspx, viewed on November 8, 2020.

West Bengal State Action Plan on Climate Change (WBSAPCC) (2012), *West Bengal State Action Plan on Climate Change 2012*, Government of West Bengal.

West Bengal State Action Plan on Climate Change (WBSAPCC) (2017), *West Bengal State Action Plan on Climate Change 2017–2020*, Government of West Bengal.

SECTION III

Income, Employment, and Credit

9

A Contemporary Study of Rural Credit in West Bengal

Pallavi Chavan, with Ritam Dutta[1]

Rural credit has been a subject of continued interest in India since the turn of the twentieth century. Historically, the focus of rural credit was on credit cooperatives, which were set up as the first formal alternative to informal sources, symbolised by the moneylender, in the Indian countryside. After Independence, particularly after the nationalisation of major private sector banks, the discussion on rural credit concerned the growing involvement of commercial banks in the provision of rural credit, particularly agricultural credit.[2] By the early-1990s, commercial banks had indeed emerged as the most important source of rural credit in India (NSSO 1998).

With the onset of financial liberalisation, however, there were distinct signs of a growing vacuum with banks retreating from the rural credit space (Ramachandran and Swaminathan 2005). There was a reduction in the number of rural bank branches and decline in the growth of rural credit in the 1990s (Chavan 2005). Banks, under the liberalised set up, were encouraged to give greater attention to profitability over redistribution and it was argued that redistribution was an objective of fiscal policy, not of monetary/credit policy (RBI 1991). It was also argued that the rural–urban divide in banking had been minimised after nationalisation, and banks' commitment to social banking could be deemed negotiable (RBI 2001).

The 1990s were also a period when various non-banking institutions

[1] The authors thank Aparajita Bakshi, Ranjini Basu and an anonymous referee for useful comments on an earlier draft. The views expressed are personal views of the authors and do not represent the views of the organisations to which the authors are affiliated.
[2] Prior to bank nationalisation, commercial banks, an institution of urban origin, were only peripherally involved in the provision of credit for agricultural marketing/processing, as envisaged by the All-India Rural Credit Survey in 1951–52 (RBI 1954).

in the form of self-regulated for-profit microfinance institutions (MFIs) made inroads into the field of rural credit (RBI 2008). Thus, the vacuum left by commercial banks in rural credit was occupied by non-banking institutions and informal sources, including moneylenders, in many parts of rural India.[3] The decade of the 1990s could thus be termed as a lost decade as far as the formal interventions in rural credit were concerned (Ramakumar and Chavan 2007).

The trend of withdrawal by commercial banks from rural credit, however, somewhat reversed since the mid-2000s. With the adoption of policy on financial inclusion, although confined by the broader commitment to financial liberalisation, banks were once again made responsible for ensuring access to formal finance for the rural masses. This was reflected in the sharp increase in the number of rural bank branches in the 2000s (Chavan 2017b). Regulated for-profit MFIs were also regarded as stakeholders alongside banks in the process of financial inclusion (RBI 2011).

The focus of financial inclusion, however, has continued to be on the provision of deposit facilities to rural areas. Although through Comprehensive Credit Policy in the mid-2000s, there was an effort to revive the flow of agricultural credit, the benefit of this revival to rural areas appeared questionable following the changes in the definition of agriculture under priority sector lending (PSL) policy (Ramakumar and Chavan 2007).[4] Limited attention is given to rural credit as part of financial inclusion, which is reflected in the persistently lopsided distribution of bank credit between rural and urban areas (Chavan 2017b).

Given the diverse nature of the Indian countryside, studies on rural credit, particularly ones based on village studies, have generally focused on features of the rural credit system in specific geographical regions/ States. This chapter is a study of the contemporary state of rural credit in the eastern Indian State of West Bengal (WB) based on surveys of three villages in addition to various secondary data sources on the State. Although WB has been mentioned in the literature on rural credit since the 1970s, studies based on systematic village surveys in the State are

[3] See NSSO (2005) for an illustration of the increased share of informal sources between the 1992 and 2002 rounds of the All-India Debt and Investment Survey (AIDIS) in various States. Also see RBI (2008) for an illustration of the growth in MFIs in India between 1992 and 2006.
[4] This policy included the commitment to raise agricultural credit flow by 30 per cent every year, financing of 100 farmers per branch, two to three new investments in agricultural projects per branch every year, and certain debt-relief measures (Ramakumar and Chavan 2007).

limited. The reference to rural credit in the 1970s and 1980s in WB, which falls in an under-banked region, is primarily in the context of oppressive informal credit relations. Studies have also referred to rural credit in the State in various other contexts, such as land reforms, decentralisation, high growth in agricultural production during the 1980s, and financial liberalisation in the 1990s, as will be discussed in a later section "Rural Credit in West Bengal".

Studying rural credit in the current context is important given the changes in rural credit policy in recent decades, notably the shift towards financial liberalisation along with an emphasis on financial inclusion. The eastern region was historically an under-banked region. Also, the setback to its rural branch network in the 1990s was more severe than in many other regions of India, thus making a study of rural credit of States from this region extremely relevant.[5] WB has witnessed the birth and growth of some of India's large MFIs in the past two decades.[6] The contribution of for-profit microfinance to rural credit in the State is also an issue of contemporary importance. Furthermore, the State is an interesting case study for agricultural credit given the predominance of small-scale farming.

The specific questions that the chapter attempts to answer are the following:

(a) What are the changes in rural credit policy in India in the recent decades and in what ways have these changes shaped the contemporary rural credit system in WB?
(b) How does WB compare in terms of the development of rural credit in the contemporary period on a national scale?
(c) What is the composition of rural credit or which major formal and informal sources provide rural credit in the State?
(d) How do these sources compare with each other in regard to their terms of credit?
(e) Which sources meet the agricultural credit needs of the State?
(f) What are the factors affecting the probability of access to agricultural credit in the study villages?

[5] See Chavan (2017b) for a regional comparison of banking development. She showed that the branch intensity was adversely affected in the north-eastern, eastern, and central regions as compared to the southern, northern, and western regions of India in the 1990s.
[6] This prominently included the Bandhan Financial Services Private Limited, a non-banking financial company (NBFC) established in WB in 2001, which later expanded its operations across the eastern and north-eastern regions.

(g) How is formal credit to agriculture distributed across various categories of cultivators?

(h) Is the provision of agricultural credit adequate in meeting the costs of cultivation across various categories of cultivators, and is it in line with the stipulated scales of finance?

The chapter answers these questions with the help of (a) secondary data on banking and household surveys, namely the All-India Debt and Investment Survey (AIDIS) and NABARD All-India Rural Financial Inclusion (NAFIS),[7] and (b) data collected through census surveys of three villages, Panahar, Amarsinghi and Kalmandasguri, from Bankura, Maldah, and Koch Bihar districts, respectively in 2010 as part of the Project on Agrarian Relations in India (PARI).[8]

The chapter is organised as follows. The second section discusses contemporary features of rural credit policy in India, with reference to West Bengal where possible. Rural credit policy in India has a long history and is well-documented in the literature (Chavan 2012b). Hence, this section focuses only on policy changes from the 1990s onwards to illustrate the present context. The third section contains a brief review of the literature, highlighting the major features of rural credit in WB since the 1970s. The fourth section analyses recent trends relating to rural credit in WB based on various data sources on rural banking, cooperative credit, and secondary household-level surveys. The fifth section discusses the rural credit system in the study villages. The sixth section analyses agricultural credit in the villages. The final section provides concluding observations.

---

[7] The AIDIS is a nation-wide decennial survey of the debt and borrowing profiles of rural and urban households conducted by the National Sample Survey Organisation (NSSO). The chapter uses data from the last three rounds of the AIDIS, namely 1991–92, 2002–03 and 2012–13. The NAFIS is a newly introduced survey by the National Bank for Agriculture and Rural Development (NABARD) in 2018 (NABARD 2018). The NAFIS covered Tier 3 to 6 centres (population of up to 50,000, including rural and portions of semi-urban centres) from 28 States. The objective of NAFIS was to obtain detailed information on various aspects of financial inclusion, including savings, insurance, and credit. The reference year was 2016–17, and the information on borrowings was canvassed for the preceding year (July–June) and also the preceding two years. Though a cultivator household in the AIDIS is defined as one cultivating a landholding of more than 0.05 acres during the survey year, the NAFIS criterion was a household whose value of produce from various agricultural activities was more than Rs 5,000. Therefore, the results from the two surveys are not comparable.

[8] The methodology for selecting the villages is discussed in the introductory chapter of this volume.

Contemporary Rural Credit Policy in India: Financial Inclusion Defined by the Contours of Financial Liberalisation

The three formal institutions currently involved in the provision of rural credit in India are commercial banks, rural credit cooperatives and regional rural banks (RRBs).[9] Among rural credit cooperatives, the long-term structure has been in a state of decay in most Indian States in the absence of requisite capital support from the Central/State Governments (Sen 2005).[10] Consequently, the share of long-term cooperatives in total cooperative credit has been reduced to very low levels in recent decades (Chavan 2013). Hence, present-day rural cooperative credit is dominated by the short-term structure comprising state cooperative banks (SCBs), district central cooperative Banks (DCCBs), and primary agricultural credit societies (PACSs). In WB, as in most States, there is a three-tier short-term structure comprising WB SCB, DCCBs, and PACSs (RBI 2017b).

The microfinance sector is also active in the contemporary rural credit system in India. At present, the microfinance sector is an unregulated one. The lending institutions in this sector include: (a) banks and non-banking financial companies (NBFC)-MFIs, which are formal institutions regulated by the Reserve Bank of India (RBI), and (b) MFIs, including non-profit companies (Section 25 companies), for-profit non-governmental organisations (NGOs), and charitable and investment trusts, which are semi-formal institutions as they are partially governed by different statutes (RBI 2008).[11] Pending the passage of the Micro Finance Institutions (Development and Regulation) Bill, there are no *uniform* regulations that govern *all* lending institutions in the microfinance sector.[12]

---

[9] See Table 1 for the present shares of these institutions in rural credit in India.

[10] The short-term cooperative credit structure has been recapitalised following the recommendations of the Task Force on the Revival of Cooperative Credit Institutions (GoI 2004). However, long-term institutions have not yet been recapitalised. In 2016, the Non-Performing Assets (NPA) ratio for State and Primary Cooperative Agriculture and Rural Development Banks (S/PCARDBs) from the long-term structure was about 17 and 37 per cent, respectively. The mounting losses due to high levels of NPAs without the requisite capital support have resulted in a slowdown in long-term cooperative credit growth in recent years (RBI 2017b).

[11] The statutes governing these entities include the Companies Act, 1956 and Indian Trusts Act, 1882/Public Trust Act, 1920 (RBI 2008). However, despite being credit institutions, their operating practices, including lending and recovery practices, are not subject to public regulation or supervision.

[12] The Micro Finance Institutions (Development and Regulation) Bill, 2012 was referred to the Parliamentary Standing Committee on Finance 2013–14, but is yet to be passed. It proposes

While microfinance is originated by the lending institutions, it is disbursed through self-help groups (SHGs) to the actual beneficiary. Effectively therefore, SHGs are the actual source of microfinance. They are affiliated either to banks under the SHG-Bank Linkage Programme (SHG-BLP) or NBFC-MFIs/other MFIs, and are responsible for the actual disbursement, monitoring and recovery of loans by individual beneficiaries. Furthermore, some SHGs even collect a margin while on-lending to individual members to maintain a contingency fund. Hence, SHGs are not merely a group of borrowers but a separate entity linking the lending institutions with borrowers. Although it may not be possible to regulate every SHG given their vast number, a uniform set of regulations applicable to all lending institutions would ensure that SHGs linked to these institutions would in effect be regulated.[13] In the absence of such regulations, SHGs need to be treated as an informal source, as has been done in this chapter. The classification of SHGs as an informal source is also justified in the case of WB given certain onerous lending and recovery practices observed in the State's microfinance sector (see section entitled "Features of Credit in the Study Villages").

Other than microfinance institutions, certain types of specialised NBFCs regulated by the RBI are also active in rural credit. More recently, Small Finance Banks (SFBs) and Payments Banks too have been introduced to provide small-sized retail credit, deposit, and payments facilities.[14]

Over the years, with commercial banks emerging as the leading institution in the provision of rural credit, rural credit policy in India has become almost synonymous with the banking policy. Thus, financial liberalisation – an important area of structural reforms driving banking policy since the early 1990s – has significantly influenced the contemporary state of rural credit in India.[15]

---

a regulatory framework for the entire microfinance sector making RBI as the registration, regulatory and supervisory authority for the sector (GoI 2014).

[13] There are 1.8 and 8.6 million SHGs that are credit- and saving-linked with banks, respectively (RBI 2017a). Furthermore, there are a number of SHGs not linked to the banking system for which no credible estimate is available.

[14] Of the 10 SFBs that were granted licenses by RBI, six had started operations by 2016–17 (RBI 2017b). However, the progress of payments banks has been much slower. Of the seven entities that were given license to operate as payments banks, five had started operations by 2017–18, and the remaining two in 2018–19 (RBI 2018a).

[15] See "Introduction" in Ramachandran and Swaminathan (2005) for the effect of financial liberalisation on rural credit in India.

Given the influence of banking policy on the contemporary rural credit policy, this section focuses on the recent changes in (rural) banking policy. While banking policy covers various aspects of banking operations, this section only includes policies closely influencing operations in rural areas, particularly with regard to bank branches and credit penetration, and also includes a brief discussion on relevant policy measures related to credit cooperatives and RRBs.

Changes in the Existing Policies

Branch licensing policy

Branch licensing policy has directly affected the spread of rural branches in India. After bank nationalisation, the policy was used as a major tool to strengthen banking operations in rural areas. Banks were guided by the branch licensing norm of 1:4, that is, opening four branches in unbanked rural areas for every branch opened in metropolitan or port areas (Copestake 1985). In 1992, with the objective of liberalising banking operations, they were given the autonomy to rationalise their branch network by abolishing the 1:4 norm (RBI 2008).[16]

Branch licensing policy was then replaced by branch authorisation policy whereby instead of granting licenses for individual branches, banks were allowed to open branches through an annual authorisation by the RBI.[17] In 2011, guided by the idea of financial inclusion, this authorisation was subjected to a restriction that, of the total number of branches to be opened during a year, at least 25 per cent would be located in unbanked rural centres (a revenue unit having a population of less than 10,000).[18] Another restriction introduced was that the total number of branches opened during the year in urban plus metropolitan centres (with a population of 0.1 million or above) could not exceed the number of branches opened in the non-urban and non-metropolitan centres i.e., rural (with a population not exceeding 10,000) and semi-urban (10,000 to

---

[16] Banks were permitted to shift their existing branches within the same locality, open certain types of specialised offices and convert existing "non-viable" rural offices into satellite offices without the prior approval of RBI (Chavan 2017b).

[17] See "Liberalised Branch Authorisation Policy," September 8, 2005, available at https://rbi.org.in/scripts/NotificationUser.aspx?Id=2503&Mode=0, viewed on May 22, 2020.

[18] "Branch Authorisation Policy - Opening of Branches in Unbanked Rural Centres," July 15, 2011, available at https://rbi.org.in/scripts/NotificationUser.aspx?Id=6613&Mode=0, viewed on May 22, 2020.

0.1 million) centres, as well as all centres in the north-eastern States and Sikkim.[19]

In recent decades, branch licensing policy for RRBs too has been liberalised on similar lines as commercial banks. Since 2013, RRBs have also been guided by the norm of opening at least 25 per cent of their new branches in unbanked rural centres. However, unlike commercial banks, they have to obtain RBI's approval for opening branches in urban/metropolitan centres, as they are essentially rural-centric banks.[20]

There have been striking implications of the aforementioned policy changes for rural branches, such as a reduction in the number of rural branches (of commercial banks and RRBs) in the 1990s (Ramakumar and Chavan 2011).[21] The reduction was followed by a recovery in the number of rural branches after 2008 with the increase being more rapid after 2011 (Chavan 2017b).

Priority sector lending policy
After bank nationalisation, PSL policy was also used as an important tool to extend bank credit to under-served sectors/sections. Under this policy, commercial banks were mandated to allocate at least 40 per cent of their credit to certain priority sectors, including agriculture (with a sub-target of 18 per cent). Furthermore, 10 per cent of the credit had to be allocated to "weaker sections", which included various socio-economically backward sections such as Scheduled Castes and Tribes (SCs/STs) and small and marginal farmers.[22]

With the onset of financial liberalisation, there was a recommendation to phase out the PSL policy (RBI 1991). Notwithstanding the recommendation, the PSL policy was retained without any changes to the targets. However, major changes were made in the definitions of priority sectors during this

[19] See "Relaxation in Branch Authorisation Policy," October 21, 2013, available at https://www.rbi.org.in/Scripts/BS_CircularIndexDisplay.aspx?Id=8518, viewed on May 22, 2020.
[20] "Master Circular on Branch Licensing" for Regional Rural Banks (RRBs), July 1, 2015, available at https://www.rbi.org.in/SCRIPTs/BS_ViewMasCirculardetails.aspx?id=9817, viewed on May 22, 2020.
[21] Ramakumar and Chavan (2011) analysed the number of bank branches from the *Basic Statistical Returns of Scheduled Commercial Banks* (*BSR*) in India, an annual banking publication of RBI that includes data on both commercial banks and RRBs.
[22] The PSL target was first calculated as a proportion of net bank credit, which was later changed to adjusted net bank credit; see RBI Master Circulars on PSL for computation of adjusted net bank credit.

period, particularly of agriculture and weaker sections (Ramakumar and Chavan 2007; Chavan 2012a).

Under agriculture, the definitions of both "direct" (credit given directly to farmers/producers in agriculture and allied activities) and "indirect" (institutions supporting production in agriculture and allied activities, such as, input and storage dealers, and warehouse operators) forms of agricultural credit were widened significantly (Ramakumar and Chavan 2007).[23] The definitional changes resulted in a shift in the distribution of agricultural credit towards (a) indirect agriculture, (b) large-sized agricultural loans, and (c) agricultural credit given to urban areas. These changes also seemed to help banks increase the flow of agricultural credit in the 2000s, and more specifically, meet the high growth targets set under the Comprehensive Credit Policy between 2004 and 2007. However, the benefit of this growth to rural areas in general, and small farmers in particular, appeared questionable (Ramakumar and Chavan 2014).

The definitional changes need to be seen as part of a shift in public policy on agriculture to promote large-scale, commercial, and capital-intensive forms of agricultural production and post-production activities as part of economic reforms (*ibid.*). Moreover, they were also an integral part of financial liberalisation to make PSL commercially viable for banks.[24]

---

[23] There were additions made under "weaker sections" too. Several newer categories were made eligible for PSL, including SHGs and minority communities engaged in specific occupations, while retaining the target at 10 per cent (Chavan 2012a).

[24] This would be ensured by bringing down the costs by making a few large loans to corporations or institutions as part of direct or indirect lending instead of several small loans to a large number of farmers. Coupled with the definitional changes, newer means for meeting agricultural credit were also introduced in the recent decades to further enhance commercial viability of PSL. Some of these means included (a) outright purchases of agricultural loans by banks from other banks, (b) securitisation of agricultural loans, and (c) priority sector lending certificates (PSLCs). Initially, the Rural Infrastructure Development Fund (RIDF) was used by banks to invest funds equivalent to their PSL shortfalls in this fund. By inversely linking the rate of interest with the extent of shortfall, RIDF was designed to act as a deterrent against any PSL shortfall; see "RIDF and Other Funds," December 10, 2014, available at https://www.rbi.org.in/Scripts/NotificationUser.aspx?Id=9397&Mode=0, viewed on May 22, 2020. With an objective of creating a market-based mechanism for providing an interest rate subsidy to banks that were lending to priority sectors, the Committee on Financial Sector Reforms recommended the institution of PSLCs (GoI 2009). PSLCs were meant to treat PSL like any other portfolio applying similar yardsticks of costs and returns. Hence, instead of every bank lending to priority sectors to minimise default, this mechanism encouraged a few banks to specialise in PSL by acting as sellers and to trade their PSL portfolio at a premium to others who could not meet the PSL targets; see details of the PSLC mechanism in "Priority Sector Lending Certificates," available

The more recently introduced sub-target for small and marginal farmers as part of PSL reflects the commitment to financial inclusion.[25] This change was expected to recognise the credit due to small and marginal farmers more formally than before, although it is still early to comment on its actual impact (Chavan 2017a). Another recent change in the interest of farmers was to cover loans only up to Rs 20 million per borrower to corporate/partnership firms engaged in agriculture and allied activities as part of PSL. This diverged from earlier policy of including loans even above Rs 20 million as part of PSL, although as part of indirect agricultural credit.[26]

While introducing the two aforementioned changes, however, the RBI removed the distinction between direct and indirect agricultural credit in 2015.[27] This made agricultural credit a single homogenous category subject to an overall target of 18 per cent as against the earlier cap on indirect credit of 4.5 per cent within the overall target. The distinction between direct and indirect credit was consciously preserved till then to nudge banks to prioritise farmers over institutions and corporate borrowers.[28] However, while merging the two categories, banks were encouraged to maintain the share of credit going to non-corporate entities (i.e., farmers), at least at the systemic average share for the previous three years.[29] The last change was expected to preserve the focus of PSL on farmers to some extent. Evidently, the frequency and nature of changes in PSL policy in recent years indicates efforts to constantly rebalance the objectives of

at https://rbi.org.in/scripts/NotificationUser.aspx?Id=10339&Mode=0, viewed on May 22, 2020. Interestingly, though the trade valuation and premiums realised by banks from PSLCs have been rising since their introduction, it is questionable whether this increase has translated into an increase in the underlying volume of loans to priority sectors (RBI 2018a).

[25] This target was placed at eight per cent, to be achieved in a phased manner and applicable to domestic banks by 2017 and foreign banks with 20 branches or more from 2018 (see "Master Circular on Priority Sector Lending Targets and Classification," July 1, 2015, available at https://m.rbi.org.in/Scripts/BS_ViewMasCirculardetails.aspx?id=9857, viewed on May 22, 2020.

[26] See "Priority Sector Lending – Targets and Definitions," April 23, 2015, available at https://rbi.org.in/scripts/NotificationUser.aspx?Id=9688, viewed on May 22, 2020.

[27] Ibid.

[28] It was also preserved to ensure the growth in agricultural production (RBI 2004). Furthermore, the distinction between direct and indirect credit may also be necessary in the interest of financial inclusion. Unlike institutions/corporates, who may enjoy other sources of funds, farmers without bank credit may find themselves financially excluded and left at the disposal of informal sources.

[29] See "Priority Sector Lending – Targets and Classification," July 16, 2015, available at https://www.rbi.org.in/Scripts/NotificationUser.aspx?Id=9948&Mode=0, viewed on May 22, 2020.

credit redistribution and profitability. This is the hallmark of the financial inclusion policy in the period of financial liberalisation.

PSL policy for RRBs has been liberalised to a much greater extent than commercial banks in recent decades. The changes for RRBs relate not only to redefining priority sectors on similar lines as commercial banks but also have entailed lowering PSL targets over time.[30]

Interest Rate Policy

Interest rate policy was another regulatory control used by RBI after bank nationalisation for ensuring redistribution of bank credit at regulated rates of interest to priority sectors. The Differential Rate of Interest scheme was also notified to provide loans for production-related activities to economically weaker sections at rates lower than the commercial rates.

There has been a gradual deregulation of both deposit and lending rates of commercial banks since the early 1990s, whereby banks received complete functional freedom in pricing their products.[31] At present, the only exceptions within priority sectors wherein interest rate subventions are offered are the following: (a) direct agricultural credit up to Rs 0.3 million and (b) loans given to SHGs up to Rs 0.3 million, which are included as part of loans to "weaker sections" under PSL. While the interest rate subvention on agricultural loans was introduced in 2006–07 to direct credit to farmers at regulated rates of interest, the subvention for SHGs was introduced in 2013–14 to benefit women belonging to economically weaker sections from the backward districts in the country.[32]

---

[30] The PSL target of RRBs was reduced from 100 per cent (i.e., lending *only* to PSL sections) to 40 per cent in 1997, and subsequently raised to 60 per cent in 2002 and 75 per cent in 2015. See "Priority Sector Lending- Targets and Classification," December 3, 2015, available at https://www.rbi.org.in/Scripts/NotificationUser.aspx?Id=10155&Mode=0, viewed on May 22, 2020.

[31] See RBI (2008) for a discussion on the liberalisation of deposits rates and Mohanty (2010) for the chronology of interest rate liberalisation.

[32] The scheme for direct agricultural credit provides further rebate to farmers who repay on time. See "Interest Subvention Scheme for Short-Term Crop Loans During the Year 2017–18," August 16, 2017, available at https://rbi.org.in/Scripts/NotificationUser.aspx?Id=11098&Mode=0, viewed on May 22, 2020. As for the second scheme, women SHGs in rural areas are provided bank credit at 7 per cent per annum. Moreover, for a select set of backward districts, women SHGs were eligible to get a further rebate of 3 per cent on prompt repayment, bringing down the effective interest rate to 4 per cent. See "Deendayal Antyodaya Yojana–National Rural Livelihoods Mission (DAY-NRLM)–Aajeevika–Interest Subvention Scheme," October 18, 2017, available at https://rbi/org.in/Scripts/NotificationUser.aspx?Id=11150&Mode=0, viewed on May 22, 2020.

Similar to commercial banks, there has been liberalisation of the interest rate policy for RRBs as well.[33] Furthermore, SCBs and DCCBs too have been given freedom to determine their lending rates subject to a floor of 12 per cent per annum (NAFSCOB 2014). Direct agricultural credit and credit to women SHGs are the only two sectors where, similar to commercial banks, interest rate subventions are applicable to RRBs, SCBs and DCCBs.[34]

Thus, apart from the definitional changes in priority sectors, the rates of interest on priority sector loans were also liberalised ending preferential treatment to these loans in terms of pricing. It reaffirmed the concept of commercially viable financial inclusion in a liberalised set up.

New Policy Initiatives

Thrust on non-branch means of banking

Another important development during the phase of financial inclusion has been the increasing thrust on non-branch means of banking. The non-branch means include off-site Automated Teller Machines (ATMs), mobile vans, and business correspondents (BCs) equipped with hand-held devices to offer banking services to remote rural areas (Chavan 2017b). Over time, the list of BCs has been widened to include both not-for-profit and for-profit entities (including telecom companies and non-deposit taking NBFCs), and BCs have, in fact, emerged as the most important non-branch means of banking in recent years.

Since 2010, financial inclusion objectives are being formalised in the form of three-yearly Financial Inclusion Plans (FIPs) by banks. An analysis of the progress achieved under the FIPs suggest that banks have been more than successful in meeting targets for serving unbanked villages. It also shows that BCs have been responsible for covering the largest number of unbanked villages (RBI 2018a).

---

[33] See "Priority Sector Lending- Targets and Classification" dated December 3, 2015, available at https://www.rbi.org.in/Scripts/NotificationUser.aspx?Id=10155&Mode=0, viewed on May 22, 2020.

[34] For the applicability of interest rate subvention for short-term agricultural credit to RRBs and credit cooperatives, see "Cabinet Approves Interest Subvention to Banks on Short-Term Crop Loan to Farmers," June 14, 2017, available at http://pib.nic.in/newsite/PrintRelease.aspx?relid=165625, viewed on May 22, 2020. For subvention to women SHGs, see "NRLM/NULM (Deendayal Antyodaya Yojana)," available at https://www.nabard.org/content.aspx?id=582, viewed on May 22, 2020.

BCs act as retail agents of a bank.[35] Their assigned functions clearly suggest that they must be in close proximity and have connectivity to the nearby branch of the bank they represent.[36] However, in 2017, RBI modified branch authorisation policy and coined a new definition of a fixed point "banking outlet" providing delivery of banking services for a minimum of four hours per day and for at least five days a week operated by a BC or bank staff.[37] Banks are now governed by the new definition of "banking outlets" to meet their targets set under the FIPs. In particular, this definition is applicable to the previously mentioned condition of opening at least 25 per cent of new branches (now, banking outlets) in a year in unbanked rural centres.[38] It is expected that replacing a (brick and mortar) branch by a fixed-point banking outlet with limited business hours would reduce the costs of financial inclusion for banks.

Evidently, given that a bank branch would now be replaced by a banking outlet, BCs would be treated not as agents but as part of the banking staff. This change in the treatment of BCs enhances the need to (a) urgently address the concerns about BCs with regard to their mobile/telecom connectivity and safety (Bansal and Srinivasan 2009; Kishore 2012), and (b) ensure adequate remuneration to these entities so that they are viable and can sustain the delivery of banking services in their areas of operation.

It is early to comment on the outcomes of the recent change in using banking outlets instead of branches to meet various financial inclusion targets. However, key questions that beg answers are as follows. (a) Is there a need for such a change in policy at a time when banks have been successful in meeting financial inclusion targets with regard to branch

[35] They perform various functions such as identification of borrowers, collection, and preliminary processing of loan applications, submission of applications to banks, follow-up for recovery, disbursal of small value credit, recovery of principal/collection of interest, and collection of small-value deposits, apart from promotional functions like creating financial awareness and education, and promoting and monitoring SHGs/joint liability groups (JLGs) (RBI 2010).

[36] Hence, RBI laid down distance criteria for BCs and base branches for various centres. See "Financial Inclusion by Extension of Banking Services - Use of Business Correspondents," June 24, 2014, available at https://www.rbi.org.in/scripts/BS_CircularIndexDisplay.aspx?Id=8955, viewed on May 22, 2020.

[37] See "Rationalisation of Branch Authorisation Policy – Revision of Guidelines," May 18 2017, available at https://www.rbidocs.rbi.org.in/rdocs/notification/PDFs/NOTI3062319C9C94C33494794C2B5271CF92878.PD, viewed on May 22, 2020.

[38] In the process, the other restriction of the number of newly opened banking outlets in the urban/metropolitan centres not exceeding the banking outlets in non-urban/metropolitan centres in a year has been removed.

expansion in rural areas (either through brick and mortar branches or BCs connected to such branches)? (b) At a time when banks provide round-the-clock banking facilities in a cost-efficient manner through mobile/internet banking in urban areas, is limiting the business hours in un/under-banked rural areas justified on grounds of equity and cost cross-subsidisation? Evidently, the recent change is also aimed at facilitating commercially viable financial inclusion.

Greater thrust on deposit mobilisation than credit provision
Financial inclusion is expected to provide a bouquet of financial services, including deposit, payments/remittances, credit, and insurance to under-served sections (Chakrabarty 2013). Of these services, the thrust on providing deposit, and possibly payment/remittance services, has till now been much greater than the provision of credit.

Consequently, through the FIPs implemented by banks since 2010, which were later aligned with the objectives of the Pradhan Mantri Jan-Dhan Yojana (PMJDY) introduced in 2015, there has been a direct push to open deposit accounts in rural areas. Thus, in addition to the number of newly banked villages, another metric used to judge the progress of the FIPs and PMJDY is the number of newly opened basic savings bank deposit accounts (BSBDA) (earlier called no-frill accounts). As per this metric, there has been a striking increase in the number of newly opened BSBDA since 2010 (RBI 2018a).[39]

For encouraging retail payments/remittances, initially, banks introduced the National Electronic Fund Transfer (NEFT) and Immediate Payment Switch (IMPS) and, the more recent Unified Payment Interface (UPI) application (RBI 2017b).[40] The RuPay debit cards launched by banks is also a means to encourage retail digital payments as part of the PMJDY. There has been a striking growth in the usage of UPI and issuance of the RuPay debit cards in recent years.[41]

---

[39] At the end of March 2018, banks opened 536 million BSBDAs through branch and non-branch means (*ibid.*). However, there was a simultaneous rise in the percentage of population with inactive accounts (Chavan 2020). In 2017, about 48 per cent of the adult Indian population had inactive accounts.

[40] Various non-bank players, including prepaid payment instruments providers, are also active in the retail electronic payments' field through mobile and e-wallets (*ibid.*).

[41] About 246 million RuPay debit cards have been issued as part of PMJDY till September 2018; see "Progress Report Pradhan Mantri Jan-Dhan Yojana," April 15, 2020, available at https://www.pmjdy.gov.in/, viewed on May 22, 2020.

By contrast, under the FIPs as well as the PMJDY, the only credit-related initiative has been a small overdraft facility of Rs 5,000 per account (increased to Rs 10,000 in 2018).[42] Given that the overdraft is a small amount subject to fairly stringent conditions, the progress under this facility has been slower than the other performance metrics for financial inclusion discussed earlier (RBI 2018a).[43] Evidently therefore, rural credit initiatives have not garnered as much importance as rural deposits in the official discussion on financial inclusion till now.[44]

The thrust on rural deposits can be justified as a way of formalising the unbanked population by first inculcating a basic saving habit in them and providing credit only in the second stage. Though this may be true, the mobilisation of rural deposits also makes greater commercial sense for banks than rural credit in the pursuit of financial inclusion in a liberalised set up. First, retail deposits are a cheaper and more stable source of funding than wholesale deposits. As part of financial inclusion, banks are, in fact, encouraged to mobilise these deposits from the point of view of both costs and stability (Khan 2011). Second, as against the benefits from mobilising retail deposits, small-sized credit of any form, apart from the usual credit risks, also imposes higher transaction costs (of screening, monitoring and enforcement) on banks.

Creation of new differentiated financial institutions
The recent decades have seen the creation of new types of differentiated financial institutions for financial inclusion, including MFIs, small finance

---

[42] Upon the successful operation of the BSBDA for at least six months, the overdraft is granted. It carries an interest rate not exceeding two per cent above the base rate of a bank; see "Pradhan Mantri Jan-Dhan Yojana Overdraft up to Rs 5,000/- in PMJDY Accounts," available at https://www.pmjdy.gov.in/files/QuickLinks/Overdraft-facility.pdf, viewed on May 22, 2020.

[43] The other metric of monitoring progress in rural credit under the FIPs has been the number of Kisan Credit Cards (KCCs) and amount of credit given against these cards. However, two points about KCCs need to be noted: First, the KCC scheme has been in existence since 1998 and is not strictly a product of the financial inclusion policy. However, RBI revised it as part of its financial inclusion efforts (see "Revised Kisan Credit Card Scheme" on May 11, 2012, available at https://rbidocs.rbi.org.in/rdocs/notification/PDFs/CRB5100512KC.pdf viewed on May 22, 2020. Second, KCCs by themselves do not ensure greater access to or increase in the flow of agricultural credit. These cards provide a single-window facility to cultivators to increase the pace of dissemination of agricultural credit.

[44] See Sriram (2018) who also highlighted the emphasis on deposit mobilisation under financial inclusion. He suggests that this stands in contrast to the credit-centric approach taken after bank nationalisation.

banks (SFBs), and payments banks. MFIs entered the rural credit space in the early 1990s. The original approach was to not formally regulate their operations in order to encourage them to grow freely and flexibly.[45] Originally, SHGs promoted and financed by banks (under the SHG-BLP) was the fastest growing model of microfinance in India (RBI 2008).[46] In WB, PACSs were also encouraged to register SHGs as members, thereby symbolising a model linking credit cooperatives with SHGs.[47]

Over time, the Bank-MFI linkage model gathered considerable momentum. As the size of the MFIs grew, their demand for borrowed resources increased, as they could not mobilise deposits like banks. Consequently, their reliance on private equity investments increased and a few even raised capital through public issuances of shares. There was pressure on these institutions to post higher returns on equity to be an attractive investment proposition for private investors. A higher return implied higher interest rates and low default rates. As a result, the rates of interest charged by most MFIs were higher than the comparable commercial bank rates. Also, some MFIs resorted to coercive recovery practices to ensure low defaults (Ramakumar 2010).

The onerous practices of the MFIs came under severe criticism follow-ing reports of suicides by female borrowers in Andhra Pradesh (*ibid.*). This resulted in a change in the approach towards MFI-led microfinance from a self-regulated to a (partially) regulated one. Following the recommendations of the sub-committee constituted by RBI to study issues and concerns in the microfinance sector, a new category of NBFC-MFIs was created, and most large companies (other than Section 25 companies) active in the field of microfinance were placed under stricter RBI control.[48]

[45] The task force set up by NABARD to look into the issues of regulation and supervision of MFIs had observed that "in view of the changing environment in the financial sector of the country towards decentralisation and privatisation, [the task force] strongly feels that self-regulation would be a more appropriate mode for the microfinance sector" (NABARD 1999, p. 4). Hence, MFIs followed a voluntary code of conduct broadly on governance, transparency, handling of customer grievances, staff conduct and recovery practices; see "Core Values and Voluntary Mutual Code of Conduct for Micro Finance Institutions," available at http://www. bfil.co.in/wp-content/themes/sks/public/downloads/sa_dhan_core_values.pdf, viewed on May 22, 2020.

[46] The involvement of commercial banks distinguished the Indian model of microfinance from the NGO-based model of microfinance in Bangladesh spearheaded by Grameen Bank.

[47] See "Self Help Groups," available at http://coopwb.in/shg.html, viewed on May 22, 2020.

[48] This category of companies was based on a set of conditions, including the extent of exposure of these institutions to microfinance (defined as the provision of small-value loans to

Various regulatory controls, including caps on the annual margin and interest rates, were imposed on NBFC-MFIs to be eligible for priority sector credit from banks.[49]

The interest rate controls marked a clear deviation from the basic principle of market-determined interest rates under liberalisation. Notwithstanding these controls, NBFC-MFIs charged interest rates that were significantly higher than those charged by formal sources, as also shown through the village studies discussed in this chapter. Moreover, over time, the interest rate controls on the NBFC-MFIs have been relaxed, giving them more freedom to determine rates based on their costs of funds.[50]

SFBs and payments banks were introduced in 2015 and 2016, respectively. SFBs provide small-sized deposit and credit facilities, whereas payments banks provide only small-sized deposit and payment facilities. Given that SFBs and payments banks have been introduced only recently, it is early to comment on their performance.

The private sector character of SFBs, payments banks, and MFIs – the new-generation-differentiated institutions – separates them from RRBs, the old-generation-differentiated public sector institutions created for extending credit to the financially excluded or under-served sections. These new-generation-differentiated institutions are essentially products of financial liberalisation and have been created for the pursuit of financial inclusion in a commercially viable manner.

Rural Credit in West Bengal: Some Insights from the Literature since the 1970s

Common observations that emerge from studies on rural credit in WB since the 1970s are summarised in this section.

---

pre-dominantly low-income borrowers on an unsecured basis mainly for income-generating activities) (RBI 2011).

[49] See "Bank Loans to MFIs- Priority Sector Status," May 3, 2011, available at https://www.rbi. org.in/scripts/NotificationUser.aspx?Id=6381&Mode=0, viewed on May 22, 2020.

[50] Against the cap of 26 per cent on individual loans, interest rates charged by NBFC-MFIs were to be the lower of (a) the cost of funds plus a capped margin and (b) the average base rate of the five largest commercial banks by assets and multiplied by 2.75, see "Master Circular- 'Non-Banking Financial Company-Microfinance Institutions' (NBFC-MFIs) – Directions," July 1, 2015, available at https://www.rbi.org.in/scripts/BS_ViewMasCirculardetails.aspx?id=9827, viewed on May 22, 2020.

An Underdeveloped Formal System of Rural Credit

Systematic village studies covering issues on rural credit have been limited in the case of WB, as already noted. However, the available evidence from various parts of the State unequivocally indicates the underdeveloped character of the rural credit system (Bhattacharyya 1996; Bhaumik and Rahim 1998 cited in Rawal 2006; Rawal 2005 and 2006).[51]

Studies have noted a distinct expansion in bank branches and supply of bank credit in rural WB following bank nationalisation (Rawal 2005). Even though this closed the gap between WB and India to a considerable extent in the 1970s and 1980s, the State still performed poorly with respect to the national averages related to banking development. Notably however, formal credit at the State level was more equally distributed than at the national level (Bhattacharyya 1996). Studies have highlighted the role of panchayats in improved targeting of formal credit under the Integrated Rural Development Programme (IRDP) and access of small and marginal farmers to formal credit in the 1980s (Swaminathan 1990; Rawal 2005; Bardhan and Mookherjee 2006).[52]

The decline in formal credit in WB in the 1990s and early 2000s has also been discussed (Rawal 2005; 2006). The decline was evident from a fall in the number of rural branches, growth in rural credit and share of agricultural credit in total bank credit. The decline caused the State to fall further down the national scale in terms of banking development.

Shift from Landlords to Traders as Sources of Informal Credit

Studies have noted the existence of professional/agriculturist moneylenders and landlords as key sources of rural credit in WB in the 1970s (Rudra 1975). Landlords mainly catered to the consumption-related needs of tenant cultivators and agricultural labourers. Following land reforms in the State, the hold of moneylenders and landlords over the rural credit system weakened considerably (Bhattacharyya 1996; Rawal 2006). Bhattacharyya (1996) using the AIDIS data argued that the decline in moneylending in WB villages in the 1970s was far greater than that at the all-India level, underlining the "institutionalisation" of the rural credit market in the State (p. 181).

---

[51] For a detailed review of the literature on rural credit in WB, see Rawal (2006).

[52] The IRDP was introduced in 1980 as a nation-wide credit-based rural poverty alleviation programme. It was later integrated as part of the Swarnajayanti Gram Swarozgar Yojana.

During the phase of high growth in agricultural production in the 1980s, the State witnessed the rise of agricultural traders as sources of credit (Bhaumik and Rahim 1998 cited in Rawal 2006; Rajeev and Deb 1998). The rise of traders was seen as a fallout of the growing demand for agricultural credit during the high growth phase apart from being associated with the decline of landlords (Rajeev and Deb 1998).

High Interest Rates and Oppressive Practices of Informal Credit

Most studies on rural credit in the pre-land reforms period highlighted the prevalence of high interest rates and other oppressive practices of informal credit in WB. Bhaduri (1973) used examples of exploitative credit relations between landlord and tenant cultivator from WB to theorise the backwardness of agriculture under semi-feudalism. Apart from traditional property rights, the landlord derived income also from usury and prevented any agricultural investment to perpetuate indebtedness of the tenant. Rudra (1975), although countering Bhaduri's claims about agricultural backwardness, provided several illustrations of oppressive, inter-linked credit relations and high rates of interest from the WB villages he visited.[53]

The rise of traders as sources of credit allowed for the perpetuation of personalised and interlinked credit relations, but the nature and, possibly, degree of oppression through credit relations changed in rural WB. According to Rawal (2005), traders' credit filled the gap in the supply of formal credit and helped in the growth of agriculture in the post-land-reform period. Rawal also noted that traders in Panahar village – one of the villages studied in this chapter as well – used inter-linked credit relations mainly for promoting their trading businesses, and cases of overpricing inputs given on credit were rare. There were also very few cases of output traders exacting an implicit interest through such credit relations.

---

[53] Credit transactions included credit taken in crop and repaid in crop, cash credit repaid in crop, commodity repaid in crop, and crop repaid in labour. Apart from explicit references to rates being in the range of 10–20 per cent per month (120 to 240 per cent per annum), there were indications that the rates were onerous due to under-pricing crop produce and labour services (services performed at wages lower than the market rates).

Major Features of Contemporary Rural Credit in West Bengal

This section covers the major features of contemporary rural credit in WB based on nation-wide household-level surveys and data on commercial banks, RRBs and credit cooperatives.[54]

Features Emanating from the Debt Profiles of Rural Households

Weakened role of formal sources in rural credit

The household-level data from the AIDIS show a weakening of the formal sources *vis-à-vis* the informal sources in rural WB. The share of formal sources in the total debt of rural households in WB came down from about 82 per cent in 1991 to about 45 per cent in 2012 (Table 1). Though the trend was similar for most States, the decline in the share of formal sources in WB was one of the steepest (Figure 1). Although studies have noted this decline in WB in the 1990s (see previous section), it is noteworthy that the decline has persisted even in the later decades despite emphasis on financial inclusion.

As a result of the fall in the share of formal sources, formal sources contributed much less to rural credit than the informal sources in WB in 2012 (Table 1). The major informal sources of rural credit were moneylenders, and relatives and friends. Relatives and friends are generally ubiquitous and innocuous sources of credit involving no interest cost and have been a common feature of the rural credit system in WB (Bhattacharyya 1996). By contrast, moneylenders – both professional and agriculturist – whose presence declined during the 1970s and 1980s (see previous section), showed a striking rise in the subsequent decades. Interestingly, traders did not appear to be an important source of rural credit from the AIDIS data.

Using the basic indicators of extent and incidence of formal debt (average

---

[54] This section contains an analysis of commercial banks (including RRBs) using data from *BSR*. With regards to credit cooperatives, there are general concerns about the timely availability of data, particularly on PACSs (Chavan 2017a). In fact, the National Federation of State Cooperative Banks Ltd. (NAFSCOB), the only source providing updated information on PACSs, has repeated data on credit disbursed by PACSs between 2013 and 2015 for WB (see www.NAFSCOB.org). In light of the delayed availability of data, we can only draw limited inferences on the operation of credit cooperatives in the State, as has been attempted in the chapter. Finally, with regards to microfinance, particularly SHGs linked to NBFC-MFIs/other MFIs, the publicly available information is only at the national level (MFIN 2018). Hence, the chapter does not provide any State-level analysis on microfinance.

Table 1 *Share of debt outstanding of rural households, by source, WB and India, 1991–2012 and 2015–16, in per cent*

Source	1991		2002		2012		2015–16*	
	WB	India	WB	India	WB	India	WB	India
1 Formal sources	81.5	64.0	67.5	57.1	45.3	53.6	39.1	57.3
1.1 Government	11.8	6.1	11.9	2.3	3.7	1.2	–	–
1.2 Cooperative societies/ banks	20.1	21.6	14.0	27.3	14.2	24.8	3.5	6.3
1.3 Commercial banks including RRBs	41.5	33.7	35.6	24.5	20.7	25.1	26.4	46.1
1.4 Other formal sources	8.2	2.6	6.0	3.0	6.6	2.5	9.3	4.8
2 Informal sources	18.5	36.0	32.5	42.9	54.7	46.4	60.9	42.7
2.1 Landlords	0.1	4.0	0.4	1.0	–	0.7	0.1	3.4
2.2 Moneylenders	5.9	17.6	12.9	29.6	28.7	33.2	12.2	10.8
2.3 Traders	1.4	2.5	2.9	2.6	0.1	0.1	–	0.1
2.4 Relatives and friends	8.6	5.5	14.2	7.1	16.9	8.0	14.7	15.9
2.5 SHGs	–	–	–	–	5.4	2.2	33.8	11.2
2.5.1 SHGs linked to NBFC-MFIs	–	–	–	–	2.1	0.3	23.6	5.9
2.5.2 SHGs linked to banks	–	–	–	–	3.3	1.9	10.1	5.3
2.6 Others	2.0	3.2	2.0	2.3	3.6	1.9	–	0.03
2.7 Unspecified	0.3	3.2	–	–	–	–	–	–
3 All sources	100.0	100.0	100.0	100.0	100.0	100.0	100.0	100.0

Notes: – Not available.
* Data relate to amount borrowed during 2015–16 by all rural households extracted from the NAFIS database.
Source: NSSO (1998, 2005, 2016).

amount of debt per household from formal sources and percentage of households reporting at least one loan from formal sources, respectively), the contemporary formal system of rural credit in WB seemed far more underdeveloped than in most other States in India. In terms of the average amount of debt outstanding from commercial banks (including RRBs) and credit cooperatives, two key formal sources of rural credit, WB was lower than the national average in 2012 (Figure 2). There was a wide gap between WB and Kerala and Maharashtra, where the formal sector was reasonably well established. The picture was almost similar for the incidence of debt from commercial banks and credit cooperatives (Figure 3).

Figure 1 *Difference in the share of formal sector in total debt outstanding of rural households between 1991 and 2012, Indian States,* in percentage points

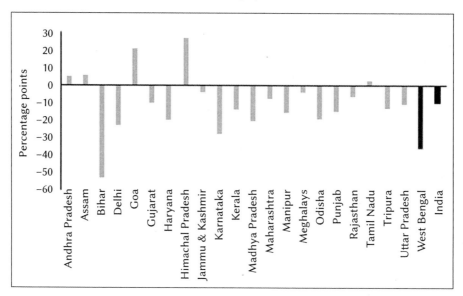

Source: NSSO (1998, 2016).

The data from the NAFIS for 2015–16 also underlined the underdeveloped formal credit system in rural WB (Table 1). Formal sources accounted for about 39 per cent of the total borrowings of rural households in WB as compared to about 57 per cent at the all-India level.[55]

Retreat of commercial banks from rural credit
The decline in the share of formal sources in the State between 1991 and 2012 was attributable to commercial banks; the share of commercial banks almost halved during this period (Table 1). Furthermore, the marginal

---

[55] The share of 57 per cent of formal sources at the all-India level is lower than the share of 69 per cent reported in NABARD (2018). The difference arises on account of the inclusion of SHGs as an informal source in this chapter, while they have been considered as a formal source in NABARD (2018). Any direct comparison of the AIDIS with the NAFIS is not feasible due to the differences in survey design and definitions of sources, as already noted. Moreover, data from the AIDIS relate to debt outstanding whereas that from the NAFIS relate to yearly borrowings. There has been a critique of the NAFIS with regard to the survey outcomes on income, savings, and investments (Swaminathan 2018). Hence, the NAFIS is used here to only provide a more recent comparison of WB with the all-India figures.

Figure 2 *Average debt per household from formal sources, Indian States, 2012,* in Rs

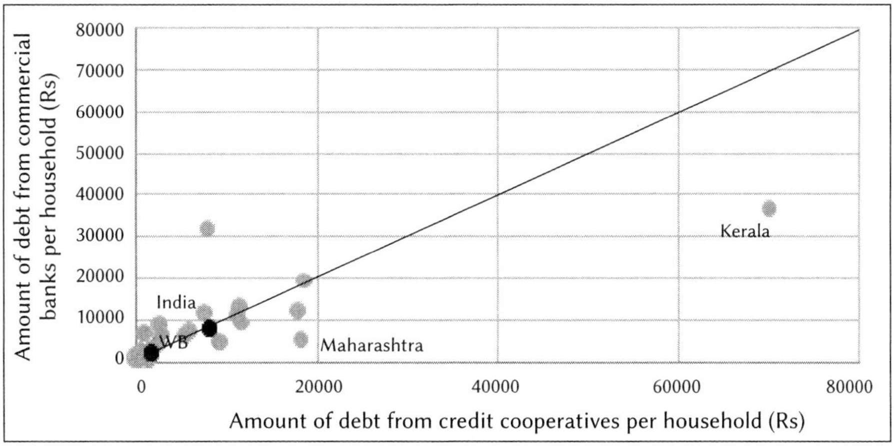

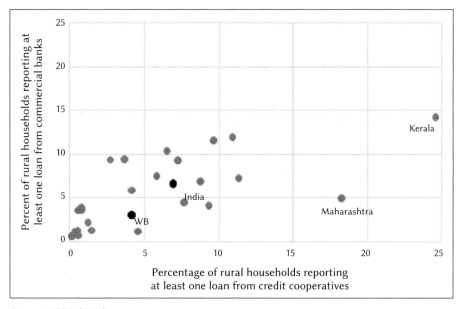

Source: NSSO (2016).

Figure 3 *Percentage of rural households reporting at least one loan from commercial banks/ credit cooperatives, Indian States, 2012,* in per cent

Source: NSSO (2016).

recovery in the share of commercial banks seen at the national level between 2002 and 2012 could not be seen at the State level. Thus, the retreat of commercial banks from the rural credit space during the phase of financial liberalisation, as noted earlier, was more striking for WB than the rest of India. As will be discussed later, there has been some revival in the intensity of bank branches after 2005 as a result of financial inclusion. However, a comparison of the AIDIS rounds of 1991 and 2012 suggests a distinct decline in the share of debt owed to commercial banks by rural households in the State.

Microfinance: an emerging source of rural credit
Microfinance – loans by SHGs linked to NBFCs, MFIs, and banks – accounted for about 5 per cent of the total debt outstanding of rural households in WB in 2012 (Table 1).[56] Data from NAFIS showed an even higher share of

Figure 4 *Average amount of debt per rural household from formal sources and microfinance, Indian States, 2012,* in Rs

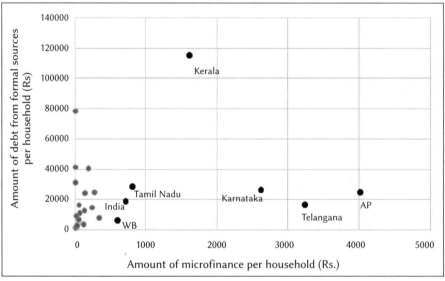

Source: NSSO (2016).

[56] While the AIDIS does not make a distinction between NBFC-MFIs and other MFIs (including NGOs and not-for- profit companies), it can be assumed that SHGs linked to NBFCs include not just SHGs linked NBFC-MFIs but also other MFIs.

microfinance of about 34 per cent in total borrowings of rural households in WB in 2015–16. A broad comparison of the NAFIS with the AIDIS bears out the striking proliferation of microfinance in rural WB in recent years. Furthermore, the NAFIS also indicates the stronghold of NBFC-MFIs over the microfinance sector in rural WB as compared to banks.

The quantum of microfinance per household, as per the AIDIS, was higher in WB than in most other States, although it ranked below the Southern States of Andhra Pradesh, Telangana, Kerala, Karnataka and Tamil Nadu, where microfinance has been a well-established source of rural credit (Figure 4).

Features Emanating from Banking and Cooperative Data

Revival in the intensity of rural bank branches

Although there was a fall in the proportion of banks in the total debt of rural households in WB between 1991 and 2012 as seen from the AIDIS, there have been distinct signs of a revival in the rural bank branch network in the State in recent years. This is evident from a steady decline in the intensity of rural bank branches (defined as the rural population per rural bank branch of commercial banks including RRBs) from 2006 onwards (Figure 5).[57] The rural population per bank branch declined over a decade from 21,600 persons in 2006 to 14,800 persons in 2016. The trend for WB was closely comparable with the all-India trend, although the branch intensity for the State remained distinctly lower than the rest of India. In 2016, there were 14,800 persons per bank branch in rural WB as compared to 10,300 persons in rural India as a whole.[58]

Growing mismatch between credit to and deposits from rural areas

Although there has been a striking revival in the bank branch intensity in rural areas, bank credit received by an average person from rural WB

---

[57] Given the difference in the definition of "rural" branches in the *BSR* (serving centres with a population of less than 10,000) and "rural" areas in the Census of India, a direct comparison of rural branches with rural areas is not recommended (Ramakumar and Chavan 2011). Hence, rural branches in this chapter are defined as "rural" plus "semi-urban" branches (branches serving rural and semi-urban centres), whereas urban branches are defined as "urban" and "metropolitan" branches (branches serving urban and metropolitan centres) as given in the *BSR*.
[58] As already discussed, there has been an emphasis on non-branch means of banking in the period of financial inclusion. However, it is hard to capture their growth in WB in the absence of any State-level data on such means.

Figure 5 *Rural population per rural branch, WB and India, 1975 to 2016,* in thousands

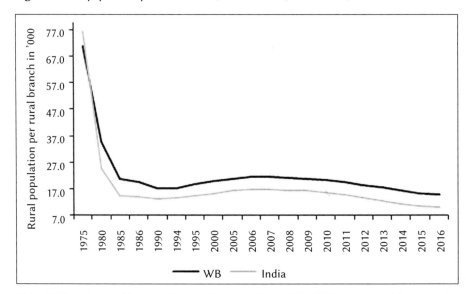

Notes: (i) There is a problem in a time-series comparison of the *BSR* data on bank branches by population groups, namely "rural", "semi-urban", "urban", and "metropolitan". This is because centres and branches serving these centres tend to shift upward on account of an increase in the size of their population, whenever the data from the new population Census are applied for classification of centres/branches in the *BSR* (Ramakumar and Chavan 2011). The *BSR* followed the Census of India of 1971 for the classification of centres up to its publication of 1985. The classification was based on the Census of 1981 between 1986 and 1994; the Census of 1991 between 1995 and 2005; and the Census of 2001 from 2006 onwards. This figure shows only end-points of comparable periods till 2005. After 2005, the data are comparable till 2016, and have been reported on an annual basis to bring out the recent trends in greater detail.
(ii) Rural refers to the total of "rural" and "semi-urban" branches in the *BSR*.
Source: RBI (various issues).

remains much lower than the deposits contributed by her to the banking system. Moreover, this mismatch between rural credit and rural deposits has been growing over time (Table 2). In 2016, the ratio of credit to deposits was only about 28 per cent in WB; the ratio at the all-India level was 61 per cent and has been on a rising trend in recent years.

Another way of bringing out the poor allocation of bank credit to rural areas is to compare the ratio of rural to urban credit with the ratio of rural to urban deposits. In 2016, an average person in rural WB received only about 8 per cent of the credit received by an average person from urban areas of the State. Compared to this, an average person from rural

Table 2 *Ratio of rural credit per capita to rural deposits per capita, WB and India, 1975 to 2016,* in per cent

Year	WB	India	Year	WB	India
1975	20.4	49.8	2007	36.8	56.2
1980	26.2	49.7	2008	36.7	56.2
1985	32.2	60.7	2009	33.2	52.9
1986	31.4	31.5	2010	32.4	55.0
1990	41.0	54.2	2011	33.0	56.0
1994	32.3	43.8	2012	32.1	59.4
1995	33.2	43.5	2013	33.4	61.4
2000	21.4	37.1	2014	28.6	61.6
2005	28.9	47.3	2015	25.6	60.8
2006	35.9	52.5	2016	27.9	61.4

Notes: (i) The separation of years indicates years that are comparable with each other after accounting for changes in definition of "rural", "semi-urban", and "urban" and "metropolitan" branches in the *BSR*. See note (i) of Figure 5. (ii) Rural refers to total "rural" and "semi-urban" branches, and urban refers to total "urban" and "metropolitan" branches as reported in the *BSR*. *Source*: RBI (various issues); www.census.gov.in.

Figure 6 *Ratio of rural credit/deposits per capita to urban credit/deposits per capita, WB, 1975–2016,* in per cent

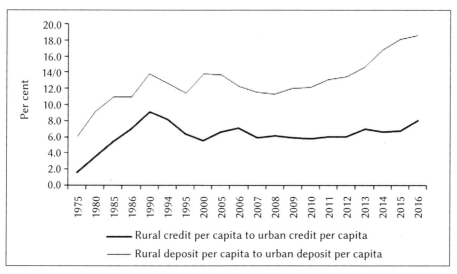

Note: See Figure 5 for notes.
Source: RBI (various issues).

WB contributed about 19 per cent of the deposits mobilised from urban areas of the State (Figure 6). The gap between the two ratios widened with a spurt in the relative contribution of rural areas to bank deposits as compared to their relative share in bank credit. This once again underlines the rural–urban divide in banking in the State, which has been a common feature of banking in India (Chavan 2017b).

Weakened link between agricultural credit and rural areas

Agricultural credit has been an integral part of rural credit in India. However, as discussed earlier, since the early-1990s, the character of agricultural credit has changed considerably weakening the link between agricultural credit and rural areas. WB too witnessed a sharp decline in the allocation of agricultural credit, particularly direct agricultural credit, to its rural areas during the 2000s. By 2012, rural areas accounted for less than half of the total/direct agricultural credit in WB; the remaining was accounted for by urban areas (Figures 7 and 8).

Notably, the disconnect between agricultural credit and rural areas

Figure 7 *Share of rural branches in total agricultural credit, WB, India and Kolkata, 1990–2016,* in per cent

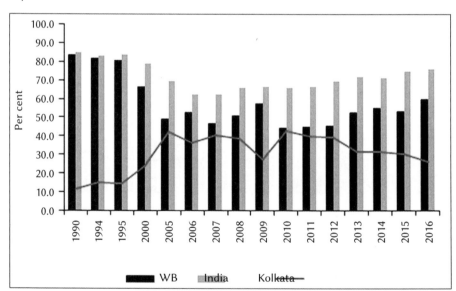

Notes: See Figure 5 notes.
Source: RBI (various issues).

widened during the period of high growth in agricultural credit in the State. The 2000s, particularly the period between 2000 and 2005, was a phase of very high growth in agricultural credit (and also direct agricultural credit) in WB (Table 3). This high growth in agricultural credit is likely to be attributed to the implementation of Comprehensive Credit Policy. As noted in a discussion on PSL policy in a previous section, there were several changes in the definition of agriculture under this policy, which partly facilitated the achievement of the growth targets set under Comprehensive Credit Policy for banks. However, these definitional changes also modified the character of agricultural credit in India. The shift of agricultural credit away from rural areas was one such change, and as suggested by the analysis presented in this chapter, this change was rather significant in WB in the 2000s.

After 2012, the trend has somewhat reversed with rural areas in the State regaining their share in total (and direct) agricultural credit. However, the share of rural areas in total (and direct) agricultural credit in WB continues to be much lower than at the all-India level. Agricultural

Figure 8 *Share of rural branches in direct agricultural credit, WB, India and Kolkata, 1990–2016, in per cent*

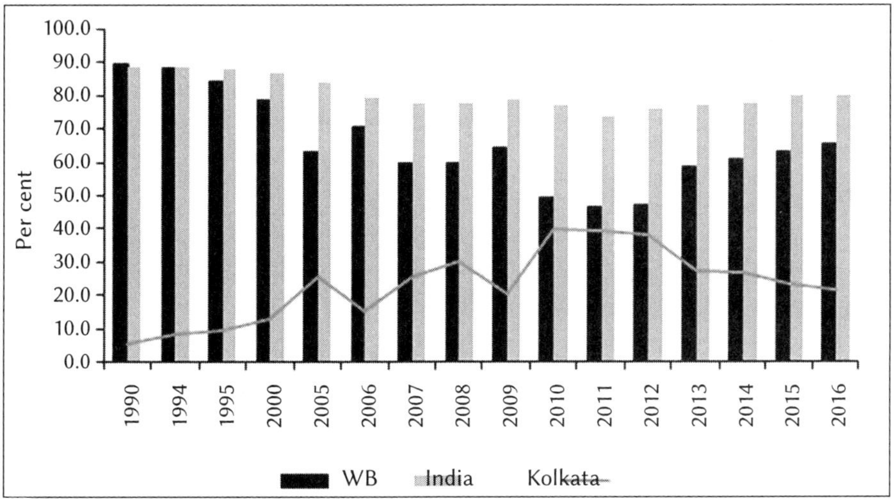

Note: See Figure 5 for notes.
Source: RBI (various issues).

Table 3 *Rate of growth of total and direct agricultural credit, WB, 1990–2015,* in per cent per annum

Category	1990–95	1995–2000	2000–05	2005–10	2010–15
Direct agricultural credit	16.2	−1.0	36.6	23.1	4.9
Total agricultural credit	15.7	−2.0	32.9	23.9	5.9

Notes: (i) Growth rates are worked out after deflating agricultural credit figures using the State net domestic product (SNDP) deflator.
(ii) The growth rates are worked out till 2015 as data on SNDP for the later years are not available.
Source: RBI (various issues), RBI (2018b).

credit in the State, therefore, remains more urban than in other parts of India (Figures 7 and 8).[59]

A related feature of the distribution of agricultural credit in WB has also been a high concentration of total and direct agricultural credit in Kolkata, a district with only "metropolitan" centres and branches, as per *BSR.* Interestingly, Kolkata accounted for about 26 per cent of the total agricultural credit in WB in 2016, and its share in direct agricultural credit was about 22 per cent (Figures 7 and 8). As there is little agricultural activity in Kolkata, its share was likely owing to corporate borrowers/institutions from the district who are engaged in production/post-production activities in agriculture and allied sectors. The concentration of agricultural credit in Kolkata is also evident from the district-level analysis of banking presented in the following sub-section.

Inter-district disparity in the distribution of bank credit
The district-wise distribution of banking is closely associated with the state of rural credit in WB. On the one hand, as discussed earlier, Kolkata is a district with only "metropolitan" branches as per the *BSR.* On the other hand, a majority of the remaining districts have only "rural" or "semi-urban" branches. Hence, the distribution of banking across districts offers another dimension of the rural–urban divide in the State.

Firstly, in terms of the intensity of bank branches (defined as total population per bank branch), the gap between Kolkata and the remaining districts is significantly wide. Of the 19 districts in the State, 16 had an intensity of bank branches equal to or lower than the State average in

[59] Also see Ramakumar and Chavan (2014) for a similar point about WB.

Table 4 *District-wise indicators of banking development, WB, 2013*

District	Total population per bank branch ('000)	Rural population per rural bank branch ('000)	Bank credit as % of bank deposits	Rural credit as % of rural deposits	Bank credit per capita as % of DNDP per capita	Total agricultural credit per capita as % of agricultural DNDP per capita
	(1)	(2)	(3)	(4)	(5)	(6)
Bankura	18	18	24	28	8 (6)	9 (7)
Birbhum	16	14	24	24	9 (7)	8 (7)
Barddhaman	14	14	32	26	17 (13)	19 (14)
Koch Bihar	20	18	47	47	11 (7)	8 (7)
Dakshin Dinajpur	21	23	48	72	11 (9)	7 (6)
Darjiling	11	15	49	25	26 (18)	11 (8)
Hugli	15	13	18	24	10 (7)	16 (12)
Haora	15	10	20	14	11 (8)	8 (6)
Jalpaiguri	21	19	36	41	10 (6)	7 (6)
Kolkata	3	–	94	–	478 (440)	3,884 (2,649)
Maldah	24	22	41	38	10 (8)	6 (5)
Purba Medinipur	20	19	32	31	7 (6)	9 (8)
Paschim Medinipur	17	18	35	47	14 (11)	17 (13)
Murshidabad	23	21	35	37	9 (7)	7 (6)
Nadia	20	17	31	34	12 (10)	11 (10)
Puruliya	23	23	41	49	14 (12)	20 (20)
Uttar Dinajpur	29	31	46	49	10 (8)	7 (5)
North 24-Parganas	15	18	25	31	23 (18)	16 (13)
South 24-Parganas	22	18	40	46	13 (10)	7 (6)
West Bengal	15	18	62	33	48 (42)	16 (13)
India	11	13	79	61	60 (51)	40 (35)

Notes: (i) Figures in brackets in column (5) indicate the ratio of total credit excluding retail loans per capita to DNDP per capita.
(ii) Figures in brackets in column (6) indicate the ratio of direct agricultural credit per capita to agricultural DNDP per capita.
Source: RBI (various issues); GoWB (2015).

2013 (Table 4).[60] Secondly, the disparity in banking among districts was also evident from the bank credit to district net domestic product (DNDP) ratio. For most districts in the State, the ratio was less than 20 per cent as compared to 478 per cent for Kolkata in 2013. In simple terms, only about one-fifth of the contribution to the State's domestic product by each of the districts other than Kolkata was financed by banks. For Kolkata, by contrast, credit from banks was more than four times the district's contribution to the State's domestic product.[61]

Thirdly, the credit to deposit ratio for all districts other than Kolkata was less than 50 per cent. This indicates that credit received by the districts was only up to half the deposits contributed by the districts. As already noted, most of the districts had primarily "rural" or "semi-urban" branches; this reaffirms the earlier point about a mismatch between the credit extended to rural areas and the deposits mobilised from these areas. Fourthly, Kolkata received agricultural credit to the tune of about 3,884 per cent of its contribution to the State's agricultural domestic product in 2013. Importantly, the ratio of even direct agricultural credit (going to direct producers in agriculture and allied activities) to agricultural product for Kolkata was as high as 2,649 per cent in 2013. This corroborates the earlier observation about the urban-centric nature of agricultural credit in WB.

The inter-district gap was relatively narrow in terms of the intensity of rural branches (rural population per rural bank branch) and the ratio of rural credit to deposits. This, however, is expected as Kolkata is dropped from the analysis because it does not have any rural branches.

The study districts of Bankura, Maldah, and Koch Bihar have a relatively underdeveloped banking system, as can be seen from all the indicators of banking development discussed here. However, among the three, branch intensity was the highest for Bankura, followed by Koch Bihar and Maldah in 2013. As is the case with most districts in WB, the branch network in the three study districts was primarily rural in nature in 2013.[62]

---

[60] The year 2013 has been purposively chosen for the inter-district comparison, as the latest data for DNDP for WB are available only for this year.

[61] Total bank credit also includes retail loans. Retail loans are meant for consumption and do not contribute directly to income generation. Even after excluding retail loans, the disparity amongst districts remained stark with Kolkata leading with a ratio of about 440 per cent of bank credit (excluding retail loans) to DNDP in 2013.

[62] In Koch Bihar, there were no "urban" or "metropolitan" branches as per the BSR. In Maldah and Bankura, there were "urban" branches but the proportion of such branches was less than 11 per cent in 2013.

Decline in cooperative credit

There has been a trend of decline in cooperative credit in WB in the recent decades, except for a spurt in the first half of the 2000s. Between 1995 and 2000, credit disbursed by PACSs (adjusted for inflation) posted a modest growth of about 3 per cent per annum (Table 5).[63] Cooperative credit in the State grew at a much higher rate of about 14 per cent between 2000 and 2005, which was likely attributable to Comprehensive Credit Policy discussed earlier. After 2005, cooperative credit in the State has shown an absolute fall.

Owing to the decline in credit, there has been a severe reduction in the size of cooperatives in WB after 2005. The average size of a cooperative society (defined as the amount of credit disbursed per PACS) was only about 12 per cent of the average size of a cooperative society at the all-India level in 2015, declining from 41 per cent in 2005 (Table 5). Here, PACSs were purposively chosen to represent cooperative credit, as they form the ground-level tier in the short-term structure of rural cooperatives. As already noted, the long-term structure, saddled with high NPAs, has been on a decline across India such that the present-day cooperative credit is almost equivalent to the credit provided by short-term cooperatives.

Table 5 *Rate of growth of credit from PACSs, WB, 1995–2015,* in per cent per annum

Category	1995–2000	2000–05	2005–10	2010–15
Credit growth	3.2	14.3	−1.2	−5.1
	(48.9)	(41.2)	(23.2)	(11.7)

Notes: (i) Growth rates are worked out after deflating credit figures using the State net domestic product (SNDP) deflator.
(ii) The growth rates are worked out till 2015 as data on SNDP for the later years are not available.
(iii) Given the repetition of data for the years between 2013 and 2015 by NAFSCOB, figures reported against 2010–15 need to be treated with caution.
(iv) Figures in brackets relate to the average size of a cooperative society in WB as per cent of the average size of a cooperative society in India reported for the end-year in each period.
Source: RBI (2018b), www.nafscob.org.

---

[63] Interestingly, according to Rawal (2005), the second half of the 1990s marked a revival from the slowdown in cooperative credit that had set in right from the 1970s.

Features of Credit in the Study Villages

An Underdeveloped System of Formal Credit

All three villages had a relatively underdeveloped formal system of credit in 2010. Of the fresh borrowings by all households during the survey year, less than half were from formal sources in Amarsinghi (Maldah district, 47 per cent) and Kalmandasguri (Koch Bihar district, 37 per cent) (Table 6). In Panahar (Bankura district), the share of formal sources was 62 per cent. However, this was inflated owing to a single loan of Rs 1.4 million from an NBFC by one household for the purchase of trucks for its trading business. If this is considered an outlier and excluded, the share of formal sources in total borrowing was about 43 per cent (Table 6).

The shares of formal sources in total debt outstanding were much higher in all three villages than their corresponding shares in total borrowings (Table 7). Generally, borrowings during the survey year (including amount borrowed and repaid during the year itself) are a better indicator of the fresh flow of credit than the stock of debt outstanding (including principal and interest outstanding) on the date of the survey, as the latter may also include old unsettled loans.[64] Thus, even if formal sources appeared to be well-established in the three villages taking their shares in debt outstanding, this impression could be misleading, as these sources added more to the stock of debt than to the flow of borrowings. This may partly reflect the poor repayment of formal sector loans.[65] By contrast, the shares of informal sources, particularly SHG loans/microfinance, in total borrowings were higher than their shares in total debt outstanding, indicating better repayment and higher turnover of these loans. The issue of repayment of microfinance will be discussed later in this section.

The low incidence of formal sector borrowing (percentage of households reporting at least one fresh loan during the survey year from any of the formal sources) too underlined the limited spread of the formal sector. In

---

[64] We rely on debt outstanding while analysing the AIDIS data in the earlier section, because data on borrowings are not available for the AIDIS round of 2012.

[65] Although the data on repayments are not separately collected as part of the survey, repayments can be broadly conjectured using the difference between debt outstanding and amount borrowed. Another possible reason for formal sources having a larger share in debt outstanding was the longer duration of loans extended by these sources. However, this point cannot be adequately substantiated as data on duration of loans have not been collected as part of the surveys.

Table 6 *Amount borrowed during the survey year, study villages in WB, 2009–10,* in Rs

Source	Panahar	Amarsinghi	Kalmandasguri
1 Formal sources	25,81,800	3,61,500	7,29,000
	(62.0)*	(47.4)	(37.1)
1.1 Commercial banks/RRBs	8,49,800	2,97,500	6,49,000
	(20.4)	(39.0)	(33.1)
1.2 Credit cooperatives	1,82,000	62,000	80,000
	(4.4)	(8.1)	(4.1)
1.3 Other formal sources	15,50,000	2,000	–
	(37.2)*	(0.3)	–
2 Informal sources	15,80,255	4,00,408	12,34,555
	(38.0)	(52.6)	(62.9)
2.1 Friends and relatives	4,23,100	1,10,725	1,28,600
	(10.2)	(14.5)	(6.5)
2.2 Landlord/ rich peasants	22,060	–	–
	(0.5)	–	–
2.3 Other peasants	1,14,550	64,000	2,15,000
	(2.8)	(8.4)	(10.9)
2.4 Moneylenders	48,000	–	58,000
	(1.2)	–	(3.0)
2.5 Traders/other service providers	5,90,145	2,01,933	1,32,030
	(14.2)	(26.5)	(6.7)
2.6 SHGs	1,79,600	16,000	6,34,025
	(4.4)	(2.1)	(32.3)
2.6.1 SHGs linked to NBFC-MFIs	1,69,000	3,000	5,40,125
	(4.1)	(0.4)	(27.5)
2.6.2 SHGs linked to banks	10,600	13,000	93,900
	(0.3)	(1.7)	(4.8)
2.7 Other informal sources	2,02,800	7,750	66,900
	(4.9)	(1.0)	(3.4)
3. All sources	41,62,055	7,61,908	19,63,555
	(100.0)	(100.0)	(100.0)

Notes: Figures in brackets indicate percentage share in total.
* For Panahar, there was one large loan of Rs 1.4 million from NBFCs that inflated the share of "All formal sources" and "Other formal sources". Excluding this as an outlier brought down the shares to 43 per cent and 5 per cent, respectively
– No borrowing/debt.
Source: PARI survey (2010).

2010, not more than 15 per cent of households in any of the three villages reported a loan from the formal sector. The incidence of informal sources was considerably higher than formal sources (Table 8). In Panahar and Amarsinghi, about 65–67 per cent of the households had taken a loan from informal sources, particularly traders. In Kalmandasguri, there was a high incidence of informal sector loans on account of SHG loans/microfinance.

A Bank-Based System of Formal Credit

Commercial banks (including RRBs) were the most important source of rural credit in all three three villages in 2010. Panahar seemed to be an exception but this was on account of one large NBFC loan outlier, as noted earlier. Commercial banks were mainly into financing production-related needs of households, particularly agricultural credit needs (Table 9). However, Panahar again appeared to be an exception with a much lower share of about 39 per cent of bank credit taken for directly income generating activities, but again, this was due to two large-sized bank loans taken for house construction (Table 9).[66]

All three villages were served by public sector bank branches located in close vicinity. Panahar was served by two branches of public sector banks, both located at about three kilometres from the village. Amarsinghi was served by a public sector bank branch at a distance of about six kilometres. Kalmandasguri too was served by two public sector bank branches located three and seven kilometres from the village as well as an RRB branch.

There were also credit cooperatives serving the three villages, although their share in the total household borrowing did not exceed eight per cent in any of the villages (Table 6). The average size of a cooperative loan too was much smaller than that of commercial banks, particularly in Panahar and Kalmandasguri (Table 10). The overall incidence of formal sector borrowing was low in all three villages, as already discussed, but it was particularly low for cooperative credit, even though each of these villages had a functioning cooperative society/bank operational in their vicinity.

Panahar was served by a PACS, the Deopara Cooperative Society Limited, which was located barely one kilometre away, and by a branch of the West Bengal State Cooperative Bank Limited located about three

---

[66] The two loans were of Rs 0.3 and Rs 0.4 million.

Table 7 *Amount of debt outstanding, study villages in WB, 2009–10, in Rs*

Source	Panahar	Amarsinghi	Kalmandasguri
1 Formal sources	69,81,104	7,16,951	9,61,528
	(81.9)*	(63.3)	(39.7)
1.1 Commercial banks/RRBs	35,01,298	6,19,331	8,86,780
	(41.1)	(54.6)	(36.6)
1.2 Credit cooperatives	2,13,581	75,821	65,710
	(2.5)	(6.7)	(2.7)
1.3 Other formal sources	32,66,225	21,799	9,038
	(38.3)*	(1.9)	(0.4)
2 Informal sources	15,45,926	4,16,352	14,58,305
	(18.1)	(36.7)	(60.3)
2.1 Friends and relatives	4,23,550	85,625	1,19,100
	(5.0)	(7.6)	(4.9)
2.2 Landlord/ rich peasants	25,700	–	–
	(0.3)	–	–
2.3 Other peasants	2,25,225	1,30,560	5,76,500
	(2.6)	(11.5)	(23.8)
2.4 Moneylenders	72,460	1,500	49,726
	(0.8)	(0.1)	(2.1)
2.5 Traders/ other service providers	4,79,169	1,84,028	1,81,366
	(5.6)	(16.2)	(7.5)
2.6 SHGs	1,09,960	9,489	3,73,163
	(1.3)	(0.9)	(15.4)
2.6.1 SHGs linked to NBFC-MFIs	86,660	434	2,87,750
	(1.0)	(0.1)	(11.9)
2.6.2 SHGs linked to banks	23,300	9,055	85,413
	(0.3)	(0.8)	(3.5)
2.7 Other informal sources	2,09,862	5,150	1,58,450
	(2.5)	(0.5)	(6.5)
3 All sources	85,27,030	11,33,302	24,19,833
	(100.0)	(100.0)	(100.0)

Notes: (i) Figures in brackets indicate percentage share in total.
(ii) * For Panahar, there were two large loans of Rs 1.4 and 1.2 million each from NBFCs that inflated the share of "All formal sources" and "Other formal sources". Excluding these as outliers brought down the shares to about 74 per cent and 11 per cent, respectively.
(iii) – No borrowing/debt.
Source: PARI survey (2010).

Table 8 *Incidence of borrowing, study villages in WB, 2009–10,* in per cent

Source	Panahar	Amarsinghi	Kalmandasguri
1 Formal sources	12.9	11.0	15.0
1.1 Commercial banks/RRBs	5.2	8.7	12.2
1.2 Credit cooperatives	6.5	1.6	2.7
1.3 Other formal sources	1.2	0.8	–
2 Informal sources	67.3	64.6	83.0
2.1 Friends and relatives	7.7	15.0	14.3
2.2 Landlord/ rich peasants	2.4	–	–
2.3 Other peasants	8.9	2.4	6.1
2.4 Moneylenders	2.0	–	3.4
2.5 Traders/other service providers	25.4	37.0	12.2
2.6 SHGs	8.8	3.9	42.1
2.6.1 SHGs linked to NBFC-MFIs	7.6	0.8	26.5
2.6.2 SHGs linked to banks	1.2	3.1	15.6
2.7 Other informal sources	4.8	–	6.3
3 All sources	55.2	59.1	58.5

Note: – No borrowing/debt.
Source: PARI survey (2010).

kilometres away.[67] Households in Amarsinghi accessed credit from a branch of the Maldah District Central Cooperative Bank Limited located in the vicinity of the village. Kalmandasguri too was served by Uttar Bararangras Krishi Unnoyan Limited, which was affiliated to the Coochbehar District Co-operative Bank. The PACSs and SCB branches in the study villages provided credit for income generating activities, mainly agriculture (Table 9).

The overall evidence from WB on cooperative credit has been mixed suggesting differences in the extent of cooperative development across districts/villages (Rawal 2006). The findings from the three study villages suggested the existence of functioning credit cooperatives contributing to the supply of formal credit, although in a limited way.

---

[67] In 2010, a large number of village households reported loans from the Deopara society. This finding differs from the observation made by Rawal (2005), who in 2002 did not find any functioning society in Panahar.

Table 9 *Share of borrowing during the survey year, by purpose, study villages in WB, 2009–10,* in per cent

Source	Panahar		Amarsinghi		Kalmandasguri	
	Directly income-genera-ting activities	Not directly income-generating activities	Directly income-genera-ting activities	Not directly income-generating activities	Directly income-genera-ting activities	Not directly income-generating activities
1 Formal sources	74.3	25.7	96.0	4.0	100.0	–
1.1 Commercial banks/ RRBs	38.7	61.3	95.1	4.9	100.0	–
1.2 Credit cooperatives	100.0	–	100.0	–	100.0	–
1.3 Other formal sources	90.3	9.7	100.0	–	–	–
2 Informal sources	49.1	50.9	49.2	50.8	35.2	64.8
2.1 Friends and relatives	47.8	52.2	28.8	71.2	9.7	90.3
2.2 Landlord/ rich peasants	17.4	82.6	–	–	–	–
2.3 Other peasants	52.7	47.3	15.6	84.4	–	100.0
2.4 Moneylenders	69.0	31.0	–	–	17.5	82.5
2.5 Traders/other service providers	77.3	22.7	92.1	7.9	44.2	55.8
2.6 SHGs	31.6	68.4	–	100.0	58.0	42.0
2.6.1 SHGs linked to NBFC-MFIs	34.2	65.8	–	100.0	66.8	33.2
2.6.2 SHG linked to banks	–	100.0	–	100.0	12.3	87.7
2.7 Other informal sources	14.0	86.0	7.6	92.4	18.5	81.5

Note: – No borrowing/debt.
Source: PARI survey (2010).

Table 10 *Loan size, study villages in WB, 2009–10,* in Rs

Source	Panahar	Amarsinghi	Kalmandasguri
1 Formal sources	90,550*	23,133	28,174
1.1 Commercial banks/RRBs	62,954	25,727	29,900
1.2 Credit cooperatives	13,917	20,667	16,667
1.3 Other formal sources	5,16,667*	2,000	–
2 Informal sources	7,623	4,593	8,743
2.1 Friends and relatives	18,905	4,948	5,200
2.2 Landlords/ rich peasants	2,300	–	–
2.3 Other peasants	3,359	21,333	26,375
2.4 Moneylenders	8,400	–	10,000
2.5 Traders/other service providers	7,101	4,048	6,224
2.6 SHGs	6,636	2,750	8,129
2.6.1 SHGs linked to NBFC-MFIs	7,153	3,000	10,084
2.6.2 SHGs linked to banks	3,533	2,667	4,041
2.7 Other informal sources	4,993	958	14,375
3 All sources	19,717*	7,754	11,763

Notes: * For Panahar, there was one large loan of Rs 1.4 million from NBFCs that inflated the amount of "All sources", "All formal sources", and "Other formal sources". Excluding this as an outlier brought down the loan size to Rs 12,490, Rs 42,052, and Rs 75,000 for "All sources", "All formal sources", and "Other formal sources", respectively.
– No borrowing/debt.
Source: PARI survey (2010).

Decline in the Formal System of Credit in Amarsinghi and Kalmandasguri

Between 2005 and 2010, there was a distinct decline in the share of formal sources in total debt outstanding of households in Amarsinghi and Kalmandasguri.[68] As per the survey findings presented in Rawal (2006), formal sources accounted for 78 per cent of the total debt in Amarsinghi in 2005, which was remarkably high considering the fact that the village belonged to a relatively under-banked district of Maldah (Table 11). In 2010, the share of formal sources had declined to 63 per cent in Amarsinghi. In

---

[68] Given that debt outstanding on the survey date could have originated either during the survey year or any time before that, ideally, the comparison should be made between the amount borrowed during the two survey years. However, such a comparison is not feasible as the data on borrowings are not available from Rawal (2006).

Kalmandasguri, the share of formal sources was about 45 per cent in 2005, which fell to 40 per cent in 2010.

However, the decline in formal sources between 2005 and 2010 was not entirely due to commercial banks but possibly due to credit cooperatives. The decline in formal sources seemed to have been compensated by traders' credit in Amarsinghi and NBFC-led microfinance in Kalmandasguri.

NBFCs: New Conduits of Rural Credit

Commercial banks and credit cooperatives can be reckoned as the traditional sources of rural credit in India, whereas NBFCs are new entrants into the field and have generally grown in areas under-served by the traditional sources. This observation was also true for the study villages. The presence of NBFCs was stronger in Kalmandasguri where the traditional formal sources were underdeveloped. NBFCs operated as vehicle and housing finance companies (captured under "Other formal sources" in Tables 1, 6, 7, 8, 9, 10, 12 and 13), and as NBFC-MFIs. Unlike the other NBFCs which directly extended credit to the village households, NBFC-MFIs operated through SHGs. Hence, their share in total borrowings/debt in the three villages is reflected in Tables 1, 6, 7, 8, 9, 10, 12 and 13 under "SHGs linked to NBFC-MFIs".

The two NBFC-MFIs active in Kalmandasguri were Bandhan Financial Services Private Limited (henceforth Bandhan) and SKS Microfinance. In Panahar too, microfinance was provided by Bandhan.

Banks were also involved in providing microfinance through SHGs in the three villages; their share is captured under "SHGs linked to banks" in Tables 1, 6, 7, 8, 9, 10, 12 and 13. However, they accounted for a smaller share in the total volume of microfinance in the village than NBFC-MFIs.

Table 11 *Share of different sources in total debt outstanding, Amarsinghi and Kalmandasguri, 2005 and 2010*, in per cent

Source/Year	Amarsinghi		Kalmandasguri	
	2005	2010	2005	2010
1 All formal sources	78.1	63.3	44.7	39.7
1.1 Commercial banks	56.0	54.6	29.2	36.6
2 All informal sources	21.8	36.7	55.3	60.3
2.1 Traders/other service providers	2.1	16.2	8.5	7.5

Source: Rawal (2005) and PARI survey (2010).

It can, thus, be concluded that microfinance in the villages was more NBFC-led than bank-led.

NBFC-led Microfinance: An Accessible but Onerous Source of Credit

Microfinance rendered through NBFC-MFIs was accessible to the economically weaker sections but was onerous in many ways.[69] Some of the features of NBFC-led microfinance are the following:

First, there were notable differences between the microfinance rendered through NBFCs and through banks.

(a) The average size of NBFC-led microfinance was much higher than that from banks; the difference was particularly large in Kalmandasguri, where the penetration of NBFC-led microfinance was striking (Table 10);
(b) The rate of interest on NBFC-led microfinance was lower than bank-led microfinance (Table 12). This observation is somewhat at odds with the literature on microfinance, which suggests that the transaction costs (cost of group formation/promotion and cost of credit delivery) tend to be generally higher for NBFCs than for banks (Satyasai 2008). Furthermore, the cost of funds for NBFCs is also generally higher than banks as they do not have recourse to public deposits. Hence, the rate of interest on NBFC-led microfinance is expected to be higher than bank-led microfinance;
(c) Contravening the basic principle of microfinance of being collateral-free in nature, there were cases in Kalmandasguri of banks providing collateralised loans to SHGs. NBFC-led microfinance, however, was totally uncollateralised. The ability of NBFC-MFIs to offer microfinance at cheaper rates and without collateral possibly explained the ease of access of NBFC-led microfinance in the study villages.

Secondly, NBFC-MFIs catered to diverse credit needs of the village households (Table 9). These included not just activities that were directly income generating but also what may be called as consumption-related activities. These included expenses on housing, health, education, ceremonies, and other household requirements, such as purchasing durable domestic assets and repaying old loans.

---

[69] It is important to note that these surveys were conducted before RBI issued the regulatory guidelines on NBFC-MFIs. As noted in the previous section "Contemporary Policy on Rural Credit in India", it issued the guidelines in 2011 in response to the concerns raised about the coercive nature of NBFC-MFIs from Andhra Pradesh.

The fact that NBFC-led microfinance did not distinguish between borrowers based on the purpose of loans was another reason for its easy accessibility for the economically poorer sections.[70] This also ensured a better reach of the NBFC-MFIs over banks and credit cooperatives, which were primarily involved in financing various production-related activities (Table 9).[71] Further, it also enabled NBFC-led microfinance to easily substitute the credit from the traditional formal and informal sources. To illustrate, in Kalmandasguri where the traditional formal sources were relatively underdeveloped, a major part of the NBFC-led microfinance was given to fulfil production-related needs of households (Table 9).

Thirdly however, NBFC-led microfinance, although meant for the economically weaker sections, was more expensive than traditional formal finance rendered to individual borrowers by commercial banks and credit cooperatives (Table 12).[72] In 2010, the weighted average rates of interest on NBFC-led microfinance were around 14.5 per cent per annum across all three villages, which were close to twice the corresponding rates charged by formal sources in the three villages.[73]

Fourthly, NBFC-MFIs ensured perpetual indebtedness amongst borrowers. They organised women into groups and provided individual loans to all members of the groups. At any given time, therefore, all members of the group were indebted to the given NBFC-MFI. The perpetual indebtedness to NBFCs typically distinguished the NBFC-led microfinance from the bank-led microfinance. Banks organised women into groups and provided individual loans on the basis of the demands raised by group members and hence, it was not necessary that at any given point in time, all members were indebted to the given bank.

In the case of NBFCs, when a loan was repaid, the borrower had to take

[70] In the literature on rural credit, purpose has been reckoned as a factor responsible for the segmentation of the rural credit system into formal and informal segments (Swaminathan 1991). It has been argued that the formal sources lend exclusively for production-related activities. However, as the consumption needs of the poor often outweigh their production credit needs, they often end up relying on informal sources.

[71] The correlation coefficient between the amount borrowed for production activities and formal sector credit taken by households ranged between 0.96 and 0.99 in the three villages.

[72] An exception was the weighted average rate charged by credit cooperatives in Kalmandasguri of 16.3 per cent. However, this was due to an exceptionally high interest loan of Rs 20,000 at 36 per cent per annum, which was an outlier. If this loan was removed, then the weighted average interest was seven per cent per annum.

[73] In the revisit to the villages in 2015, Bandhan had increased its rate of interest from 14.5 to 22.9 per cent.

Table 12 *Weighted average and modal rate of interest, study villages in WB, 2009–10,* in per cent

Source		Weighted average rate of interest		
		Panahar	Amarsinghi	Kalmandasguri
1	Formal sources	9.7	8.0	8.6
1.1	Commercial banks/RRBs	9.9	8.2	7.7
1.2	Credit cooperatives	7.2	7.0	16.3
1.3	Other formal sources	9.8	7.0	–
2	Informal sources	36.8	37.0	21.0
2.1	Other peasants	31.4	36.4	–
2.2	Moneylenders	51.0	–	57.8
2.3	Traders/other service providers	38.2	24.0	45.0
2.4	SHGs	16.3	19.3	16.2
2.4.1	SHGs linked to NBFC-MFIs	14.6	14.5	14.7
2.4.2	SHGs linked to banks	28.0	20.5	23.3
2.5	Other informal sources	97.8	10.0	74.0
3	All sources	12.4	10.6	14.2
	Modal rate of interest			
1	Formal sources	7.0	7.0	7.0
2	Informal sources	60.0	24.0	60.0
2.1	SHGs	14.5	18.0	14.5
2.1.2	SHGs linked to NBFC-MFIs	14.5	14.5	14.5
2.1.3	SHGs linked to banks	24.0	18.0	24.0
3	All sources	7.0	7.0	14.5

Note: – No borrowing/debt.
Source: PARI survey (2010).

another loan immediately. If the next loan was not taken, the borrower's membership was liable to get cancelled, ensuring that she would not be eligible for a future loan. As a result, borrowers were forced to take loans even when there was no immediate need, to avoid disqualification leading to a kind of debt trap for the borrowers.

Fifthly, repayments were made by all members strictly on a weekly basis. The instalments had to be paid by all borrowers on a specified day of the week, at a specified time and place in the village itself. Early repayment was not even an available option. In case a borrower failed to repay, other borrowers from the village were required to mobilise money for the repayment. There were several instances observed during the survey of Kalmandasguri where borrowers had to sell assets, including, two cases of land, to make repayments (Ramachandran 2008). Moreover, after their repayments, all such borrowers were disqualified from obtaining future loans from the NBFC. In case the borrower fled from the village, the NBFC traced her through its network of branches and collection officers and ensured recovery. By ensuring that all members borrowed from the NBFC and were repaying on a weekly basis, the NBFC ensured a continued relation with the borrowers. Moreover, the strict repayment schedule also led to a high turnover of loans taken from NBFC-MFIs, as noted earlier.

Sixthly, loans were often linked to compulsory savings or insurance schemes. This enabled the NBFC to indemnify itself against default or made it the first claimant on any insurance payment to be made to the borrower (*ibid.*).

Near-Absence of Moneylenders and Landlords

Moneylenders accounted for a small share in the total borrowings of households in the villages. The incidence of loans from moneylenders was also minuscule. Their near-absence seemed to be in complete contrast to their striking rise in rural WB as suggested by the AIDIS rounds since 1991 (Tables 6 and 1).

With regard to moneylenders, the three study villages from WB appeared to also be different from the PARI villages from Andhra Pradesh, Rajasthan, and Bihar (Chavan and Das 2015). Unlike professional moneylenders as defined by the AIDIS, i.e., those who pursue moneylending as their primary profession, moneylenders in WB villages were mostly persons engaged in other professions but lent money as a secondary activity. In most cases, these moneylenders operated from outside the villages.

Typical of informal sources, moneylenders met various kinds of credit needs of village households. In Kalmandasguri, they met various consumption-related credit needs, whereas in Panahar, they lent for potato cultivation, supplementing crop loans from formal sources (Table 9).

There was a total absence of landlords and rich peasants as sources of credit in the study villages. This was in line with previous observations about the decline of landlords as sources of credit in WB after land reforms (see previous section, "Rural Credit in West Bengal"). The absence of landlords was not just a feature of the rural credit system in the three villages but also of the general class structure in the villages (see Chapter 3 in this volume).

Prevalence of Traders' Credit

Credit from traders was a common form of informal credit in all three villages. This point has been highlighted in the literature as well (see previous section, "Rural Credit in West Bengal"). The share of traders in total borrowings was the highest in Amarsinghi (Table 6). In most cases, traders' credit was in the form of fertilisers supplied on credit to potato cultivators. Such credit was generally free of interest. The price of fertilisers was pre-determined and settled after the sale of the crop produce. However, there were cases in Panahar and Kalmandasguri, wherein such loans carried an explicit interest.

There were cases, although very few, where potato dealers extended cash credit to cultivators in lieu of the promise to sell their produce. This credit was generally taken for meeting working capital needs in agriculture. Although these loans appeared to be generally interest-free, some cultivators reported an implicit burden, wherein they had to sell their potato produce to the same dealer immediately after harvest at a rate lower than the market rate.

Apart from the input and output dealers, cement traders supplied cash loans in Kalmandasguri. The loans from these traders were for housing; this explained the high share of "not directly income generating activities" in total credit taken from traders in Kalmandasguri (Table 9).

Features of Agricultural Credit in the Study Villages

Low Incidence of Formal Credit for Agriculture

There was a strong correlation between formal credit and agricultural credit in all three villages, indicating the predominance of formal sources in meeting agricultural credit needs.[74] Commercial banks and credit cooperatives primarily financed agriculture in all the three villages (Table 9). Similarly, of the total borrowings for agriculture and allied activities by households in Amarsinghi and Kalmandasguri during the survey year, over 80 per cent was from formal sources (Table 13).[75]

However, the source-wise distribution of agricultural credit was

---

[74] See footnote 72.

[75] For Panahar, the share was much lower, at 48 per cent. This was due to a fairly high share of informal sources, namely traders' loans. In all, five households took loans for potato cultivation during the survey year ranging between Rs 20,000 and Rs 75,000 each, all adding up to Rs 0.35 million.

misleading, as it did not convey the unequal distribution of formal credit for agriculture across households. The percentage of households reporting a formal sector loan for agriculture was extremely low in all three villages (Table 13). Only about 8–12 per cent of the households in each village reported a formal sector loan for agriculture during the survey year despite the fact that 2009–10 was a normal agricultural year for WB. It was already noted in the previous sub-section, "An Underdeveloped System of Formal Credit," that the overall incidence of formal sector borrowing was low in all the three villages. The incidence for formal sector borrowing for agriculture was even lower. This implied that very few households managed to get relatively large-sized loans for agriculture in the villages.

The incidence of borrowing for agriculture from formal sources was characterised as "manifested access" to formal credit and its determinants were analysed using a logistic regression model as follows:

FormalSectorAccess$_i$ = {1 if household 'i' reported at least one formal sector loan at the time of the survey (commercial bank/credit cooperative/RRB/ any other formal source) for agriculture and allied activities; 0 otherwise}.

Various factors related to the social and economic (agricultural) profiles of households were taken as the determinants of access as follows:

(1) Basic socio-economic characteristics: (1.1) LandOperated$_i$ – the land operated during the survey year by household 'i'; (1.2) SocialGroup$_i$ – the social group of a household (if SC/ST/Muslim = 0; Otherwise = 1); (1.3) YearofSchooling$_i$ – the average years of schooling of all members (above 16 years of age); (1.4) Tenancy$_i$ – 1 if the household had not leased in land during the survey year for cultivation, 0 otherwise; (2) Crop diversification: (2.1) CommercialCrop$_i$ – whether the household cultivated a commercial crop (potato/jute) during the survey year; (2.2) IrrigationIndex$_i$ – Gross irrigated area as per cent of gross cropped area by the household during the survey year; (3) alternative sources of funds: (3.1) TraderLoans$_i$ – the amount of borrowing from traders for agriculture during the survey year in Rupees; (3.2) SHGMembership$_i$ – Whether at least one member of the household was a member of any SHG. The village specific factors were controlled through village dummies.[76]

---

[76] Two dummies for Amarsinghi and Kalmandasguri were introduced in the model taking Panahar as the base category. The presence of multi-collinearity was expected to be minimal given the moderate to weak degree (less than +/– 0.5) of pair-wise correlation between the variables used in the model. The descriptive statistics for the quantitative variables are provided in Appendix Table 2 in Appendix.

Table 13 *Distribution of agricultural credit by source, study villages in WB, 2010,* in per cent

Source	Panahar	Amarsinghi	Kalmandasguri
	Distribution of amount of agricultural credit		
1 Formal sources	47.5	80.0	81.5
1.1 Commercial banks	31.1	61.9	77.5
1.2 Credit cooperatives	16.4	17.5	4.0
1.3 Other formal sources	–	0.6	–
2 Informal sources	52.5	20.0	18.5
2.1 Friends and relatives	6.0	2.8	1.5
2.2 Landlord/rich peasants	0.2	–	
2.3 Other peasants	2.8	2.8	–
2.4 Moneylenders	2.8	–	
2.5 Traders/other service providers	34.7	14.3	2.4
2.6 SHGs	2.4	–	14.6
2.6.1 SHGs linked to NBFC-MFI	2.4	–	13.6
2.6.2 SHGs linked to banks	–		1.0
2.7 Other informal sources	3.7	–	
3 Total agricultural credit	100.0	100.0	100.0
	(10,14,585)	(3,53,533)	(7,28,500)
	Incidence of agricultural credit (% of households reporting at least one loan for agriculture)		
1 Formal sources	8.9	7.9	12.2
1.1 Commercial banks	4.0	5.5	10.9
1.2 Credit cooperatives	4.8	1.6	1.4
1.3 Other formal sources	–	0.01	–
2 Informal sources	30.6	36.2	17.0
2.1 Friends and relatives	2.0	3.1	2.0
2.2 Landlord/rich peasants	0.4	–	
2.3 Other peasants	3.2	0.01	–
2.4 Moneylenders	0.8	–	
2.5 Traders/other service providers	16.5	32.2	5.4
2.6 SHGs	1.6	–	9.5
2.6.1 SHGs linked to NBFC-MFIs	1.6	–	6.1
2.6.2 SHGs linked to banks	–		3.4
2.7 Other informal sources	6.0	–	
3 Total agricultural credit	39.9	44.1	29.3

Notes: – No borrowing/debt
Figures in brackets indicate the total amount of borrowing for agriculture in Rs.
Source: PARI survey (2010).

As expected, the availability of land increased the probability of access to formal credit for agriculture (Table 14). The importance of land as a determinant of access to formal credit is generally due to its role as collateral as well as in deciding the availability of agricultural credit.[77] The role played by land in the Indian credit system has been well established in the literature (Swamy 1980a and 1980b). The importance of land in deciding the availability of agricultural credit stems from the crop credit scheme implemented by formal sources, wherein the crop credit limit sanctioned to any cultivator is linked to the land operated under a given crop and scale of finance for the crop.

Average years of schooling were also positively correlated with the probability of access to agricultural credit but were not statistically significant. Selection of the variable was taken as a control for the extent of financial literacy and awareness of the household, which are often argued to be important determinants in dealing with formal sources of credit (Grohmann, Klühs, and Menkhoff 2018).

The social group of borrowers also had a significant effect on their probability of access under the Baseline Model; backward social groups had a lower probability than other groups. The low probability of access for backward social groups was intuitively understandable considering their general marginalisation in India's rural credit system (Chavan 2012a). Among the three villages, Panahar and Amarsinghi showed a distinctly lower representation of backward social groups in their rural credit systems. For every Rs 100 of formal sector credit received by a caste Hindu household during the survey year, an average backward social group household (SCs, STs, and Muslims taken together) received less than Rs 16 in the two villages. The picture was different in the case of Kalmandasguri, where an average backward social group household received Rs 93 for every Rs 100 received by a caste Hindu household.[78]

The probability of tenant cultivators gaining access to formal credit was lower than owner cultivators; its impact was not statistically significant.

The ability of a household for crop diversification through the cultivation of commercial banks was analysed under Model II. Given both greater credit needs and the higher scale of finance fixed for commercial crops,

---

[77] Although we considered land operated and not land owned, the correlation of both these variables with access to formal credit was similar.

[78] The share of backward social groups in Kalmandasguri was pushed up by SC households, who reported remarkably high borrowings from formal sources compared to caste Hindu households.

Table 14 *Modelling the access to agricultural credit from formal sources, study villages in WB, 2010*

Explanatory variable	Dependent variable: FormalSectorAccess$_i$ (Access to agricultural credit from formal sources at the time of the survey – 1 if access; 0 if no access)		
	(1)	(2)	(3)
	Baseline model	Model II: Control for crop diversification	Model III: Control for alternative sources of funds
LandOperated$_i$	0.434**	0.203*	0.202*
	(0.179)	(0.097)	(0.116)
SocialGroup$_i$	0.790**	0.380	0.380
	(0.352)	(0.367)	(0.368)
YearsofSchooling$_i$	0.092	0.053	0.055
	(0.060)	(0.065)	(0.066)
Tenancy$_i$	0.231	0.056	0.068
	(0.391)	(0.396)	(0.413)
CommercialCrop$_i$		3.033***	3.021***
		(1.023)	(1.003)
IrrigationIndex$_i$		0.017***	0.017***
		(0.004)	(0.005)
Constant	Yes	Yes	Yes
Village dummies	Yes	Yes	Yes
Controls for alternative sources of funds	No	No	Yes
No of observations	522	522	522
P-value (χ^2)^	0.21	0.99	0.99

Notes: Figures in parentheses are robust standard errors
*** p <0.01, ** p<0.05, * p<0.1.
^ gives the p-value for the null hypothesis that the specified model fits the data.
Source: Estimated from PARI survey (2010).

the presence of commercial crops significantly enhanced the probability of a household accessing formal credit in the study villages. The irrigation index, which also enabled expanding the crop mix for a household, had a positive and significant relationship with the probability of access, although its coefficient had a fairly small value.

Model III used the controls for alternative sources of agricultural credit. Traders played an important role in providing agricultural credit in Panahar and Amarsinghi, and SHGs financed agriculture in Kalmandasguri, as will be discussed later in the section. The model yielded negative signs for both access to SHGs and traders' loans but the impact of these variables was not statistically significant (not separately reported in Table 14). Evidently, even though both traders and SHGs were involved in financing agriculture, the degree of substitutability between these two sources and the formal sources seemed weak in the three villages.

Given that all three models satisfied the goodness-of-fit test, we could conclude that the models fitted the data.

Traders: A Major Source of Agricultural Credit in Panahar and Amarsinghi

Most households in Panahar and Amarsinghi turned to traders for agricultural credit. In Panahar, the incidence of traders' credit was relatively low at about 17 per cent. However, their share in total agricultural credit was 35 per cent indicating that traders in the village extended fairly large-sized loans for agriculture. About one-third of the households in Amarsinghi reported having borrowed from traders for agricultural needs in the survey year (Table 13).

In 2015, a resurvey of select households in Panahar revealed the presence of PepsiCo, a multinational corporation, involved in contract farming for potato. Seed forms the single-largest item of cost in potato cultivation (Pandit *et al.* 2007). The commission agents appointed by PepsiCo in Panahar were involved in distribution of seeds on credit to potato cultivators. The case studies of potato cultivators contracted by PepsiCo did not show overpricing of seeds when the company settled farmers' dues after harvest. As the price of the potato was pre-fixed, under-pricing the produce was also ruled out. Apart from seeds, the resurvey did not reveal any other form of credit exchanging hands between the commission agents and potato cultivators in 2015. According to Pandit *et al.* (2007), traders were an important source of finance in WB villages for potato cultivators and their credit came at fairly high rates of interest. However, the evidence from Panahar and Amarsinghi did not support this observation.

Microfinance Supplementing Agricultural Credit Needs in Kalmandasguri

In Kalmandasguri, microfinance helped in meeting the agricultural credit needs of village households. As discussed earlier, microfinance was being used not only for meeting consumption-related needs but also production-related needs in the village (Table 9). SHGs provided about 15 per cent of the total agricultural credit in the village in the survey year (Table 13).

Availability of Formal Credit for Small Cultivators Higher in Amarsinghi and Kalmandasguri than Panahar

In 2010, Amarsinghi and Kalmandasguri were characterised by the presence of cultivators with small-sized holdings (Table 15).[79] Cultivators with operational holdings of less than four acres accounted for about 93 and 90 per cent of the total land operated in these two villages, respectively. The concentration of land was particularly striking in Amarsinghi, where cultivators operating upto two acres accounted for about 66 per cent of the total land operated in the village. The land size classes in this chapter were designed to effectively capture the agricultural credit situation in the villages. A comparison of the land size classes with the socio-economic classes used in other chapters in this volume suggested that households operating up to two acres of land in Amarsinghi and Kalmandasguri were primarily concentrated in the peasant and manual labour categories. A

Table 15 *Distribution of households by land size classes, study villages in WB, 2010*, in per cent

Land size		Panahar		Amarsinghi		Kalmandasguri	
		% of total number of cultivator households	% of land operated by cultivator households	% of total number of cultivator households	% of land operated by cultivator households	% of total number of cultivator households	% of land operated by cultivator households
1	0 < size <0.5	48.7	9.4	36.5	10.0	17.1	4.8
2	0.5 < size <1	19.7	10.7	19.2	14.1	40.0	19.2
3	1 < size <2	9.2	10.9	32.7	41.8	17.1	19.2
	0 < size <2	77.6	31.0	88.5	66.0	74.3	43.1
4	2 < size <4	15.8	30.3	9.6	26.9	22.9	47.0
	0 < size <4	93.4	61.3	98.0	92.8	97.1	90.1
5	4 < size	6.6	38.7	1.9	7.2	2.9	9.9
6	All households	100.0	100.0	100.0	100.0	100.0	100.0

Source: PARI survey (2010).

[79] In fact, all three villages from WB are essentially "small-farmer-dominated" villages; this was evident from a comparison of the landholding pattern of these villages with villages from other States, done by Chavan (2017a), who defined "small farmers" as households having five standard (irrigated) acres of operational landholding during the survey year.

few of these households also reported income from petty business and self-employment (Appendix Table 1).

The pattern of land distribution in favour of small-scale cultivators or peasants also reflected in the higher availability of agricultural credit from formal sources to these classes in Amarsinghi and Kalmandasguri than in Panahar. About 67 per cent of the agricultural credit taken by cultivators operating up to two acres of land in Amarsinghi and Kalmandasguri was from formal sources as compared to 22 per cent in Panahar (Table 16). The incidence of agricultural credit among small-scale cultivators was also better in the two villages than in Panahar (Table 16). In Panahar, the concentration of land was more skewed in favour of higher land size classes. Cultivators operating more than four acres of land accounted for about 39 per cent of the total land operated in the village (Table 15); this land size class in Panahar primarily included landlords/capitalist farmers (Appendix Table 1).

Credit to Costs Ratio Higher for Small Cultivators in Kalmandasguri

Apart from the enhanced availability of formal credit to small-scale cultivators, the average formal credit to costs ratio in agriculture was higher in Kalmandasguri than in Amarsinghi or Panahar.[80] Though the cost of cultivation can itself be circumscribed by the availability of formal credit for any cultivator, the formal credit to costs ratio can indicate how much of the given costs in a year can be met with the help of the formal credit available to the cultivator. It can, thus, be regarded as a broad proxy to determine the adequacy of formal credit. In Amarsinghi and Kalmandasguri, the average formal credit to costs ratio for cultivators operating up to two acres of land was 17 and 39 per cent, respectively; the corresponding ratio was about nine per cent in Panahar (Table 17). Notwithstanding the relative differences, the formal credit to costs ratio for small-scale cultivators was less than 40 per cent in all three villages, suggesting a general inadequacy of formal credit.

Interestingly, in Kalmandasguri, the ratio of total (formal and informal) credit to costs was remarkably high, at 60 per cent, for small-scale cultivators. Evidently, these cultivators managed the shortfall in formal

---

[80] Here, costs refer to the paid out costs on cultivation (A2 as defined by the Commission for Agricultural Costs and Prices) averaged across all cultivators in a given land size category and normalised by the total land operated by the given land size class. Similarly, formal credit for agriculture refers to the total agricultural credit sought by the given land size class from all formal sources during the survey year and normalised by the land operated by the size class.

Table 16 *Proportion of households borrowing for agriculture from the formal sector, by land size category, study villages in WB, 2010,* in per cent

Land size category (acres)	Panahar		Amarsinghi		Kalmandasguri	
	Formal agricultural credit/total agricultural credit	Households reporting at least one formal sector agriculture loan/total households in each category	Formal agricultural credit/total agricultural credit	Households reporting at least one formal sector agriculture loan/total households in each category	Formal agricultural credit/total agricultural credit	Households reporting at least one formal sector agriculture loan/total households in each category
1 0 < size < 0.5	21.0	4.7	42.0	2.6	67.0	6.3
2 0.5 < size < 1	32.0	12.1	63.0	8.7	54.0	7.9
3 1 < size < 2	16.0	6.3	74.0	20.8	79.0	23.5
0 < size <2	22.1	6.5	67.4	9.4	66.5	9.7
4 2 < size < 4	76.0	42.9	14.0	20.0	90.0	57.1
0 < size < 4	46.9	10.8	63.6	10.0	78.0	15.4
5 4 < size	49.0	33.3	100.0	100.0	–	–
6 All households	48.0	8.9	80.0	7.9	78.0	12.2

Note: - = No borrowing/debt.
Source: PARI survey (2010).

Table 17 *Formal credit for agriculture to cost of cultivation, by land size category, study villages in WB, 2010, in per cent*

Land size class (acres)	Panahar		Amarsinghi		Kalmandasguri	
	Agricultural credit/ cost of cultivation	Agricultural credit from formal sources/cost of cultivation	Agricultural credit / cost of cultivation	Agricultural credit from formal sources/cost of cultivation	Agricultural credit/ cost of cultivation	Agricultural credit from formal sources/cost of cultivation
1 0 < size < 0.5	45.0	9.0	24.0	10.0	109.0	73.0
2 0.5 < size < 1	29.0	9.0	24.0	15.0	67.0	36.0
3 1 < size < 2	44.0	7.0	26.0	19.0	44.0	35.0
0 < size <2	39.0	9.0	25.0	17.0	59.0	39.0
4 2 < size < 4	35.0	27.0	5.0	1.0[*]	81.4	77.0
0 < size < 4	37.0	17.0	19.0	12.0	71.0	59.9
5 4 < size	26.0	13.0	196.0	196.0	0.0	0.0
6 All households	33.0	16.0	32.0	24.0	67.0	38.0

Source: PARI survey (2010).

credit by borrowing from informal sources, particularly SHGs, for their agricultural needs.

In Panahar, the reliance of informal sources among the small-scale cultivators was most prominent. There was a wide gap between the total agricultural credit to costs (39 per cent) and formal credit to costs ratio (9 per cent) for these cultivators.

Inadequacy of Crop Credit for Potato Cultivators in Panahar

A possible explanation for the greater reliance on informal sources among small-scale cultivators in Panahar was the cultivation of potato. Potato, cultivated extensively in the village during the survey year, is a capital-intensive crop and its initial investment at the time of planting, including seeds, is generally substantial (Pandit *et al.* 2007). The average cost of cultivation (A2) for potato in Panahar in 2010 was Rs 23,415 per acre. The costs broadly showed an inverse relation with the size of landholding. In other words, costs per acre were higher for relatively small-scale potato cultivators (Table 18). By contrast, the ratio of crop credit received for potato cultivation (from commercial banks and credit cooperatives) to costs on potato cultivation was distinctly lower for small-scale cultivators.[81]

Table 18 *Formal credit to costs of cultivation for potato, Panahar, 2010*

	Land size (acres)	Cost of cultivation per acre of land operated under potato (Rs)	Crop credit for potato per acre of land operated under potato (Rs)	Crop credit/cost of cultivation (%)
1	0 < size < 0.5	21,596	6,406	29.7
2	0.5 < size < 1	24,799	2,658	10.7
3	1 < size < 2	24,991	–	–
	0 < size <2	24,002	2,925	12.2
4	2 < size < 4	24,474	13,754	56.2
	0 < size < 4	24,271	8,922	36.8
5	4 < size	22,061	11,250	51.0
6	All households	23,415	9,800	41.9

Note: – No borrowing/debt.
Source: PARI survey (2010).

[81] Crop credit from commercial banks and credit cooperatives for potato refers to the credit received as per the stipulated scale of finance for potato cultivation from these two sources. It is a subset of the formal credit for agriculture used in Tables 16 and 17, wherein it refers to

Table 19 *Case studies of potato cultivators, Panahar, 2010*

Cultivator no.	Land size (acres)	Crop credit for potato per acre of land operated under potato (Rs)	Crop credit/Scale of finance (%)
1	0 < size < 0.5	–	–
2	0 < size < 0.5	–	–
3	0.5 < size < 1	–	–
4	0.5 < size < 1	–	–
5	1 < size < 2	–	–
6	1 < size < 2	–	–
7	2 < size < 4	14,286	54.9
8	2 < size < 4	31,250	120.2
9	4 < size	16,667	64.1
10	4 < size	17,500	67.3

Notes: The scale of finance by the Bankura District Central Cooperative Bank for potato in 2009–10 was reported as Rs 26,000 per acre
– No borrowing/debt.
Source: PARI survey (2010).

On average, crop credit covered only about 12 per cent of the costs of cultivation for potato cultivators operating up to two acres of land as compared to 51 per cent for cultivators operating more than four acres.

Apart from the fact that the crop credit was not adequate to cover the costs, the crop credit received was also much lower than the stipulated scale of finance. Taking case studies of the two smallest cultivators in each land size class, we calculated the ratio of crop credit received by these cultivators with the per-acre scale of finance (fixed by the Bankura District Central Cooperative Bank for potato in 2009–10), which was used for sanctioning crop credit to potato cultivators in Panahar.

The smallest cultivators in each of the land size classes up to two acres did not report any crop credit from commercial banks/credit cooperatives for potato cultivation (Table 19). Evidently, these cultivators largely relied on informal sources for credit. Those cultivating more than two acres reported taking crop credit but the amount of credit received was lower

---

the total agricultural credit taken from all formal sources not only as crop credit against the stipulated scales of finance for various crops but also credit sought for fixed capital formation in agriculture and for allied activities.

than the per-acre scale of finance, although the ratio broadly increased as we moved to higher land size classes.[82]

Concluding Observations

The chapter discussed various features of the contemporary rural credit system in WB. The leading institutions of rural credit in the State, as in most other States of India, are commercial banks (including RRBs). However, the development of banking in rural WB has not been monotonic – it has shown significant variations over time following the changes in the rural credit policy. After bank nationalisation, there was a striking increase in the presence of banks in rural WB. The expansion of banking in the 1970s and 1980s could be seen in the form of increased bank branch penetration and supply of bank credit to rural areas of the State.

Notwithstanding this expansion, the State remained a relatively less-banked State on the national scale. The backwardness of WB's rural credit system could be seen from the dominance of landlords (replaced by traders after land reforms in most parts of the State) as sources of informal credit and the persistence of exploitative practices, including high rates of interest and interlinked credit transactions.

The initiation of economic reforms in the early-1990s resulted in the liberalisation of the banking sector. Most of the banking sector regulations, including branch licensing, priority sector lending and interest rate regulations, instituted with the objective of redistributing banking services, were liberalised during this period. During the 1990s, WB witnessed a decline in the rural branch network and the relative supply of credit to its rural areas *vis-à-vis* urban areas.

While commercial banks retreated in the 1990s, credit cooperatives – the other formal agency of rural credit – also could not provide the necessary succour to the rural population in the State. Firstly, the long-term structure of credit cooperatives has been in a state of decay in WB, as in most other States. Secondly, credit growth from PACSs – the lowest tier in the short-term structure – has also been slowing down except

---

[82] Here, the crop credit estimate was based only on the existing scale of finance. However, as per the crop credit scheme, commercial banks/credit cooperatives also add a component for post-harvest/consumption requirements, maintenance expense on assets, and small investment credit requirements while fixing the crop credit limit over and above the scale of finance. Hence, the ratio presented here was more likely to be an overestimate; the difference between the actual crop credit and the crop credit due to a cultivator could have been even wider.

during a sporadic policy-driven push in first half of the 2000s. Certain structural/operational factors may have constrained the growth of credit cooperatives in the State, but such factors were not discussed in this chapter due to limited availability of data on cooperatives for WB.

Policy changes in the period of financial liberalisation have also definitively influenced the working of cooperatives in WB as well as in other States. To illustrate, the prudential regulations were made applicable to rural credit cooperatives but without any capital support from the Central/State Government. High NPAs and the resultant provisioning constrained the credit creating capacity of the rural credit cooperatives. Till date, the long-term cooperatives have not been recapitalised (RBI 2017b). For the short-term cooperatives, the conditional capital support was provided but with a delay affecting the working of these institutions in many States in the interim period (Satish 2007). This, in part, explained the moribund state of long-term cooperatives and the slowdown in credit from the short-term cooperatives in WB in recent decades.

The surveys conducted in Panahar Amarsinghi, and Kalmandasguri in 2010 indicated the presence of credit cooperatives. Expectedly however, their contribution to rural credit in these villages was limited. A comparison of the 2010 surveys of Amarsinghi and Kalmandasguri with the 2005 surveys showed a perceptible decline in the share of formal sources in the total debt outstanding of village households; this decline was not just on account of commercial banks but possibly credit cooperatives as well.

After 2005, the financial inclusion policy, although constrained by the commitment to financial liberalisation, resulted in some positive changes in the rural credit system in WB. There was a notable revival in the rural branch network and the relative flow of bank credit to rural areas.

Yet, on the national scale, the State continued to be less-banked. There was also a widening gap between credit to and deposits from rural areas over time, as banks laid greater thrust on mobilising low-cost retail deposits than providing small-sized loans in their pursuit of commercially viable financial inclusion. Furthermore, there was a growing disconnect between rural areas and agricultural credit in the State. Agricultural credit was concentrated in urban areas, particularly in Kolkata – a metropolitan district with little agricultural activity. This was partly a fallout of the widened definition of agriculture under the PSL policy, again in an effort to make inclusion more viable. The definitional changes encouraged financing large-scale commercial forms of agricultural production and post-production activities. Hence, even though agricultural credit in WB achieved a striking growth in the 2000s following Comprehensive Credit Policy, the benefits of this growth to rural areas of the State remained questionable.

The effort to make financial inclusion commercially viable also resulted in encouraging various for-profit forms of microfinance. The vacuum left by commercial banks and credit cooperatives in rural credit was filled not just by the traditional informal sources, such as traders and moneylenders, but also by private NBFC-MFIs.

Microfinance in rural WB was primarily led by NBFC-MFIs and not by banks as was the case in other States. NBFC-MFIs grew rapidly during the 2000s. NBFCs/SHGs were a major source of rural credit in the study villages in 2010, particularly in Kalmandasguri.

Unlike formal sources, microfinance from NBFC-MFIs was accessible for all purposes and was entirely uncollateralised. Hence, it enjoyed a wide reach among the economically backward sections, particularly poor women. However, the interest rates charged by NBFC-MFIs were significantly higher than formal sources in all three villages. Moreover, the lending and recovery practices of these institutions were fairly onerous and ensured perpetual indebtedness among borrowers.

Agriculture was primarily financed by formal sources, although NBFC-MFIs and traders were also involved in meeting agricultural credit needs in the villages. The availability of land significantly increased the probability of accessing formal credit among village households. It did not, however, imply that every landed household in the village sought formal credit. In fact, only 8-12 per cent of the households in the villages reported a fresh borrowing for agriculture during the survey year. The low incidence was perplexing in the case of Amarsinghi and Kalmandasguri given the relatively widespread access to land in the two villages.

The low incidence of formal credit for agriculture was partly a reflection of the underdeveloped character of the village credit systems. All the three villages were well-endowed in terms of the presence of both bank branches and credit cooperatives. Yet, neither the presence of formal sources nor the availability of land translated into widespread formal sector borrowings among households.

In part, the low incidence of formal credit could also be explained by the rise in (unregistered) fixed tenancy in the villages (see 'Case study of the largest landlord household in Panahar' by Ranjini Basu in chapter 3, this volume). Unregistered tenants unlike the registered sharecroppers were not assured formal credit for agriculture. The low incidence in the case of owner cultivators could have been due to an informal sub-division of land between generations without a legal transfer.[83] There were also some instances of informal transfers to third parties of patta land received under land reforms. As formal credit was given against the hypothecation of land, it could not be obtained by cultivators with a *de facto* ownership of land.

There could have also been other constraints in getting a timely and adequate access to formal credit for cultivators, although it was not easy to capture these through the survey data. There was anecdotal evidence to suggest that most of the KCCs, meant to ensure quick and easy access to crop credit, were not being actively used by cultivators. Furthermore, crop credit obtained by cultivators was not in line with the stipulated scale of finance. In fact, the case studies of potato cultivators from Panahar showed that not all obtained crop credit for potato cultivation, and those who did, had to contend with an amount much lower than the scale of finance. Importantly, potato was a commercial crop with a relatively high scale of finance. If the stipulated finance did not reach the cultivators for commercial crops, the possibility of it reaching for other crops seemed even less likely. The inability to extend credit in line with the scale of finance reflected the poor implementation of credit policies by formal sources, and could have deterred cultivators from approaching these sources in the first place.

Furthermore, on an average, the availability of formal credit was far lower than the cost of cultivation. For an average cultivator, formal credit in the survey year could meet at the most 50 per cent of the cost of cultivation in the three villages. If costs were taken as a proxy for adequacy, the available formal credit seemed inadequate.

Needless to say, small-scale cultivators in all the three villages were worse off than their large-scale counterparts in terms of the adequacy of formal credit. However, the small-scale cultivators in Amarsinghi and Kalmandasguri were better off than their counterparts in Panahar; both Amarsinghi and Kalmandasguri were dominated by small-scale cultivators.

To conclude, the chapter revealed several areas of possible reform in the rural credit system of WB. Firstly, it may be necessary to effectively implement crop credit scheme to draw in more cultivators into the fold of formal credit. Secondly, controlling the diversion of agricultural credit to non-farmer categories may be necessary to reduce the stark disconnect

[83] Typically, the land was held in the name of the father but was sub-divided between the sons in a *de facto* but not *de jure* manner.

between rural areas and agricultural credit in the State. This may also help in reducing the wide inter-district disparity in bank credit in the State. Thirdly, the recapitalisation of long-term credit cooperatives may be essential for revitalising the cooperative system in the State.

Fourthly, the surveys discussed in the chapter were conducted in 2010, after which stricter regulations were imposed on NBFC-MFIs by RBI. We expect that some of the onerous practices of these institutions discussed in the chapter, would have been checked on account of the controls. However, it may be necessary not to dilute the controls on NBFC-MFIs given the for-profit nature of these institutions serving an economically poor clientele. Finally, going forward, a uniform regulatory control over the entire microfinance sector in India may be necessary. It may be argued that NBFC-MFIs and banks, the two segments accounting for a major share of India's microfinance are under the regulatory control of RBI (MFIN 2018). However, standardising the operating procedures of the remaining MFIs and the myriad SHGs associated with these institutions may also be necessary. Given that microfinance deals with the vulnerable segments of the population, market share cannot be used as the sole criterion for deciding the regulatory perimeter.

References

Bansal, Yeshu and Srinivasan, Narasimhan (2009), "Business Correspondents and Facilitators: The Story So Far," *CAB Calling*, no. 33, April–June.

Bardhan, Pranab and Mookherjee, Dilip (2006), "Pro-poor Targeting and Accountability of Local Governments in West Bengal," *Journal of Development Economics*, January.

Bhaduri, Amit (1973), "A Study in Agricultural Backwardness Under Semi-Feudalism," *Economic Journal*, Royal Economic Society, vol. 83, no.329, pp. 120–37, March.

Bhattacharyya, Sudipta (1996), "Evolution of the Agricultural Credit Markets in West Bengal Since 1977: A Journey from Peasant Class Differentiation to Agriculture-Led Development," in Ajitava Raychaudhuri and Debjani Sarkar (eds.), *Economy of West Bengal: Problems and Prospects*, Allied Publishers, Calcutta.

Bhaumik, Sankar Kumar and Rahim, Abdur (1998), "Structure and Operation of Rural Credit Markets: Some Results Based on Field Surveys in West Bengal," paper presented at the State level seminar on Decentralisation: Devolution and Participation, November 20-22, Calcutta.

Chakrabarty, Kamalesh Chandra (2013), "Financial Inclusion in India – Journey So Far and Way Forward," September 6, Speeches, available at https://www.bis.org/review/r130909c.pdf, viewed on May 22, 2020.

Chavan, Pallavi (2005), "Banking Sector Reforms and Growth and Distribution of Rural Banking in India," in V. K. Ramachandran and Madhura Swaminathan (eds.), *Financial Liberalisation and Rural Credit*, Tulika Books, New Delhi.

Chavan, Pallavi (2012), "Debt of Rural Households in India: A Note on the All-India Debt and Investment Survey," *Review of Agrarian Studies*, vol. 2, no. 1.

Chavan, Pallavi (2012a), "The Access of Dalit Borrowers in India's Rural Areas to Bank Credit," *Review of Agrarian Studies*, vol. 2, no. 2, July–December.

Chavan, Pallavi (2012b), "A Study of Rural Credit in Maharashtra – The Resurvey of a Village from Western Maharashtra," PhD thesis submitted to the University of Calcutta, Kolkata.

Chavan, Pallavi (2013), "Credit and Capital Formation in Agriculture: A Growing Disconnect," available at http://www.macroscan.org/anl/nov13/Pallavi_Chavan. pdf, viewed on May 22, 2020.

Chavan, Pallavi (2017a), "Formal Credit and Small Farmers in India," in Madhura Swaminathan and Sandipan Baksi (eds.) *How Do Small Farmers Fare: Evidence from Village Studies in India*, Tulika Books.

Chavan, Pallavi (2017b), "Public Banks and Financial Intermediation in India: The Phases of Nationalisation, Liberalisation, and Inclusion," in Christoph Scherrer (ed.), *Public Banks in the Age of Financialisation: A Comparative Perspective*, Edward Elgar Publishing Limited.

Chavan, Pallavi and Das, Amalendu (2015), "Contemporary Rural Credit System in India: Some Insights from Village Surveys," Paper presented at FAS Annual Conference, Kochi, available at https://fasconference2014.files.wordpress. com/2014/01/fas-rural-credit_revised.pdf, viewed on May 22, 2020.

Chavan, Pallavi (2020), "Women's Access to Banking in India: Policy Context, Trends, and Predictors", *Review of Agrarian Studies*, vol. 10, no. 1.

Copestake, James G. (1985), "The Transition to Social Banking in India: Promises and Pitfalls," *Development Policy Review*, no. 6.

Government of India (GoI) (2004), *Draft Final Report of the Task Force on the Revival of Cooperative Credit Institutions (Short Term)* (Chair: A. Vaidyanathan), Mumbai.

Government of India (GoI) (2009), *Report of the Committee on Financial Sector Reforms* (Chair: Raghuram G. Rajan), New Delhi.

Government of India (GoI) (2014), *The Microfinance (Institutions) Development and Regulation Bill – 2012, 84th Report*, available at http://www.prsindia.org/uploads/ media/Micro%20Finance%20Institutions/SCR-%20Micro%20finance%20bill.pdf, viewed on May 22, 2020.

Government of West Bengal (GoWB) (2015), *Statistical Abstract – 2015*, Bureau of Applied Economics and Statistics, Department of Planning, Statistics and Programme Monitoring, Kolkata.

Grohmann, Antonia, Klühs, Theres, and Menkhoff, Lukas (2018), "Does financial literacy improve financial inclusion? Cross country evidence," *World Development*, Elsevier, vol. 111(C), pp. 84–96.

Khan, Harun Rashid (2011), "Financial Inclusion and Financial Stability: Are They Two Sides of the Same Coin?," November 14, Speeches, available at https://rbi.org.in/scripts/BS_SpeechesView.aspx?Id=623, viewed on May 22, 2020.

Kishore, Anupam (2012), "Business Correspondent Model boosts Financial Inclusion in India," https://www.minneapolisfed.org/publications/community-dividend/business-correspondent-model-boosts-financial-inclusion-in-india, viewed on May 22, 2020.

Microfinance Institutions Network (MFIN) (2018), *Micrometer – Data as on 30 September 2018*.

Mohanty, Deepak (2010), "Perspectives on lending rates in India," Speeches, Kolkata, June 11, available at https://www.rbi.org.in/scripts/BS_SpeechesView.aspx?id=508, viewed on May 22, 2020.

National Bank for Agriculture and Rural Development (NABARD) (1999), *Task Force on Supportive Policy and Regulatory Framework for Micro Credit*, Mumbai.

Narayana, D. (1988), "A Note on the Reliability and Comparability of the Various Rounds of the AIRDIS and AIDIS," unpublished paper, Centre of Development Studies, Thiruvananthapuram.

National Bank for Agriculture and Rural Development (NABARD) (2018), *NABARD All India Rural Financial Inclusion Survey 2016-17*, Mumbai.

National Federation of State Cooperative Banks Ltd. (NAFSCOB) (2014), "50 Years of NAFSCOB, NAFSCOB Journal – Editorials: A Compendium – 1990–91 to 2013–14," NAFSCOB, Navi Mumbai.

National Sample Survey Organisation (NSSO) (1998), "Household Assets and Indebtedness of Social Groups as on 30-06-91," Report No. 432 (Part II), National Sample Survey 48th round, Ministry of Statistics and Programme Implementation, Government of India, New Delhi, available at http://www.mospi.gov.in/sites/default/files/publication_reports/432_part2_final.pdf, viewed on May 22, 2020.

National Sample Survey Organisation (NSSO) (2005), "Household Indebtedness in India as on 30.06.2002," Report No. 501, National Sample Survey 59th round, Ministry of Statistics and Programme Implementation, Government of India, New Delhi, available at http://www.mospi.gov.in/sites/default/files/publication_reports/501_final.pdf, viewed on May 22, 2020.

National Sample Survey Organisation (NSSO) (2016), "Household Indebtedness in India," Report No. 577, National Sample Survey 70th round, Ministry of Statistics and Programme Implementation, Government of India, New Delhi, available at http://mospi.nic.in/sites/default/files/publication_reports/nss_577.pdf, viewed on May 22, 2020.

Pandit, Arun, Pandey, N.K., Lal, Barsati, Chandran, K.P., and Rana, Rajesh K. (2007), "Financing Agriculture: A Study of Bihar and West Bengal Potato Cultivation," *Indian Journal of Agricultural Economics*, January.

Ramachandran, V. K. (2008), "Agrarian Relations and Village Studies," Radha Kamal Mukherjee Lecture at the ISLE's 50th Annual Conference, December 13–15, Lucknow.

Ramachandran, V. K. and Swaminathan, Madhura (eds.) (2005), *Financial Liberalisation and Rural Credit in India*, Tulika Books, New Delhi.

Ramakumar, R. (2010), "A Route to Disaster," *Frontline*, vol. 27, no. 24, November 20–December 3.

Ramakumar, R. and Chavan, Pallavi (2007), "Revival in Agricultural Credit in the 2000s: An Explanation," *Economic and Political Weekly*, vol. 42, no. 52, December 29–January 4.

Ramakumar, R. and Chavan, Pallavi (2011), "Changes in the Number of Rural Bank Branches in India, 1991 to 2008," *Review of Agrarian Studies*, vol. 1, no. 1.

Ramakumar, R. and Chavan, Pallavi (2014), "Agricultural Credit in the 2000s: Dissecting the Revival", *Review of Agrarian Studies,* vol. 4, no. 1, February–June.

Rajeev, Meenakshi and Deb, Sharmistha (1998), "Institutional and Non-Institutional Credit in Agriculture: Case Study of Hugli District of West Bengal," *Economic and Political Weekly,* vol. 33, no. 47/48, pp. 2997–3002.

Rawal, Vikas (2005), "Banking and Credit Relations in Rural West Bengal," in V. K. Ramachandran and Madhura Swaminathan (eds.), *Financial Liberalisation and Rural Credit*, Tulika Books, New Delhi.

Rawal, Vikas (2006), Indebtedness in Rural West Bengal, report submitted to the Development and Planning Department, Government of West Bengal.

Reserve Bank of India (RBI) (1954), *All India Rural Credit Survey: The General Report – Vol. 2*, Bombay.

Reserve Bank of India (RBI) (1991), *Report of the Committee on the Financial System*, Mumbai.

Reserve Bank of India (RBI) (2001), "Developmental Issues in Micro-credit", Speech by Jagdish Capoor, *RBI Bulletin*, March.

Reserve Bank of India (RBI) (2004), *Report of the Advisory Committee on Flow of Credit to Agriculture and Related Activities from the Banking System* (Chair: V. S. Vyas), RBI, Mumbai.

Reserve Bank of India (RBI) (2008), *Report on Currency and Finance -2006-08*, Mumbai.

Reserve Bank of India (RBI) (2010), "Discussion Paper on Engagement of 'for-profit' Companies as Business Correspondents", Mumbai, available at https://www.rbi.org.in/scripts/bs_viewcontent.aspx?Id=2234, viewed on May 22, 2020.

Reserve Bank of India (RBI) (2011), *Report of the Sub-Committee of the Central Board of Directors of the Reserve Bank of India to Study Issues and Concerns in the MFI Sector* (Chair: Y. H. Malegam), Mumbai.

Reserve Bank of India (RBI) (2017a), "Non-Banking Finance Companies in India's Financial Landscape," *RBI Bulletin*, vol. 71, no. 10, October.

Reserve Bank of India (RBI) (2017b), *Report on Trend and Progress of Banking in India – 2016-17,* Mumbai.

Reserve Bank of India (RBI) (2018a), *Report on Trend and Progress of Banking in India – 2017-18*, Mumbai.

Reserve Bank of India (RBI) (various years), *Basic Statistical Returns of Scheduled Commercial Banks in India*, Reserve Bank of India, Mumbai.

Reserve Bank of India (RBI) (2018b), *Handbook of Statistics on Indian States – 2017-18*, RBI, Mumbai.

Rudra, Ashok (1975), "Loans as a Part of Agrarian Relations – Some Results of a Preliminary Survey in West Bengal," *Economic and Political Weekly*, vol. 10, no. 28, July 12, pp. 1049–53.

Satish, P. (2007), "Agricultural Credit in the Post-Reform Era," *Economic and Political Weekly*, vol. 42, no. 26, June 30–July 6.

Satyasai, K. J. S. (2008), "Rural Credit Delivery in India: Structural Constraints and Some Corrective Measures," Agricultural Economics Research Review, vol. 21.

Sen, Abhijit (2005), "Rural Cooperative Banks – Their Present Problems," in V. K. Ramachandran and Madhura Swaminathan (eds.), *Financial Liberalisation and Rural Credit*, Tulika Books, New Delhi.

Sriram, M.S. (2018), *Inclusive Finance India Report 2017*, SAGE Publications Pvt. Ltd., New Delhi.

Swaminathan, Madhura (1990), "Village Level Implementation of IRDP: Comparison of West Bengal and Tamil Nadu," *Economic and Political Weekly*, vol. 25, no. 13, March 31.

Swaminathan, Madhura (1991), "Segmentation, Collateral Undervaluation, and the Rate of Interest in Agrarian Credit," *Cambridge Journal of Economics*, vol. 15, no. 2, June.

Swaminathan, Madhura (2018), "NABARD National Financial Inclusion Survey (NAFIS) – 2: Are Rural Households Really Saving?," available at http://fas.org.in/blog/nabard-national-financial-inclusion-survey-nafis-2/, viewed on May 22, 2020.

Swamy, Dilip S. (1980a), "Land and Credit Reforms in India: Part One," *Social Scientist*, vol. 8, no. 11, June, pp. 3–13.

Swamy, Dilip S. (1980b), "Land and Credit Reforms in India: Part Two," *Social Scientist*, vol. 8, no. 12, July, pp. 46–64.

APPENDIX

Appendix Table 1 *Share of households, across socio-economic classes and land size classes, study villages in WB, 2010, in per cent*

Socio-economic class	Amarsinghi						Kalmandasguri						Panahar					
	0 < size <=0.5	0.5< size <=1	1< size <=2	2< size <=4	4< size	All	0 < size <=0.5	0.5< size <=1	1< size <=2	2< size <=4	4< size	All	0 < size <=0.5	0.5< size <=1	1< size <=2	2< size <=4	4< size	All
Landlord/capitalist farmer	–	–	–	–	–	–	–	–	–	–	–	–	0	0	0	0	78	3
Upper peasant	9	74	100	100	–	43	13	63	65	79	100	39	47	91	88	90	22	58
Poor peasant	–	–	–	–	–	–	3	13	18	7	0	7	–	–	–	–	–	–
Manual worker	61	13	0	0	0	38	62	16	6	0	0	37	37	0	0	0	0	25
Major income from artisanal work	3	0	0	0	0	2	–	–	–	–	–	–	–	–	–	–	–	–
Major income from small and petty business/self employed	–	–	–	–	–	–	16	3	6	7	0	10	–	–	–	–	–	–
Major income from business	15	9	0	0	0	10	–	–	–	–	–	–	5	6	0	10	0	5
Major income from pension	4	0	0	0	0	2	4	0	0	0	0	2	–	–	–	–	–	–
Major income from remittances/small rent	5	0	0	0	0	3	–	–	–	–	–	–	2	0	0	0	0	1
Major income from salaries	3	4	0	0	0	2	3	5	6	7	0	4	5	3	13	0	0	5
Major income from other sources	–	–	–	–	–	–	–	–	–	–	–	–	3	0	0	0	0	2
All households	100	100	100	100	100	100	100	100	100	100	100	100	100	100	100	100	100	100

Note. – Not applicable; Size is expressed in acres.
Source: PARI survey (2010).

Appendix Table 2 *Descriptive Statistics of variables used in the logistic model, study villages in WB, 2010*

Variable	Mean	SD	Maximum	Minimum
Land Operatedi	0.78	1.45	19.2	0
Years of Schoolingi	3.62	3.26	14.5	0
Irrigation Indexi	44.41	47.42	100.0	0
Trader Loansi	808.62	4,901.87	75,000	0

Source: PARI survey (2010).

10

The Nature of and Changes in Labour and Employment in Rural West Bengal

Niladri Sekhar Dhar, Shruti Nagbhushan, and Subhajit Patra[1]

Introduction

This chapter addresses various aspects of labour and employment of the working population in the three study villages and in West Bengal based on three sets of data – the village-level household-level surveys conducted in 2010 and 2015 under the Project on Agrarian Relations in India (PARI), and the Census of India. It looks into levels of employment and unemployment among the manual-worker and peasant households in rural West Bengal in general and in the study villages of Panahar, Amarsinghi, and Kalmandasguri in particular. It discusses different aspects of proletarianisation of the peasantry, wherein its poorer section participates in the rural labour market to gain wage employment. Furthermore, it explores some characteristics of the working poor, such as their social group affiliation and the work participation of women from different classes. Features of the employment received by the two main classes dependent on wage employment – manual workers and small peasants – are also discussed, including the number of days of employment received, nature/form of work, importance/dependence on agriculture for wage work, and gender gap in employment. Lastly, it discusses the pattern of labour use in crop production and the factors instrumental in the change of labour use between 2009–10 and 2014–15.

[1] The section titled "Male Out-migration from Rural West Bengal" is written with extensive inputs from Yasodhara Das, Rakesh Kumar Mahato, and Yoshifumi Usami. We are grateful to them. We are also grateful to Arindam Das for support in data analysis and preparation of the initial draft of this paper.

The Class of Manual Workers

Labour in the rural production process is primarily provided by the class of proletariat and a section of the semi-proletarianised peasantry. In this section, we focus on characteristics of the class of manual workers. A manual-worker household is defined using income criterion, wherein the major share of the household income is derived from wage employment in agricultural and non-agricultural activities because manual workers do not have ownership or access to the means of production. Such households are not exclusively engaged in wage employment; they did have multiple sources of income such as that from crop production in small plots of owned or leased-in land, animal resources, salaries and trade, and transferred incomes such as pensions, remittances, and scholarships. These sources of income constitute a minor share of their total household income. In any rural economy, members of manual-worker households are the most significant source of labour in various economic activities undertaken by other agrarian and non-agrarian socio-economic classes.[2]

In the study villages of West Bengal, the number of manual workers was high, especially in Amarsinghi and Kalmandasguri, where 38 per cent and 37 per cent of all households belonged to this class, respectively, and at least two members from each manual-worker household worked as wage workers in the village production system and occasionally in neighbouring villages or towns. In Panahar, one-fourth of all households belonged to this class, with two members from each manual-worker household participating in wage work. Given the average number of members per manual-worker household, almost 50 per cent household members from each manual-worker household participated in the rural wage labour market.

To understand the socio-economic characteristics of the class of manual workers vis-à-vis other socio-economic classes, we have considered three indicators: the ratio of workers to non-workers, the incidence of youth participation in the labour market, and the extent of female participation in economic activities.

The ratio of workers to non-workers among those aged 15 years and above (i.e., the working-age population) was the highest for manual-worker households of all socio-economic classes in the study villages (see Table 1). In Panahar, the ratio was 6:1 for manual workers, whereas

---

[2] See chapter 3 in this volume for a description of socio-economic classes in the three villages.

Table 1 *Ratio of worker to non-worker, by socio-economic class, study villages, 2009–10 and 2014–15*

Socio-economic class	2009–10			2014–15		
	Panahar	Amar-singhi	Kalman-dasguri	Panahar	Amar-singhi	Kalman-dasguri
Landlord/capitalist farmer	4:01	NA	NA	3:01	NA	NA
Peasant I	2:01	–	6:01	2:01	–	3:01
Peasant II	5:01	7:01	12:01	5:01	9:01	7:01
Manual worker	6:01	10:01	12:01	5:01	5:01	13:01
Others	2:01	4:01	4:01	3:01	3:01	4:01

Notes: The ratios are calculated for the population belonging to the age group of 15 years and above. Households dependent on rents, remittances, and salaries have been clubbed together in "Others."
– Undefined.
NA = Not applicable.
Source: PARI surveys (2010 and 2015).

it was 5:1 for peasant II class. In Amarsinghi, the ratio for the class of manual workers was 10:1, whereas it was 7:1 for the peasant II class.[3] In Kalmandasguri, this ratio for the class of manual workers was very high at 12:1, the same as that of the peasant II class. For other socio-economic classes, the ratio was low.

The incidence of youth participation in the labour market for different socio-economic classes is presented in Table 2. The table depicts the worker-to-student ratio among those aged 15–24 years.[4] This is the age group when youths either participate in labour market or enrol themselves for higher or vocational education to access better job opportunities in the future. Taking the study villages together, the data suggest only 28 per cent of youths were enrolled in any educational institutions, with variation across the socio-economic classes in attaining higher educational achievements.

---

[3] The figures for 2015 are based on a sample. For comparison between the two survey years, we use the classification of households based on sample stratification. See chapter 1 for a discussion on the sampling method. The peasant I class refers to peasants who owned more than 2.5 acres of land, peasant II refers to peasant households owning more than 2.5 acres of land, and all non-agricultural classes are grouped as others.
[4] The United Nations defines "youth" as the population in 15–24 years' age group, wherein one is expected to enter the labour market after completing compulsory education (United Nations 1996).

Table 2 *Ratio of worker to student among the population aged 15–24 years, by socio-economic class, study villages, 2009–10 and 2014–15*

Socio-economic class	2009–10			2014–15		
	Panahar	Amar-singhi	Kalman-dasguri	Panahar	Amar-singhi	Kalman-dasguri
Landlord/capitalist farmer	0.5:1	NA	NA	6:01	NA	NA
Peasant I	0.3:1	0.7:1	1.3:1	NA	1.7:1	1.1:1
Peasant II	1.9:1	1.4:1	2.8:1	2.1:1	2:01	1.6:1
Manual worker	5.6:1	2.7:1	3.8:1	4.4:1	1.7:1	1.2:1
Others	0.7:1	2.5:1	2.3:1	0.4:1	10.5:1	3:01

Notes: Households dependent on rents, remittances, and salaries are grouped together in "Others."
NA = not applicable.
Source: PARI surveys (2010 and 2015).

In Panahar, the ratio for the class of manual workers was very high at 5.6:1, whereas it was 1.9:1 for the peasant II class. In Amarsinghi, the ratio for manual workers was 2.7:1, the highest among all the socio-economic classes. This suggests that the probability of participating in the labour market rather than enrolling in higher or vocational education was very high for youth from manual-worker households, followed by those belonging to the impoverished section of the peasantry. The reason for such high incidence among these sections is the lack of control over the means of production and low household income; this compelled a large proportion of youths from the manual-worker class and lower section of the peasantry to enter the labour market at an early age.

For young women aged 15–24 years, a significantly large share was exclusively engaged in household activities and never participated in any economic activities. In Panahar, 35 per cent of women of this age group were neither students nor workers – the highest among all the study villages (the corresponding figures were 18 and 26 per cent in Amarsinghi and Kalmandasguri, respectively). The share of this age group of women who were already married was remarkably high. For example, in Panahar, 33 out of 38 of these young women were already married, and a similar pattern was observed in other villages. These women neither participated in the labour market nor enrolled in any educational institution for higher or vocational education and were exclusively engaged in household chores.

To summarise, four points can be made. Firstly, the lack of ownership of the means of productive assets congregates a large number of households into the class of manual workers. The most important economic opportunity for this class was participating in the wage labour market and working for other socio-economic classes. Secondly, the work participation of members of manual-worker households was high in all study villages. Thirdly, the withdrawal of youth from education lowered their probability of receiving more remunerative jobs when they entered the job market. Household economic conditions compelled them to enter the wage labour market early without education and technical specialisation, thus hindering their occupational mobility. In turn, they reproduced the class of manual workers. Fourthly, a large section of young women did not participate in any economic activity, and their early ages of marriage further aggravated the problem; this raises serious questions on the status of human resource development in the State.

Purview of the Rural Wage Labour Market and Its Constituents

Generally, the class of manual workers constitutes a lion's share of wage labour markets in capitalist agrarian systems. In addition, a strong tendency of proletarianisation of the peasantry has been observed in the Indian agrarian economy in general and West Bengal in particular.[5] Marxian literature has argued that the class of wage labour did not primarily own agricultural land and other means of production, and were compelled to sell their labour power to earn their livelihood. However, in different parts of India, a section of the peasantry is the net seller of their labour power to the rural labour market, and wage labour has been a major source of its income. Rising input costs and unfavourable market conditions under the global neoliberal regime make small-scale farming almost unviable (Bakshi and Modak 2017). Given income poverty among poorer sections and even the middle peasantry due to unsustainability of farming, the section of the peasantry engaging in wage labour crowded and significantly expanded the rural labour market. This crowding by the peasantry has further intensified the crisis of employment (Mishra 2007). By 2011–12, nearly 47 per cent of all rural households in West Bengal were dependent on wage

---

[5] For a detailed dissuasion on various aspects of proletarianisation of the peasantry, see Ramachandran (2019).

Table 3 *Manual-worker and poor-peasant households, study villages, 2009–10,* in per cent

Village	Manual-worker households as a proportion of all households	Poor peasants as a proportion of all households	Share of landless households among manual worker households	Share of landless households among all households
Panahar	25	38	59	43
Amarsinghi	38	28	58	35
Kalmandasguri	38	26	33	22

Source: PARI survey (2010).

labour (NSSO 2012). Thus, it becomes important to understand the features of wage employment of this vast and expanding workforce.

Table 3 shows that manual-worker and poor-peasant households comprised more than 60 per cent of all households in the study villages. Despite the fact that Panahar had the highest extent of landlessness among the three villages, it had the smallest share of manual-worker households because Panahar residents had diversified income sources. Among manual-worker households in Kalmandasguri, only 33 per cent were landless, and though the remaining owned some land, they were mainly dependent on wage work.

Proletarianisation of the Peasantry

The main feature of peasant households in pre-capitalist and early capitalist societies was subsistence farming and the deployment of family labour to cultivate their own land, upon which peasant household members performed all or some of the major manual tasks. The process of subjugation of small peasants/subsistence farmers to the market led them to deploy more hired labour than family labour on their farms and to sell their labour power for a livelihood – a process described as proletarianisation of the peasantry (Ramachandran 2019).

Proletarianisation of the peasantry is an important aspect of the process of differentiation of the peasantry, which proceeds along with the development of capitalism in agriculture. One form commonly discussed in the literature is proletarianisation due to dispossession or de-peasantisation, wherein cultivating peasants who have lost their land are forced to sell their labour power for a livelihood (Ramachandran 2019). The progress of capitalist development and modernisation of agriculture was envisaged as the process of de-peasantisation and proletarianisation of the peasantry, as it has historically occurred in developed countries. It was expected that the traditional small peasant, who was seen as unproductive and incapable of adopting new technologies, would exit agriculture and join the ranks of the industrial workforce (Bakshi and Modak 2017). However, increasingly, sections of the peasantry, whilst cultivating their own land, are also being drawn into the labour market to sustain themselves, given that incomes from cultivation alone are not enough. This has been discussed by Ramachandran (2019) as a less-analysed form of proletarianisation. In all three of the West Bengal villages, the peasantry was being proletarianised, but there was no accompanying de-peasantisation.

In this chapter, proletarianisation of the peasantry has been explored through three major aspects that have been discussed in Ramachandran (2019) – deployment of labour time on one's own farm, labour time spent on one's own farm versus wage work, and expansion of the rural labour market by increased participation in wage labour. Each of these aspects is discussed in the subsections below.

High dependence on hired labour
Traditionally, peasants were those purely dependent on family labour for cultivation. In the study villages, there were no traditional peasants, and middle and even small peasants hired labour for various tasks. In fact, there was not a single poor-peasant household in Amarsinghi that did not use hired labour on their farm. Given that these were predominantly rice-cultivating villages, hired labour was mainly deployed for transplanting and harvesting operations. In the villages, poor peasants predominantly used family labour for crop production, although in Amarsinghi, the share of family labour in total labour use was the lowest among the three. In contrast to Panahar and Kalmandasguri, poor peasants in Amarsinghi used a higher proportion (more than 40 per cent) of hired labour on their farms. This means that even though poor peasants in Amarsinghi were spending some of their own labour time on their fields, they still had to hire labour.

The middle and large peasants (upper peasants) in all three villages, as in other villages across India, were primarily dependent on hired labour on their farms, owing to their larger operational holdings compared to the poor-peasant households.[6] However, in Kalmandasguri, the share of

---

[6] Upper peasants in Panahar operated more than two acres per household on average, whereas poor peasants operated less than 0.5 acre per household. In Amarsinghi, upper peasants operated two acres per household, whereas poor peasants operated one acre.

Table 4 *Family farm labour days as a proportion of all farm labour (family + hired) days, by class, study villages, 2009–10,* in per cent

Village	Upper peasant	Poor peasant	Manual worker
Panahar	33	79	89
Amarsinghi	18	59	82
Kalmandasguri	45	75	79

Source: PARI survey (2010).

family labour in the total labour used by upper peasants was nearly 45 per cent; this could be explained by the fact that these peasants only had small landholdings (an average of 2.4 acres per household).

Extent of labour time spent on own farm and wage work
To study another feature of proletarianisation of small peasants, we look at the labour deployment ratio – the ratio of the aggregate number of days that peasant households worked on their own farms to the number of days they worked as hired farm and non-farm workers. Across all three villages, this ratio for poor peasants was less than 50 per cent, meaning that poor-peasant households spent less than 50 per cent of their labour time cultivating their own land. In Panahar and Kalmandasguri, this proportion was even lower – poor peasants spent more than 70 per cent of their labour time selling their labour power for wages. One important factor contributing to the low labour deployment ratio, particularly in the case of Panahar, was the high participation of women from poor-peasant households in the wage labour market. The labour deployment ratio for upper peasants in Amarsinghi was low because they deployed their own labour time in non-agricultural wage labour and relied heavily on hired labour for work on their own farms.

Table 5 *Family labour days as a proportion of all labour (family + wage) days, by class, 2009–10,* in per cent

Village	Upper peasant	Poor peasant	Manual worker
Panahar	60	17	2
Amarsinghi	47	49	8
Kalmandasguri	77	30	6

Source: PARI survey (2010).

Expansion of the rural wage labour market

If we look at the total days of wage employment in a given village and disaggregate them by the major socio-economic classes, we find that in each of the three villages, the rural wage labour market had expanded beyond the class of manual workers. All sections of the peasantry participated in wage employment, particularly poor peasants. In Panahar, poor peasants comprised nearly 45 per cent of the rural wage employment received in the village. There were also some non-agricultural classes participating in wage employment, especially in Amarsinghi, where households whose major source of income came from small businesses and shops (such as barbers and vendors) were also engaged in non-agricultural wage employment.

It is clear that the poorer sections of the peasantry in all three villages were being proletarianised. There were, however, important differences in the process/extent of proletarianisation between Panahar, Amarsinghi, and Kalmandasguri. In Panahar, where the extent of landlessness and inequality was high, proletarianisation of the peasantry had proceeded to a larger extent. In fact, with respect to deployment of labour and participation in the wage labour market, the boundary between small peasants and manual workers was almost blurred.

Table 6 *Share of selected classes in total days of wage employment, study villages, 2009–10,* in per cent

Village	Upper peasant	Poor peasant	Manual worker	All other classes	Total
Panahar	8 (21)	45 (38)	46 (25)	2 (16)	100
Amarsinghi	4 (14)	15 (28)	71 (38)	10 (20)	100
Kalmandasguri	4 (20)	29 (26)	59 (37)	8 (17)	100

Note: The figure in brackets gives the household share of each class group.
Source: PARI survey (2010).

Work participation of women in wage employment. Women from manual-worker households participated almost equally as men in the wage labour market in all three villages. In all three villages, more than 35 per cent of women from the class of manual workers were engaged in wage employment (Table 7). Their work participation rate in wage employment was higher in Panahar and Amarsinghi because the proportion of landless households among manual workers was higher in these villages (Tables 7 and 3). Although overall landlessness in both villages was fairly low,

Table 7 *Work participation rate in wage employment of manual-worker and poor-peasant households, by sex, study villages, 2009–10, in per cent*

Work participation rate	Manual worker		Poor peasant	
	F	M	F	M
Panahar	42	56	37	53
Amarsinghi	44	59	8	43
Kalmandasguri	35	45	31	49

Note: To calculate the work participation rate, the population aged above 15 years was considered as the denominator.
Source: PARI survey (2010).

particularly in Amarsinghi, the majority of landless households were dependent on manual wage work for their livelihood.

The participation of women from poor-peasant households in wage employment was lower than those from manual-worker households, particularly in Amarsinghi (Table 7). However, in Panahar and Kalmandasguri, the difference between poor-peasant and manual-worker households in terms of women's work participation rate in wage employment was minimal – this could be due to the availability of non-agricultural employment for women. The high work participation rate of women from poor-peasant households further validates that Panahar had a high degree of proletarianisation of its peasantry.

Days of employment. The average days of employment per worker for all workers (both men and women) in the three villages was either less than or around 100 days. Women received merely 60 days per worker in Amarsinghi and Kalmandasguri, the lowest number of employment days across all of the PARI study villages (Nagbhushan 2020). Employment received by men on average was at least 1.5 times than that for women in all three villages.

In Panahar, the high number of employment days per worker among women may be due to the availability of non-agricultural employment for women. Women engaged in wage employment here received more days of wage employment from the non-agricultural sector than from agriculture. NREGS (National Rural Employment Generation Scheme) as well as a market for hired domestic work within the village contributed to their high share of non-agricultural wage employment; one woman even worked as van driver in the village. This pattern was reversed for male wage

Table 8 *Average annual days of employment per worker, by sex, study villages, 2009–10, in number*

Village	F	M	All
Panahar	78	118	102
Amarsinghi	59	83	75
Kalmandasguri	61	119	98

Note: This table includes average days of employment received by workers of all classes.
Source: PARI survey (2010).

Table 9 *Share of employment days in agriculture and non-agriculture, by sex, study villages, 2009–10, in per cent*

Village	Female			Male		
	Agriculture	Non-agriculture	Total	Agriculture	Non-agriculture	Total
Panahar	44	56	100	57	43	100
Amarsinghi	90	10	100	47	53	100
Kalmandasguri	97	3	100	30	70	100

Source: PARI survey (2010).

workers in Panahar, where 60 per cent of the total employment received by them came from agriculture. This mostly included transplanting and harvesting of rice and sowing and harvesting of potato.

In Amarsinghi and Kalmandasguri, women's dependence on agriculture was much higher than in Panahar. Here, women received more than 90 per cent of wage employment from agriculture, particularly within the villages. Men, on the other hand, particularly those in Kalmandasguri, were largely dependent on the non-agricultural sector. They engaged in NREGS work in the village as well as earth- and construction-related activities in the nearby towns and villages.

While non-agricultural employment in Amarsinghi and Kalmandasguri was fairly low, NREGS played a significant role. As mentioned earlier, NREGS was particularly important for women workers in Panahar. Of all women wage workers from manual-worker households, 75 and 49 per cent in Panahar and Amarsinghi, respectively, reported doing NREGS work (See Appendix Table 4).

Features of Labour Use in Crop Production
in the Study Villages

In the villages, crop production through both self-employment and wage employment was the major source of employment for the agrarian socio-economic classes. In this section, we discuss features of labour use in crop production. The level of labour use in crop production is determined by the extent of land operated and the nature of crop practices adopted by cultivators of the different socio-economic classes. Total labour use in Panahar was 24,298 labour days on 215 acres of operated land. Rice cultivation in the pre-kharif and kharif seasons absorbed 22 and 41 per cent of the total labour days, respectively, whereas rabi crops (potato, mustard, and sesame) absorbed 36 per cent.[7]

In Amarsinghi, total labour use in crop production was 9,386 labour days on 72.39 acres of land (130 labour days per acre per year). The major crops here were jute in pre-kharif season, rice in both kharif and rabi seasons, and potato in rabi season. The pattern of labour absorption was well distributed across two crop seasons: kharif and rabi crops absorbed 39 and 48 per cent of the total labour use, respectively. Jute cultivated in the pre-kharif season absorbed only 9 per cent of the total labour use.

In Kalmandasguri, labour use in crop production amounted to 12,400 labour days. As in Amarsinghi, labour deployment was well distributed by season: pre-kharif (mainly jute), kharif (mainly rice), and rabi (mainly potato) crops absorbed 19, 33, and 41 per cent of total labour use, respectively.

The sources of human labour for crop production were family members of cultivating households, hired labour, and any form of non-wage labour. The latter, such as exchange labour, have almost ceased to exist in the study villages. The use of family labour was the lowest in Panahar at 38 per cent of the total labour use. In Panahar and Amarsinghi, a large share of labour use for crop production came from the village wage labour market. In Kalmandasguri, 57 per cent of the total labour use came from the cultivating households belonging to different socio-economic classes.

Daily wage and piece-rated contracts were the two most prevalent labour contracts. In Panahar, 70 per cent of the total hired labour use was deployed on daily wage contracts, whereas in Amarsinghi, 56 per cent was deployed on piece-rated contracts. In Kalmandasguri, the composition of both types of contracts was 53 and 47 per cent, respectively.

---

[7] See chapter 5 for a description of the cropping pattern in the villages.

Table 10 *Total labour use, by season, study villages, 2009–10, in per cent*

Village	Pre-kharif	Kharif	Rabi	Others	Total labour days (number)
Panahar	22	41	36	0	24,298
Amarsinghi	9	39	48	3	9,386
Kalmandasguri	19	33	41	7	12,400

Source: PARI survey (2010).

Table 11 *Composition of total labour use, study villages, 2009–10, in per cent*

Village	Family labour	Hired labour	Exchange labour	Total labour days (number)
Panahar	38	59	3	24,298
Amarsinghi	42	58	0	9,386
Kalmandasguri	57	43	1	12,400

Source: PARI survey (2010).

Table 12 *Composition of hired labour use, by type of contract, study villages, 2009–10, in per cent*

Village	Daily-wage contract	Piece-rated contract	Total hired labour (number)
Panahar	70	30	14,336
Amarsinghi	44	56	5,444
Kalmandasguri	53	47	5,332

Source: PARI survey (2010).

Labour Absorption by Crop

The choice of crops along with the production organisation plays an important role in determining the level of labour absorption. In Panahar, kharif rice in the kharif season absorbed 44 per cent of the total labour use in crop production, followed by potato in the rabi season (31 per cent of the total labour use) and rice in the pre-kharif season (20.6 per cent of the total labour use). In rice cultivation, the average labour use per acre of land was 60 and 53 labour days in the pre-kharif and kharif seasons, respectively. However, the labour intensity of potato cultivation was highest in the village, at 73 labour days per acre. The overall labour use per acre of crop cultivated declined by 32 per cent between 2009–10 and 2014–15. For instance, labour use in potato cultivation declined by 29 per cent in this period. All forms of labour declined, specifically family labour (see Appendix Tables 1 and 2). Between 2009–10 and 2014–15, the area under rice cultivation in the rabi season declined by 29 per cent, whereas the extent of land under sesame cultivation increased by 123 per cent. Because the labour use pattern suggests labour absorption in sesame cultivation was much lower than that in rice and potato, increased cultivation of the former might have reduced overall labour use in rabi season.

In Amarsinghi, the three major crops in terms of total labour absorption were rice in rabi, rice in kharif, and jute in pre-kharif (in ascending order). They accounted for 79.8 per cent of the total labour use and resulted in an average labour use per acre ranging between 58 and 69 labour days. Furthermore, the data suggest that potato cultivation required 103 labour days per acre, which was the highest among all crops, but it was only cultivated on a small extent of land. Thus, though the labour intensity per acre was high, the total labour use for potato was not as significant as it was for rice or jute. In comparing labour use per acre for different crops for 2009–10 and 2014–15, we first note that overall labour use per acre declined from 58 to 47 labour days per acre. Among rice and jute in kharif and potato in rabi, jute showed a significant decline in labour absorption. More importantly, the composition of family labour and different forms of hired labour were also altered (see Appendix tables 1 and 2). For jute cultivation, the use of family labour doubled and hired labour on piece-rated contracts almost tripled between 2009–10 and 2014–15. In fact, hired labour use on piece-rated contracts increased for all crops cultivated in Amarsinghi. Except for family labour use in jute, all other crops showed a significant decline in the use of family labour and hired labour on daily wage contracts. The data suggest that cultivators have moved towards piece-rated contracts that do not require much supervision and are considered more efficient than daily wage contracts.

In Kalmandasguri, jute was extensively cultivated and absorbed 33.7 per cent of the total labour use, followed by vegetable cultivation – gourds, cluster beans, cauliflower, okra, chilli, cabbage, cucumber, and others absorbed 29 per cent of the total labour use – and finally kharif rice, which absorbed 24 per cent of the total labour use. Importantly, the labour absorption capacity of vegetable production was significant at 111

Table 13 *Average labour use per acre of land operated, by crop, study villages, 2009–10 and 2014–15*, in eight-hour days

Village	Crop	2009–10	2014–15
Panahar	Paddy (pre-kharif)	60	42
	Paddy (kharif)	53	40
	Potato	73	52
	Sesame	17	25
Amarsinghi	Jute	58	67
	Paddy (kharif)	59	51
	Potato	103	82
Kalmandasguri	Jute	82	55
	Paddy (kharif)	50	45
	Potato	67	51
	Vegetables	111	117

Source: PARI surveys (2010 and 2015).

labour days per acre, compared to that of pre-kharif jute and kharif rice at 82 and 50 labour days, respectively. Overall labour use per acre declined by 18 per cent between 2009–10 and 2014–15 for all crops except vegetables. In particular, jute, rice (kharif), and potato (rabi) declined significantly; for instance, labour days in jute cultivation declined from 82 to 55. Family labour use declined significantly across all crops and was replaced by hired labour both on daily wage and piece-rated contracts, however, in the case of jute, there was no clear pattern regarding hired labour use on daily wage and piece-rated contracts. In vegetable cultivation, labour use under daily wage contracts increased significantly, from 14 to 41 labour days per acre, whereas for potato cultivation, labour use under piece-rated contracts increased significantly, from 2 to 13 labour days per acre. Hired labour use on daily wage contracts for vegetable cultivation increased as some agricultural tasks for these crops required more care and precision rather than rapid completion.

Employment in Non-Agricultural Work

A continuous shift in occupational structure from agriculture to non-agriculture has been taking place in India, as well as in West Bengal. The share of workers in agriculture has declined and that in non-agriculture such as the construction and services sector has increased. Given this increase, we now discuss the distribution of wage employment generated in the non-agricultural sector in 2009–10 and 2014–15 in the study villages. Male employment in non-agriculture increased in Panahar (from 10,953 to 11,448 person days) and Amarsinghi (from 5,527 to 6,623 person days) and substantially declined in Kalmandasguri (from 10,645 to 6,830 person days). Employment in manufacturing was more prevalent in Amarsinghi and Kalmandasguri than in Panahar. Construction absorbed substantial male labour: in 2014–15, person days in this sector increased in Panahar and Amarsinghi (1,953 to 3,514 and 710 to 2,761 person days, respectively), whereas in Kalmandasguri, person days decreased from 6,172 to 4,083. (see Appendix tables 3–5).

In Panahar, job creation for male workers was observed in various State departments, and private sector expansion of business and trade activities, whereas female workers were employed as Anganwadi workers, auxilliary nurse and midwives (ANMs), domestic workers, and MDM (mid-day meal) cooks. In Amarsinghi, employment for male workers increased due to opportunities at a plywood factory (saw mill). In Kalmandasguri, male employment in services sector increased due to the expansion of the fish business as well as recruitment in government departments for various positions for men (such as peon at post office, community health guide, tax collector at panchayat) and ANMs, Anganwadi workers, mid-day meal cooks, and integrated child development services (ICDS) workers for women. Female work participation in the non-agricultural sector was limited to MGNREGA (The Mahatma Gandhi National Rural Employment Guarantee Act) and services. In Panahar, female employment in this sector decreased, mainly due to the failure of MGNREGA. As a result, women who received employment in MGNREGA in 2009–10 had to return to agriculture or leave the economic activity.

The classes of manual workers and peasant II have predominantly participated in manual work in non-agricultural occupations. Tables 14–16 indicate the number of wage workers, the number of days of employment in non-agricultural works, and the average number of days of employment per person in 2009–10 and 2014–15. The number of male workers in non-agricultural occupations for the classes of manual workers and peasant II decreased drastically: from 166 to 96 in Panahar, 102 to 53 in Amarsinghi, and 106 to 52 in Kalmandasguri. With this decline, the average number of days of work per person has increased, even though the absolute number of employment days in non-agriculture decreased; the decline in number of workers was sharper than that in the absolute number of employment days. The average number of employment days per person increased during the five-year period: from 62.4 to 96.8 person days in Panahar, 47.2 to 119.4 in Amarsinghi, and 99.5 to 126.3 in Kalmandasguri.

The number of female workers belonging to the manual-worker and peasant II classes decreased in all three villages: from 76 to 57 in Panahar, 50 to 46 in Amarsinghi, and 69 to 47 in Kalmandasguri. Employment in non-agricultural sectors for female wage workers declined, and the number of wage workers, the total number of employment days, and the average number of employment days per person decreased in all villages. In Panahar, the failure of MGNREGA in 2014–15 resulted in a drastic decline in wage work.

With a decline in the participation of workers of peasant II households in the non-agricultural wage labour market, these workers' number of employment days did not substantially increase as was observed for those from the class of manual workers. For instance, in Kalmandasguri, between 2010 and 2015, the number of peasant II workers declined by 60 per cent, but the number of employment days per worker increased by 57 per cent. Among manual-worker households, the number of workers declined by 39 per cent, but the number of employment days per worker increased by 202 per cent. A similar pattern was observed in Panahar. In Amarsinghi, both the number of workers and number of employment days per worker declined in the same period.

Two observations can be made. Firstly, the lack of employment

Table 14 *Days of wage employment, by class and sex, Panahar, 2009–10 and 2014–15*, in number

Year	Class	Female			Male		
		Number	Total labour days	Days/ person	Number	Total labour days	Days/ person
2010	Manual worker	46	3,179	69	62	4,810	78
	Peasant II	65	2,505	38	104	5,542	53
	Total	111	5,684	51	166	10,352	62
2015	Manual worker	21	1,834	89	63	6,859	109
	Peasant II	5	52	11	33	2,434	74
	Total	26	1,886	75	96	9,293	97

Source: PARI surveys (2010 and 2015).

Table 15 *Days of wage employment, by class and sex, Amarsinghi, 2009–10 and 2014–15*, in number

Year	Class	Female			Male		
		Number	Total labour days	Days/ person	Number	Total labour days	Days/ person
2010	Manual worker	31	259	8	57	2,695	47
	Peasant II	8	93	12	45	2,117	47
	Total	39	352	9	102	4,812	47
2015	Manual worker	NA	NA	NA	35	4,999	142
	Peasant II	2	107	50	18	1,329	74
	Total	2	107	50	53	6,328	119

Note: NA = Not applicable.
Source: PARI surveys (2010 and 2015).

Table 16 *Days of wage employment, by class and sex, Kalmandasguri, 2009–10 and 2014–15*, in number

Year	Class	Male			Female		
		Number	Total labour days	Days/ person	Number	Total labour days	Days/ person
2010	Manual worker	51	7,106	139	11	70	6
	Peasant II	55	3,442	63	10	61	6
	Total	106	10,548	66	21	131	6
2015	Manual worker	24	4,876	203	10	291	30
	Peasant II	28	1,694	60	3	28	10
	Total	52	6,570	126	13	319	26

Source: PARI surveys (2010 and 2015).

opportunities discouraged workers from peasant II households to seek wage work in non-agricultural jobs. Secondly, the opportunity cost of searching from the limited number of available jobs resulted in a smaller number of days of employment, that is, peasant II workers preferred to abstain from regular job market visits and concentrated more on cultivating their own land. However, this was not the case for manual-worker households – they were compelled to seek jobs even at a higher opportunity cost to maintain household income. The reduced participation of peasant II households and their unwillingness to claim jobs helped workers from manual-worker households obtain more days of employment.

Male Outmigration from Rural West Bengal

Some Results from the Census of India

Consecutive rounds of the Census of India show that the rate of outmigration from West Bengal increased rapidly after 1991. The proportion of male outmigrants decreased from 11.6 per cent of the total male population in 1971 to 9.5 per cent in 1991, after which it continually increased in the next two decades to 19.4 per cent in 2011. Here, outmigrants are defined as those whose last residence differs from their place of enumeration, and includes intra-state, interstate, and international migrants.

A large section of male outmigrants were intra-state migrants – however, male interstate migration has also increased from 1.2 per cent in 1991 to 2 per cent in 2011. According to the Census, of the total male outmigrant population from West Bengal in 2011, 41.4 and 35.4 per cent were from rural and urban areas, respectively (the last residence of the remaining 23.2 per cent were unspecified). The highest rates of male outmigration were from North 24 Parganas, Darjiling, Hugli, Nadia, Barddhaman, and Jalpaiguri districts – male outmigrants from these districts comprised more than 20 per cent of their district's population (Table 18). The districts in which the three PARI villages were located – Bankura, Maldah, and Koch Bihar – had outmigration rates below the State average.

Table 17 *Male outmigration, West Bengal, 1971–2011*, in number and per cent

Year	Population	Outmigrants	Share of outmigrants (%)
1971	23,435,987	2,859,938	11.6
1981	28,560,901	3,314,456	11.6
1991	35,510,633	3,371,248	9.5
2001	41,465,985	5,665,356	13.7
2011	46,809,027	9,077,853	19.4

Note: This table was computed by Yoshifumi Usami.
Source: Census of India.

Table 18 *Male outmigration by location, West Bengal districts, 2011*, in per cent

District	Rural	Urban	Total
North 24 Parganas	29.6	33.3	31.7
Darjiling	26.5	21.3	24.4
Hugli	21.2	27	23.5
Nadia	20.9	25.8	22.3
Barddhaman	22.3	20.7	21.7
Jalpaiguri	19.9	26	21.6
Haora	27.4	13.9	18.8
Kolkata	–	6.5	16.5
South 24 Parganas	10.5	23.6	13.8
Koch Bihar	10.9	34.1	13.2
Dakshin Dinajpur	12	18.4	12.9
Birbhum	9.8	25.7	11.8
Murshidabad	10.4	14.9	11.3
Bankura	7.6	47.7	10.9
Uttar Dinajpur	9.4	20.7	10.8
Maldah	9.4	14.8	10.1
Paschim Medinipur	6.2	20	7.8
Purba Medinipur	6.2	13.6	7
Puruliya	4.3	17	5.9

Source: Computed from Table D-6, Census of India, 2011.

Outmigration from the Three Villages

In the PARI surveys, information of household members residing outside the village for most of the year was collected. There are significant differences in the PARI and Census definitions of a migrant. The former follows the concept of "current migration" – only those household members who spend part of the year in the village and the remaining part outside are enumerated as migrants. Therefore, female members who migrate out of the village after marriage are not considered as current migrants in PARI surveys. Similarly, members who permanently reside outside the village are not considered as migrants. Migrants listed in PARI surveys are usually household members who migrate out for employment or education.

The 2010 survey defined current migrants as "people who have been staying out of the village for a period of six months or more." In 2015, noting the importance of shorter-term outmigration from the three villages, the definition of migration was broadened to include members who stayed out of the village for less than six months. An additional questionnaire was also canvassed in households reporting migrant members to collect information on previous migrations of members, the purpose of migration, the living conditions at the destination, and the networks that enabled members to find work outside.

In the 2010 survey, the proportion of migrants in the total population was 5 per cent for Amarsinghi and Kalmandasguri, whereas it was lower in case of Panahar (3 per cent). Not counting marriage migration in the definition of migrants, the PARI survey in the three villages revealed more male than female migrants. In the 2015 sample survey, the proportion of migrants in the sample population was 2.1 per cent for Panahar, 9 per cent for Amarsinghi, and 6.2 per cent for Kalmandasguri. This does not necessarily imply an increase in migration from Amarsinghi and

Table 19 *Distribution of migrants, by sex, study villages, 2010,* in number and per cent

	Panahar			Amarsinghi			Kalmandasguri		
	F	M	All	F	M	All	F	M	All
Population	538	545	1,083	289	286	575	334	367	701
Migrants	4	30	34	5	23	28	5	33	38
Share of migrants (%)	0.7	5.5	3.1	1.7	8	4.9	1.5	9	5.4

Source: PARI survey (2010).

Table 20 *Distribution of migrants, by sex, study villages, 2015,* in number and per cent

	Panahar			Amarsinghi			Kalmandasguri		
	F	M	All	F	M	All	F	M	All
Population (sample size)	229	256	485	123	132	255	119	124	243
Migrants (sample estimate)	1	9	10	1	22	23	0	15	15
Share of migrants in sample (%)	0.4	3.5	2.1	0.8	16.7	9	0	12.1	6.2

Source: PARI survey (2015).

Kalmandasguri, given that the definition of migrants is different in the two survey rounds. Also, the 2015 sample survey used the 2010 survey list as the sampling frame and hence was not a representative sample for the villages. Thus, we cannot draw population estimates from the 2015 survey. Due to this empirical limitation, we focus, instead, on the features of male outmigration from each of the villages.

Panahar

Outmigration from Panahar was primarily for salaried employment or higher education. Of the 30 male outmigrants here in 2010, 10 were in salaried occupations, 9 were students, 6 were in skilled/semi-skilled wage employment, and 5 were in unskilled wage work. The skilled/semi-skilled workers were drivers, carpenters, factory workers, whereas the unskilled workers worked as guards and in shops. No workers worked in construction work. In 2015, of the nine male migrants, four were in salaried occupations, one was a student, and the remaining four migrated to semi-skilled and manual-wage employment as cooks, helpers, and in shops. Again, no one worked in the construction sector. In Panahar, manual wage employment in agriculture and non-agriculture was readily available in the village or in nearby urban centres, so outmigration for manual wage work was not very common.

Outmigration from Panahar was primarily pull migration of the educated and skilled workforce for regular and remunerative jobs in cities and towns. Due to the nature of this employment, long duration migration from the village was common – 40 per cent of migrants migrated for more than a year. It is worth noting that most migrants from Panahar were from caste Hindu and Muslim households – 53 and 21 per cent, respectively, in 2010. These households owned most of the land and assets in the village and constituted the classes of landlords/capitalist farmers and upper peasants. Members of these households invested in higher education and found salaried employment in Kolkata and other urban centres. Furthermore, Scheduled Castes (SCs) were under-represented in migration – though SCs comprised 49 per cent of Panahar's population, only 21 per cent of outmigrants were SCs.

Most outmigrants' destination was Kolkata, though a few migrated to other parts of the State as well. Only two had migrated outside the State in 2010. In 2015, there may have been an increase in interstate migration as the number of interstate migrants had increased to four.

Amarsinghi

The nature of migration from Amarsinghi (as well as Kalmandasguri) was different from Panahar. Male outmigrants engaged in mainly two types of occupations – unskilled manual and semi-skilled/skilled work. Half of the male outmigrants in 2010 and 6 out of 22 in 2015 were unskilled manual workers and worked in the construction sector, as gardeners, and as daily labourers in shops and mills in Delhi, Haryana, and Mumbai. Semi-skilled/skilled work consisted of work in factories, workshops, and manufacturing such as jewellery-making units. The data seem to indicate that outmigration for such type of employment increased between 2010 and 2015, whereas migration for manual work declined, but we cannot draw clear conclusions due to the limitations of the data. There was no migration from Amarsinghi for salaried formal sector jobs in either survey year. Interstate migration was most common, primarily to Delhi and more recently to Haryana, and the duration was very short – 60 per cent of all male current migrants migrated for less than six months in 2015 (Table 21). There was an equal number of SC and caste Hindu migrants; this corresponded to the village population consisting of 45 per cent SCs and 55 per cent caste Hindus.

The migration route from Amarsinghi to Delhi is quite old and has been noted in earlier studies as well. Bakshi (2010) remarked that a number of trains between Maldah and Delhi were initiated by the erstwhile Minister of Railways Ghani Khan Chowdhury and continued through the years. However, there seems to be a shift in the occupations of outmigrants. In 2005–06, village outmigrants migrated to Delhi and worked as gardeners and in jewellery workshops in Delhi (Bakshi 2010). In the 2010 survey, most migrants were engaged in unskilled wage employment, whereas in the 2015 survey, more migrants worked in factories and workshops. The type of employment was always of a short duration in nature.

Labour contractors facilitated the migration network in Amarsinghi and the adjoining villages. Interviews with migrants in 2015 revealed that labour contractors who hired migrant workers for temporary employment were based in Kaliachak town, 65 kilometers from Amarsinghi and located in the administrative division of Maldah Sadar subdivision of Maldah district. These contractors had "assistants" in villages such as Amarsinghi who were responsible for hiring workers who agreed to work on construction sites in Delhi and Haryana on a contract basis. This contract was usually for two months and could be renewed, depending on the work available at the destination. According to these contracts, half of the wages are paid in advance at the place of origin, i.e., Amarsinghi, and the rest paid after completion of the contract.

Kalmandasguri

Like Amarsinghi, migration from Kalmandasguri was mainly for unskilled and skilled/semi-skilled wage employment. Of the 33 migrants from the village in 2010, 15 were in unskilled work and 11 in skilled/semi-skilled wage work. Unskilled workers primarily engaged in construction work, whereas skilled/semi-skilled workers worked in a variety of occupations such as factory workers, masons, blacksmiths, and cooks. There were only two who migrated for salaried jobs, both in the defense services. The remaining 5 were students. In 2015, 13 out of 15 male migrants engaged in manual wage work – all but one were employed in construction work. Most migration from Kalmandasguri was interstate migration, though there was some to the neighboring country of Bhutan for construction activities. In Kalmandasguri, 26 per cent of male migrants migrated for less than 6 months and 47 per cent migrated for 6 to 12 months in 2015 – thus, a substantial portion was short duration migration. Lastly, migrants belonged to all social groups in the village.

When surveyed in 2010, Kalmandasguri had a well-established migration network with Kerala – migrants there were engaged in the construction sector. In the 2015 sample survey, there were five workers who had migrated to Kerala, mostly for work in construction and cashew nut factories. One such migrant surveyed in 2015, 22-year-old Yacoub Miya, had already migrated eight times to Kerala and Bhutan for construction work. He started migrating at age 16 and regularly does so for short durations. Joydeb Debnath, another migrant, was a potato cultivator who migrated to work in construction in Kerala and Karnataka during the lean agricultural season.

Migration from the village was facilitated by a network of agents and labour contractors. Of the 15 outmigrants in 2015, 7 reported that they were recruited by such agents or contractors. Family members and relatives who found employment outside the village also helped other members to migrate. We also asked household members who had not migrated in 2014–15 to report previous migrations. The earliest reported male migration in the sample was of Enajuddin Miya, aged 56 in 2015, who was recruited by a labour contractor and migrated to Thimpu in Bhutan for construction work in 1995.

To sum up, a number of outmigrants were observed in all three villages,

Table 21 *Distribution of outmigrants (current), by duration of stay at destination, study villages, 2015*, in number

Duration of stay	Panahar	Amarsinghi	Kalmandasguri
Unspecified	2	4	0
≤ 6 months	3	10	4
> 6 months and ≤ 12 months	1	5	7
> 1 year	4	4	4
Total	10	23	15

Source: PARI survey (2015).

Table 22 *Distribution of male outmigrants, by occupation, study villages, 2010 and 2015*, in number

Occupation/activity status	Panahar		Amarsinghi		Kalmandasguri	
	2010	2015	2010	2015	2010	2015
Salaried	10	4	0	0	2	1
Skilled/semi-skilled worker	6	1	7	12	11	1
Unskilled manual worker	5	3	12	6	15	13
Business	0	0	1	0	0	0
Student	9	1	2	1	5	0
Unspecified	0	0	1	3	0	0
Total	30	9	23	22	33	15

Source: PARI surveys (2010 and 2015).

Table 23 *Distribution of male outmigrants, by destination of migration, study villages, 2010 and 2015*, in number

Destination of migration	Panahar		Amarsinghi		Kalmandasguri	
	2010	2015	2010	2015	2010	2015
Intra-state	26	5	3	1	9	2
Interstate	2	4	20	21	22	11
International	0	0	0	0	2	2
Unspecified	2	0	0	0	0	0
All	30	9	23	22	33	15

Source: PARI surveys (2010 and 2015).

in varying degrees. Due to limitations of the data, we cannot state whether the rate of migration from the villages increased between 2010 and 2015. The pattern of male outmigration from Panahar was remarkably different from the other two villages – it was of longer duration, for education or salaried/more regular employment, and within the State. There was a higher tendency of migration among the better-off caste Hindu and Muslim households than among SC households, and none of the Panahar migrants were engaged in construction work in 2010 or 2015. In contrast, Amarsinghi and Kalmandasguri saw push migrations necessitated by inadequate employment and incomes within the villages. Migration was for short durations and primarily for semi-skilled and unskilled wage employment outside the State, where construction served as a major source of employment. Outmigration was prevalent among all social groups in these two villages. The well-established migration networks were from Amarsinghi to Delhi and from Kalmandasguri to Kerala, often mediated by agents and labour contractors.

Note on MGNREGA

In this section, we discuss the availability of MGNREGA work and its impact on the household income of labouring households. Figure 1 shows the trends in MGNREGA employment over time for India and West Bengal. At the all-India level, total employment increased from 1,063 million person days in 2008–09 to 2,283 million person days in 2010–11 but plateaued thereafter at 2,300 million person days, except in 2014–15 when employment fell substantially. In West Bengal, employment grew from 35 million person days in 2008–09 to 312 million person days in 2010–11, with declines in 2014–15 and 2016–17. Given this background, the role of MGNREGA in Panahar, as well as in Amarsinghi and Kalmandasguri, became irrelevant in 2015. In fact, in the 2015 sample survey in Amarsinghi, not a single household reported receiving employment under MGNREGA for 2014–15, compared to 152 people who did receive it in 2009-10. In Kalmandasguri, very few people received employment under MGNREGA in 2015, and there is minimal impact of MGNREGA on household income.

In Panahar, the decline in the number of MGNREGA beneficiaries was very sharp over the five-year period. Only 21 women received employment in 2014–15, compared to 105 in 2009–10, a decline of 80 per cent. For their male counterparts, there was a decline of 74 per cent. Male and female workers from the classes of peasant II and manual workers were

Figure 1 *Days of employment generated in MGNREGA, all-India and West Bengal, 2008–18, in* number

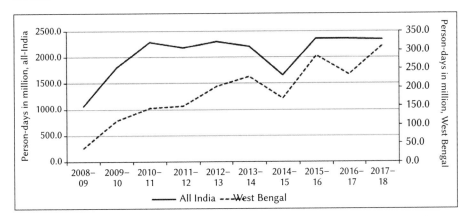

Source: MIS reports, MGNREGA, Ministry of Rural Development, Government of India, available at http://164.100.129.6/netnrega/MISreport4.aspx?fin_year=2013-2014&rpt=RP, viewed on January 16, 2021.

Table 24 *Female MGNREGA workers and their share among all female workers, by socio-economic class, Panahar, 2009–10 and 2014–15*, in number, per cent, and annual earnings in Rs

Socio-economic class	2009–10				2014–15			
	Worker	Per cent	Days/ worker	Earnings/ worker	Worker	Per cent	Days/ worker	Earnings/ worker
Landlord/ capitalist farmer	0	0	0	0	0	0	0	0
Peasant I	1	2	49.4	4,349	0	0	0	0
Peasant II	59	31.7	30.9	2,784.3	5	9.6	10.2	1,557
Manual worker	44	51.2	32.2	2,900.2	16	23.9	7.7	896.4
Others	1	2.1	24	2756	0	0	0	0
Total	105	27.1	31.6	2,847.5	21	15.2	8.3	1,053.7

Source: PARI surveys (2010 and 2015).

Table 25 *Male MGNREGA workers and their share among all male workers, by socio-economic class, Panahar, 2009–10 and 2014–15*, in number, per cent, and annual earnings in Rs

Socio-economic class	2009–10				2014–15			
	Worker	Per cent	Days/ worker	Earnings/ worker	Worker	Per cent	Days/ worker	Earnings/ worker
Landlord/ capitalist farmer	1	4.5	12	986	2	10.5	4.5	702
Peasant: I	4	9.1	18.1	1675.3	0	0	0	0
Peasant: II	95	54.3	30.9	2809.8	17	32.1	11.9	1996.4
Manual labour	51	64.6	29.9	2662.6	20	27.8	8.5	1036.4
Others	3	6.4	26	2480	NA	NA	NA	NA
Total	154	42	30	2713.3	39	27.1	9.8	1477.5

Note: NA = Not applicable.
Source: PARI surveys (2010 and 2015).

Table 26 *Distribution households and earnings per household, by socio-economic class, Panahar, 2009–10*, in number and Rs

Socio-economic class	2009–10		2014–15	
	Households	Earnings/ household	Households	Earnings/ household*
Landlord/ capitalist farmer	1	986	1	937.2
Peasant I	4	2,762.5	0	0
Peasant II	93	4,636.6	17	1,638.4
Manual worker	49	5,375.6	25	936.4
Others	4	2,549	NA	NA
Total	151	4,747.3	43	1,214.4

Notes: * Earnings/household in 2014–15 is deflated by the consumer price index for agricultural labour (CPI-AL) of 2009.
NA = Not applicable.
Source: PARI survey (2010).

the worst affected, given that these two classes were heavily dependent on wage employment. In terms of the number of days of employment, a female worker received, on average, 31.6 days of employment in 2009–10, which declined to merely 8.3 days of work in 2014–15. For male workers, the number of employment days declined from 30 days to 9.8 days. The steep fall in the number of days of employment certainly added to the already persistent problem of underemployment in Panahar. Evidently, MGNREGA earnings per worker in 2014–15, for both male and female workers, were halved since 2009–10, even in nominal terms.

Furthermore, the contribution of MGNREGA in household income substantially declined. Table 26 suggests that in 2009–10, 151 households received some income from MGNREGA. A total of 142 households from the classes of peasant II and manual worker benefitted, as 17 per cent of their household income was derived from MGNREGA work in 2009–10. In 2014–15, only 42 households from the peasant II and manual-worker classes earned 8 per cent and 3 per cent of their total household income from MGNREGA work, respectively. More specifically, 76 out of 93 peasant II households lost access to MGNREGA work and the remaining 17 households that received MGNREGA work lost two-thirds of their MGNREGA earnings between 2009–10 and 2014–15 (at 2009–10 prices). In the case of the class of manual workers, 25 of 49 households lost access to MGNREGA work and the remaining 24 households that received MGNREGA work lost four-fifths of their earnings (at 2009–10 prices).

Conclusions

This chapter dealt with the employment and unemployment situation of the rural workforce in the three study villages of West Bengal. Wage employment was an important source of livelihood in all the villages because manual-worker and poor-peasant households constituted more than 60 per cent of all households. Four major conclusions can be drawn regarding employment among the manual-worker and poor-peasant households. Firstly, all sections of the peasantry participated in the wage labour market. Though participation of manual-worker households was the highest, as expected, it was almost matched by the small peasants, particularly in Panahar. Secondly, women from manual-worker households participated almost equally with men in the wage labour market. However, the participation of women from small-peasant households was low, except in the case of Panahar. Thirdly, the average number of employment days per worker was less than 100 in all the three villages – however, it was lowest in Amarsinghi, where the average was clearly brought down by the low number of days of employment for women. Men in all villages received more than 1.5 times the average number of employment days received by women. This low number indicates underemployment among male and female workers, more so for the latter.

Lastly, agriculture provided the majority of employment to women in Amarsinghi and Kalmandasguri, whereas men in both villages primarily depended on MGNREGA and construction-related activities. In Panahar, the pattern was reversed because women mainly received employment in MGNREGA and hired domestic work, whereas men were mainly engaged in agricultural activities. Women in Panahar also engaged in agricultural activities such as transplanting/sowing of rice and harvesting of rice, potato, and jute. Moreover, female workers were mostly confined to MGNREGA and other low-remunerative, non-agricultural occupations. Between 2010 and 2015, overall employment opportunities for female workers absolutely declined, which forced them either to be confined to cultivating their own land and animal husbandry or to withdraw from the workforce.

As the data suggest, non-agricultural employment increased in Panahar and Amarsinghi but decreased in Kalmandasguri. In 2009–10, MGNREGA provided a sizable employment in the study villages but became irrelevant in Amarsinghi and Kalmandasguri in 2014–15. In Panahar, the number of MGNREGA workers declined sharply over the five-year period. The cessation of MGNREGA in Panahar in 2014–15 severely affected female employment. Consequently, the contribution of MGNREGA to household income substantially declined for peasant II and manual-worker households. The households that received employment under MGNREGA in 2014–15 lost more than 67 per cent of their MGNREGA income between 2009–10 and 2014–15. This reduction in income has serious consequences on rural poverty especially among manual workers and the impoverished section of the peasantry.

The decline in employment opportunities, both in agricultural and non-agricultural activities, along with the failure of the State-sponsored MGNREGA have seriously curtailed livelihood options for manual workers and the poorer section of the peasantry. The result of such a severe employment crisis in village production systems compels the working population to migrate to various places in the country.

References

Bakshi, Aparajita (2010), "Rural Household Incomes," unpublished PhD thesis, University of Calcutta, Kolkata.

Bakshi, Aparajita, and Modak, Tapas Singh (2017), "Incomes of Small Farmer Households," in Madhura Swaminathan and Sandipan Baksi (eds.), *How Do Small Farmers Fare: Evidence from Village Studies in India,* Tulika Books, New Delhi, pp. 126–70.

Mishra, Surjya Kanta (2007), "On Agrarian Transition in West Bengal," *The Marxist*, vol. 23, no. 2, pp. 1–22.

Nagbhushan, Shruti (2020), "Employment and Unemployment in Manual Worker Households," in Madhura Swaminathan, Shruti Nagbhushan, and V. K. Ramachandran (eds.), *Women and Work in Rural India*, Tulika Books, New Delhi, pp. 221–33.

National Sample Survey Organisation (NSSO) (2012), *Surveys of Employment and Unemployment, 68th Round (July 2011–June 2012)*, National Sample Survey Organisation, Ministry of Statistics and Programme Implementation, Government of India, New Delhi.

Ramachandran, V. K. (2019), "Aspects of the Proletarianisation of the Peasantry in India," in A. Narayanamoorthy, R.V. Bhavani, and R. Sujatha (eds.), *Whither Rural India? Political Economy of Agrarian Transformation in Contemporary India*, Tulika Books, New Delhi, pp. 69–83.

United Nations (1996), General Assembly, Fiftieth Session. A/RES/50/81, available at https://undocs.org/en/A/RES/50/81, accessed on September 5, 2020.

APPENDIX

Appendix Table 1 *Average labour use in per acre of land operated, by crop, study villages, 2009–10*, in eight-hour days

Village	Crop	Family labour	Hired labour		Total
			Daily-rate	Piece-rate	
Panahar	Paddy (pre-kharif)	29	21	11	60
	Paddy (kharif)	18	20	15	53
	Potato	33	27	13	73
	Sesame	7	9	1	17
Amarsinghi	Jute	10	39	8	58
	Paddy (kharif)	22	21	16	59
	Potato	41	52	10	103
Kalmandasguri	Jute	48	12	22	82
	Paddy (kharif)	29	8	13	50
	Potato	28	37	2	67
	Vegetables	91	14	6	111

Source: PARI Survey data (2010).

Appendix Table 2 *Average labour use in per acre of land operated, by crop, study villages, 2014–15*, in eight-hour days

Village	Crop	Family labour	Hired labour		Total
			Daily-rate	Piece-rate	
Panahar	Paddy (pre-kharif)	14	21	7	42
	Paddy (kharif)	12	19	8	40
	Potato	23	19	10	52
	Sesame	17	6	2	25
Amarsinghi	Jute	20	25	23	67
	Paddy (kharif)	11	17	24	51
	Potato	24	47	11	82
Kalmandasguri	Jute	32	13	9	55
	Paddy (kharif)	19	7	19	45
	Potato	16	23	13	51
	Vegetables	70	41	6	117

Source: PARI survey (2015).

Appendix Table 3 *Distribution of manual work in non-agricultural work, by sex, Panahar, 2009–10 and 2014–15, in number*

Year	Sex		Manual work in non-agriculture					
		Cons-truction	MGN-REGA	Trade	Manu-facture	Trans-port	Other	Total
2009–10	Male	1,953	4,731	300	263	2,606	1,100	10,953
	Female	56	3,404	0	0	47	1,413	4,920
	Total	2,009	8135	300	263	2,653	2,513	15,873
2014–15	Male	3,514	396	263	924	3,217	3,134	11,448
	Female	0	175	0	0	0	1,735	1,910
	Total	3,514	571	263	924	3,217	4,869	13,358

Source: PARI surveys (2010 and 2015).

Appendix Table 4 *Distribution of manual work in non-agricultural work, by sex, Amarsinghi, 2009–10 and 2014–15, in number*

Year	Sex		Manual work in non-agriculture					
		Cons-truction	MGN-REGA	Trade	Manu-facture	Trans-port	Other	Total
2009–10	Male	710	879	454	1,543	1,356	585	5,527
	Female	0	352	0	0	0	64	416
	Total	710	1,231	454	1,543	1,356	649	5,943
2014–15	Male	2,761	0	34	1,711	1,536	581	6,623
	Female	0	0	0	0	0	107	107
	Total	2,750	0	34	1,711	1,536	688	6,730

Source: PARI surveys (2010 and 2015).

Appendix Table 5 *Distribution of manual work in non-agricultural work, by sex, Kalmandasguri, 2009–10 and 2014–15,* in number

Year	Sex	Manual work in non-agriculture						
		Cons-truction	MGN-REGA	Trade	Manu-facture	Trans-port	Other	Total
2009–10	Male	6,172	531	30	1,858	1,604	450	10,645
	Female	0	152	0	0	0	0	152
	Total	6,172	683	30	1,858	1,604	450	10,797
2014–15	Male	4,083	347	612	296	584	908	6,830
	Female	176	118	0	0	0	25	319
	Total	4,259	465	612	296	584	933	7,149

Source: PARI surveys (2010 and 2015).

Appendix Table 6 *Share of female workers among manual-worker households who reported MGNREGA work, study villages, 2009-10,* in per cent

Village	Share of women among all MW HHs
Panahar	75
Amarsinghi	49
Kalmandasguri	23

Source: PARI survey (2010).

11

Wage Rates in Rural West Bengal
Insights from Three Villages

Arindam Das

Introduction

There has been a rapid rise in rural wages in most Indian States after 2006–07, and West Bengal was no exception (Himanshu 2017; Himanshu and Kundu 2016; Gulati, Jain, and Satija 2013). Despite the State's 7 percent growth in real wages between 2007–08 and 2014–15, it continues to have lower wage rates than other States in the country (Das and Usami 2017; Usami 2011). Furthermore, wage employment continues to be an important source of income for rural households in West Bengal. Data from the three study villages surveyed by the PARI in 2010 showed that more than 40 per cent of rural households were manual worker households, whose main source of income was casual wage work.[1] Therefore, it is important to examine wage rates in both the State as a whole and also in these villages, as movements in wages have far-reaching implication for the well-being of a wide section of rural households in West Bengal. This chapter discusses the level and pattern of wage rates for agricultural operations and non-agricultural occupations of manual workers in the three villages in 2009–10 and 2015–16.

PARI surveys collected disaggregated data on wage rates by crop, crop operation, and season; by type of wage contract; by mode of payment (cash and in kind); and by demographic characteristics of workers such as sex and age (i.e., adult or child); the data can also be disaggregated by social group and socio-economic class. Such detailed data on rural wages are not available from any secondary sources. For example, the *Wage Rates in*

---

[1] See chapter 3 in this book.

Rural India (WRRI), published by the Labour Bureau, only provides data on average wages of certain occupational groups.[2] The PARI data cover the two types of wage contracts prevalent in the villages: piece-rated and time-rated. In piece-rated contracts, wages are paid based on the volume of the task assigned, and for agricultural production, piece rates are based on crop acreage or the volume of production. Time-rated wage contracts may be hourly or daily and even annual contract depending on the nature of the task. It is essential to note that official sources on wage rates do not provide data on piece-rated contracts, nor do they report hours of work under daily contracts.

Wage Rates in Agricultural Operations

In this section, I examine wage rates by crop operations and type of wage contract in the study villages. Using the simple average (unweighted mean) of the reported wage rates, we analyse how wage rates have varied across operations for male and female workers in both survey years.

Aside from piece-rated contracts in agriculture, time-rated contracts were either daily-rated or long-term/annual contracts – the latter were only observed in Panahar village. One of the major limitations of official data on wages is that they lack information on wage contracts such as the wages other than daily rates. Thus, these sources cannot capture significant changes in the type of wage contracts, from daily to piece rates, that are predominant across rural India. In the study villages, more than 40 per cent of hired labour days in agriculture were covered under piece-rated contracts (Table 1). These contracts were extensively prevalent in the two triple-cropped villages of Amarsinghi and Panahar as well as in the rainfed village of Kalmandasguri.

From the village survey data, types of wage contract were reported as daily wage rates and have not been adjusted for labour hours. That is, these wages were received for the customary labour-day in the villages, not for a standard eight-hour labour day. According to survey data, the duration of the labour-day varied by crop operation (generally longer for harvesting and shorter for sowing/transplanting and weeding), and between male and female workers. Furthermore, though male and female workers would be hired for the same operation or even by the same employer, they were paid different wages. Daily wages were paid

---

[2] An analysis of WRRI data in West Bengal is given in the Appendix Note.

Table 1 *Proportion of total hired labour-days in agriculture, by type of wage contract, study villages, 2009–10,* in per cent

Village	Daily-rated	Piece-rated
Panahar	57	43
Amarsinghi	56	44
Kalmandasguri	51	49

Source: Dhar (2017).

in cash, in kind, and with meals. Between the 2009–10 and 2014–15 surveys, payments became monetised, and in-kind payments had almost disappeared in all the villages.

Panahar

The major crops in Panahar were *aman* paddy (kharif), potato (winter), and *boro* paddy or sesame (summer). Though sesame was cultivated largely by family labour, there was substantial use of hired labour in transplanting, weeding, and harvesting of paddy, and sowing, harvesting, and packing of potatoes. In 2009–10, the prevailing wage rates for various operations were Rs 70–95 for male workers and Rs 70–85 for female workers (Table 2). In addition to a meal of rice, dal, and vegetables (and fish curry, occasionally), male workers received tea, puffed rice as snacks or breakfast, and *bidi.* The variation in cash wages paid to these male workers were often related to the type and frequency of meals provided. For example, the daily cash wage was Rs 60 when two meals were provided or Rs 70–80 when only one was provided. Working hours for daily-rated work were six to seven hours, depending on the crop operation, crop, and employer. Male workers generally worked from 8 a.m. to 3 p.m. with a one-hour break. Wage rates for female workers in similar operations were only slightly lower than their male counterparts – female to male wage ratios ranged between 0.89 and 0.99 for different operations. A wage disparity was more pronounced for paddy transplanting than for weeding and harvesting.

Upon resurvey in 2014–15, wages had been completely monetised and male workers no longer received cooked food as part of their wages. Wages were uniform across crop operations, and for both male and female workers, at Rs 200 per day (Table 3). Despite these changes, working hours remained the same in 2014–15 at six to seven hours.

Piece-rated contracts were widespread in Panahar for paddy transplanting and harvesting, and potato packing (Table 4). These

Table 2 *Daily wage rates, by crop operation and sex, Panahar, 2009–10*, in Rs per day (at current prices)

Crop	Operation	Male		Female	
		Cash	Kind	Cash	Kind
Aman paddy	Transplanting	80–85	Meal + bidi + tea	70–85	NA
	Weeding	80–85	Meal + bidi + tea	70–85	NA
	Harvesting	80–85	Meal + bidi + tea	70–85	NA
Boro paddy	Transplanting	80–90	Meal + bidi + tea	80–85	NA
	Harvesting	80–90	Meal + bidi + tea	80–85	NA
Potato	Sowing	85–95	Meal + bidi + tea	70–85	NA
	Harvesting	70–85	Meal + bidi + tea	70–85	NA

Note: NA = Not applicable.
Source: PARI survey (2010).

Table 3 *Daily wage rates, by crop operation and sex, Panahar, 2014–15*, in Rs per day (at current prices)

Crop	Operation	Male		Female	
		Cash	In kind	Cash	In kind
Aman paddy	Transplanting	200	–	200	–
	Weeding	200	–	200	–
	Harvesting	200	–	200	–
Boro paddy	Transplanting	200	–	200	–
	Harvesting	200	–	200	–
Potato	Sowing	200	–	–	–
	Harvesting	200	–	–	–

Source: PARI survey (2015).

contracts were fixed on a per acre basis, and work under them was done by groups of workers led by a labour contractor who mediated between landowners and workers. The groups generally consisted of 10–20 workers, depending on the extent of land under the contract. In the case of transplanting, groups comprised male and female workers (in a 3:5 ratio), wherein male workers were hired for making and distributing bundles of seedlings and female workers for planting seedlings. Piece-rated work hours were generally greater than those under daily-rated wage work, lasting for 10 hours (8 a.m. to 6 p.m.) in the summer and 9 hours (8 a.m. to

---

Box 1

AM is a Scheduled Caste (SC) agricultural worker from Panahar. In the 2009–10 agricultural year, she worked for 300 days in various agricultural operations such as land preparation, sowing, transplanting, weeding, harvesting, and post harvesting of paddy (*aman* and *boro*), potato, sesame, and rapeseed. She worked in Panahar and the nearby villages of Koalpara and Deopara. The daily wage rate was Rs 85, without any in-kind payment, and her total wage earnings for the year amounted to Rs 26,000.

Her husband, SM, is also an agricultural worker who participated in various agricultural operations throughout the year. He worked for 330 days in agriculture on a daily-rated contract and received Rs 28,000 as his total earnings. His daily wage rate for ploughing with the employers' bullock was Rs 90–100, and for all other operations, it was Rs 85, without any in-kind payment such as cooked food.

---

5 p.m.) in the winter. Furthermore, piece rates often varied by the size of the group under contract; a larger group could complete the task faster. For example, in 2009–10, the wage rate for paddy transplanting varied between Rs 700 per acre and Rs 1,000 per acre – the latter was for a group of four workers, who could complete 1.5–2 *bigha*s per day.[3] For paddy harvesting, piece-rated wage rates were slightly higher at Rs 1,000–1,500 per acre. Potato packing wage rates were Rs 6–8 per bag in 2010 and Rs 12 per bag in 2015 – a worker could pack about 8–10 bags per day.

By 2014–15, piece-rated wage contracts became more common for most crop operations in Panahar. A combine harvester was introduced for paddy harvesting and post harvesting, and hence these operations were mechanised to some extent. Wage rates for major paddy operations increased from Rs 2,000 per acre to Rs 2,500 per acre. Though the piece-rated wage payment increased two- to three-fold, the total number of workers in the group remained the same, and thus the share received by individual workers increased. For example, the piece-rated wage for a paddy crop operation was Rs 340 per *bigha* in 2009–10, and a group of four workers could complete 1.5 *bigha* (roughly 8 cottah per worker) in a day (8–9 hours) – each worker earned Rs 127.5 per day. In 2014–15, the wage rate and duration of work for paddy (transplanting and harvesting)

---

[3] 1 acre = 2.5 *bigha*.

Table 4 *Piece-rated wages, by crop operation, Panahar, 2009–10 to 2014–15, in Rs*

Crop	Season	Operation	2009–10	2014–15
Paddy	*Aman, Boro*	Transplanting	700–1,000/acre	2,000–2,500/acre
		Harvesting	1,000–1,500/acre	2,000–2,500/acre
Potato	Winter	Packing	6–8/bag	12/bag

Source: PARI surveys (2010 and 2015).

increased to Rs 800 per *bigha* and 10 hours, respectively. With group strength remaining the same, individual workers completed eight cottah per day – individual wages increased proportionally to Rs 320 per day.

Amarsinghi

In Amarsinghi, the major crops cultivated by hired labour were *aman* paddy and *boro* paddy, whereas family labour performed major operations in other crops – jute and vegetables. Wage rates for major crop operations in Amarsinghi are reported in Table 5.

In Amarsinghi, workers received 1–1.25 kg of raw rice as part of their wages, instead of cooked food. As it is surrounded by villages with large proportion of Muslim households, Hindu workers from Amarsinghi preferred to take raw rice instead of cooked food. The equal presence of Hindus and Muslims among workers and employers, and traditional practices of untouchability, have led to the custom of paying workers in rice equivalent to a meal, rather than cooked meal. Hindu workers even refused tea and snacks from Muslim employers, whereas they accepted them from Hindu employers. In 2009–10, wage rates for *aman* paddy

Table 5 *Daily wage rates for male and female workers, by crop operation, Amarsinghi, 2009–10, in Rs per day (at current prices)*

Crop	Operation	Male		Female	
		Cash	Kind	Cash	Kind
Paddy	Ploughing	100	1 meal		
Aman paddy	Transplanting	80–100	1–1.25 kg*	50–80	1–1.25 kg*
	Weeding	80–100	1–1.25 kg*	50–80	1–1.25 kg*
Boro paddy	Transplanting	60–100	1–1.5 kg*	50–100	1–1.25 kg*
	Weeding	50–80	1–1.5 kg*	50–60	1–1.25 kg*

Note: *Rice
Source: PARI survey (2010).

operations were Rs 80–100 with 1–1.25 kg of rice for male workers and Rs 50–80 with 1–1.25 kg of rice for female workers. In the case of *boro* paddy operations, there were significant variations in wage rates across that year – for example, male workers received Rs 60–100 and 1–1.25 kg of rice for transplanting, and Rs 50–80 and 1–1.25 kg of rice for weeding, whereas female workers' wages for the respective operations were Rs 50–100 and 1–1.25 kg of rice, and Rs 50–60 and 1–1.25 kg of rice. For all operations, female agricultural workers received lower wages than their male counterparts.

Paddy harvesting in Amarsinghi was done on piece-rated contracts wherein workers received a share of produce as wages – agricultural labourer households needed the paddy received as wages to ensure household food security. For this reason, landless workers often offered to work at wages below the market wage in other operations when offered a harvesting contract paid in paddy share.

In 2014–15, maximum cash wage rates for all agricultural operations increased to Rs 200 and Rs 150 for male and female workers, respectively. Wages were completely monetised and did not include rice or any other in-kind payment, barring tea given to workers transplanting *aman* paddy.

Under piece-rated contracts, paddy harvesting and post harvesting wages consisted of a share of the produce. Such contracts for harvesting, threshing, winnowing, and loading remained prevalent in 2015, with the wage share increasing from one-sixth to one-fifth of total produce between

---

Box 2

SM is an agriculture labourer in Amarsinghi. He participated in land preparation, sowing, weeding, plant protection, and weedicide operations for paddy (*aman* and *boro*) on a daily-rated wage contract. Other than paddy, he was also hired for weeding vegetables and land preparation operations for mustard. The wage rates he received for *aman* paddy and *boro* paddy were Rs 80 and 1 kg of rice and Rs 60 and 1.2 kg of rice, respectively, and his total days of employment for these respective crops were 32 and 18 days. His total earnings from daily-rated work in agriculture was Rs 4,617.

SD is an agricultural labour who was employed only for weeding and paddy and jute transplanting on a daily-rated wage contract, wherein she received Rs 70 and 1.5 kg of rice.

Table 6 *Daily wage rates, by crop operation and sex, Amarsinghi, 2014–15,* in Rs per day (at current prices)

Crop	Operation	Male		Female	
		Cash	Kind	Cash	Kind
Paddy	Ploughing	200			
Aman paddy	Transplanting	200	Tea	150	Tea
	Weeding	150–200		120–150	
Boro paddy	Transplanting	200		150	
	Weeding	NA		NA	

Note: NA = Not applicable.
Source: PARI survey (2015).

Box 3

MM and her family comprising her son, daughter-in-law, and a brother-in-law performed paddy (*aman* and *boro*) harvesting, threshing, and winnowing in 2009–10 under a piece-rated contract of one-sixth of the total harvested production. They received 349 kg of *aman* paddy and 395 kg of *boro* paddy, after spending roughly 20 days during each harvesting season to complete the work.

2010 and 2015. These contracts were generally undertaken by families (husband, wife, parents, and children), and the paddy wage received was used for household consumption needs. Harvesting contracts were undertaken by SC families (Parihar, Manjhi, and Das sub-castes) in the village and lasted for 20 days to one month in the season.

Kalmandasguri

Major crops in Kalmandasguri were paddy, jute, and potato, and most operations were undertaken on daily wage contracts. The daily-rated work was predominantly performed by male workers, whereas both male and female workers were hired for piece-rated operations. In 2009–10, cooked food was included in wage contracts – male workers received meals as in-kind wages whereas female workers received only tea (Table 7). Ploughing with animals, done mainly by male workers, was the most remunerative among all agricultural operations, with wage rates ranging from Rs 120 to Rs 150 with a meal. For other operations, male and female workers' wages were Rs 70–100 with a meal and Rs 60–100 with tea, respectively. Male workers' meals consisted of cooked rice, dal, and vegetables or beaten rice with jaggery. The difference in male and female workers' in-kind wage payment was partly due to duration of their respective work – female workers generally worked from 7 a.m. to 1 p.m., whereas male workers' hours were from 8 a.m. to 4 p.m. with a one-hour break. Weeding was the primary operation in this high-rainfall region and absorbed both female and male workers.

In the 2014–15 survey, major land preparation operations were mechanised, so ploughing was done with a tractor under a piece-rated contract. Cooked food was no longer included in the wage contract, and cash wage rates increased to Rs 200 for male workers and Rs 150 for female workers – these wages were uniform across operations. The working hours remained the same for both survey rounds.

A gender differential in wage rates was observed in Kalmandasguri –

Box 4

BN is an agricultural labourer and the head of his household in Kalmandasguri. His household owned 1.5 *bigha*s of agricultural land, and their main sources of income were wages from manual work and crop production. His wife MN also worked as an agricultural labourer, and his son RN migrated to Bhutan for construction work. BN and MN worked from 7.30 a.m. to 1 p.m., and 3 p.m. to 4.30 pm. During the paddy harvesting season, they worked from 5 a.m. to 7.30 pm, for threshing and harvesting thereafter. His son's and wife's daily wage rates were reported to be Rs 100 and Rs 60, respectively. BN's cooked food component under the daily-rated wages consisted of either rice, dal, and vegetables or beaten rice, or both (meal and beaten rice), depending on the negotiation and relationship with his employers. In 2009–10, he and his wife performed various agricultural operations (sowing, transplanting, weeding, harvesting, threshing, and winnowing) of jute, *aman* paddy, and potato. In addition, he was hired for operations of sugarcane that a juice seller was cultivating on a very small scale – he made the furrows (three days), did weeding (three days), and loaded the sugarcane (six days) at a rate of Rs 100 per day

As one of the heads of the labour gangs in the village, BN's gang completed both jute weeding and harvesting on 60–65 *bigha*s and paddy transplanting on 65 *bigha*s of land in 2009–10.

Table 7 *Daily wage rates, by crop operation and sex, Kalmandasguri, 2009–10, in Rs per day (at current prices)*

Crop	Operation	.Male		Female	
		Cash	In kind	Cash	In kind
All	Ploughing	120–150	Meal		
Jute	Weeding	70–100		60–100	
	Harvesting	70–100		60–100	
Aman paddy	Transplanting	80–100	Meal	70–90	Tea
	Weeding	70–100	Meal	60–90	Tea
	Harvesting	70–100	Meal	60–90	Tea
Potato	Sowing	80–100		60–80	
	Harvesting	70–100		60–100	

Source: PARI survey (2010).

Table 8 *Daily wage rates, by crop operation and sex, Kalmandasguri, 2014–15, in Rs per day (at current prices)*

Crop	Operation	Male		Female	
		Cash	In kind	Cash	In kind
All	Ploughing	200			
Jute	Weeding	200		150	
	Harvesting	200		150	
Aman paddy	Transplanting	200	Tea	150	Tea
	Weeding	200	Tea	150	
	Harvesting	200	Tea	150	
Potato	Sowing	200		150	
	Harvesting	200		150	

Source: PARI survey (2015).

wage rates for female workers were three-fourths of male wage rates for all major agricultural operations. High female work participation rates, low crop intensity, and limited access to non-farm employment could be reasons for this gap.

In Kalmandasguri, workers also performed weeding and transplanting of paddy on piece-rated contracts (Table 9). The piece rate for these operations varied between Rs 900 per acre and Rs 1,200 per acre in

Table 9 *Piece-rated wage rates for paddy, Kalmandasguri, 2009–10 to 2014–15,* in Rs per acre

Operation	2010		2015	
	Cash	Kind	Cash	Kind
Transplanting	900–1,200	–	2,400–3,000	–
Weeding	900–1,200	–	–	–
Harvesting	1,200–1,500	–	2,400–3,000	–

Note: In 2015, there were very few observations in Kalmandasguri.
Source: PARI surveys (2010 and 2015).

2009–10 and depended on factors such as the male–female ratio in the group, time taken to finish the operation, difficulty of the task, terrain, and distance to the worksite. For paddy transplanting and harvesting under these contracts, the wage rate increased from Rs 2,400 to Rs 3,000 between 2010 and 2015.

Wage Rates in Non-Agriculture

In Panahar, participation in non-agricultural wage work was largely confined to MGNREGS, for both male and female workers. MGNREGS daily wages were Rs 82–104 in 2009–10, equal to the notified wage rates in West Bengal. Only male workers also found employment in construction work, wherein their wages were slightly higher at Rs 90–120 in 2009–10. Wages increased substantially between 2009–10 and 2014–15: the MGNREGS wage increased to Rs 150–170 per day and that of construction increased to Rs 150–200.

In Amarsinghi, construction jobs in nearby small towns such as Samsi was the dominant wage work available for male workers – wages for general construction workers and masons were Rs 100 and Rs 150, respectively, in 2010. There were also a few instances of MGNREGS-related wage work with a daily wage of Rs 80 for both male and female workers in 2010. In 2014–15, there was no MGNREGS employment and, hence, no non-agricultural wage employment for women. For male workers, daily wages of the general construction workers and masons increased to Rs 150 and Rs 300, respectively, in 2014–15.

In Kalmandasguri, the non-agricultural sector – mainly house construction, brick kilns, and other construction-related work – played an important role for male workers. Increased employment in the construction sector was due to urbanisation in nearby towns such as Koch

Table 10 *Daily wage rates, by non-agricultural occupation and sex, Panahar, 2009–10 and 2014–15*, in Rs per day

Occupation	Male		Female	
	2010	2015	2010	2015
MGNREGS	82–104	150–170	82–104	150–170
Construction	90–120	150–200		
Mason		300		

Source: PARI surveys (2010 and 2015).

Table 11 *Daily wage rates, by non-agricultural occupation and sex, Amarsinghi, 2009–10 and 2014–15*, in Rs per day

Occupation	2010		2015	
	Male	Female	Male	Female
MGNREGS	80	80	NA	NA
Construction	100	NA	150	NA
Mason	150	NA	300	NA

Note: NA = not applicable.
Source: PARI surveys (2010 and 2015).

Bihar, Alipurduar, and Siliguri. In addition, fishing, particularly among Muslim households,[4] and migration to Kerala, Uttar Pradesh, Delhi, and Bhutan for non-agricultural employment were also substantial sources of income. Participation of women in non-agricultural work was limited, except for work under MGNREGS. A total of 99 workers (75 male and 24 female) were engaged in MGNREGS work in 2009–10, which declined to 41 (31 male and 10 female), as estimated from the 2014–15 survey.

The daily wages for different kinds of construction work ranged from Rs 100 to Rs 120 in 2009–10, whereas those of masons were higher at Rs 170–200 per day. Wages increased substantially in 2015 – construction wages almost doubled to Rs 200 per day and that of masonry increased by more than 50 per cent, at Rs 300 per day.

---

[4] Even though fishing is an activity allied to agriculture, we report it here as a non-agricultural occupation.

Box 5

HR is a construction worker in Kalmandasguri who used to work in the nearby town of Alipurduar. He received 225 days of employment with a daily wage of Rs 100 in construction. According to the 2014–15 survey, he received a daily wage of Rs 300 as a mason in Alipurduar. His days of employment declined to 180 in 2014–15, indicating stagnation in construction work.

Table 12 *Daily wage rates, by non-agricultural occupation and sex, Kalmandasguri, 2009–10 and 2014–15, in Rs per day*

Occupation	Male		Female	
	2010	2015	2010	2015
MGNREGS	100	100	169	169
Fence-making	100	200		
Fishing	100	200		
Masonry	170–200	300		
Construction	100–120	200		

Source: PARI surveys (2010 and 2015).

Observations on Wage Earnings of Manual Worker Households

This section deals with wage earnings of manual workers in the three study villages. We define manual worker households as those whose major sources of income is from manual wage employment in agriculture and/or non-agriculture. There were 63 such households in Panahar, 48 in Amarsinghi, and 55 in Kalmandasguri. Wage earnings are calculated as total wage earnings from daily- and piece-rated work, divided by number of standard (eight-hour) days of employment. Because the PARI database also provides data on actual work hours, we can calculate the number of standard days of employment for each worker. Wage payments received in kind such as cooked food have been converted to a cash value and added to the wage earning. To compare between the two survey years, the monetary wages of 2014–15 were deflated by the consumer price index for agricultural labourers (CPI-AL) for agricultural work and by the consumer price index for rural labourers (CPI-RL) for non-agricultural work in 2009–10. The results are summarised in Tables 13, 14, and 15.

Table 13 *Average wage earnings in agricultural operations, by sex and type of wage contract, study villages, 2009–10*, in Rs per eight-hour labour day

Village	Male		Female		Gender gap	
	Daily rated	Piece rated	Daily rated	Piece rated	Daily rated	Piece rated
Panahar	93	133	90	129	0.97	0.97
Amarsinghi	93	93	85	92	0.91	0.99
Kalmandasguri	104	130	78	100	0.75	0.77

Source: PARI survey (2010).

Table 14 *Average wage earnings in agricultural operations, by sex and type of wage contract, study villages, 2014–15*, in Rs per eight-hour labour day, at 2009–10 prices

Village	Male		Female		Gender gap	
	Daily-rated	Piece-rated	Daily-rated	Piece-rated	Daily-rated	Piece-rated
Panahar	135	156	133	142	99	91
Amarsinghi	132	108	109	100	83	93
Kalmandasguri*	144	130			NA	NA

Notes: * There were very few observations for piece-rated contracts for female workers in Kalmandasguri. Hence, average wage earnings could not be calculated.
NA = Not applicable.
Source: PARI survey (2010).

Table 15 *Change in wage earnings, study villages, 2009–10 to 2014–15*, in per cent (at 2009–10 prices)

Village	Daily-rated		Piece-rated		Gender gap	
	Male	Female	Male	Female	Daily-rated	Piece-rated
Panahar	43	47	32	10	Unchanged (0.98)	Increased (0.99 to 0.91)
Amarsinghi	42	28	16	8	Increased (0.92 to 0.82)	Increased (0.99 to 0.85)
Kalmandasguri	39	37			Unchanged (0.75)	

Source: PARI surveys (2010 and 2015).

Daily-Rated versus Piece-Rated Contracts in Agriculture

Wage earnings varied significantly with the type of wage contract. In Panahar, average wage earnings for male workers were Rs 113 under a piece-rated contract and Rs 93 under a daily-rated contract. In Kalmandasguri, male workers' average wage earnings under the respective contracts were Rs 130 and Rs 104. This difference was not significant in Amarsinghi. In all three villages, wages were similar for female workers, and they earned higher wages under piece-rated contracts.

Thus, the data show that workers received higher wages under piece-rated contracts than time-rated contracts, particularly in Panahar and Kalmandasguri. In these two villages, workers formed groups and collectively undertook contracts for a given task, and payment was based mostly on the extent of land on which they worked (transplanting or harvesting). Being formed into groups seemed to allow workers to negotiate for higher wages. Workers also had an added incentive to quickly execute the task to undertake work on more land and maximise their earnings. Thus, enhanced wage bargaining and intense physical exertion could have resulted in higher wage earnings in piece-rated contracts.

In Amarsinghi, piece-rated contracts were undertaken by families rather than labour gangs. The fact that harvesting contracts were mostly undertaken by SC households indicated the traditional employer–worker relationship, wherein families undertook such contracts to earn foodgrains for their annual consumption needs. Wage earnings here were not higher under piece-rated contracts.

Between 2009–10 and 2014–15, average wage earnings increased for all types of contracts, and for both male and female workers. In Panahar and Amarsinghi, the increase in time-rated wage earnings was much higher than wages under piece-rated contracts.

Daily Wage Earnings in Agriculture Below the Minimum Wage Rate

The average daily wage earnings from agriculture was lower than the official minimum wage rate in 2009–10 and 2014–15 for both male and female workers in the Amarsinghi and Kalmandasguri. In Panahar, the average wage earning was higher than the notified minimum wage rate for piece-rated wage contracts, but it was lower than the minimum wage for time-rated contracts. The minimum wage in agriculture in West Bengal was Rs 112 and Rs 201 in 2010 and 2014, respectively. Papola and Kannan (2017) showed that 56 per cent of male casual workers in the agricultural sector in West Bengal received wages lower than the minimum wage, compared to 5 per cent in Kerala and all-India 47 per cent.

Minimal gender gap in agricultural wage earnings
The official data on wage rates show that the gender gap in agricultural wage rates was relatively small in West Bengal, compared to the rest of India (see Appendix Note). The village data showed that the gap is relatively small in the irrigated multi-cropped villages of Panahar and Amarsinghi and large in the rainfed, single-crop village of Kalmandasguri. A gender gap in wage earnings was observed under both daily- and piece-rated wage contracts – in the latter, female workers received much lower average daily wage earnings compared to male workers. The 2014–15 data showed that the male–female wage disparity did not decline over the previous five years in all villages.

Changes in wage rates
The data show a significant increase in real wage rates for agriculture under both daily- and piece-rated contracts between 2009–10 and 2014–15. Across all operations in the three villages, the absolute increase in real wage earnings was from Rs 15 to Rs 40 in 2014–15 (a 13–40 per cent increase) for male workers and from Rs 8 to Rs 23 (an 8–47 per cent increase) between 2009–10 to 2014–15 for female workers. The increase

Table 16 *Average daily wage earnings, by non-agricultural occupation and sex, study villages, 2010 and 2015,* in Rs per day (at 2009–10 prices)

Village	Task	Male			Female		
		2010	2015	Change (%)	2010	2015	Change (%)
Panahar	Construction	91	112	23			
	MGNREGS	90	93	3	89	83	−7
Amarsinghi	Mason	150	198	32			
	Construction	100	116	16			
	MGNREGS	84	NA	NA	80	NA	
Kalmandasguri	Mason	180	198	10			
	Construction	110	132	20			
	MGNREGS	100	112	12			

Note: NA = not applicable.
Source: PARI surveys (2010 and 2015).

was highest in Panahar, followed by Kalmandasguri and Amarsinghi.

For male workers in Kalmandasguri and Amarsinghi, wage earnings in construction were higher than those in agriculture. Real wage rates in construction increased by 23, 16, and 20 per cent in Panahar, Amarsinghi, and Kalmandasguri, respectively. Non-agricultural activities for female workers were limited, except those under MGNREGS.

The rapid growth in agricultural and non-agricultural wages in West Bengal between 2009–10 and 2014–15 was also observed in the three villages (see Appendix Note). This increase was higher in non-agricultural occupations than in agricultural operations.

Conclusion

This chapter examined the levels of and changes in wage rates in the three study villages in West Bengal in and between 2009–10 and 2014–15. The following changes in wages and wage contracts in agriculture were observed in the interim period. Firstly, the increase in real agricultural wages paid under daily- and piece-rated contracts was 28–64 per cent for men and 8–32 per cent for women, for different agricultural operations. Secondly, village data showed that although daily wages were more common, piece rates were also widespread and covered crop operations like paddy harvesting in Amarsinghi, paddy transplanting and harvesting in Panahar, and weeding and harvesting in Kalmandasguri. By 2014–15, there had been a shift from daily wages to piece-rated wages for most crop operations in Panahar and Amarsinghi. Thirdly, in-kind payments such as cooked food, tea, and rice formed a part of wage payments in all the three villages in 2009–10. Five years later, wages had been completely monetised in Panahar and Kalmandasguri. The same was true of wages for crop operations in Amarsinghi, except in the case of paddy harvesting wages, which were paid in kind (one-sixth of the total production).

The increase in piece-rated contracts has implications for the gender gap in wages. Village data showed that the ratio of male to female daily wages in agriculture remained unchanged between 2009–10 and 2014–15 but increased for piece-rated operations in Panahar and Amarsinghi. Female workers were at a disadvantage under piece-rated contracts, and thus the increase in piece-rated operations also meant an increase in the male–female wage disparity.

Construction wages increased for male workers in all the three villages, with the magnitude of increase ranging between 10 and 32 per cent. Female workers did not participate in construction work and only performed MGNREGS work as non-agricultural wage employment in 2010. In 2015, employment in MGNREGS had declined by seven per cent in Panahar and halted altogether in Amarsinghi and Kalmandasguri.

References

Das, Arindam, and Usami, Yoshifumi (2017), "Wage Rates in Rural India, 1998–99 to 2016–17," *Review of Agrarian Studies*, vol. 7, no. 2, July–December, pp. 4–38, available at http://www.ras.org.in/wage_rates_in_rural_india_1998, viewed on January 12, 2020.

Dhar, Niladri Sekhar, with Patra, Subhajit (2017), "Labour in Small Farms: Evidence from Village Studies," in Madhura Swaminathan and Sandipan Baksi (eds.), *How Do Small Farmers Fare? Evidence from Village Studies in India*, Tulika Books, New Delhi, pp. 62 – 94.

Gulati, Ashok, Jain, Surbhi, and Satija, Nidhi (2013), "Rising Farm Wages in India: The 'Pull' and 'Push' Factors," Discussion Paper No. 5, Commission for Agricultural Costs and Prices, Department of Agriculture and Cooperation, Ministry of Agriculture, Government of India, New Delhi.

Government of India (GoI) (various issues), *Wage Rates in Rural India*, Ministry of Labour and Employment, Labour Bureau, Government of India.

Himanshu and Kundu, Sujata (2016), "Rural Wages in India: Recent Trends and Determinants", *The Indian Journal of Labour Economics*, vol. 59, no. 2, 217–44.

Himanshu (2017), "Growth, structural change and wages in India: recent trends," *Indian Journal of Labour Economics*, vol. 60, no. 3, 309–31.

Papola, T. S., and Kannan, K. P. (2017), "Toward an India Wage Report," ILO Asia Pacific Working Paper Series, ILO Regional Office for Asia and the Pacific.

Ramachandran, V. K. (2019), "Aspect of the Proletarianization of the Peasantry in India," in A. Narayanamoorthy, R. V. Bhavani, and R. Sujatha (eds.), *Whither Rural India? Political Economy of Agrarian Transformation in Contemporary India*, Tulika Books, New Delhi, pp. 68–83.

Usami, Yoshifumi (2011), A Note on Recent Trends in Wage Rates in Rural India, *Review of Agrarian Studies*, Volume 1, no. 1, available at http://ras.org.in/a_note_on_recent_trends_in_wage_rates_in_rural_india, viewed on January 12, 2020.

APPENDIX NOTE

Trends in Agricultural and Non-Agricultural Wages in Rural West Bengal

In this note, we examine the trends in real wage rates for various agricultural operations and non-agricultural occupations in rural West Bengal and compare the trends with the national averages. The major empirical analysis is based on WRRI as reported in the *Indian Labour Journal*, a monthly publication of the Labour Bureau, Government of India. WRRI data are collected from a sample of villages on a monthly basis for different agricultural operations and non-agricultural occupations in 18 major States and include wage rates by sex. Methodological issues in the WRRI database are discussed in Usami (2011) and Usami and Das (2017). To analyse wage rate trends, we made three adjustments to the data. Firstly, though WRRI reports agricultural wages by individual operation, for ease of analysis, we aggregated these operation into three major groups – ploughing, sowing/weeding/transplanting (SWT), and harvesting/threshing/winnowing (HTW). To understand the trends in non-agricultural wages, we only discussed two occupations – masonry and unskilled work. Secondly, WRRI publishes monthly wage rates, whereas we have used annual wage rates. Following Usami (2011), we have used the arithmetic mean of wages (for each operation/occupation) for the entire agricultural year (May to April) to arrive at annual wage rates. Thirdly, nominal wage rates were deflated by the CPI-AL for agricultural operations and by the CPI-RL for non-agricultural occupations at the 2009–10 base period.

Levels in Agricultural and Non-Agricultural Wage Rates

As a low-wage State, West Bengal's wage rates in most occupations for male workers were lower than the all-India averages (Appendix Table 1) (Usami 2011). Among agricultural operations, ploughing in West Bengal earned slightly higher wages than the all-India value, but SWT and HTW wage rates were lower than the national average. In non-agricultural occupations, the wage rate for unskilled workers in West Bengal was similar to the national average, whereas that of masons was lower by Rs 88.

For all occupations, female workers' wage rates in the State were similar to the national averages. It is worth noting that the male–female wage gap was smaller in West Bengal than in India. For agricultural operations, the male to female wage ratio was 1.13 for SWT and 1.11 for

Appendix Table 1 *Wage rates for agricultural and non-agricultural occupations, West Bengal and India, 2018-19*

Occupation	Male		Female		Male:Female wage ratio	
	West Bengal	India	West Bengal	India	West Bengal	India
Ploughing	330.6	323.8				
SWT	261.8	290.1	232.6	239.8	1.13	1.21
HTW	259.0	285.8	233.8	244.5	1.11	1.17
Mason	382.9	470.7				
Unskilled labour	287.7	286.7	218.6	216.4	1.32	1.32

Source: GoI (various issues).

HTW in West Bengal, compared to the respective national figures of 1.21 and 1.17. For unskilled work, the ratio was the same for West Bengal and India, at 1.32.

Broad Changes in Rural Wages

Dividing 1998–99 and 2016–17 into three sub-periods indicates noteworthy trends in wages. The first sub-period, between 1998–99 and 2006–07, saw stagnation or decline in most agricultural operations and non-agricultural occupations at the all-India level. This stagnation can be attributed to the multiple years of drought, low agricultural prices, and relatively low minimum support price MSP during this period. This was followed by a sharp increase in all-India wages in the second sub-period between 2007–08 and 2014–15 for both male and female workers in most occupations. The years after 2014–15 showed a decline in the growth of wage rates (Das and Usami 2017).

Growth in real wage rates in West Bengal followed a slightly different pattern from the national trend. Real wages in major agricultural operations and non-agricultural occupations stagnated in the State between 2002–03 and 2009–10, after which they sharply increased. Agricultural wage rates for both male and female workers rose substantially between 2009–10 and 2014–15: from Rs 133 to Rs 192 for ploughing (male), Rs 92 to Rs 140 for SWT (male), Rs 82 to Rs 130 for SWT (female), Rs 90 to Rs 141 for HTW (male), and Rs 79 to Rs 131 for HTW (female) (Appendix Figure 1). After 2014–15, growth in female workers' wages for SWT and HTW, and male workers' wages for ploughing slowed down.

Appendix Figure 1 *Real wage rates for various agricultural operations, West Bengal, 2007–08 to 2018–19* in Rs per day (at 2009–10 prices)

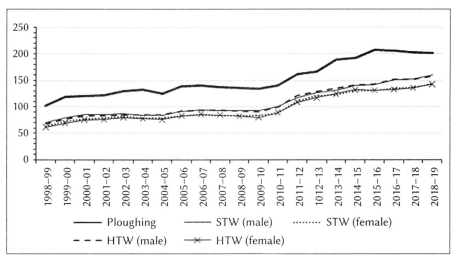

Source: GoI (various issues).

Appendix Figure 2 *Real wage rates for unskilled non-agricultural labour, by sex, West Bengal, 2007–08 to 2018–19* in Rs per day (at 2009–10 prices)

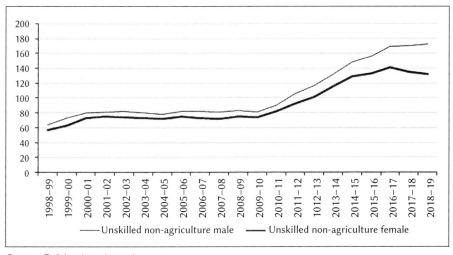

Source: GoI (various issues).

Appendix Table 2 *Average annual growth rates of real wages in two agricultural operations and unskilled non-agricultural labour, by sex, West Bengal, 2001–02 to 2015–16, in per cent*

Period	Ploughing	HTW		Unskilled labour	
	Male	Male	Female	Male	Female
2001–02 to 2009–10	1.17	1.35**	1.01	0.14	0.2
2009–10 to 2015–16	9.4**	6.80**	7.63**	11***	10.8***

Note: * 0.05 level of significance, ** 0.01 level of significance, *** 0.001 level of significance.
Source: GoI (various issues).

Wage rates for non-agricultural occupations showed a similar pattern to that of agricultural wages. In West Bengal, real wage rates for major non-agricultural occupations saw a moderate rise between 1998–99 and 2004–05, followed by a period of stagnation till 2009–10 and then a sharp rise till 2015–16. For example, between 2009–10 and 2015–16, masonry wages increased from Rs 131 to Rs 212 (at 2009–10 prices), and unskilled workers' wages increased from Rs 82 to Rs 157 (male) and Rs 74 to Rs 133 (female) (Appendix Figure 2). After 2015–16, there was a decline in female unskilled workers' wages and a slowdown in those of their male counterparts.

We have fitted linear trend and calculated the average annual growth rate of real wages between 2009–10 to 2015–16 (Appendix Table 2). In this period, wage rates for agricultural operations grew by more than 7 per cent annually in West Bengal; this growth rate was higher for female workers. For unskilled non-agricultural labour, wage growth rates were 11 and 10.8 per cent for males and females, respectively. Thus, growth in wages were higher for unskilled non-agricultural occupations than those for agricultural operations. Das and Usami (2017) noted that the increase in agricultural and non-agricultural wages for all major occupations after 2007–08 was a remarkable, nationwide phenomenon. In West Bengal, this increasing trend of wages was delayed; wage growth rates post 2009–10 were impressive, but later slowed down after 2015–16. We have not calculated the growth rates after 2015–16, as there are only four data points.

12

Income Diversification in West Bengal Villages

Aparajita Bakshi and Tapas Singh Modak

Introduction

By analysing the sources of household income in the three study villages, this chapter specifically focuses on the nature, importance, and limitations of the non-farm sector in rural incomes. In spite of broad access to agricultural land and crop production, income from agriculture constituted less than half the total household income in these villages. We argue that the dominance of non-agricultural income in the household income portfolio compounded by the incidence of pluri-active households show that diversification to non-agriculture in the villages is due to the general limitation of smallholder agriculture and income stress. Households engaged in labour in the non-agricultural sector in the study villages comprised three sections: a large section dependent on low non-agricultural wages; a very small section that was able to diversify to high-income, regular-salaried employment; and a sizeable section employed in heterogeneous, self-employment activities. The growing importance of non-agricultural income, in our view, presages significant changes in class formation and class interests in the three villages, and rural life in West Bengal in general.

Secondary data sources confirm that West Bengal has a large and growing rural non-farm sector. NSS Employment and Unemployment Survey estimates after 1980 indicate that West Bengal had a higher proportion of rural non-agricultural workers than most other States in India (Chandrasekhar 1993; Bhaumik 2002; Kashyap and Mehta 2007). In 2009–10, only 55 per cent of rural workers in West Bengal were employed in agriculture, hunting, and forestry sectors, and 1.2 per cent in fishing, by usual status of employment.[1] All other States, except Goa, Kerala, Manipur, and Tripura, had a higher share of rural workers in agriculture, forestry, and fishing (NSSO 2011). Consequently, non-farm income forms a significant share of rural household income in West Bengal. According to the Situation Assessment Survey (SAS) of Farmers of 2003, 60.9 per cent of the average household income of farmer households in West Bengal in 2002–03 came from wage earnings and non-farm business activities (NSSO 2005). Ten years later, the SAS of Agricultural Households of 2013 reported that 70 per cent of the average monthly income of agricultural households in West Bengal was sourced from wages and non-farm business; the corresponding figure for India was only 40 per cent (NSSO 2014).

After this introductory section, the rest of this chapter is organised as follows. In the second section we describe the levels of income and income inequality, followed by a discussion on the sources of income and composition of household income in the third section. In the fourth section we analyse some of the features of the income diversification process. Here, we first discuss a very important feature of diversification – the "pluri-activity" of households in these three villages. Pluri-activity refers to households receiving income from more than one source, a feature not limited to these three villages but also observed throughout rural India (Bakshi and Modak 2017; Djurfeldt 2019; Djurfeldt and Sarkar 2017; Heyer 2019).[2] We then try to understand if there are differences in the patterns of pluri-activity and income composition between socio-economic classes in the villages, particularly focusing on diversification of income among the peasant classes. Finally, we decompose the income inequality index by sources of income to understand which sources currently drive income inequalities. In the fifth and final section of the chapter, we describe the changes that have taken place in the three villages in terms of levels and composition of income between 2010 and 2015.

For collecting data on household income, the Foundation for Agrarian Studies (FAS) has designed an elaborate methodology that provides reliable estimates. The details of the methodology can be obtained from

---

[1] NSS defines usual status employment as the activity status of a person during the reference period of 365 days preceding the date of survey.

[2] The term "pluri-activity" is defined in two ways in the literature on income and occupational diversification. Household-level pluri-activity is observed when a single household earns from multiple income sources/occupations. Individual-level pluri-activity refers to a single worker engaging in multiple occupations in a given reference period. In this chapter, we are only concerned with the pluri-activity of households.

the income calculation manual, "Calculation of Household Incomes – A Note on Methodology" (FAS 2015). A short note on the methodology can be found in Appendix Note 1.

Levels of Income and Income Inequality

Levels of Income

Average income across the villages was quite similar in 2010 (Table 1). In all three villages, the median was lower than the mean, indicating that income was unevenly distributed across households. Panahar showed the highest variation in per capita income, ranging from Rs −4,065 to Rs 1.6 lakh, and the households with maximum and minimum income in 2010 were also in this village.

In Panahar, two households incurred negative income in the reference year, primarily due to losses in crop cultivation, and about 27 per cent of cultivator households had negative farm business income, due to losses in potato cultivation.[3] In Amarsinghi and Kalmandasguri, 4 per cent and 10 per cent of cultivator households respectively incurred crop production losses, but were compensated by supplementary income from other sources.

Table 1 *Descriptive statistics on per capita annual household income, study villages, 2010, in Rupees*

Statistic	Panahar	Amarsinghi	Kalmandasguri
Mean	11,796*	10,204	11,815
Median	6,931*	7,610	9,874
Minimum	−4,065	817	1,200
Maximum	1,57,113	57,190	59,256
Households with negative income	2	0	0

Note: * The mean and median in Panahar excludes two households that incurred negative income.
Source: PARI survey (2010).

Income Inequality

Land and asset inequalities were relatively high in Panahar, and income inequality was the highest in this village (Appendix Table 1a). The Gini coefficient of total household income was 0.643 and per capita income was

---

[3] See chapter 5 for more details.

0.552. The richest decile received 54.2 per cent of the household income, whereas the bottom 50 per cent of the households received only 14 per cent of the total village income. It is worth noting in Panahar that only the top income decile (consisting of landlord/capitalist farmer households, upper-peasant 1 households, and a few upper-peasant 2 and salaried households) households received a high-income share. The income levels of even the ninth decile were fairly modest: Rs 12,391–23,833 per capita per annum (Rs 1,000–2,000 per capita per month). In Amarsinghi and Kalmandasguri, which had no landlord class, many households had gained land through land reforms, and income inequality was quite low – the Gini coefficients being 0.372 and 0.386, respectively (Appendix tables 1b and 1c). Similar to these values, the Gini coefficients for per capita household income were 0.37 and 0.331 for Amarsinghi and Kalmandasguri, respectively. In both villages, the top income decile received 27 and 28 per cent of total income, and the bottom 50 per cent of the households received 28 and 29 per cent of total income, both respectively.

Though the landlord/capitalist farmer households in Panahar constituted only 5.7 per cent of the total population, their income share was 27.3 per cent of total village income (Table 2). All other classes in the village, except the upper-peasant 1 and salaried class, either received an income share equal to or less than their share in total population.

As mentioned above, there were no landlord households with

Table 2 *Representation of classes in total population and household income, Panahar, 2010,* in per cent

Class	Share in total population	Share in total income
Landlord/capitalist farmer	5.7	27.3
Upper peasant 1	5.9	13.4
Upper peasant 2	19.6	14.2
Poor peasant	33.7	18.9
Manual worker	24	12.1
Major income from business	5.4	3.9
Major income from remittances/rent	0.7	1.0
Major income from salaries	4.4	9.2
Major income from other sources	0.7	0.2
All households	100	100

Source: PARI survey (2010).

Table 3 *Representation of classes in total population and household income, Amarsinghi, 2010, in per cent*

Class	Share in total population	Share in total income
Upper peasant 1	3.8	11.6
Upper peasant 2	9.9	15.2
Poor peasant	29.0	24.7
Manual worker	38.1	27.1
Major income from business	11.8	13.3
Major income from remittances	3.0	1.9
Major income from salaries	2.1	4.7
Major income from pension	0.7	0.4
Major income from artisanal work	1.6	1.1
All households	100	100

Source: PARI survey (2010).

Table 4 *Representation of classes in total population and household income, Kalmandasguri, 2010, in per cent*

Class	Share in total population	Share in total income
Upper peasant	17.1	21.7
Poor peasant: small self-employment	7.4	7.0
Poor peasant: semi-proletarian	23.4	22.0
Manual worker	36.4	26.7
Major income from business	10.7	11.0
Major income from salaries	4.4	11.2
Major income from pension	0.6	0.4
All households	100	100

Source: PARI survey (2010).

large landholdings in Amarsinghi and Kalmandasguri. Upper peasant households, with small to medium landholdings, received income higher than their share in population (Tables 3 and 4). Classes other than salaried households received income similar to or less than their share in population.

Income inequalities across social and religious groups largely follow the class position of households. In Panahar, the landlord households were Muslim and had an average income of Rs 64,769 per capita per annum, which was almost four times higher than the average income of caste Hindu households and ten times higher than that of Scheduled Caste (SC) and Scheduled Tribe (ST) households. Income inequalities between social and religious groups were less apparent in the other two villages. In Amarsinghi, the average income of caste Hindu households were marginally higher than that of SC households. In Kalmandasguri, the average income of SC and ST households were in fact higher than caste Hindus and Muslims. This was because the Rajbangshis, an SC group, were the predominant caste group in the village in terms of land ownership (Appendix Table 2).

Sources of Income

The villages differed from each other in terms of agricultural development as well as their location within industrial and urban development in the State. These aspects had specific implications for the sources and composition of income in the villages.

Panahar

Panahar in Bankura district was the first among the three villages to use green revolution technology and irrigation in its agriculture. Furthermore, its proximity to the urban and industrial centres of Hugli and Kolkata and general road connectivity influenced non-farm employment, agricultural marketing, and development dimensions such as education.

Of the total household income, primary sector activities contributed 37.7 per cent, secondary and tertiary activities 53.8 per cent, and other sources including transfers and remittances 8.5 per cent. Despite the lower share of the primary sector in the household income portfolio, 97.2 per cent of households in the village received income from it, 86.3 per cent received income from secondary and tertiary sectors, and 26.6 per cent from other sources.

About 15.7 and 14.6 per cent of primary sector income was sourced from cultivation and agricultural wages, respectively. Animal resources, of which fish cultivation was significant, formed 4.8 per cent of total income. Several families (mostly of the same social group) owned and settled around large fishing ponds, each holding tiny shares of ownership of a given pond. Though they fished collectively and shared the total produce, most of the catch was used for household consumption. Three landlord/capitalist farmer and some peasant households earned income from the commercial sale of fish.

It is interesting to note that the shares of income from salaries as well as from business and trade were higher than that from crop cultivation. Average income from salaries (Rs 136,342) and business and trade (Rs 50,194) were also significantly higher than that from crop production (Rs 11,554). Though losses in potato cultivation in the survey year may have depressed crop incomes and reduced the share of crop production in households' income portfolio, Panahar's connectivity to urban locations enabled residents to earn a higher share of their income through salaries and business and trade. Though salaries constituted 21.9 per cent of total income, only 9.3 per cent of households received them. Among salaried employees, most held government jobs such as teachers at higher secondary and primary schools, clerks at government offices, employees at the State transport department and worked in Panahar as well as in the towns of Kotulpur, Jairambati, Kamarpukur, Barddhaman, and Bankura. Locally in the village, there were also a few Integrated Child Development Services (ICDS) and (Accredited Social Health Activist (ASHA) workers.

Table 5 *Distribution of total household income by source, Panahar, 2010*

Income source	Households (%)	Share in total income (%)	Average income (Rs.)
Crop income	78.6	15.7	11,554
Trees	36.7	0.7	1,100
Animal resources	79.4	4.8	3,473
Fisheries	32.3	1.6	2,798
Agricultural labour	62.1	14.6	13,612
Rental income from agricultural land	11.7	2.6	12,961
Total primary sector	97.2	37.7	22,445
Non-agricultural labour	69.4	10.1	8,397
Salaries	9.3	21.9	1,36,342
Business and trade earnings	21.8	18.9	50,194
Artisanal and caste-based work	0.4	0	2,400
Rent from machinery and other assets	8.1	2.9	20,804
Total secondary and tertiary sectors	86.3	53.8	36,024
Other sources	26.6	8.5	18,258
Transfers and remittances	25.8	8.4	17,794
Total income	–	100	57,903

Source: PARI survey (2010).

Private sector employment was limited; only seven people received monthly salaries from private companies, working as drivers and helpers in shops and dairy farms in nearby Kotulpur and Jairambati. The income received from such jobs were also lower than those from regular public sector employment. In addition, 18.9 per cent of household income was derived from business and trade, primarily in retail. Finally, rent from agricultural machinery and other assets such as tractors, tillers, and tubewells was also a component of income.

Amarsinghi

Situated in the Gangetic plains, Amarsinghi village of Maldah district is characterised by varied agricultural production, rich alluvial soil, and small landholdings. In addition to paddy and jute as the main crops, a large variety of vegetables were cultivated. Households also owned mango orchards (a crop which the district is famous for) and bamboo groves, which added to crop incomes. The village was once irrigated with diesel-powered, shallow tubewells, but after agricultural electrification in 2007, these were replaced by electric medium tubewells (locally referred to as "mini"). The majority of households engaged in primary sector activities, which contributed to 47 per cent of total household income. Income shares from these activities included 25.2 per cent from crop production (including fruits, vegetable, bamboo, and other tree crops) and 13.4 per cent from agricultural wages.

Maldah is well connected to Delhi by train, a legacy of the erstwhile Minister of Railways Ghani Khan Chowdhury, who hailed from the region.[4] Thus, there have been long-standing migration links to Delhi, and village residents have seasonally migrated to work as gardeners and other manual workers. In the nearby towns of Samsi, Ratua, Chanchol, Baidyanathpur, and Gajole, they migrate to work as *pandal* workers, drivers, loaders and unloaders, and van pullers as well as in construction, plywood factories, and jute mills. The majority of households received income from non-agricultural wages, which formed 10.5 per cent of total income. Some households also engaged in petty trade – owning small shops, selling sugarcane juice, or working as barbers (a caste-based occupation), jute merchants, and MDM (mid-day meals) cooks through self-help groups (SHGs) in nearby villages; these earnings were the second largest

---

[4] A. B. A. Ghani Khan Chowdhury was the Minister of Railways from 1982 to 1984 and Minister of Programme Implementation from 1985 to 1987.

Table 6 *Distribution of total household income by source, Amarsinghi, 2010*

Income source	Households (%)	Share in total income (%)	Average income (Rs.)
Crop income	74.0	25.2	14,948
Trees/mango orchards	38.0	1.9	1,710
Animal resources	80.3	7.4	4,023
Agricultural labour	52.0	13.4	11,311
Rental income from agricultural land	11.8	1.0	3,741
Total primary sector	94.5	47.0	21,817
Non-agricultural labour	81.9	10.5	5,631
Salary	9.4	9.4	43,806
Business and trade earnings	33.0	19.8	26,304
Artisanal and caste-based work	1.6	0.8	23,350
Rent from machinery and other assets	8.7	3.2	16,294
Total secondary and tertiary sectors	95.3	43.7	20,182
Other sources	43.3	9.3	9,286
Transfers and remittances	43.3	9.1	15,141
Total income	–	100	43,937

Source: PARI survey (2010).

component of household income (19.8 per cent). Lastly, salaries or regular employment and other sources (including transfers and remittances) constituted 9.4 and 9.1 per cent of total household income, respectively.

Kalmandasguri

Of the villages, Kalmandasguri was the most disadvantaged in terms of employment opportunities, both in agriculture and non-agriculture. The village was remote, accessible only by a narrow kutcha road leading to the nearest bus stop, seven kilometres away at Pundibari, and electrified for both domestic and agricultural use only in 2013. Agriculture was largely unirrigated – jute in pre-monsoon and *aman* rice in kharif season. In rabi season, some land under potato cultivation was irrigated by diesel-powered, shallow tubewells, but incidence of irrigation was low. Consequently, crop production constituted only 17.9 per cent of total household income, even though 88.4 per cent of the households engaged in this work. In 2010, the average income from crop production was Rs 11,327.

Animal resources were almost as important as crop production; its share in total income was 15.9 per cent in 2010, with 93.6 per cent households having received income from this source. Fish cultivation, in particular, was an important source of income. Residents formed SHGs and collectively engaged in fish cultivation for eight to ten months in 2010. These groups generally did not lease in the pond for fish cultivation but instead took contracts for harvesting fish from pond owners and sold their catch in nearby towns. At Rs 18,211 per household, average annual income from fish cultivation was higher than crop production, but only 12.9 per cent of households had access to this income source. In total, primary sector income contributed 45.3 per cent of total household income.

The major sources of non-agricultural income in Kalmandasguri were non-agricultural labour and business and trade earnings, each contributing around 18 per cent to total income. Those engaged in non-agricultural wage employment (80.3 per cent of all households) worked in Pundibari, Alipurduar, Birpara, and Koch Bihar towns as construction workers, loaders and unloaders, brick kiln workers, van pullers, auto

Table 7 *Distribution of total household income, by source, Kalmandasguri, 2010*

Income source	Households (%)	Share in total income (%)	Average income (Rs)
Crop income	88.4	17.9	11,327
Trees	76.2	1.5	1,065
Animal resources	93.6	15.9	9,440
Fisheries	12.9	4.2	18,211
Agricultural labour	72.8	11.2	8,622
Rental income from agricultural land	5.4	0.3	3,524
Total primary sector	98.0	45.3	25,697
Non-agricultural labour	80.3	18.6	12,849
Salary	4.1	8.4	1,14,700
Business and trade earnings	34.0	14.1	23,088
Artisanal and caste-based work	0.7	0.2	16,000
Rent from machinery and other assets	6.8	1.5	12,601
Total secondary and tertiary sectors	94.6	42.8	25,185
Other sources	44.9	11.9	14,950
Transfers and remittances	44.2	11.9	35,077
Total income	–	100	55,874

Source: PARI survey (2010).

drivers, and helpers in shops. Those engaged in petty trade and business activities operated small shops, sold wood and bamboo, were potato and jute merchants, and sold fish in the village and its surrounding areas.

An important feature of this village was outmigration of its workforce outside the State. Migrant workers travelled to Kerala, Rajasthan, Delhi, Assam, and Bhutan to work as construction or unskilled factory labour. Other income sources, primarily remittances, formed 12 per cent of total household income.

Some Observations on the Sources of Income

From our description of income sources in the villages, four major points emerge. First, in each village, the share of primary sector activities was less than half of the total income, despite the fact that almost all rural households (94 to 98 per cent) were engaged in these activities. The legacy of land reforms in West Bengal continues to be reflected in the fact that 74 to 88 per cent of households received income from crop production, thus they maintained access to land by ownership or tenancy.

Despite widespread access to agricultural land and engagement in crop production, only 10 households (six in Panahar, three in Amarsinghi, and one in Kalmandasguri) depended entirely on income from self-employment in agriculture (crop production, animal resources, and rental income from land) in 2010. Regarding purely "agricultural" households in the villages, that is, households solely dependent on income from primary sources – cultivation, animal resources, agricultural labour, and agricultural land rents – there were only 22 (16 in Panahar, 4 in Amarsinghi, and 2 in Kalmandasguri), 6.5 per cent of all households. This shows the general limitation of agriculture in generating adequate income and employment.

Secondly, non-agricultural wage employment was the most common form of non-agricultural occupations. In all three villages, participation in non-agricultural labour was 69.4 per cent in Panahar, 81.9 per cent in Amarsinghi, and 80.3 per cent in Kalmandasguri, all of which were higher than the corresponding values for agricultural labour. This can, to some extent, be attributed to the National Rural Employment Guarantee Act (NREGA), which was implemented in the villages in varied degrees in 2010. Despite the high levels of participation, the share of non-agricultural wages in total income was very low – about 10 per cent in Panahar and Amarsinghi and 18.4 per cent in Kalmandasguri. Average wages earned per household from non-agricultural labour was lower than those earned from agricultural labour in Panahar and Amarsinghi because fewer days of employment (per capita and total) were available for non-agricultural manual work. In Kalmandasguri, though average wages earned per household from non-agricultural labour was higher than those earned from agricultural labour, the number of days of employment in non-agricultural manual work was comparable with that in agricultural labour.[5]

Thirdly, regular-salaried employment was the most remunerative source of income – average annual income per household was Rs 1,36,342 in Panahar, Rs 1,14,700 in Kalmandasguri, and Rs 43,806 in Amarsinghi. However, a minimal portion of households, around 9 per cent in Panahar and Amarsinghi and only 4 per cent in Kalmandasguri, received salaries.

Fourthly, non-agricultural self-employment activities formed a significant share of the income portfolio, and average income from these activities was higher than that from all other sources except salaries. However, not all households received a substantial amount of income from such activities. In fact, more than half received less than Rs 25,000 per annum and only a handful in each village received more than Rs 1,00,000 in 2010. The scale of enterprises was small, a fact also reflected in the Sixth Economic Census.[6] Large variations in household assets and access to resources is reflected in the heterogeneity of non-agricultural self-employment activities – in the nature of entrepreneurial activities and the income generated. Thus, annual income from non-agricultural self-employment ranged from Rs 200 in Kalmandasguri to Rs 6,00,000 in Panahar. Some types of business activities such as street vending, women's SHG work as MDM cooks in schools, and men's SHG work in leasing in ponds for fishing were not very different from manual labour and required low investments. On the other end of the spectrum, landlord households diversified to running medium and small businesses such as shops and in real estate. For example, 44 per cent of the income of the richest household in Panahar was sourced from non-agricultural sources

---

[5] This is discussed in some detail in chapter 10 in the context of days of employment for manual-worker households.

[6] The Economic Census is a census of all units (establishments) engaged in the production and/or distribution of goods and services not for the purpose of sole consumption. It excludes crop production, plantation, public administration, defence, and compulsory social security. According to the Sixth Economic Census of West Bengal in 2012–13, 86.35 per cent of the rural establishments in West Bengal were own-account establishments (that is, establishments that did not hire any labour), and the average number of persons employed per establishment was only 1.77. The highest number of establishments was in the retail trade sector, constituting 28.5 per cent of all rural enterprises (GoWB 2016).

– businesses and salaries – which included cattle trading, operating a paddy mill, and one member who was a college lecturer.

Finally, the composition of income in the villages was influenced by their urban linkages, which determined the types of employment opportunities households could access. In Panahar, the share of salary in income was high because the village was well-connected to a number of urban centres. In fact, among the three villages, the share of income from secondary and tertiary sector activities was the highest in Panahar. In Amarsinghi, the largest share of non-agricultural income was from business and trade, and in Kalmandasguri, it was from wages. Amarsinghi's urban links were primarily with nearby small towns and semi-urban areas that did not present many opportunities of salaried employment. As previously mentioned, Kalmandasguri was remote, and hence, the opportunities to earn non-agricultural income were limited.

Income Diversification

Pluri-activity of Households

Pluri-activity, that is, households having multiple sources of income and employment, is a common feature observed in all the PARI (Project on Agrarian Relations in India) villages (Bakshi and Modak 2017; Bakshi and Das 2017). The Bengal villages particularly reflected widespread pluri-activity and diversification of household income portfolios.

To understand income diversification and pluri-activity in the proceeding analysis, we have applied the following six-fold classification of household income:

I. Agricultural income
    i. *Self-employment in agriculture*: all income from crop cultivation including tree crops (fruits or timber), agricultural land rent, livestock, and pisciculture
    ii. *Agricultural wage income*: income received from casual and long-term wage employment in agriculture
II. Non-agricultural income
    i. *Self-employment in non-agriculture*: income from business, trade, owning non-agricultural establishments, renting out machinery, buildings, etc.
    ii. *Non-agricultural wage income*: income from manual wage labour in non-agriculture

Table 8 *Distribution of households by number of income sources, study villages, 2010*, in number

Number of income sources	Panahar		Amarsinghi		Kalmandasguri	
	Households (number)	Share of all households (%)	Households (number)	Share of all households (%)	Households (number)	Share of all households (%)
1	14	5.6	5	3.9	3	2.1
2	66	26.6	27	21.3	18	12.2
3	115	46.4	45	35.4	60	40.8
4	49	19.8	38	29.9	51	34.7
5	4	1.6	12	9.5	15	10.2
All	248	100	127	100	147	100

Source: PARI survey (2010).

iii. *Salaries*: income from regular, skilled wage employment in non-agriculture

iv. *All other sources*: income from pensions, scholarships, cash transfers, remittances, interest, financial income, and any other source

A small proportion of households (5.6 per cent in Panahar, 3.9 per cent in Amarsinghi, and only 2 per cent in Kalmandasguri) received income from only one source (Table 8). The mode of the number of sources of income for households in each of the villages was three; in other words, three sources provided income for 46.4 per cent of households in Panahar, 35.4 per cent in Amarsinghi, and 40.8 in Kalmandasguri. More than 85 per cent of households received income from two to four sources.[7]

Income Composition by Classes

Differential access to sources of income based on social and material wealth of households is both a cause and effect of income deprivation. Households with larger asset holdings are able to diversify to more remunerative and stable sources of income that further enhance their income. On the other hand, households with meagre assets are unable

[7] It is worth mentioning here that in the PARI villages surveyed in Uttar Pradesh, Maharashtra, Rajasthan, and Karnataka, a majority of the households received income from two to three sources (Bakshi 2015; Bakshi and Das 2017). Thus, individual households had to rely on more sources of income in West Bengal than in other States.

to access such remunerative options and are forced to diversify to risky and low-paid income sources. There is a close correspondence between household socio-economic class and the total value of their assets; landlords/capitalist farmers have the highest value of assets and manual workers the least. We now discuss major observations regarding the income composition of the different socio-economic classes in the villages (Appendix tables 3a, 3b, and 3c).

The most asset- and income-rich households in Panahar were among landlord/capitalist farmer households. This class received the highest income share from agricultural self-employment among all classes in the village, and more than half of their total income was sourced from salaries and non-agricultural self-employment. As we discussed earlier, there were variations in income from non-agricultural self-employment in the villages. However, landlord households in Panahar invested in remunerative forms of business and trade opportunities and received high incomes from such sources; they did not receive any wage income.

For the upper-peasant households in the three villages, non-agricultural self-employment was the second most important source of income, after agriculture, and included earnings from being input dealers, commission agents, and merchants of agricultural commodities; owning small shops and businesses; selling fish; rental income from agricultural machinery; and tuitions. Upper-peasant households in Panahar and Amarsinghi also received salaries, but the income share from salaries was much higher for upper-peasant 1 households (30.2 per cent in Panahar, and 33.4 per cent in Amarsinghi) than the upper-peasant 2 households (6 per cent in Panahar, and 4.8 per cent in Amarsinghi). Such opportunities were unavailable for upper peasants in Kalmandasguri. Upper-peasant 2 households in Panahar and Amarsinghi and upper-peasant households in Kalmandasguri received a small fraction of their income from non-agricultural wages. Upper-peasant 2 households in Amarsinghi did not engage in agricultural wage employment, whereas those in Panahar sourced 5.5 per cent of their household income from agricultural wages. Thus, the share of wage income was low for these households, their major source being agricultural and non-agricultural self-employment.

Poor-peasant households that had small landholdings and a few assets were more dependent on wage income than other peasant households. In Panahar, 60 per cent of income for poor-peasant households was from agricultural and non-agricultural wages. In Amarsinghi and Kalmandasguri, these households received the largest income share from agriculture (54.9 and 48.1 per cent, respectively) but also received a sizeable portion of their income from wages. Wages were the major source of income for manual-worker households, though they also received income from agricultural and non-agricultural self-employment. Thus, in the villages, we see the asset-poor, such as poor peasants and landless/near landless manual workers, are highly dependent on wage employment, whereas the relatively asset-rich can diversify to salaried work and self-employment in non-agriculture. This is true of most of the PARI villages.

Income Diversification and Income Inequality

One of the commonly used methods in economic analysis to understand the contribution of individual sources of income to income inequality is the decomposition of an income inequality index such as the Gini coefficient, variance, or coefficient of variation. An income inequality index is naturally decomposable if the index can be written as a weighted sum of incomes. In such cases, total inequality can be expressed as the weighted sum of the different components of income. Income itself is the sum of different components, that is, of income received from different sources. We have decomposed the income inequality measure, GE(2), by different sources of income to understand the contribution of each source in total inequality (the methodology is explained in Appendix Note 2). In the proceeding analysis of the impact of different sources of income on inequality, we have used the six-fold classification of income sources previously given.

Table 9 summarises the results of the decomposition exercise. In Panahar, the major contributors to income inequality were salaries and self-employment in agriculture, respectively contributing 38.81 and 36.92

Table 9 *Decomposition of GE(2) by sources of income, study villages, 2010*

Village	Agri self-employ-ment (%)	Agri wages (%)	Non-agri wages (%)	Salary	Non-agri self-employed (%)	Other (%)	All (%)	GE(2)
Panahar	36.92	−1.15	−0.54	38.81	22.52	3.44	100	2.265
Amarsinghi	32.63	−1.74	0.52	34.4	31.99	2.21	100	0.308
Kalmandasguri	18.59	−0.59	−1.23	24.98	16.68	41.57	100	0.425

Source: PARI survey (2010).

per cent of the GE(2) income inequality index. The other major contributor was self-employment in non-agriculture, which formed 22.52 per cent of income inequality. These three income sources in Panahar were dominated by the asset-rich households, i.e., the large and medium landowners who also diversified to salaried employment and business and trade. Land inequalities were perpetuated through other forms of capital, including human capital via education, and differential access to remunerative income opportunities. On the other hand, we see that income from wages had a small but equalising effect on household income. The magnitude of this equalising force was small because of the low levels of income received from these sources. Nevertheless, it indicated the importance of wage employment in counteracting asset-based inequalities in rural India.

Amarsinghi also provides a similar picture – income from self-employment and salaries were the major drivers of income inequality, contributing 32 per cent and 34 per cent of GE(2), respectively. Agricultural wages had a small and negative impact on income inequality, and interestingly, non-agricultural wages increased inequality due to the nature of non-agricultural wage employment. NREGA implementation was poor, unlike in the other two villages. Non-agricultural wage employment opportunities were few and difficult to obtain and, to a large extent, consisted of specialised, semi-skilled labour such as *pandal* work or seasonal work outside the State.

The distinguishing feature in Kalmandasguri, compared to Panahar or Amarsinghi, was that the major source of income inequality was "other" sources – mainly remittances – that contributed 41.57 per cent of the inequality index. Small agricultural landholdings and low incomes from crop production were a result of limited irrigation. The lack of opportunities drove a significant section of the village workforce to other States, and thus remittances from migrant workers played a significant role in household livelihood strategies and also contributed to income inequalities.

The analysis brings to light new dynamics in inequality and class relations in West Bengal. Though land-based inequalities that manifest through agricultural income remain important in two of the three villages, the major drivers of inequality were different forms of non-agricultural income sources. Our analysis of the income composition of socio-economic classes show that the landowning classes – the landlords and rich peasants – successfully exploited remunerative non-agricultural income opportunities. Thus, while the dominance of these classes in the socio-economic hierarchy remain, the importance of agriculture and land wealth as the source of dominance has diminished. The decline of agriculture and emergence of non-agriculture as the major source of income inequality change and shape class relations in important ways and define new class interests.[8]

Sources of Income Growth, 2010–2015

In 2015, we conducted a follow-up survey of a sample of 209 households (103 in Panahar, 54 in Amarsinghi, and 52 in Kalmandasguri) to understand the changes the villages underwent. For the purpose of sampling, we used a simplified stratification (see chapter 1), where the strata corresponded with the 2010 aggregated class structure of the villages. In this section, we discuss some of the major changes in household income between 2010 and 2015, comparing only *panel households surveyed in both years*. We have not computed village-level estimates for 2015 due to methodological constraints of the data.[9] We must reiterate that the statistics for the panel households in 2010 closely correspond to the village-level statistics discussed earlier, but are not exactly the same.

Table 10 *Changes in per capita income, study villages, 2010–15, in Rs*

	Panahar	Amarsinghi	Kalmandasguri
Average per capita household income, 2010 (in 2015 prices)	22,747	16,947	18,124
Average per capita household income, 2015	19,885	18,388	18,625
Change per annum (%)	−2.5	2	0.3

Note: Data are for households that were sampled in 2010 and 2015 and constitute a panel, which contained 103 households in Panahar, 54 households in Amarsinghi, and 52 households in Kalmandasguri.
Source: PARI surveys (2010 and 2015).

[8] We have discussed the changing nature of classes and class relations in West Bengal and in the three villages in chapter 3.

[9] The 2015 sample was drawn from the list of households surveyed in 2010. We did not enumerate households in 2015; thus, without a sampling frame, we could not determine village-level estimates in that sample. However, a comparison of panel households could give us an idea of the direction, rather than the exact magnitude, of change. Please note, the statistics obtained from the panel households in 2010 may vary from those in the census-type survey as reported in previous sections. The analysis in this section is strictly limited to the panel of households surveyed in both years.

To compare income across the two years, we inflated the 2010 income by 2015 prices using the consumer price index for rural labourers. Table 10 shows that mean per capita income declined in Panahar (−2.5 per cent per annum), increased in Amarsinghi (2 per cent per annum), and stagnated in Kalmandasguri (0.3 per cent per annum) (see the subsection below, "Who Gained and Who Lost?").

Changes in Income from Different Sources

The changes in the composition of rural incomes (Table 11) reveal a few important features. First, the share of income from agricultural self-employment, which comprised income from crop production, animal resources, and rent from agricultural land, declined significantly in Panahar and Kalmandasguri villages. For example, in Panahar, strikingly, the share of income from agricultural self-employment declined from 28.4 per cent in 2010 to 15 per cent in 2015. This occurred despite the fact that cultivator households incurred substantial losses in potato cultivation due to a crash in potato prices in 2010. The reason for the large decline in crop income was the substantial increase in input cost – particularly costs of fertilizers, pesticides, and irrigation – whereas prices remained stagnant. For example, the village data show that in *boro* paddy cultivation, the real paid-out costs increased by 11 per cent, whereas the real prices declined. Similarly, the paid-out costs of all major crops increased in the period without a commensurate increase in output prices, resulting in a decline in crop income.

In Kalmandasguri, income from agricultural self-employment declined from 40.6 per cent in 2010 to 21.4 per cent in 2015. Jute was one of the major crops in the village and constituted about 27 per cent of total gross cropped area in 2010. The real price for jute received by farmers in the village declined sharply from Rs 3,039 to Rs 2,174 per quintal, which was much lower than the minimum support price of jute in 2015 (Rs 2,700). Additionally, the drastic decline in net income from jute cultivation, from Rs 18,478 to Rs 7,092 per acre, resulted in falling income from crop production between 2010 and 2015 in the village. Though the share of crop income in total household income declined, there was an increase in the share from fish cultivation in all the three villages, which implied diversification within agricultural activity.

Secondly, the share of primary sector income declined in all the three villages. The decline was minimal in Amarsinghi (47.1 to 43.2 per cent) and much larger for Panahar and Kalmandasguri. In the latter two villages, primary sector income declined by more than 13 and by 18 percentage

Table 11 *Changes in composition of income, 2010 and 2015*, in per cent

Income source	Panahar		Amarsinghi		Kalmandasguri	
	2010	2015	2010	2015	2010	2015
Agricultural self-employment	28.4	15	35.5	34.8	40.6	21.4
Fisheries	2.0	4.4	0	0.6	7.9	8.4
Agricultural labour	10.8	11.8	11.6	8.4	7.4	8.0
Total primary sector	39.2	26.8	47.1	43.2	48	29.4
Self-employment in non-agriculture	21.1	32.9	25.5	32.2	15.4	29.2
Rental income	3.8	11.5	3.3	3.0	1.8	6.6
Non-agricultural labour	6.6	8.4	8.1	11.5	15.3	19.6
Salary	25.0	22.3	11	7.3	9.5	9.0
Transfers and remittances	8.0	9.6	8.2	5.8	11.6	12.8
Total secondary and tertiary	60.7	73.2	52.8	56.8	51.8	70.6
Other sources	0.1	0	0.1	0	0.2	0
All sources	100	100	100	100	100	100

Note: Data are for households sampled in 2010 and 2015, constituting a panel of 103 in Panahar, 54 in Amarsinghi, and 52 in Kalmandasguri.
Source: PARI surveys (2010 and 2015).

points, respectively, indicating a rapid transformation in the composition of income.

Thirdly, of all income sources, non-agricultural self-employment in all three villages witnessed the largest increase in its share of household income: from 21.1 to 32.9 per cent in Panahar, from 25.5 to 32.2 per cent in Amarsinghi, and almost doubling from 15.4 to 29.2 per cent in Kalmandasguri. Within this category, rental income from other assets, particularly from agricultural machinery, increased substantially in Panahar and Kalmandasguri. In Panahar, renting out tractors for both agriculture and non-agricultural purposes and selling water from private tubewells for irrigation constituted the major share of rental income from other assets. In Kalmandasguri, two modern technologies were introduced in agriculture during the intervening period. In the first case, a rich-cultivator household purchased a tractor and thresher in 2012 and 2014, respectively, which established a rental market for these machines. In the second, electrification in 2013 resulted in electric pumpsets replacing some diesel pumps and the subsequent initiation of a water market for irrigation, though it was not very extensive in 2015.

Fourthly, the share of salaries in household income did not increase anywhere and rather declined in Panahar and Alooks fmarsinghi. Thus, no new opportunities in regular employment were created. Finally, though the share of non-agricultural wages showed only small increases of two to three percentage points in the villages, there was a marked increase in average wages. Average non-agricultural wages per household (for those who received income from non-agricultural wage employment) increased from Rs 12,532 to Rs 21,080 in Panahar, Rs 7,694 to Rs 23,374 in Amarsinghi, and Rs 19,394 to Rs 33,794 in Kalmandasguri. The increase in average wages without commensurate increase in income shares indicates a fall in days of employment. There was a decline in NREGA activities in Panahar and Kalmandasguri, and as a result, fewer households could find non-agricultural wage employment.[10]

Who Gained and Who Lost?

In this section, we discuss the changes in income between 2010 and 2015 across different socio-economic classes. However, the classification of households used in this section differs from that used in the previous section because the smaller 2015 sample size necessitated the use of aggregated categories to classify households for statistical estimation. The landlord/capitalist farmer and manual-worker classes are identical in both surveys, whereas all non-agricultural classes are aggregated into a single class titled "others." In the case of the peasant classes, there are two broad categories: "peasant I," households owning 2.5 acres of land or more, and "peasant II," households owning less than 2.5 acres.

Panahar

In Panahar, all three agricultural classes – landlord/capitalist farmer, peasant I, and peasant II – witnessed a significant decrease in mean per capita income between 2010 and 2015 (Table 12). The greatest decline was for peasant II households (35 percentage points), followed by peasant I households (16 percentage points), and landlord/capitalist farmer households (24 percentage points). Thus, though all these classes experienced a decline in crop income, poor-peasant households were the worst hit.

---

[10] The decline in NREGA could have also led to an increase in average non-agricultural wage rates of participating households, as NREGA wages are generally lower than wages received in other non-agricultural activities.

The decrease in per capita income was primarily due to major decline in income from crop production across agricultural classes, which consist of landlord/capitalist farmers, peasant I, and peasant II classes. For all major crops in Panahar, there was substantial increase in the cost of cultivation (cost A2) and a simultaneous decline in the output prices of all commodities obtained by farmer households between the two surveys. For instance, the average per acre cost of cultivation for potato increased from Rs 40,323 in 2009–10 (at 2014–15 prices) to Rs 46,031 in 2014–15 (an increase of 14 per cent), yet the average price received by farmers declined from Rs 320 to Rs 261 per quintal. This was the case for all crops in Panahar, which led to a significant decline in income from crop production.[11]

The landlord/capitalist farmer class diversified to non-agricultural self-employment activities. Though their share of income from agricultural self-employment activities decreased from 48.9 to 32.4 per cent in 2015, that from non-agricultural self-employment increased from 16.1 to 41.6 per cent.

Manual-worker households also experienced a decline in average per capita income (three percentage points). The survey data revealed that the number of employment days in agriculture had declined sharply in Panahar. During the five-year period, there was a shift in cropping pattern, particularly during the summer season, from water-intensive *boro* paddy to dry sesame cultivation. Given that sesame cultivation is

Table 12 *Change in income by class, Panahar, 2010 and 2015*, in Rs

Class	Average per capita annual income		Change (%)
	2010 (at 2015 prices)	2015	
Landlord/capitalist farmer	1,27,909	1,04,227	−19
Peasant I	39,557	29,998	−24
Peasant II	14,120	9,192	−35
Manual worker	11,661	11,338	−3
Others	21,556	29,749	38

Note: Data are for households sampled in 2010 and 2015, constituting a panel of 103 in Panahar, 54 in Amarsinghi, and 52 in Kalmandasguri.
Source: PARI surveys (2010 and 2015).

[11] See chapter 5 for details.

less labour-intensive, this shift negatively affected employment. Days of employment in non-agriculture also declined due to a decline in NREGA employment, despite an increase in wages.

In Panahar, the only classes that showed an increase in income were the non-agricultural classes ("others" in Table 12). Within these classes, however, households dependent on salaries and pensions gained due to an increase in government payments, whereas those receiving income from business and trade gained only marginally.

Amarsinghi

The income growth in Amarsinghi was largely driven by manual-worker households whose income increased by 39 percentage points during the five years (Table 13). The survey data revealed that this was primarily on account of increased non-agricultural wages in the plywood factory and construction work.

The agricultural classes did not experience a substantial growth in income. Though the peasant I class, which had marginally larger landholdings, witnessed a small increase in income, the peasant II class witnessed a decline in income. There were no major changes in the composition of income of peasant households.

Table 13 *Change in income by class, Amarsinghi, 2010–15,* in Rs

Class	Average per capita annual income		Change (%)
	2010 (in 2015 prices)	2015	
Peasant I	52,493	53,763	2.4
Peasant II	17,060	16,506	−3.3
Manual worker	9,934	13,805	39.0
Others	15,679	17,163	9.5

Note: Data are for households sampled in 2010 and 2015, constituting a panel of 103 in Panahar, 54 in Amarsinghi, and 52 in Kalmandasguri.
Source: PARI surveys (2010 and 2015).

Kalmandasguri

In Kalmandasguri, agricultural households experienced a decline in real income. To some extent, this decline is exaggerated due to losses in crop production in 2015. Agricultural mechanisation increased during the period, and some households among the peasant I class were able

Table 14 *Change in income by class, Kalmandasguri, 2010–15*, in Rs

Class	Average per capita annual income		Change (%)
	2010 (in 2015 prices)	2015	
Peasant I	15,303	13,959	−8.8
Peasant II	15,984	13,451	−15.8
Manual worker	16,779	20,614	22.9
Others	27,739	24,845	−10.4

Note: Data are for households sampled in 2010 and 2015, constituting a panel of 103 in Panahar, 54 in Amarsinghi, and 52 in Kalmandasguri.
Source: PARI surveys (2010 and 2015).

to diversify their income sources by renting out agricultural machinery. Other non-agricultural households also witnessed income losses due to decline in salaries and wages in non-agricultural wage labour (particularly NREGA). Manual-worker households had substantially higher per capita income by 22.9 percentage points between 2010 and 2015, on account of an absolute increase in non-agricultural wages.

Thus, we find that peasant income declined in all three villages between 2010 and 2015. Significantly, the profitability of all major crops declined due to increased production costs and falling output prices. Peasants were unable to cope with these increasing costs without commensurate increases in output prices. On the other hand, manual-worker households made income gains due to increased wages, but there was no indication that days of employment in non-agricultural wage employment increased likewise. In fact, the number of NREGA employment days declined in Panahar and Kalmandasguri. Though unviable agriculture pushed the peasantry towards proletarianisation, wage employment opportunities within the State were limited, thus leading income-distressed peasantry to out-migrate to other States. The rest of the workforce, the large reserve army of surplus workers, tried to earn a meagre living through a variety of odd jobs and non-agricultural self-employment activities.

Conclusions

This chapter analysed the sources of household income and patterns of income diversification in the three villages surveyed in West Bengal. The results reveal some of the pertinent questions and dilemmas regarding structural transformation and agrarian relations in the State.

The majority of the households in the villages, 70 to 78 per cent, had access to land through ownership and tenancy – a legacy of land reforms in the State – and 74 to 88 per cent of the households received income from crop production. However, the income share from crop production constituted less than 50 per cent of household income. In 2010, annual per household income from crop production was less than Rs 12,000 in Panahar and Kalmandasguri and close to Rs 15,000 in Amarsinghi.

The village data presented a complex situation in terms of income generation, particularly for the small peasantry. Income from agriculture was meagre and non-agricultural wage and salaried employment opportunities were limited; rural households thus engaged in multiple activities, generating income from two to four activities on average. This pluri-activity represented a kind of income stress among most households, rather than diversification incentivised through accumulation. There was, however, some accumulation, for example in the case of the landlord/capitalist farmer households in Panahar that invested in businesses and in educating the next generation for salaried employment or those who invested in agricultural machinery, particularly in Amarsinghi and Kalmandasguri. The majority, however, diversified to various non-agricultural sources to supplement their meagre income from agriculture.

A substantial proportion of households (69 per cent in Panahar, 82 per cent in Amarsinghi, and 80 per cent in Kalmandasguri) received income from non-agricultural wage work, but the share of this source in the total income portfolio was minimal. The major source of income outside agriculture was non-agricultural self-employment, but income from this source varied from being steady and decent to more periodic and limited. Landlords in Panahar and the upper peasantry in all villages diversified to non-agricultural self-employment, whereas the poor peasantry received income from both self-employment and manual labour wages in non-agriculture. A select few households had access to salaried employment.

A decomposition analysis of income inequalities in the three villages in 2010 by source of income revealed that though agricultural self-employment constituted about one-third of total income inequality, the major drivers of inequality were non-agricultural income sources. Agricultural wage income in all three villages and non-agricultural wages in Panahar and Kalmandasguri (both villages that had generated wage employment under NREGA in 2010) had equalising effects towards income inequality. Though land wealth and agricultural income most often determined access to remunerative sources of non-agricultural income, the growing importance of non-agricultural income sources are bound to shape class positions and relations in significant ways.

Between 2010 and 2015, the share of income from crop production further declined (agricultural income declined in absolute terms in Panahar), and most of the peasantry witnessed a decline in real income. Despite major political changes in the State in the two survey years, distress in agricultural production only intensified. Manual workers and salaried employees experienced a rise in their real incomes due to increased wages and government salaries. There was, however, no indication of increased days of employment in non-agricultural wage employment, at least within the State, nor any sign of more regular employment in private or government sectors. Significantly, the share of income from non-agricultural self-employment increased in all three villages. Thus, though West Bengal was and has remained a petty-producer economy, the nature of production continues to gradually, but definitely, shift from agriculture to small-scale trade and services.

References

Bakshi, Aparajita (2015), "Nature of Income Diversification in Village India with Special Focus on Dalit Households," Project Report submitted to Indian Council for Social Science Research, Foundation for Agrarian Studies, Bangalore.

Bakshi, Aparajita, and Das, Arindam (2017), "Household Incomes in the Three Study Villages," in Madhura Swaminathan and Arindam Das (eds.), *Socio-economic Surveys of Three Villages in Karnataka: A Study of Agrarian Relations,* Tulika Books, New Delhi, pp. 218–49.

Bakshi, Aparajita, and Modak, Tapas Singh (2017), "Incomes of Small Farmer Households," in Madhura Swaminathan and Sandipan Baksi (eds.), *How Do Small Farmers Fare: Evidence from Village Studies in India,* Tulika Books, New Delhi, pp. 126–70.

Bhaumik, Shankar Kumar (2002), "Employment Diversification in Rural India: a State level analysis," *The Indian Journal of Labour Economics,* vol. 45, no. 4.

Chandrasekhar, C. P. (1993), "Agrarian Change and Occupational Diversification in Non-Agricultural Employment and Rural Development in West Bengal," *Journal of Peasant Studies,* vol. 20, no. 2, pp. 205–70.

Djurfeldt, Goran (2019), "No Place for Family Farms? Agrarian Transformation in India," in A. Narayanamoorthy, R. Sujatha, and R. V. Bhavani (eds.), *Whither Rural India? Political Economy of Agrarian Transformation in Contemporary India, A Festschrift for Venkatesh Athreya,* Tulika Books, New Delhi, pp. 22–28.

Djurfeldt, Goran, and Sircar, Srilata (2017), *Structural Transformation and Agrarian Change in India,* Routledge, London.

Foundation for Agrarian Studies (FAS)(2015), "Calculation of Household Incomes - A Note on Methodology," available at http://fas.org.in/wp-content/themes/zakat/pdf/Survey-method-tool/Calculation%20of%20Household%20Incomes%20-%20A%20Note%20on%20Methodology.pdf, viewed on August 16, 2018.

Government of West Bengal (GoWB) (2016), *Sixth Economic Census West Bengal 2012–2013*, Bureau of Applied Economics and Statistics, Department of Planning, Statistics and Programme Monitoring, Kolkata.

Heyer, Judith (2019), "The Role of Agriculture in the Process of Industrialization: Lessons from a Case Study from Western Tamil Nadu," in A. Narayanamoorthy, R. Sujatha, and R. V. Bhavani (eds.), *Whither Rural India? Political Economy of Agrarian Transformation in Contemporary India, A Festschrift for Venkatesh Athreya*, Tulika Books, New Delhi, pp. 29–55.

Kashyap, S. P., and Mehta, Niti (2007), "Non-Farm Sector in India: Temporal and Spatial Aspects," *The Indian Journal of Labour Economics*, vol. 50, no. 4, pp. 611–32.

Morduch, Jonathan and Sicular, Terry (2002), "Rethinking Inequality Decomposition, With Evidence from Rural China", *The Economic Journal*, vol. 112, January.

National Sample Survey Office (NSSO) (2005), *Income, Expenditure and Productive Assets of Farmer Households,* Ministry of Statistics and Programme Implementation, New Delhi.

National Sample Survey Office (NSSO) (2011), *Key Indicators of Employment and Unemployment in India 2009–10*, Ministry of Statistics and Programme Implementation, New Delhi.

National Sample Survey Office (NSSO) (2014), *Key Indicators of Situation of Agricultural Households in India*, Ministry of Statistics and Programme Implementation, New Delhi.

Appendix Note 1

Methodology of Income Calculation
(Extracted from Bakshi and Modak 2017)

FAS has developed a detailed methodology to gather data and arrive at reasonably accurate estimates of household income. The methodology can be obtained from the income calculation manual (FAS 2015). Here, we highlight a few positive aspects of the income calculation methodology.

a. Income is a derived variable, hence detailed and disaggregated data on all sources of income are collected. The FAS–PARI interview schedule uses separate modules for different income sources. The following 12 sources of income are reported for each household:
   1. Crop production
   2. Animal resources (including rental income from animals)

3. Wage labour
    a. Agricultural labour (casual)
    b. Agricultural labour (long-term)
    c. Non-agricultural labour (casual)
    d. Non-agricultural labour (monthly/long-term)
4. Salaried jobs
    a. Government salaried jobs
    b. Other salaried jobs
5. Business and trade
6. Moneylending
7. Income from savings in financial institutions and equity
8. Pensions and scholarships
9. Remittances and gifts
10. Rental income
    a. From agricultural land
    b. From machinery
    c. From other assets
11. Artisanal and caste-based work
12. Any other sources

b. Household income includes all cash and kind flows. Kind flows are valued at annualised local market prices or reported valuation by respondents. Price data from local markets and reliable respondents are collected separately.

c. To the extent possible, an accounting framework is adopted to collect data on income from self-employment activities such as crop production, raising livestock, and non-farm business. Income is defined as gross value of output less paid-out costs of production.

d. Concepts and definitions followed by the Commission for Agricultural Costs and Prices of the Government of India are broadly adhered to for estimating income from crop production. Crop income is gross value of output (main and by-products) less cost A2. Cost A2 excludes the cost of family labour and rental value of owned land and includes all paid-out costs, including the imputed value of depreciation of own machinery and interest on working capital.

e. Data are collected at various levels of disaggregation to assist in more accurate reporting and better recall from respondents. For example, crop income and costs of production are reported and calculated for each crop and crop-mix during the agricultural year. Livestock income is calculated for each type of livestock. Wage income is calculated for each type of wage employment by every member of household.

f. The reference period is the agricultural year.

APPENDIX NOTE 2

Decomposition of GE(2) by Sources of Income

The inequality index can be naturally decomposed to analyse how different sources of income contribute to total income inequality. Thus, if the index is naturally decomposable, then

$$I = \sum_f S_f$$

where, S_f depends on income from source f. Thus, the contribution of each source f to total income inequality is $s_f = S_f/I$.

We use the general entropy measure of power 2, or GE(2) measure of inequality, for our decomposition analysis. We have used this measure for the following reason: Since we are dealing with single time point data, there are households with net losses in income or in specific sources of income (particularly crop production and animal husbandry) during the survey year. Inequality measures such as the Gini coefficient, which is based on cumulative income shares, are difficult to calculate in the presence of negative income. On the other hand, GE(2), which is simply half the squared coefficient of variation, can be calculated even when there are negative values in the distribution. Thus,

$$GE(2) = \frac{1}{2}\left(\frac{sd(y)}{mean(y)}\right)^2$$

and the decomposition rule for the coefficient of variation and GE(2) is given by

$$s_f = \frac{S_f}{I} = \frac{covariance(y_f, y)}{variance(y)}$$

where s_f is the share of component f in total income inequality (Morduch and Sicular 2002).

The value of s_f may be positive or negative since the covariance can be positive or negative. A negative value of s_f indicates that the specific component has an equalizing effect on decomposition, that is, it reduces income inequality.

Appendix Tables

Appendix Table 1a *Distribution of total and per capita household income by income deciles, Panahar, 2010* in per cent

Per capita income deciles (Rs.)	Share of total household	Share of total household income	Share of per capita income
≤ 1,918	10	0.7	0.9
1,919–3,360	10	1.7	2.3
3,361–4,718	10	3	3.4
4,719–5,738	10	3.8	4.5
5,739–6,853	10	4.9	5.2
6,854–8,076	10	5.2	6.5
8,077–9,464	10	5.6	7.5
9,465–12,390	10	8.7	9.5
12,391–23,833	10	12.2	14.1
≥ 23,834	10	54.2	46.1
Total	100	100	100

Gini coefficient of total income = 0.643
Gini coefficient of per capita income = 0.552

Source: PARI survey (2010).

Appendix Table 1b *Distribution of total and per capita household income by income deciles, Amarsinghi, 2010,* in per cent

Income deciles	Share of household number	Share of total household income	Share of per capita income
≤ 3,594	10	3	2.6
3,594–4,956	10	5	4.5
4,956–5,847	10	6.2	5.4
5,847–6,617	10	7.1	5.8
6,617–7,447	10	6.6	7.2
7,447–9,300	10	9.9	8.5
9,300–11,266	10	10.1	9.8
11,266–14,290	10	11.4	13
14,290–17,444	10	14.1	15.8
≥ 17,445	10	26.6	27.4
Total	100	100	100

Gini coefficient of total income = 0.372
Gini coefficient of per capita income = 0.37

Source: PARI survey (2010).

Appendix Table 1c *Distribution of total and per capita household income by income deciles, Kalmandasguri, 2010*, in per cent

Income deciles	Share of total household	Share of total household income	Share of per capita income
≤ 4677	10	3.2	3.2
4,678–6,342	10	5.2	4.8
6,343–7,566	10	6.3	6.1
7,567–8,553	10	7.1	6.4
8,554–9,874	10	7.8	7.7
9,875–11,142	10	9.1	9.2
11,143–12,695	10	11.2	9.7
12,696–15,000	10	9.4	11.8
15,001–17,651	10	13.5	13.9
≥ 17,652	10	27.2	27.2
Total	100	100	100

Gini coefficient of total income = 0.386

Gini coefficient of per capita income = 0.331

Source: PARI survey (2010).

Appendix Table 2 *Mean per capita household income by social and religious groups, 2010*, in Rs

Social group	Panahar		Amarsinghi		Kalmandasguri	
	Households (Number)	Mean (Rs.)	Households (Number)	Mean (Rs.)	Households (Number)	Mean (Rs.)
Caste Hindu	92	16,632	69	10,542	27	12,656
Muslim	6	64,769	–	–	61	9,167
Scheduled Caste	133	6,539	57	9,845	49	14,081
Scheduled Tribe	17	6,365	1	7,395	10	14,598

Source: PARI survey (2010).

Appendix Table 3a *Composition of household income by class, Panahar, 2010, in per cent*

Class	Self-employment in agriculture	Agricultural wage	Non-agricultural wage	Salaries	Self-employment in non-agriculture	Other sources	Total
Landlord/capitalist farmer	41.7	0	0.1	26.8	28.9	2.5	100
Upper peasant 1	29.3	0	0.2	30.2	36.4	3.9	100
Upper peasant 2	27.2	5.5	7.9	6.0	30.1	23.3	100
Poor peasant	13.4	39.5	21.3	12.2	4.9	8.7	100
Manual worker	5.7	51.1	38.3	0.8	2.0	2.1	100
Major income from business	8	0.2	2.6	0	88.8	0.4	100
Major income from other sources	5.3	5.9	0	0	35.7	53.1	100
Major income from salaried person	3.5	1.5	1.3	79.7	0.8	13.2	100
Major income from remittances/rent	7.9	0	0	0	0	92.1	100
All households	23.1	14.6	10.1	21.9	21.8	8.5	100

Source: PARI survey (2010).

Appendix Table 3b *Composition of household income by classes, Amarsinghi, 2010, in per cent*

Class	Self-employment in agriculture	Agricultural wage	Non-agricultural wage	Salaries	Self-employment in non-agriculture	Other sources	Total
Upper peasant I	43.5	0	0.1	33.4	23.0	0	100
Upper peasant II	51.9	0	7.1	4.8	31.7	0	100
Poor peasant	54.9	5.8	11.7	1.7	21.4	4.5	100
Manual worker	16.3	40.3	19.5	0.7	3.7	19.5	100
Major income from business	13.9	6.6	8.7	0	68.2	2.6	100
Major income from remittances/ rent	17.4	7.3	1.8	0	2.0	71.5	100
Major income from salaries	6.7	0	0	88.0	2.8	2.5	100
Major income from pension	0.4	0	3.7	0	0	95.9	100
Major income from artisanal work	9.9	0	0.8	14.6	0	74.7	100
All households	33.6	13.4	10.5	9.4	23.8	9.3	100

Source: PARI survey (2010).

Appendix Table 3c *Composition of household income by class, Kalmandasguri, 2010, in per cent*

Class	Self-employment in agriculture	Agricultural wage	Non-agricultural wage	Salaries	Self-employment in non-agriculture	Other sources	Total
Upper peasant	52.5	0.9	3.0	0	9.7	33.9	100
Poor peasant: small self-employment	45.9	5.0	1.1	0	46.0	2.0	100
Poor peasant: semi-proletarian	48.1	16.5	24.3	0.6	4.9	5.6	100
Manual worker	20.1	23.7	40.1	0	6.8	9.3	100
Major income from business	17.6	5.6	9.2	0	66.2	1.4	100
Major income salaries	13.1	0.3	5.7	73.8	0	7.1	100
Major income from pension	50.9	14.8	5.6	0	0	28.7	100
All household	34.1	11.2	18.6	8.4	15.8	11.9	100

Source: PARI survey (2010).

Appendix Table 4a *Change in shares of sources of household income by class, Panahar, 2009–10 and 2014–15,* in percentage points

Class	Self-employment in agriculture	Agricul-tural wage	Non-agricultural wage	Salaries	Self-employment in non-agriculture	Other sources
Landlord/capitalist farmer	−16.5	0	0.1	−10.6	25.4	1.6
Peasant I	−1.1	0	19.5	−24.6	9.3	−3.1
Peasant II	−25.9	9.8	4.3	−16.9	44.2	−15.5
Manual worker	4.2	−4	−3.7	−1.6	−0.4	5.6
Others	−3.3	−2.1	−1	6.9	−20.7	20.2
All	−13.4	1.1	1.8	−2.7	11.8	1.5

Note: Data are for households that were sampled in 2010 and 2015 and constitute a panel, which contained 103 households in Panahar, 54 households in Amarsinghi, and 52 households in Kalmandasguri.
Source: PARI surveys (2010 and 2015).

Appendix Table 4b *Change in shares of sources of household income by class, Amarsinghi, 2009–10 and 2014–15,* in percentage points

Class	Self-employment in agriculture	Agricul-tural wage	Non-agricultural wage	Salaries	Self-employment in non-agriculture	Other sources
Peasant I	10.2	0	−0.2	−10.8	0.8	0
Peasant II	−5.5	−0.4	−2.5	1.4	7.1	0
Manual worker	1.8	−16.2	16.6	–	5.7	−7.9
Others	−3.2	−2.5	2.7	–	18.1	−5.1
All	−0.6	−3.2	3.4	−3.8	6.7	−2.5

Note: Data are for households that were sampled in 2010 and 2015 and constitute a panel, which contained 103 households in Panahar, 54 households in Amarsinghi, and 52 households in Kalmandasguri.
Source: PARI surveys (2010 and 2015).

Appendix Table 4c *Change in shares of sources of household income by class, Kalmandasguri, 2009–10 and 2014–15,* in percentage points

Class	Self-employment in agriculture	Agricul-tural wage	Non-agricultural wage	Salaries	Self-employment in non-agriculture	Other sources
Peasant I	−77.1	1.1	0.7	16.3	66.2	−7.1
Peasant II	−5.4	4.9	4.7	0.2	−1.6	−2.8
Manual worker	−6.8	−3.9	14.7	1.5	−0.7	−4.8
Others	6	1.1	−8.9	−17.2	3.4	15.6
All	−19.2	0.6	4.3	−0.5	13.8	1

Note: Data are for households that were sampled in 2010 and 2015 and constitute a panel, which contained 103 households in Panahar, 54 households in Amarsinghi, and 52 households in Kalmandasguri.
Source: PARI surveys (2010 and 2015).

SECTION IV

Poverty

13

Aspects of Poverty in the Three Villages

Aparajita Bakshi and Shamsher Singh

In this chapter we analyse the different forms of poverty experienced by households in the three villages in West Bengal. We explore deprivation along four dimensions: incomes, assets, education, and housing and basic amenities. We use suitable indicators to measure deprivation along each of these dimensions and report the levels of deprivation, i.e. the proportion of deprived households or populations in each village. The differential forms and intensities of deprivation experienced by households in different socio-economic classes and social–religious groups in the villages are also examined. Our analysis primarily uses data from the 2010 survey of the villages. Though we do not extensively discuss the changes after 2010, we do highlight some noteworthy developments.

Income Deprivation

Levels of Income and Income Poverty

Conventionally, the literature on poverty has used the metric of income to translate minimum commodity requirements of individuals at the poverty threshold to an income poverty line. However, in many developing economies including India, income flows are difficult to measure due to the nature of the economy, nature of occupations, and seasonal and temporal patterns of income flows.[1] Due to these difficulties, the National Sample

---

[1] See Bakshi (2010) for a detailed discussion on the problems of measurement of household incomes, and Rawal and Swaminathan (2011) on underestimation of poverty using the consumption poverty line in India.

Surveys in India use consumption expenditure surveys to determine and update the poverty line in the country at regular intervals.

The focus of the PARI surveys was to ascertain household incomes. Though it is true that household incomes of rural households and agricultural households in particular tend to vary across seasons and years and that single-year surveys may not adequately capture the poverty status of households, the data do reveal income vulnerability of rural households. Low incomes, losses in agriculture, and inability to find adequate days of employment for various reasons even for a single year cause serious income stress for most households, and such income vulnerabilities have long-term implications on household strategies of income, investments, and spending. Thus, we argue that even a single-year income profile of households can indicate the extent of material deprivation and precariousness of rural households' livelihoods.

Table 1 describes the average levels of household income in the three villages in 2010. The mean household income ranged from Rs 55,874 in Kalmandasguri to Rs 57,903 in Panahar. The median income, however, was much lower than the mean – particularly in Panahar, due to high inequality in the distribution of incomes. Compared to the other two villages, Panahar had more unequal income distribution and extreme values in the income distribution. Vertical income inequality was relatively higher, with the Gini coefficient of household income being 0.643. In Amarsinghi and Kalmandasguri, the household income Gini coefficients were 0.372 and 0.386, respectively.[2]

As stated earlier, the official poverty line in India is based on consumption expenditure. Hence, the official poverty line cannot be used as a benchmark to assess the extent of income poverty in the study villages. Thus, we have used an alternate measure based on minimum wages in agriculture,[3] which was Rs 112.5 in West Bengal in 2010 (Labour Bureau 2015). Assuming that one working member of the household received minimum wage employment in agriculture for at least 300 days a year, the poverty line is defined at the annual household income of Rs 33,750.[4] Using this poverty line, we observed a fairly high degree of

[2] See chapter 12 in this book.
[3] See Bakshi and Modak (2017) for a more elaborate explanation of the minimum-wage-based poverty line.
[4] The minimum wage calculation is based on a family of two adults and one child. However, in our use of the minimum wage poverty line, we have not adjusted for household size.

Table 1 *Descriptive statistics of household income, study villages, West Bengal, 2010,* in Rs

	Panahar	Amarsinghi	Kalmandasguri
Mean	57,903	43,937	55,874
Median	25,461	36,390	43,356

Source: PARI survey (2010).

Table 2 *Households below minimum wage poverty line, study villages, West Bengal, 2010,* in per cent

Village	Proportion of poor households
Panahar	62.1
Amarsinghi	48.0
Kalmandasguri	32.7

Source: PARI survey (2010).

poverty in all three villages, much higher than the official headcount ratio of the State in 2010. According to official estimates, 28.8 per cent of the population in the State was below the poverty line. However, we found that 62.1 per cent of the households in Panahar, 48 per cent households in Amarsinghi, and 32.7 per cent households in Kalmandasguri received incomes below the poverty benchmark (Table 2).

Income Deprivation across Socio-Economic Classes and Social–Religious Groups

The incidence of poverty is highest among manual-worker households in all the three villages – 65.1 per cent of the manual-worker households in Panahar, 60.4 per cent in Amarsinghi, and 40 per cent in Kalmandasguri received incomes below the poverty line (Appendix Table 1). Poor-peasant households in the three villages also had high incidence of poverty compared to other socio-economic classes. This reflects the problems of small-scale agriculture and points to the fact that households with very small landholdings do not make adequate incomes from agriculture, even when they labour out for wages.

It is important to note that there are poor households in all socio-economic classes, with only two exceptions – landlord/capitalist households in Panahar and business households in Amarsinghi. This shows that income deprivation is widespread in West Bengal and there is general suppression of incomes in the economy. Not only are general levels of income poverty high in all villages, but there is also a sizeable section of poor, at least one-fourth of households, in most socio-economic classes.[5] Thus, even when households are in occupations other than agriculture, their incomes are not remarkably higher than that received from agriculture. The fact that households receiving major incomes from business or salaries do not receive incomes much higher than the minimum wage in agriculture reiterates the problem of low incomes, particularly

Table 3a *Households below minimum wage poverty line, by socio-economic class, Panahar, 2009–10*, in per cent

Class	Poor households
Landlord/capitalist farmer	0
Upper peasant	53.8
Poor peasant	74.2
Manual worker	65.1
Major income from business	53.8
Major income from salaries	25.0
Major income from other sources	100.0
Major income from remittances/rent	33.3
All	62.1

Source: PARI survey (2010).

Table 3b *Households below minimum wage poverty line, by socio-economic class, Amarsinghi, 2009–10*, in per cent

Class	Poor households
Upper peasant	27.8
Poor peasant	52.8
Manual worker	60.4
Major income from business	0
Major income from salaries	33.3
Major income from artisanal work	50.0
Major income from remittances	75.0
Major income from pension	100.0
All	48.0

Source: PARI survey (2010).

[5] The exceptions are capitalist-landlord/farmer households in Panahar, business households in Amarsinghi, and salaried households in Kalmandasguri.

Table 3c *Households below minimum wage poverty line, by socio-economic class, Kalmandasguri, 2009–10*, in per cent

Class	Poor households
Upper peasant	26.3
Poor peasant: small self-employment	27.3
Poor peasant: semi-proletarian	28.9
Manual worker	40.0
Income from small and petty business/ self-employed	20.0
Major income from salaries	16.7
Major income from pension	100.0
All	32.7

Source: PARI survey (2010).

in the three villages, and in the rural economy of West Bengal, in general.

The general pattern in most PARI village surveys as well as in India as a whole is that poverty is higher among Scheduled Caste (SC) and Scheduled Tribe (ST) households than caste Hindu households. The same is broadly true of the three West Bengal villages (Table 4). The proportion of income-poor households among SC and ST households was higher than among caste Hindu households. However, poverty among caste Hindu households was also high, particularly in Panahar and Amarsinghi. Horizontal inequalities in income in India are most often mediated through large inequalities in ownership of land and means of production, and SC households are largely excluded from ownership of the means of production. Such deep-rooted inequalities in ownership structures are not prominent in rural West Bengal, where land reforms eliminated the class of large landlords and granted access to land to the smaller peasantry and landless from all social–religious groups.[6] However, in recent times, demographic pressures have diminished the size of landholdings and the economic importance of land. Thus, we find high incidence of poverty among all social–religious groups in the villages, including caste Hindus. Muslim households in Panahar were able to retain relatively large landholdings; hence the incidence of poverty among them was lower than other social–religious groups. On the other hand, Muslim households reported the highest level of poverty in Kalmandasguri.

[6] See chapter 4 in this book.

Table 4 *Households in poverty based on minimum wage poverty line, by social–religious group, study villages, 2009–10,* in per cent

Social–religious group	Panahar	Amarsinghi	Kalmandasguri
Caste Hindu	50	44.9	18.5
Muslim	33.3	NA	39.3
SC	69.9	50.9	32.7
ST	76.5	100*	30.0
All	62.1	48	32.7

Notes: * There was only one ST household in Amarsinghi.
NA = Not applicable.
Source: PARI survey (2010).

Asset Poverty

Asset Values and Composition of Assets

The value of assets owned by households not only signifies the household's stock of wealth but also its capacity to earn income, make productive investments including in education, recover from income shocks, and ensure consumption levels. The major household assets for which PARI surveys collected data are: agricultural land, non-agricultural land and buildings, means of production (such as agricultural and non-agricultural tools and machinery), trees, animal resources, means of transport, domestic durable goods (such as furniture and household appliances), and inventories (such as unsold agricultural outputs or stocks in shops and commercial establishments). Data on financial assets and gold were not collected due to the sensitive nature of such information. Based on local market conditions, respondents self-reported the value of these assets in most cases.

The average value of assets owned by households in 2010 was 6.2 lakhs in Panahar, 4.4 lakhs in Amarsinghi, and 2.9 lakhs in Kalmandasguri (Table 5). These values are comparable with the levels reported in the NSSO's All-India Debt and Investments Surveys (AIDIS), 2013. According to the AIDIS, the average value of assets in rural West Bengal in December 2012 was Rs 4,07,297 per household,[7] which was significantly lower than the average value for rural India in 2012 – Rs 10,06,985.

[7] AIDIS includes shares, deposits, and amount receivable in total asset value. As mentioned earlier, information on such financial assets were not collected in the PARI surveys. However, the share of such assets in the asset portfolio of rural households was rather small, about 1.85 per cent in rural India and 3.98 per cent in rural West Bengal in 2012.

There was a large increase in asset values at current prices between 2010 and 2015 in the range of two to five times. Even if we account for inflation, the increase is substantial. This rapid increase was largely driven by the increase in land values. The average value of agricultural landholdings of households increased 1.4 times in Panahar, 2.75 times in Amarsinghi, and 4 times in Kalmandasguri. In our experience, land prices shoot up in villages when there are major changes that enhance the strategic locational position of the village, such as a new highway, airports or industry, or expansion of an urban agglomeration, or there is investment, particularly in irrigation, that improves productivity and hence the real value of land. Improvements in irrigation in Amarsinghi and electrification in Kalmandasguri may have played a role in the increase in land prices in these two villages. This increase may also be indicative of the scarcity value of land due to increasing population density and competitive demands on land.

The major asset owned by rural households was land – agricultural land comprised 58 to 65 per cent of the asset portfolio of households, whereas non-agricultural land and buildings comprised an additional

Table 5 *Households and average value of assets, study villages, 2010 and 2015*, in number and Rs

Village	N	2010	2015
Panahar	248	6,27,578	13,84,254
Amarsinghi	127	4,43,632	18,78,863
Kalmandasguri	147	2,97,303	11,95,901

Source: PARI surveys (2010 and 2015).

Table 6 *Composition of assets, study villages, 2010*, in per cent

Category of asset	Panahar	Amarsinghi	Kalmandasguri
Agricultural land	58	65.0	62.0
Non-agricultural land, buildings, and trees	36	29.0	31.5
Animals	1	2.0	2.7
Means of production	1	0.34	0.7
Means of transport	1	0.43	0.4
Other assets	3	3.0	2.5
All	100	100.0	100.0

Source: PARI survey (2010).

29 to 36 per cent (Table 6). Hence, agricultural and non-agricultural land, buildings, and trees constituted almost 95 per cent of the asset portfolio of households. Animals formed another 1 to 3 per cent of asset values, whereas means of production (other than land) comprised only 0.3 to 1 per cent. This shows that beyond land and buildings, households in the three villages owned very little, which is true for rural India as a whole. According to the AIDIS, land and buildings constituted 92 and 94 per cent of asset values in rural West Bengal and India, respectively, in 2012.

Along with the lack of diversification of asset portfolios, there was substantial inequality in asset ownership across households. Panahar had a Gini coefficient of asset ownership of 0.8, and the richest decile here owned 72 per cent of the total value of assets (Appendix Table 1). Gini coefficients of asset value in Amarsinghi and Kalmandasguri were 0.6 and 0.55, respectively, and the wealthiest deciles owned 40 per cent and 38 per cent of total asset value, respectively. At the other end of the spectrum, the bottom 50 per cent of households owned only 3 per cent of total assets in Panahar, 10 per cent in Amarsinghi, and 13 per cent in Kalmandasguri. This underlines the fact that along with substantial concentration of asset ownership in the villages, a large proportion of households were relatively deprived of assets. Even though we say "relatively" deprived, in reality, the poorest households barely owned any assets that could be a source of income or provide security during periods of vulnerability. To illustrate this point, we present case studies of asset-poor households in the villages.

Asset profiles of the poorest households
The poorest households in each of the villages owned no agricultural land. In Panahar, they owned neither homestead land nor houses and lived in shared accommodations with extended family. Their only assets were a few domestic durables and bicycles, all worth less than Rs 500 in 2010. Among the households in the bottom wealth decile, those who owned homesteads had small pieces of land and kutcha houses, few household durables, and bicycles that constituted their asset portfolio, amounting to Rs 20,000 or less. The level of destitution can be understood by the fact that household net worth fell short of the poverty line income of Rs 33,750. Thus, even if households liquidated all their assets, they would not be able to sustain for a whole year.

The asset profile of the poorest households in Amarsinghi was similar to Panahar. They did not own land, houses, or homesteads, and their only assets were a few household durables. Households in the bottom wealth decile generally did not own any agricultural land, any means of production; they owned small pieces of house sites, kutcha houses, or consumer durables. The asset value of the poorest decile was Rs 31,000 and below, which is lower than our estimated poverty line of annual income.

Due to the specific habitation pattern of Kalmandasguri, homesteads were larger than those in the other villages, which allowed the poor to grow trees and keep cattle. Thus, the asset portfolio of the poorest households in Kalmandasguri consisted of homesteads (only two of these households did not own any), kutcha houses, trees, livestock, bicycles, and household durables. Households in the poorest decile has an asset value of Rs 39,000 and below, just about a year's minimum wage income, which we consider our poverty benchmark.

Thus, we find that the total value of assets of the poorest households in the three villages at best equalled a year's poverty line income. Such low value of assets provided very little security for households during major events such as marriage, illness, or death of an earning member. Nor could the assets provide a sustained source of income, as households did not own any productive assets such as agricultural land. The only worthy asset for them was the sheer labour power that would enable them to earn wages.

Ownership of Specific Assets

As discussed in the previous section, assets have two important economic functions. They serve as insurance or security that allows households to smooth consumption flows by liquidating assets at times of distress. Secondly, assets such as land, trees, cattle, and machinery also have an important role in production and income generation. When households do not own specific assets, they are deprived of livelihood choices and security. Table 7 presents the number and proportion of households not owning important assets such as land, means of production (excluding land), and means of transport to assess the scale and dimensions of asset deprivation in the villages.

The proportion of households not owning any land or buildings (in this case, land includes agricultural and non-agricultural land and homesteads) ranged from 1.4 to 3.1 per cent of all households. The proportion of households not owning any agricultural land is, of course, much higher.[8] Livestock is the second most important asset for agricultural households, and 28 per cent households in Panahar, 22 per cent in Amarsinghi, and

---

[8] See chapter 4 of this book.

Table 7 *Households not owning specific assets, study villages, 2010*, in number and per cent

Village	Land		Livestock	
	Households	Proportion	Households	Proportion
Panahar	5	2.0	71	28.6
Amarsinghi	4	3.1	28	22.0
Kalmandasguri	2	1.4	21	14.3
Village	Means of production (excluding land)		Means of transport	
	Households	Proportion	Households	Proportion
Panahar	136	54.8	51	20.6
Amarsinghi	90	70.9	34	26.8
Kalmandasguri	96	65.3	21	14.3

Source: PARI survey (2010).

14 per cent in Kalmandasguri did not own any livestock. The majority of households – 55 per cent households in Panahar, 71 per cent in Amarsinghi, and 65 per cent in Kalmandasguri – did not own any other means of production excluding land. Other means of production include agricultural and non-agricultural tools and machinery and trees. In the villages, 14 to 27 per cent of the households did not own any means of transport, and the majority of those who did, owned bicycles. Very few households owned any motorised means of transport.

Asset Ownership by Socio-Economic Class and Social–Religious Group

Asset poverty, like other forms of deprivation, has a specific relation to the socio-economic location of households on the basis of class and social–religious group. As Tables 8a, 8b, and 8c show, in each of the three villages, the most asset-poor (in terms of the average value of asset holdings) were households in the manual-worker class. Though only a few in each village, households dependent on pensions were also severely deprived of assets. Households in these two classes had the lowest value of asset holdings, were largely excluded from ownership of agricultural land and other means of production, and did not even own house sites or houses in some cases (Appendix Table 2). They may have owned some livestock, but the value of that was much lower than that owned by the peasant classes. The proportion of manual-worker households that did not own any transport (namely bicycles) was higher than other classes, and understandably, none of the pensioner households owned any means of transport.

A large proportion of households in the non-agricultural classes, specifically those who received major incomes from businesses, did not own any means of production excluding land and buildings. Ownership of any kind of means for non-agricultural production was largely absent – there was no non-agricultural production in the villages – and the major non-agricultural enterprise was petty trade.

Table 8a *Average value of asset holdings, by class, Panahar, 2010*

Class	Households	Mean (Rs)	As ratio to manual-worker class' average value of asset holdings
Landlord/capitalist farmer	7	94,25,157	208.9
Upper peasant	52	12,36,541	27.4
Poor peasant	93	1,10,447	2.4
Manual worker	63	45,126	1.0
Business	13	4,45,636	9.9
Rents/remittances	3	1,03,355	2.3
Salaried person	12	4,99,008	11.1
Others	5	31,439	0.7
All	248	6,27,578	13.9

Source: PARI survey (2010).

Table 8b *Average value of asset holdings, by class, Amarsinghi, 2010*

Class	Households	Mean (Rs)	As ratio to manual-worker class' average value of asset holdings
Upper peasant	18	16,03,053	12.8
Poor peasant	36	4,48,589	3.6
Manual worker	48	1,24,919	1.0
Major income from business	13	1,56,008	1.2
Major income from salaries	3	7,31,553	5.9
Major income from pension	3	32,363	0.3
Major income from remittances/small rent	4	1,45,926	1.2
Major income from artisanal work	2	1,15,213	0.9
Total	127	4,42,002	3.5

Source: PARI survey (2010).

Table 8c *Average value of asset holdings, by class, Kalmandasguri, 2010*

Class	Households	Mean (Rs)	As ratio to manual-worker class' average value of asset holdings
Upper peasant	19	8,53,474	8.0
Poor peasant: small self-employment	11	3,20,028	3.0
Poor peasant: semi-proletarian	38	2,72,769	2.5
Manual worker	55	1,07,098	1.0
Income from small and petty business/self-employed	15	2,16,440	2.0
Major income salaried person	6	7,25,203	6.8
Major income from pension	3	37,933	0.4
Total	147	2,97,303	2.8

Source: PARI survey (2010).

The average value of assets owned by landlord/capitalist farmers in Panahar was 208.9 times that owned by manual workers, whereas the value of assets owned by peasants was 27.4 times that owned by manual workers, reflecting the large inequalities in asset ownership in the village. Such stark differences in asset levels were not observed in Amarsinghi or Kalmandasguri.

The relationship between asset deprivation and social–religious group is not straightforward, and can only be explained by understanding the relation between land ownership and class locations of households from different social–religious groups. Only in Panahar did we observe clear differences in asset ownership across social–religious groups. Muslim and caste-Hindu households owned landholdings and other means of production, whereas SC/ST households were largely landless or had small landholdings. SC/ST households also had less ownership of the means of production and animals compared to that of caste Hindu and Muslim households (Appendix Table 3). The average value of assets of SC/ST households were significantly lower than that of caste Hindus and Muslims in the village (Table 9a).

SC households in Amarsinghi had a lower average value of assets than that of caste Hindus, and a higher proportion of SC households than caste Hindu households did not own any means of production or livestock (Tables 9b and Appendix Table 3). It is interesting to note that all tubewells in Amarsinghi were owned by members of caste Hindu households.

Table 9a *Average value of asset holdings, by social–religious group, Panahar, 2010,* in Rs

Social–religious group	Household	Mean
Caste Hindu	92	11,27,749
SC	133	80,226
ST	17	1,02,881
Muslim	6	65,77,916
Total	248	6,27,578

Source: PARI survey (2010).

Table 9b *Average value of asset holdings, by social–religious group, Amarsinghi, 2010,* in Rs

Social–religious group	Household	Mean
Caste Hindu	69	5,69,709
SC	57	2,94,088
ST	1	61,305
Total	127	4,42,002

Source: PARI survey (2010).

Table 9c *Average value of asset holdings, by social–religious group, Kalmandasguri, 2010,* in Rs

Social–religious group	Household	Mean
Caste Hindu	27	3,78,711
SC	49	4,43,209
ST	10	2,65,407
Muslim	61	1,49,295
Total	147	2,97,303

Source: PARI survey (2010).

The case of Kalmandasguri is distinct, as SC households were not among the most asset-deprived; rather, they had the highest average value of asset holdings (Table 9c). Only 2 per cent of SC households did not own livestock, and 47 per cent did not own any other means of production – these proportions are the lowest among all social–religious groups in the village (Appendix Table 3). The elevated position of SC households in

Kalmandasguri can be attributed to the specific history of Rajbanshis in Koch Bihar district.

Thus, it is not difficult to identify the socio-economic characteristics of the asset-poor households. These households depend on manual work, partly because they are excluded from owning land and other means of production. In most villages, these households belong to caste groups that have been historically excluded from land ownership – the SCs.

Deprivation in Education

Educational Attainment

Education not only has intrinsic value to enhance human capability but also has instrumental value to obtain higher incomes, better livelihoods, and enhanced well-being. In the present phase of services-led economic growth and structural change in India, educational achievements are important determinants of access to remunerative non-farm employment (Lanjouw and Shariff 2004). Household-data-based studies have shown that inequalities in educational achievement increase rural income inequalities in India (Bakshi 2010, 2015; Lanjouw and Shariff 2004). To the extent that education increases access to remunerative income, particularly in the non-farm sector, the role of education in rural livelihoods, incomes, and income inequalities would be important in a State such as West Bengal, which has a significant rural non-farm sector.

Table 10 shows some basic indicators of education in the three study villages. Literacy rates of the population aged seven years and above was significantly low compared to the national average, and abysmally low for the female population – about half of them were illiterate. Adult literacy rates were even lower – only one-third of women and 53 to 67 per cent of men could read and write.

Educational attainment was also low. Median years of schooling ranged between zero to two years for women and four to five years for men. In Panahar, 41.8 per cent of the adult population never went to school; in Amarsinghi, this figure was 28.6 per cent. Surprisingly, in Kalmandasguri, there was no adult person who reported not having attended school. There were only a few college graduates in the villages – 34 in Panahar, 3 in Amarsinghi, and 6 in Kalmandasguri, constituting 4.8, 0.8, and 1.5 per cent of the adult population, respectively. There were only four women graduates in Panahar, none in Amarsinghi, and two in Kalmandasguri.

Table 10 *Educational achievement, study villages, 2010,* in per cent and years

Village	Indicator	Female	Male	All
Panahar	Literacy rate	49	60	54
	Adult literacy rate	37	53	45
	Median years of schooling	0	4	2
Amarsinghi	Literacy rate	54	72	63
	Adult literacy rate	39	67	53
	Median years of schooling	2	5	4
Kalmandasguri	Literacy rate	50	61	56
	Adult literacy rate	34	55	45
	Median years of schooling	2	4	3

Note: The literacy rate refers to the population aged seven years and above, whereas the adult literacy rate and median years of schooling refer to the population aged 18 years and above. *Source*: PARI survey (2010).

Schooling

Each village had accessible government schooling infrastructure, i.e., a primary school within the village and middle and high schools within a distance of five kilometres. In Panahar, the high school was situated in Deopara, about half a kilometre away. In Amarsinghi, the secondary school at Baidyanathpur and several high schools in Samsi were situated about two and five kilometres away, respectively. Post-primary students in Kalmandasguri could access Hatidhura Junior High School and Bararangrash High School situated one and five kilometres away, respectively. In brief, access to government schools was not an impediment to children's schooling in any of the villages.

Each of the villages showed a cent per cent enrolment rate among children aged 6 to 10 years, the primary-school-going age group (Table 11). Though this is an achievement, school attendance fell after age 10 in all villages. In Panahar, school attendance among those in the 11–14 age group was 100 and 97 per cent for girls and boys, respectively. In the secondary school age group of 15 to 16 years, the respective attendance rates were 87 per cent and 67 per cent, showing a greater decline for boys. At the high school age of 17 to 18 years, girls' and boys' attendance rates further declined to 53 and 56 per cent, respectively. Thus, boys began dropping out earlier, at the secondary school level, but by the higher secondary level, attendance rates were lower for girls by three percentage points.

Table 11 *School-going children, by age group and sex, study villages, 2010,* in per cent

Village	Age group (years)	Female	Male	Total
Panahar	6–10	100	100	100
	11–14	100	97	99
	15–16	87	67	81
	17–18	53	56	54
	All	91	90	90
Amarsinghi	6–10	100	100	100
	11–14	93	96	95
	15–16	95	100	96
	17–18	20	57	38
	All	84	90	86
Kalmandasguri	6–10	100	100	100
	11–14	95	90	93
	15–16	80	74	76
	17–18	29	57	45
	All	84	83	84

Source: PARI survey (2010).

In Amarsinghi, school attendance for girls and boys were similar and above 93 per cent till the age of 15 to 16 years, after which there was sharp decline: at 17 to 18 years, the respective attendance rates were 20 and 57 per cent. This was the case despite the fact that there were separate government high schools for girls and boys in Samsi, just five kilometres away.

In Kalmandasguri, there was steady attrition from school at every level for both girls and boys. The decline in attendance rates was steepest for girls aged 17–18, falling from 80 to 29 per cent. Among boys, attendance rates declined from 90 to 74 per cent in the 15–16 age group and further to 57 per cent in the 17–18 age group.

Thus, by the age of 18, only 56–57 per cent of boys remained in school; the situation was worse for girls. We classified children aged 17–18 by their primary occupations to understand the occupation status of out-of-school children. Except for one, all out-of-school girls reported domestic duties or "housework" as their primary occupation.[9] It is also important

[9] The sole exception, a 17-year-old in Panahar, reported tutoring younger children as her primary occupation.

to note that of the 32 out-of-school girls in the 17–18 age group in all the villages combined, 18 (i.e., 56 per cent) were married. With the exception of two out-of-school boys (one in Panahar and one in Amarsinghi who owned a shop), all were workers in crop production on their family farms or agricultural and non-agricultural workers (none were married). Thus, it is very clear that boys dropping out of school at higher school levels immediately joined the labour market, though that was not the case for girls. Low attendance rates among girls and the steep decline in their enrolment after age 16 was due to socio-cultural factors that restricted girls' education and encouraged their underage and early marriages.

Caste and Class Dimensions of Educational Attainment and Schooling

In each of the indicators of educational attainment and schooling, the village data show clear divisions on the lines of caste and class. Literacy rates in Panahar and Amarsinghi were significantly lower among SC/ST households, compared to caste-Hindu and even Muslim households. In Kalmandasguri on the other hand, Muslim and ST households had lower literacy rates than caste Hindu and SC households (Appendix Table 5).

The variations became clearer when we analysed educational indicators across socio-economic classes. Manual-worker and poor-peasant households fared the worst for all indicators. For example, literacy rates for members of these two classes in Panahar were only 35 and 40 per cent, respectively, whereas the rates for members of landlord/capitalist farmer and upper-peasant households were 84 and 76 per cent, respectively (Appendix Table 4). The same pattern was observed in the other two villages. In all villages, literacy rates were highest for those from the landlord/capitalist farmer and salaried classes, slightly lower among the upper-peasant and business and trade classes, and significantly lower among the manual-worker and poor-peasant classes. This class-based pattern holds true for the other educational indicators – adult literacy rates and mean and median years of schooling. There was not a single graduate in any manual-worker household in the three villages.

The overall school attendance rates of children were among the lowest among children from manual-worker and poor-peasant households (Appendix Table 6), and a more worrying fact is that these children dropped out of school at earlier levels. Attrition from school generally began after the age of 16 (roughly after secondary level), with a few exceptions. For children from manual-worker households in all villages, attrition began in the 11–14 age group, that is, immediately after primary school. The case was similar for children from poor-peasant households in Amarsinghi and Kalmandasguri, whereas there was 100 per cent attendance among such children in Panahar.

Amarsinghi and Kalmandasguri had higher overall enrolment rates for SC/ST children than that of caste Hindu children. In Kalmandasguri, enrolment rates among Muslim children was the lowest. On the other hand, SC/ST children in Panahar had lower enrolment rates than that of caste Hindu children.

In a study of ten villages in West Bengal in the late 1980s and early 1990s, Ramachandran, Swaminathan, and Rawal (2003) tried to determine the factors affecting educational achievement of children aged 6–16 and concluded that "class barriers to school attendance have become less significant; other social and regional features of educational deprivation persist" (p. 18). Our results contradict this position: there were significant differences in enrolment rates of children across socio-economic classes. Differences in enrolment rates across social–religious groups exist in Panahar, this is not the case in Amarsinghi and Kalmandasguri. The latter two villages are quite distinct, having low levels of inequality in land and asset ownership and income.

To sum up, educational deprivation is most severe among the manual-worker and poor-peasant classes in the three villages. The fact that children from such households also drop out of school at early ages indicates the severity and obstinacy of the problem and its long-term impacts.

Access to Housing and Basic Amenities

Quality of and access to housing and amenities such as electricity, water, and lavatories determine health outcomes, which affect productivity and human development. In this section, we discuss housing conditions and household access to selected basic amenities. Because the housing environment is a combination of many factors, an overall housing quality indicator, "integrated housing," which considers various amenities in addition to the structure itself, has been developed and discussed.

Housing

The most common and basic indicator used for housing quality is whether the structure is pucca/permanent or kutcha/temporary, which is determined by the construction material. Table 12 shows the proportion of households living in a fully pucca dwelling, i.e., wherein all components of the structure – walls, roof, and floors – are made of pucca material.[10] The data show 15 per cent of all households in Panahar, more than 20 per cent in Amarsinghi, and merely 3 per cent in Kalmandasguri lived in fully pucca structures, while the remaining households lived in semi-pucca or kutcha structures. In terms of housing materials used, asbestos sheets, wood, and bamboo for roofs, and mud and bamboo for walls were the most common in Panahar; burnt tiles and bamboo for roofs and mud for walls were the most common materials in Amarsinghi; and metal sheets and wood for roofs, and bamboo and jute sticks with mud for walls were used in Kalmandasguri.

Inequalities based on caste and class were clearly visible due to differences in housing. For instance, in Panahar, only 3 per cent of SC households lived in pucca structures, while 50 per cent of Muslims (the major landowning group in Panahar) and 33 per cent of caste Hindus lived in pucca houses (Appendix Table 8). In Amarsinghi, 11 per cent of SC households had pucca housing, against 33 per cent of caste-Hindu households. In Kalmandasguri, this proportion was eight and zero per cent for SC and caste Hindu households, respectively, and only two per cent for Muslim households. Data from the 2015 survey showed some improvements in Kalmandasguri – 10 per cent of households lived in pucca houses, more than triple the proportion in 2010. SC households living in pucca houses in 2015 had doubled to 16 per cent, while the figure for caste Hindu households increased from zero to 12 per cent. The housing situation in the other two villages remained unchanged over the five-year period. Across all villages, most households owning pucca dwellings were from landlord/capitalist-farmer and peasant classes; no more than 5 per cent of manual-worker households lived in pucca houses.

Availability of living space is an important aspect of housing conditions. This is usually measured in terms of either floor/carpet area or number of rooms in the dwelling. Other than living space, availability of homestead land gives an idea of how much space (including open space) households have for non-residential purposes such as keeping cattle and storing grain and straw. Data on homestead land presented in Appendix Table 9 show that households have sizeable homesteads in all three villages, with the largest plots in Kalmandasguri. Here, SC, ST, and Muslim households

---

[10] It is important to note that this definition is different from that used by the government (as per the Census of India and the NSSO), which takes into consideration only the materials used in the construction of roofs and walls.

owned sizeable homesteads, and there was less disparity between SC and caste Hindu households in this regard.

The proportion of households living in single-room structures raises the issue of crowdedness in dwellings. The 2010 data show a situation far from satisfactory in terms of availability of living space in dwellings – over a quarter of households in Panahar, one-third of households in Amarsinghi, and almost half of households in Kalmandasguri lived in single-room structures. The majority of the households in all villages had five or more members of different ages, sexes, and marital status; it is not difficult to imagine the inconvenience members face living in such a condition. Furthermore, though homestead plots were reasonably sized, the built space was relatively smaller in all villages.

In Panahar, 59 and 32 per cent of ST and SC households, respectively, lived in single-room dwellings, while among caste Hindu households, this figure was 18 per cent (Appendix Table 10). Such inequality in housing was not pronounced in the other two villages. In all villages, a larger proportion of small-peasant and manual-worker households than other classes lived in single-room houses.

Provision of a kitchen or separate cooking space enables the separation of cooking from the living space and other domestic activities. This is important for maintaining hygiene and has a positive impact on the health of the residents. A significant proportion of households in the study villages had a kitchen in their houses: 49 per cent in Panahar, 61 per cent in Amarsinghi, and the highest in Kalmandasguri at 92 per cent (Table 12). In most cases, a typical kitchen consisted of a small room in the corner of the compound and was made of tin sheets and a bamboo roof with mud or jute stick walls. It is important to note here that a cooking space separate from the living space is critical, given that the majority of households (seven exceptions) in the villages used firewood and dung cakes as their primary cooking fuel source. These sources, being unclean or smoke-generating, pose a severe health threat to those performing cooking activities.

Differences across social–religious groups in having a separate kitchen was quite pronounced in Panahar and Amarsinghi (Appendix Table 11). In Panahar, all Muslim households and 66 per cent of caste Hindu households had separate kitchens, while the proportion for ST and SC households were only 27 and 38 per cent, respectively. In Amarsinghi, 72 per cent of caste Hindu households compared to 42 per cent of SC households had separate kitchens. Such was not the case in Kalmandasguri, where over 90 per cent of households of all groups had separate kitchens.

Table 12 *Selected indicators of housing quality, study villages, 2010*, in per cent

Village	Households in *pucca* houses[1]	Households in single-room structures	Households having a kitchen	Average availability of homestead land (sq. ft)[2]
Panahar	15	28	49	2,134
Amarsinghi	22	33	61	2,613
Kalmandasguri	3	48	92	6,142

Notes: [1] Classification of construction material is that used by the Census of India and NSSO. *Pucca*/permanent materials are cement, concrete, oven-burnt bricks, hollow cement/ash bricks, stone, stone blocks, jack boards (cement-plastered reeds), metal sheets (iron, metal, etc.), timber, tiles, slate, corrugated iron, asbestos cement sheet, veneer, plywood, artificial wood of synthetic material, and polyvinyl chloride (PVC) material; *kutcha*/temporary materials are any others.
[2] Area reported here is the actual extent of land, and not floor space or built area.
Source: PARI survey (2010).

Access to Basic Amenities: Electricity, Water, and Lavatories

Electricity for domestic use is an important household amenity. Our survey data reveal a grim situation regarding household access to electricity in the study villages. Table 13 shows that less than three-fourths of Panahar households and more than one-third of Amarsinghi households had access to domestic electricity. Kalmandasguri was entirely non-electrified during the 2010 survey; only four households (two ST and two Muslim) situated close to a neighbouring village with an electricity distribution line had authorised connections.

The 2015 survey showed considerable improvement in household access to electricity. Data from this round (Appendix Table 13) showed that 97 per cent of households in Panahar, and all SC households and 97 per cent of caste Hindu households in Amarsinghi had access to electricity.

Table 13 *Household access to domestic electricity, drinking water within homestead, and a lavatory, study villages, 2010*, in per cent

Village	Domestic electricity connection	Drinking water source within homestead	Lavatory
Panahar	71	21	28
Amarsinghi	37	2	42
Kalmandasguri	3	84	71

Source: PARI survey (2010).

In Kalmandasguri, more than 90 per cent of households reported having an authorised electricity connection. Kalmandasguri residents stated that electrification of villages in that area had been in the pipeline for the past few years and eventually was completed in their village in 2015.

There are three important aspects of drinking water sources: the type or quality of source(s) used (open or covered), the nature of ownership over the source(s) (individual or common/public), and distance of the source from the house. Almost all households in the study villages used a covered source, mostly a handpump. None of the villages had a public, piped water supply provision; however, there were public handpumps installed by the panchayats in different parts of the villages.

National and international norms on water for drinking and other domestic uses recommend a tapped connection inside the house or premise for exclusive household use, i.e., personal access to piped water within house premise. In Panahar, only around one-fifth of households reported having a water source within the dwelling premise, whereas in Amarsinghi, this was the case for only 2 per cent of households (all of which were caste Hindu). The situation was better in Kalmandasguri, where 84 per cent of households had a drinking water source within their premises (Table 13); the village panchayat installing handpumps was a significant factor for better access here.

In Indian society, access to drinking water has been governed by notions of 'purity' and 'pollution' – resulting in certain social–religious groups, usually SCs, being restricted from accessing public water sources. In our surveys, SC households did not report any incidence of discrimination in accessing water. In Panahar, a higher proportion of caste Hindu and Muslim households than SC/ST households had a drinking water source within the housing premise. The 2015 survey showed marginal improvement in Amarsinghi for all households. In Kalmandasguri, a higher proportion of SCs over other social–religious groups had a water source within their house premise due to government intervention as noted earlier.

Having access to functional lavatories is crucial for personal and public hygiene, environmental safety, and individual dignity. The absence of a lavatory provision at the household level compromises individual safety and health outcomes for the entire society. Table 13 shows a dismal picture of household- and village-level sanitation in Panahar and Amarsinghi, where only 42 and 28 per cent of all households reported having access to a lavatory, respectively; access was particularly low for SC households

(Appendix Table 13). Kalmandasguri's situation was better but not satisfactory – only 71 per cent of households had a lavatory in 2010.

Through the village panchayat, a significant proportion of households in Kalmandasguri reported receiving some government benefits related to housing and amenities: 59 per cent of all households – 75 per cent ST, 51 per cent SC, 76 per cent Muslim, and 37 per cent caste Hindu – received assistance for house construction, homestead land, a handpump, or a lavatory. These interventions played a major role in households achieving improved standards for certain indicators.

Data from the 2015 survey showed no change in household-level sanitation in Panahar (Appendix Table 13) and an improvement in Amarsinghi and Kalmandasguri. Three-fourths of all households in Amarsinghi reported having access to a lavatory, however, there was a disparity between caste-Hindu and SC households – 90 per cent of the former had access compared to about half of the latter. In Kalmandasguri, there was an increase in household access, from 71 to 79 per cent.

Integrated Housing

Considering the concept of adequate housing, which suggests that housing is not just a matter of four walls and a roof but something that should provide basic safety and certain amenities, a broader definition of housing based on a set of criteria was proposed by Singh, Swaminathan, and Ramachandran (2013). According to their definition, a house meeting the following criteria was defined as adequate:

> (1) pucca roof, walls, and floors; (2) two rooms; (3) a source of water inside or immediately outside the house; (4) an electricity connection (authorised or unauthorised); and (5) a functioning latrine. (p. 64)

This definition helps to gauge the quality of housing in an integrated way by combining aspects of housing structure and the provision of basic household amenities.

Table 14 shows extremely high levels of overall deprivation in housing and amenities in the study villages. Only 8 per cent of all households in Panahar, one household in Amarsinghi, and none in Kalmandasguri fulfilled our criteria of integrated housing. Needless to say, households that enjoyed integrated housing were those with higher incomes and who belonged to the landholding classes, but were not necessarily all economically well off. In Panahar, all landlord/capitalist farmer and upper-peasant households (as well as one poor-peasant household) reported

Table 14 *Households living in a fully pucca house of at least two rooms and having electricity, water within or immediately outside house, and a functional lavatory; by social–religious group, survey villages, 2010, in per cent*

Village	Social–religious group				
	ST	SC	Muslim	Caste Hindu	All
Panahar	0	0	50	17	8
Amarsinghi	0	0	NA	1	1
Kalmandasguri	0	0	0	0	0

Note: NA = Not applicable.
Source: PARI survey (2010).

living in integrated housing. Similarly, in Amarsinghi, the one household living in integrated housing belonged to the upper-peasant class. When overall deprivation was the norm in a given village, there were no SC/ST households fulfilling the integrated housing criteria. A distressing factor was that a significant number of households across the study villages did not have even one or had only one of the mentioned provisions.

Improvements in housing conditions were observed between 2010 and 2015. In Panahar, 11 per cent of all households fulfilled the integrated housing norm in 2015, a marginal increase of three percentage points from 2010. However, SC/ST households were excluded from this improvement, and only Muslim and caste Hindu households benefited. In Amarsinghi, which previously had only one household with integrated housing, nine per cent of all households (5 and 13 per cent of SC and caste-Hindu households, respectively) now met the criteria in 2015. In Kalmandasguri, this proportion increased from zero to eight per cent of all households (11, 4, and 12 per cent of SC, Muslim, and caste-Hindu households, respectively). ST households across all study villages had integrated housing only in 2015 (Appendix Table 12), and no manual-worker households (except two in Panahar) had it even in 2015.

Multiple Dimensions of Deprivation in the Three Villages

In this chapter, we have tried to understand the multiple types of deprivation that households in the three villages experienced, including the depth of deprivation and differences across social–religious groups and classes. We quantified and analysed deprivation in four dimensions

– income, education, asset ownership, and housing and basic amenities. Though the experience of and implications for each dimension varied among the households, we use data visualisation in this section to present an overall picture and summary of the results.

The four axes in Figures 1–7 present the four indicators of deprivation, one for each dimension analysed. Income deprivation is quantified by the proportion of households not receiving minimum wage income; asset deprivation is quantified by the proportion of households without access to productive assets such as agricultural land, livestock, or other means of production; deprivation in education is quantified by the proportion of illiterates in the adult population; and deprivation in basic amenities is quantified by the proportion of households lacking more than three of the five amenity criteria for integrated housing – a fully pucca house, at least two rooms, electricity, a covered water source (within or near the homestead), and a functioning lavatory.

Figure 1 reveals that the levels of deprivation were highest in Panahar, where 62 per cent of households were income-poor, 66 per cent lacked amenities, 55 per cent of adults did not know how to read and write, and 16.5 per cent did not own any productive assets. Levels of deprivation in

Figure 1 *Deprivation in four dimensions, study villages, 2010*

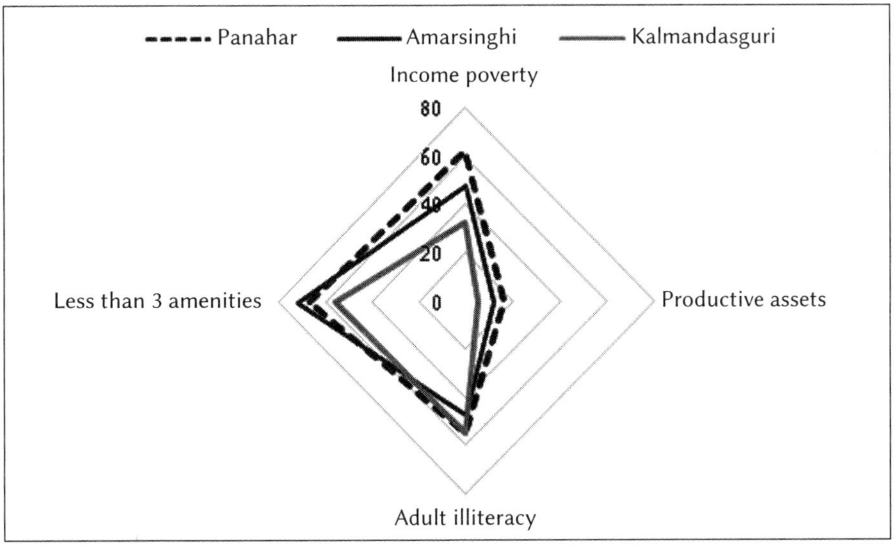

Source: PARI survey (2010).

Amarsinghi were lower for income poverty, asset poverty, and literacy, whereas 77 per cent of households here lacked access to basic amenities. Households in Kalmandasguri showed relatively low levels of deprivation in all dimensions, except adult literacy: 33 per cent were income-poor, only 5 per cent lacked productive assets, 55 per cent lacked basic amenities, and 55 per cent adults were illiterates.

Comparing across dimensions, deprivation in education and access to amenities was most widespread in the villages – more than 50 per cent of households/population were deprived in these two dimensions. However, we must reiterate that though adult literacy was low, the State made progress in educational indicators for children. All three villages reflected universal enrolment at the primary school level and above 90 per cent enrolment in the 11–14 age group. Dropouts after the age of 14 are a concern that needs to be addressed. The Trinamool government did initiate schemes such as Kanyashree in 2013 to arrest school dropouts and marriages of girls under the age of 18. However, no such initiatives exist for boys, though our village data shows a significant number of dropouts among boys after the age of 14.

Asset poverty was low in the villages, and less than 20 per cent of households lacked productive assets. However, the value of these assets were low. The AIDIS data showed that the average value of assets in rural West Bengal was about 40 per cent of the national average. Productive assets mainly consisted of land and livestock; access to agricultural machinery was low, and tools and machinery for non-agricultural production were almost non-existent.

In the years after 2010, data from the three villages showed improvement in the proportion of households living in pucca dwellings and having access to electricity and a lavatory and, as a result, improvement in integrated housing in varying degrees. However, these improvements remained concentrated within capitalist-farmer and peasant households, leaving the conditions of manual-worker and poor-peasant households unchanged. Though there was some improvement in the literacy rates and years of schooling between 2010 and 2015, high dropout rates after secondary school do not bode well for the State's future growth.

Panahar was characterised by high levels of deprivation and inequality. This was the only village with a class of landlords/capitalist farmers that owned large landholdings, agricultural machinery, and other assets and received significantly higher incomes than other classes. The average asset holdings of landlord households was 208 times higher than those of

Figure 2 *Deprivation in four dimensions, by socio-economic class, Panahar, 2010*

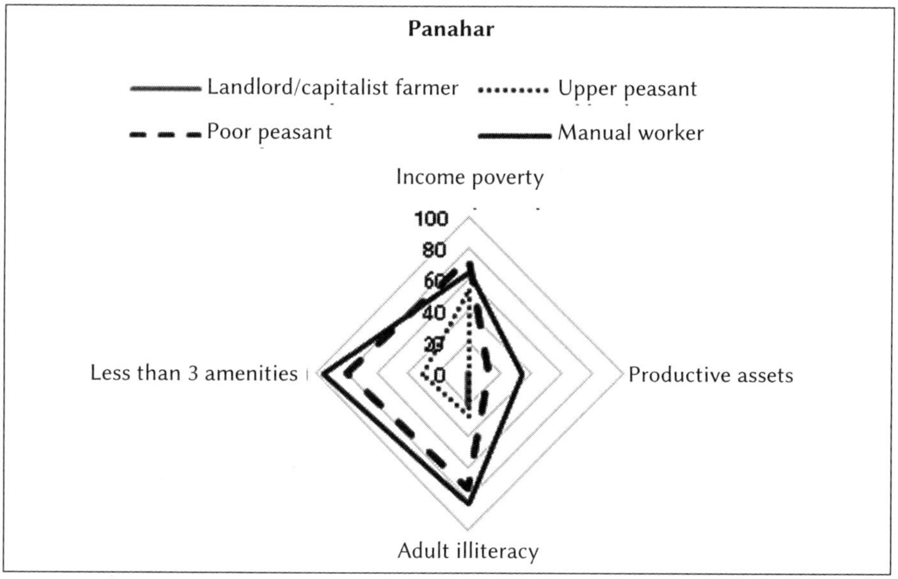

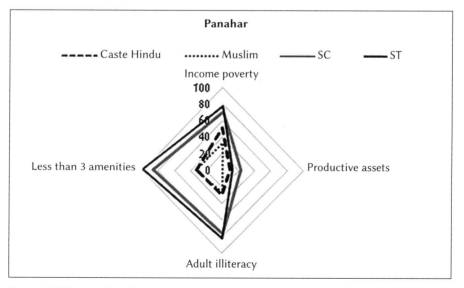

Source: PARI survey (2010).

Figure 3 *Deprivation in four dimensions, by social–religious group, Panahar, 2010*

Source: PARI survey (2010).

manual workers, reflecting the extent of inequality. Not a single landlord household faced deprivation in income, amenities, or assets, though there was some deprivation in literacy – six caste Hindu adults were not literate, four of them being women.

At the other end of the spectrum, 65 and 74 per cent of manual-worker and poor-peasant households, respectively, were income-poor, and 95 and 81 per cent of these respective households lacked basic amenities. These two classes also fared the worst in the educational indicators of adult literacy and school enrolment rates. Our analysis revealed a disturbing trend of school dropouts after the age of 14, among one-third and one-fourth of children from manual-worker and poor-peasant households, respectively; a large proportion of dropouts were boys entering the workforce.

The landlord/capitalist farmers were Muslims and caste Hindus, while a large proportion of SC/ST households belonged to the manual-worker and poor-peasant classes. The deprivation among SC/ST households in Panahar was most alarming – more than 70 per cent of these households were income-poor, illiterate, and lacked basic amenities.

Given that there are no landlord/capitalist-farmer households in Amarsinghi, all cultivators were small and marginal farmers, and inequalities in land ownership, incomes, and assets were lower than those in Panahar. Levels of deprivation in income, education, and basic amenities were high for manual-worker households (Figure 4) – about 60 per cent were income-poor, 96 per cent lacked basic amenities, and 66 per cent adults were illiterates. Poor-peasant households also experienced high levels of deprivation in these dimensions – 53 per cent were income-poor, 67 per cent lacked basic amenities, and 41 per cent adults were illiterates. Deprivation among upper-peasant households was relatively lower.

There was one landless ST household in Amarsinghi and that was deprived in all aspects (Figure 5). Though caste Hindu households fared better than SC households with regard to amenities, access to productive assets, and education, the levels of income poverty were similar in the two groups – 45 and 51 per cent of caste Hindu and SC households, respectively. An interesting feature of this village was that school enrolment rates were better for SC children (89 per cent) than caste Hindu children (83 per cent). Particularly in the 16–18 age group, 33 per cent of caste Hindu children were enrolled, compared to 45 per cent of SC children.

Economic inequality was the lowest in Kalmandasguri. The implementation of land reforms in the region had decisively broken the stronghold of the old landlord class and democratised the ownership of

Figure 4 *Deprivation in four dimensions, by socio-economic class, Amarsinghi, 2010*

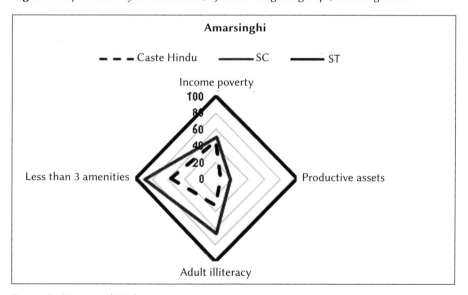

Source: PARI survey (2010).

Figure 5 *Deprivation in four dimensions, by social–religious groups, Amarsinghi 2010*

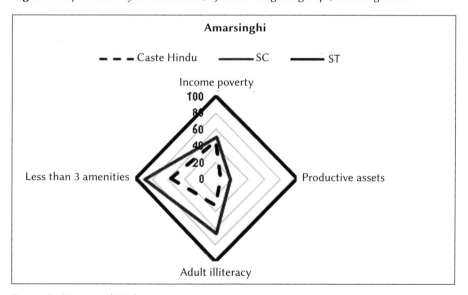

Source: PARI survey (2010).

land. Members of the erstwhile landlord household here, a Muslim family living in an adjacent village, were small peasants by 2010, with no social–religious or economic influence in the village.[11] Ceiling surplus land was redistributed to sharecroppers and landless households, a majority of which were Muslims and Rajbanshis (SC) as well as some caste-Hindu and ST households (Basu 2015). There were also significant government interventions in areas such as drinking water and sanitation.

Kalmandasguri was the least developed among the three villages in 2010 – agriculture was largely unirrigated, there was no mechanisation of operations, production and productivity were low, there was no electricity for domestic use or for agriculture, and there was no pucca road or transport services connecting the village to the nearest market. Outmigration of workers to other States in India and to neighbouring countries for manual wage work and remittances formed a significant share of total household income. Yet, levels of income and asset deprivation were also low.

The proportion of income-poor households in Kalmandasguri ranged from 26 per cent among upper-peasants to 40 per cent among manual workers (Figure 6). About 9 per cent of manual workers did not own productive assets, whereas all upper-peasant households owned some productive assets. Access to amenities was also better here, though conditions were worse for manual-worker and poor-peasant classes than peasant classes. Educational indicators were also worse for these two classes than the upper-peasant classes – there was universal enrolment among peasant children till the age of 16 and dropouts after primary school among children from manual-worker and poor-peasant households.

There were very little differences between SC and caste Hindu households in Kalmandasguri. Income poverty was slightly lower among caste Hindus, but in all other aspects – land ownership, amenities, and education – SC households showed similar levels as that of caste Hindus. School enrolment was much higher for SC children than caste Hindus, with 100 per cent enrolment till the age of 16. Muslim households faced high levels of deprivation in all dimensions, whereas ST households faced deprivation in amenities and education.

By the 2015 survey, an important change occurred in Kalmandasguri, namely electrification. Nascent changes in irrigation and agricultural mechanisation were underway, though their impact was still not visible. Rather, visible improvements were made in housing conditions.

---

[11] See chapter 4 in this book.

Figure 6 *Deprivation in four dimensions, by socio-economic class, Kalmandasguri, 2010*

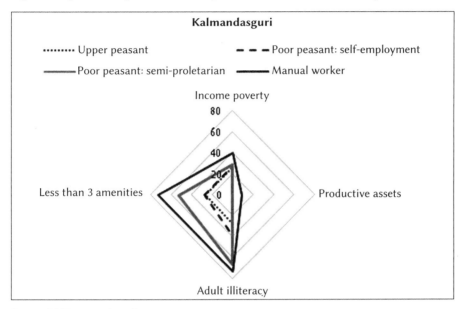

Source: PARI survey (2010).

Figure 7 *Deprivation in four dimensions, by social–religious group, Kalmandasguri, 2010*

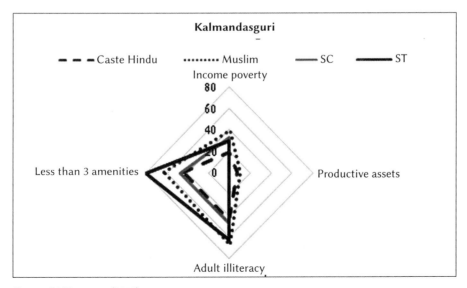

Source: PARI survey (2010).

Conclusion: Looking Back, Looking Ahead

The material conditions of households in the three villages surveyed by the FAS in 2010 and 2015 portrayed, in a way, the achievements and failures of the decades-long Left Front government, as well as the limitations of and future potential for the State's development.

The weakening of feudal relations of production and democratisation of land through land reforms were perhaps the greatest achievements of the Left Front government. No village in the State was untouched by land reforms. In chapter 4 of this book, Basu documents the long history of land reforms in each village and establishes how its implementation after prolonged peasant struggles curbed the economic and social power of the landlords and empowered tenant cultivators and the landless. The landlord class retained only limited land operations in some places – Panahar was one such village. In the other two villages, there were no large landowners. The success of land reforms also meant the weakening, though not complete absence, of caste-based inequalities, as we see in Amarsinghi and Kalmandasguri.

Land reforms had an immediate and positive impact on agricultural production and productivity in the 1980s, as discussed at length in chapter 2 of this book. However, land reforms also created a large class of small peasantry. During the 2010 survey, most households consisted of small and marginal farmers, owning less than one hectare of land. In chapter 3 of this book, Bakshi, Modak and Das show that there was a small segment of landlord and capitalist-farmer households retaining large landholdings in Panahar and the absence of landlords, capitalist farmers, in Amarsinghi and Kalmandasguri. A few rich peasants and medium peasants constituted the upper peasantry. The largest section of the peasantry was semi-proletarianised poor peasants who significantly depended on manual wage employment.

Small-scale production posed several challenges to crop production and farm business incomes. In chapter 5, Sarkar clearly shows the limitations of production faced by small farmers. Average farm business incomes decreased progressively with size of landholdings, and small peasant households depended heavily on other sources of income for subsistence. Small peasants were also subjected to price volatility and had limited access to markets and storage facilities for crops such as potato in the case of Panahar. In chapter 7, Modak narrates how misconceived policies adversely affected access to groundwater irrigation and increased irrigation costs for peasant households. In dhapter 9, Chavan and Dutta show the inadequacy of formal-sector credit reaching small-scale cultivators. Thus, though land reforms reduced rural inequalities and brought remarkable increases in production and productivity in the State as a whole, the absence of any further thrust to support and enrich small-scale production or improve the economic condition of rural households has left the problem of high deprivation in material conditions of life unresolved.

The net result from our 2010 data is that households were trapped in income and asset deprivation, though inequalities were not high, except in the case of Panahar. Poverty was particularly high for poor-peasant and manual-worker households. Households owned very few assets other than land, and ownership of modern tools and machinery for agricultural or non-agricultural production was also scant.

There were also high levels of deprivation in basic amenities and education. In our view, widespread deprivation in education and amenities in the villages showcases the greatest weaknesses of public policy in the three decades of the Left Front rule in West Bengal. Though some gains were made in the later years, particularly in near universal school enrolment rates till the age of 14 and the accessibility of government schools in the villages, the high incidence of school dropouts after the age of 14 reflect the lost potential. Deprivation in education and basic amenities was high among all social–religious groups, with few exceptions (such as Muslim and caste-Hindu households in Panahar). Differences across socio-economic classes were more pronounced – small-peasant and manual-worker households faced higher levels of deprivation than peasant and landlord/capitalist-farmer households did.

Investments in human development, such as those in education, housing, and basic amenities, have long-term implications for the economy and polity, as well as for the quality of labour. Inadequate efforts and achievements in human development have reduced the State's capacity to consolidate the gains made from land reforms and agricultural growth in rural areas and further progress. The development path of the State in recent years, which reflects rapid proletarianisation and increase in outmigration of manual workers, is perhaps the result of this policy failure.

The three villages bear testimony to the processes of proletarianisation of the rural workforce, the rising importance of wage employment in household incomes and livelihoods, and the challenges to obtaining gainful employment in a capital-scarce economy. In the villages, the classes of manual workers and poor-peasants sourcing a major portion of their income from agricultural and non-agricultural wages constituted more than 60 per cent of the households.

Dhar, Nagbhushan and Patra's analysis in chapter 10 discusses the employment crisis faced by manual workers wherein they received less than 100 days of wage employment in the agricultural year. In his analysis of wages in chapter 11, Das notes that manual workers' average daily wages in agricultural operations were below the minimum wage, thus clearly showing that the highest incidence of poverty lies in this class. Male children from manual-worker and poor-peasant households dropped out from school early to join the labour force to supplement household income. Furthermore, the lack of agricultural and non-agricultural wage employment opportunities within or near the village forced workers from Amarsinghi and Kalmandasguri to migrate for short periods to urban centres within and outside the State – chapter 10 describes male outmigration from these villages.

The description of male outmigration from the villages is also instructive regarding the importance of education on the rural labour supply. Male outmigration from Amarsinghi and Kalmandasguri was for short durations in the lean seasons for different types of manual wage work such as construction that did not require a highly educated workforce and was performed by all social–religious groups and classes. Male outmigration from Panahar, on the other hand, was primarily done by educated workers for salaried and regular employment, long-term, and largely concentrated among caste-Hindu and Muslim households. The short-term migration witnessed in Amarsinghi and Kalmandasguri might have mitigated short-term household income stress, but cannot necessarily resolve chronically low incomes and poverty.

During the 2010 survey, we witnessed low levels of income and assets, and widespread deprivation in education and access to basic amenities. The situation did not show noticeable improvement in 2015. Our analysis indicates that the future of the State is crucially linked to rethinking agriculture in a way that benefits small and marginal cultivators, creating alternate livelihoods outside agriculture, and investments in education and basic amenities to improve the living and working conditions of rural labour.

References

Bakshi, Aparajita (2010), "Rural Household Incomes," unpublished PhD thesis, University of Calcutta, Kolkata.

Bakshi, Aparajita (2015), *Nature of Income Diversification in Village India with Special Focus on Dalit Households*, Project report submitted to Indian Council for Social Science Research, Foundation for Agrarian Studies, Bangalore.

Bakshi, Aparajita and Modak, Tapas Singh (2017), "Incomes of Small Farmer Households," in Madhura Swaminathan and Sandipan Baksi (eds.), *How Do Small Farmers Fare: Evidence from Village Studies in India*, Tulika Books, New Delhi, pp. 126–70.

Basu, Ranjini (2015), "Land Tenures in Cooch Behar District, West Bengal: A Study of Kalmandasguri Village," *Review of Agrarian Studies*, vol. 5, no. 1, January–June, pp.88–111.

Labour Bureau (2015), *Report on the Working of the Minimum Wages Act, 1948 for the Year 2013*, Ministry of Labour and Employment, Government of India, Chandigarh.

Lanjouw, Peter and Shariff, Abusaleh (2004), "Rural Non-Farm Employment in India: Access, Incomes and Poverty Impact," *Economic and Political Weekly*, vol. 39, no. 40, October, pp. 4429–46.

Ramachandran, V. K., Swaminathan, Madhura, and Rawal, Vikas (2003), "Barriers to Expansion of Mass Literacy and Primary Schooling in West Bengal: A Study Based on Primary Data from Selected Villages," CDS working paper no. 345, Centre for Development Studies, Thiruvananthapuram.

Singh, Shamsher, Swaminathan, Madhura, and Ramachandran, V.K. (2013), "Housing Shortages in Rural India," *Review of Agrarian Studies*, vol. 3, no. 2, July–January, pp. 54–72.

Swaminathan, Madhura and Rawal, Vikas (2011), Income Inequality and Caste in Village India, *Review of Agrarian Studies*, vol. 1, no. 2.

Appendix

Appendix Table 1 *Share of asset values, by decile and Gini coefficient of asset value, study villages, 2010*

Asset decile	Panahar	Amarsinghi	Kalmandasguri
D1	0.2	0.4	1
D2	0.4	1.1	2
D3	0.6	1.9	2
D4	0.8	2.7	3
D5	1.1	4.1	5
D6	1.6	5.6	7
D7	2.7	7.8	9
D8	5.1	12.8	13
D9	15.3	23.3	20
D10	72.2	40.4	38
Gini coefficient	0.8	0.6	0.55

Source: PARI survey (2010).

Appendix Table 2 *Households not owning specific assets, by class, 2010*, in per cent

Class	Land and buildings	Livestock	Means of production	Means of transport
Panahar				
Landlord/capitalist farmer	0	0	0	0
Upper peasant	0	9.6	5.8	0
Poor peasant	1.1	29.0	57.0	24.7
Manual worker	4.8	34.9	92.1	28.6
Major income from business	0	30.8	53.8	7.7
Major income from salaries	0	66.7	58.3	16.7
Major income from other sources	20.0	60.0	100.0	100.0
Major income from remittances/rent	0	66.7	100.0	66.7
All classes	2.0	28.6	54.8	20.6
Amarsinghi				
Upper peasant	0	5.6	16.7	16.7
Poor peasant	2.8	11.1	41.7	11.1
Manual worker	2.1	31.3	97.9	41.7
Major income from business	0	15.4	100.0	0
Major income from salaries	0	33.3	100.0	33.3
Major income from pension	66.7	66.7	100.0	100.0
Major income from remittances/ small rent	0	50.0	100.0	50.0
Major income from artisanal work	0	50.0	100.0	50.0
All classes	3.1	22.0	70.9	26.8
Kalmandasguri				
Upper peasant	0	0	15.8	0
Poor peasant: small self-employment	0	18.2	72.7	0
Poor peasant: semi-proletarian	0	10.5	52.6	18.4
Manual worker	1.8	16.4	89.1	20.0
Income from small and petty business/self- employed	0	33.3	80.0	0
Major income from salaries	0	0	16.7	0
Major income from pension	33.3	33.3	100	100
All classes	1.4	14.3	65.3	14.3

Source: PARI survey (2010).

Appendix Table 3 *Households not owning specific assets, by social–religious group, 2010,* in per cent

Social–religious group	Land and buildings	Livestock	Means of production	Means of transport
Panahar				
Caste Hindu	3.3	25	33.7	9.8
Muslim	0	16.7	16.7	0
SC	1.5	31.6	72.2	27.1
ST	0	29.4	47.1	35.3
All	2	28.6	54.8	20.6
Amarsinghi				
Caste Hindu	2.9	18.8	59.4	20.3
SC	3.5	24.6	84.2	33.3
ST	0	100	100	100
All	3.1	22	70.9	26.8
Kalmandasguri				
Caste Hindu	0	25.9	66.7	14.8
Muslim	1.6	18	77	24.6
SC	2	2	46.9	2
ST	0	20	80	10
All	1.4	14.3	65.3	14.3

Source: PARI survey (2010).

Appendix Table 4 *Population (aged seven and above) that can read and write, by class and sex, 2010*, in per cent

Village	Class	Female	Male	All
Panahar	Landlord/capitalist farmer	78	88	84
	Upper peasant	73	79	76
	Poor peasant	32	48	40
	Manual worker	31	39	35
	Major income from business	60	83	73
	Major income from salaries	75	89	82
	Major income from remittances/rent	50	0	33
	Major income from other/miscellaneous sources	0	25	13
	All	49	60	54
Amarsinghi	Upper peasant	69	97	83
	Poor peasant	65	74	69
	Manual worker	41	58	49
	Major income from business	52	84	71
	Major income from salaries	75	100	82
	Major income from artisanal work	75	60	67
	Major income from pension	0	0	0
	Major income from remittances/small rent	38	33	36
	All	54	72	63
Kalmandasguri	Upper peasant	71	88	79
	Poor peasant: small self-employment	56	75	65
	Poor peasant: semi-proletarian	38	60	50
	Manual worker	41	41	41
	Major income from business	60	63	61
	Major income from salaries	82	93	88
	Major income from pension	0	0	0
	All	50	61	56

Source: PARI survey (2010).

Appendix Table 5 *Population (aged seven and above) that can read and write, by social–religious group and sex, 2010*, in per cent

Village	Social–religious group	Female	Male	All
Panahar	Caste Hindu	69	79	74
	Muslim	60	80	70
	SC	31	45	38
	ST	32	36	34
	All	49	60	54
Amarsinghi	Caste Hindu	65	81	73
	SC	43	62	51
	ST	0	50	33
	All	54	72	63
Kalmandasguri	Caste Hindu	48	75	63
	Muslim	44	49	46
	SC	60	70	64
	ST	36	53	45
	All	50	61	56

Source: PARI survey (2010).

Appendix Table 6a *School-going children, by age group and class, Panahar, 2010*, in per cent

Age group (years)	Landlord/ capitalist farmer	Upper peasant	Poor peasant	Manual worker	Major income from business	Major income from salaries	All others	All
6–10	100	100	100	100	100	100	NA	100
11–14	100	100	100	96	100	100	100	99
15–16	100	100	75	63	100	NA	NA	81
17–18	100	82	50	0	60	NA	NA	54
All	100	96	89	85	85	100	100	90

Note: NA = Not applicable.
Source: PARI survey (2010).

Appendix Table 6b *School-going children, by age group and class, Amarsinghi, 2010*, in per cent

Age group (years)	Upper peasant	Poor peasant	Manual worker	Major income from business	Major income from salaries	All others	All
6–10	100	100	100	100	100	100	100
11–14	100	100	91	100	NA	67	95
15–16	100	100	91	100	NA	100	96
17–18	50	50	22	50	NA	0	38
All	88	90	85	88	100	63	86

Note: NA = Not applicable.
Source: PARI survey (2010).

Appendix Table 6c *School-going children, by age group and class, Kalmandasguri, 2010*, in per cent

Age group (years)	Upper peasant	Poor peasant: small self-employment	Poor peasant: semi-proletarian	Manual worker	Major income from business	Major income from salaries	All
6–10	100	100	100	100	100	100	100
11–14	100	100	94	87	100	100	93
15–16	100	100	82	50	80	100	76
17–18	80	60	36	25	38	50	45
All	97	88	77	85	71	86	84

Source: PARI survey (2010).

Appendix Table 7 *School-going children, by age group and social–religious group, study villages, 2010*, in per cent

Village	Age group (years)	Caste Hindu	Muslim	SC	ST	All
Panahar	6–10	100	NA	100	100	100
	11–14	97	100	100	100	99
	15–16	93	0	71	100	81
	17–18	75	NA	29	100	54
	All	94	50	87	100	90
Amarsinghi	6–10	100	NA	100	100	100
	11–14	100	NA	90	NA	95
	15–16	93	NA	100	NA	96
	17–18	33	NA	45	NA	38
	All	83	–	89	100	86
Kalmandasguri	6–10	100	100	100	100	100
	11–14	86	91	100	100	93
	15–16	75	53	100	100	76
	17–18	50	24	73	50	45
	All	80	77	95	88	84

Note: NA = Not applicable.
Source: PARI survey (2010).

Appendix Table 8 *Households living in pucca houses, by social–religious group, study villages, 2010 and 2015**

Village	Social–religious group				
	Caste Hindu	Muslim	SC	ST	All
Amarsinghi	32 (41)	NA	11 (14)	0 (0)**	22 (28)
Kalmandasguri	0 (12)	2 (4)	8 (16)	0 (0)	3 (10)
Panahar	33 (37)	50 (100)	3 (6)	0 (0)	15 (19)

Notes: (i) The classification of construction material is that used by the Census of India and NSSO. *Pucca*/permanent materials are cement, concrete, oven-burnt bricks, hollow cement/ash bricks, stone, stone blocks, jack boards (cement-plastered reeds), metal sheets (iron, metal, etc.), timber, tiles, slate, corrugated iron, asbestos cement sheet, veneer, plywood, artificial wood of synthetic material, and PVC material; *kutcha*/temporary materials are any others.
(ii) * 2015 figures are in parenthesis; ** There was only one ST household in the village.
NA = Not applicable
Source: PARI surveys (2010 and 2015).

Appendix Table 9 *Average homestead land, by social–religious group, study villages, 2010*, in sq. feet

Village	Social–religious group				
	Caste Hindu	Muslim	SC	ST	All
Panahar	2,919	4,922	1,525	1,481	2,134
Amarsinghi	3,179	NA	1,960	2,875	2,613
Kalmandasguri	7,405	4,225	7,623	6,926	6,142

Notes: Area reported here is the actual extent of land, not floor space.
NA = Not applicable.
Source: PARI survey (2010).

Appendix Table 10 *Households living in single-room structures, by social–religious group, study villages, 2010*, in per cent

Village	Social–religious group				
	Caste Hindu	Muslim	SC	ST	All
Panahar	18	0	32	59	28
Amarsinghi	28	NA	39	0	33
Kalmandasguri	41	57	37	60	48

Note: NA = Not available.
Source: PARI survey (2010).

Appendix Table 11 *Households having a kitchen, by social–religious group, study villages, 2010*, in per cent

Village	Social–religious group				
	Caste Hindu	Muslim	SC	ST	All
Panahar	66	100	38	27	49
Amarsinghi	77	NA	42	0	61
Kalmandasguri	93	90	94	90	92

Note: NA = Not applicable.
Source: PARI survey (2010).

Appendix Table 12 *Households having a domestic electricity connection, by social–religious group, study villages, 2015* by per cent

Village	Social–religious group				
	Caste Hindu	Muslim	SC	ST	All
Panahar	100	100	96	83	97
Amarsinghi	97	NA	100	NA	98
Kalmandasguri	100	91	85	100	91

Note: NA = Not applicable.
Source: PARI survey (2015).

Appendix Table 13 *Households having access to a lavatory, by social–religious group, study villages, 2010 and 2015*, in per cent

Village	Social–religious group									
	Caste Hindu		Muslim		SC		ST		All	
	2010	2015	2010	2015	2010	2015	2010	2015	2010	2015
Panahar	65	67	67	100	5	4	0	0	28	29
Amarsinghi	57	93	NA	NA	24	53	NA	NA	42	74
Kalmandasguri	77	57	59	87	84	84	60	67	71	79

Note: NA = Not applicable.
Source: PARI surveys (2010 and 2015).

Appendix Table 14 *Households living in a fully pucca house of at least two rooms and having electricity, water within or immediately outside house, and a functional lavatory, by social–religious group, survey villages, 2015*, in per cent

Village	Social–religious group				
	Caste Hindu	Muslim	SC	ST	All
Panahar	25	100	0	0	11
Amarsinghi	13	NA	5	0	9
Kalmandasguri	12	4	11	0	8

Note: NA = Not applicable.
Source: PARI survey (2015)

Contributors

APARAJITA BAKSHI, Associate Professor, R. V. University, Bengaluru.

RANJINI BASU, Programme Officer, Focus on the Global South, New Delhi.

PALLAVI CHAVAN, Economist working on rural credit, Mumbai.

ARINDAM DAS, Joint Director, Foundation for Agrarian Studies, Bengaluru.

NILADRI SEKHAR DHAR, Associate Professor, Asian Development Research Institute, Patna.

RITAM DUTTA, Junior Research Fellow, Economic Analysis Unit, Indian Statistical Institute, Bengaluru.

T. JAYARAMAN, Senior Fellow, M. S. Swaminathan Research Foundation, Chennai.

SANDEEP MAHATO, Research Scholar, Tata Institute of Social Sciences, Mumbai.

TAPAS SINGH MODAK, Associate Fellow, Foundation for Agrarian Studies, Bengaluru.

KAMAL KUMAR MURARI, Assistant Professor, Tata Institute of Social Sciences, Mumbai.

SHRUTI NAGBHUSHAN, Research Scholar, School of Oriental and African Studies, London.

SUBHAJIT PATRA, Senior Data Analyst, Foundation for Agrarian Studies, Bengaluru.

BIPLAB SARKAR, Associate Professor, P. E. S. University, Bengaluru.

DIBYENDU SEN, Assistant Professor, St. Xavier's College (Autonomous), Kolkata.

SHAMSHER SINGH, Assistant Professor, FLAME University, Pune.